THE COMPLETE ENCYCLOPEDIA OF
BASKETBALL

Author acknowledgements

Ira Winderman: Thanks to Mark Pray, Director of Public Relations, WNBA;
Tim Donovan, Vice President Public Relations, Miami Heat; Rob Wilson,
Assistant Director of Sports Media Relations, Miami Heat; Robin J. Deutsch,
Director of Publishing and New Media, Basketball Hall of Fame.

Mary Schmitt Boyer: I would like to thank my husband, Gene Boyer,
who put up with the stacks of research scattered around our house, and
also Tracy Dodds, my backup proofreader!! Thanks.

THIS IS A CARLTON BOOK

This edition published in 2001

10 9 8 7 6 5 4 3 2 1

Copyright © Carlton Books Limited 2001

A CIP catalogue record for this book is available from the British Library

ISBN 1 84222 114 0

Project editor Martin Corteel
Project art direction Mark Lloyd
Picture research Debora Fioravanti
Production Lisa French
Designed by Simon Mercer

Printed in Dubai

(Opposite) CROSSING BOUNDARIES: *Vince Carter's spectacular play has been a huge factor in the success of the Toronto Raptors.*

THE COMPLETE ENCYCLOPEDIA OF
BASKETBALL

Ron Smith, Ira Winderman & Mary Schmitt Boyer

CARLTON
BOOKS

CONTENTS

INTRODUCTION 6

FOREWORD 8
by Dr. Jack Ramsay

THE HISTORY
OF THE NBA 12

THE NBA TEAMS 32
Atlanta Hawks 34
Boston Celtics 36
Charlotte Hornets 38
Chicago Bulls 40
Cleveland Cavaliers 42
Dallas Mavericks 44
Denver Nuggets 46
Detroit Pistons 48
Golden State Warriors 50
Houston Rockets 52
Indiana Pacers 54
Los Angeles Clippers 56
Los Angeles Lakers 58
Miami Heat 60
Milwaukee Bucks 62
Minnesota Timberwolves 64
New Jersey Nets 66
New York Knicks 68
Orlando Magic 70
Philadelphia 76ers 72
Phoenix Suns 74
Portland Trail Blazers 76
Sacramento Kings 78
San Antonio Spurs 80
Seattle SuperSonics 82
Toronto Raptors 84
Utah Jazz 86
Vancouver Grizzlies 88
Washington Wizards 90

LEGENDS
OF THE NBA 92
Kareem Abdul-Jabbar 94
Charles Barkley 96
Rick Barry 98
Elgin Baylor 100
Larry Bird 102

Wilt Chamberlain	104
Bob Cousy	106
Julius Erving	108
Patrick Ewing	110
Walt Frazier	112
John Havlicek	114
Elvin Hayes	116
Magic Johnson	118
Michael Jordan	120
Karl Malone	122
Moses Malone	124
George Mikan	126
Hakeem Olajuwon	128
Shaquille O'Neal	130
Bob Pettit	132
Oscar Robertson	134
Dennis Rodman	136
Bill Russell	138
John Stockton	140
Jerry West	142

THE GREAT PLAYERS — 144

THE GREAT COACHES — 270

Red Auerbach	272
Billy Cunningham	274
Chuck Daly	276
Red Holzman	278
Hank Iba	280
Phil Jackson	282
John Kundla	284
Don Nelson	286
Jack Ramsay	288
Pat Riley	290
Adolph Rupp	292
Dean Smith	294
Pat Summitt	296
Lenny Wilkens	298
John Wooden	300

THE NBA'S SECOND SEASON — 302

THE NBA ALL-STAR GAME — 360

THE NBA DRAFT — 376

THE ARENAS — 386

OLYMPIC GAMES — 406

INTERNATIONAL BASKETBALL — 422

THE WNBA — 444

COLLEGE BASKETBALL — 466

THE RULES OF BASKETBALL — 488

THE BUSINESS OF THE NBA — 498

THE HALL OF FAME — 508

NBA RECORDS — 548

CHRONOLOGY OF PROFESSIONAL BASKETBALL — 560

GLOSSARY OF TERMS — 566

INDEX — 568

(*Opposite*) **HOT PROPERTY:** *Alonzo Mourning (right) has been a star for the Miami Heat.*

(*Top*) **L.A. STORY:** *Kobe Bryant is one of the Los Angeles Lakers' young stars.*

(*Middle*) **LARRY THE LEGEND:** *Larry Bird enjoyed success as a player and as a coach.*

(*Bottom*) **GOLDEN NUGGET:** *Denver's Antonio McDyess helped the U.S. team win the gold medal at the 2000 Olympic Games.*

INTRODUCTION

The NBA has lost Bill Russell, Wilt Chamberlain, Larry Bird, Magic Johnson and Michael Jordan, but the league endures.

A funny thing happened when Michael Jordan retired from the National Basketball Association on January 13, 1999.

Nothing. The game endured. The San Antonio Spurs replaced Jordan's Chicago Bulls as NBA champions, Vince Carter emerged as the league's next great highwire act, and Allen Iverson scored as frequently from the Philadelphia's 76ers' backcourt as Jordan scored from Chicago's for all 13 of his brilliant seasons.

It has been that way throughout the game's history. When one legend departs, another arrives.

Among NBA legends there were Russell and Chamberlain, a duo that gave way to the holy trinity of Magic, Bird and Jordan. These days there is the cosmic brilliance of Carter, Iverson and Kobe Bryant.

It has been that way at all levels. From the UCLA dynasty under John Wooden evolved Duke's annual march to the Final Four under Mike Krzyzewski. From female pioneers such as Cheryl Miller and Nancy Lieberman have emerged women's stars of today such as Lisa Leslie, Cynthia Cooper and Chamique Holdsclaw.

Basketball, on any level, is more than a game. It is a continuum. It is one legend setting the bar and another legend coming around to raise it.

It is why the college game has been able to endure through gambling scandals, the pro game through early disinterest, the women's game through initial skepticism, and the Olympic game through the injustice of 1972 in Munich.

The greatest event in basketball? You can argue college basketball's Final Four, the NBA's championship series, the Dream Team at the Olympics, and, to some mothers and daughters, the hope delivered by the WNBA season.

The Complete Encyclopedia of Basketball explores the entire passion that is basketball, the game Dr. James Naismith invented, John Wooden taught and Michael Jordan well may have perfected. It goes to the roots of the college, professional and women's games. It explores the Olympics, international game and the Hall of Fame.

Quite simply, it delves into what has become a passion for so many, from those who pack Pauley Pavilion for UCLA games to those who shed tears when Boston Garden and Chicago Stadium were razed.

It evokes debate about who stands as the greatest players in the game, about why some could dare to consider Dennis Rodman a legend, while others had no patience for one of the most colorful personalities in the sport.

It explores coaching genius not only on the professional level, but also on the collegiate level and in the women's game. In this tome, these coaching legends are lined up on consecutive pages, but think of the privilege it would be to be a part of a meeting of the minds of John Wooden, Pat Riley, Red Auerbach, Dean Smith and Pat Summitt.

If you listened carefully it probably would become clear why the game's pioneers were willing to endure such primitive conditions in the sport's early days, why women accepted male chauvinism for so many years, why college players would travel for days by train for the opportunity to play at Madison Square Garden, why the first professionals accepted playing in dance halls and armories.

The sport, you see, always has been about more than individual stars. It has been about a never-ending search for a better way to get a big ball through a small basket. It has endured through wars, segregation, point shaving and the crass intrusion of television and big-money marketing.

For in the end, there remain champions, tears, joy.

There are Red Auerbach victory cigars, Dream Team perfection and Final Four euphoria.

Michael Jordan plays no more. He watches, like the rest of us, from the stands. He is a businessman now, one charged with running the operations of the NBA's Washington Wizards as team president. Like the rest of us, he second-guesses the greats, debates the sideline strategy of the league's shrewdest minds, and scours the college game in hopes of unearthing the next great talent.

And still the game endures. MJ is gone, but there always has been more than enough in the basketball alphabet to keep the game moving forward. From peach baskets, basketball has harvested a following rivaled worldwide by few other games.

It is the simplest of sports—a ball, a basket and a single individual are it takes to get started. Yet the complexities can be maddening. In the following pages, we list the greatest players, coaches and moments from the pro, college, women's, international and Olympic games. We have tried to meet our goal to be "complete." But we realize the difficulty of that task.

It is a big basketball world out there, a universe of thrills and drama that constantly is expanding.

Michael Jordan left. The basketball world did not spin out of orbit. Only now can we realize how resilient, how remarkable and how relentlessly evolving this game can be.

Ira Winderman
Fort Lauderdale, Fla.

(Opposite) HIS AIRNESS: *Chicago's Michael Jordan took the league to new heights.*

FOREWORD BY
Dr. JACK RAMSAY

The Complete Encyclopedia of Basketball is a wonderful, beautifully illustrated source of total information about the sport. It is an updated and expanded version of The Ultimate Encyclopedia of Basketball, itself an excellent reference, but one that was limited mostly to the history of the National Basketball Association and its teams, players and coaches. However, this new edition, although using The Ultimate Encyclopedia as a foundation, examines all facets of the game—not only its professional aspects.

The Complete Encyclopedia has enlarged on the description of the NBA – updating information, statistics, photographs and anecdotes about players, teams, playoff competition, and newly constructed arenas. It adds to the list of legendary players and other great performers in the game, then reaches out to detail the history and growth of men's college basketball; the history of Olympic competition in the sport; the development of the game on an international scale; and the development of women's basketball competition leading to the formation of the Women's National Basketball Association. It is the most thorough work on the game that I've ever read.

Twenty-five players are in the "Legends of the Game" section. They include 12 who played in the early years of the NBA (George Mikan, Bob Pettit, Elgin Baylor, Bill Russell, Bob Cousy, Wilt Chamberlain, Oscar Robertson, Jerry West, Walt Frazier, Elvin Hayes, John Havlicek and Rick Barry); eight who played more recently, but who are now retired form the game (Charles Barkley, Larry Bird, Julius Erving, Kareem Abdul-Jabbar, Moses Malone, Magic Johnson, Dennis Rodman and Michael Jordan); and five who are still playing (Patrick Ewing, Karl Malone, Hakeem Olajuwon, Shaquille O'Neal and John Stockton).

THE DOCTOR IS IN: *Dr. Jack Ramsay possesses a wealth of basketball information.*

It is extremely difficult to make these kinds of selections—not so much in choosing players, but in limiting the number to 25. Many great players are overlooked. Those chosen are all great players and worthy of legendary status—although Rodman's presence might come as a surprise to some. But each of these players had special skills that took him to the elite level, and Rodman is regarded as the game's greatest rebounder for his size (6–8) and an excellent team player—despite his often zany behavior on and off the court. This part of the book describes the contributions of each of these players, augments those details with pertinent quotes and excellent

photographs—which fit perfectly with the player and his role with his team.

The section on "Great Coaches" adds college legends (Hank Iba, Adolph Rupp, Dean Smith, John Wooden and women's coach Pat Summitt) to a list of the Top Ten NBA coaches; namely Red Auerbach, Billy Cunningham, Chuck Daly, Red Holzman, Phil Jackson, John Kundla, Don Nelson, Pat Riley, Lenny Wilkens, and yours truly. Highlights from the careers of all of the coaches are presented, and the information on active coaches is updated.

There are fascinating insights into the coaching mystique of Auerbach; the different, but highly successful approach by Jackson; the ferocity and depth of

Riley's determination; and the calm demeanor of Wilkens, the NBA's all-time leader in team wins.

Readers will also become aware of the impact on the game of the college coaches, although none had professional experience. The four men's coaches are held in such high regard that their principles on how the game should be played are accepted at all levels. Their styles of play, methods of conducting practice, and strategies of the game have been emulated by coaches all over the world, including those of the NBA. There are still college, international and NBA teams that utilize Iba's defensive concepts, Rupp's and Wooden's basic half-court offenses, and Smith's "four-corners" ball control tactics at the end of a game. Pat Summitt has put her indelible stamp on the women's game that will remain as long as women play the sport. Vivid descriptions of the personal make-up of each of these coaches are provided that make it easy to understand why they achieved such success.

There are descriptions of over 250 players—past and present—in "The Great Players", and all information on current players has been updated through the 2000 season. It's nice to see that players from the early years are not overlooked. Joe Lapchick, one of game's first versatile big men while playing for the Original Celtics in the 1920s, is represented; as is Tom Gola, who played a similar game three decades later on teams that won NIT and NCAA championships at La Salle University, and an NBA title at Philadelphia. Other outstanding old-timers include: a group of great playmaking guards—Bob Davies, Larry Costello, Andy Phillip, Al Cervi and Slater Martin; prolific rebounders Bill Bridges and Cliff Hagan; and high-scoring forwards Joe Fulks, Bernard King and George Yardley. Identifying these players and culling the information on them represents a marvelous piece of research.

Some of the more remote, but truly great players of the more recent period are also singled out for recognition in this section. Little guys like Spud Webb, Michael Adams, Muggsy Bogues and Calvin Murphy – all well under 6-feet tall

and possessing huge competitive hearts, are saluted for their accomplishments in a big man's game.

Again, some might question the selection of a few of these players – in particular current players Gheorghe Muresan, Shawn Bradley and Bryant Reeves – to whom the term "great" might apply more to their physical size than to their performances on the court. But overall, the players included are well-deserving and the information provided on each of them is presented in an interesting manner.

The Hall of Fame section contains descriptions of all members – players and coaches, men and women, professional and amateur, national and international – not just those with NBA affiliations. This affords basketball fans the opportunity to read about players whose impact on the game was strong when it was just getting organized ... men like Dutch Dehnert, Bennie Borgmann, Nat Holman and Barney Sedran; to meet international star players Kresimir Cosic, Sergei Belov and Uljana Semenova, a 7-foot Latvian woman; as well as Afro-Americans who reached the Hall of Fame without NBA affiliations: Tarzan Cooper, Pop Gates

and Marques Haynes; and women stars Nancy Lieberman, Cheryl Miller, Carol Blazejowski, Lusia Harris and Ann Meyers. This is a splendid segment of the book that is certain to retain the attention of the most avid basketball follower.

"College Basketball" details the history of basketball at the intercollegiate level and contains a description of playoff competition that started with the first National Invitation Tournament in 1938 (won by Temple) and the first National Collegiate Athletic Association tournament the following year (won by Oregon). Readers might be surprised to learn that the two tournament winners played a championship game in Madison Square Garden for a few years until the NCAA put restrictions on its members to assure their participation in its own post-season tournament. This move, which required conference champions to participate in the NCAA tourney, had long-range effects. It reduced the NIT to secondary status, led to the development of regional playoffs, and ultimately to the Final Four format in 1952. The NCAA Final Four has since become collegiate athletics' major annual event.

This fascinating section also delves into the gambling scandals that rocked college basketball in the early 1950s and takes interesting looks at the racism that was once prevalent in college sports and the problems that accompanied efforts toward racial integration in the 1960s. It follows UCLA on its amazing 88-game winning streak; tells the story of each NCAA Finals game from 1990 through the 2000 season; and contains interesting details about "small college" competition as well. This work required painstaking research, and it is splendidly presented to make those efforts well worth the while.

"The Arenas" section describes the growth of the pro game from hotel ballrooms, armories, and high school gyms to the construction of the mammoth, new venues of the NBA – and the decision-making process that accompanied several of them as well. The reader gets a personalized tour of the

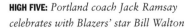

HIGH FIVE: *Portland coach Jack Ramsay celebrates with Blazers' star Bill Walton*

great new buildings—the playing courts, locker rooms, lounges, restaurants, and parking facilities. Of special interest is the description of Indiana's Conseco Fieldhouse, a fabulous basketball facility in downtown Indianapolis, which retained the characteristics of the traditional elements of a basketball gymnasium, so typical throughout the State of Indiana. Conseco even contains a bleacher section in the upper end zone as a reminder of days past.

"The Rules of Basketball" starts with Dr. James Naismith's basic 13 rules and follows the changes in both the amateur and professional games. Considerable attention is given to the efforts of the NBA to provide its fans with a game that is attractive to watch and one that allows its players to perform at their highest levels. The NBA has made many changes to assure that this happens. Among them are the banning of the zone defense;

widening the free throw lane; division of the game into four 12-minute periods; introducing the 24-second clock and 3-point shot; limiting the time of possession in the back-court and in the free throw lane for both the offense and defense; increasing the number of personal fouls allowed per player in a game, but limiting the number per team in a period; as well as the time of possession for a post player with his back to the basket. These adjustments have helped to bring NBA popularity to an all-time high.

There's also attention given to NBA individual and team record performances, and an interesting chronology of significant events in professional basketball.

There are marvelous morsels of basketball information sprinkled liberally throughout this opus. One such item is that Wilt Chamberlain, known primarily as an unstoppable scoring force (he once averaged 50.4 points a game for an NBA

season and scored 100 points in a single game—both in 1962) sat out only 8 minutes of play in that entire season! (I have since discovered through a conversation with Philadelphia's Harvey Pollock—a living legend among pro basketball statisticians—that Wilt only missed those minutes because he was ejected from a game for protesting a call by the official, Norm Drucker. Without that incident, Wilt would have played every minute of every game the Philadelphia Warriors played in the 1962 season!)

Another is that the first Olympic basketball competition in Berlin, Germany in 1936, was played out of doors on a makeshift, sand and clay tennis surface, that the rules initially limited competitors to a height of 6-feet, 2-inches; that squads were limited to 7 players; that the championship game was played in a driving rainstorm, in which the

United States defeated Canada, 19–8!

There are also heart-warming details about the fund-raising efforts of Dikembe Mutombo, who raised $750 million to help fund the building of a hospital in his hometown in Zaire (Congo), his native land; the long road traveled by international players to reach the NBA, the ultimate level of the game; and the efforts to promote women's professional basketball that led to the formation of the WNBA.

Other tidbits relate that City College of New York (CCNY) won both the NIT and NCAA tournaments in the same year (1950) under the direction of former playing great, Nat Holman—only to lose the glory of those accomplishments when many of its players became implicated in the gambling scandal of the time.

And that Utah also won both tournaments—the NCAA in 1944, with a lineup of youngsters who averaged just more than 18 years of age; and the NIT in

'47 with essentially the same players, who had returned to college after completing their military service commitments during the Second World War.

This is simply a marvelous book on basketball. It will satisfy any fan's hunger for information about the game at every level but the scholastic, while allowing intimate glimpses into teams, players and coaches. Ron Smith did a formidable job laying the groundwork for this work with *The Ultimate Encyclopedia of Basketball*.

Ira Winderman, who writes about NBA basketball for *the Fort Lauderdale Sun Times*, has done a masterful job in researching and writing the new segments of *The Complete Encyclopedia of Basketball*. Winderman displays a sharp sense of awareness of the history and developments of the NBA game, and offers interesting insights on its players and coaches. He gives proper attention to the college game and its coaches, to

basketball as an Olympic sport, and provides pertinent details about the growth of the WNBA.

Mary Schmitt Boyer, an NBA journalist like Winderman, who chronicles the events of the Cleveland Cavaliers for the *Cleveland Plain Dealer*, also did outstanding work in rewriting and updating facts and general information on existing NBA players, teams and arenas and added the international information.

This book is exactly what it purports to be: a complete encyclopedia of the game of basketball.

Jack Ramsay

Jack Ramsay
Naples, Fla.

WINGING IT: *Sacramento's Jason Williams shows off the flashy passing that fans love.*

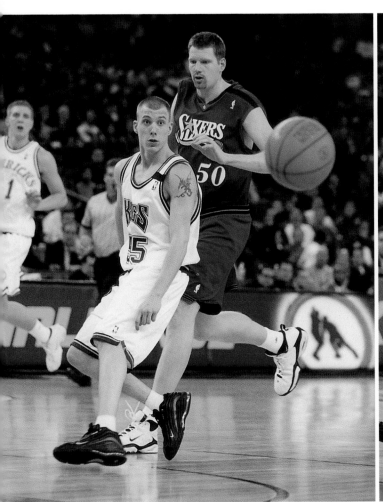

THE HISTORY OF THE NBA

Nobody knows who made the first shot in basketball history, but it happened on a December day in 1891. One of 18 students who were trying out a new game invented by their Canadian-born professor claimed the honor by throwing a soccer ball into one of two peach baskets hanging from a gymnasium balcony railing at the Young Men's Christian Association Training School in Springfield, Mass.

Shooting for the stars

For Dr. James Naismith, "basket ball" was a simple matter of expediency. Forced to deal with testy students who were bored with the winter physical education routines of calisthenics and gymnastics, he decided to invent an indoor game that would give them a competitive outlet. Naismith, a future Presbyterian minister who played on the school's football team for legendary coach Amos Alonzo Stagg, envisioned a contest that would promote the subtler sporting arts of finesse, agility and teamwork over brute strength and power.

But when he nailed his two peach baskets to a 10-foot-high railing at opposite ends of the gym, assigned ball retrievers to stand on ladders near the baskets and divided his gym class into two nine-man squads, little did he suspect the almost instantaneous craze he would touch off in a sports-hungry society.

The basic elements of Naismith's game were not all that different from those that govern the basketball played today. But the early rules dictated a slow, plodding, almost stationary game that mirrored the rural, take-life-as-it-comes society it would entertain in the early stages of its existence. As society evolved, so did basketball—into the fast, high-tech, above-the-rim sport that has captured worldwide affection more than a century later.

Less than a month after "basket ball's" humble introduction, Naismith's rules were printed in the school newspaper and on February 12, 1892, two branches of the Springfield YMCA met for the first organized game—a 2–2 tie that was witnessed by a crowd of about 100. Naismith, sensing the enormity of his invention, began staging exhibitions

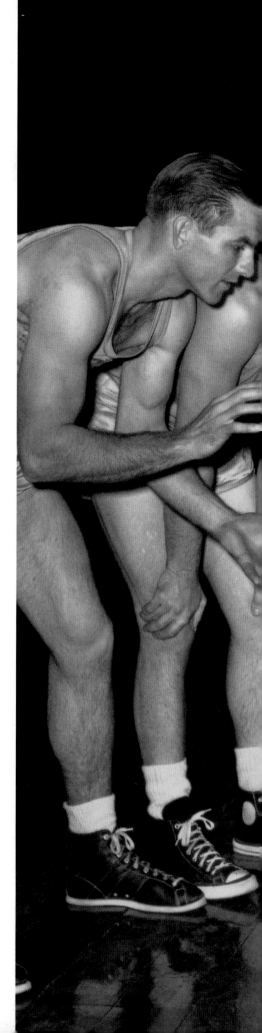

SIMPLY THE BEST: *The Minneapolis Lakers were the league's first dynasty.*

PICTURE PERFECT: *A sketch shows how the first game of "basket ball" was played.*

and word of the new game spread like wildfire. By 1893, "basket ball" had become so popular that the Hartford, Conn., YMCA organized a five-team league that drew more than 10,000 spectators over one winter.

Almost overnight, the game spread its roots into high schools and colleges, where enamored students clamored for "basket ball" almost to the exclusion of all other sports and activities. Amateur teams and leagues began forming and regional rivalries developed. The game even transcended gender barriers, giving girls an outlet they could not enjoy through the all-male team sports of football and baseball.

The Professionals

Necessity was the mother of professional basketball. As more and more amateur teams began competing for time and space at the local YMCAs throughout the Northeast, other sports and activities were being shortchanged. Complaints from long-time members forced YMCA officials to limit playing time.

On one such occasion in 1896, a team from Trenton, N.J., looked for an alternative rather than cancel its scheduled game. The solution was simple. The club rented the local armory, tacked up baskets and charged admission to

cover expenses. The game attracted enough spectators to pay the rent and give each player a $15 bonus. The game's professional roots were in place.

Buoyed by such spectator interest, the first known professional league was formed in 1898 by teams in the Philadelphia area. The National Basketball League lasted until 1903 and spawned a series of other professional circuits that flourished briefly, mostly in the East. The early professional leagues were regional configurations and teams hired their players on a game-to-game basis and played their games in local

armories and dance halls. A typical team might have two or three local players and several imported stars. This practice allowed the era's better players to sell their services to the highest bidder and even play for two or more teams at a time. It also led to fan confusion and displaced loyalties.

The professional game of the early 1900s more closely resembled a football scrimmage than a basketball contest. Players punished each other with hard body checks and anybody who dared leave his feet while shooting could count on being undercut. Offensive maneuvers were limited to two basic shots—the layup and a two-handed set or push. And layups were limited by a defensive strategy that placed a "standing guard" in the free-throw lane.

Another professional innovation was a cage that enclosed the court, keeping the ball in play and protecting the players from rowdy fans. While the cage did speed up the game, it also cut and bruised players who bounced off its wire and steel mesh sides as often as the ball.

"The ball was always in play in those cages, and only the brave went into the corners to get it," Joe Lapchick, an early professional star and long-time college and professional coach, told The Sporting News in 1963. "The boys stayed out while the men drove in. A fellow would come out of the corner of a wire cage

TRENDSETTERS: *Basketball's "first team" in 1891. Dr. James Naismith is wearing a suit.*

A Different Kind of Basketball

They have entertained millions of fans in hundreds of countries as the "Clown Princes of Basketball." They have performed for the Pope, penetrated the Iron Curtain and served as the subject of two motion pictures. The Harlem Globetrotters have, in every sense, conquered the world.

The Globetrotters were organized in 1927 by Chicago promoter Abe Saperstein as an all-black barnstorming team. They traveled through the rural Midwest, booking games where they could and piling up victories against overmatched local teams. In order to assure return invitations, the Globetrotters began putting on a different kind of show, turning basketball clowning into an artform that would carry them to international fame.

Players like Goose Tatum, dribbling wizard Marques Haynes and Meadowlark Lemon combined comedy with first-rate basketball skills and became hot attractions—so hot that Saperstein extended the team's travels from coast to coast and eventually fulfilled his goal: spreading the basketball message all around the world.

The Globetrotters' famous warmup routine, performed to the music of "Sweet Georgia Brown," is the signature for an act that has spread that message, loud and clear, beyond even Saperstein's wildest imagination.

DOWN ON THE FARM *The Original Celtics were a barnstorming team from New York.*

striped like a zebra, after being sandwiched against the wire. All he would get out of it was a jump ball.

"Another difference in construction with the cages was the basket. With net cages, there were open hoops without backboards, which of course demanded precise shooting. With the chicken-wire setup, the basket was 6 to 10 inches from the backboard."

Many fans, denied courtside access to visiting players, would bring hairpins, nails and other sharp items to jab them through the wire. The cage remained popular in many professional cities through the 1920s.

Leagues weren't the only product of the early professional game. Barnstorming teams were put together and traveled from city to city, taking on all comers. Touring teams had the advantage of good players performing together over a long period. The Buffalo Germans, who compiled a 792–86 record from 1895 to 1929, were the best of the early barnstormers.

Moving Forward

As the nation plunged into the industrial revolution and the joys of big-city life, the recreational pursuits of Americans became more defined and their sports affections more lasting. Baseball already was the national pastime and football was gaining appeal as the physical choice of the masses, but basketball was being played throughout the country and as far away as Europe and Australia.

By 1915, the game's evolution had passed infancy. Tailored basketballs had replaced soccer balls, backboards were required and baskets with wire or metal rims and open bottoms were being used. Five-man teams were standard, free-throw lines were 15 feet from the basket, players were allowed either four or five fouls before disqualification and field goals counted two points. But other rules kept the game in a relative dark age. A debate raged over dribbling—two hands,

one hand or not at all. If allowed, should a player be permitted to shoot after dribbling? A more limiting rule required a center jump after every basket, giving teams with a tall leaper an advantage. That rule would not be changed until 1937, a decision that would open up the game and set it on course toward prosperity.

That course was nudged forward ever so subtly in 1918, when a nation emerging from the depths of World War I got its first look at a talented and colorful barnstorming team that would have an impact on basketball's future. The team, which was formed by New York promoter Jim Furey, was called the Original Celtics because the owner of the New York Celtics, a team disbanded during the war, refused to relinquish rights to the name. With a lineup featuring Pete Barry, Ernie Reich, Joe Trippe, Eddie White, Mike Smolick, Swede Grimstead, Horse Haggerty and Dutch Dehnert, the Celtics became the dominant team of the East. Such subsequent additions as the 6-foot-5 Lapchick, Nat Holman, Chris Leonard, Johnny Beckman and Davey Banks extended that dominance to regions beyond.

The Celtics operated without a coach and were unlike any team fans had ever seen. The players, who were signed to exclusive season-long contracts, were

ONE OF A KIND: *Stanford star Hank Luisetti pioneered the one-handed shot in 1937–38.*

innovative and dazzled spectators with their brilliant passing, ballhandling and shot-making. The Celtics pioneered the zone defense and the give-and-go passing play, using the center as the hub for their offense. They usually overmatched the independent teams they played.

When the American Basket-ball League opened play in 1925 as the first truly "national" professional circuit, the Celtics were conspicuously absent. That was fine with ABL organizers, who feared

the Celtics might kill spectator interest with their dominance. But when the ABL completed its first season without any sustained signs of prosperity, ABL President Joe Carr and other officials did an about-face and decided they could not survive without the Celtics.

Getting the Celtics to join, however, was another matter. A simple invitation might not be enough, so the league's executive committee banned all ABL teams from playing the Celtics in exhibitions, thus cutting off their primary source of competition. Facing the prospect of a weaker schedule and smaller crowds, the Celtics joined the ABL five games into the 1926–27 season and went on to claim consecutive titles— in dominating fashion.

With the Celtics in the fold, the ABL took major steps in the advancement of professional basketball. Exclusive player contracts were required and roster-jumping was outlawed. Standard-sized backboards were mandatory, two-handed dribbling was banned, caged courts were outlawed and other rules, which had varied from region to region and from the college game to the pros, were standardized to conform to the Amateur Athletic Union. The standardized rules, most notably the conformity of dribbling techniques, made it easier for college athletes to adjust to the professional game.

"The monkey dribble was a two-handed dribble and it could be started and stopped as often as desired," said Lapchick, referring to a rule that never gained widespread use at the college level. "The ball did not have to be passed or shot after breaking the first dribble. The monkey dribble was a possession device."

And the product of a ball not fit for extensive dribbling.

"The ball might be any old thing," Lapchick said. "It started new as a leather cover of approximately round shape, with a bladder that was laced inside. The inflation tube often protruded. The ball might be used two or three years, with occasional aid from the shoemaker when a tear or scruffed spot developed. The ball got slick, it stretched out of shape and it inevitably got larger in size, reducing the chance of a basket."

The Cleveland Rosenblums, led by

Honey Russell, captured the ABL's first championship. But the next two seasons belonged to the flashy Celtics, which rankled league officials. So when Furey was convicted of embezzlement and sent to prison after the 1927–28 season, ABL officials seized the opportunity and broke up the Celtics, dispatching their players to teams around the league.

The ABL lasted three more seasons, with the Rosenblums, bolstered by the addition of four Original Celtics, winning two more championships. But the once-ambitious circuit, which had stretched from New York to Chicago, fell on hard economic times after the great stock market crash of 1929 and disbanded in 1931, with the nation in the grips of the great Depression.

The next six years would belong to college basketball. The professional game was dominated once again by regional industrial leagues and barnstormers— gifted teams like the revived Original Celtics and all-black powerhouses like the New York Renaissance Five (the Rens) and the Harlem Globetrotters, who still perform their magic today in a less-competitive manner. It wasn't until 1937 that pro basketball returned with serious major league designs and a rules change that would help make those designs a reality.

Try, Try Again

As the professional game remained in hibernation through the Depression years, college basketball flourished. Constructive rules changes made the college game cleaner, faster and more popular and promoter Ned Irish brought the sport into the spotlight by booking doubleheaders at New York's Madison Square Garden. His innovation was a financial bonanza and triggered similar promotional ventures throughout the East and Midwest.

Fans enthusiastically embraced a more streamlined game that now included a more functional, laceless ball, uniform baskets and backboards, two referees per game and a 10-second line that forced teams into their offensive frontcourts and minimized stalling tactics. A three-second rule limited players from camping under the basket and the 1937 elimination of the center jump made the game less tedious and more competitive. Another 1937–38 innovation was the introduction of the one-handed shot by Stanford star Hank Luisetti during a game at Madison Square Garden.

"That was when fast, modern basketball began," Lapchick said, referring to Luisetti as well as the 10-second and center-jump rules. "The general concept of the game also changed. The Celtics and all other outstanding teams of the old times stressed a ball-holding game on the floor. The modern team still must control the ball, but the idea now is a sort of possession in the air, in the ability to capture rebounds, and that means height."

Former Celtics teammate and long-time City College of New York coach Nat Holman agreed. "That was the greatest thing that ever happened to basketball. Elimination of the center jump speeded up the game, made it more colorful for the spectator and helped us all."

Amazingly, when the National Basketball League began play in 1937 with 13 teams stretching from Buffalo and Pittsburgh in the East to Kankakee, Ill., and Oshkosh, Wis., in the Midwest, it failed to embrace the rules that had made the college game so popular. After arguing the merits of the center-jump rule in a league organizational meeting, it was decided to let the home team determine which way to play it. Uneven scheduling combined with non-uniform rules to make the NBL's first season difficult.

But the NBL, older and wiser, eliminated those problems before the 1938–39 season and thus pioneered a professional game that mirrored the blossoming college game. Finally operating under the same rules as the National Collegiate Athletic Association, the NBL began attracting graduating college stars familiar to fans on both a regional and national level.

With a streamlined field of eight teams and rules that encouraged faster play, the NBL began to flourish. But in 1941, just when the future began to look bright, progress was halted by the Japanese attack at Pearl Harbor, thrusting the United States into World War II. In 1942–43 and 1943–44, the NBL was operated as a four-team league and prospects did not improve until players began returning from war-time duty.

Two-handed set shot artist Bobby McDermott finished the 1944–45 season for the champion Fort Wayne Pistons with a 20.1-point scoring average and other stars were emerging. The Rochester Royals captured the 1945–46 championship with a backcourt featuring playmaker Bob Davies and Red Holzman.

Former DePaul University star George Mikan arrived in 1946, and he was the biggest force, literally, the basketball world had ever seen.

Mikan was a 6–10 giant who looked at the world through thick-rimmed glasses and cleared paths to the basket with nasty elbows. Mikan, who decided to stay in his hometown and signed with the NBL's Chicago Gears, missed the 1945–46 regular season and playoffs as he completed his college career, but he was eligible for the world professional tournament, an annual event open to all

WHAT A SPECTACLE: *Minneapolis' George Mikan (99) was the Lakers' big star.*

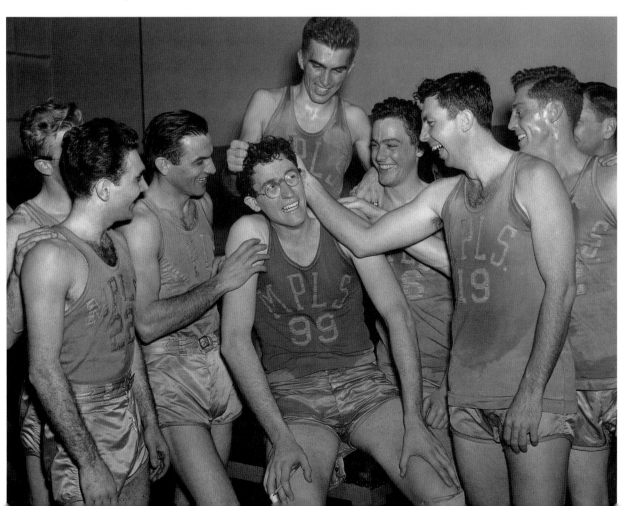

18

comers. The Gears reached the semifinals and Mikan served notice by scoring 100 points in five games, winning MVP honors.

But Mikan's presence would not be felt immediately in 1946–47. He sat out six weeks in a contract dispute before joining a team mired in fifth place. When the big man arrived, the Gears stormed to a playoff berth and powered their way to a championship with a three-games-to-one victory over Rochester.

Just when it appeared the foundation for an NBL dynasty was in place, Maurice White, owner of the American Gear Company, changed the course of pro basketball. When White tried to form his own league around Mikan, the plan failed and his team collapsed. Mikan's rights were assigned to a first-year Minneapolis team and he combined with Jim Pollard to lead the Lakers to the 1947–48 NBL title.

Early Success, by George

Despite the fortuitous arrival of Mikan in 1946, the NBL still found itself on shaky ground. As Mikan was preparing for his first professional season, a new league arrived on the block complete with deep-pocketed owners, big-city arenas and a desire to promote a slicker game fed by the more-popular college players.

The Basketball Association of America, with Maurice Podoloff as president, was formed in 1946 with 11 teams—Boston, New York, Philadelphia, Providence, Toronto and Washington in the Eastern Division; Chicago, Cleveland, Detroit, Pittsburgh and St. Louis in the West. The league clearly boasted the bigger cities and better arenas, but the NBL still had the better players—a division that became clear over the BAA's first two seasons.

The Washington Capitols, coached by young Red Auerbach, grabbed regular-season honors with a 49–11 record, but Philadelphia, coached by Eddie Gottlieb and featuring jump-shooting Joe Fulks, won the first league championship. The Baltimore Bullets, a team imported from the American Basketball League when Detroit, Toronto, Cleveland and Pittsburgh folded, won the second-year title.

But it wasn't until 1948 that the BAA was able to enhance its status. Right before the league's third season was to begin, officials made the stunning announcement that four teams—Fort Wayne, Minneapolis, Rochester and Indianapolis—were defecting from the NBL, giving the BAA a 12-team circuit and instant status as the best basketball money could buy. Four of the NBL's best teams were in the fold and, more importantly, its best player—Mikan.

Devastated by the defection, the NBL managed to piece together one more season while the Lakers were winning their first BAA championship. When the season ended, the NBL went out of business and six of its teams joined the BAA, creating a new 17-team circuit. It was renamed the National Basketball Association.

But even without serious competition, the NBA struggled. Its new 17-team format was awkward and many of the inherited teams were based in small cities. After the 1949–50 season, six dropped out and a seventh folded in January 1951, leaving a more manageable 10 teams divided into two divisions with deeper and more talented rosters.

And despite such emerging stars as Max Zaslofsky, Dolph Schayes, Pollard, Ed Macauley, Slater Martin, Neil Johnston, Bob Cousy, Bill Sharman and Paul Arizin, the games often were rugged, foul-filled, plodding yawners without much pace and little sustained excitement.

Much of the period was spent trying to beat the Lakers, who rode Mikan's broad shoulders to five championships in six seasons (1949–54), yielding only to Rochester in 1951. Mikan was the powerful centerpiece for a team that also featured forwards Pollard and Vern Mikkelsen and point guard Martin. Mikan was an offensive force who averaged 22.6 points per game over nine professional seasons, but he also was a ferocious rebounder and many other things.

"Big George reminds me of Babe Ruth," Knicks coach Lapchick said in 1953. "When the Babe was hitting home runs, everyone forgot he'd once been an exceptional pitcher. Everyone also forgets that Mikan is the best feeder from out of the pivot that the game ever had. He

V-DAY *Boston's Red Auerbach celebrates the 1965 NBA Championship.*

MR. DEFENSE: *Bill Russell (6) set a new standard for defense.*

whips in a bounce pass to cutting teammates that can't be stopped.

"He creates all kinds of situations. Cover him normally and he kills you with his scoring. Cover him abnormally, and he murders you with his passing. We've tried every known defense on him and nothing works."

Surprisingly, Mikan and the Lakers had to work for everything they won. They were challenged throughout the Mikan era by West Division-rival Rochester, which featured a talented lineup of center Arnie Risen, Holzman, Davies and Bobby Wanzer. Syracuse, with Schayes and Alex Hannum, and New York, coached by Lapchick and featuring Zaslofsky, Sweetwater Clifton and Harry Gallatin, also came close. But Rochester's 1951 title was the only chink in the Lakers' six-year dynasty.

After the 1954 championship, Mikan stunned the league by announcing his retirement—at age 30. He had almost single-handedly given a struggling new league status while drawing excited fans to the game every time he played. He also had given the Lakers franchise a special place in professional basketball history.

Oh Shoot!

The 1950s dawned with a dark cloud hanging over the basketball world. Players for Manhattan College, City College of New York, New York University, Long Island University and other schools had been implicated in point-shaving scandals that rocked the college game and opened a door of opportunity for the NBA.

But that threshold would not be crossed without a serious restructuring of a professional game that was slow, conservative and filled with fouls and stalling tactics. NBA officials tried to address the dominance of Mikan in 1951 by widening the lane from 6 feet to 12, theoretically getting him away from the basket. But the change had little effect. That wasn't the case with two 1954 rules changes that pointed the NBA on the road to prosperity.

The most radical change was proposed by Syracuse owner Danny Biasone, who wanted a clock to put a time limit on ball possession. Biasone arrived at 24 seconds by dividing the number of seconds in a 48-minute game (2,880) by the average number of shots (120). Amazingly, his arbitrary formula has withstood the test of time.

The other rule limited the number of fouls any team could commit in a quarter. Anything over six would give the free-throw shooter three shots instead of two. The effects of the rules, the 24-second shot clock in particular, were felt immediately.

In the opening game of 1954, the Royals beat Boston, 98–95, and the eight teams produced a season average of 93.1 points per game. The 1954–55 Celtics became the first team to average 100 points and the other teams soon followed. The NBA game suddenly was faster, more fluid and exciting.

"It was the most important rules change in the last 50 years," former Boston coach and current Vice Chairman of the Board Red Auerbach said.

Auerbach's affection for the clock is understandable because it also fueled one of the great dynasties in sports history. With the running game as their trademark and the great Cousy to quarterback a devastating fast break, Auerbach's Celtics would win their first championship in 1957 and set the stage for an incredible 10 titles in 11 years from 1959–69.

The Dynasty of all Dynasties

Auerbach had his Celtics running and gunning in 1955–56, but a second-place Eastern Division finish was followed by a first-round playoff loss to Syracuse—the team's sixth consecutive early playoff failure. The Celtics, featuring the explosive backcourt of Cousy and Sharman, averaged 106 points per game but they gave up 105.3.

Auerbach knew that trend would continue unless he could beef up a frontcourt that was mobile offensively, but soft defensively and on the boards. When Auerbach discussed his problem with Bill Reinhart, his former coach at George Washington University, Reinhart provided a quick, concise answer—Bill Russell.

Auerbach, who did not enjoy the luxury of today's sophisticated scouting system, was only vaguely familiar with the name. He knew Russell played for the University of San Francisco and had led the Dons to the 1955 NCAA championship, but not much else. When Reinhart described Russell as a ferocious rebounder and defender with limited offensive skills, the decision was made: Auerbach would maneuver into position to get Russell in the 1956 draft.

In a series of moves that would impact the NBA for the next decade and a half, Auerbach grabbed Holy Cross sensation Tom Heinsohn with a territorial pick leading off the draft and then traded Ed Macauley and the rights to 1953 draftee

LUCKY NO. 13: *Philadelphia's Wilt Chamberlain was a remarkable specimen.*

Cliff Hagan to the St. Louis Hawks for their third selection—Russell. When Rochester picked Sihugo Green with the No. 2 selection, Auerbach had his man.

The only hitch was that Russell had committed to playing for the 1956 U.S. Olympic team and would not be available until December. But the Celtics were not exactly shorthanded, with beefy Jim Loscutoff manning the middle in Russell's absence, Heinsohn anchoring one forward position and Frank Ramsey, who was returning from military duty, at the other.

When Russell arrived, the pieces were in place for Boston's first championship. And the 6–9 center was everything Auerbach had hoped—and more. He was ferocious on the boards, intimidating defensively and intense beyond imagination. When the scowling Russell stepped onto the court, the entire Boston team took on another personality.

Told by Auerbach to concentrate on rebounding, triggering the Celtics' running game and playing defense, Russell blossomed. So did his teammates, who were able to release quickly on the

break and cheat defensively, knowing Russell was in the middle to cover up their mistakes. And cover up he did—with an above-the-rim shot-blocking presence that ushered in a new era of defensive basketball.

Offensively, Russell's contributions were limited to tip-ins and short jump hooks. But that didn't matter to Auerbach, who watched the Celtics defeat Bob Pettit and St. Louis in the 1957 NBA Finals, lose to the Hawks in a six-game Finals the next season and then roll off an incredible eight straight championships.

Over those eight seasons, the Celtics averaged 57.6 victories and won seven division crowns. They were extended to the seven-game limit in only three final series. As good as the Celtics were in the regular season, they lifted their game in the playoffs to a different—and higher—level.

And they did it with an ever-changing cast of characters, courtesy of Auerbach's genius. Cousy arrived in 1950, Sharman in 1951, Ramsey in 1954, Russell and Heinsohn in 1956, Sam Jones in 1957, K.C. Jones in 1958, Tom Sanders in 1960, and John Havlicek and Don Nelson in 1962. From December 1956, the one constant was Russell.

"Russell is the greatest center who ever lived," said Auerbach in the midst of the title run. "The defense he plays is fantastic. He has a wonderful sense of timing. He may not be the greatest rebounder of all time, but he's the greatest in the clutch.

"No center in the history of basketball could run with this guy. George Mikan? He'd eat him up. Russell would drive Mikan crazy. Bill would take him outside, give him the shot, then block it."

When Auerbach moved full-time into the Celtics' front office after the 1966 championship, he named Russell as his successor—the first black coach in the history of the NBA. Russell, performing double duty as a player and coach, watched the record-setting Philadelphia Warriors win the 1967 title but then took the aging Celtics to consecutive titles to close out the decade. When the big man retired after the 1968–69 season, the Boston dynasty came to an unofficial end.

Brute Force

While the 1959–60 Celtics were galloping to their second consecutive championship, another force was sending shock waves through the NBA. A 7–1 giant named Wilt Chamberlain arrived on the Philadelphia scene, and he began ravaging the record books like a hurricane in a paper factory.

Chamberlain, an unstoppable offensive scorer and rebounder, tore through the league with an amazing 38.6-point rookie average. But that was just an appetizer. Chamberlain's offensive showcase was 1961–62 when he averaged a whopping 50.4 points and 25.7 rebounds while playing 3,882 minutes—of a possible 3,890. He also scored a record 100 points in a game against the Knicks.

Ironically, Chamberlain's second

Up and Over The Color Barrier

When the Basketball Association of America became the NBA before the 1949–50 season, there were no blacks listed on any of the league's rosters.

Desegregation would begin in the spring of 1950, and with the professional game's first blacks would come hope for a whole new generation of Americans.

The first black to sign a professional contract was Nat (Sweetwater) Clifton, a 6–7 forward who would play eight seasons with New York and Detroit. Clifton, a former Harlem Globetrotter, signed with the Knicks for an estimated $10,000.

But the honor of breaking pro basketball's color barrier belonged to Earl Lloyd, who signed with the Washington Capitols and scored six points in his NBA debut—a day before Clifton and Boston's Chuck Cooper took the court for the first time. The 6–5 Cooper, the first black player drafted out of college, played six NBA seasons and the 6–6 Lloyd nine.

By 1958, every NBA team had at least one black player. The last to integrate was St. Louis, which acquired Sihugo Green from Rochester in the 1958 season.

showcase season was 1966–67, when his scoring average dropped to 24.1. He was the centerpiece for a 76ers team (Billy Cunningham, Hal Greer, Chet Walker, Wali Jones) that produced a regular-season record 68 victories and ended the Celtics' championship run during an 11–4 postseason romp.

The 1960s also introduced a bevy of new stars who would light up the NBA arenas. Names such as Elgin Baylor, Dave Bing, Jerry Lucas, Oscar Robertson, Nate Thurmond, Jerry West, Willis Reed and Wes Unseld would help the league rise to a new level of popularity.

Franchise shifts and expansion also brought the NBA to new, fertile markets. The Lakers moved to Los Angeles in 1960, the Warriors shifted to San Francisco in 1962 and the Nationals relocated to Philadelphia in 1963, changing their name to 76ers. By 1970, the NBA, under Commissioner Walter Kennedy, was operating as a 17-team circuit with its first solid franchise in Chicago (the Bulls) and clubs in Seattle, Portland, Milwaukee, Atlanta, Buffalo, San Diego, Phoenix, Baltimore and Cleveland.

A Changing of the Guard

The 1969–70 season marked a transition for the NBA. When center Reed, forward Bill Bradley and guard Walt Frazier led the New York Knicks to their first championship, they officially closed Boston's decade of domination. Eight different teams would claim titles in the new decade, giving credence to the league's claim of parity.

The 1969–70 season also introduced the game's next dominating center—a skinny 7–2 gazelle who would drop his sky hooks on helpless defenders for 20 record-setting seasons and lead his teams to six NBA titles. Kareem Abdul-Jabbar claimed his first championship ring in 1971 when, as Lew Alcindor, he led the three-year-old Milwaukee Bucks to 66 regular-season victories and a 12–2 playoff romp. But his greatest success would come in the 1980s, when he combined with Magic Johnson to lead the Los Angeles Lakers to five titles in nine seasons.

That domination was presaged by the Lakers' lone title of the 1970s—pre-

BUCK SHOT: *Milwaukee's Lew Alcindor (33) shoots over the Warriors' Nate Thurmond.*

Jabbar. The center for that team was an aging Wilt Chamberlain, who helped the Lakers put together a phenomenal 33-game winning streak en route to a regular-season-record 69 victories. The Lakers needed only 15 postseason games to win their first title.

Such dramatics were played out amid a confrontational atmosphere. The NBA received its first serious challenge from a rival league when the upstart American

Basketball Association, which seemed to drop out of nowhere, began play in 1967 without much of a product or any definitive game plan. With the tumultuous 1960s forming a perfect backdrop and George Mikan serving as the league's commissioner, 11 teams began operation on shoestring budgets from coast to coast.

At first, the NBA looked at its rival with understandable scorn. But what the

GARDEN PARTY: *The Boston Celtics raise yet another NBA Championship banner.*

ABA lacked in substance, it made up for with creativity. Everybody laughed at the circuit's red-white-and-blue ball, but soon no respectable American playground was without one. The ABA also introduced the three-point shot and the slam-dunk contest, innovations that eventually would become NBA fixtures.

The ABA played nine seasons before small crowds and without a television contract. And it spent much of its existence fighting expensive courtroom battles and bidding against the NBA for top players. But before it died, the ABA made serious inroads in talent acquisition, primarily through its signing of underage college players—a tactic that incurred the wrath of the NCAA and NBA. Such players as Rick Barry, George McGinnis, George Gervin, Moses Malone, Artis Gilmore, Mel Daniels, Connie Hawkins, Spencer Haywood, Dan Issel and Julius Erving gave the league more than a passing respect.

The ABA also gave Erving, the flashy Dr. J, a forum for a theatrical playing style that eventually would influence the conservative NBA and elevate its game above the rim. Erving dazzled fans and fellow players with his spectacular dunks and aerial wizardry, the kind of showmanship the game badly needed.

When Erving was traded by financially

strapped Virginia to the New York Nets in 1973, the wheels for an eventual ABA–NBA merger were set in motion. As the New York media and fans took note of the colorful Erving, so did new NBA Commissioner Larry O'Brien. On June 17, 1976, the ABA's New York, Indiana, San Antonio and Denver franchises merged with the NBA, increasing the field to 22 teams.

Bird and the Magic Man

As the NBA approached a new decade, officials were searching for answers. Television ratings, never outstanding, were on the decline and the league's top stars were viewed with indifference by would-be fans. The image problem was compounded by the sagging fortunes of teams in the NBA's leading markets: In 1978–79, New York and Boston had finished fourth and fifth, respectively, in the Atlantic Division, Chicago last in the Midwest and Los Angeles third in the Pacific.

In an effort to brighten up its game, NBA officials resurrected an ABA gimmick they once had chastised as cosmetic: the 3-point shot. It would be an instant success, a new weapon to open up offenses and add excitement in the final minutes. But two even more deadly weapons were discovered in the annual NBA draft.

When the Celtics selected 6–9 Indiana State forward Larry Bird and the Lakers went for 6–9 Michigan State point guard Earvin (Magic) Johnson, the league began a new era of prosperity. The two college stars had met in the recent NCAA Tournament finals, Michigan State, led by Johnson, winning the highest-rated basketball telecast in history. They were stars of the first magnitude, the kind of players a league could mold a marketing plan around.

Their contrasts were as important as their talents. Bird was a blue-collar worker from the farming community of French Lick, Ind. He represented the common man, earning everything he got with a determination more impressive than his physical abilities. Johnson was a

GREEN GIANT: *Larry Bird had the skills and tenacity.*

slick-passing, fast-talking city kid who could light up a court with his ever-present smile and flashy style. If Bird was a good fit for Boston and the East Coast, then Johnson was perfect for Los Angeles and the West Coast. Every time they played, fans flocked through the turnstiles.

And they didn't disappoint. The Lakers, with Magic running the show and Abdul-Jabbar dominating the middle, won five championships in the 1980s, beating Boston in the Finals two times. Boston, with Bird joining center Robert Parish and forward Kevin McHale, countered with three championships, beating Los Angeles in the 1984 Finals.

The Bird–Johnson magic vaulted the

NBA to a new level of affection. Suddenly TV networks were interested, fans were flocking to games and more young stars were flashing their acrobatic talents. Michael Jordan arrived in 1984 to revive a sagging Chicago franchise and 7-foot Patrick Ewing arrived a year later to carry the Knicks back into the New York spotlight. They joined a growing cast of stars that gave the NBA its most attractive product in history: Hakeem Olajuwon, Isiah Thomas, Charles Barkley, Clyde Drexler, Karl Malone, Dominique Wilkins, David Robinson, John Stockton, James Worthy and many others.

And when David Stern took the reins in 1984 as the NBA's fourth commissioner, he built an ambitious marketing plan that would carry the league's message beyond American borders. By the end of the decade, NBA stars Bird, Johnson, Jordan and Barkley would rank among the most recognized athletes in the world and NBA merchandise would generate millions of dollars in previously untapped revenue. The former eight-team league would number 27 with rumors of even more expansion in the not-too-distant future.

The most fortuitous development of the mid-1980s was the arrival of Jordan, who combined an Erving-like style with an intensity and flair that won over a whole new legion of fans and attracted hungry television sponsors and promoters. Jordan quickly established himself as the dominant player in the league en route to a record-tying seven straight scoring titles, three Most Valuable Player awards and three NBA championship rings. Then, at age 30, he retired—suggesting he had no more basketball worlds to conquer.

Beyond Michael

He was wrong. Shortly after Jordan's retirement, the NBA expanded to 29 teams, with franchises in two Canadian cities, Toronto and Vancouver. By the time the Raptors and Grizzlies began play in 1995–96, Jordan was back, trading his baseball pursuits for another Bulls uniform.

Jordan was still king of the court, but he had to work hard to maintain that status. Like the fastest gun in the west, he was being tested every day by a whole new generation of skywalkers. Shaquille

MAKING MAGIC: *The Lakers' Magic Johnson ran Los Angeles' "showtime" style of play.*

O'Neal was the new center of attention, physically and commercially. And attractions such as Chris Webber, Shawn Kemp, Alonzo Mourning, Reggie Miller, Kenny Anderson, Grant Hill, Jamal Mashburn and Anfernee Hardaway were not far behind.

But while dozens of stars could

perform Jordan-like exploits on the court, nobody could match his dominance as a winner. In 1995–96, the Bulls' 72–10 regular-season mark broke the Los Angeles Lakers' 24-year record of 69 wins en route to an NBA Finals victory over Seattle. A year later, Chicago ended 69–13, Jordan won a ninth scoring crown, and the Bulls made it five NBA titles in seven years.

Jordan was no less impressive a season later—a season in which he turned 35. Another scoring title, another MVP award, another championship ring and another Finals MVP as the excellent but aging Karl Malone and John Stockton looked doomed to be remembered as two of the greatest stars never to win an NBA title.

Professional basketball's popularity continues to zoom toward the top of the charts. And as the game heads for a new century and incredible financial success, many predict a future as the No. 1 sport of America—if not the world. Nothing it seems is out of reach for those who can fly.

The lockout

That is not to say there weren't problems. The storm clouds had been forming for a couple of years. There was a lot of rhetoric on both sides, and it grew increasingly antagonistic as time went on.

But it still came as something as a surprise when the NBA owners locked out players and missed the start of the 1998–99 season. After all, this was a league that always prided itself on its labor relations, that had always been ahead of the game when it came to business dealings. This was a league that had seen the effects of strikes in baseball, football and hockey, had witnessed the fallout from the work stoppages and saw how long it took for the fans to forgive and forget.

Surely, the NBA was not going to go down the same road, was it?

Even when the owners locked the players out over the summer and into training camp, no one thought they'd actually let things go on so long that

DOUBLE TROUBLE: *The Lakers were the team of the 1980s with five titles in nine years.*

23/45: *The only change fans noticed when Michael Jordan returned in 1995 was a new number.*

was a lot of pressure from both parties. Both parties decided we had to do something to save the season."

The players agreed to set limits for the amount of money a player could make in a season, while the owners increased the amount of basketball-related income shared with the players. Even after agreeing in principle, it still took about two weeks for all the details to be worked out. By the time the two sides signed the final documents, the lockout had stretched 204 days and cost 928 games and untold millions of dollars, including at least $500 million in lost salaries.

Then came the hard part.

"We know we have some winning back of fans to do, and we're going to do it," Stern said. "We're glad to be back, and we'll do whatever we have to do to demonstrate that."

Some of the players were more direct.

"We've got to clean up the garbage we've dumped at fans feet the last six months," Mutombo said.

"We've got to get out and apologize to the parking lot attendant and the guy who sells nachos," added New Jersey's Jayson Williams. "We've got to say, 'We're sorry,' and mean it sincerely. The fans did nothing to deserve this."

The problem of winning the fans back would prove to be a tricky one. Polls taken during the lockout indicated

games were in jeopardy. And even if the owners stood firm, wouldn't the players cave in eventually?

In fact, the owners locked the players out for more than the first two months of the season, and the players were presenting a united front. It was the first time in the league's 52-year history that games were lost because of a work shortage, and it appeared the NBA would become the first league to lose an entire season because of labor woes.

Then, 29 hours from the deadline NBA commissioner David Stern had set to cancel the season, there was a breakthrough. Billy Hunter, the executive director of the NBA Players Association, phoned Stern and the two met in Stern's Fifth Avenue office. They stayed up all night, finally reaching a tentative deal about 6 a.m. on January 6.

"We sat down and all of a sudden we started talking like never before, " Hunter said. "It was just time. I don't know what

happened. It was probably something intangible. But for whatever reason, there was a deal in the air."

Word of the agreement spread like wildfire through the ranks of the players who had gathered in New York to vote on whether to support the union negotiating committee's recommendation to reject the owner's final proposal. Similarly, the owners were gathering for their regularly scheduled Board of Governors meeting, at which time Stern was prepared to recommend cancelling the season.

But instead of parting ways, the two sides agreed to continue working together.

"We were at a very critical period of time," said Atlanta Hawks center Dikembe Mutombo, a member of the union's negotiating committee. "There

LOCKOUT ENDS: *Billy Hunter, ex-Director of the NBA Players Association, speaks out.*

tremendous apathy on the part of basketball fans in particular and the public in general. In order to try and counter that, the teams invited fans to a free open scrimmage during training camp and a free exhibition game as well. In addition, owners were asked to make some $10 seats available for every game.

Checks of the crowds at the free events often found fans and families who considered themselves NBA fans but couldn't afford tickets to exhibition or regular-season games. Despite their attendance, there was still a healthy dose of skepticism, which continued into the season.

Not that it wasn't warranted. With shortened training camps, the beginning of the season was filled with errors as players worked themselves—and their games—back into shape. By the time the San Antonio Spurs beat the New York Knicks to claim their first NBA championship, it seemed things were just about back to normal—but it did not appear interest in the league was as intense as it was before the lockout. Whether that was because of the labor situation or the subsequent retirement of Michael Jordan is not clear. But as the league entered the 21st century, some things had changed. Television ratings had declined. Empty seats became more prevalent around the league—even in places where sellouts had been assured—like Salt Lake City and Sacramento.

It also will be interesting to watch the long-term effects of the new collective bargaining agreement. It's possible that with the increasingly complex salary rules, players will stay in one place longer than they have been. At least that was the view of Danny Ferry, the Cleveland Cavaliers player representative whose first 10 seasons were spent in Cleveland.

Even more profound changes could result in the 2001-02 season, when an escrow system goes into effect. If total salaries and benefits exceed 55 percent of basketball-related income, individual player salaries could be reduced by up to 10 percent to bring the salaries and benefits back to 55 percent of basketball-related income. If that is still not enough, teams will pay a dollar for dollar tax for any amount above that level.

This is a concentrated effort by the

owners to keep expenses in check, but it could be a rude awakening not only for players but for owners who will pay for past indulgences. Only then will both sides be able to judge whether the lockout was worthwhile and whether the new collective bargaining agreement was a good one. At the time, though, everyone seemed happy.

"I'm just glad they came to their senses," Miami guard Dan Majerle said. "Both sides gave up a little. In the long

SLAM JAM: *The Lakers' Shaquille O'Neal emphatically makes his point.*

run, the fans get basketball back and we get to go play. So everybody wins."

Clothes H-O-R-S-E

Stars have come and gone, and styles of play have changed over the years. So, too, have the uniforms.

The main differences are in the materials used and in the length of the shorts, according to Chris Tripucka of Champion, which has manufactured athletic uniforms since the 1920s.

"Uniforms have gone from silk materials made in the 1940s and 1950s to the nylon stretch mesh of today," Tripucka

told the *Cleveland Plain Dealer*. "Today's materials are lighter and less absorbent than they were years ago."

Gary Briggs, former trainer for the Cleveland Cavaliers, remembered how long it took for the old uniforms to dry—and how tough it was to get out the odor.

"When I first came (to Cleveland in 1982) the uniforms were 100 percent nylon," Briggs told the Plain Dealer. "When they got wet, they stayed wet. We'd put them in the dryers at halftime and still could not get them dry. The material in those uniforms of the early 1980s locked odors in. Today, if I were to get a Bobby Wilkerson uniform from 1982, I'd bet that the smell of cologne would still be in it."

Briggs had to laugh when he thought about some of those smelly old uniforms—and the short shorts that were part of them. Looking back, some of the shorts worn in the early days were almost obscene by today's standards.

"I don't know how they played in shorts that were as tight as those were," Briggs said.

Michael Jordan may not have created the fuller shorts, but he did want his NBA shorts baggy enough so he could wear the shorts from his North Carolina college uniform underneath. Jordan, who was going prematurely bald, also was one of the first NBA players to shave his head, setting off another trend. That did start to reverse itself after his retirement, when players began to let their hair grow back, often wearing braids or cornrows or the afros made popular in the 1970s.

Jordan also helped revolutionize the shoes worn by athletes. The first players wore canvas hightops with very little support. With increased support came leather and suede uppers. Now, of course, there are dozens of different high-tech models made from a variety of synthetic and natural materials, and every player who is anybody has a shoe contract.

Among the other most popular fashion accessories in the league these days are tattoos popularized by Dennis Rodman and headbands popularized by Cliff Robinson.

(Opposite) FASHION PLATE: *Allen Iverson's tattoos and cornrows are part of his style.*

BASKETBALL ASSOCIATION OF AMERICA
The long, long road to stability

In the beginning there were Celtics, Knickerbockers and Warriors. But there also were Stags, Falcons, Huskies and Capitols. We can only surmise that fans of power basketball probably enjoyed watching the Ironmen and the Steamrollers. And that proponents of outside shooting might have supported the Bombers. Non-conformist fans most likely identified with the Rebels.

The 1946–47 Basketball Association of America was a colorful collection of professional wannabes, if not a bastion of franchise stability. But it also was the humble beginning for the National Basketball Association, a league that eventually would soar to great heights and prosperity.

The BAA was content to crawl in 1946–47 when it opened play with 11 teams, survived a shaky first season and then watched four franchises drop by the wayside. Four more of the original 11 would be gone by the end of the fifth season

NATIONAL OBSESSION: *Syracuse joined the BAA in 1950–51.*

with only New York (Knickerbockers), Boston (Celtics) and Philadelphia (Warriors) able to bridge the long-term gap from the BAA to the NBA.

From the moment the Basketball Association of America was conceived, it stood a level above the 9-year-old National Basketball League in scope and viability. The NBL, which was born under the flag of corporate sponsorship, had been operating since the 1937–38 season in the Midwest obscurity of small cities and dingy, makeshift arenas. The BAA had much bigger dreams and the means to make them come true.

All 11 of the original BAA franchise owners were members of the Arena Managers Association of America, an organization that controlled dates for the major arenas in the nation's biggest cities. All 11 owned an arena, were tied closely to hockey and were looking for events to provide extra revenue.

With 5-foot-2 Maurice Podoloff serving as its first president, the BAA opened with franchises in Boston, New York, Philadelphia, Chicago (Stags), Cleveland (Rebels), Detroit (Falcons), Pittsburgh (Ironmen), Providence (Steamrollers), St. Louis (Bombers) and Washington (Capitols). The 11th team took the BAA above and beyond national boundaries—the Toronto Huskies.

The Huskies, the Rebels, the Ironmen and the Falcons folded after one season, forcing Podoloff to scramble for reinforcements. Podoloff talked the Baltimore Bullets into making the jump from the American Basketball League, a minor East Coast circuit, giving the BAA a manageable eight-team configuration. Such was the talent level of the early BAA that the Bullets captured the league's second-year championship.

Such growing pains would be eased with one quick maneuver that fortified the BAA's status and sent the NBL tumbling toward oblivion before the 1948–49 season. Podoloff talked four NBL franchises—the Fort Wayne Pistons, Rochester Royals, Minneapolis Lakers and Indianapolis Jets—into jumping leagues, bringing with them such talent as Bob Davies, Arnie Risen, Jim Pollard and, most important, the greatest basketball drawing card in the nation—6–10 giant George Mikan.

Indianapolis and Providence folded after the 1948–49 season, but the 1949 BAA/NBL merger into the NBA briefly expanded the league's roster to 17 members located in large and small cities from the East Coast as far west as Denver (the Nuggets). It took only one season to pare the field back to 11 with the loss of the Nuggets, the Anderson Packers, the Sheboygan Redskins and the Waterloo Hawks as well as two BAA originals—the St. Louis Bombers and Chicago Stags.

When the 1950–51 season opened, the ever-changing cast included BAA originals Boston, New York, Philadelphia and Washington; the former ABL Bullets; Minneapolis, Fort Wayne and Rochester, three of the four teams that made the 1948 NBL jump; the Syracuse Nationals and Tri-Cities Blackhawks, two NBL refugees; and the Indianapolis Olympians, a 1949–50 newcomer composed mostly of former University of Kentucky and 1948 Olympics stars.

The configuration would change again in January of '51 when the Capitols folded in midseason. And Tri-Cities made history after the season when it performed the NBA's first franchise shift—from Moline, Ill., to the more populous Milwaukee market—and also shortened its nickname, from Blackhawks to Hawks.

When the Olympians ceased operations after the 1952–53 season and the Bullets followed suit after 1953–54, the NBA's franchise-juggling act came to a merciful end. Never again would a franchise go out of business because of financial or other difficulties. But the mid-1950s NBA was still many miles from stability—the miles its teams would log moving from one city to another.

When the NBA opened play as an eight-team circuit in 1954–55, only three cities could claim uninterrupted tenure from the BAA's first season and Philadelphia would soon lose that distinction. In the ensuing years, the alignment that now included Boston, Fort Wayne, Milwaukee, Minneapolis, Rochester, New York, Philadelphia and Syracuse would shift dramatically, in city identity if not in substance.

The Hawks started the relocation ball rolling by shifting to St. Louis after the 1954–55 campaign and other moves followed quickly: Rochester to Cincinnati and Fort Wayne to Detroit after 1956–57; Minneapolis to Los Angeles after 1959–60; Philadelphia to San Francisco after 1961–62; and Syracuse to Philadelphia (as the 76ers) after 1962–63. Even the NBA's 1961 expansion to Chicago was short-circuited by the never-ending search for greener pastures. The Chicago Packers/Zephyrs packed their bags after two seasons and moved to Baltimore as the reincarnated Bullets.

The relocation bug continued to bite the league for two more decades (St. Louis to Atlanta, Cincinnati to Kansas City to Sacramento, San Francisco to Oakland—as Golden State—etc.), but another growth trend was more positive. When the Chicago Bulls were admitted to the league in 1966, the NBA stood at 10 teams and the time was right to expand its horizons. The San Diego Rockets (who moved to Houston after the 1970–71 season) and Seattle SuperSonics began play in 1967–68 and two more teams—the Phoenix Suns and Milwaukee Bucks—joined the circuit a year later. The

1970–71 arrival of the Portland Trail Blazers, the Cleveland Cavaliers and the Buffalo Braves (the future San Diego/Los Angeles Clippers) brought the league population to seventeen.

The 1974–75 addition of the New Orleans Jazz preceded by two years the arrival of four ABA teams—San Antonio, New York, Indiana and Denver. Dallas was admitted in 1980–81, setting the stage for the next wave of expansion to Charlotte and Miami (in 1988–89) and Minnesota and Orlando (1989–90). The Canadian markets of Vancouver and Toronto were added in 1995–96.

JIM DANDY: *Jim Pollard was one the league's first big stars.*

WHATEVER HAPPENED TO…?

Forty-four teams have called the NBA home. Some, like the Anderson (Indiana) Packers and Cleveland Rebels, lasted one season. Others, like the Boston Celtics and New York Knicks, have been along for the whole ride. Then there are teams like the Hawks, who started out as the Tri-Cities Blackhawks in 1949–50, moved to Milwaukee from the 1951–52 season through the 1954–55 season, relocated in St. Louis through the 1967–68 season and then settled into Atlanta for the 1968–69 season.

Here's a brief look at the history of the NBA franchises, including those that started in the Basketball Association of America, the forerunner of the NBA.

The following teams lasted only one season: The Anderson (Indiana) Packers, 1949–50; Cleveland Rebels, 1946–47; original Denver Nuggets, 1949–50; Detroit Falcons, 1946–47; Indianapolis Jets, 1948–49; Pittsburgh Ironmen, 1946–47; Sheboygan (Wisconsin) Redskins, 1949–50; Toronto Huskies, 1946–47, and Waterloo (Iowa) Hawks, 1949–50.

Several more teams survived a few years longer. The original Baltimore Bullets played from 1947–48 until disbanding on November 27, 1954. The Chicago Stags lasted from 1946–47 until 1949–50. The Indianapolis Olympians made it from 1949–50 until 1952–53. The Providence Steamrollers played from 1946–47 to 1948–49. The Bombers called St. Louis home from 1946–47 until 1949–50, while the Washington Capitols lasted from 1946–47 through January 9, 1951.

While the Celtics and the Knicks are the only two teams to have remained in the same city and the same league for the entire duration, several teams aren't far behind in terms of length of time in the NBA. The Warriors, for instance, started in Philadelphia in the 1946–47 season through the 1961–62 season, played in San Francisco from 1962–63 through 1970–71 and then became the Golden State Warriors in the 1971–72 season.

The Pistons played in Fort Wayne, Indiana, from the 1948–49 season through the 1956–57 season and then moved to Detroit for the 1957–58 season.

The Lakers were more aptly named when they played in Minneapolis (Minnesota is known as The Land of 10,000 Lakes) from 1948–49 until moving to Los Angeles for the 1960–61 season.

Similarly, the Jazz nickname better suited the New Orleans basketball team from its expansion debut in 1974–75 until moving to Salt Lake City, Utah, for the 1979–80 season.

Among the more well-travelled clubs are the Washington Wizards, who joined the league as the expansion Chicago Packers in 1961–62, were renamed the Zephyrs for the 1962–63 season, moved to Baltimore through 1972–73, spent one season as the Capital Bullets and 23 as the Washington Bullets before changing their name again for the 1997–98 season. Also, the Sacramento Kings were born the Rochester Royals in 1948–49, moved to Cincinnati from 1957–58 through 1971–72, spent three seasons as the Kansas City/Omaha Kings, shortened that to the Kansas City Kings for the next 10 years before moving to Sacramento for the 1985–86 season.

Less complicated moves involved the Syracuse Nationals, who started in 1949–50 and became the Philadelphia 76ers in 1963–64; the San Diego Rockets, who started in 1967–68 and moved to Houston for the 1971–72 season, and the Los Angeles Clippers, formed as the Buffalo Braves in 1970–71 until the 1978–79 move to San Diego, where they were renamed the Clippers. They moved to Los Angeles for the 1984–85 season.

The NBA and American Basketball Association merged in 1976–77, which brought in the Indiana Pacers, San Antonio Spurs (who had played as the Dallas Chaparrals or Texas Chaparrals from 1967–68 through 1972–73), Denver Nuggets (who had played as the Denver Rockets from 1967–68 through 1973–74) and the New Jersey Nets (who started out as the New Jersey Americans in 1967–68 and became the New York Nets from 1968–69 through 1976–77.) Through expansion the league welcomed the Chicago Bulls in 1966–67, Seattle in 1967–68, Milwaukee and Phoenix in 1968–69, Cleveland and Portland in 1970–71, Dallas in 1980–81, Charlotte and Miami in 1988–89, Minnesota and Orlando in 1989–90 and Toronto and Vancouver in 1995–96.

CENTER OF ATTENTION: *Wilt Chamberlain (13) often drew a crowd.*

AMERICAN BASKETBALL ASSOCIATION

It's as simple "as A–B–A"

WHAT'S UP DOC? *Julius Erving (Nets) was one of the ABA's finest.*

When the NBA opened its doors to the San Antonio Spurs, New York Nets, Indiana Pacers and Denver Nuggets as part of a 1976 merger agreement, it brought down the curtain on the nine-year-old American Basketball Association and its game of musical franchises.

By the end of its run, the ABA had changed its once patriotic colors to a war-weary black and blue and basketball fans were left to piece together a franchise-shifting puzzle that put the early NBA to shame. In the beginning, there were 11 ABA teams; at the end there were six. The in-between was a blur of cities, near-empty arenas and team nicknames that scored high for originality if not endurance.

The ABA opened play with franchises in Anaheim, Denver, Indianapolis, Pittsburgh, Louisville, Minneapolis, New Orleans, Oakland, Houston, Dallas and the booming metropolis of Teaneck, N.J. The New Jersey Americans, in keeping with the spirit of the patriotic ABA, wore red, white and blue uniforms and played their games in an armory. The Denver Rockets, owned by the Rocket Truck Lines, were more interested in the long haul than an instant takeoff.

While the red, white and blue basketball, the innovation of Commissioner George Mikan, became the enduring symbol of the ABA, the colorful nicknames became its legacy. The Amigos (Anaheim), Chaparrals (Dallas), Oaks (Oakland), Pacers (Indiana), Mavericks (Houston), Colonels (Kentucky), Muskies (Minnesota), Buccaneers (New Orleans) and Pipers (Pittsburgh) gave the ABA a personality that changed faster than Jekyll and Hyde.

The Amigos, for instance, were Amigos for only one season. They spent their second and third seasons as the Los Angeles Stars and their fourth and fifth as the Utah Stars before folding 16 games into their sixth campaign. Their demise came less than two years after winning an ABA championship.

Likewise, two other franchises refused to let success force stability. The Pipers claimed the ABA's first championship, moved to Minnesota for their second season and back to Pittsburgh for their third. In season No. 4, club officials, apparently bored again with life in Pittsburgh, changed the team name to "Condors" and struggled through two more seasons before folding. The Oakland Oaks won the ABA's second title, moved cross country to Washington the next

season and relocated a few miles south to Virginia the next. From 1970 to the ABA's demise in 1976, the team played as the "Squires" in the Virginia cities of Norfolk, Hampton and Richmond.

And so life went in the unpredictable ABA. The Houston Mavericks transformed magically into the Carolina Cougars and later the St. Louis Spirits. The New Orleans Buccaneers relocated to Memphis after three seasons and tried on a series of nicknames: Pros, Tams and Sounds. The Dallas Chaparrals tried their luck for a season as the Texas Chaparrals before moving to San Antonio. And the Minnesota Muskies survived one season before relocating to Miami as the Floridians. Minnesota will go down in ABA annals as the city that welcomed and lost two different teams in consecutive seasons.

The ABA even had an expansion team—the San Diego Conquistadors, who began play in 1973 and competed for three seasons before becoming the "Sails." Another team, the Baltimore Claws (remnants of the defunct Memphis franchise), folded a few days before playing its first game.

When all was said and done, six franchises remained standing— Indiana, Denver, San Antonio, New York, Kentucky and St. Louis. Five of the six were originals and three competed the entire nine seasons in the same city—the Pacers, Rockets/Nuggets and Colonels.

Not surprisingly, the six final teams accounted for six of the nine ABA championships, proving, after all, there is something to be said for stability.

THE NBA TEAMS

In the spectacular world of reverse slam dunks, no-look passes and 3-point jump shots, the unspectacular bottom line can be found on the scoreboard. Individuals excite fans with their above-the-rim theatrics and showmanship but teams bring them back to arenas with their ability to outscore opponents and successfully achieve the common goal— victory.

The essence of sports is winning and losing, and winning most often is accomplished within the framework of a team. Success is determined by such mundane functions as fundamentals, rebounding, ball movement and defense.

Wilt Chamberlain always will be revered as the most spectacular offensive machine in NBA history, but while he was carving out his own special section of the record book, the Boston Celtics, dedicated to Coach Red Auerbach's principles of teamwork and defense, were claiming championship after championship.

Many consider Oscar Robertson to be the most complete player in basketball history, but a championship eluded him until he joined forces with a young Kareem Abdul-Jabbar at Milwaukee near the end of his career.

And Michael Jordan, one of the game's ultimate offensive and defensive weapons, was a helpless superstar for an average Chicago team—until the Bulls management got him a championship-caliber supporting cast.

Chamberlain, Robertson, Jordan—any of the game's brightest stars—will tell you statistics are nice, but championship rings define the ultimate success of a career. And long-term team success defines the ultimate goal of every franchise.

Team success like the Boston Celtics' 16 overall championships or the Lakers' 12 titles and 24 appearances in the NBA Finals. Like the 11 championship rings won by Boston center Bill Russell, the prototypical team player, whose last two titles came as a player-coach.

Like the Chicago Bulls of Michael Jordan, Scottie Pippen and Phil Jackson, who carved out their historical niche as the team of the 1990s with six championships in eight seasons.

(Opposite) MONSTER MASH: *Jamal Mashburn was a big part of Miami's success in his three-plus seasons with the Heat.*

34 ATLANTA HAWKS

Somewhere in-between has been their fate

NOT SO EASY RIDER: *Isaiah Rider was more trouble than he was worth for the Hawks.*

If nothing else, the Hawks have been consistent. Only once have they ranked among the NBA's muscle men. Only occasionally have they ranked among its weaklings. Most of their St. Louis and Atlanta existence has been spent somewhere in between.

In the 40 seasons from 1955 through 1995, the Hawks finished within 10 games of .500 19 times, qualified for the playoffs 31 times and lost before reaching the NBA Finals 27 times. Only in one four-year span did they fail to reach the playoffs in consecutive seasons.

Not that the Hawks have been a bland, colorless franchise. From 1956 to '61, gifted forward Bob Pettit won a pair of scoring titles while leading the team to five consecutive Western Division titles and its only NBA championship—a six-game 1958 victory over the powerful Boston Celtics.

From 1966 to '74, Sweet Lou Hudson combined with Zelmo Beaty, Bill Bridges, Joe Caldwell and Pete Maravich over a run that produced two division titles and six second-place finishes.

And from 1985 to '89, high-flying Dominique Wilkins was the centerpiece for a Hawks team that recorded 50 or more victories in four consecutive seasons.

The Hawks trace their NBA roots back to 1949, when they joined the league as the Tri-Cities Blackhawks. The franchise, one of six survivors when the National Basketball League folded, spent six losing seasons in Moline, Ill., and Milwaukee before moving to St. Louis in 1955.

The 1954 arrival of Pettit was the franchise's first step forward. The Hawks joined the NBA elite in 1956 when Owner Ben Kerner pulled off a draft-day trade that brought future Hall of Famers Ed Macauley and Cliff Hagan from Boston for a first-round draft pick. Pettit, Macauley and Hagan led the Hawks to four NBA Finals; the Celtics used their

Conference/Division	Eastern/Central Division			
First Year in NBA	1949–50			
Arenas (Capacity)	Philips Arena (19,445)			
Former Cities/Nicknames	Tri-Cities Blackhawks, 1949–51,			
	Milwaukee Hawks, 1951–55,			
	St. Louis Hawks, 1955–68			
NBA Finals Appearances	1957, 1958, 1960, 1961			
NBA Championships	1958			
Playing Record	G	W	L	Pct.
Regular Season	4,010	2,049	1,961	.511
Playoffs	272	119	153	.438

pick on center Bill Russell, who led them to 11 championships.

By 1965, Macauley was long gone, Pettit was ready to retire and Hagan was a year away. But new coach Richie Guerin was reloading his offensive arsenal around swingman Hudson, backcourt ace Lenny Wilkens, 6-foot-9 center Beaty and Bridges, a rebounding forward. Guerin's teams advanced to the Western Division finals four times in five seasons and that success carried through the franchise's 1968 move from St. Louis to Atlanta.

When Guerin left after the 1971–72 campaign, the Hawks fell on hard times. But they revived to win 50 games in 1979–80 and became a 1980s power under Mike Fratello. Wilkens provided the glitter and firepower for Fratello's Hawks, never averaging below 25.9 points from 1984 to 1994, when he was traded to the Clippers. Wilkens created excitement with his above-the-rim theatrics, which rivaled the shows being staged in other cities by Julius Erving and Michael Jordan.

The current-edition Hawks are in good hands. Lenny Wilkens, the NBA's all-time winningest coach, took over the coaching reins in 1993–94 and has rebuilt the team with a talent base that features defensive specialist Dikembe Mutombo at center. Teamed with standout guards Mookie Blaylock and Steve Smith, Mutombo led the Hawks to a 50–32 record in 1997–98 only to fall victim to a first round upset at the hands of Charlotte in the playoffs.

The Hawks were hoping that would be a springboard for the 1998–99 season. But injuries plagued the team all year. LaPhonso Ellis, who signed as a free agent before the season, missed the last 30 games with a hernia. Alan Henderson missed 12 games with back spasms, a bruised tailbone and a left eye abrasion. Smith missed 14 games with knee injuries.

Still, the Hawks, who set an NBA record for fewest points allowed per game (83.4), qualified for the playoffs for the seventh straight year. This time they defeated the Pistons, 3–2, in the first round but were swept by the New York Knicks, 4–0, in the Eastern Conference semifinals.

Atlanta moved into a new building, the Philips Arena, for the 1999–2000 season, but the team struggled through its worst season in years. In an effort to remake the team, the Hawks traded Smith to Portland for Isaiah Rider and Jim Jackson. It proved to be a volatile move. Rider created much turmoil with his antics on and off the court. He did lead the Hawks with 19.3 points a game, and also averaged 4.3 rebounds and 3.7 assists, none of which was worth the trouble.

The Hawks eventually were forced to cut him, but by that time they were on their way to a 28–54 record, their worst record since going 29–53 in 1975–76.

They missed the playoffs and Wilkens resigned under pressure.

Shortly thereafter, the team turned to Lon Kruger, a college coach who had never been a head coach in the NBA. Kruger coached at Pan American, Kansas State, Florida and Illinois. The Florida State alumnus was a ninth-round pick of the Hawks in 1974.

STILL WAITNG: *Dikembe Mutombo hasn't put the Hawks over the top*

36 BOSTON CELTICS

The winning formula was developed by Auerbach

Red Auerbach, Bill Russell, John Havlicek, Larry Bird. The names form an historical link of basketball generations. They fit together like "Abbott and Costello," "Peter, Paul and Mary," "NBA" and "championship" and "Boston" and "Celtics."

The common denominator, of course, is Auerbach, the coaching genius who fit together the pieces of the NBA's most storied franchise. He began his work in 1950, when he took over as coach of the 4-year-old Celtics, one of the BAA/NBA's original teams.

Auerbach's dream was to mold a team of rabbits that could run and gun its way past the more conservative teams of the era. He built a foundation by picking up forward Ed Macauley and guards Bob Cousy and Bill Sharman.

It took a brilliant 1956 draft-day maneuver to provide the puzzle's biggest piece. Auerbach traded Macauley and the rights to Cliff Hagan, two future Hall of Famers, to St. Louis for Russell, the Hawks' first-round draft pick.

The beefed-up Celtics were on their way. With Russell rebounding, playing maniacal defense and triggering an explosive fast break from his center position, they raced to the 1957 NBA championship, the franchise's first, and ran off a record string of eight consecutive titles from 1959–66. It was the longest championship streak in team-sports history. Through the run, Auerbach surrounded Russell with a steady stream of excellent supporting players: Cousy, Sharman, Sam Jones, Tom Heinsohn, K.C. Jones, Tom Sanders, Havlicek and Don Nelson.

The end of the streak was only a temporary setback. Russell, who had taken over the coaching reins after the 1965–66 season, played two more years and collected two more championship rings, his 10th and 11th in 13 seasons. When he retired after the 1969 victory, the Celtics were forced to reload.

They did it quickly with Heinsohn as coach and Havlicek, the Celtics' former "Sixth Man," as the go-to star. Auerbach brought in center Dave Cowens, guards Jo Jo White and Charlie Scott, and rebounder Paul Silas, who combined with Havlicek to win five consecutive Atlantic Division titles and two more NBA championships from 1971–76. Again it was time to reload.

This time Auerbach reloaded with a first-round draft pick that he used to select Indiana State's Bird—after his junior season. The Celtics languished in the division basement in 1978–79 while Bird was playing his senior season, but the 6–9 forward would be worth the wait.

LUCK OF THE IRISH: *Antoine Walker is the latest player to star for the Celtics.*

Auerbach complemented Bird with center Robert Parish, forward Kevin McHale and guards Dennis Johnson and Danny Ainge. Under Bill Fitch and K.C. Jones, the Celtics won eight division titles and three more championships in the 1980s, bringing their record total to 16. When Bird was forced to retire in 1992 with a chronic back problem, the Celtics fell back into the pack.

After hitting rock bottom with a team record 67 losses in 1996–97, the team signed former University of Kentucky coach Rick Pitino to a lengthy contract to rebuild the once-proud franchise. Pitino, a brilliant motivator who preaches the up-tempo, fast-break style of basketball loved in Beantown, inherited a roster of talented but misguided players and began planning for the future. Antoine Walker looked like an All-Star in waiting, while Ron Mecer made the All-Rookie first team as the Celtics improved to 36–46.

Despite adding highly regarded rookie

FACTS & FIGURES				
Conference/Division	Eastern/Atlantic Division			
First Year in BAA/NBA	1946–47			
Arena (Capacity)	FleetCenter (18,600)			
Former Cities/Nicknames	None			
NBA Finals Appearances	1957, 1958, 1959, 1960, 1961, 1962, 1963, 1964, 1965, 1966, 1968, 1969, 1974, 1976, 1981, 1984, 1985, 1986, 1987			
NBA Championships	1957, 1959, 1960, 1961, 1962, 1963, 1964, 1965, 1966, 1968, 1969, 1974, 1976, 1981, 1984, 1986			
Playing Record	G	W	L	Pct.
Regular Season	4,183	2,527	1,656	.604
Playoffs	461	272	189	.590

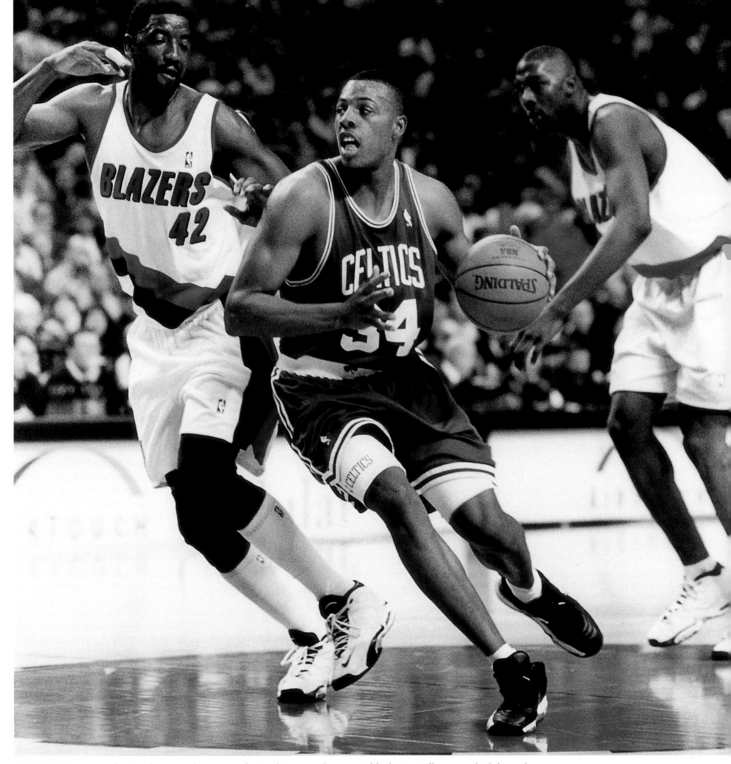

ON THE MEND: *Boston is hoping for a speedy recovery by Paul Pierce, who was stabbed repeatedly in a nightclub incident.*

Paul Pierce from Kansas for the 1998-99 season, the Celtics actually took a step backward that season, finishing 19-31.

Pierce ranked third on the team in points (16.5), second in rebounding (6.4) and first in steals (1.71) and was a unanimous choice to the Schick All-Rookie first team. Walker led the team in scoring for the third straight season at 18.7 points per game.

In the middle of the season, the Celtics acquired Vitaly Potapenko from the Cleveland Cavaliers in exchange for Andrew DeClercq and a first-round draft choice. Boston was hoping the physical Potapenko would bolster their inside game. But that was not enough to keep the Celtics from finishing with a losing record for the sixth straight year.

They made it seven by going 35-47 in 1999-2000. Walker again led the team in scoring, at 20.5 points per game, with Pierce right behind at 19.5. Although Pitino's teams pride themselves on defense,

the Celtics gave up more than 100 points per game.

The Celtics' failure to progress actually had Pitino at least considering leaving, but he opted to remain and vowed improvement. He made many moves in his first three seasons with the club, and that can be expected to continue until he finds the kind of success he's been used to at the college and pro level.

The stabbing of Paul Pierce set Pitino's Celtics back before the 2000-01 season.

38 CHARLOTTE HORNETS

Expanding horizons are the team's buzzwords

THE NEXT STEP: *Elden Campbell and the Hornets are looking forward to success.*

One of the best stories of the 1996–97 NBA season was the Charlotte Hornets. Entering preseason, many experts thought a .500 season would be a success because the Hornets had a new coach (Dave Cowens) and two new players (Anthony Mason from New York and Vlade Divac from the Lakers) who had been acquired by Charlotte because they weren't wanted in their old homes. And, even though the year ended with a playoff sweep at the hands of the New York Knicks, Cowens led the Hornets to a franchise-record 54 wins, forward Glen Rice was the MVP of the All-Star Game, and Mason had emerged as one of the league's toughest competitors.

One year later, after posting a 51–31 regular season record, the Hornets went one better in the playoffs, surprising Atlanta in the first round before bowing out to Chicago in five games. Those playoff appearances were but a distant dream for North Carolina fans in 1987 when the NBA Board of Governors announced that Charlotte and Miami would begin play in 1987–88.

Charlotte's ticket to success was Alonzo Mourning, who arrived out of Georgetown University as the second overall pick of the 1992 draft. Mourning, a 6-foot-10 leaper with a nice blend of offensive, defensive and rebounding skills, was the perfect fit for the youthful Hornets.

Mourning joined forces with 6–7 Larry Johnson in one of the league's most potent frontcourts and concluded his first season with 21-point and 10.3-rebound averages and 271 blocked shots. Not surprisingly, the Hornets improved from 31 to 44 victories, posted their first winning record and made their first trip to the playoffs. They capped a rewarding season by disposing of Boston in a first-round series before losing to the rugged New York Knicks.

The Hornets came back to post a 41–41 record in 1993–94 when Johnson missed 31 games with a bad back, but they shed their expansion cloak in 1994–95, winning a franchise-record 50 games. An inspiring regular season was followed by a playoff disaster as the Chicago Bulls, with Michael Jordan back, swatted the Hornets in a quick first-round series.

But that disappointment was nothing compared to the news that greeted fans as the team prepared for its eighth NBA campaign. Mourning and management were engaged in a bitter contract hassle that finally resulted in the big center turning down a $20-million deal and demanding a trade. Shortly before the season, he was sent to Miami for forward Glen Rice, 7-foot center Matt Geiger and guard Khalid Reeves.

A midseason deal brought ball-handling wizard Kenny Anderson to Charlotte. The new-look Hornets were stronger on the perimeter, but softer and less intimidating in the paint. Not even the offseason acquisition

FACTS & FIGURES				
Conference/Division	Eastern/Central Division			
First Year in NBA	1988–89			
Arena (Capacity)	Charlotte Coliseum (24,042)			
Former Cities/Nicknames	None			
NBA Finals Appearances	None			
NBA Championships	None			
Playing Record	G	W	L	Pct.
Regular Season	952	452	500	.475
Playoffs	29	10	19	.345

of Lakers' center Divac could ease the pain.

And when the team dealt Johnson to the Knicks for Mason, a hard-nosed forward, few fans in Charlotte thought the combination of Mason and Divac would make them forget Mourning and Johnson. But first-year coach Cowens, a former great player with the Boston Celtics, instilled a winning attitude in his team and they responded immediately.

However, Divac, a free agent, left for Sacramento before the 1998-99 season started, and Mason missed the entire 1998-99 season with a ruptured tendon in his right biceps. Rice missed the first 16 games with bone fragments in his right elbow. Once he recovered, he, J.R. Reid and B.J. Armstrong were traded to the Los Angeles Lakers for Eddie Jones and Elden Campbell.

In addition to those problems, Cowens resigned 15 games into the season and was replaced by Paul Silas. Silas led the team to a 22-13 record but that was not good enough to make the playoffs.

Jones wound up leading the Hornets with 17.0 points per game, while Campbell wound up second leading in rebounding, averaging 9.4, and blocked shots, averaging 1.78.

Tragedy struck the Hornets in 1999-2000. Popular veteran Bobby Phills was killed in a car accident outside the Charlotte Coliseum on January 12. He and teammate David Wesley were racing their sports cars after the team's shootaround in preparation for that night's game against Chicago.

The team, which also had suffered through an earlier auto accident involving Derrick Coleman and Eldridge Recasner, was devastated and it took quite some time for the Hornets to recover. But with Jones having an All-Star season and averaging 20.1 points per game, the Hornets finished 49-33 and advanced to the playoffs where they lost to the Philadelphia 76ers.

Coleman averaged 16.7 points per game, and Wesley recovered enough emotionally to average 13.6 points per game, ironically, the same thing Phills was averaging before his death.

A TIME TO UNITE: *Anthony Mason and the Hornets are trying to get a handle on things.*

40 CHICAGO BULLS

Up, up and away followed by down in the dumps

History for Chicago fans begins in 1984, the season Michael Jordan was plucked out of the NBA draft with the third overall pick. That was the point at which they could separate hope from futility.

The question, after Jordan and his magnificent allies of coach Phil Jackson, Scottie Pippen and Dennis Rodman led the Bulls to a sixth championship in eight years in 1998, was how much longer they would be able to enjoy the sublime skills of arguably the game's best ever player. That same championship concluded with the four main protagonists talking of retirement or moving on.

Jordan brought excitement and acceptance to a city that had not always embraced the professional game. The Chicago Stags lasted four seasons as 1946 charter members of the Basketball Association of America. The Chicago Packers/ Zephyrs joined the league in 1961 and lasted two seasons before moving to Baltimore.

The Bulls made their NBA debut as an expansion team in 1966 and began charting a course through the rough Chicago waters. The Bulls made their first serious foray into the NBA's upper stratosphere in 1970–71 when young coach Dick Motta guided them to a 51–31 record and a second-place finish in the Midwest Division. With forwards Chet Walker and Bob Love providing points, guard Norm Van Lier directing the offense and forward

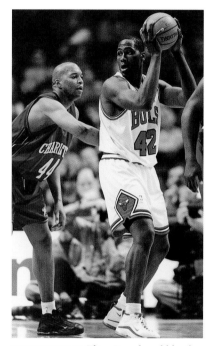

BRAND NEW START: *Elton Brand could be the key to bringing the Bulls back.*

Jerry Sloan supplying defense, the Bulls won more than 50 games in four straight seasons and their first Midwest Division title. But four playoff appearances resulted in first-round failures, two others ended in the Western Conference Finals and the next nine seasons would produce only two playoff appearances and a low position in the 1984 draft.

In 1986–87, Jordan earned the first of seven consecutive scoring titles. In

1987–88, he won the first of four MVPs. But try as he might, Jordan alone couldn't give the Bulls what everybody wanted most—playoff success.

Help finally arrived in 1987 when the Bulls acquired Pippen and drafted Horace Grant, two athletic front-court players, on the same day. In their first season with Jordan, the Bulls won 50 games and tied for second in the Central Division. Three years later, under second-year coach Jackson, the Bulls won 61 times, cruised through the Eastern Conference playoffs and overpowered the Lakers in a five-game NBA Finals. The Bulls powered their way to a second straight championship in 1992 and became the third NBA team to pull off a three-peat a year later. Jordan capped the 1993 title by retiring to pursue a baseball career.

Life beyond Jordan was predictable. The Bulls sank in the standings and were headed toward an early playoff ouster in 1995 when Jordan, revitalized and ready to play, came out of retirement for the final 17 games. He wasn't enough to get the Bulls past the second round, but the Jordan–Pippen reunion and Chicago's acquisition of rebounding master Rodman set the stage for an unprecedented 1995–96 season. The Bulls rolled to a 72–10 regular-season mark and posted their fourth championship in six years. A year later, the team "slumped" to 69–13 (tied for the second greatest season ever), then won 15 of 19 playoff games to make it five titles in the decade.

In was more of the same in 1997–98, when the same team repeated the three-peat ending the regular season 62–20 and again beating the Utah Jazz in the finals. All that changed when Jackson resigned and Jordan retired before the 1998–99 season. Pippin was traded to Houston and Rodman, a free agent, left the team.

Jordan's career averages of 31.5 points, 6.3 rebounds and 5.4 assists per game

FACTS & FIGURES

Conference/Division	Eastern/Central Division		
First Year in NBA	1966–67		
Arena (Capacity)	United Center (21,711)		
Former Cities/Nicknames	None		
NBA Finals Appearances	1991, 1992, 1993, 1996, 1997, 1998		
NBA Championships	1991, 1992, 1993, 1996, 1997, 1998		
Playing Record	**G**	**W**	**L**	**Pct.**
Regular Season	2,755	1,447	1,278	.536
Playoffs	153	147	106	.581

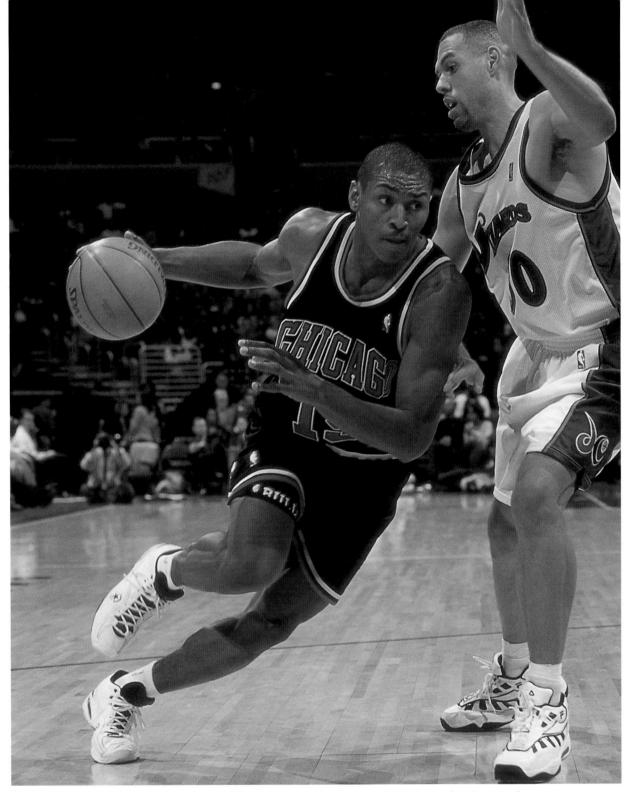

STORM WARNING: *Rookie Ron Artest, coming out of St. John's, did his best to complement fellow rookie Elton Brand.*

don't come close to reflecting what he meant to the Bulls and the city of Chicago. In leading the team to six titles, he won five MVP awards and was named the MVP in the finals six times. He clearly was the most dominant player of his era—and may have been the best ever.

New coach Tim Floyd suffered through a 13-37 debut in the lockout-shortened season. Holdovers Toni Kukoc and Ron Harper led the team averaging 18.8 and 11.2 points per game, respectively. But that did earn the Bulls the No. 1 draft choice in 1999.

That proved to be Duke forward Elton Brand, who averaged 20.1 points and 10 rebounds to lead the Bulls and earned co-Rookie of the Year honors for the 1999-2000 season with Steve Francis of Houston. Even with fellow rookie Ron Artest out of St. John's contributing 12 points a game, the Bulls could do no better than 17-65.

After losing free agent Harper to the Lakers and trading Toni Kukoc to Philadelphia in the middle of the season, all vestiges of the Bulls' championship teams were gone. But the memories remained. Now Coach Floyd has the difficult task of trying to add some of his own.

42 CLEVELAND CAVALIERS

The long and difficult road to respectability

When the NBA gave birth to the Cleveland Cavaliers in a three-team 1970 expansion, nobody could have imagined the pain and heartache that would track the unfortunate franchise through its first quarter century. But early omens should have put league officials and fans on red alert.

The Cavs opened their first season with 15 consecutive losses and dropped 34 of their first 36 games—the only two victories coming against Buffalo and Portland, their expansion mates. A final 15–67 record showed how thin their first-year roster really was.

Still, coach Bill Fitch saw reason for optimism. John Johnson had finished a solid rookie season with a 16.6-point average and the Cavs grabbed hot-shooting Notre Dame guard Austin Carr with the first pick of the 1971 draft. The second-year Cavs improved to 23 victories, the third-year Cavs won 32 and Fitch added a pair of muscular draft picks, 6-foot-9 Jim Brewer and 6–8 Campy Russell.

When 6–11 center Jim Chones arrived from the ABA in 1974 and veteran guard Dick Snyder was acquired in a trade, Fitch had the pieces in place for a championship run. And indeed the 1975–76 Cavaliers posted a franchise-record 49 victories, won their first Central Division title and

STILL A STRUGGLE: *Even the presence of All-Star Shawn Kemp couldn't help the Cavs.*

made their playoff debut a successful one, advancing to the Eastern Conference Finals.

But just when everything appeared to be falling into place, misfortune began to dog the franchise. The 1976 playoff run was deflated when Chones broke his ankle, making the Cavs easy prey for a veteran Boston team.

Never again would the Cavaliers win a division title. It would take 16 years before they would win another playoff series. The franchise would struggle through inept play in the late 1970s, near-disastrous mismanagement by owner Ted Stepien in the early 1980s and bad luck and injury problems in the 1990s. The wheeling and dealing Stepien so disfigured the 1981–82 Cavs that they sank back to expansion form with 15 victories.

When Stepien finally sold the franchise to George and Gordon Gund, the NBA had to guarantee the new owners four bonus first-round draft picks to help rebuild the team. With solid ownership in place, the Cavs began the slow climb back to respectability.

The breakthrough came in a lucrative 1986 draft that brought 7-foot center Brad Daugherty, shooting guard Ron Harper and point guard Mark Price to Cleveland. That talented threesome soon was joined by 6–11 Hot Rod Williams and 6–10 Larry Nance in a lineup that Lakers guard Magic Johnson labeled the "Team of the '90s."

And indeed the young Cavs appeared to be headed in that direction under the steady hand of Lenny Wilkens, who arrived in 1986 and coached the team to 285 victories over a six-season stretch that included another trip to the conference finals.

Wilkens was replaced by Mike Fratello, who made the Cavs one of the league's top defensive teams only to launch a major

Conference/Division	Eastern/Central Division			
First Year in NBA	1970–71			
Arena (Capacity)	Gund Arena (20,562)			
Former Cities/Nicknames	None			
NBA Finals Appearances	None			
NBA Championships	None			
Playing Record	G	W	L	Pct.
Regular Season	2,428	1,096	1,332	.451
Playoffs	77	28	49	.364

FACTS & FIGURES

rebuilding project after a run of five straight playoff appearances ended in 1996–97. Two major trades, each involving three teams, saw All-Star forward Shawn Kemp arrive from Seattle and Wesley Person from Phoenix. A 47–35 record and valiant losing effort against Indiana in the playoffs suggested the Cavs' history of mismanagement was well behind them.

Things did not go exactly as the Cavs had hoped the next season. Kemp reported to camp overweight and by the time he was able to play himself into shape, the Cavs were already behind the eight ball. Another major blow came early in the season when Zydrunas Ilgauskas suffered a broken bone in his left foot, missing his third season in four years. The team had been depending on him to take some of the pressure off Kemp inside after watching the 7-3 Lithuanian play well enough to make the all-rookie team in 1997-98.

Although Kemp put up solid numbers with 20.5 points and 9.2 rebounds, he missed the last eight games with a sprained left foot and the Cavs missed the playoffs.

In a surprising move a month after the season, the Cavs fired Fratello and hired one of his former players, Randy Wittman, to replace him. A rookie head coach who had been a longtime assistant in the league, Wittman directed the Cavs to a 32-50 record, missing the playoffs once again.

Kemp again was the team's leading scorer with 17.8 points and 8.8 rebounds. But Ilgauskas missed yet another season when his left foot failed to heal and he needed surgery in January.

The best news for the Cavs was the development of first-round draft choice Andre Miller, a point guard from the University of Utah. He moved into a starting spot after an injury to Brevin Knight and finished averaging 11.1 points and 5.8 assists per game.

Bob Sura rebounded from a couple of injury-filled seasons and displayed the kind of athleticism that made him the team's No.1 draft choice in 1995. But he was traded away to the Golden State Warriors before the start of the 2000–01 season.

NEW KID: *Andre Miller averaged more than 25 minutes per game in his rookie season.*

DALLAS MAVERICKS

Back to the future is the best way to go

It wasn't much fun, but at least it was understandable. The newborn Mavericks, trying to take their first NBA steps under coach Dick Motta, stumbled, tottered and wheezed en route to a curtain-raising 15–67 record.

That was 1980–81 and management could take consolation in the belief that expansion teams are supposed to suffer; that the organization never again would experience such a low.

Now, fast-forward to the 1990s and the Mavs showed just how fickle NBA life can be. After crashing to records of 11–71 and 13–69 in the 1992–93 and 1993–94 seasons, Mavs owner Donald Carter saw his team seemingly start to rise again from the ashes. Building through the draft, the Mavericks fashioned an exciting back-court with Jim Jackson and Jason Kidd and two-thirds of a frontcourt with inside/out scorer Jamal Mashburn and rebounder Popeye Jones. The young team experienced a 36-victory revival in 1994–95, but the success was very short-lived.

The next two seasons saw the franchise beset by big-time problems, both on and off the court. They slumped to 26–56 and 24–58 seasons and traded away Jackson, Kidd, Mashburn and Jones. They finished the 1996–97 season without a proven star, and entered yet another rebuilding period in their short history.

That manifested itself early in the 1997–98 season when General Manager

THE RIGHT STUFF: *Michael Finley has all the tools to become one of the NBA's new stars.*

Don Nelson took over coaching duties and immediately appointed his son Donnie Head Coach in waiting with his reign due to start in the 2000–01 season.

A major revival would not be unlike the dramatic rise Dallas executed in the 1980s. From their 15-victory debut, Motta's

Mavericks jumped to 28 wins and improved in each of their first seven seasons. In 1983–84, they posted the franchise's first winning mark (43–39), finished second in the Midwest Division and won a first-round playoff series against Seattle.

The Mavericks were being rightly hailed as the model expansion franchise. Management had pulled all the right strings, building a solid foundation in a 1981 draft that produced guard Rolando Blackman and forwards Mark Aguirre and Jay Vincent. Guard Derek Harper was drafted in 1983 and forwards Sam Perkins and Detlef Schrempf in 1984 and '85.

When 7-foot-2 center James Donaldson was acquired in 1985 and rebounding ace Roy Tarpley was drafted in '86, the Mavericks appeared to have all the pieces for a championship run. They won 55 games and their first Midwest title in 1986–87 and followed with a 53-win campaign under new coach John MacLeod. The Mavs beat Houston and Denver in 1988 playoff series before losing a seven-game Western Conference Finals heart-breaker to the Lakers.

But just when it appeared the Mavs were on the brink, the bottom fell out. First Tarpley suffered a severe knee injury and a series of drug-related suspensions. Then Aguirre and Schrempf were traded and Donaldson suffered a knee injury.

Even under the experienced hand of Nelson senior, 1997–98 was a miserable campaign with the Mavs struggling to a 20–62 record.

Things were not much better the next season when the Mavericks finished 19-31. The major bright spot was Michael Finley, who led the team in scoring at 20.2 points per game and minutes at 41 per game, which ranked him third in the NBA. He was the only guard in the league to average at least 20 points and five rebounds and was one of just 10 players to score 1,000 points in the shortened season.

Dallas stood pat heading into the 21st century and it paid off as Nelson guided the team to a strong finish and a 40–42 record in the 1999–2000 season. The biggest glitch for the Mavs was the signing of quirky forward Dennis Rodman for a 12-game stint in the middle of the season. The Mavericks quickly realized their mistake as Rodman disrupted their progress. After one too many run-ins, Nelson cut him loose.

For a third straight season, Finley led the team in scoring, averaging 22.6 points, 6.3 rebounds and 5.3 assists and being named an All-Star for the first time. Young forward Dirk Nowitzki added 17.5 points per game and looked like the kind of player who would blossom in the future. Shawn Bradley, the 7-foot-6 center, averaged 2.47 blocked shots per game, ranking fifth in the league.

THE FUTURE: *Dirk Nowitzki fits right into the Mavericks' style of play.*

46 DENVER NUGGETS

A franchise on the run and in search of playoffs

ANOTHER REJECTION: *Raef LaFrentz's defensive talents shone after his 1999 knee injury.*

FACTS & FIGURES

Conference/Division	Western/Midwest Division			
First Year in ABA/NBA	1967–68/1976–77			
Arena (Capacity)	Pepsi Center (19,300)			
Former Cities/Nicknames	Denver Rockets, 1967–74			
NBA Finals Appearances	None			
ABA/NBA Championships	None			
Playing Record	**G**	**W**	**L**	**Pct.**
ABA Regular Season	744	413	331	.555
NBA Regular Season	1,936	897	1,039	.463
ABA Playoffs	62	27	35	.435
NBA Playoffs	98	39	59	.398

If you measure franchise success by NBA Finals appearances and championships, the Denver Nuggets have been two-decade failures. But if you judge a franchise by its star-quality players, competitive teams, exciting style and fan appeal, the Nuggets have been NBA giants.

Consider: In their first 20 NBA seasons, the Nuggets led the league in scoring seven times and finished in the top four 12 times; they showcased high-flying forwards David Thompson, Alex English and Dan Issel; they flashed their way to four Midwest Division titles; and they laid claim to one of the most stunning playoff upsets in league history.

The Nuggets came into being as the Denver Rockets, one of the 11 original American Basketball Association franchises in 1967. It quickly became apparent Denver would become one of the ABA's most stable teams. They posted winning records in their first two seasons and stunned the basketball world in 1969 by signing NBA-ineligible Spencer Haywood, a high-scoring forward who had just finished his sophomore season at the University of Detroit.

Haywood would play only one season in Denver before bolting to the NBA, but the Rockets had clearly established a front-office tenacity. Denver's stock rose dramatically in the ABA's final two seasons when the Rockets/ Nuggets (they changed their nickname in 1974) won 125 games, advanced to the league's final championship series (a loss to the New York Nets) and opened plush McNichols Arena, one of the best basketball facilities in the country.

It was no coincidence that the Nuggets were one of the four ABA teams invited to join the NBA in 1976. And it was no fluke that Denver raced to 50 victories and the Midwest Division title in its first season—the best finish ever for a new NBA entrant.

The Nuggets, coached by Larry Brown, were potent scorers with the acrobatic Thompson, Issel and forward Bobby Jones. Denver lost to Portland in the Western Conference semifinals, but returned to claim a second division title in 1977–78 and advanced to the conference finals.

Brown departed in 1978 and Thompson's career faded shortly after. But a short lull was followed by the 1981 arrival of coach Doug Moe, who gave the Nuggets a running start toward a new era of prosperity. Literally.

Moe preached run-and-shoot basketball with little regard for defense and the Nuggets spent most of the 1980s piling up gaudy statistics and moderate success. The top gun in Moe's arsenal was the 6–7 English, but Kiki Vandeweghe, Calvin Natt and Lafayette (Fat) Lever also provided significant firepower.

Moe left after the 1989–90 season and the Nuggets began assembling first-round draft picks: guards Jalen Rose and Mahmoud Abdul-Rauf, forwards LaPhonso Ellis and Antonio McDyess and 7–2 center Dik-embe Mutombo. Abdul-Rauf and Rose were traded for veteran guards Mark Jackson and Ricky Pierce after the 1995–96 season.

The Nuggets went through coaching and management shake-ups in 1996–97 and 1997–98, which saw the team post depressing records of 21–61 and 11–71. The latter season saw them at one stage flirt with the possibility of collecting the worst ever regular season record. They avoided that embarrassment but general manager Dan Issel entered the summer of 1998 looking for a new coach and, hopefully, a brighter future.

He selected Mike D'Antoni, who lasted only one season after the Nuggets finished 14–36 and missed the playoffs for the fourth straight season. The good news was that the Nuggets actually won more games than they had the year before, joining Toronto and Golden State as the only teams to do that in the lockout-shortened season.

Denver's main problem was a 2–23 record on the road, where they averaged 12 fewer points than they averaged at home, the fifth-largest point differential in NBA history.

UNCOVERING A NUGGET: *Nick Van Exel always made his point with the Nuggets.*

McDyess, who returned as a free agent, led the Nuggets, averaging 21.2 points per game, while Nick Van Exel, obtained in a trade with the Lakers, averaged 16.5 points per game.

Issel returned to the coaching reins himself in the 1999–2000 season, and the Nuggets improved to 35–47, although that was still not good enough to reach the postseason.

McDyess led the team with 19.1 points and 8.5 rebounds per game. Trades brought Ron Mercer from Boston. He finished averaging 18.3 points per game before being traded to Orlando for Chris Gatling and Tariq Abdul-Wahad as the Nuggets remade their team yet again.

In addition, forward Raef LaFrentz of Kansas, who missed almost all of his rookie season with a torn ACL in his left knee, returned to average 12.4 points, 7.9 rebounds and 2.22 blocked shots per game, which ranked him eighth in the league. Behind LaFrentz, the Nuggets actually led the league in blocked shots averaging 7.54 per game. The Nuggets are moving in the right direction and the playoffs are no longer a distant dream.

48 DETROIT PISTONS

Blue-collar basketball and the "Bad Boys"

They were brought into the world by a blue-collar owner in a blue-collar city and given a blue-collar name. Fittingly, the Pistons have played blue-collar basketball through an existence that spans more than half a century.

It began in 1937 when Fred Zollner organized a team that he named after his Fort Wayne, Ind., factory that manufactured automobile pistons. The team barnstormed during its early years, played in the National Basketball League after World War II and then jumped to the Basketball Association of America (the pre-NBA) before the 1948–49 season.

For the first six seasons of its Fort Wayne existence, the team posted only three winning marks, never finished higher than third in the Western Division and won only seven of 21 playoff games.

But life after George Mikan proved more rewarding. The Pistons, powered by forward George Yardley, guard Max Zaslofsky and bruising center Larry Foust, won three straight division titles and advanced to the 1955 and '56 NBA Finals.

But success would be fleeting. When Zollner fled Fort Wayne for more populous Detroit in 1957, the franchise began more than two decades of futility. For their first 13 Detroit seasons and 23 of their first 26, the Pistons failed to record a winning record. Over that span, they won three playoff series and compiled a 23–36 postseason record.

There were a few bright spots. Such talented players as guard Gene Shue, forwards Bailey Howell, Dave DeBusschere and Terry Dischinger and center Walter Dukes passed through. And two of the franchise's all-time best players, smooth guard Dave Bing and 6–11 center Bob Lanier, lifted the Pistons' pulse during a 45-win 1970–71 season and a 52-win 1973-74 campaign.

But Detroit's first brush with success would not come until the 1983 arrival of coach Chuck Daly and it would be rooted in the old blue-collar ethics—hard work and defense. Daly inherited a team with one of the game's best point guards of all-time, Isiah Thomas, and a physical center, Bill Laimbeer. The rest of the puzzle was filled in through the draft and trades: center James Edwards, guard Joe Dumars, sixth man Vinnie Johnson and forwards Mark Aguirre, Dennis Rodman and John Salley.

By the late 1980s, the defensive-minded Pistons were playing with a bruising, no-holds-barred style that earned them a reputation as the game's "Bad Boys." Beginning in 1987–88, they bullied their way to three straight Central Division titles and NBA Finals. The Pistons lost in 1988 to Los Angeles, but they beat the Lakers in 1989 and Portland in 1990 to become the NBA's second repeat champions in more than two decades.

In Daly's nine-year tenure, the Pistons never won fewer than 46 games, never

MOTOWN BLUES: *After Detroit fell in the first round in 2000, Grant Hill left for Orlando.*

finished below third in the division and compiled a 71–42 postseason mark.

But after Daly's 1992 departure, new coach Doug Collins brought only a fleeting improvement, despite the Pistons boasting one of the NBA's new generation of pin-up boys in versatile forward Grant Hill. Problems with Hill, as Detroit missed the playoffs with a 37–45 regular season record in 1998, eventually cost Collins his job and Alvin Gentry was handed the task of returning the Pistons to the game's upper echelons.

Gentry was well-liked by the players but his appointment did not necessarily translate into success on the court.

In 1998–99 the Nuggets finished 29-21, advancing to the playoffs, where they lost to the Hawks, 3-2, in the first round. Hill was named All-NBA second team for the third time in his career after leading the team in points, rebounds and assists for the third time in four seasons.

The team entered the 1999–2000 season without beloved veteran Joe Dumars, who had retired. By the end of the season, Gentry was gone as well, replaced by his assistant, George Irvine. Irvine, too, was popular with the players,

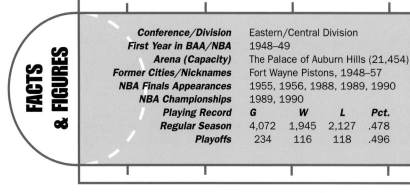

and the Pistons did finish the season 42–40 to advance to the playoffs. But when Hill fractured an ankle the Pistons lost to Miami in a three-game sweep in the first round. That was the ninth straight season the team failed to advance to the second round, including four seasons in which the team did not make the playoffs.

Hill, again, led the team with 25.8 points, 6.6 rebounds, 5.2 assists and 1.39 steals. The Pistons also received a big boost from Jerry Stackhouse, who chipped in 23.6 points per game and received strong consideration for the league's most improved player award. It was Stackhouse's best season since being traded to the Pistons from the Sixers in the middle of the 1997–98 season.

MOTOWN MOVER: *Jerry Stackhouse came into his own during his second season in Detroit.*

50 GOLDEN STATE WARRIORS

California dreaming

Their NBA journey has passed through three cities and covered thousands of miles. It has produced championships, scoring titles and dominant personalities and performances. When the Warriors look back on a half century of basketball, it's easy to detect two unmistakable trends.

First, Warriors players have won a record 14 scoring titles—all in the franchise's first 22 seasons. Joe Fulks won two, Paul Arizin two, Neil Johnston three, Wilt Chamberlain six and Rick Barry one. No Warrior has won another for more than a quarter of a century.

Second, the Warriors have won three championships and played in three other NBA Finals—all in their first three decades. In their last two, they have never advanced beyond the second round of the playoffs and didn't even qualify for the postseason from 1977–86.

The Philadelphia Warriors, the creation of Eddie Gottlieb, were one of 11 charter 1946 franchises that began play in the Basketball Association of America, the league that evolved into the NBA. The team carved the first notch in the NBA's record book when it captured the new league's first championship.

But the Warriors would not win again until 1956, when the unstoppable inside-out combination of Johnston and Arizin combined to average 46.3 points per game. The franchise's final title, choreographed

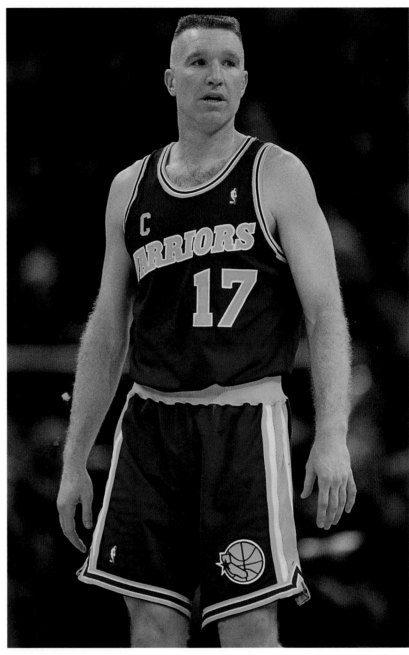

GOLDEN BOY: *Chris Mullin helped get the Warriors back on track after some lean years.*

by the high-scoring Barry and coached by former guard Al Attles, was earned in 1975, 13 years after the Warriors made a coast-to-coast move from Philadelphia to San Francisco and four years after they became the "Golden State" Warriors with a move across the Bay to Oakland.

The 7–1 Chamberlain re-wrote the NBA record books during his five-plus

FACTS & FIGURES

Conference/Division	Western/Pacific Division
First Year in BAA/NBA	1946–47
Arena (Capacity)	The Arena in Oakland (19,596)
Former Cities/Nicknames	Philadelphia Warriors, 1946–62; San Francisco Warriors, 1962–71
NBA Finals Appearances	1947, 1948, 1956, 1964, 1967, 1975
NBA Championships	1947, 1956, 1975

Playing Record	G	W	L	Pct.
Regular Season	4,178	1,967	2,211	.471
Playoffs	214	99	115	.463

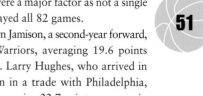

seasons with the Warriors, but he couldn't get his team a championship. The man who averaged an incredible 50.4 points in his third NBA season did come close in 1964, but the Warriors lost a five-game NBA Finals series to Boston. A year later Chamberlain was traded to Philadelphia, with center duties turned over to Nate Thurmond.

While the Warriors ranked among the NBA elite for their first three decades, the last two have been a different story. When they lost in the second round of the 1977 playoffs, that signaled the beginning of a bleak nine-year period in which they managed only two winning records and failed to generate momentum with a changing cast that included big men Robert Parish, Joe Barry Carroll and Ralph Sampson and long-range bombers Purvis Short and World B. Free. Prospects remained grim until Don Nelson took the coaching reins in 1988.

Nelson crafted his revival around 6–7 forward Chris Mullin, adding guards Mitch Richmond, Tim Hardaway and Latrell Sprewell and 6–10 forward Chris Webber. The Warriors vaulted to 55 victories in 1991–92 and 50 two years later, but Nelson's foundation was ripped apart when he feuded with Webber and traded the big man to Washington, a move that cost him his job early in 1995.

Personnel problems arose spectacularly with new coach P.J. Carlesimo in 1997–98, a season after the Warriors had slipped to a last-place finish. Sprewell attacked the coach during practice, earning a record 12-month suspension and dragging the Warriors' name into the headlines for all the wrong reasons. Against that backdrop, it was no surprise the team won only 19 games.

Carlisimo lasted through the next lockout-shortened season but the Warriors finished just 21-29. John Starks was one of just three players to play all 50 games that season, leading Golden State by averaging 13.8 points per game.

Although the Warriors averaged just 88.3 points per game—fifth worst in the NBA—their defensive average of 90.8 points per game, ranked 12th in the league. But the Warriors never completely recov-

WEST COAST WARRIOR *Antawn Jamison was just getting warmed up for Golden State.*

ered from the Sprewell-Carlisimo situation, and a coaching change was made early in the 1999-2000 season.

General Manager Garry St. Jean came down from his office to assume the coaching reins. Effervescent and gregarious, St. Jean had been a head coach in Sacramento for four years. His 159 regular season victories ranked first overall among head coaches in the club's Sacramento era. He was not able to lead the Warriors to similar heights and they finished 19-63.

Injuries were a major factor as not a single player played all 82 games.

Antawn Jamison, a second-year forward, led the Warriors, averaging 19.6 points per game. Larry Hughes, who arrived in midseason in a trade with Philadelphia, wound up scoring 22.7 points per game in the last part of the season.

St. Jean had intended to remain as coach, but after the season announced Dave Cowens as his replacement. The former Charlotte coach has his hands full.

HOUSTON ROCKETS

52

A dream come true for the franchise center

When the San Diego Rockets joined the NBA in 1967 as an expansion team, everybody anticipated a difficult road to respectability. But respectability, it turned out, would be much easier attained than a championship ring.

Respectability, in fact, would come in the 1968 draft with the selection of 6-foot-9 scoring machine Elvin Hayes. With the rookie Hayes averaging 28.4 points and 17.1 rebounds, the Rockets jumped from a 15-victory debut season to 37 and even qualified for the 1969 playoffs.

But that championship dream would not be realized for more than a quarter of a century. In 1993–94, 7-foot center Hakeem Olajuwon, appropriately nicknamed "The Dream," carried Houston's Rockets to the first of consecutive titles under the direction of coach Rudy Tomjanovich, a star forward in the Hayes era.

Hayes was merely the first forward step on the Rockets' evolutionary trail. He led the team to a franchise-best 40 victories in 1970–71, but he was traded to Baltimore a year later after feuding with coach Tex Winter. Ironically, Hayes, a college star at the University of Houston, was dealt away one season after the Rockets had moved to Houston because of sagging attendance in San Diego.

Hayes' departure was even more unfortunate because the Rockets had added two outstanding prospects in the 1970

draft. The 6–8, 220-pound Tomjanovich joined Hayes at one forward slot and Calvin Murphy began his career as one of the best off-guards in NBA history.

FIRST YEAR HERO: *Steve Francis shared rookie of the year honors with Elton Brand.*

The Rockets' fortunes did not improve dramatically until 1976, when 21-year-old center Moses Malone arrived after two ABA seasons. The Rockets won their first

Central Division title in 1976–77 and advanced to the Eastern Conference Finals before losing to Philadelphia. In 1980–81, the Rockets advanced all the way to the NBA Finals, but lost to Boston.

Malone departed after a quick 1982 playoff loss and so did the Rockets' momentum. But, operating on the notion that bigger is better, the Rockets drafted 7–4 Ralph Sampson in 1983 and Olajuwon in '84. The "Twin Towers" and hard-nosed forward Rodney McCray carried Houston to the 1985–86 Midwest Division title and another visit to the NBA Finals, but again the Rockets lost to the Celtics.

It wasn't until the team was handed to Tomjanovich in 1991 that the final puzzle began taking shape. Olajuwon matured into the game's best all-around big man, and with a supporting cast that included point guard Kenny Smith and forward Otis Thorpe, the 1993–94 Rockets cruised through the playoffs before defeating the Knicks in a rugged seven-game Finals. A year later, Olajuwon was reunited with his former college teammate Clyde Drexler and that combination led the way to the Rockets' second straight NBA title, a four-game sweep of the Orlando Magic.

Charles Barkley arrived in Houston two years later and experts predicted another crown but the future Hall of Fame trio of Olajuwon, Drexler and Barkley were beset by injuries over the coming seasons, losing to Utah in the Western Conference Finals of 1997 and the same team in the first round a year later. The summer of 1998 saw Drexler retire and the Rockets plan a major rebuilding program.

It looked as if acquiring Scottie Pippin in a trade with the Chicago Bulls would have been the key to that rebuilding, but things didn't quite work out that way. Pippin did play in every game and averaged 14.5 points, 6.5 rebounds and a team high 5.9 assists. He was named to the NBA's all-defensive first team for the

Conference/Division	Western/Midwest Division		
First Year in NBA	1967–68		
Arena (Capacity)	Compaq Center (16,285)		
Former Cities/Nicknames	San Diego Rockets, 1967–71		
NBA Finals Appearances	1981, 1986, 1994, 1995		
NBA Championships	1994, 1995		
Playing Record	**G**	**W**	**L**	**Pct.**
Regular Season	2,674	1,331	1,343	.498
Playoffs	199	100	99	.503

THE DREAM CENTER: *Hakeem Olajuwon had an amazing combination of power and finesse.*

eighth straight year. Olajuwon averaged 18.9 points and 9.5 rebounds, while Barkley averaged 16.1 points and 12.3 rebounds —second in the NBA.

But the mixture did not prove to be a winner, and the Rockets lost to the Lakers in the first round of the playoffs, 3-1. In the wake of that, some discord developed between Pippin and Barkley, and heightened after Pippin criticized Barkley's work

habits in a nationally televised interview. Sensing the two could no longer play together, the Rockets shipped Pippin to Portland in a multi-player deal.

The Rockets also obtained Steve Francis, the second player taken in the 1999 draft, from Vancouver. Francis led the Rockets' youth movement by averaging 18 points, 5.3 rebounds, 6.6 assists and 1.53 steals in earning co-rookie of the

year award with Chicago's Elton Brand.

The development of the Rockets' younger players was crucial because Barkley suffered a career-ending injury 20 games into the season. He suffered a ruptured tendon in his left quadriceps. Also, Olajuwon missed 38 games with a variety of injuries, including a hernia.

Houston finished 34-48, failing to make the playoffs for the first time in eight years.

54 INDIANA PACERS

A little NBA fish swims with the sharks

A CUT ABOVE: *Rik Smits and the Pacers shaved their heads during one playoff run.*

FACTS & FIGURES

Conference/Division	Eastern/Central Division		
First Year in ABA/NBA	1967–68/1976–77		
Arena (Capacity)	Conseco Fieldhouse (18,345)		
Former Cities/Nicknames	None		
NBA Finals Appearances	2000		
ABA/NBA Championships	1970, 1972, 1973 (all ABA)		
Playing Record	G	W	L	Pct.
ABA Regular Season	744	427	317	.574
NBA Regular Season	1,936	923	1,013	.477
ABA Playoffs	111	58	53	.523
NBA Playoffs	75	36	39	.480

For nine seasons, the Indiana Pacers were the biggest fish in the ABA pond. Over the next two decades, they were little more than tadpoles lost in the NBA ocean. Now, with a legendary player turned coach (native Hoosier Larry Bird) and two veteran stars (Reggie Miller and Rik Smits) they seem to have the tenacity to swim among the league's sharks.

They certainly illustrated that in the 1998 playoffs where they became the first team in six years to push the mighty Chicago Bulls to a full seven game series before agonizingly losing the Eastern Conference Finals. It took an heroic performance from Miller and an astute coaching display from Bird to take the Pacers that far but it was a sign of Bird's legendary competitive edge that he was far from satisfied with a season that ended short of Indiana's first ever Finals appearance.

Born in 1967 as a charter member of the ABA, the team stepped into an Indiana market that had enjoyed only two brief associations with the professional game—the Jets (1948–49) and the Olympians (1949–53). The Pacers won over skeptics by assembling a team that dominated the league from 1970 to '73 and produced some of its brightest stars.

The cornerstone of the early Pacers was 6-foot-9 center Mel Daniels, a bulldog rebounder and scorer. Fiery coach Bob (Slick) Leonard filled in the pieces around Daniels—forward Roger Brown, guards Billy Keller and Freddie Lewis—and the 1969–70 Pacers stormed to 59 victories and the first of three ABA championships.

When George McGinnis, a 6–8 former star at Indiana University, joined Brown and Daniels in an explosive frontcourt, the 1972 and '73 Pacers became the ABA's first back-to-back champions.

But the remainder of the Pacers' ABA tenure would be spent cutting costs in a desperate battle against red ink. By the time the ABA–NBA merger was forged, only McGinnis remained and even he would be gone before the franchise played its first NBA game. The Pacers, New York Nets, San Antonio Spurs and Denver Nuggets were accepted into the NBA in 1976—at a stiff price. The cash-short Pacers were required to pay a $3.2-million entry fee, forfeit television rights for four years and sit out the 1976 college draft. To stay afloat, they had to deal valuable future draft picks for journeyman players and entered the league with a soft, depleted roster.

Recovery from that shaky NBA debut would be painful. Over the next 17 years, the franchise was hindered by shaky ownership, unwise draft choices, bad trades and the inability to produce star-quality players. In 17 seasons from 1976–77 through 1992–93, the team never won more than 44 games, missed the playoffs 11 times and won only four post-season games. Playmaking guard Don Buse, high-scoring Billy Knight and power forward Clark Kellogg were the brightest stars in an ever-changing cast of players and coaches. From 1989 through 1993, the Pacers employed five coaches before the arrival of Larry Brown.

With Miller emerging as one of the league's premier shooters and clutch performers, and the 7–4 Smits' development into one of the league's better centers, the Pacers piled up 52 victories and their first Central Division title in 1994–95. They reached the Eastern Conference Finals twice in the mid-90s, only to lose seventh-game heartbreakers to New York and Orlando.

In the lockout-shortened 1998–99 season, the Pacers stayed together and many of the players continued to work out in Indianapolis. Observors thought this would give them an advantage when the regular season finally started because they were already so used to playing together. And in fact, Indiana tied for the best record in the Eastern Conference (33–17) with Miami and Orlando. They also won their second Central Division championship.

For the 10th straight season, Miller led the Pacers in scoring at 18.4 points per game. He also led the league in free throw shooting at .915 (226 of 247). Mark Jackson was second in the league in assists-to-turnover ratio at 3.90–1, and Chris Mullin was second in the league in three-point percentage at a Pacer record .465.

Still, the Pacers wound up losing to the New York Knicks in the Eastern Conference finals in six games.

As the 1999–2000 season began, Indiana knew this was its last chance to win under Bird, who had announced he would step down as coach at the end of the season.

Once again, Indiana won the Eastern Conference and Central Division titles. But this year it was young Jalen Rose who led the Pacers in scoring, inching past Miller, 18.2 points to 18.1. Miller was second in the league in free throw shooting at .919 (373 of 406).

But Miller took over in the playoffs, and this year the Pacers beat the Knicks in six games in the Eastern Conference Finals to advance to the NBA Finals. Unfortunately for Indiana, the Pacers lost in six games to Shaquille O'Neal and the Los Angeles Lakers. Though Miller remained, many changes followed.

MILLER TIME: *Reggie Miller raised his game in the playoffs, pointing the way forward.*

56 LOS ANGELES CLIPPERS

Sailing against the wind has become a trademark

It hasn't been pretty. It hasn't even been close. For more than a quarter century, the Clippers have been giving new meanings to the word "futility." Among some of the more embarassing statistics, the Clippers have managed five winning seasons while stumbling through one 12- and three 17-victory campaigns and qualified for postseason play five times, but only three times since 1976.

The Clippers have won less than 37 percent of their games and no division titles, so maybe it is not quite so surprising that they have employed 18 coaches and made five in-season changes.

It certainly has not helped the franchise that they have played in three cities including Los Angeles, where the Clippers are overshadowed by the high-profile Lakers. The highlight— lowlight maybe— came in a bizarre 1978 deal, when team owner John Y. Brown traded his Buffalo Braves for Irv Levin's Boston Celtics.

The Clippers began their NBA life in 1970 in Buffalo as part of a three-team expansion that also included Portland and Cleveland. The Braves should have realized something was wrong when the team was sold one day before its first-ever game.

The first glimmer of hope arrived in 1972 when new coach Jack Ramsay grabbed high-scoring Bob McAdoo with the second overall pick of the draft and surrounded his 6-foot-9 center with guards Randy Smith and Ernie DiGregorio and

THE CANDY MAN: *Michael Olowokandi was a sweet pick for the Clippers in 1999.*

forwards Jim McMillian and Garfield Heard. McAdoo won three consecutive scoring titles and the Braves earned three consecutive playoff berths, advancing to the second round in 1976.

But that glimmer flickered into darkness after the 1976 playoffs when Ramsay departed for Portland and McAdoo was inexplicably traded to the Knicks in an unpopular deal that foreshadowed the bleakest and most futile 15-year period for any team in NBA history.

Over those 15 seasons, the Clippers managed only one winning record and one campaign with more than 36 victories. It would not qualify for postseason play. After the 1977–78 campaign, when the owners traded franchises, the Braves were relocated to San Diego—Levin's base—as the Clippers and six years later they moved to Los Angeles. A lot of offense (World B. Free, Terry Cummings, Bill Walton, Freeman Williams, Tom Chambers) passed through the franchise, but less defense—and even fewer victories.

Relief finally appeared at the end of the 1991–92 season when Larry Brown took the coaching reins and quickly returned the team to respectability. Brown's Clippers, featuring guard Ron Harper and forwards

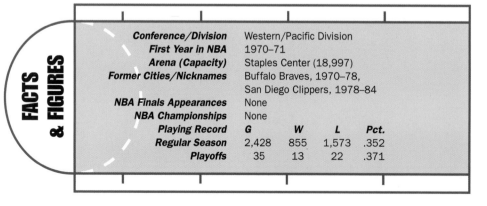

FACTS & FIGURES

Conference/Division	Western/Pacific Division			
First Year in NBA	1970–71			
Arena (Capacity)	Staples Center (18,997)			
Former Cities/Nicknames	Buffalo Braves, 1970–78,			
	San Diego Clippers, 1978–84			
NBA Finals Appearances	None			
NBA Championships	None			
Playing Record	G	W	L	Pct.
Regular Season	2,428	855	1,573	.352
Playoffs	35	13	22	.371

Danny Manning and Ken Norman, finished 45–37 and 41–41 in his two seasons, although they did make quick playoff exits on both occasions. With the Lakers in a rebuilding mode, the Clippers were at last out of their illustrious neighbors' shadow. But the franchise quickly returned to its sad, familiar ways.

Brown left for Indiana after the 1993 playoffs and was followed in quick order by Harper (free agent), Manning (traded) and Norman (free agent). The 1994–95 Clippers, under new coach Bill Fitch, sank back to 17 victories before improving to 36 wins and a playoff appearance two years later.

Fitch had built that team around power forward Loy Vaught but when he missed most of the 1997–98 season after back surgery, the Clippers slipped back to the cellar with a 17–65 record, a year that cost Fitch his job and wrote another unpredictable chapter in the team's inconsistent history.

Chris Ford, fired by the Milwaukee Bucks, became the latest coach to try to turn around the Clippers when he took the helm for the 1998-99 season. His luck was no better than any of his predecessors', and the team finished 9-41.

Maurice Taylor emerged as one of the top young power forwards in the league, averaging 16.8 points and 32.7 minutes, both team highs. He also shot .461 from the field, another team high. Rookie Michael Olowokandi, the first pick in the 1999 draft, led the Clippers in rebounding with 7.9 a game, and blocked shots at 1.22.

Ford lasted long enough to help the Clippers move into the brand new Staples Center in Los Angeles, but no so long as to finish out the 1999–2000 season. He was replaced in midstream by assistant Jim Todd, who fared no better as the hapless Clippers finished 15–67.

Taylor led the team in scoring with 17.1 points per game while Olowokandi added 9.8 points and 8.2 rebounds. Newcomer Derek Anderson, obtained in a trade with Cleveland, added 16.9 points, 4 rebounds and 3.4 assists.

Amazingly, the Clippers averaged 13,652 fans at their games in 1999–2000, despite extending their hapless streak to only one playoff appearance in seven years.

FULL CLIP: *Lamar Odom impressed a lot of people in his rookie season.*

LOS ANGELES LAKERS

58

The best in the west, thanks to the biggest gun

THE BIG DADDY: *Shaq was the MVP as the Lakers won the NBA title in 2000.*

They ruled the NBA through the first half of the 1950s, served as bridesmaids during the '60s, made a cameo appearance in the '70s and performed basketball Magic in the '80s. The Lakers might not be the game's most storied franchise, but they're close.

Franchise success is defined by the Boston Celtics, owners of 16 NBA championships, 19 conference titles, 24 division titles and the highest winning percentage in league history. But consider: The Lakers have won 11 championships, 24 conference titles and 25 division titles while winning more than 60 percent of their games. They have failed to reach the playoffs four times.

The Lakers' amazing consistency has been the product of three distinct eras: the George Mikan years with John Kundla as coach (1948–54); the Elgin Baylor–Jerry West period with Fred Schaus (1960–73), and the Magic Johnson-Kareem Abdul-Jabbar run with Pat Riley (1980–91).

The Lakers were based in Minneapolis when they abandoned the National Basketball League in favor of the two-year-old Basketball Association of America in 1948. Mikan, a bruising 6-foot-10, 245-pounder, redefined how the center position should be played, scoring and rebounding almost at will against smaller opponents. With Mikan winning four consecutive scoring titles and getting support from Jim Pollard, Vern Mikkelsen and playmaker Slater Martin, the Lakers rolled to four division titles and five championships in six years.

Mikan retired after the 1954 champi-

onship and the next push started with the 1958 draft selection of Baylor, a classy 6–5 forward. When Baylor, Mr. Inside, was joined in 1960 by guard Jerry West, Mr. Outside, the Lakers were primed for another run.

The Baylor-West show opened on the West Coast, where the Lakers moved after the 1959–60 season. From 1962 to 1970, the Lakers won five division titles and reached the NBA Finals seven times. But without a center to compete against Bill Russell or Willis Reed, they lost six series to the powerful Celtics and one to the Knicks.

Baylor, plagued by knee problems, made only a cameo appearance for a 1972 Lakers team that finally broke through. With an aging Wilt Chamberlain playing center and West sharing backcourt duties with high-scoring Gail Goodrich, the 1971–72 Lakers piled up an incredible 33-game winning streak en route to an NBA-record 69 victories and bulled their way through a 12–3 playoff run.

The framework for the next run was built around 7–2 center Abdul-Jabbar, a 1975 acquisition from Milwaukee, and 6–9 point guard Magic Johnson, a 1979 draft pick. With Riley pulling the strings and Abdul-Jabbar and Johnson getting support from James Worthy, Byron Scott, Michael Cooper and Jamaal Wilkes, the Lakers won the 1980 championship and added four more before the decade closed. They also lost three times in the Finals.

With Abdul-Jabbar and Johnson retiring, and Riley moving on, the Lakers fell on hard times in the early 1990s. A 53-win season in 1995–96 gave a ray of hope, then the signing of free agent Shaquille O'Neal in the summer of 1996 lifted the Lakers and ushered in a new era in Los Angeles. Despite a second round exit in the 1996–97 playoffs and a harrowing 4–0 sweep at the hands of Utah in the Conference Finals a year later, the Lakers

FACTS & FIGURES

Conference/Division	Western/Pacific Division
First Year in BAA/NBA	1948–49
Arena (Capacity)	Staples Center (18,997)
Former Cities/Nicknames	Minneapolis Lakers, 1948–60
NBA Finals Appearances	1949, 1950, 1952, 1953, 1954, 1959, 1962, 1963, 1965, 1966, 1968, 1969, 1970, 1972, 1973, 1980, 1982, 1983, 1984, 1985, 1987, 1988, 1989, 1991, 2000
NBA Championships	1949, 1950, 1952, 1953, 1954, 1972, 1980, 1982, 1985, 1987, 1988, 2000

Playing Record	G	W	L	Pct.
Regular Season	4,073	2,507	1,566	.616
Playoffs	563	332	231	.590

NOTHING BUT A NUMBER: *Kobe Bryant has quickly grown into one of the team's key players, despite his tender years.*

look ahead with a nucleus of O'Neal, Eddie Jones, and teen-age sensation Kobe Bryant as one of the more entertaining and talented teams in the NBA.

Finding a coach for this group has proved to be the hard part. Gentlemanly Del Harris put in four seasons but just 12 games into the lockout-shortened 1998–99 season he was replaced for one game by longtime assistant Bill Bertka and then former player Kurt Rambis took a turn at the reins. Rambis did finish the season 24–13, and the Lakers beat the Rockets, 3–1 in the first round of the playoffs. But they were swept out of the Western Conference semifinals by the San Antonio Spurs and Rambis was not asked to come back for the next season.

O'Neal led the Lakers by averaging 26.3 points (second in the league) and 10.7 rebounds (eighth in the league). O'Neal's .576 field goal percentage (510 of 885) led the league.

The Lakers opened the 1999–2000 season with a new coach, Phil Jackson, and a new arena, Staples Center. Jackson, renewed after a one-year hiatus from coaching, looked as if he had picked up with the Lakers where he had left off with the Bulls, who had won six championships in eight years under his guidance.

Los Angeles finished with the best record in the league, 67–15. O'Neal, who shared the All-Star Game MVP with Tim Duncan and came within one vote of becoming the first unanimous selection for Most Valuable Player honors, averaged 29.7 points, 13.6 rebounds, 3.8 assists and 3.03 blocked shots per game. Even his free throw percentage improved to .524

(432 of 824), his best free throw shooting in five seasons.

O'Neal continued his domination in the playoffs, and the Lakers needed every point and rebound as they had a hard time putting away teams. They needed five games to beat Sacramento in the best-of-five first round, five games to beat Phoenix in the best-of-seven second round, seven games to beat Portland in the Western Conference Finals and six games to beat Indiana in the NBA Finals.

In the finals, O'Neal averaged 38 points and 16 rebounds to win the Finals Most Valuable Player award, becoming just the third player in NBA history to sweep the All Star, regular season and Finals MVP awards, joining New York's Willis Reed (1970) and Chicago's Michael Jordan (1996 and 1998.)

60 MIAMI HEAT

Growing pains and gains

GOOD MOURNING: *Miami's Alonzo Mourning has been the heart and soul of the Heat.*

In the fragile early years of every expansion franchise, there comes a moment of truth— the point where opportunity knocks, the door to success opens and management faces a difficult decision.

The Miami Heat faced their moment of truth in 1995—twice. First they gave the New York Knicks a precious 1996 No. 1 draft pick to let Pat Riley out of the final year of his contract. Then they settled the Charlotte Hornets' $20-million feud with center Alonzo Mourning by trading three players for the 6-foot-10 star.

And just like that, Miami began heating up the NBA's Atlantic Division. Mourning quickly became the centerpiece for Riley's puzzle and within two seasons the Heat reached the Eastern Conference finals. Riley did so by rejuvenating point guard Tim Hardaway into a First Team All-Star.

He turned power forward Isaac Austin into the league's Most Improved Player and plucked Voshon Lenard out the CBA and made him a valuable offensive contributor. Riley's creation was so good they won 61 games in 1996–97 and defeated the Magic and Knicks in the playoffs, before succumbing to the powerful Bulls in five games.

The sudden makeover was shocking for Miami fans who had watched management build the team sensibly and patiently through the draft. Center Rony Seikaly and forward Grant Long, a pair of 1988 picks, were starters during the Heat's 15-victory expansion season (1988–89) and their 42-win 1993–94 campaign. Long-range bomber Glen Rice was drafted in 1989 and guard Steve Smith in 1991.

The Heat's early stability was the product of a solid ownership group pieced together by former NBA player and coach Billy Cunningham. The group was awarded a franchise in April 1987 as part of a four-team expansion that also included Charlotte, Minnesota and Orlando. The Heat and Hornets began play in 1988–89, the Timberwolves and Magic a year later.

The Heat took their first NBA steps on wobbly legs under coach Ron Rothstein. They won 15 games in their debut season, 18 the next year and 24 in year three. Rothstein was replaced by Kevin Loughery in 1991–92 and the young team, which featured Seikaly, Rice, Smith and Long, showed signs of life. They jumped to 38 wins and became the first of the four expansion teams to qualify for a playoff berth—a quick sweep by Chicago. The 1993–94 winner was a cause for celebration.

But everything unraveled in 1994–95. Just before the season opened, Miami shipped Seikaly to Golden State for Billy Owens and followed quickly by dealing Long and Smith to Atlanta for Kevin

FACTS & FIGURES

Conference/Division	Eastern/Atlantic Division			
First Year in NBA	1988–89			
Arena (Capacity)	American Airlines Arena (19,600)			
Former Cities/Nicknames	None			
NBA Finals Appearances	None			
NBA Championships	None			
Playing Record	**G**	**W**	**L**	**Pct.**
Regular Season	952	448	504	.470
Playoffs	48	20	28	.416

Willis. Rice and 7-footer Matt Geiger were part of the 1995 package that brought Mourning.

Much like his teams in New York, Riley's Heat play a physical, relentless defense combined with an uncompromising desire to win at all costs. There were few tears shed around the league, therefore, when the Heat mystifyingly followed a 1997–98 55–27 regular season record with a first round playoff exit at the hands of Riley's fomer club New York.

Mourning just continued to get better. In the lockout-shortened 1998–99 season, he averaged 20.1 points, 11 rebounds (sixth in the league), and an amazing 3.91 blocked shots (which led the league.) His .511 field goal percentage (324 of 634) ranked fourth in the league. He was named the league's Defensive Player of the Year and was named to the All-NBA first team and the All-Defensive first team. Miami finished that short season with a record of 33–17, tying Indiana and Orlando for the best record in the Eastern Conference. But for the third straight season, the Heat lost a five-game first round series to the New York Knicks.

Riley did not make any significant roster changes for the 1999–2000 season, although the team did relocate to the new American Airlines Arena, a short distance from the old Miami Arena. And even though the Heat lost Tim Hardaway for 30 games with a variety of injuries, Miami still finished 52–30 to win the Atlantic Division title. Mourning averaged 21.7 points, 9.5 rebounds and 3.72 blocked shots per game, tops in the league. He was, once again, named Defensive Player of the Year. Jamal Mashburn picked up the slack in Hardaway's absence, averaging 17.5 points per game, his highest since joining the Heat in the 1996–97 season.

In the playoffs, the Heat swept the Detroit Pistons in the first round before running into the Knicks yet again. This time the Knicks won a seven-game second-round series, the fourth straight season the Knicks had eliminated Riley's Heat.

THUNDER DAN: *Dan Majerle has been unable to get the Heat past the New York Knicks.*

62 MILWAUKEE BUCKS

The flip of a coin transformed a young team

One year they were expansion babies, inexperienced and naïve in the ways of the NBA. The next year they were title-contending giants, confident and capable of mixing it up with the game's elite.

All it took to transform the Milwaukee Bucks from a caterpillar into a butterfly was the flip of a coin and a stroke of luck that instantly changed the NBA's balance of power and the future course of two franchises.

The Bucks struggled to a 27–55 first-year record, the worst in the Eastern Division. The Phoenix Suns, Milwaukee's expansion mates, finished 16–66, last in the West. A coin flip determined the first pick of the 1969 draft and the prize was 7-foot-2 UCLA center Lew Alcindor.

When the Suns made the wrong call, the Bucks moved into the NBA stratosphere. Alcindor, who later would change his name to Kareem Abdul-Jabbar, averaged 28.8 points and 14.5 rebounds in his rookie season and Milwaukee won 56 games, more than double its victory total of 1968–69.

The Bucks, suddenly thrust into the championship picture, quickly surrounded their big man with veteran talent. Venerable Oscar Robertson, still looking for his first NBA title, was brought in to run the show and he was joined in a talented backcourt by Jon McGlocklin and Lucius Allen. Abdul-Jabbar was

flanked in the frontcourt by Greg Smith and rebounding ace Bob Dandridge.

The 1970–71 season was no contest. Abdul-Jabbar won the first of consecutive scoring titles en route to league MVP honors and Milwaukee rolled to 66 victories. In a 12–2 postseason, the 3-year-old Bucks brushed past San Francisco, Los Angeles and Baltimore for their first NBA championship.

Although Milwaukee continued to dominate the Midwest Division with 192 victories over the next three seasons, there would be no more titles. Abdul-Jabbar carried them to the 1974 NBA Finals—a seven-game loss to the Boston Celtics—but the Bucks cleaned house after an injury-plagued 1974–75 campaign and Abdul-Jabbar was sent to Los Angeles for four young players.

The rebuilding program began paying dividends in 1979–80, when Don Nelson coached his young team to the first of seven consecutive Midwest and Central Division titles. From 1980–81 through 1986–87, Milwaukee victory totals ranged from 50 to 60 and the Bucks advanced deep into the playoffs every season from 1983 to '87.

But a strong team built around such players as Terry Cummings, Quinn Buckner, Bob Lanier, Junior Bridgeman, Marques Johnson and Sidney Moncrief could not get past Eastern Conference powers Boston and Philadelphia and the

FACTS & FIGURES

Conference/Division	Eastern/Central Division			
First Year in NBA	1968–69			
Arena (Capacity)	Bradley Center (18,633)			
Former Cities/Nicknames	None			
NBA Finals Appearances	1971, 1974			
NBA Championships	1971			
Playing Record	G	W	L	Pct.
Regular Season	2,592	1,410	1,182	.544
Playoffs	177	87	90	.492

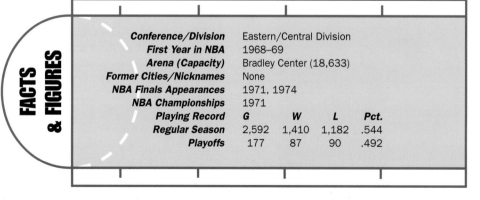

HOUSE TRAINED: *Glenn Robinson has been the "Big Dog" for the Milwaukee Bucks.*

Bucks never reached the NBA Finals.

The end of the decade was filled with 40+-win seasons under coach Del Harris, but the 1990s began with another rebuilding program that is finally showing results.

Chris Ford led the Bucks to 33 wins in 1996–97, their best season in five years, and went three wins better a year later after structuring a major three-team trade that took Vin Baker to Seattle and brought in Tyrone Hill and Terrell Brandon from Cleveland. At least young forward Glenn Robinson finally began to fulfill some of his enormous potential but the Bucks are still some way from returning to their Championship years.

Coach George Karl moved up the timetable somewhat after his arrival for the 1998-99 season. Chris Ford's firing and Karl's hiring came late in the summer, long after such moves are commonly made. Then there was the long wait for the lockout to end and the season to start.

But Karl didn't waste any time in impressing his style upon the floundering Bucks. He recorded the most successful first season for the Bucks in the history of the franchise when he finished with a record of 28–22, putting the team in the playoffs for the first time since the 1990–91 season.

Robinson averaged a team high 18.4 points, 5.5 rebounds, 2.1 assists and 1 steal per game. He shot .459 from the field, .392 from three-point range and .870 from the foul line, the last two career highs. He was ably assisted by Ray Allen, who averaged 17.1 points, 4.2 rebounds, 3.6 assists and 1.07 steals, with career highs from the free throw line (.903) and the field .(.450).

After being swept out of the playoffs by the Pacers, in three games in the first round, the Bucks came back in 1999–2000 determined to improve. Allen led the charge with 22.1 points per game while Robinson added 20.9. The Bucks survived a midseason swoon to finish 42–40 and again advance to the playoffs, where they once more faced the Pacers.

The Bucks lost again, but this time it took five games, after which Indiana veteran Reggie Miller said he wasn't sure the best team won.

HE'S GOT GAME: *Ray Allen provided some help in the backcourt for the Bucks.*

MINNESOTA TIMBERWOLVES

Out of the wilderness and into the playoffs

ON GUARD: *Point guard Terrell Brandon has directed the Wolves' attack since 1999.*

Prior to the 1996–97 season, it would have been fair to call the Minnesota Timberwolves offensively-challenged. Or defensively-challenged. Or, to cover the full spectrum of their first seven seasons, basketball-challenged.

But two of the league's youngest players, Kevin Garnett and Stephon Marbury helped change all that. That season, the T-Wolves were one of the league's nicest stories, reaching the 40-win plateau and grabbing their first playoff berth. Those improvements continued in 1997–98, despite the loss to injury for much of the second half of the season of influential forward Tom Gugliotta.

Garnett and Marbury took the team on their young shoulders as Minnesota reached 45 wins and won their first ever playoff games, scaring fancied Seattle before going down in five games.

When the Timberwolves made their debut in 1989–90, they were greeted by a highly excited Minneapolis contingent that envisioned a rekindling of past glories. Four decades earlier, in the fledgling years of the League, the Minneapolis Lakers, featuring super center George Mikan, had begun an impressive run that produced five NBA championships in six seasons.

It seemed only fitting that Mikan, who had retired before the Lakers made their 1960 move to Los Angeles, was part of a task force that helped bring professional basketball back to the Twin Cities. And it appeared to be a good omen when the first-year 'Wolves, playing under the disciplined, defensive-minded umbrella of coach Bill Musselman, won 22 games—more than any of the other expansion beginners.

Musselman's second-edition team produced 29 victories and more encouragement, but as fans filled the new Target Center and embraced their young team with fanatical enthusiasm, an unsteady foundation began to crumble. Musselman was fired and replaced by Jimmy Rodgers, whose up-tempo style was not a good fit for the plodding Timberwolves.

It turned out to be a disastrous choice. Minnesota sagged to 15 victories in 1991–92 and Rodgers departed 29 games into the next season, a 63-defeat nightmare. Rodgers' successor, Sidney Lowe, did not fare any better as the Timberwolves suffered through a record four consecutive 60-loss seasons and became the doormat of the Midwest Division.

But losing does have an upside, which has given Minnesota fans reason for optimism. Early stars such as Pooh Richardson, Isaiah Rider and Christian Laettner are gone, as are 7-foot draft flops Felton Spencer and Luc Longley.

Donyell Marshall, the 1994-first-rounder, was traded to the Golden State Warriors for Tom Gugliotta, a hard-working power forward who turned into a scoring threat with the Wolves. A year later, the team showed its commitment to patience and player development with their draft selection of 6–11 Garnett, who bypassed college and stepped in the NBA wars right out of a Chicago high school. Garnett, who improved steadily in his rookie season under coaches Bill Blair and Flip Saunders, was teamed a year later with another teen-ager, Marbury.

An all-American point guard as a

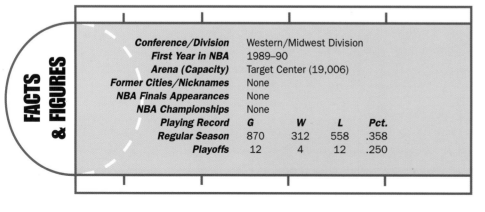

FACTS & FIGURES

	G	W	L	Pct.
Conference/Division	Western/Midwest Division			
First Year in NBA	1989–90			
Arena (Capacity)	Target Center (19,006)			
Former Cities/Nicknames	None			
NBA Finals Appearances	None			
NBA Championships	None			
Playing Record	G	W	L	Pct.
Regular Season	870	312	558	.358
Playoffs	12	4	12	.250

freshman at Georgia Tech, Marbury was the No. 4 selection in 1996 draft and finished second in the rookie-of-the-year balloting and guided the Wolves with the savvy of a five-year veteran.

It looked as if the Timberwolves were set for years of success. But little by little their best-laid plans began to fall apart. First Gugliotta signed as a free agent with the Phoenix Suns before the 1998–99 season. In the middle of the year, Marbury, concerned at playing second fiddle to Garnett, forced a trade that sent him to the New Jersey Nets. That left Saunders with Garnett to build around—not a bad starting point.

The lanky 6–11 forward led the team in scoring and rebounding with 20.8 points 10.4 rebounds per game. He finished 13th in the league in blocked shots at 1.77 and 20th in steals at 1.66. Newcomer Terrell Brandon, obtained in a trade with Milwaukee, led the team with 8.6 assists per game and led the league in assists-to-turnover ratio at 4.18–1.

In spite of all the changes, the Wolves finished 25–25 and made the playoffs. There they faced—and lost to—the San Antonio Spurs in the first round, but they did take a game off the team that would be crowned NBA Champions at the end of the playoffs.

The 1999–2000 season brought continued improvement and the team finished 50–32, winning 50 games for the first time in the 11-year history of the franchise. Garnett blossomed into a complete player and one of the league's new superstars. He averaged 22.9 points, 11.8 rebounds, 5.0 assists, 1.56 blocks and 1.48 steals. He proved to be so versatile that he almost persuaded All-Star coach Phil Jackson to use him at point guard.

Brandon averaged 17.1 points and 8.9 assists, while rookie Wally Szczerbiak scored 11.6 points per game while shooting a team high .511 (342 of 669). In the playoffs, however, they still failed to advance past the first round, losing to Portland. Again, the Wolves managed just one victory in the best-of-five series, but it seemed as if it would be just a matter of time before they broke through to the next level.

SHOOTING STAR: *Rookie Wally Szczerbiak was soon a valuable part of the Wolves' attack.*

66 NEW JERSEY NETS

A long and winding road that leads to nowhere

During its three nomadic decades, the team has played home games in six arenas, represented two states in two leagues and sported two nicknames. Its wandering path through New York City and New Jersey has been mirrored by its aimless journey through the NBA standings.

The team began play in the American Basketball Association in 1967 as the New Jersey Americans and played its first season in colorful red, white and blue uniforms in a dingy armory in its home base of Teaneck, N.J.

The Americans moved to Long Island's Commack Arena and adopted a new name (New York Nets) before their second season, but a blueprint for success would not be drawn until 1970 when Roy Boe bought the team, brought in very popular Lou Carnesecca as coach and acquired high-scoring Rick Barry from the Virginia Squires. The Nets, now playing in Island Garden Arena and armed with their first superstar attraction, qualified for the 1972 playoffs with a 44–40 record and advanced to the ABA Finals before losing to Indiana.

When a federal judge shocked the Nets by ordering Barry to take his 31.5-point average back to the NBA after the 1972 playoffs, Boe simply reloaded. He brought in Kevin Loughery as coach, acquired young forward Julius Erving from the Squires and signed a pair of talented draft picks in Larry Kenon and John Williamson. The 1973–74 Nets bolted to a 55–29 regular-season record, stormed to a 12–2 playoff mark and captured the first of two ABA championships in three years. The second would come in 1976, the ABA's final campaign.

The championship success and the excitement generated by the acrobatic Dr. J secured the Nets' inclusion in the 1976 ABA-NBA merger. But the financial responsibilities that accompanied the jump secured a long, grueling existence in the lower reaches of the Atlantic Division standings. In order to pay the bills, Boe was forced to sell Erving's contract to the Philadelphia 76ers, dooming his club to a long dry spell.

Over their first 16 NBA seasons, the Nets would post but four winning records (1981–82 through 1984–85) and win six playoff games. Five of the post-season wins came in 1984 when coach Stan Albeck led the Nets in their only advance past the opening round.

The early years were not a total disaster. The Nets moved back to New Jersey in 1977, spent four seasons playing at the Rutgers Athletic Center and finally moved into the plush new Meadowlands Arena, their current home. But on-court hope did not arrive until 1992 when Chuck Daly took over as coach.

Daly brought Nets fans their first winning record in seven seasons with a lineup that featured 6–10 Derrick

HORN O'PLENTY: *Keith Van Horn should be a key piece in the New Jersey Nets' future.*

FACTS & FIGURES

Conference/Division	Eastern/Atlantic Division			
First Year in ABA/NBA	1967–68/1976–77			
Arena (Capacity)	Continental Airlines Arena (20,049)			
Former Cities/Nicknames	New Jersey Americans, 1967–68,			
	New York Nets, 1968–77			
NBA Finals Appearances	None			
ABA/NBA Championships	1974, 1976 (both ABA)			
Playing Record	G	W	L	Pct.
ABA Regular Season	744	374	370	.503
NBA Regular Season	1,936	776	1,160	.400
ABA Playoffs	69	37	32	.536
NBA Playoffs	39	9	30	.231

Coleman, hot-shooting Drazen Petrovic and point guard Kenny Anderson. But Petrovic's tragic death in a 1993 automobile accident was a major setback, as was Daly's 1994 departure after his second straight winning season.

The Nets began another rebuilding project in 1996 when they named John Calipari as Head Coach. A success in college at UMass, Calipari struggled in his first year as he oversaw a huge restructuring of his roster. But Kendall Gill, All-Star Jayson Williams, Kerry Kittles and rookie Keith Van Horn formed an impressive young nucleus that brought about a dramatic change in fortune in 1997–98, leading the Nets into the playoffs and a first round defeat at the hands of Chicago.

Neither the success nor Calipari lasted very long. In fact, when the Nets started the 1998–99 season, with a 3–17 record, he was fired and replaced by Don Casey.

The Nets' biggest problem was losing Williams with a fractured right leg for the last 20 games of the season. Van Horn missed a total of eight games with a sprained right ankle and broken left thumb. Newcomer Jim McIlvaine was lost for 27 games with a shoulder injury.

Casey did guide the Nets to a 13–17 finish and they won 11 of their last 21 games, still falling short of the playoffs. Amazingly, the Nets had the top scoring duo in the league with Van Horn averaging 21.8 points and Stephon Marbury, obtained in a trade with Minnesota, adding 21.3.

After exploring several other possibilities, the Nets rehired Casey for the 1999–2000 season, but the team continued to struggle, finishing 31–51. Williams missed the entire season, leaving Marbury and Van Horn in charge. Marbury averaged 22.2 points and Marbury 19.2 points, to no good end. When the Nets missed the playoffs for the fifth time in six season, Casey was history.

However, the Nets did win the No. 1 pick in the NBA lottery, giving them some hope for the future.

POINT OF HONOR: *Stephon Marbury also has been a key acquisition for the franchise.*

NEW YORK KNICKS

A dedication to defense grows in the Garden

SHOPPING SPREE: *New York's Latrell Sprewell has been a bargain for the Knicks.*

The Knicks began play as a BAA/NBA original in 1946, but fans prefer to ignore the first 23 seasons. For them it began in 1970, when one of the most perfectly sculpted teams in league history rose to the top of the basketball world.

The middle of that team was dominated by 6–10 Willis Reed, a hard-working center who had arrived as a second-round 1964 draft pick. The perimeters were manned by Bill Bradley, who later became a U.S. Senator, and sharp-shooting Dave DeBusschere. The frontcourt was manned by Dick Barnett and Walt Frazier.

In retrospect, the 1969–70 Knicks might have been a team of destiny. Boston's Bill Russell had retired after the 1969 playoffs, officially ending the Celtics' 13-year dynasty, and New York was positioned perfectly for a run at its first NBA championship. With coach Red Holzman espousing the principles of patience, discipline and defense, the Knicks rolled to 60 victories, captured their first Eastern Division title in 16 years and advanced to the NBA Finals, where they defeated the Lakers in seven games.

The Knicks returned to the top of the Eastern Division in 1970–71 and advanced to the NBA Finals in 1972 and again in '73. With fast-shooting guard Earl Monroe now in the mix, the 1973 Knicks earned their second title with a five-game victory over the Lakers.

That four-year, two-title run provided Madison Square Garden with a touch of the magic that had been missing through New York's formative years. The early Knicks contended for Eastern supremacy under coach Joe Lapchick and reached the NBA Finals three times, but were no match for the bigger Rochester and Minneapolis teams. After that moderate success, the Knicks went through 11 seasons (from 1955–56 to 1965–66) without winning a playoff game.

The 1970s success was followed by another lull marked by constant change.

The Knicks tried their luck with such players as Bob McAdoo, Bill Cartwright and Campy Russell, but it wasn't until the 1985 draft yielded 7-foot Georgetown center Patrick Ewing that the team regained momentum.

Serious title thoughts returned to the Garden in 1991 when Pat Riley arrived to mold a winner around the intimidating Ewing. Surrounding him with physical players such as Charles Oakley and Derek Harper gave the Knicks a fierce defensive presence that bullied opponents and made high-scoring games obsolete. The Knicks became the most unpopular team in the NBA, but they laughed all the way to three straight Atlantic Division titles and a four-year average of 56 victories.

But when a disillusioned Riley left after the 1995 playoffs, all he had to show for his New York tenure was a 1994 trip to the NBA Finals and a seven-game loss to Houston. Jeff Van Gundy, a Riley understudy who took over the coaching reins in February 1996, led Ewing and newcomers Larry Johnson, Allan Houston and Chris Childs to a 57–25 regular-season record in 1996–97 before the team blew a 3–1 lead in the second round to Riley's Miami.

FACTS & FIGURES

Conference/Division	Eastern/Atlantic Division
First Year in BAA/NBA	1946–47
Arena (Capacity)	Madison Square Garden (19,763)
Former Cities/Nicknames	None
NBA Finals Appearances	1951, 1952, 1953, 1970, 1972, 1973, 1994, 1999
NBA Championships	1970, 1973

Playing Record	G	W	L	Pct.
Regular Season	4,179	2,156	2,023	.515
Playoffs	345	177	168	.513

Even greater disappointments came a year later when a hand injury forced Ewing to miss all but 26 games of the regular season. There was the consolation of upsetting Riley's new team Miami in the first round of the playoffs but a heavy loss to Indiana in round two left Ewing and the Knicks no closer to their first title in a quarter of a century.

Ewing came back strong from his injury and averaged 17.3 points to help the Knicks finish the 1998-99 season at 27-23. After faltering early, the Knicks hung on to claim the eighth and last spot in the Eastern Conference playoffs. They relied heavily on newcomer Latrell Sprewell, who arrived with a questionable reputation after his suspension for choking Golden State Coach P.J. Carlisimo. The New York fans welcomed him with open arms and responded by averaging 16.4 points in the regular season and 20.4 points in the playoffs to help the Knicks upset the top-seeded Miami Heat in five games in the first round.

However, Ewing suffered a heel injury in the second round against Indiana and could only watch as the Knicks defied the odds to advance to the NBA finals against the San Antonio Spurs. The Spurs prevailed in five games.

Ewing missed another 20 games with injuries in 1999–2000, but the Knicks were stronger and finished 50-32. Houston led New York averaging 19.7 points while Sprewell contributed 18.6. For the better part of two seasons, questions were raised about whether the team might be better off without Ewing. But Van Gundy remained steadfastly in the veteran center's corner and used him whenever his health permitted.

The Knicks swept the Toronto Raptors in the first round of the playoffs and then the Heat in a seven-game classic in the conference semifinals before losing to the Indiana Pacers in six games in the Eastern Conference Finals.

That would prove to be the last playoffs for the New York Knicks as we knew them. In the off-season, they traded Patrick Ewing to the Seattle SuperSonics after a 15-year career with the team.

LEADING MAN: *Point guard Charlie Ward has played a leading role in the Knicks' success.*

70 ORLANDO MAGIC

A Magical mystery tour conducted on the court

PERMISSION GRANTED: *Free agent Grant Hill opted to leave Detroit and signed with Orlando.*

Do you believe in Magic? Orlando basketball fans do, and with good reason. They're still trying to figure out the sleight of hand General Manager Pat Williams used to turn a tottering expansion team into an NBA powerhouse. Those same fans can now only hope that GM John Gabriel, and coach Doc Rivers, can perform the same trick and build on the franchise's 1999-2000 success.

The first transformation began in 1992 when Orlando, coming off a 21-victory season, struck gold in the Draft Lottery— a drawing to determine order of selection in the annual college draft. The stakes were high, with the lucky winner gaining rights to 7-foot-1, Louisiana State University center Shaquille O'Neal.

With the drawing weighted heavily toward the league's weaker teams, it was not a major surprise that the Magic became instant winners of the Shaquille sweepstakes; Orlando possessed the second to worst record in the NBA in the 1991–92 season. But what transpired just one year later sent shock waves through the NBA.

Orlando rose to a 41–41 record and barely missed qualifying for the 1993 playoffs, despite its 20-game improvement in the victory column. The Magic did, however, qualify again for the draft sweepstakes—this time with a 1-in-66 chance of landing the No. 1 pick. Amazingly, they won the lottery and selected 6–10 Michigan star Chris Webber as a prelude to a draft-day trade that would plot a quick course to the NBA Finals.

Many Magic fans drooled at the thought of a front line with O'Neal and Webber, but Williams, looking for a swing player with Michael Jordan-type abilities, shipped Webber to Golden State for Anfernee Hardaway, the Warriors' first-round pick, and three future No. 1 selections.

The young and talented Magic, with O'Neal controlling the middle, Hardaway scoring from everywhere on the court and Nick Anderson and Dennis Scott providing long-range scoring punch, powered their way to 50 victories in 1993–94 and a second-place finish in the Atlantic Division. A first-round playoff loss to Indiana only whetted a young team's growing appetite.

Williams added another big piece to the puzzle in 1994 by signing Horace Grant, a powerful rebounder for the 1991, '92 and '93 Chicago championship teams. The 1994–95 Magic rolled to 57 victories, captured their first division title en route to an NBA Finals. But the Houston Rockets pulled off a stunning four-game sweep and a 60-victory 1995–96 effort

Conference/Division	Eastern/Atlantic Division			
First Year in NBA	1989–90			
Arena (Capacity)	TD Waterhouse Centre (17,248)			
Former Cities/Nicknames	None			
NBA Finals Appearances	1995			
NBA Championships	None			
Playing Record	G	W	L	Pct.
Regular Season	870	438	432	.503
Playoffs	45	21	24	.466

FACTS & FIGURES

was followed by a conference-finals loss to Chicago and the shocking departure of O'Neal to Los Angeles with the biggest free-agent contract in history.

O'Neal's departure paved the way for Hardaway to emerge as the team leader—both on and off the court. And when the team struggled during the first half of the 1996–97 season, Hardaway was a key figure in the ousting of Brian Hill as head coach. Hill was replaced by assistant Richie Adubato and the Magic players responded with a strong finish before losing to the Miami Heat in the playoffs.

Magic's future was then put in the hands of Chuck Daly, a proven winner in his days with the Pistons. But his relationship with Hardaway was uncomfortable during the 1997–98 season, when Penny missed several games due to injury, and the team even considered trading their ubiquitous star.

In fact, after the 1998–99 season Daly and Hardaway were gone. Daly led the Magic to a 33–17 record, tying them for the Eastern Conference title with heavyweights Miami and Indiana. But after the lightly regarded Magic lost in four games to Philadelphia, Daly stepped down.

The oft-injured Hardaway, who averaged 15.8 points in playing all 50 games, was traded to Phoenix later that summer for Danny Manning, Pat Garrity and two first-round draft choices. Also traded was Nick Anderson, a member of the original Magic team.

It was against that backdrop that popular ex-player Glenn (Doc) Rivers was hired as coach by Gabriel. The Magic's rebuilding plan included accumulating as much money as possible under the salary cap in order to lure high-priced free agents.

Instead, Rivers led his odd assortment of players to a 41–41 record, losing the last playoff spot to the Milwaukee Bucks on the last day of the regular season.

For his efforts, Rivers beat out Lakers Coach Phil Jackson to win Coach of the Year honors while Gabriel was named the NBA Executive of the Year.

Gabriel continued his aggressive play in 2000, aquiring both Grant Hill and Tracy McGrady, making the Magic a likely contender once more.

PENNY FOR YOUR THOUGHTS: *Penny Hardaway's career in Orlando did not include a title.*

72 PHILADELPHIA 76ERS

Playing in the shadows

As one of seven NBA franchises within 50 of 2,000-plus regular-season victories, the 76ers have been surprisingly inefficient. The Celtics, Lakers and Knicks, the three other biggest winners, have combined for 29 championships and 50 NBA Finals appearances. The 76ers have won three titles in eight Finals.

Since making their debut in 1949–50 as the Syracuse Nationals, the Nats/76ers have posted 31 winning records, qualified for postseason action 37 times, including one stretch of seven straight 50-win seasons. The 1966–67 76ers compiled an amazing 68–13 record—the third-best mark in NBA history.

But too often the team's success has been lost in the shadow of other teams' accomplishments. Much of the Nationals' 14-year Syracuse stay was spent bumping heads with the Minneapolis Lakers and Rochester Royals. The Nationals, led by high-scoring forward Dolph Schayes, lost to the Lakers in the 1950 and '54 Finals before claiming their only title in 1955, the year after Minneapolis center George Mikan retired.

When the team relocated to Philadelphia in 1963, a year after the Warriors had moved from Philadelphia to San Francisco, winning became a matter of trying to keep up with the powerful Celtics, who were in the midst of their incredible run of 11 titles in 13 seasons.

The 76ers rose up to win three straight

SNOW DAY: *Eric Snow has taken over the point guard duties in Philadelphia.*

Eastern Division titles and copped the 1967 championship under Alex Hannum with one of the most powerful lineups ever assembled. The 1966–67 team featured Wilt Chamberlain at center, Billy Cunningham, Chet Walker and Luke Jackson at forward, and Wali Jones and Hal Greer at guard.

The 76ers' championship ended Boston's run of eight straight titles, but the

Celtics returned to the throne in 1967–68 despite Philadelphia's 62-victory campaign. Amazingly, the 76ers would gradually sink to a 9–73 record five years later—the lowest win total in NBA history.

But just as quickly as they had faded, the 76ers rose back into prominence. The next glory period began in 1976 with the arrival of Julius (Dr. J) Erving and ended in 1985 with the departure of Cunningham as coach. In between, the 76ers won four Atlantic Division titles, topped 50 victories in nine of 10 seasons, reached the NBA Finals four times and won the franchise's third and final championship—a 1983 sweep of the Lakers. The title puzzle was completed with the insertion of center Moses Malone into a lineup with the fantastic Dr. J, Andrew Toney, Maurice Cheeks and Bobby Jones.

The post-championship era began with the arrival of Charles Barkley, a fiery

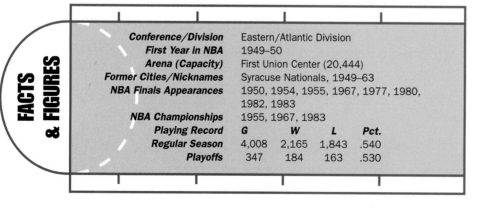

FACTS & FIGURES

Conference/Division	Eastern/Atlantic Division			
First Year in NBA	1949–50			
Arena (Capacity)	First Union Center (20,444)			
Former Cities/Nicknames	Syracuse Nationals, 1949–63			
NBA Finals Appearances	1950, 1954, 1955, 1967, 1977, 1980, 1982, 1983			
NBA Championships	1955, 1967, 1983			
Playing Record	G	W	L	Pct.
Regular Season	4,008	2,165	1,843	.540
Playoffs	347	184	163	.530

power forward who kept the 76ers competitive for eight seasons with his rebounding and scoring. But Barkley didn't get much help and his 1992 trade to Phoenix signaled the beginning of a serious rebuilding program.

Top draft selections Clarence Weatherspoon, Jerry Stackhouse and 1997 Rookie of the Year Allan Iverson will give new head coach Larry Brown a talented but undisciplined trio of stars to start another 76ers rebuilding plan. A much-traveled coach with a proven track record, Brown's goals are to ensure that the whole of his team is at least equal to the sum of its misguided parts, as well as to revive hope for a quick return to the NBA's upper stratosphere.

It took Brown just one season to get the 76ers back into the playoffs.

With Iverson leading the way by averaging a league best 26.8 points per game, Philadelphia finished 28-22 in the regular season, then knocked off Orlando in the first round of the playoffs before losing to Indiana 4-0 in the second round. Iverson, who had been moved from point guard to shooting guard, actually averaged 28.5 points in the playoffs but did not have enough help to get the Sixers past the veteran Pacers.

In an effort to provide that help, the 76ers obtained veteran forward Tony Kukoc from the Bulls during the 1999-2000 season. In 32 games with Philadelphia Kukoc did add 12.4 points and 4.5 rebounds a game. But it was still Iverson's show. After making his first All-Star appearance, the flashy guard wound up average 28.4 points, 3.8 rebounds, 4.7 assists and 2.06 steals as the Sixers finished 49-33.

In the first round of the playoffs the 76ers dispatched the Charlotte Hornets, setting up another meeting with the Pacers. When Indiana built a 3–0 lead it looked as if the series were over. But the gutsy Sixers won the next two games before eventually succumbing in six. Those two games, however, showed the Sixers how far they had come.

Heartened by that, the team stood pat, making few changes for the 2000–01 season.

I ON THE BALL: *Allen Iverson has thrilled fans in Philadelphia with his on-court creativity.*

74 PHOENIX SUNS

Suns rise in the west and burn their opponents

When the Suns selected 6-foot-10 Florida center Neal Walk with their first pick of the 1969 draft, they set an unspectacular course that would lead them toward the higher elevations of the NBA. But it's tempting to look back and wonder what might have been—if, for instance, the Suns had won the annual coin flip to earn rights to the first overall pick in 1969.

Phoenix had finished its expansion season of 1968–69 in the Western Division basement; their expansion cousins, the Milwaukee Bucks had finished in the same position in the East. The coin-flip winner would walk away with draft rights to 7–2 UCLA center Lew Alcindor.

With Alcindor, the Bucks became champions in their third NBA season. Without him, the Suns became consistent contenders who always seemed to be a big man away from a championship. The absence of a dominating center became a recurring theme.

In the early 1970s, Alcindor would have been a perfect fit for a team that featured Connie Hawkins, Dick Van Arsdale, Charlie Scott and Paul Silas. In 1975–76, a Suns team coached by John MacLeod won a modest 42 games but upended Seattle and Golden State in playoff series and advanced to the NBA Finals, where it lost in six games to Boston. That Suns team featured Paul Westphal, Alvan Adams, Van Arsdale and Curtis Perry with Garfield Heard at center.

From 1977 to 1983, the Suns averaged more than 51 victories but failed to get past the Western Conference finals. Westphal, Adams and Davis provided the firepower, 6–10 Larry Nance and 6–7 Truck Robinson the muscle. Again the Suns came up short in the middle.

During a four-year rebuilding period in which they did not win a playoff game, the Suns reloaded their guard and forward positions but failed to find the big man who could take them to the next level.

From 1988–89, under coach Cotton Fitzsimmons, Phoenix began a seven-year run of 50-plus victory seasons. Guard Kevin Johnson and forwards Eddie Johnson and Tom Chambers keyed the early charge, but it wasn't until the 1992 arrivals of Westphal as coach and Charles Barkley as top gun that the Suns could return to the NBA Finals.

Barkley, a 6–6 power forward, came over from Philadelphia and led guards Johnson and Danny Ainge, swingman Dan Majerle and frontcourt players Cedric Ceballos and Oliver Miller through to a franchise-record 62-victory season that was followed by an inspired 1993 playoff drive. But the Suns, soft in the middle, were thwarted by the Chicago Bulls.

The Suns appeared primed for another drive in 1994–95, but the season fell apart as Barkley and newcomer Danny Manning suffered a season-ending knee injury and Barkley battled career-threatening back

BURNING BRIGHT: *Tom Gugliotta hopes to overcome injuries and shine for the Suns.*

FACTS & FIGURES

Conference/Division	Western/Pacific Division
First Year in NBA	1968–69
Arena (Capacity)	America West Arena (19,023)
Former Cities/Nicknames	None
NBA Finals Appearances	1976, 1993
NBA Championships	None

Playing Record	G	W	L	Pct.
Regular Season	2,592	1,422	1,170	.548
Playoffs	197	94	103	.477

and knee problems.

Westphal was fired during a mediocre 1995–96 season and a year later Danny Ainge took over a team that had started 0–13 and led them to a playoff berth. Ainge, true to the pattern, built his second half success around a small talented team led by newcomers Jason Kidd and Robert Horry and veterans Kevin Johnson and Danny Manning. The improvements continued in the following regular season but another serious knee injury to Manning, a first round playoff loss to San Antonio and the release of "K.J." made for a disappointing end.

Ainge kept the ship on course through the lockout-shortened 1998–99 season when the Suns finished 27–23. Newcomer Tom Gugliotta, who signed as a free agent, led the team in scoring with 17 points per game and rebounding with 8.9 per game. Kidd was right behind in scoring, with a career high of 16.9 points per game. Kidd also led the NBA in assists with 10.8, becoming the first Suns player to accomplish that feat.

Although the Suns qualified for the playoffs for the 11th straight season, the fourth-longest streak in the league, they were swept by Portland in the first round, 3–0.

In one of the biggest deals in franchise history, the Suns obtained Penny Hardaway from Orlando the next summer in exchange for Danny Manning, Pat Garrity and two first-round draft picks. The move paid immediate dividends even though Hardaway missed 22 games with injuries. He still averaged 16.9 points, 5.8 rebounds, 5.3 assists per game. Cliff Robinson led the Suns with 18.5 points per game while Rodney Rogers added 13.8 to win the league's Sixth Man Award.

By that time, however, Ainge had resigned and was replaced by assistant Scott Skiles, who led the Suns to a 39–21 finish and a 53–29 record overall. The Suns beat the defending champion San Antonio Spurs in the first round of the playoffs before falling to the Lakers in the second round. It was no help to the Suns that they were without Gugliotta, who'd suffered a broken leg. But they expected him to come back for the 2000–01 season as strong as ever.

KIDDING AROUND: *Jason Kidd is recognized as one of the league's best point guards.*

76 PORTLAND TRAIL BLAZERS

Fairy tale season is a magical memory

BLAZING TRAILS: *Steve Smith (8) gets into position to snatch another rebound for Portland.*

Bill Walton. Maurice Lucas. Lionel Hollins. Dave Twardzik. Bobby Gross. Larry Steele. The names are frozen in the memory of Portland fans who watched their 1976–77 Trail Blazers live out a fairy tale. For one glorious NBA season, Cinderella wore glass sneakers.

The script opened in 1970 when Portland began play with Buffalo and Cleveland as part of a three-team expansion. And true to expansion form, the Blazers spent their first six seasons looking for a .500 season and a coach with a plan.

Jack Ramsay had more than a plan when he arrived in 1976 as the six-year-old franchise's fifth coach. He had a magic wand. He also had the 6-foot-11 Walton, who finally was healthy after two injury-plagued seasons. Walton, the former UCLA center, was ready to take his place in the middle of a Portland lineup that included Lucas, a frontcourt enforcer acquired by Ramsay, and Hollins, a talented guard.

With a healthy Walton scoring, rebounding and swatting away shots, the Blazers jumped from 37 to 49 victories and a second-place Pacific Division finish. Their first playoff appearance produced surprising first and second-round victories over Chicago and Denver. But the best was yet to come.

Portland swept the powerful Lakers and Kareem Abdul-Jabbar in the Western Conference finals and completed its shocking championship run by the Julius Erving led 76ers in six games. The fairy tale was complete.

Over the next two decades, Portland would make two more trips to the NBA Finals—and lose both times. The Blazers used the momentum of their 1977 success to build one of the NBA's most competitive franchises, but they never could match it.

The 1977–78 Blazers picked right up where they had left off, posting a franchise-record 58 victories. But Walton suffered a foot injury late in the season and hobbled through a quick playoff exit. The big redhead sat out the entire 1978–79 season and signed with San Diego a year later. Without Walton, the Blazers remained competitive, but seldom escaped the first playoff round.

It was during Ramsay's tenure that the Blazers made their best and worst decisions. The 1983 draft brought acrobatic guard Clyde Drexler, who would become one of the league's flashiest performers. In the 1984 draft, Portland selected 7–1 center Sam Bowie, passing up such future stars as Michael Jordan and Charles Barkley.

The Blazers stepped back into the spotlight in 1989–90 under Rick Adelman. A lineup featuring Drexler, master rebounder Buck Williams and point guard Terry Porter posted consecutive seasons of 59, 63, 57 and 51 victories and made two more visits to the NBA Finals. One resulted in a five-game 1990 loss to Detroit, the other a six-game 1992 loss to Chicago.

Adelman departed after the 1994 playoffs and new coach P.J. Carlesimo rebuilt the team around fresh characters such as guard Kenny Anderson, forward Rasheed Wallace and center Arvydas Sabonis. Despite improving the team's record each of his three years, Carlesimo was replaced by Mike Dunleavy who secured a major coup late in the 1997–98 season by signing homegrown point guard Damon Stoudamire from Toronto and taking the Blazers into the playoffs where they lost to the LA Lakers in the first round.

Dunleavy also obtained troubled guard Isaiah Rider from Minnesota. He averaged 19.7 and 13.9 points in his first two seasons, but as had been the case previously, his off-court antics distracted from his wealth of talent.

It was Brian Grant who emerged as the team's leader averaging 11.5 points and 9.8 rebounds per game. Rasheed Wallace shot .508 from the field, sixth best in the league.

After finishing the regular season 35–15 to win the Pacific Division, the Blazers swept the Suns in the first round and knocked off the Utah Jazz in six games in the second round before losing to the San Antonio Spurs, 4–0, in the Western Conference finals.

Having come that close, the Blazers decided to remake their team for the 1999–2000 season. They obtained Scottie Pippin from Houston, Steve Smith from Atlanta, and signed free agent Detlef Schrempf in an effort to make a more serious run at a title.

Wallace led the team in scoring with 16.4 points per game, followed by Smith at 14.9, Stoudamire at 12.5 and Pippin at 12.5. The Blazers finished with a record of 59-23, the second best record in the league. The Blazers beat Minnesota in the first round of the playoffs and Utah in the second round before advancing to the Western Conference Finals against the Lakers, the only team with a better record during the regular season.

When the Lakers took a commanding 3–1 lead, it looked as if the series would be a short one. But the Blazers roared back to take Games 5 and 6 and force a deciding Game 7 in Los Angeles, where the Lakers rallied from 15 points down to win.

Portland showed their desire for revenge by adding Shawn Kemp and Dale Davis in the 2000 off-season.

MAN-TO-MAN: *Rasheed Wallace (left) tries to shoot past Shaquille O'Neal.*

78 SACRAMENTO KINGS

A tale of five cities

They've logged more miles, lost more games and frustrated more fans than any team in NBA history. They've been "Royals", they've been "Kings" and they've been disappointments in five "home" cities on a long westward journey that took them south in the standings.

And the very things this itinerant franchise has been seeking—respect and success—are what it left behind when it moved from Rochester, N.Y., its first NBA home, to Cincinnati in 1957.

As the Rochester Royals, one of four National Basketball League franchises that jumped to the Basketball Association of America in 1948, Les Harrison's team had the tools to compete for a championship—center Arnie Risen and outstanding guards Bob Davies and Bobby Wanzer. But it didn't have big George Mikan, a barrier that would prove difficult to cross.

In three of the Royals' first four BAA/NBA seasons, they beat or tied Minneapolis for the division's best record. But that regular-season success translated into only one championship (1951) as Mikan and the Lakers captured five in six years.

After six consecutive winning seasons under Harrison, the Royals struggled through three losing campaigns and began looking elsewhere for relief. That "else-

DIVIDED REACTION: *Flashy Jason Williams has his fans and detractors.*

where" in 1957 turned out to be Cincinnati, which offered a larger population base, a more spacious arena and, most importantly, the opportunity to land University of Cincinnati all-everything guard Oscar Robertson with a territorial draft pick three years down the road.

The wait would be difficult, but worthwhile. After three disastrous seasons (33, 19 and 19 victories), the 6-foot-5 Robertson arrived with a 30.5-point rookie performance. Not surprisingly, the Royals jumped 14 games in the win column. In the Big O's second season, he averaged an incredible triple-double—30.8 points, 12.5 rebounds and 11.4 assists.

The Robertson era lived up to its billing for individual achievement, but fell short of team success. Despite surrounding Robertson with outstanding center Jerry Lucas and forwards Jack Twyman and Wayne Embry, the Royals managed only one big season—a 55–25 campaign that was short-circuited by powerful Boston in the 1964 Eastern Division finals.

Lucas was traded at the beginning of the 1969–70 season and Robertson was dealt a few months later, signaling the end of the Cincinnati era. Attendance dropped

FACTS & FIGURES

Conference/Division	Western/Pacific Division			
First Year in BAA/NBA	1948–49			
Arena (Capacity)	Arco Arena (17,317)			
Former Cities/Nicknames	Rochester Royals, 1948–57,			
	Cincinnati Royals, 1957–72,			
	Kansas City-Omaha Kings, 1972–75,			
	Kansas City Kings, 1975–85			
NBA Finals Appearances	1951			
NBA Championships	1951			
Playing Record	G	W	L	Pct.
Regular Season	4,073	1,863	2,210	.457
Playoffs	129	50	79	.388

with the departure of the franchise's biggest stars and the journey west resumed in 1972.

For the next three seasons, the franchise operated as the Kansas City/Omaha Kings, splitting home games between the two midwestern cities. In 1975, the "Omaha" was dropped, but the losing continued. Despite such fine players as center Sam Lacey, guards Nate (Tiny) Archibald, Phil Ford and Reggie Theus and forward Scott Wedman, the Kings managed only four winning records and five post-season appearances in 13 years.

Since moving to Sacramento in 1985, the Kings have been able to reward their great fans with just one playoff appearance, in 1996. Recent seasons, in particular 1997–98, have been huge disappointments for the Kings who decided in the summer of 1998 to trade the cornerstone of their franchise, All-Star guard Mitch Richmond, after years of trade speculation. He went to Washington, along with Otis Thorpe, for the brilliant but unpredictable Chris Webber as Sacramento attempted to breathe new life into its franchise.

That was exactly what happened. In fact, even the Kings had to be somewhat surprised at the incredible turnaround their franchise made.

With new coach Rick Adelman at the helm for the 1998-99 season, the Kings surprised the league by finishing 27-23. Webber led the league in rebounding with 13 per game and also averaged 20 points per game to earn second team All-NBA honors. He finished second in the league in double-doubles with 36 and became the first NBA player who was not a center since Charles Barkley in 1986-87 to average at least 20 points and 13 rebounds.

But it was flashy rookie Jason Williams who epitomized the new-look Kings. The cocky point guard and his signature wild passes made the Kings the darlings of the league as they pushed the veteran Utah Jazz to five games before losing in the first round.

The Kings came back for more in 1999-2000, but opponents were ready. Despite Webber's 24.5 points per game, the Kings finished with a regular season record of 44-38 and lost to the Los Angeles Lakers in the first round of the playoffs.

RIGHT AT HOME: *Chris Webber has played better in Sacramento than anywhere else.*

80 SAN ANTONIO SPURS

"Iceman" and "The Admiral": A tale of two eras

LITTLE BIG MAN: *Point guard Avery Johnson always looks to Tim Duncan or David Robinson.*

Before 1995, the San Antonio Spurs had never even won two playoff series in the same season. When the postseason rolls around, they have been known to drop to the bottom of the playoff pool like a wet blanket.

But, oh the regular season! That is the time to watch bastketball in San Antonio. Exciting. Fast. Lots of points. Lots of victories. Fun. "Iceman" and "The Admiral."

If NBA success were measured by regular-season results, the Spurs would rank among the game's most prestigious franchises. Since moving to the NBA in 1976, after nine unspectacular seasons in the ABA, the Spurs have won eight Central and Midwest Division titles, finished second four times and posted 47 or more victories 11 times. And they've done it with flair. They led the league in scoring three of their first four NBA seasons and ranked anywhere from first to third for eight consecutive years.

From 1976, the year the ABA Dallas Chaparrals moved to San Antonio, through 1985, many of those points came from 6–7 scoring machine George Gervin, alias "Iceman." Gervin, who liked to attack the basket with his silky, mesmerizing moves and beat his defender with a never-ending assortment of shots, won four scoring titles with averages ranging from 27.2 to 33.1 while helping the Spurs win five division titles.

Gervin was the centerpiece for a cast that included Larry Kenon, Billy Paultz, Ron Brewer, Mike Mitchell and Alvin Robertson. But never did he play with a dominating big man, which probably explains why the 1976–85 Spurs could do no better than three trips to the Western Conference finals.

Four years after Gervin's departure, San Antonio finally got that big man. The Spurs, coming off a 28-win season, grabbed 7–1 Navy center David Robinson with the first overall pick of the 1987

FACTS & FIGURES

Conference/Division	Western/Midwest Division			
First Year in ABA/NBA	1967–68/1976–77			
Arena (Capacity)	Alamodome (20,662)			
Former Cities/Nicknames	Dallas Chaparrals, 1967–70, 1971–73, Texas Chaparrals, 1970–71			
NBA Finals Appearances	1999			
NBA Championships	1999			
Playing Record	**G**	**W**	**L**	**Pct.**
ABA Regular Season	744	378	366	.508
NBA Regular Season	1,936	1,080	856	.558
ABA Playoffs	49	17	32	.347
NBA Playoffs	149	72	77	.483

draft and then struggled through two more difficult seasons while Robinson completed his military commitment. The wait was worthwhile.

"The Admiral" arrived in 1989 and Larry Brown's Spurs stormed to 56 wins (35 more than the previous season) and a Midwest Division title. With able help from Terry Cummings, J.R. Reid, Dennis Rodman, Willie Anderson, Sean Elliott and Avery Johnson, the Spurs averaged more than 54 wins over the next six seasons and claimed three more Midwest titles.

The capper was a 62-victory cruise in 1994–95 under new coach Bob Hill. Robinson averaged 27.6 points and claimed league MVP honors and led the Spurs to playoff wins over Denver and the Lakers before losing to Houston in the West Finals. A year later, the Spurs won 59 games but were eliminated in the second round of the postseason by Utah.

The 1996–97 season was a disaster from the start with Robinson ruled out for all but six games with injuries. They managed just 20 wins with general manager Gregg Popovich taking over coaching duties from Hill. The consolation came with the No. 1 draft pick Tim Duncan who linked superbly with Robinson and led the Spurs to an amazing turnaround, a 56–26 record, in 1997–98. There was also a promising first round playoff win over Phoenix before defeat at the hands of Utah.

It was Duncan who became the Spurs star in his second season. He led the team in scoring at 21.7 points per game, rebounding at 11.4 per game, and blocked shots at 2.52 per game. Robinson, accepting a secondary role for the good of the team, still averaged 15.8 points, 10 rebounds, 2.43 blocked shots and a team best 1.4 steals per game.

With the Spurs finally fairly injury free, they finished the regular season 37–13,

first in the Midwest Division. They rolled through the playoffs, beating the Timberwolves 3–1 in the first round, the Lakers 4–0 in the second round and the Blazers 4–0 in the Western Conference finals to advance to the NBA finals for the first time in their history.

Duncan averaged 27.4 points, 14 rebounds, 2.4 assists, 2.2 blocks and 45.8 minutes in the playoffs and was named the finals Most Valuable Player as the Spurs beat the Knicks in five games.

Duncan continued his dominance in 1999–2000, averaging 23.2 points and 12.4 rebounds per game—third in the league—as the Spurs finished 53–29. But with their young star nursing a knee injury, the Spurs were upset by the Phoenix Suns in the first round of the playoffs.

TWIN TOWERS: *Tim Duncan (left) and David Robinson have been towers of strength for the San Antonio Spurs.*

82 SEATTLE SUPERSONICS

Somewhere between great and run-of the mill

They came out of nowhere to claim professional basketball's biggest prize, then quietly slipped back into middle-of-the-pack mediocrity. Now, nearly two decades later, the Seattle Sonics are still searching for that elusive second NBA championship.

In 1978 and '79 the Sonics exploded into prominence without warning, earning consecutive NBA Finals appearances and their only championship. But nothing in the team's 30-year history has come without the element of surprise. When the team seemed set for a championship in 1993–94 after posting a 63–19 record, it was humbled by Denver in the biggest opening-round playoff upset in league history.

Nothing in the Sonics' first 10 seasons prepared anybody for the shock of 1977–78. Born with the San Diego Rockets in 1967–68 as part of a two-team expansion, the Sonics struggled through their first seven seasons without qualifying for the playoffs and posted three winning records in their first 10. Five coaches tried their luck over that span, including former Boston great Bill Russell.

But it wasn't until Lenny Wilkens replaced Bob Hopkins after 22 games in 1977 that the team began to take shape.

MOVE FORWARD: *Vin Baker, obtained in the Shawn Kemp trade, has disappointed.*

Wilkens, a former guard who had served as a player-coach for three of Seattle's early seasons, guided the team through a 42–18 stretch run that resulted in a 47–35 record and third-place finish in the Pacific Division.

With a frontcourt that included Jack Sikma and Marvin Webster and a guard rotation of Gus Williams, Dennis Johnson and "Downtown" Freddie Brown, the surprising Sonics shocked powerful Los Angeles, Portland and Denver in the early playoff rounds and fell just short of a championship in a seven-game NBA Finals loss to Washington.

There was no element of surprise in 1978–79 when the Sonics won 52 games, claimed their first division title and advanced again to the NBA Finals, where they beat the Bullets in five games. The franchise had its first championship in its 12th NBA season.

Wilkens coaxed a 56-win record out of the Sonics in 1979–80, but just as quickly as they had arisen from the dead, they slipped back into the pack. Players like Tom Chambers, Dale Ellis and Xavier McDaniel sparkled in the 1980s, but the team did not make any more championship noise until George Karl arrived in 1991–92. And this time, expected to win, the Sonics stumbled badly.

Karl pieced together a fast-paced team that played furious defense and won 55 regular-season games in 1992–93. Guards Ricky Pierce and Gary Payton, forwards Shawn Kemp, Derrick McKey and Eddie Johnson and center Sam Perkins keyed a postseason effort that won two playoff series and extended Phoenix to Game 7 of the Western Conference finals.

Over the next four seasons, Payton and Kemp led the Sonics to an average of 60 wins per season, but only one Western Conference title. In 1995–96, Seattle posted a club-record 64 victories and won three playoff series before losing to

FACTS & FIGURES

Conference/Division	Western/Pacific Division			
First Year in NBA	1967–68			
Arena (Capacity)	Key Arena at Seattle Center (17,072)			
Former Cities/Nicknames	None			
NBA Finals Appearances	1978, 1979, 1996			
NBA Championships	1979			
Playing Record	G	W	L	Pct.
Regular Season	2,674	1,441	1,233	.539
Playoffs	201	99	102	.493

Chicago in six games in the NBA Finals. A year later, another Pacific Division title followed but the Sonics were upset by Houston in the second round.

A year later, following the trade of Kemp to Cleveland in a deal that brought Milwaukee's Vin Baker, the Sonics turned in another poor playoff showing, losing 4–1 to the LA Lakers in the second round. It was a result that cost Karl his job and left Seattle fans wondering when all that promise would turn into success.

The more laid-back Paul Westphal replaced Karl as the Sonics attempted to change their fortunes. But the newcomer could do no better than a 25-25 mark in his first season. Seattle missed the playoffs for the first time since the 1989-90 season.

Gary Payton did lead Seattle, averaging 21.1 points—sixth best in the NBA—and a career high 8.7 assists per game—fourth best in the NBA. His 2.18 steals ranked seventh in the NBA. But far too often he was a one-man show in Seattle.

That was still the case in the 1999-2000 season but the Sonics managed to finish 45-37 and advance to the first round of the playoffs before losing to Utah.

The fiery Payton was often critical of his coach and his teammates, and let them know his opinions in no uncertain terms. After averaging a career high 24.2 points per game, he could afford to speak out. He also averaged a career high 8.9 assists.

Baker, however, was a disappointment, averaging just 16.2 points and 7.7 rebounds. He acknowledged late in the season that he had been troubled by depression, which accounted for many of his problems on the court.

After the season ended on such a sour note, the Sonics decided to shake things up. In the off-season, they pulled the trigger on a deal to obtain center Patrick Ewing from the New York Knicks. The Sonics saw Ewing—a veteran of 15 seasons in New York—still could provide leadership, as well as the desire to win an NBA Championship sooner than later.

PAY DAY: *Point guard Gary Payton is the glue that holds the SuperSonics together.*

84 TORONTO RAPTORS

Oh Canada! Border Warfare, NBA-Style

KISSING COUSINS: *Family ties didn't stop Tracy McGrady–Vince Carter's cousin–moving on.*

Isiah Thomas, who always made the right decisions as a 13-year point guard for the Detroit Pistons, had to doubt his first big player move as part owner and rookie general manager of the expansion Toronto Raptors. Momentarily, at least.

When NBA Commissioner David Stern announced to the record draft crowd of 21,268 at Toronto's SkyDome that the hometown Raptors had selected 5-foot-10 Arizona point guard Damon Stoudamire

with the seventh overall pick, boos cascaded through the arena like a swarm of hockey players through the crease.

But less than a year later, Isiah Thomas the front-office guru was already looking every bit as sharp as Isiah Thomas the playmaker. Stoudamire, a fast-shooting, ball-handling wizard sculpted in Thomas' basketball-playing image, completed his first NBA campaign as the league's outstanding rookie. He averaged 19 points and 9.3 assists per game, captured the hearts of the formerly skeptical Toronto fans with his exciting play and provided the hope and foundation for a bright future.

Stoudamire was the centerpiece for a first-year team that exceeded expectations and won 21 games, six more than expansion mate Vancouver. The Raptors' roster had been stocked with reputed problem players made available by existing teams in the expansion draft, waiver-wire pickups and draft picks. Critics said the Raptors were short on size, long on immaturity and destined for a painful opening act.

But that was not the case. Stoudamire got help from 6–9 center Oliver Miller and rookie coach Brendan Malone got encouraging performances from 6–11 forward Sharone Wright and guard Doug Christie.

The one glitch in Toronto's debut was detected the day after the 1995–96 season ended. The 54-year-old Malone was replaced by 35-year-old assistant Darrell

Walker, a former teammate of Thomas in Detroit. It gave the Raptors a younger presence on the bench.

At the 1996 Draft, the Raptors selected 6–9 forward Marcus Camby from UMass, who performed nearly as brilliantly as Stoudamire in his rookie season. Christie emerged as a dependable No. 2 guard and the Raptors improved by nine wins to finish 30–52, a better record than six other teams. On any given night, the Raptors were capable of giving the NBA's best teams a tough struggle. The highlight of the season was home victories over Chicago, Utah, the Lakers and Houston.

But the real measure of Toronto's two-year success was provided by the same fans who had booed Thomas and Stoudamire on draft day 1995. The team played to sellouts on most nights and was challenging the Maple Leafs as the hottest ticket in a hockey-obsessed town.

Sadly for those fans, Thomas severed his ties with the team at the start of the 1997–98 season, a move that eventually led to Stoudamire leaving for the Portland Trail Blazers before the trading deadline. After such big improvements in 1996–97, a 16-win year was not what the Toronto public were looking for and the Raptors future is now in the hands of Butch Carter, who was promoted from interim to Head Coach at the end of the campaign.

It was another Carter who would provide the Raptors with the biggest thrills in their brief history.

North Carolina star Vince Carter was the fifth pick of the 1998 draft by the Golden State Warriors, who traded him to the Raptors for Antawn Jamison on draft day. It may be a move the Warriors regret for the rest of their existence. The explosive 6-6 swingman drew comparisons to Michael Jordan with his high playing acrobatic act. He averaged 18.3 points, 5.7 rebounds and 3 assists a game to earn the Rookie of the Year award in 1999.

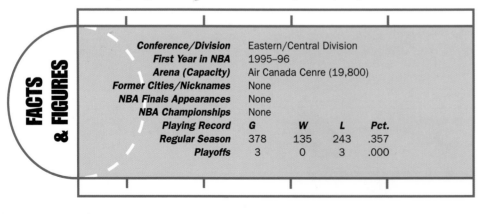

FACTS & FIGURES				
Conference/Division	Eastern/Central Division			
First Year in NBA	1995–96			
Arena (Capacity)	Air Canada Cenre (19,800)			
Former Cities/Nicknames	None			
NBA Finals Appearances	None			
NBA Championships	None			
Playing Record	**G**	**W**	**L**	**Pct.**
Regular Season	378	135	243	.357
Playoffs	3	0	3	.000

Although the Raptors finished with a record of 23–27 that season, hopes were high for 1999–2000, and Carter did not disappoint.

He averaged 25.7 points, 5.8 rebounds, 3.9 assists and 1.34 steals. Voted into the All-Star starting lineup in just his second season, Carter also wowed the crowd in the Oakland Arena by winning the slam dunk title with a flashy array of moves during the All-Star weekend.

Tracy McGrady, Carter's cousin, also emerged as a star averaging 15.4 points per game, but joined Orlando in the off season.

Toronto finished the season with a 45–37 record and its first berth in the playoffs. The Raptors lost in the first round to the New York Knicks.

VIN-SANITY: *Vince Carter's slam dunks made him one of the NBA's more popular players.*

86 UTAH JAZZ

A different kind of jazz plays well in Utah

Before it had a nickname, before it even had a coach, the expansion New Orleans team had a superstar. When Pistol Pete Maravich arrived as the foundation for the NBA's 18th franchise in 1974, he provided an instant following, if not a long-range blueprint for success.

The flamboyant Maravich, one of the greatest ballhandling magicians ever to put on a uniform, had been a collegiate scoring machine at Louisiana State University and promised New Orleans fans excitement, if not victories. But he did not come cheaply.

To acquire Maravich from Atlanta, the team had to surrender two players and four draft picks—two No. 1s and 2s. Maravich indeed brought an entertaining, swashbuckling style to New Orleans, but without draft picks, management could never provide him with help. Pistol Pete won one NBA scoring title in five New Orleans seasons, but the team never won more than 39 games and was doomed to failure.

With Maravich in the lineup, management settled on a nickname that would reflect the spirited nature of the city and its famed French Quarter. But, ironically, when new ownership bought the team and relocated it to Salt Lake City in 1979, a city that was politically, religiously and socially conservative inherited a team and nickname that was none of those things.

JAZZ MAN *John Stockton is widely recognized as one of the NBA's best-ever point guards.*

But life in Utah agreed with the Jazz, a team that had gone through three coaches in its inaugural season and four in five years. The new ownership quickly began overhauling the roster, trading for high-scoring forward Adrian Dantley and letting a disgruntled Maravich buy out his contract.

From 1980 through 1985, the Jazz stocked their roster with a succession of outstanding draft picks. Guard Darrell Griffith came in 1980, forward Dominique Wilkins in 1982, 6-foot-11 Thurl Bailey in 1983, point guard John Stockton in 1984 and 6–9 Karl Malone, a.k.a. The Mailman, in 1985. Only a judgment error kept the Jazz from becoming a dominant team: Wilkins was traded to Atlanta for Freeman Williams and John Drew, a pair of aging guards.

After four unproductive seasons in Utah, the Jazz suddenly blossomed into playoff contenders. The transformation took place in 1983–84 under Frank Layden, who guided Utah to the franchise's first Midwest Division title and first playoff berth after nine misses.

The Jazz would not miss again, either under Layden or Jerry Sloan, his successor. Dantley and Griffith provided the firepower for a few years. Then Malone and Stockton developed into one of the best inside-outside combinations ever to play. Malone was devastating around the basket and Stockton, the greatest assist and steal man in NBA history, got him the ball.

Under Sloan, the Jazz topped 50 victories in eight of his first nine years, including a team-record 64–18 mark in 1996–97. And, after losing in the Western Conference Finals in 1992, '94, and '96, they finally took the next step by defeating Houston in six games in the '97 conference finals. Malone, Stockton and guard Jeff Hornacek led the veteran group into

FACTS & FIGURES

Conference/Division	Western/Midwest Division
First Year in NBA	1974–75
Arena (Capacity)	Delta Center (19,911)
Former Cities/Nicknames	New Orleans Jazz (1974–79)
NBA Finals Appearances	1997, 1998
NBA Championships	None

Playing Record	G	W	L	Pct.
Regular Season	2,018	1,080	938	.535
Playoffs	169	86	83	.509

the NBA Finals before losing to Chicago in six games.

Sadly, the reputation of Malone, Hornacek and Stockton as nice guys destined to finish last was not helped a year later when, after an impressive 4–0 sweep of the LA Lakers in the Western Conference Finals, the Jazz lost to a tired Chicago, again in six games.

That would prove to be as close as the Jazz got for some time. Malone won the league's Most Valuable Player award in 1998–99, averaging 23.8 points and 9.4 rebounds while shooting .493 from the field.

The Jazz finished 37–13, winning the Midwest Division. They held off the determined Sacramento Kings, 3–2, in a thrilling first-round playoff series before falling to the Trail Blazers, 4–2, in the Western Conference semifinals.

The next season followed a similar script. Malone showed no signs of slowing down, averaging 25.5 points, 9.5 rebounds and 3.7 assists in 35.9 minutes per game. Stockton averaged 12.1 points and 8.6 assists, while Hornacek flirted with the all-time free throw percentage record all season. He finished at .950 (171 of 180) just missing Calvin Murphy's single season record of .958 set in 1980–81.

Although the Jazz finished 55–27 to win the Midwest Division crown again, they could get no farther than the second round of the playoffs. After beating Seattle, they fell to Portland, 4–1.

Fourteen-year veteran Hornacek announced his retirement at the end of the season, perhaps signaling the start of a changing of the guard.

Malone and Stockton remained, however, and the Jazz brought in an interesting pair of newcomers for the 2000–01 season—veterans John Starks and Donyell Marshall. In fact, 19-year-old shooting guard DeShawn Stevenson, a first round pick, is the only new face with age on his side. The Jazz certainly won't have the youngest roster in the NBA, but the policy in Utah has to be the future is now, especially if Malone and Stockton are to get the championship their stellar play merited throughout the 1990s.

OH, SHOOT: *John Hornacek's outside shooting perfectly complemented Karl Malone's inside game and will be hard to replace.*

88 VANCOUVER GRIZZLIES

Bearing Down in the Great Northwest

They suffered through a 23-game losing streak, the second longest in the history of the NBA, and another of 19 games. They won only 15 times, tying Dallas and Miami for the fewest victories by a first-year expansion team. At times they looked totally overmatched and out of synch. At others they appeared lost in the shadows of their NBA brethren. But through it all, Vancouver players, team officials and fans refused to let themselves get discouraged. Things couldn't get any worse in their second season, or could it?

The Grizzlies won just 14 games in 1996–97, which included a 15-game losing streak, the firing of coach Brian Winters, and the team winning back-to-back games just once. Things scarcely improved a year later when new coach Brian Hill led them to a 19–63 mark.

With a solid season-ticket base of more than 13,500 at the 20,004-seat General Motors Place and patient fans who seem understanding and willing to let the franchise take a natural expansion course, the Grizzlies appear to be founded on solid ground. The holes on their roster are obvious and the talent from top to bottom is precariously thin, but they do still have some reasons for optimism.

One is burly Bryant Reeves, who averaged 13.1 and 16.2 points while showing steady improvement throughout his first two seasons. "Big Country," the 1995 draft's sixth overall pick, more than lived up to the team's expectations.

But if there's a potential superstar in Vancouver's future it comes in the form of 6–10 forward Shareef Abdur-Rahim, the No. 3 overall selection in the 1996 draft. Abdur-Rahim, who left college after his freshman season, led the team in scoring

at 18.7 and received strong rookie-of-the-year consideration. Combined with Reeves, the Grizzlies may have at least two pieces of their long-term puzzle in place.

The Vancouver franchise was awarded in April 1994, more than five months after expansion mate Toronto had broken the long NBA border barrier. The Toronto Huskies had played for one season (1946–47) as charter members of the Basketball Association of America, but no other franchise had existed outside the United States for almost five decades until the Raptors were born. The Vancouver market was viewed as enthusiastic and fertile, qualities that were confirmed in the Grizzlies' first season.

But nothing came easy in the team's formative process. After preparing more than a year for the expansion and college drafts, the Grizzlies made their choices and then had to endure an owners' lockout that kept them from even contacting their new players. The two expansion teams also were hobbled by an $18 million salary cap— about three-quarters of what the other teams had to work with—and they were not allowed a lottery No. 1 pick until 1999. So goes life in the expansion world.

But, everything considered, things could have been worse. Vancouver headed into their uncertain future with patient fans, a 7-foot center who should only get better and the front-office backing to buy free-agent players and time for the evolutionary process to work naturally.

That's a lot more than many long-existing franchises have to work with.

There were more growing pains in 1998–99. Coach Brian Hill could do no better than an 8–42 record. The .160 winning percentage was the lowest in the team's history, and the Grizzlies went 1–24 on the road, losing their last 23 games away from home.

Abdur-Rahim led the team in scoring, and his 23-point average ranked fourth in

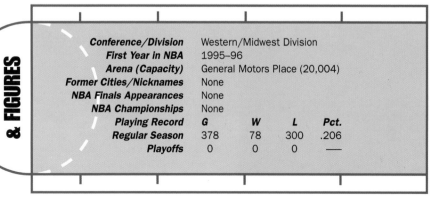

EIGHT BALL *Michael Dickerson is making fans forget the departure of Steve Francis.*

FACTS & FIGURES				
Conference/Division	Western/Midwest Division			
First Year in NBA	1995–96			
Arena (Capacity)	General Motors Place (20,004)			
Former Cities/Nicknames	None			
NBA Finals Appearances	None			
NBA Championships	None			
Playing Record	G	W	L	Pct.
Regular Season	378	78	300	.206
Playoffs	0	0	0	—

the league. He actually finished in the league's top 40 in six different categories, scoring in double figures in all 50 games.

It looked as if the Grizzlies were about to get him a running mate when they drafted Maryland's Steve Francis with the second pick in the 1999 draft. But Francis made good on his predraft claim that he would not play for a Canadian team and forced a trade to the Houston Rockets.

Hill was fired early in the 1999–2000 and replaced by assistant Lionel Hollins. For a brief time it appeared the team might rally around Hollins. Instead, the Grizzlies finished 22–60.

A total overhaul was in order with a new owner, a new executive team led by Dick Versace and a new coach, Sidney Lowe. Lowe was a one-time head coach of the Minnesota Timberwolves but more recently had been an assistant in Cleveland and Minnesota. It remains to be seen if any of these experiences prepared him adequately for Vancouver.

PAPA BEAR *Shareef Abdur-Rahim has been just right for the Vancouver Grizzlies.*

90 WASHINGTON WIZARDS

Shooting for the stars

When the team made its debut in 1961 as the NBA's first expansion franchise, nobody realized the road it would travel in search of an identity. From the aromatic stockyards of Chicago to the more traditional venues of Baltimore and Washington D.C., the Bullets' NBA journey has been both bumpy and exciting.

The team entered the NBA as the Chicago Packers and played its games in the Chicago Amphitheater, which was located next to the stockyards. Perhaps believing that a little west wind might dissipate the smell of hogs, cattle and the team's shoddy play, management changed the nickname from Packers to Zephyrs for its second season.

But not even the outstanding rookie play of center Walt Bellamy in 1961–62 or the arrival of forward Terry Dischinger in 1962–63 could sell Chicago fans on NBA life and the need for a new arena. So team owners packed up their franchise and moved it to the more friendly confines of Baltimore. Playing their third season with their third nickname, the Bullets topped the 30-victory mark for the first time and began building for a promising future.

STRICTLY SPEAKING: *Rod Strickland and the Wizards have continued to struggle.*

FACTS & FIGURES

Conference/Division	Eastern/Atlantic Division			
First Year in NBA	1961–62			
Arena (Capacity)	MCI Center (20,674)			
Former Cities/Nicknames	Chicago Packers, 1961–62, Chicago Zephyrs, 1962–63, Baltimore Bullets, 1963–73, Capital Bullets, 1973–74 Washington Bullets, 1974–97			
NBA Finals Appearances	1971, 1975, 1978, 1979			
NBA Championships	1978			
Playing Record	G	W	L	Pct.
Regular Season	3,155	1,467	1,688	.465
Playoffs	166	69	97	.416

That future began to take shape in 1967 with three big developments: the arrival of coach Gene Shue, the drafting of guard Earl (The Pearl) Monroe and a switch to the Eastern Division. When the Bullets grabbed a 6–foot-7, 245-pound wide body named Wes Unseld in 1968, they positioned themselves for the most glorious decade in franchise history.

With Monroe and Kevin Loughery in the backcourt and Gus Johnson, Jack Marin and Unseld up front, the 1968–69 Bullets rolled to their first winning record (57–25), their first division championship and a play-off appearance that ended in a first-round sweep. But that was merely an appetizer.

Over the next 10 seasons, the Bullets would win six more division titles, finish second three times and make four appearances in the NBA Finals. They also would win the franchise's lone championship—a 1978 Finals victory over Seattle. That team was coached by Dick Motta and still featured the rugged Unseld in the middle. It also included high scoring Elvin Hayes, rebounding ace Bob Dandridge, Mitch Kupchak and guards Kevin Grevey and Phil Chenier. When the Sonics avenged that loss with a five-game 1979 Finals victory over the Bullets, the team's era of prominence came to an end.

The Bullets moved to Washington in 1973 and spent one season as the Capital Bullets before becoming Washington Bullets through 1996–97. In 1997–98, they will be the more gentle Washington Wizards.

The team self-destructed in the 1980s, beginning with the retirement of Unseld and the 1981 trade of Hayes. In 1996–97 under new coach Bernie Bickerstaff, a Washington assistant in the glory days of the 1970s, the Bullets reached just their fourth winning season (44–38) in the last 17 years.

Sadly, that self-destruct mechanism was again at work in 1997–98 when, despite the arrival of point guard Rod Strickland, the Wizards failed to make the playoffs. More was expected of a team that also featured a frontcourt of Chris Webber and Juwan Howard but Washington finally decided at the end of the season that the future lay elsewhere, trading the volatile Webber for the Kings' veteran All-Star guard Mitch Richmond.

Even those changes could not reverse the Wizards' spell.

Stickland continued to be the team's best player, averaging 15.7 points and 9.9 assists per game—second in the league. Richmond did lead the team in scoring at 19.7 points per game, three-pointers made (70) and free throw percentage at .857. Yet the team could do no better than an 18-32 record.

Such a performance actually got two coaches fired that season. Bickerstaff was removed after going 13-19, and his successor, Jim Brovelli, was shown the door

after finishing 5-13.

Washington was hoping the distinguished Gar Heard would bring back respectability in the 1999-2000 season, but he did not last the year.

Richmond averaged 17.4 points to lead the team, followed by Howard at 14.9 and Stickland at 12.6 points and 7.5 assists. Even the addition of Michael Jordan as president of basketball operations failed to get the Wizards back on

track. Although they played better under Jordan's choice of Coach Darrell Walker, they still finished out of the playoffs with a 29-53 record.

It will remain to be seen if Jordan can have anywhere near the impact he had with the Bulls. Many think he'll have to join the lockeroom for that to happen.

NO NEW TRICKS: *Juwan Howard has been unable to work his magic for the Wizards.*

LEGENDS OF THE NBA

Like thieves in the night, they sneak into our consciousness, steal our hearts and slip away all too soon, leaving only memories of their wondrous feats. They leave traces of their basketball brilliance scattered throughout the NBA record book and they provide a stronger foundation upon which a whole new generation can build.

Nothing illuminates a sport more dramatically than its brightest stars and the NBA's have come in many shapes, sizes and forms. Wilt Chamberlain electrified fans with his size, strength and offensive skills; Bob Cousy dazzled them with his ballhandling wizardry. Bill Russell was a devastating rebounder and shot-blocker; Jerry West was a long-range shooting machine. Oscar Robertson could do all of the above, as could Magic Johnson, the tallest point guard in league history.

And they lit up NBA arenas with their charisma and their style as well as their athletic skills. Who will forget the above-the-rim theatrics of Julius Erving and Michael Jordan? Or the championship presence of John Havlicek, Larry Bird and Kareem Abdul-Jabbar? And what serious fan can help but appreciate the defensive brilliance of Walt Frazier or the power and domination of big man George Mikan?

Winning teams and championships are at the heart of professional basketball, but star power is its soul. It's the stuff legends are made of.

That has become more and more obvious in recent seasons. Allen Iverson and Vince Carter, for example, were huge stars before their teams, the Philadelphia 76ers and the Toronto Raptors, respectively, ever challenged for playoff spots.

LIVING LEGENDS: *A once-in-a-lifetime photo of the NBA's 50 greatest players.*

Kareem Abdul-Jabbar
The Sky Is the Limit

Charles Barkley
The Round Mound of Rebound

Rick Barry
A Golden Warrior

Elgin Baylor
The Lakers' Mr. Inside

Larry Bird
The Birdman of Boston

Wilt Chamberlain
The Offensive Machine

Bob Cousy
The Razzle-Dazzle Man

Julius Erving
Dr. J

Patrick Ewing
New York's Middle Man

Walt Frazier
The Knicks' Clyde

John Havlicek
Keep on Running

Elvin Hayes
Stats can do

Magic Johnson
Weaving a Magic Spell

Michael Jordan
His Royal Highness

Karl Malone
The prototypic power forward

Moses Malone
Finding the Promised Land

George Mikan
The First Big Man

Hakeem Olajuwon
The Dream Lives On

Shaquille O'Neal
The bigger, the better

Bob Pettit
Soaring With the Hawks

Oscar Robertson
The Big O

Dennis Rodman
Flair for the theatric

Bill Russell
Celtics' Cornerstone

John Stockton
A passing fancy

Jerry West
The Lakers' Mr. Outside

KAREEM ABDUL-JABBAR

"If there's been anyone any better, he'd have to be a heck of an athlete."

Bob Lanier, former Milwaukee and Detroit center.

Statistics

BORN: *April 16, 1947, New York*
HEIGHT: *7–2*
WEIGHT: *267*
COLLEGE: *UCLA*
PRO TEAMS: *Milwaukee Bucks, 1969–75; Los Angeles Lakers, 1975–89*
NBA CAREER AVERAGES: *24:6 ppg; 11.2 rpg; 3.6 apg*
NBA PLAYOFF AVERAGES: *24.3 ppg; 10.5 rpg; 3.2 apg*

HANDS DOWN: *The young Lew Alcindor presented a real defensive challenge.*

He entered the NBA in 1969 as Lew Alcindor and left it 20 years later as Kareem Abdul-Jabbar. Over the course of 20 record seasons, he piled up more games (1,560), more minutes (57,446), more points (38,387) and more blocked shots (3,189) than any player in history.

While it's difficult to proclaim the 7-foot-2 Abdul-Jabbar as the best center in history, it's not a stretch to call him the most durable and consistent.

Three things set Abdul-Jabbar apart from previous big men: his agility around the basket, a dedication that allowed him to play until age 42 and, of course, the "sky hook."

Abdul-Jabbar fought his first NBA battles in 1969–70 for the Milwaukee Bucks. He had led UCLA to an unprecedented three consecutive national championships and he arrived amid predictions of Wilt Chamberlain-like offensive numbers.

He did nothing to discourage such talk in his first four Milwaukee seasons. Unveiling his unstoppable sky hook, Abdul-Jabbar averaged 28.8 points and 14.5 rebounds en route to 1970 Rookie of the Year honors and followed that with two scoring titles. He also led the 3-year-old Bucks to a 1971 championship.

But when the Bucks complied with Abdul-Jabbar's trade request in 1975 and sent him to the Lakers, critics were pointing to a scoring average that had dipped into the mid-20s and a playing style that relied on finesse.

He never won a scoring title with the Lakers, but the team won five championships, all after Magic Johnson arrived in 1979. With Johnson running the show and Abdul-Jabbar playing his consistent all-around game, the Lakers

became the scourge of the 1980s.

"I always appreciated his talents," said Bob Lanier, a Hall of Fame center for Detroit and Milwaukee. "The perfection of that one shot enabled him to endure time"

Abdul-Jabbar would get the ball on either side of the paint, back his defender toward the basket, pivot and extend either of his long arms to deliver a hook that seldom missed.

When Abdul-Jabbar retired in 1989, he might have been the most honored athlete in NBA history: six MVP awards; 10 first-team All-NBA selections; two playoff MVPs. And, of course, those six precious championship rings.

(Opposite) THE SKY'S THE LIMIT: *Kareem Abdul-Jabbar rose to new heights with the Lakers.*

CAREER HIGHLIGHTS

1969 Closed out college career after leading UCLA to three NCAA championships; selected by Bucks with first overall pick of draft.

1970 Made first of record 18 appearances in All-Star Game; named Rookie of the Year.

1971 Led Bucks to NBA championship; named regular-season MVP for first of six times; named NBA Finals MVP.

1974 Led Bucks to NBA Finals and earned third MVP award.

1975 Traded to Lakers as part of blockbuster six-player deal.

1980 Helped Lakers win NBA championship, the first of five they would win in the decade; named to NBA 35th Anniversary All-Time Team.

1984 Scored career point 31,420 to break Wilt Chamberlain's all-time record.

1989 Retired after record 20 seasons.

1995 Elected to the Naismith Memorial Hall of Fame.

CHARLES BARKLEY

> **"I want to win an NBA championship. Not a day goes by that I don't think about it. I will get it someday, or I'll die trying."**
>
> *Charles Barkley*

Statistics

BORN: Feb. 20, 1963, Leeds, Ala.;
HEIGHT: 6–6
WEIGHT: 252
COLLEGE: Auburn (three years)
PRO TEAMS: Philadelphia 76ers, 1984–92; Phoenix Suns, 1992–96; Houston Rockets, 1996–2000
NBA CAREER AVERAGES: 22.1 ppg; 11.7 rpg; 3.90 apg
NBA PLAYOFF AVERAGES: 23.0 ppg; 12.9 rpg; 3.9 apg

JUST CALL HIM SIR: *The outspoken Charles Barkley was focused on winning a title.*

He's brash, arrogant, cocky, outspoken and controversial. But whenever Charles Barkley speaks, people listen.

On the court, he speaks to the NBA's big men with a dominating game that belies his 6-foot-6 (some claim he's only 6–4) height. What he lacks in height, he makes up for with a solid 250-pound girth that he uses to clear away defenders and a quick leaping ability that he uses to pull down rebounds and score points. But his greatest asset is a fierce determination to succeed.

"Hey, all I want to do is win," says Barkley. "Anybody who doesn't like that can just get out of the way."

From the time Barkley was drafted by Philadelphia in 1984, it was apparent he liked to win. He had done so at Auburn before leaving after his junior season. And he would do so with the 76ers, adding muscle to a lineup that included Julius Erving and Moses Malone. The

CAREER HIGHLIGHTS

1984 Gave up final year of college eligibility and was selected by 76ers with fifth overall pick of draft.

1987 Became shortest player to lead league in rebounding, averaging 14.6; selected to first All-Star Game.

1988 Earned first of four consecutive All-NBA first-team selections with 28.3-point and 11.9-rebound averages.

1991 Grabbed 22 rebounds and earned All-Star Game MVP honors.

1992 Traded to Suns for three players; played for U.S. on gold medal-winning Dream Team at Barcelona Olympic Games.

1993 Finished season with league-leading six triple-doubles; led Suns to NBA Finals, where they lost six-game battle to Bulls; named regular-season MVP.

1994 Scored career-high 56 points in first-round playoff game against Golden State.

1996 Played for Dream Team III in the Atlanta Olympic Games.

1996 Traded to Houston

2000 Retired after rupturing tendon in left quadricep.

76ers won 58 games in Barkley's rookie season and 54 in 1985–86, when the youngster averaged 20 points and 12.8 rebounds.

Free to express his basketball talents, Barkley began muscling with the big boys and running with the little guys, demonstrating a surprising shooting range from the paint to the 3-point line. His all-around talent was impressive: In 1986–87, Barkley became the shortest rebounding champion in NBA history; in 1992–93, he led the league with six triple-doubles.

With the departure of Malone in 1986 and Erving in '87, the 76ers became Barkley's team. He earned All-NBA first-team honors four straight seasons and performed his duties with a fervent emotion that made fans, and opponents, take note.

"He can do anything he wants to on a floor," said Mychal Thompson, a former Portland and Los Angeles forward. "When he gets the ball, he's as close to unstoppable as any player I've seen."

Chuck Daly, former coach at Cleveland, Detroit and New Jersey, agreed, "He's one of a handful of players who can go out and win a game by himself," he said

That's almost what Sir Charles had to do in Philadelphia. Not blessed with a lot of help after Erving's departure, Barkley kept the 76ers respectable but couldn't get them deep into the playoffs. In 1992, he was traded to Phoenix and he tuned up for his new beginning by playing for the U.S. Dream Team in the Barcelona Olympics.

Barkley enjoyed his best season in 1992–93 when he earned MVP honors and led the Suns to the NBA Finals where they lost in six games to Chicago. After entertaining thoughts of retirement, Barkley chased his elusive dream in 1994 and '95, but the Suns were beset by injuries and sank in the standings.

A trade to Houston—teaming him with fellow future Hall of Famers Hakeem Olajuwon and Clyde Drexler—rekindled the championship desire in Barkley but his first two seasons with the new team were hampered by injury. He played just 53 and 68 games in 1996–97 and '97–98.

He was able to play 42 games in the lockout-shortened 1998–99 season, but an injury ended his career in the 1999–2000 season.

Barkley had announced 1999–2000 would be his last season anyway, but on December 8, 1999, when the Rockets were playing—ironically enough—in Philadelphia, he ruptured a tendon in his left quadriceps, putting a premature end to that final season. He could have gone quietly into retirement, but that was never his style. Instead Barkley returned for a cameo appearance in the Rockets' final game of the season, getting two points, a rebound, an assist and a blocked shot in a six-minute stint.

UP AND OVER: *Charles Barkley could shoot the ball over the tallest of opponents.*

RICK BARRY

> ## "There is no doubt Rick's on-court demeanor hurt his image. But, boy, he sure could play."

Butch Beard, former Warriors teammate.

Statistics

BORN: March 28, 1944, at Elizabeth, N.J.

HEIGHT: 6–7   **WEIGHT:** 220

COLLEGE: Miami (Fla.)

PRO TEAMS: San Francisco/Golden State Warriors, 1965–67, 1972–78; Oakland Oaks/ Washington Capitols (ABA), 1968–70; New York Nets (ABA), 1970–72; Houston Rockets, 1978–80

NBA CAREER AVERAGES: 23.2 ppg; 6.5 rpg; 5.1 apg

NBA PLAYOFF AVERAGES: 24.8 ppg; 5.6 rpg; 4.6 apg

It was no coincidence that Rick Barry looked familiar to NBA opponents when he took his first dribbles toward Rookie of the Year honors with the San Francisco Warriors in 1965–66.

"Barry is a young Elgin Baylor," said Boston defensive ace Tom (Satch) Sanders at the time. "Rick gives you that quick little fake and then he's gone."

"I'm no Baylor," responded Barry, a 6-foot-7 forward, "but I'd like to be. Most of the moves I've got I copied from Elgin. I've been studying Baylor's floor game for a long time. But my shots are my own. I've always been able to shoot."

Nobody could dispute that claim. Barry shot his way to a collegiate national scoring title (37.4 points per game) as a senior at the University of Miami. After his Rookie of the Year campaign, he led the NBA with a 35.6-point average and combined with 6–11

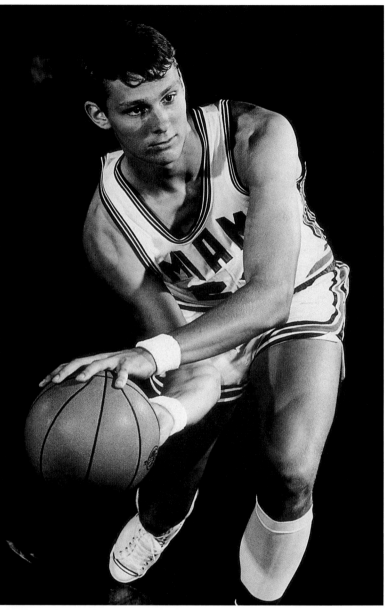

HOT SHOT: *Rick Barry led the nation in scoring as a senior at Miami of Ohio.*

CAREER HIGHLIGHTS

1965 Closed college career by leading nation with a 37.4-point average; picked by Warriors in first round of NBA draft.

1966 Averaged 25.7 points and 10.6 rebounds while earning Rookie of the Year honors.

1967 Named MVP in All-Star Game; won scoring title with 35.6 average; led Warriors to NBA Finals; signed as free agent with ABA's Oaks; sat out 1967–68 season under court order.

1969 Captured ABA scoring title with 34-point average and led Oaks to ABA championship.

1970 Traded by Capitols to Nets.

1972 Returned to NBA's Warriors; earned first free-throw percentage title.

1975 Led Warriors to championship; named NBA Finals MVP; led league with 2.85 steals per game; earned fourth of five All-NBA first-team citations.

1978 Signed with Rockets as free agent.

1980 Retired with ABA/NBA combined point total of 25,279.

1986 Elected to Hall of Fame.

center Nate Thurmond to lead the Warriors to the 1967 NBA Finals, where they lost to Wilt Chamberlain and the Philadelphia 76ers.

The intense and outspoken Barry was on his way to stardom, the toast of San Francisco. But with greatness at his fingertips, Barry made a controversial decision that would tarnish his Golden Boy image. He agreed to a free-agent contract with the rival ABA's Oakland Oaks, touching off a long and bitter legal tussle that would not be forgotten for years.

Barry was forced to the sideline in 1967–68, while the NBA and ABA were haggling in court. But he returned to action with a vengeance in 1968–69, leading the ABA with a 34-point average and propelling the Oaks to the ABA championship.

From that point on, Barry became a self-described basketball gypsy. The next three ABA seasons would take him to Washington, New York and back to the NBA, via court order. When he rejoined the renamed Golden State Warriors for 1972–73, he was greeted by unsympathetic fans who perceived him as a traitor and criticized the emotional playing style they had once found endearing.

Not only could Barry create shots and instant points in the long-admired Baylor style, he was one of the game's best passing forwards, a clutch rebounder and a quick defender who led the league one season in steals. He was unmatched as a free-throw shooter, using his throwback underhand style to hit an NBA-record 90 percent of his career tosses.

Barry's best NBA season came in 1974–75, when he averaged 30.6 points and 6.2 assists while leading an overachieving Golden State team to its only West Coast championship. When the Warriors swept heavily-favored Washington in the Finals, he was named MVP.

Barry retired in 1980 after two seasons with Houston. Over 14 years, he carried a 24.8 professional scoring average and the distinction of being the only player to lead both the NBA and ABA in scoring. He also was a five-time All-NBA first-team selection and a six-time free-throw percentage champion.

GOLDEN BOY: *Rick Barry was a shooting star for San Francisco, Golden State and Houston.*

ELGIN BAYLOR

"Sometimes you think he's got to eat the ball, but he's still hanging up there in the air, shooting or passing."

John Kundla, former Minneapolis Lakers coach.

Statistics

BORN: Sept. 16, 1934, Washington, D.C.
HEIGHT: 6-5
WEIGHT: 225
COLLEGE: The College of Idaho; Seattle
PRO TEAM: Minneapolis/Los Angeles Lakers 1958-72
NBA CAREER AVERAGES: 27.4 ppg; 13.5 rpg; 4.3 apg
NBA PLAYOFF AVERAGES: 27.0 ppg; 12.9 rpg; 4.0 apg

LAKERS LEGEND: *Elgin Baylor had a wide range of offensive skills.*

All he needed was a tiny hole, a defensive crack that most players would not even notice. Suddenly, before anybody realized what was happening, Elgin Baylor would slice through, make an impossible cut to the basket and deliver two points.

Or Baylor would use his burly 6-foot-5 frame to back a helpless defender into the paint, turn and hang in the air until an opening developed for his deadly jump shot. Or he would simply post up the defender and fire a turn-around jumper; or a pinpoint pass to an open teammate. Whatever Baylor needed, he would simply dip into his bag of offensive tricks.

"He just floats," marveled John Kundla, Baylor's coach when he joined the Minneapolis Lakers in 1958. "For a man who weighs 225 pounds, I've never seen that kind of timing. The man amazes me."

Baylor, who spent his entire 14-year career with the Lakers, amazed more than Kundla. He averaged 24.9 points and 15 rebounds en route to Rookie of the Year honors in 1958–59 and increased his totals dramatically over his first four seasons, posting eye-popping totals of 38.3 points, 18.6 rebounds and 4.6 assists in 1961–62. And when he got into the scoring groove, he was virtually unstoppable.

He broke the NBA single-game record when he scored 64 points against Boston in 1959 and lifted the mark to 71 a year later against New York. In a 1962 NBA Finals game against the Celtics,

Baylor poured in a record 61.

After leading the University of Seattle to the NCAA Tournament final in 1958, Baylor was selected first overall by the Lakers in the draft. He immediately lifted the sagging Minneapolis franchise back to respectability and when the team moved to Los Angeles in 1960, he was joined by hot-shooting guard Jerry West.

The Baylor/West tandem became synonymous with Lakers basketball and soon Los Angeles was a serious title contender. But the road to an NBA championship traveled through Boston in the 1960s and the Celtics proved more than the Lakers could handle. Eight times Baylor/West teams reached the NBA Finals and eight times they lost, seven to the Celtics. The closest Baylor came to a championship was 1972, a career-ending season in which he played only nine games, none in the playoffs, while the Lakers won their first title since moving to Los Angeles.

By that time, Baylor was only a shell of his former self, a victim of knee problems that plagued him consistently from the early 1960s until the end of his career. He finished with 27.4-point and 13.5-rebound averages, Hall of Fame numbers in anybody's book.

After teaming with West for so long, the two became rivals while directing the two Los Angeles teams–West with the Lakers and Baylor with the Clippers.

(Opposite) UNSTOPPABLE: *Baylor gave nightmares to many an over-matched defender.*

CAREER HIGHLIGHTS

1958 Led Seattle to finals of NCAA Tournament, where it lost to Kentucky; selected first overall by Lakers in NBA draft.

1959 Named All-Star Game co-MVP; set NBA single-game scoring record with 64 points against Boston; led Lakers to first of eight NBA Finals appearances (all losses) in 12 years; named Rookie of the Year; became All-NBA first-team selection for first of 10 times.

1960 Scored NBA-record 71 points against New York.

1962 Averaged 38.3 points for season, second only to Chamberlain's 50.4 mark of same season; scored NBA Finals-record 61 points in game against Boston.

1972 Played only nine games because of knee problems and watched Lakers capture first NBA championship; retired with 23,149 career points and 11,463 rebounds.

1976 Elected to Naismith Memorial Hall of Fame.

1980 Named to NBA 35th Anniversary All-Time Team.

LARRY BIRD

"Bird is the best passer I've ever seen. In fact he's so good, he makes his teammates look good."

Bob Cousy, former Boston great.

Statistics

BORN: *Dec. 7, 1956, West Baden, Ind.*

HEIGHT: *6–9*

WEIGHT: *220*

COLLEGE: *Indiana State*

PRO TEAM: *Boston Celtics, 1979–92*

NBA CAREER AVERAGES: *24.3 ppg; 10.0 rpg; 6.3 apg*

NBA PLAYOFF AVERAGES: *23.8 ppg; 10.3 rpg; 6.5 apg*

When NBA scouts took their first look at Larry Bird, they had to wonder what all the commotion was about. The Indiana State star could not jump well, his foot-speed was average and his quickness was suspect. But, still, there was something intriguing about the 6-foot-9 forward.

Maybe it was his 30.3 collegiate scoring average, much of it amassed off a deadly outside jump shot. Maybe it was his uncanny ability to get the ball to the open man, often with blind passes that had no business threading their way through the crowded lane. Or maybe it was the success of the Bird-powered Sycamores, who were on their way to an NCAA Tournament finals berth opposite Magic Johnson and Michigan State.

Boston President Red Auerbach saw plenty he liked and grabbed Bird after his junior season with the sixth pick of the '78 draft. The Celtics had to wait an entire season, but the payoff was big.

"You know if you're open, you'll get the ball," marveled center Dave Cowens, who watched rookie Bird carry the Celtics from a 29-victory disaster to 61 in 1979–80. And his Rookie of the Year performance also included 21.3 points and 10.4 rebounds per game. In his second season, Bird combined with center Robert Parish and forward Cedric Maxwell to carry the Celtics all the way to an NBA championship.

That was the first of three that Bird and the Celtics would win in the 1980s. Before his career was derailed by back problems that would force a premature

BORN WINNER: *Larry Bird was driven to succeed for the Celtics.*

retirement, Bird also would earn three MVP awards, nine consecutive first-team All-NBA selections, three All-Defensive Team nods and two citations as the outstanding player of the NBA Finals.

"The ultimate beauty of the kid is that he'll do anything to win," Auerbach gushed early in Bird's career.

And that, perhaps, is the quality that stands out more than any other. His lightning reflexes, his pinpoint passes, his incredible instincts and his sixth-sense feel for the court all combined to lift his teammates to a different level. Bird was always there at crunch time, but he could not have won without over-achieving teammates.

And he couldn't have done it without the most consistent jump shot ever launched by an NBA forward. He finished his career with a 24.3 average, almost 2,000 of his 21,791 points coming on 3-point jumpers. If Bird wasn't the best all-around player to grace the NBA arenas, he was close.

His skill level was matched by his basketball charisma, but Bird was forced to the sideline by back problems after the 1991–92 season and made only one more appearance in uniform—as a member of the 1992 U.S. Olympic Dream Team.

Given his intense competitive nature, it should have come as no surprise that after a five-year sabbatical from the sport, he returned in 1997 as Head Coach of the Indiana Pacers. In his rookie season he led the Pacers to the Eastern Conference Finals and won Coach of the Year honors.

CAREER HIGHLIGHTS

1978 Selected by Celtics as sixth overall pick of NBA draft after junior season of college.

1979 Led Indiana State to NCAA Tournament final, where Sycamores lost to Magic Johnson and Michigan State; finished college career with 30.3-point average.

1980 Finished first season with 21.3 scoring average and earned Rookie of the Year honors; earned first of nine consecutive All-NBA first-team selections.

1981 Helped Celtics win first NBA championship since 1974.

1982 Scored 19 points and captured NBA All-Star Game MVP honors.

1984 Led Celtics to NBA championship and earned NBA Finals MVP; won first of three consecutive regular-season MVP awards.

1985 Scored career-high 60 points in game against Atlanta.

1986 Helped Celtics win third championship of decade with six-game Finals victory over Houston.

1992 Retired because of chronic back problem; finished with career total of 21,791 points; member of gold medal-winning U.S. Dream Team at Barcelona Olympic Games.

1997 Appointed coach of his home state Indiana Pacers

LARRY LEGEND: *It was Bird's competitive nature that made him such a dangerous opponent.*

That may have surprised some, but not Auerbach, who said, "I've decided, quite frankly, that he's the greatest player ever to put on a uniform."

In 1998–99, the Pacers lost to the New York Knicks in the conference finals, but in 1999–2000 they defeated the Knicks in six games to advance to their first NBA Finals. Bird had already announced that he was to finish coaching after just three seasons in Indiana, but the Pacers could not send him out with a championship, eventually losing to the Los Angeles Lakers in six games.

WILT CHAMBERLAIN

"If you or I went to the gym alone, it would take us a half hour to make enough for 100 points."

Frank McGuire, Warriors coach, after Chamberlain's 100-point game.

Statistics

BORN: Aug. 21, 1936, Philadelphia
HEIGHT: 7–1
WEIGHT: 275
College: Kansas (three seasons)
PRO TEAMS: Philadelphia/San Francisco Warriors, 1959–65; Philadelphia 76ers, 1965–68; Los Angeles Lakers, 1968–73
NBA CAREER AVERAGES: 30.1 ppg; 29.9 rpg; 4.4 apg
NBA PLAYOFF AVERAGES: 22.5 ppg; 24.5 rpg; 4.2 apg

By the time Wilt Chamberlain brought his 7-foot-1, 275-pound body to the NBA wars in 1959, fans and players were comfortable with the idea of dominating centers. George Mikan, the first center to dominate with offense, had retired five years earlier and Bill Russell, a defensive and rebounding terror, already had led Boston to two championships. How could Chamberlain, coming off a season with the Harlem Globetrotters, compete with that?

What the basketball world witnessed in 1959–60 was the unveiling of the greatest offensive machine the game would ever produce. Not only was "Wilt the Stilt" big and amazingly strong, he could run the court like a gazelle, had the stamina of a mule and the quickness and determination to score and rebound almost at will.

His rookie numbers for the Philadelphia Warriors were 37.6 points and 27 rebounds per game. Only two players had topped 2,000 points in a season; Chamberlain scored 2,707. Only Russell had previously topped 1,500 rebounds; Chamberlain grabbed 1,941. And he was just getting started.

Chamberlain averaged 38.4 points and 27.2 rebounds per game in 1960–61 to set the stage for the greatest offensive season in history. In 1961–62, he put his fadeaway jumper into full gear and averaged an incredible 50.4 points and 25.7 rebounds, exploding for a record 100 points in a game against New York.

Through his first seven NBA seasons, Chamberlain's scoring average never dipped below 33.5. But the Warriors never won a championship. Despite his record- shattering exploits and tremendous drawing power, he became a much-maligned superstar, a scoring machine who couldn't take a team to the highest level. He bristled at the suggestion.

"It's human nature," said Chamberlain, a four-time MVP. "No one roots for Goliath."

Ironically, Chamberlain's first taste of success came in 1967, after a campaign in which he averaged a career-low 24.1 points. In his second season after the transplanted San Francisco Warriors had traded him back to Philadelphia, he helped the 76ers end Boston's bid for a ninth consecutive championship. His only other title came in 1972 with the Los Angeles Lakers.

The biggest controversy, one that still rages on, pits Wilt against Russell, the offensive genius versus the defensive enforcer. Russell often gets the nod because of the Celtics' 11 championships.

But not everyone agrees. "To me, he's one in history," former Utah coach Frank Layden said. "One Babe Ruth. One Willie Mays. One Wilt."

After the 63-year-old Chamberlain died of a heart attack on Oct. 12, 1999, Russell eulogized him this way: "I feel unspeakably injured. I've lost a dear and

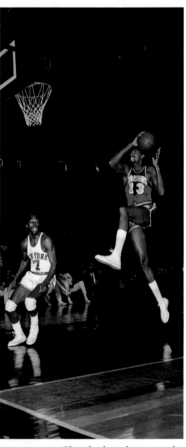

WILT THE STILT: *Chamberlain driving to the basket was an awesome sight.*

CAREER HIGHLIGHTS

1959 Drafted by Warriors as territorial pick in first round.

1960 Set single-game record with 55 rebounds against Boston; completed season with record 37.6-point scoring and 27-rebound averages; named Rookie of the Year; earned first of four regular-season MVPs; earned first of seven All-NBA first-team selections.

1961 Finished season with record 2,149 rebounds and 3,033 points.

1962 Had 100-point game against Knicks; scored record 4,029 points, averaging season-record 50.4 points.

1967 Led 76ers to NBA championship.

1968 Led league with 702 assists.

1972 Earned NBA All-Defensive Team; led Lakers to NBA championship.

1973 Retired with 31,419 points and 23,924 rebounds.

1978 Elected to Naismith Memorial Hall of Fame.

1980 Named to NBA 35th Anniversary All-Time Team.

1997 Named one of the 50 greatest players in league history.

1999 Died of a heart attack.

exceptional friend and an important part of my life. Our relationship was intensely personal. Many have called our competition the greatest rivalry in the history of sports. We didn't have a rivalry; we had a genuinely fierce competition that was based on friendship and respect. We just loved playing against each other. The fierceness of the competition bond us as friends for eternity ... Wilt was the greatest offensive player I have ever seen. I've seen none better. Because his talents and skills were so super human, his play forced me to play at my highest level."

TREADING THE BOARDS: *Wilt Chamberlain was the NBA's rebound leader 11 times.*

BOB COUSY

"You know, he looks one way, feints a second and passes a third. He bounced quite a few off my head before I adjusted."

Bill Sharman, former Celtics teammate.

Statistics

BORN: Aug. 9, 1928, New York
HEIGHT: 6–1
WEIGHT: 175
COLLEGE: Holy Cross
PRO TEAMS:
Boston Celtics, 1950–63; Cincinnati Royals, 1969–70
NBA CAREER AVERAGES: 18.4 ppg; 5.2 rpg; 7.5 apg
NBA PLAYOFF AVERAGES: 18.5 ppg; 5.0 rpg; 8.6 apg

For 13 confounding seasons, Bob Cousy flitted and floated through the National Basketball Association like a horse fly in a stable. Frustrated opponents swatted, waved and thrashed at no-look passes, behind-the-back dribbles and other seemingly magical ball-handling feats that set up teammates for easy baskets time after time.

Cousy was the "Houdini of the Hardwood," a 6-foot-1 New Yorker who arrived on the NBA scene in 1950 after four outstanding seasons at Holy Cross. He brought with him a sleight-of-hand artistry that would lift the concept of playmaking guard to a new level. Now you see it, now you don't. The Cooz was a magician with a jump shot.

"The first game we played together, he bounced a pass off my head," said Bill Sharman, Cousy's Boston Celtics backcourt mate from 1951 to '61. "It was a continual adjustment, a continual amazement."

In retrospect, Cousy was a forerunner to the razzle-dazzle basketball that has been played by such worthy successors as Pete Maravich, Magic Johnson and John Stockton. But in the 1950s, when professional basketball was still in its learning stage, he must have seemed like something from another planet.

"I used to stay awake all night thinking about him before I had to play him," said former Minneapolis Lakers guard Slater Martin.

When Cousy emerged from Holy Cross, he was selected by Tri-Cities in the first round of the draft and traded to Chicago. When the Stags folded before the 1950–51 season, the team's players were dispersed and Cousy's name was drawn out of a hat by disappointed Boston Coach Red Auerbach, who was hoping to get Max Zaslofsky or Andy Phillip.

Auerbach's bad luck was Boston's salvation. Cousy was the perfect fit for the running game Auerbach wanted to install at Boston Garden. In his rookie season, Cousy averaged 15.6 points and

HOUDINI OF THE HARDWOOD: *His hands were what made Bob Cousy such a success.*

CAREER HIGHLIGHTS

1950 Selected in first round of NBA draft by Tri-Cities Blackhawks and traded to Chicago Stags; NBA rights drawn out of hat by Boston in dispersal of Chicago franchise.

1952 Earned first of 10 consecutive All-NBA first-team citations.

1953 Earned first of eight consecutive assist titles with average of 7.7 per game; scored playoff-record 50 points in Boston's four-overtime first-round victory over Syracuse.

1954 Scored 20 points and earned first of two All-Star Game MVPs.

1957 Played on first of six NBA championship teams; named NBA regular-season MVP.

1963 Retired with career totals of 16,960 points and 6,955 assists.

1969 Made brief seven-game comeback attempt after taking over as coach of Cincinnati Royals, a job he held four-plus seasons.

1970 Elected to Naismith Memorial Hall of Fame; named to NBA 25th Anniversary All-Time Team.

1980 Named to NBA 35th Anniversary All-Time Team.

4.9 assists as the Celtics improved from 22 victories to 39. In his third season, Cousy averaged 19.8 points and began a string of eight consecutive seasons as the league's assist leader.

But more importantly, he fueled a Celtics fast-break offense that would carry the franchise to six championships before his retirement in 1963. The first title came in 1957, when Cousy earned MVP honors. The Celtics went on to win championships every year from 1959–63.

When Cousy retired, he owned career regular-season averages of 18.4 points and 7.5 assists and playoff marks of 18.5 and 8.6. He had played in the All-Star Game every one of his 13 seasons. But his outstanding career still was defined by the championships and the hocus-pocus he used to constantly amaze fans as well as opponents and teammates.

The Celtics had taller stars, but not bigger ones.

THE TOAST OF BEANTOWN: *The 6-1 Cousy played a large part in the Celtics success.*

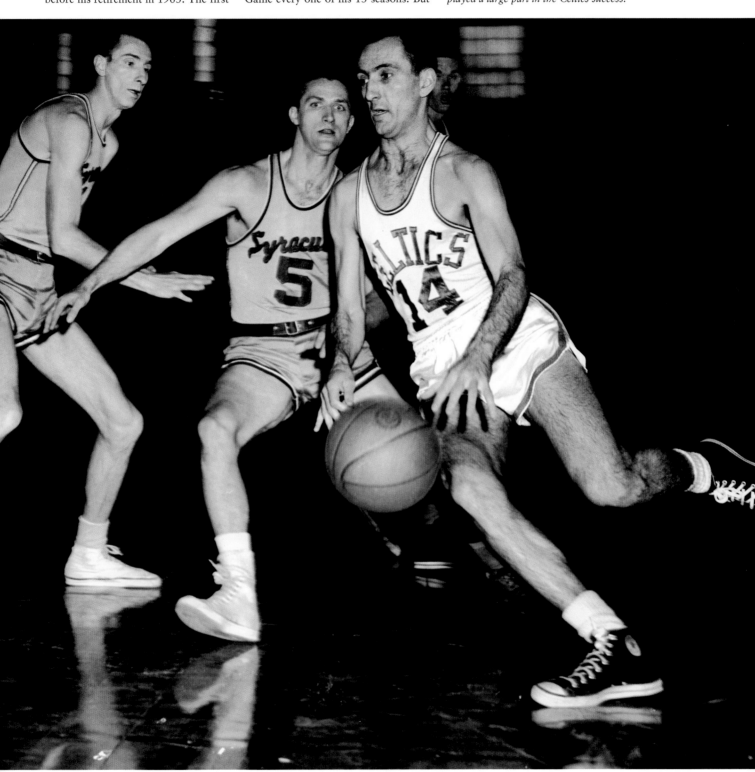

JULIUS ERVING

"I used to watch games on TV and I'd dream up fantastic moves and then go out on the court and try them."

Julius Erving

Statistics

BORN: *Feb. 22, 1950, Roosevelt, N.Y.*

HEIGHT: *6–7*

WEIGHT: *210*

COLLEGE: *Massachusetts (left after junior season)*

PRO TEAMS: *Virginia Squires (ABA), 1971–73; New York Nets (ABA), 1973–76; Philadelphia 76ers (NBA) 1976–87*

NBA CAREER AVERAGES: *22.0 ppg; 6.7 rpg; 3.9 apg*

NBA PLAYOFF AVERAGES: *21.9 ppg; 7.0 rpg; 4.2 apg*

CALL THE DOCTOR: *Julius Erving makes another house call on the road.*

He flew through the air with the greatest of ease and if Julius (Dr. J) Erving wasn't the best player in basketball history, he at least was its most eloquent.

At first glance, there was nothing unusual about Erving, a 6-foot-7 forward with thin, muscular legs and huge hands. But as soon as the clock began ticking, a spectacular transformation took place. He would glide around the court, palming the ball like a tiny grapefruit. He would soar above the crowd like a rim-seeking missile and drop the ball through from one of several impossible angles. He would drive the lane, hang in the air and either pass or shoot while mere mortal defenders returned to earth.

In an era where players left their feet only to shoot or defend, Dr. J wrote a special prescription for fan-pleasing showmanship.

"I'm a Pisces. I have a wild imagination and I've always been one to exper-

CAREER HIGHLIGHTS

1971 Signed as free agent with ABA's Squires.

1972 Earned first of four ABA All-Star first-team citations.

1973 Won first of three ABA scoring titles with 31.9 average; traded to New York Nets.

1974 Led Nets to first of two ABA championships, capturing playoff MVP honors; claimed first of three consecutive ABA regular-season MVPs.

1976 Completed ABA career with

28.7-point and 12.1-rebound averages; sold by Nets to NBA's 76ers.

1977 Made first of 11 appearances in NBA All-Star Game, scoring 30 points and earning MVP honors; led 76ers to first of four NBA Finals appearances in seven years.

1978 Earned first of five All-NBA first-team citations.

1980 Named to NBA 35th Anniversary All-Time Team.

1981 Named NBA's regular-season MVP.

1983 Led 76ers to first NBA championship since 1967.

1987 Retired with combined ABA/NBA point total of 30,026.

1993 Elected to Naismith Memorial Hall of Fame.

iment," Erving explained. "I dunk the ball a lot of different ways because I know dunking excites people."

Dr. J signed with the American Basketball Association after his junior season at Massachusetts. The struggling ABA badly needed a star and Erving needed room to operate. Unshackled from the conservative college game, Dr. J unleashed a spectacular air show that left fans, coaches and players gasping.

In five ABA seasons with the Virginia Squires and New York Nets, Erving did everything imaginable to win fans and games. He scored (28.7 points per game), rebounded (12.1) and passed (4.8 assists). He also earned three ABA MVPs and carried the Nets to a pair of championships. When the ABA folded after the 1975–76 season and the Nets were admitted to the NBA for a hefty fee, Erving's contract was sold to the Philadelphia 76ers.

It was love at first sight, both in Philadelphia and around the NBA. "The things he does when he's airborne will never be done again," marveled former Portland Coach Jack Ramsay. "He takes off at the top of the circle, goes into the air and there are about six things that can happen."

Over the next 11 seasons, Erving transformed professional basketball from ground zero to an above-the-rim experience. Fans loved it and so did officials and coaches, who began unshackling other showmen. The stage was set for such future high-wire acts as Dominique Wilkins and Michael Jordan.

Erving led the 76ers to four NBA Finals and a 1983 championship. He finished his career in 1987 with a combined ABA/NBA total of 30,026 points, which ranks No. 3 on the all-time list.

But the legend of Dr. J was built on style, not numbers. Former ABA and NBA star Dan Issel watched Erving operate for 14 seasons. "If the NBA fans could have seen Julius in his ABA years," he said, "they would have thought he was the greatest player who ever put on basketball shoes."

ONE OF A KIND: *Julius Erving was always known for his dignity and class.*

PATRICK EWING

"I've always said I thought he was the best center in the league."

Pat Riley, former New York Knicks coach.

Statistics

BORN: Aug. 5, 1962, Kingston, Jamaica

HEIGHT: 7–0

WEIGHT: 240

COLLEGE: Georgetown

PRO TEAMS: New York Knicks, 1985–2000, Seattle Supersonics, 2000–present

NBA CAREER AVERAGES: 22.8 ppg; 10.4 rpg; 2.0 apg

NBA PLAYOFF AVERAGES: 20.6 ppg; 10.5 rpg; 2.0 apg

Away from the court, Patrick Ewing is a gentle giant: soft spoken, unassuming, quick to flash a reassuring smile. But when he puts on a jersey, Dr. Patrick turns to Mr. Hyde.

He scowls, he bumps and grinds, he powers his way to the basket and he physically dominates anybody who dares penetrate "his paint." There is nothing artistic about Ewing. He is a menacing 7-foot, 240-pounder who usually gets his way.

It was like that when he played for Georgetown University and led the Hoyas to a national championship and two more Final Four appearances. And it was like that in 1984, when he helped the U.S. win an Olympic gold medal at Los Angeles. When the Knicks grabbed him with the first overall pick of the 1985 draft, they thought they had the center-piece for a championship-filled future.

It wouldn't be that easy. He averaged 20 points and nine rebounds in 1985–86 en route to Rookie of the Year honors, but he also missed 32 games as the Knicks finished last in the Atlantic Division. Ewing, in fact, would not pay dividends until 1989–90, his fifth NBA season, when he blossomed both physically and mentally, averaging 28.6 points and 10.9 rebounds while blocking 327 shots.

But the Knicks would not blossom until two years later, when Pat Riley took over as coach and began molding a team around his big center. Soon, the Knicks would reflect the qualities of Ewing— methodical on offense, menacing on defense and physically intimidating. New York opponents drove the lane at their own risk and scores of Knicks games seldom reached triple figures.

Riley's game plan was a triumphant success but a public relations nightmare. Ewing was dominating in the half-court game and the Knicks became instant title contenders, but the physical battering they handed opponents cast them in the role of villains. Ewing was unfairly labeled a thug and the team's defensive style criticized. But Riley responded:

"I played with Chamberlain and coached Kareem and never did they get criticism like Patrick does. He handles it better than anyone."

New York reeled off consecutive seasons of 51, 60, 57 and 55 victories. But twice they lost to the title-bound Chicago Bulls in early playoff rounds and in 1993– 94 they advanced to the NBA Finals, only to lose to Houston.

Riley departed after the 1995 playoffs, but Ewing remained the heart and soul of the Knicks. In 1996, they seemed poised to dethrone the Bulls in the East, but lost in the semis to Miami, despite taking a 3–1 lead.

Ewing's career has been filled with accomplishment and disappointment— none more so than in 1997–98 when a hand injury limited him to 26 regular season games before returning briefly for a convincing play-off loss to Indiana— but few could argue the fact that Patrick Ewing has only had winning on his mind.

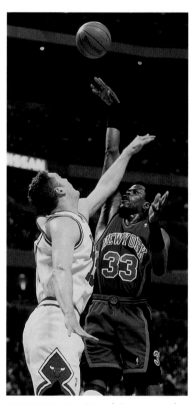

NOT JUST A PLAYER: *Patrick Ewing was the heart and soul of the Knicks.*

CAREER HIGHLIGHTS

1985 Led Hoyas to third NCAA Tournament final in four seasons; selected by Knicks with first overall pick of NBA draft.

1986 Finished injury-marred rookie season with 20-point and 9-rebound averages; named Rookie of the Year.

1989 Enjoyed first career 40–20 game (44 points, 24 rebounds) in contest at Golden State.

1990 Exploded for career-high 51 points in game against Boston; scored playoff career high of 45 in game against Detroit; finished regular season with career-high 28.6 scoring average; named to All-NBA first team.

1992 Played for U.S. Dream Team at Barcelona Olympic Games.

1993 Scored 15 points and game-tying basket in his seventh All-Star Game.

1994 Blocked NBA Finals-record 30 shots as Knicks lost to Rockets.

1996 Became first Knicks player to score 20,000 points.

2000 Traded to Seattle

A heel injury kept him out of much of the 1998–99 playoffs, when the Knicks beat the Pacers to advance to the NBA Finals. As painful as his injury was, it no doubt pained him more to watch the Knicks lose to the San Antonio Spurs in five games.

More injuries cost him 20 games in the 1999–2000 regular season. But even with Ewing, the Knicks couldn't beat the Pacers this time, losing in six games in the Eastern Conference Finals.

In the summer of 2000, Ewing's 15-season career with the Knicks came to an end following his trade to Seattle.

ROAD BLOCK: *Patrick Ewing was a very hard man to get around … or over.*

WALT FRAZIER

"Walt Frazier was a premier player because he understood that basketball is a team game and he used his abilities within a team context." *Red Auerbach, Boston Celtics President.*

Statistics

BORN: *March 29, 1945, Atlanta, Ga.*
HEIGHT: *6–4*
WEIGHT: *205*
COLLEGE: *Southern Illinois*
PRO TEAMS: *New York Knicks, 1967–77; Cleveland Cavaliers, 1977–80*
NBA CAREER AVERAGES: *18.9 ppg; 5.9 rpg; 6.1 apg*
NBA PLAYOFF AVERAGES: *20.7 ppg; 7.2 rpg; 6.4 apg*

A STYLE OF HIS OWN: *Walt Frazier was as flashy on the court as he was off it.*

Walt Frazier was never difficult to recognize. At work, he wore shorts and a jersey with a large No. 10 imprinted below a lettered "New York" insignia. Away from work, he wore eye-catching clothes that made him stand out, even on the streets of the Big Apple.

"I guess I inherited my fondness for clothes from my father," Frazier once said. His nickname, Clyde, came from a former teammate who said Frazier reminded him of the slick-dressing lead character in the movie Bonnie and Clyde.

The bottom line on Frazier was simple: Anything he did, he did it with style. Especially his play for the New York Knicks and Cleveland Cavaliers over a 13-year Hall of Fame career that ended in 1980.

"Walt Frazier was unquestionably one of the great guards of his era," said Boston Celtics President and former coach Red Auerbach.

When you think of Frazier, you think about the great Knicks teams of the early 1970s. Frazier, Dick Barnett and Earl Monroe in the guard rotation. Willis Reed at center. Dave DeBusschere and Bill Bradley at the forwards. Reed provided the muscle and Bradley, DeBusschere and Barnett supplied steady scoring and defense. But it was Frazier, the quarterback, who provided the spark.

When the Knicks needed points, there was Frazier, going to the basket with either hand or launching a jump shot off a teammate's screen. When they needed a big defensive play, there was Frazier, poking the ball free with lightning-quick hands and dribbling the length of the court for a basket. He could make a pass, smother an opposing scorer or do whatever else was necessary to ensure victory. Frazier was the ultimate do-everything player.

"My specialty was trying to turn games around by intercepting a pass or poking the ball away from opponents as they dribbled," said Frazier. "Nothing would shatter a team's morale faster than a steal. Stealing the ball and making a pass that led to a basket were the part of basketball I loved most."

With "Mr. Cool" pulling the strings and Reed providing the muscle, the Knicks won 60 regular-season games in 1969–70 and advanced to the NBA Finals, where they defeated Los Angeles in seven games. Three years later, with Monroe and forward/center Jerry Lucas now in the mix, they repeated that

CAREER HIGHLIGHTS

1967 Selected by Knicks with fifth overall pick of NBA draft.
1968 Named to All-Rookie team.
1969 Earned first of seven consecutive berths on NBA All-Defensive first team.
1970 Earned first of four All-NBA first-team citations; played in first of seven All-Star Games; quarterbacked Knicks to franchise's first NBA championship.

1973 Posted playoff averages of 21.9 points and 7.3 rebounds in Knicks' run to a second NBA title.
1975 Scored 30 points and earned All-Star Game MVP award.
1977 Acquired by Cavaliers in free-agent compensation deal.
1980 Retired with 15,581 career points.
1986 Elected to Hall of Fame.

1997 Named one of the 50 greatest players in league history

scenario with a five-game Finals romp past the Lakers.

Those two championships were the pinnacle of a career that ranks Frazier among the game's great stars. He was a seven-time All-Star Game selection and the classic's 1975 MVP; he was an All-NBA first team selection four times and a member of the league's All-Defensive first team seven consecutive years; he averaged more than 20 points in six regular seasons and averaged 20.7 points, 7.2 rebounds and 6.4 assists in eight postseasons.

But beyond the numbers, Walt "Clyde" Frazier will be remembered for the style and grace he brought to basketball, both on the court and off. And in New York basketball lore, for the two championships he helped bring to a hungry city.

KING OF NEW YORK: *The Big Apple was the perfect playground for Walt Frazier.*

JOHN HAVLICEK

"If I was playing an imaginary pickup game among all the players I had ever seen, John Havlicek would be my first choice." *Bill Russell, former Boston teammate.*

Statistics

BORN: April 8, 1940, Martins Ferry, Ohio.

HEIGHT: 6–5

WEIGHT: 205

COLLEGE: Ohio State

PRO TEAM: Boston Celtics, 1962–78

NBA CAREER AVERAGES: 20.8 ppg; 6.3 rpg; 4.8 apg

NBA PLAYOFF AVERAGES: 22.0 ppg; 6.9 rpg; 4.8 apg

John Havlicek was like the Energizer Bunny: He just kept running, and running, and running. And when he finally stopped after 16 seasons, he looked back at a trail of exhausted defenders, admiring fans and NBA championships.

"I think John's a freak of nature," said Kevin Loughery, one of many former NBA players who experienced the frustration of trying to guard Havlicek. "He's constant movement. You have to chase him until you're tripping over your tongue."

Havlicek, a 6-foot-5 forward who played on Ohio State's 1960 NCAA championship team, was not blessed with Oscar Robertson-like skills, but he did offer a nice blend of speed, quickness and determination. What separated him from the pack, however, was his legendary endurance.

Havlicek was a master at moving without the ball, shaking defenders and taking quick passes for layups and short jumpers. He was a perfect fit for the fast-break Celtics and he defended with tenacity, stealing passes and fearlessly diving for loose balls. "Hondo" was the ultimate team player.

"I'll tell you what was special about John Havlicek," said former Boston coach Red Auerbach. "He didn't have a lot to say and he never made waves, but he was someone we could always count on. He got the job done. Period."

Auerbach selected Havlicek in the first round of the 1962 draft. But the Celtics had won four consecutive NBA titles and there was no room in the talent-laden starting lineup for a rookie.

So Auerbach evaluated his draft pick, noted his exceptional stamina and envisioned a supporting role that would thrust Havlicek into prominence. The youngster became Boston's "Sixth Man," a super substitute who could play either guard or forward and recharge the offense at key moments. It was a perfect fit.

Havlicek averaged 14.3 points as a rookie and 19.9 in his second season. While Bill Russell, Sam Jones, Tom Heinsohn and other Boston stars drew headlines, Havlicek also rebounded, passed and sparked the team with his defensive play. He turned his role into an art form and the Celtics rolled to six more championships in Havlicek's first seven seasons.

SUPER SUB: *John Havlicek started out as the Boston Celtics' "Sixth Man."*

CAREER HIGHLIGHTS

1960 Helped Ohio State win NCAA championship; helped Buckeyes reach NCAA finals in junior and senior seasons.

1962 Selected by Celtics in first round of NBA draft.

1963 Served as celebrated "Sixth Man" as Celtics won fifth of eight consecutive championships.

1966 Made first of 13 appearances in All-Star Game, scoring 18 points.

1971 Earned first of four consecutive All-NBA first-team citations while averaging career-high 28.9 points.

1972 Earned first of five consecutive All-Defensive team berths.

1974 Led Celtics to first post-Bill Russell championship and earned NBA Finals MVP.

1976 Played on eighth NBA championship team at age 36.

1978 Retired after 16 seasons with 26,395 points and 8,007 rebounds.

1980 Named to NBA 35th Anniversary All-Time Team.

1983 Elected to Naismith Memorial Hall of Fame.

But everything would change in 1969–70. Russell and Sam Jones retired after the 1969 championship and the Celtics dynasty crumbled fast. First-year coach Heinsohn needed an anchor for the foundering ship and he turned to Havlicek, who responded by leading the team in scoring (24.2 points per game),

rebounding (7.8) and assists (6.8). He came back the next season to average 28.9 points and 45.4 minutes per game.

Over the next five seasons, Havlicek led the rebuilt Celtics to five consecutive Atlantic Division championships and two more NBA titles, bringing his career total to eight. He won NBA Finals MVP

HOT HAND: *John Havlicek led the Boston Celtics in many different ways.*

honors in 1974 against Milwaukee.

Over the second phase of Havlicek's career, he was named to the All-NBA first team four times and to the All-Defensive Team five times.

116

ELVIN HAYES

"He's still the prototype power forward, the guy with the body who can run rebound."

Bruce Bickerstaff, NBA coach and executive.

Statistics

BORN: *Nov. 17, 1945. Rayville, La.*

HEIGHT: *6-9* **WEIGHT:** *235*

COLLEGE: *Houston*

PRO TEAMS: *San Diego Rockets, 1968-71; Houston Rockets, 1971-72; Baltimore Bullets, 1972-73; Capital Bullets, 1973-74; Washington Bullets, 1974-81; Houston Rockets, 1981-84.*

NBA CAREER AVERAGES: *21.0 ppg; 12.5 rpg; 1.8 apg*

NBA PLAYOFF AVERAGES: *22.9 ppg; 13.0 rpg; 1.9 apg*

He played with skill. He played with vigor. And he always came to play. For a power forward with such an aggressive bent for the game, Elvin Hayes missed only nine games in his 16 seasons in the NBA. An All-Star for each of his first 12 seasons, Hayes, when he left the game, had scored more points than any other player in NBA history except for Kareem Abdul-Jabbar and Wilt Chamberlain.

Hayes could score, rebound and intimidate with his defense. About the only knock during his career was an attitude that, at times, could rub teammates and coaches the wrong way.

"I'm very honest about myself," Hayes once admitted. "And that's one reason I get in trouble. I speak what I feel. Other people are more diplomatic, but I don't feel, by doing that, that I'm a man."

EASY DOES IT: *Elvin Hayes—The Big E— scores two more.*

CAREER HIGHLIGHTS

1968 Selected by San Diego Rockets in first round (first pick overall) of NBA draft.

1969 Set NBA record for minutes played by a rookie, with 3,695.

1972 Traded by Houston Rockets to Baltimore Bullets for Jack Marin and future considerations.

1975 Selected to All-NBA first team for first of three times (also in 1977 and 1979).

1978 Won NBA championship with Washington Bullets.

1981 Traded by Washington Bullets to Houston Rockets for 1981 and 1983 second-round draft choices. Departed as Bullets' all-time leading scorer, with 15,551 points and all-time blocked-shot leader, with 1,558.

1989 Elected to Basketball Hall of Fame.

1996 Selected for NBA 50th Anniversary All-Time Team.

As was the case for many NBA players, Hayes saw basketball as a means out of poverty. When he enrolled at the University of Houston, he was one of the school's first black athletes.

At Houston, Hayes was given the "Big E" moniker that would stick with him throughout his career. It was with the Cougars that Hayes might have enjoyed his ultimate basketball moment.

In 1968, Hayes and Houston faced Lew Alcindor (later to be Kareem Abdul-Jabbar) and a UCLA team that entered on a 47-game winning streak. The game was played before a crowd of 52,693 at the Astrodome in Houston and was broadcast to a national audience. With time running down in a

BULLET PROOF:
Elvin Hayes won an NBA Championship with Washington in 1978.

69–69 game, Hayes recalled, "I got the ball down low on the left side. I was going to shoot my turnaround when I was fouled. A lot of people thought I was going to miss because I was a 60-percent foul shooter. I didn't even think about being nervous, because I had the game right in my hands." He converted both attempts, as Houston won 71–69. He finished with 39 points and 15 rebounds to Alcindor's 15 points and 12 rebounds. A legend was born.

He emerged as the first overall pick of the 1968 NBA draft by the San Diego Rockets. As a rookie, he led the league in scoring at 28.4 points per game and started at center for the West in the All-Star Game.

The Rockets would later move, to of all places, Houston, where Hayes received a hero's welcome to the city he thrilled

in a previous era with his collegiate excellence. Hayes then was traded to the Baltimore Bullets.

In 1974-75, Hayes' Bullets tied the Boston Celtics for the best record in the NBA at 60-22 and advanced to the NBA Finals, where they lost in four games to the Golden State Warriors. In 1978, Hayes' Bullets made it back to the NBA Finals, to take on the Seattle SuperSonics. The rugged series went the full seven games, with the Bullets winning the title on the road, with a 105-99 victory. Hayes was ecstatic. "Finally winning the championship completes the picture," Hayes said, "because no one can ever again say that E's not a champion." Hayes took the Bullets back to the 1979 NBA Finals, but this time they lost to Seattle. Hayes finished his career back in Houston with the Rockets before settling into a life raising cattle and running a Houston car dealership. While his legacy is of scoring and rebounding, and while detractors remained in place to the end, claiming Hayes placed too much of an emphasis on statistics, those who knew him best defended his status as one of the sport's elite power players. "He's still the prototype power forward, the guy with the body who can run and rebound," said respected NBA coach and executive Bernie Bickerstaff, who was an assistant coach with the Bullets during Hayes' tenure. "Every night you could count on 20 points, 12 rebounds, two or three blocked shots. Every night, even on bad nights." Ultimately, there were few bad nights.

Upon his retirement, Hayes stood among the NBA's all-time leaders in many areas, including scoring (27,313 points, third), games played (1,303, first), minutes (50,000, first) and rebounds (16,279, third). As for where it all started, Hayes' turnaround jumper was first developed in high school, where he was recruited by more than 100 colleges. At Eula D. Britton High School in Rayville, Louisiana, Hayes averaged 35 points per game and led his team to 54 straight victories. He never looked back from that point, his game setting the benchmark for future power forwards.

MAGIC JOHNSON

"He refuses to let his team lose at the end of the game. He can beat you with the pass, shot, offensive rebound or defensive rebound." *Richie Adubato, former Dallas coach.*

Statistics

BORN: *Aug. 14, 1959, Lansing, Mich.*
HEIGHT: *6–9*
WEIGHT: *225*
COLLEGE: *Michigan State (left after sophomore season)*
PRO TEAMS: *Los Angeles Lakers, 1979–92, 1995–96*
NBA CAREER AVERAGES: *19.5 ppg; 7.2 rpg; 11.2 apg*
NBA PLAYOFF AVERAGES: *19.5 ppg; 7.7 rpg; 12.4 apg*

From the beginning, Earvin (Magic) Johnson was a basketball paradox. He handled the ball, passed it and shot it like a point guard. He ran the offense and controlled the flow of a game like a point guard. But at 6-foot-9, 225 pounds, he had the body of a power forward.

When Johnson burst into the NBA in 1979 with his infectious smile and creative genius, he helped push the stodgy game onto a new course of prosperity. Johnson was indeed Magic. As a college sophomore, he vaulted into prominence with his scintillating play in Michigan State's 1979 NCAA Tournament championship game victory over Larry Bird and Indiana State. Then, in what should have been his junior season, he dazzled NBA fans and opponents with his shocking array of talents.

"He's a point guard-center," said Richie Adubato, former Dallas coach. "He rebounds like a center, he can shoot outside and you know he can post up your 6-foot-whatever guard."

In Johnson's first season in Los Angeles, he averaged 18 points, 7.7 rebounds and 7.3 assists but lost out in Rookie of the Year voting to Bird, who was providing a similar brand of excitement in Boston. But Magic had the last laugh. The Lakers advanced to the 1980 NBA Finals and, with center Kareem Abdul-Jabbar injured and unable to play in Game 6, Johnson moved to center and scored 42 points in a championship-clinching victory over Philadelphia. He was named NBA Finals MVP, the first of three he would receive in the 1980s.

That was a tough act to follow. But over the next dozen years, Magic

TRICK AND TREAT: *Magic beat opponents— and thrilled the crowd—in so many ways.*

upgraded his game with a continuous flow of no-look passes, creative drives and clutch performances that earned him three MVP awards and nine All-NBA first-team citations. He became the game's most prolific assist man, averaging in double figures nine straight seasons, and his career averages of 19.7 points and 7.3 rebounds could have been higher.

With Abdul-Jabbar and James Worthy providing the muscle and Johnson running the show, the Lakers reached the Finals eight times in the decade and won five championships.

But Johnson's most lasting contribution won't appear in the record books. The simultaneous arrival of Magic and Bird and their battles in a championship context triggered a popularity explosion that carried the game to global heights.

Johnson retired after the 1990–91 season when he tested HIV-positive. But he reappeared in 1992 as a member of the Dream Team and rejoined the Lakers midway through the 1995–96 season as a 36-year-old power forward. His return was dynamic but brief. He retired again after the Lakers lost in the first round of the playoffs.

Before retiring as a player, he even coached the Lakers for part of a season, replacing Randy Pfund and Bill Bertka for the last 16 games of the 1993–94 season. After finishing 5–11, he also retired from coaching. Now he serves as a co-owner/vice president of the Lakers.

(Opposite) **AS GOOD AS IT GETS:** *Johnson was NBA Finals MVP in his rookie season.*

CAREER HIGHLIGHTS

1979 Led Michigan State to the NCAA championship with a finals victory over Indiana State; declared for NBA draft after sophomore season and was selected first overall by Lakers.

1980 Capped rookie season by scoring 42 points in championship-clinching victory over 76ers in NBA Finals; named Finals MVP.

1981 Led NBA with 3.43 steals per game.

1982 Earned second NBA Finals MVP award as Lakers captured second championship of decade; led league with 2.67 steal average.

1983 Earned first of five assist titles with 10.5 average; earned first of nine straight All-NBA first-team citations.

1987 Earned first of three regular-season MVP awards; helped Lakers win fourth of five championships in decade.

1991 Set NBA's all-time career assist record with 9,921; announced retirement after testing HIV-positive; left game with five NBA championships, three MVPs and 17,239 points.

1992 Played for U.S. Dream Team in Barcelona Olympic Games; came out of retirement to compete in NBA All-Star Game, scoring 25 points and winning MVP honors.

1996 Came out of retirement and helped Lakers to 53-win season

MICHAEL JORDAN

"As soon as he touches the ball, it electrifies the intensity in you."

Michael Cooper, former Los Angeles Lakers guard.

Statistics

BORN: Feb. 17, 1963, Brooklyn, N.Y.
HEIGHT: 6–6
WEIGHT: 198
COLLEGE: North Carolina (three years)
PRO TEAM: Chicago Bulls, 1984–93, 1995–1998
NBA CAREER AVERAGES: 31.5 ppg; 6.3 rpg; 5.4 apg
NBA PLAYOFF AVERAGES: 33.4 ppg; 6.4 rpg; 5.7 apg

TONGUE-TIED: *Many of Michael Jordan's moves left both players and fans speechless.*

The legend of Michael Jordan started in 1982 with a 20-foot jump shot that decided a national college championship. Over the next decade, it grew into a marketing missile that rose majestically over the NBA.

From the moment Jordan, a North Carolina freshman guard, connected on his NCAA Tournament-winning jumper against Georgetown, he was primed for greatness. He would fulfill his destiny above the rims of Chicago Stadium and the United Center, dazzling fans with his amazing grace and extraordinary athleticism, leaving opponents and coaches gasping for defensive answers and superlatives.

"Everybody knows he's going to get the ball, but you don't know what he's going to do with it," said former Los Angeles Lakers star Michael Cooper, one of the best defensive guards in NBA history.

Former Indiana Pacers Coach Dick Versace expressed a common sentiment when he called Jordan "a visitor from another planet."

Jordan's career numbers and honors lend credence to Versace's out-of-this-world description: a record ten scoring titles; record-equalling five MVP awards; 1984–85 Rookie of the Year; a

six times NBA Finals MVP; a two-time Olympic Champion.

But Jordan's crowning achievement came when he led the long-struggling Bulls to the top of the NBA mountain. It was a dream come true. Jordan's early years had been filled with scoring titles, 40 and 50-point games and individual glory, but it wasn't until the arrival of

CAREER HIGHLIGHTS

1982 Hit 20-foot shot that gave North Carolina NCAA Tournament finals victory.

1984 Selected third overall by Bulls in NBA draft; co-captain of gold medal-winning Olympic team.

1985 Named NBA Rookie of the Year.

1986 Scored NBA playoff-record 63 in double-overtime victory at Boston.

1987 Selected All-NBA first team for first of seven straight seasons; won first of seven straight scoring titles (37.1 ppg).

1988 Won first regular-season MVP; named Defensive Player of the Year.

1991 Led Bulls to first NBA championship; named Finals MVP.

1993 Averaged Finals-record 41 points as Bulls won third straight championship.

1996 Won fourth NBA Finals MVP; led Bulls to fourth 1990s championship.

1997 Won fifth NBA Finals MVP; Bulls win fifth championship of the decade

1998 Won sixth NBA Finals MVP in six attempts as Bulls capture their sixth title in eight years. Won record 10th scoring title and fifth League MVP.

Scottie Pippen, Horace Grant and John Paxson that the Bulls reached championship form. With Jordan fueling the charge, they became only the third NBA team to win three straight titles, defeating the Lakers, Portland and Phoenix from 1991–93.

Having established his credentials as an outstanding team player as well as the game's ultimate individual, a 30-year-old Jordan shocked the world in 1993 by announcing his retirement, saying he had no more basketball worlds to conquer.

But after almost two years of pursuing a second-sport career in baseball, he changed his mind, returning to his exalted position on the NBA throne. Jordan rejoined the Bulls for the final 17 games of 1994–95, and, one year later, everything was back to normal in Chicago. The Jordan-led Bulls of 1995–96 posted an unprecedented 72–10 regular season and fourth championship. A year later he led the Bulls to a 69–13 record and a fifth NBA title of the decade.

Jordan ended the 1997–98 campaign with a 31.5 career scoring average, the highest in league history. Most of those points have come off gliding, graceful jumps, hanging, double-clutching moves and in-your-face, either-hand slam dunks. His unprecedented popularity is a product of charisma and showmanship.

Jordan helped lift the league to heights of popularity never before enjoyed. His name transcends conventional marketing strategies and carries worldwide renown. The only question, as Jordan celebrated his sixth NBA title after dominating the Utah Jazz in the 1998 Finals, was for how much longer would he honor the sport with his presence.

The answer to that question was delayed somewhat by the lockout that postponed the start of the 1998–99 season. But when the NBA finally tipped off that season, it was without the man many viewed as the greatest player ever to play the game.

This time Jordan's retirement as a player was permanent. But he did move into the front office as president of basketball operations with the Washington Wizards.

RARE AIR: *Michael Jordan played the game above the rim like no other.*

122

KARL MALONE

"I've never seen a player work as hard off the floor as Karl Malone."

Jerry Sloan, Utah Jazz coach

Statistics

BORN: July 24, 1963. Summerfield, La.
HEIGHT: 6-9
WEIGHT: 259
COLLEGE: Louisiana Tech (three years).
PRO TEAMS: Utah Jazz, 1985-present.
NBA CAREER AVERAGES: 26.0 ppg; 10.6 rpg; 3.4 apg.
NBA PLAYOFF AVERAGES: 26.6 ppg; 11.2 rpg; 3.1 apg

He is the Mailman, because he always delivers. At least that's the way a writer in Louisiana put it during Karl Malone's college days.

More than a decade later, who is to argue?

Among the most sculpted of NBA power players, Malone has redefined the position of power forward during his career-long tenure with the Utah Jazz. He can barrel down the lane with the force of a raging bull. He can convert the medium-range jumper with the touch of a shooting guard. And he can rebound with the vitality of a 20-something rookie.

"I take pride in what God gave me," he said. "He gave me a body, he gave me a mind and he gave me a heart and determination to try and work and hone my body."

Malone not only has honed his physique to a bodybuilder's level, he has honed a game that is as polished now as

it was raw when he first entered the league as a little-known prospect out of Louisiana Tech.

Once a poor free-throw shooter, Malone now practically makes a living at the line, having set several NBA records for free-throw attempts. Once a

STEADY GROWTH *Karl Malone has inproved his game across the board.*

questionable defender, he now has the bulk to keep virtually any player out of the lane.

Once a good outside shooter, he now is as efficient as any forward in the league from the perimeter.

"He's made himself better in almost every aspect of his game," coach Jerry Sloan said. "When he came here his body wasn't what it is today. He changed his body. Then he changed his free throw shooting. He changed his passing. You can go on and on. He changed his inside play."

In recent seasons, the jumper has made Malone practically unstoppable.

"As time went by," he said. "I developed my offense to face my man and take him farther and farther away from the basket. I found that as I'd take the bigger guys farther out from the basket, it opened up space for me to drive around them or to shoot my jumper. And I was getting more range on my jumpers."

Perhaps his crowning moment came in 1996, when Malone and 49 other greats were honored at an NBA at 50 celebration at All-Star Weekend, commemorating the league's 50th season.

"I had some guys that played my position say, 'Hey Karl, thanks for taking our position to another level,'" he said. "And I said, 'Thanks for starting our position.'"

Those players? Hall of Fame power forwards Elvin Hayes and Bob Pettit.

Lifting himself to such levels, Malone said, was never the intended goal. "I

CAREER HIGHLIGHTS

1985 Selected by the Utah Jazz in the first round (13th pick overall) of the NBA Draft.

1989 Named MVP of the 1989 All-Star Game in Houston, with 28 points and 9 rebounds.

1990 Scored a career-high 61 points, the most by a Jazz player since the franchise moved to Utah, against the Milwaukee Bucks.

1993 Named co-MVP (with teammate John Stockton) of the 1993 All-Star Game in Salt Lake City, with 28 points and 10 rebounds.

1996 Selected as one of the 50 Greatest Players in NBA History.

1997 Appeared in first of two NBA Finals, both against Chicago Bulls.

1998 Played in 541 consecutive games before sitting out against the L.A. Clippers, and has missed only five games in his NBA career.

1999 Named NBA Most Valuable Player, becoming only the ninth player in NBA history to win the Maurice Podoloff Trophy more than once.

STRENGTH AND DETERMINATION: *The Utah Jazz power forward Karl Malone can beat you with both strength and hustle.*

never thought about making myself the best," he said. "I simply wanted to be the hardest worker at my position every time I stepped on the floor."

When paired with Jazz point guard John Stockton, Malone becomes a nightmare to guard. Not only does he set bruising screens for Stockton, but his ability to then maneuver into scoring position makes the Jazz's pick-and-roll set one of the most unstoppable offenses in basketball history. If not for Malone's ability to finish, Stockton would not stand as the NBA's all-time leader in assists.

Malone's career has been history in the making for years. He was named 1998-99 NBA Most Valuable Player, becoming only the ninth player in NBA history to win the accolade more than once.

He was named to the 1998-99 All-NBA first team, becoming the first player to be voted to 11 All-NBA first teams. He was a member of the original Dream Team that won the gold medal at the 1992 Olympics in Barcelona and the 1996 Dream Team that won the gold medal in Atlanta.

Like Stockton, Malone has spent most of his recent seasons attempting to live down the reputation of being one of the greatest players never to win a championship.

"I know a lot of people are pulling for me much like they pulled for John Elway to win an NFL championship," Malone said. "I appreciate that. And I was happy when John finally won the Super Bowl." Malone has another thing in common with Stockton—opponents believe he pushes the rules, uses his elbows and muscle for a few unfair, and illegal, advantages.Sloan said such criticisms have been unfair.

"He's under such a microscope," Sloan said. "Guys grab him and hold him and pretty soon he gets tired of it. That's human nature. I feel bad for the guy because they grab and hold and foul and, when he does something back, it's retaliation."

Mostly, though, there is praise. "He's got to be one of the top 15 players of all time," Sonics forward Vin Baker said. "The fact that Karl is so strong and he can score in the low post, the irony is he's got that jump shot mastered. He's got the whole package. A lot of guys dunk and look flashy, but Karl's got the most consistent jump shot at the power forward position."

"I don't want to say one time that I didn't give it everything I had," says Malone regarding his work ethic, "and that's just the way I am."

MOSES MALONE

> **"Everybody gave him no chance, but that changed in about two weeks, after he had dunked on everybody's head. He was one of the best rebounders I'd ever seen."** *Maurice Lucas, former ABA and NBA star.*

Statistics

BORN: *March 23, 1955, Petersburg, Va.*

HEIGHT: *6–10* **WEIGHT:** *255*

COLLEGE: *None*

PRO TEAMS: *Utah Stars (ABA) 1974–75, St. Louis Spirits (ABA) 1975–76; Houston Rockets 1976–82; Philadelphia 76ers 1982–86, 1993–95; Washington Bullets 1986–88; Atlanta Hawks 1988–91; Milwaukee Bucks 1991–93; San Antonio Spurs 1994–95.*

NBA CAREER AVERAGES: *20.6 ppg; 12.2 rpg; 1.4 apg*

NBA PLAYOFF AVERAGES: *22.1 ppg; 13.8 rpg; 1.4 apg*

From the moment he put on his first professional uniform, at the tender age of 19, Moses Malone began searching for the basketball Promised Land. He wandered for more than 20 years through an ABA/NBA maze of teams, gathering the rebounds, points and awards he will use to carve out his niche in the Hall of Fame.

Malone's resume is very impressive. He ranks third on the NBA's all-time list for points scored (27,409), third in games played (1,329), fifth in rebounds (16,212), first in offensive rebounds (6,731) and first in free throws made (8,531). And these numbers do not include two ABA seasons.

Malone won six rebounding titles and was a three-time regular-season MVP, a 12-time All-Star, a four-time All-NBA first-team selection and an NBA Finals MVP. He carried an average

A QUICK STUDY: *Malone skipped college and came to the NBA right out of high school.*

CAREER HIGHLIGHTS

1974 Signed with ABA's Utah Stars after senior year of high school.

1975 Averaged 18.8 points and 14.6 rebounds as a 19-year-old ABA rookie.

1979 Recorded career game high 37 rebounds; NBA-record 587 offensive rebounds; earned first of three regular-season MVP awards (averaging 24.8 points and 17.6 rebounds).

1981 Won second NBA rebounding title (14.8); led Rockets to NBA Finals.

1982 Career-best 53-point game

against Clippers; averaged career-high 31.1 points and earned second MVP.

1982 Set single-game record for offensive rebounds with 21.

1983 Led 76ers to NBA championship and earned Finals MVP award; won second straight regular-season MVP.

1985 Earned fourth All-NBA first-team citation.

1987 Scored 27 points in 10th All-Star Game appearance.

1995 Appeared in 17 games for Spurs, completing 21st pro season.

1995 Retired after the season.

1997 Named one of the 50 greatest players in league history.

Houston team to the NBA Finals and was the centerpiece for the Philadelphia 76ers team that won the 1983 NBA championship.

Not bad for a talented 6-foot-10 center who spent much of his career feeling unwanted.

Malone vaulted into prominence at age 19 when he gave in to big-money temptation and bypassed college, turning professional after his high school career in Petersburg, Va. He was young, inexperienced and naïve when he began banging bodies as a member of the ABA's Utah Stars.

Malone averaged 18.8 points and 14.6 rebounds in that first season, but his numbers slipped in 1975–76 when his contract was sold to the much weaker St. Louis Spirits and he discovered the realities of ABA life. When the ABA folded in 1976, he was picked up by Portland. Malone was then traded to Buffalo and Houston—before the next season had even started.

By 1978–79, the stern-faced, nononsense Moses, now stronger and quicker, was taking his place as one of the game's top centers. He won the first of six rebounding titles in seven seasons with a 17.6 average, scored 24.8 points per game and earned his first MVP. He was ferocious on the offensive boards, turning teammates' misses into quick points.

From 1980 to 1983, Malone was the most dominant force in the game. He powered the Rockets to the 1981 NBA Finals, earned his second MVP award in 1982 and combined with Julius Erving to lead the 76ers to the 1983 NBA championship. He capped his championship season by winning both the NBA regular-season and Finals MVP citations.

Malone's Philadelphia stay lasted four seasons before he began a nomadic journey around the NBA, making stops at Washington, Atlanta, Milwaukee and—finally—San Antonio. He finally called it a career in 1995, after 21 professional seasons, with a combined ABA/NBA career points total of 29,580.

INSPIRATIONAL: *Moses Malone helped lead the 76ers to the '83 championship.*

GEORGE MIKAN

"He never quit on that floor and I shall always take my hat off to George Mikan as the basketball player who ranked above all the others." *Larry Foust, former Fort Wayne Pistons star.*

Statistics

BORN: *June 18, 1924, Joliet, Ill.*

HEIGHT: *6–10*

WEIGHT: *245*

COLLEGE: *DePaul*

PRO TEAMS: *Chicago Gears (NBL), 1946–47; Minneapolis Lakers (NBL/NBA), 1947–56*

NBA CAREER AVERAGES: *23.1 ppg; 13.4 rpg; 2.8 apg*

NBA PLAYOFF AVERAGES: *24.0 ppg; 13.9 rpg; 2.2 apg*

He stood 6-foot-10, weighed 245 pounds and looked at the world through thick-rimmed glasses. Hulking George Mikan was a professor in basketball shorts and his classrooms were the big-city arenas around the NBA. He wrote a book on center-position play, held daily clinics on power basketball and taught a new league how to survive.

Mikan's short NBA tenure revolutionized pro basketball. His stature as the game's first dominating big man set the league on course to prosperity. When he joined the 2-year-old Basketball Association of America in 1948, he brought with him a deadly hook shot and the national attention and media exposure the league needed to build a solid foundation.

"He was the Babe Ruth of basketball," former Knicks coach Joe Lapchick

HE'S NO. 1: *George Mikan was the league's first dominating big man.*

CAREER HIGHLIGHTS

1945 Led nation with a 23.3 average and DePaul to NIT championship.

1946 Earned third straight All-America citation; signed with NBL's Gears.

1947 Rights awarded to Lakers when Gears franchise disbanded.

1949 Won first of four consecutive scoring titles with 28.3-point average; led Lakers to

first of five championships they would win in six years; earned first of six all-league first-team citations.

1953 Scored 22 points and earned All-Star Game MVP.

1956 Retired with record 11,764 career points.

1959 Elected to Naismith Memorial Hall of Fame.

1967 Named Commissioner of newly formed ABA.

1970 Named to NBA 25th Anniversary All-Time Team.

1980 Named to NBA 35th Anniversary All-Time Team.

liked to say. Other coaches saw it differently.

"Monster," Rochester's Les Harrison said. "He's nothing but a monster."

That's the image Mikan brought to a game previously dominated by slick ballhandling and finesse. He was bigger and stronger than the centers he played against and he used his bulk to great advantage, backing his defender into the lane and extending an elbow as protection for a deadly hook shot. The elbows also were lethal weapons in pursuit of a rebound or loose ball.

Mikan, a three-time All-American and two-time national scoring champion at DePaul, spurned the BAA for the more established National Basketball League when he turned pro amid much fanfare in 1946. But two years later, he became BAA property when his Minneapolis Lakers and three other NBL teams switched leagues.

Everywhere Mikan played, he drew big crowds and bigger headlines. And he didn't disappoint. In an era when 20-point scoring averages were seldom seen, the Lakers' big man averaged a whopping 28.3 in 1948–49 and led Minneapolis to the first of five championships in six seasons. But Mikan was more than an offensive machine. He was an outstanding rebounder and an adept passer from the post.

Mikan, who won six straight professional scoring titles, also was blessed with a strong supporting cast. Forwards Jim Pollard and Vern Mikkelsen and guard Slater Martin ranked among the best players in the league. But the key to the Minneapolis dynasty, which included three straight championships from 1952–54, was the immovable force in the middle.

Mikan, who survived double- and triple-teams as well as legislation (the lane was widened; the three-second violation) aimed at slowing him down, still managed to average 22.6 points over a nine-year professional career.

He retired in 1954 at age 30, made a brief comeback a year later and finally settled into a law career.

A LEG UP: *George Mikan was bigger and stronger than most of his opponents.*

HAKEEM OLAJUWON

"I've come to understand why Hakeem is called 'The Dream.' We all dream of playing the way he plays."

Scott Brooks, former Houston teammate.

Statistics

BORN: *Jan. 21, 1963, Lagos, Nigeria*
HEIGHT: *7-0*
WEIGHT: *255*
COLLEGE: *Houston*
PRO TEAM: *Houston Rockets, 1984–present*
NBA CAREER AVERAGES: *23.1 ppg; 11.6 rpg; 2.6 apg*
NBA PLAYOFF AVERAGES: *26.6 ppg; 11.4 rpg; 3.3 apg*

If you play him loose, he fakes one way, turns the other and hits a deadly fadeaway jump shot. Play him tight and he spins like lightning toward the basket for a dunk or jump hook. Double-team him and he finds the open man with a quick pass.

Oscar Robertson? Elgin Baylor? Larry Bird? Amazingly, this combination of power, finesse and quickness belongs to 7-foot, 255-pound Hakeem Olajuwon—the NBA's reigning center of attention.

As a total package, Olajuwon might be the best pivotman ever. Bill Russell was a master of defense, rebounding and shot-blocking; Wilt Chamberlain was an offensive machine; and Kareem Abdul-Jabbar brought finesse and durability. Olajuwon can do all of those things—and more. It's not unusual to see him block a shot at one end of the court and race to the other to finish a fast break.

"In terms of raw athletic ability, Hakeem is the best I have ever seen,"

said Magic Johnson.

The athletic ability has always been obvious, but Olajuwon's rise is the result of hard work and dedication. Amazingly, the man who led the Houston Rockets to consecutive championships in 1994 and '95, didn't even touch a basketball until age 15 and his early sports activity was limited to playing goalkeeper for a soccer team in his hometown of Lagos, Nigeria.

When Olajuwon, known then as Akeem, accepted a scholarship at the University of Houston in 1980, he was a 190-pound weakling with great leaping ability and little knowledge of the game. Cougars Coach Guy Lewis took one look and put him to work.

THE STUFF OF DREAMS: *Akeem Olajuwon was selected No.1 in the '84 draft by Houston.*

"It took him awhile to become a player," Lewis said. "He could run and jump, but that's about all the basketball skills he had. We worked him before the team got there and after the team left, but he had a desire for it."

Olajuwon bulked up and never stopped working. As a college player he was part of Houston's "Phi Slama Jama" fraternity and made three visits to the NCAA Tournament's Final Four. But he was primarily a shot-blocker and dunking machine who was still learning the fundamental skills.

Even with his on-the-job training, Olajuwon was good enough to average 20.6 points and 11.9 rebounds as a 1984–85 rookie while blocking 220 shots. A year later, he combined with fellow 7-footer Ralph Sampson to lead the Rockets to the NBA Finals, where they lost to Boston in six games. He put that wrong to rights in 1994 and '95 when he was the key figure in the Rockets' back-to-back championship victories, earning MVP honors in both Finals.

In 1996 he hoped to win a third Championship when he was teamed with Clyde Dexler and Charles Barkley, but injuries halted his and Houston's progress.

Despite those injuries, the Rockets did make the playoffs in 1998 and 1999, but that string was halted in 2000. With Olajuwon healthy enough to play in just 44 games, his averages of 10.3 points and 6.2 rebounds were the lowest of his career.

(Opposite) LIFT OFF: *Hakeem Olajuwon led the Rockets to two NBA championships.*

CAREER HIGHLIGHTS

1984 Helped Houston reach Final Four for third straight season and championship game for second; Cougars lost each year.

1984 Selected by Rockets with first overall pick of NBA draft.

1985 Averaged 20.6 points and 11.9 rebounds and finished second to Michael Jordan in Rookie of the Year voting.

1987 Earned first of three straight All-NBA first-team berths; made first of five appearances on NBA All-Defensive first team.

1988 Scored 21 points in fourth All-Star Game appearance.

1990 Recorded third quadruple-double in NBA history: 18 points, 16 rebounds, 11 blocks, 10 assists; exploded for career-high 52 points in game against Denver.

1993 Led league in blocked shots (4.17 per game) for third time in four seasons.

1994 Led Rockets to NBA championship, earning NBA Finals MVP honors; named regular-season MVP.

1995 Played in 10th All-Star Game; earned second straight NBA Finals MVP as Rockets repeated as champions.

1996 Played for Dream Team II in Atlanta Olympic Games

SHAQUILLE O'NEAL

130

> **"The most important thing for any player is talent. And my goodness, he is an unbelievable talent."**
>
> *Jerry West, former Lakers executive vice president*

Statistics

BORN: *March 6, 1972. Newark, N.J.*

HEIGHT: *7-1*

WEIGHT: *320*

COLLEGE:
Louisiana State (three years)

PRO TEAMS:
Orlando Magic, 1992-96;
Los Angeles Lakers, 1996-present.

NBA CAREER AVERAGES:
27.5 ppg; 12.4 rpg; 2.7 apg

NBA PLAYOFF AVERAGES:
27.7 ppg; 12.2 rpg; 3.2 apg

For years, he has been the most imposing presence in the NBA. Now, he also stands as the most impressive.

Shaquille O'Neal is 7 feet 1, 320 pounds of dominance. Mostly an offensive presence early in his career, he has emerged as towering defensive threat now that he has moved from the Orlando Magic to the Los Angeles Lakers. When opponents talk of limiting O'Neal, they do so almost reverentially.

Hold him to 25 points, 10 rebounds and two blocked shots, and there is a certain satisfaction as an opponent, even though those are the types of numbers that, in this league, earn you Most Valuable Player.

"He's dominant," said respected forward Maurice Taylor. "I mean he's actually right now dominating the league. There's no doubt right now that he's the best player in the league. I mean it's nothing to argue with. He's actually

the best player in the league. He's being a dominant force.

"You used to say if you stopped Shaquille O'Neal from dunking you could stop Shaquille O'Neal. But now he's adding jump hooks, turnaround jumpers, face-up jumpers. It's unbelievable the things he can do."

There is almost a universal sense of awe about what O'Neal has become. In Orlando, he was good enough to lead the Magic to the 1995 NBA Finals. But that was when he still was raw, more brawn than ability. Now he is remarkably polished for a player his size—remarkably polished for a player any size.

"Before, he was just a power player, power player," veteran NBA point guard Eric Murdock said. "You know, back to the basket, always trying to power everything up. Now, he's showing a lot of finesse, he's showing the jump hook, he's showing the turnaround jump shot, and all. He never had that in his game. Even the free throws, he seems to be concentrating a lot more and trying to do the things the coaches have been teaching."

If there is one element that has held O'Neal back from being the consummate performer, it is his foul shooting, the same limitation that left the lone black mark on the career of Wilt Chamberlain.

"I just want to hit them when we need them," he said. "Out of 100 things, I don't do one thing very well."

With such an ability to dominate, who is about to quibble about something as trivial as foul shooting? Then again, who would be willing to quibble

MASS OF MUSCLE: *Based on sheer volume, no other player can match up to O'Neal.*

about anything to O'Neal's face?

"The most dominant move is Shaq's catch and turnaround and dunk," Suns guard Jason Kidd said. "You can't defend that, unless you want to break an

CAREER HIGHLIGHTS

1992 Selected as an undergraduate by the Orlando Magic in the first round (first pick overall) of the NBA Draft.

1993 Named Rookie of the Year, and to the NBA All-Rookie first team, after averaging 23.4 points, 13.9 rebounds and 3.53 blocks.

1995 Led Orlando Magic to NBA Finals against Houston Rockets.

1996 Left Orlando Magic as free agent as franchise leader in field-goals made (3,208), free-throws made (1,602) and attempted (2,936), rebounds (3,691) and blocked shots (824).

1998 Grabbed his 5,000th career rebound, recording 15 rebounds against the Utah Jazz.

1999 Named to All-NBA second team after leading the NBA in field-goal percentage (.576).2000—Selected to participate in the NBA All-Star Game for seventh time in as many opportunities. He did not play in 1997 All-Star Game due to a left knee injury

2000 Named Most Valuable Player for both the regular season and NBA Finals.

arm or a finger or a hand."

The acclaim about O'Neal has been universal. He was a member of the second Dream Team that won the gold medal at the 1996 Atlanta Olympics and also played for the U.S. entry that won gold at the 1994 World Championship of Basketball in Toronto. Soon the debate will turn to whether O'Neal one day will stand as the game's premier big man, to eclipse the legends of players such as Chamberlain, Bill Russell and Kareem Abdul-Jabbar.

Power forward A.C. Green, who has played with both Abdul-Jabbar and O'Neal with the Lakers, sees that type of greatness in O'Neal. "Kareem had a definite role to play," Green said. "Shaq pretty much has to do everything."

Opposing teams not only double-team O'Neal when he gets they ball, they often send a third or fourth defender, as well. Then again, considering O'Neal has the strength or two or three men, there often is little impact. In a way, O'Neal comes off as a cartoon character, his might and muscle so remarkable.

"He breaks your heart," veteran NBA coach Alvin Gentry said. "You spend so much time and energy trying to figure out what you can do about Shaq. We play good defense and we try to block him out and he jumps up there and gets it back. There's nothing that anyone can do about it."

If the tone sounds familiar, it is because it is a similar tone opposing coaches would offer about Michael Jordan, a talent who also tormented.

Pat Riley has coached Abdul-Jabbar in Los Angeles, Patrick Ewing in New York and Alonzo Mourning in Miami. That makes him somewhat of an expert on big men. Yet even his expertise leaves him struggling with ways to counter O'Neal, now that he has grown into a player with a game as big as his build.

"I think he's improved probably over the last two or three years with his game, to a level where he's totally complete as an offensive player, as a passer, reads defenses very well, very patient," Riley said.

POWER UNLEASHED: *Few are foolish enough to get in the way of Shaquille O'Neal.*

132

BOB PETTIT

"There may have been greater players, but none with greater desire and dedication. Bob Pettit was the pro's pro, the owner's dream." *Ben Kerner, Hawks owner.*

SCHOOL DAYS: *Bob Pettit was a college star at Louisiana State University.*

Statistics

BORN: *Dec. 12, 1932, Baton Rouge, La.*

HEIGHT: *6–9*

WEIGHT: *215*

COLLEGE: *Louisiana State*

PRO TEAM: *Milwaukee/St. Louis Hawks, 1954–65*

NBA CAREER AVERAGES:
26.4 ppg; 16.2 rpg; 3.0 apg

NBA PLAYOFF AVERAGES:
25.5 ppg; 14.8 rpg; 2.7 apg

The Naismith Memorial Basketball Hall of Fame is full of former stars who crafted outstanding careers around natural athletic abilities. Bob Pettit is not one of them.

Pettit's Hall of Fame career was crafted without the superior athleticism he was forced to compete against. From his junior year at Baton Rouge (La.) High School (1948–49) to his final season (1964–65) with the St. Louis Hawks, Pettit captured fans and headlines with a winning combination of hard work, drive and determination.

"There's not a greater competitor in sports today than Bob Pettit," marveled Boston center Bill Russell, an intense workaholic himself. "He made second effort a part of the sports vocabulary."

Pettit needed every ounce of effort he could muster. After failing to make the

CAREER HIGHLIGHTS

1954 Finished college career with 27.4-point average and two All-America citations; selected by Hawks with the second overall pick of NBA draft.

1955 Averaged 20.4 points in first season and earned Rookie of the Year award; earned first of 10 consecutive All-NBA first-team citations.

1956 Won first of two scoring titles with 25.7-point average; earned first of two regular-season MVP awards.

1957 Averaged 29.8 points in playoffs and led Hawks to first of four NBA Finals appearances in five years.

1958 Scored 50 points against Boston in Game 6 of NBA Finals, securing Hawks' first NBA championship.

1962 Scored 25 points and grabbed 27 rebounds to earn fourth All-Star Game MVP award.

1964 Scored 19,204th point to break NBA career scoring record; became

league's first 20,000-point scorer.

1965 Retired with playoff career record for points (2,240).

1970 Elected to Naismith Memorial Hall of Fame; named to NBA 25th Anniversary All-Time Team.

1980 Named to NBA 35th Anniversary All-Time Team.

Baton Rouge varsity team as a sophomore, he combined a conditioning and coordination program with hours of practice and turned himself into a high school star. Armed with a 6-foot-9 body, a deadly push shot and the understanding that hard work makes up for physical deficiencies, Pettit accepted a scholarship to Louisiana State University, where he earned All-America honors following his junior and senior seasons.

BALL HAWK: *As a professional, Bob Pettit was a threat to score anywhere, anytime.*

When the Milwaukee Hawks made Pettit the second pick of the 1954 NBA draft, they were getting a highly motivated slasher who had a special knack for scoring points and chasing down rebounds from his forward position. Opponents quickly learned that the determined Pettit would never give them a moment's rest. "The only way to stop him is not to let him have the ball," said Lakers Coach Fred Schaus. "But he ruins that strategy by going and getting it himself."

Nobody ever accused Pettit of being artistic. But nobody ever figured out how to stop him, either. He averaged 20.4 points and 13.8 rebounds in 1954–55 en route to Rookie of the Year honors. And those were the lowest marks of his 11-year professional career.

He was an All-Star every season, a two-time MVP and a two-time scoring champion. He also led the Hawks to five division titles while forging a 26.4-point regular-season average and a 25.5 playoff mark. He became the first NBA player to reach 20,000 career points.

But the greatest testimony to Pettit's career was his almost-legendary status in St. Louis, where the Hawks moved after his rookie season. In 1956–57, the Hawks, featuring Pettit, Ed Macauley and Cliff Hagan, reached the NBA Finals, where they lost to the Celtics in a seventh-game, double-overtime thriller.

The Hawks won the Western Division title in 1957–58 and again advanced to the Finals, this time handing the Celtics a six-game defeat. Pettit carried them to a 110–109 title-clinching victory with one of the greatest performances in playoff history: 50 points, including 19 of his team's last 21. It would be the only title in the Hawks' history.

OSCAR ROBERTSON

"Oscar Robertson was probably the best guard who ever played the game of basketball."

Kevin Loughery, longtime former opponent.

Statistics

BORN: *Nov. 24, 1938, Charlotte, Tenn.*

HEIGHT: *6–5*

WEIGHT: *220*

COLLEGE: *Cincinnati*

PRO TEAMS: *Cincinnati Royals, 1960–70; Milwaukee Bucks, 1970–74*

NBA CAREER AVERAGES: *25.7 ppg; 7.5 rpg; 9.5 apg*

NBA PLAYOFF AVERAGES: *22.2 ppg; 6.7 rpg; 8.9 apg*

THE BIG O: *Offense was just one of Oscar Robertson's many skills.*

From his junior year of high school, through his 14th and final professional season, Oscar Robertson was a national celebrity. Nobody had ever seen the combination of skills and size that Robertson brought to a basketball court and he used them like an athletic surgeon carving out his Hall of Fame career.

He was a 6-foot-5 package of amazing grace. Robertson could bang with the big boys, nail 20-foot jump shots from anywhere on the court, handle the ball like a Globetrotter and deliver dazzling, pinpoint passes to disbelieving teammates. He was Bob Cousy with size and when coaches began using him as a big guard, he presented all kinds of matchup problems.

"There may be better shooters than Oscar," said Ed Jucker, Robertson's coach at the University of Cincinnati. "But for the total game—shooting, rebounding, passing, handling the ball

and, yes, defense—he's the greatest."

Basketball life started for the "Big O" in 1954 when word filtered out of Indianapolis that a new kind of prodigy was performing magic for Crispus Attucks High School. When the school won consecutive Indiana State championships, Robertson became the target of one of the most intense recruiting campaigns in college basketball history.

At Cincinnati, Robertson lived up to his reputation—and more. In his first varsity season, he led the nation with a 35.1-point average and went on to win two more scoring championships. Robertson finished his college career with a record 33.8 scoring average and an impressive .535 field-goal percentage

while leading the Bearcats to a 79–8 record.

But the best was yet to come. Robertson, who would redefine the concept of guard play with his fluid style and size, was perfect for the professional game. He was drafted by Cincinnati in 1960 as a territorial pick, stepped into the Royals' starting lineup and earned Rookie of the Year honors with averages of 30.5 points, 10.1 rebounds and 9.7 assists per game. In his second season, Robertson averaged an unprecedented triple-double—30.8 points, 12.5 rebounds and 11.4 assists. Nobody could dominate a game in so many ways and few could do damage both inside and out.

CAREER HIGHLIGHTS

1955 Led Crispus Attucks to first of consecutive Indiana State High School championships.

1958 Became first sophomore to lead nation in scoring, averaging 35.1 points for the University of Cincinnati.

1960 Closed out college career with three straight national scoring championships, a career-record 2,973 points and two Final Four appearances; selected by Royals as territorial pick in NBA draft; helped U.S. win gold medal in Rome Olympic Games.

1961 Played in first of 12 consecutive All-Star Games, earning MVP honors; finished first season with 30.5 average and named NBA Rookie of the Year; earned All-NBA first-team selection for first of nine consecutive years.

1962 Became first player in league history to average triple-double: 30.8 ppg, 12.5 rpg, 11.4 apg.

1964 Earned regular-season MVP with 31.4 ppg, 9.9 rpg, 11.0 apg; claimed third of eight career assist titles.

1970 Traded to Bucks after 10 seasons in Cincinnati.

1971 Combined with Kareem Abdul-Jabbar to lead Bucks to first NBA championship.

1974 Retired with 26,710 career points and 9,887 assists.

1979 Elected to Naismith Memorial Hall of Fame.

1980 Selected to NBA 35th Anniversary All-Time Team.

THE BUCK STOPS HERE: *Oscar Roberston finally won an NBA title in Milwaukee.*

"Oscar simply dominated the game," said Kevin Loughery, who played against Robertson for 10 seasons.

While Robertson's career statistics read like a Who's Who resume—a 25.7 scoring average, eight league assist titles, 7.5 rebounds per game, 12 All-Star Game appearances and one MVP award—one criticism dogged him during his playing days. Through 10 Cincinnati seasons, Robertson could not lead the talent-deficient Royals anywhere near a championship. But in 1970, he was traded to Milwaukee and combined with young center Kareem Abdul-Jabbar to lead the Bucks to 66 regular-season victories and the franchise's first NBA title.

The resume was complete. And Robertson retired three years later at age 36.

"On the floor, first and foremost, Dennis is an entertainer. He not only wants to play the game, he wants to put on a show."

Jack Haley, former NBA center and Rodman teammate and friend.

136

DENNIS RODMAN

Statistics

BORN: *May 13, 1961. Trenton, N.J.*

HEIGHT: *6-7* **WEIGHT:** *220*

COLLEGE: *Cooke County Junior College (one year); Southeastern Oklahoma State (three years)*

PRO TEAMS: *Detroit Pisatons, 1986-93; San Antonio Spurs, 1993-95; Chicago Bulls, 1995-98; Los Angeles Lakers, 1998-99; Dallas Mavericks 1999-2000.*

NBA CAREER AVERAGES: *7.3 ppg; 13.1 rpg; 1.8 apg*

NBA PLAYOFF AVERAGES: *6.2 ppg; 10.2 rpg; 1.3 apg*

The pierced, tattooed, foul-mouthed symbol of discontentment a fitting presence in such a pantheon of greatness?

On one hand, Rodman is a seven-time NBA regular-season rebounding champion, his streak of those seven titles the longest such run in league history. Every other player with multiple rebounding championships—with the exception of still-active Rockets center Hakeem Olajuwon and yet-to-be-eligible Moses Malone—already has been enshrined into the Basketball Hall of Fame, a group that includes Wilt Chamberlain, Bill Russell and Elvin Hayes. In fact, in the history of the NBA, only two Hall-eligible rebounding champions have not been voted in, '57 champ Maurice Stokes and '78 champ Truck Robinson.

"Dennis personifies a work ethic everyone appreciates," his former Bulls coach Phil Jackson has said. "You see a guy who does anything to retrieve the ball."

On the other hand, Rodman has not exactly cast the game in its brightest light. His off-court behavior does not precisely reach role-model standards and he nearly sank the fortunes of the Spurs during his two-year tenure in San Antonio.

The personality issues well could come into play when it is time for the Hall of Fame to debate the merits of induction. But from a purely statistical standpoint, it can be argued the NBA has never had a more dynamic rebounder. Factor in Rodman's long-

MAVERICK APPROACH: *Rodman's time in Dallas was short, as was his stint in L.A.*

recognized defensive excellence, and a personality who has made a career of standing out this time can't help but fit in.

To dismiss the excellence of Rodman would be to dismiss a two-time NBA Defensive Player of the Year. It would mean dismissing a seven-time first-team selection to NBA All-Defensive. It would mean rejecting the winner of the 1992 IBM Award, the computer formula that determines the player to make the greatest individual contribution to a team.

To Heat coach Pat Riley—who once termed Rodman "the most ridiculous thing I've ever seen," because of Rodman's on-court theatrics—that resume is too much to overlook.

"I do think he deserves Hall of Fame consideration," Riley said. "The question is whether people who choose are going to get over his personality. Is he a Hall of Fame player? Yes, he's a Hall of Fame player from the standpoint that he's in great shape, that he's been a top defender. But what's the criterion for Hall of Fame? That's what it comes down to."

Over his career, Rodman has been as much an industry as a player. Movies. Books. TV shows. And $50,000 autograph-signing appearances.

"Dennis is a real live version of a Saturday-morning cartoon superhero," Bulls Vice President of Marketing Steve Schanwald once said.

Or, as NBA Commissioner Davis Stern once said, "He may be the best

CAREER HIGHLIGHTS

1986 Selected by the Detroit Pistons in the second round (27th pick overall) of the 1986 draft.

1989 Led the NBA in field-goal percentage (.595).

1990 Named NBA Defensive Player of the Year, an award he also would win in 1991.

1992 Named to the All-NBA Third Team. Appeared in theNBA All-Star game for the second, and final, time. Won IBM statistical award for overall team contribution.

1993 Traded by the Detroit Pistons with Isaiah Morris to the San Antonio Spurs for Sean Elliott and David Wood.

1995 Traded by the San Antonio Spurs to the Chicago Bulls for Will Perdue.

1996 Named to NBA All-Defensive First Team for seventh time. Tied NBA Finals record with 11 offensive rebounds in two games of title series against Seattle.

1997 Grabbed the 10,000th rebound of his career, in game against the Washington Bullets.

1998 Led the NBA in rebounding for a record seventh consecutive season.

1999 Signed as a free agent by the Los Angeles Lakers.

2000 Signed as a free agent by the Dallas Mavericks.

media creation of his own (making) that I've ever seen in this day and age."

Long before the first tattoo, the first piercing, the first romp with Madonna, Rodman was an introverted youth from a small college in Oklahoma who hustled his way into the NBA.

His early seasons in the pros were relatively quiet, his time off the court often spent in seclusion. As "The Worm," he was part of an efficient bench that delivered two championships to the Detroit Pistons in 1989 and 1990.

However, as the personality changed, he also became a challenge.

"A certain percentage of people get a big kick out of Dennis," said former Spurs coach Bob Hill. "For a layman buying a ticket, it's fun. And if I were a layman, I'd feel the same way. But I had to coach the guy."

And at times during Rodman's career, there was no greater challenge. While Rodman thrived for three seasons under Jackson in Chicago, he was never the same after.

He burned bridges while playing for respected Del Harris with the Lakers and could not make it work under respected coach Don Nelson with the Mavericks.

By the end of the '90s, Rodman was living off his past. The rebounding was still efficient, but the defensive intensity was down and the technical fouls were up. A hard-driving life off the court had exacted a heavy toll.

Yet that cannot obfuscate more than a decade of excellence, of record-setting rebounding and total-denial defense, of enough championship rings to adorn either hand.

"He's a very complex personality and I think at times he struggles with exactly which person he really is," said Chuck Daly, his Pistons coach. "Maybe I'm taking too much of a psychological approach here, but I don't think he ever wanted or expected the kind of fame he has and he will always struggle with how to handle it."

TOP OF HIS GAME: *Rodman's commitment to rebounding helped the Bulls win it all.*

BILL RUSSELL

"Bill has great pride. He is proud of his team and proud of his own personal skills. He doesn't know what it means to play on a loser." *Red Auerbach, Boston Celtics President and former coach.*

Statistics

BORN: Feb. 12, 1934, at Monroe, La.
HEIGHT: 6–10
WEIGHT: 220
COLLEGE: San Francisco
PRO TEAM: Boston Celtics, 1956–69
CAREER AVERAGES: 15.1 ppg; 22.5 rpg; 4.3 apg
PLAYOFF AVERAGES: 16.2 ppg; 24.9 rpg; 4.7 apg

HOOP WARRIOR: *Bill Russell concentrated on rebounding and defense.*

He arrived in Boston with two NCAA Tournament championships and an Olympic gold medal. Over the next 13 seasons, he would add 11 championship rings as the centerpiece for the best team in NBA history. No player in any sport can come close to matching Bill Russell's incredible winning legacy.

The 6-foot-10 Russell vaulted into national prominence in 1955 and '56 when he dominated the middle for a San Francisco team that captured consecutive NCAA titles and won 55 straight games. He was an athletically gifted leaper who rebounded and played defense with a fiery intensity that compensated for limited offensive ability. But many questioned whether a low-scoring center could survive in the demanding professional game.

Not Auerbach. The Boston coach already had plenty of scorers; what he needed was a rebounder who could trigger the fast break and provide solid defense in the middle. He envisioned Russell getting the rebound and whipping the outlet pass to Bob Cousy or Bill Sharman, who would perform their magic on the break.

It didn't take long for Russell to justify Auerbach's faith. After leading the United States to a gold medal at the 1956 Olympic Games, Russell joined the Celtics in December and stepped right into the lineup. Auerbach gave him one instruction: "Forget about scoring and get me the ball."

Russell averaged 19.6 rebounds in his rookie season and played an intimidating defense never before seen in the NBA. If an opponent missed a shot, Russell was there to grab the rebound and ignite the break. If a teammate made a defensive mistake, Russell was there to cover up. He turned the blocked shot into an art form, often using it like an outlet pass. With Russell smothering the middle, the Celtics rolled to their first championship in 1957.

Over the next 12 seasons, Russell would average a modest 15.1 points and a not-so-modest 22.5 rebounds. He would earn five MVP citations, play in the All-Star Game 12 times and set defensive standards beyond even Auerbach's wildest dreams. But his biggest contribution would be as the ultimate team player, the one constant in the 13-year Boston dynasty that produced eight straight titles and 11 overall.

"Russell put aside personal glory for the good of the team," Auerbach said. "Russell is the greatest center who ever lived."

Auerbach made that assessment despite the overpowering presence of Wilt Chamberlain. Auerbach thought so highly of Russell that he chose him as his coaching successor in 1966. The first black coach in team sports his-tory, Russell led the Celtics to two more titles in three years. He later coached at Seattle and Sacramento.

(Opposite) PRICELESS: *The Celtics wouldn't have been so dominant without Russell .*

CAREER HIGHLIGHTS

1956 Led San Francisco to second consecutive NCAA Tournament championship and school's 55th straight victory; led U.S. to gold medal in Melbourne Olympics; selected by Hawks with third overall pick of draft; traded to Celtics.

1957 Grabbed record 32 rebounds in one half against Philadelphia; won first of five rebounding titles (19.6 average); led Celtics to first NBA championship.

1958 Earned first of 12 All-Star Game selections and first of five regular-season MVP awards.

1959 Averaged 16.7 points and 23 rebounds as Celtics won second NBA championship and first of record eight straight; averaged NBA Finals record 29.5 rebounds in series against Lakers.

1960 Set NBA record with 51 rebounds in game against Syracuse.

1966 Named player/coach of Celtics, becoming first black coach in a major team sport.

1968 Coached and powered Celtics to 10th NBA title in 12 years.

1969 Retired as player and coach after guiding Celtics to second straight title and 11th in 13 seasons.

1970 Named to NBA 25th Anniversary All-Time Team.

1973 Began four-year stint as coach/general manager of Seattle SuperSonics.

1974 Elected to Naismith Memorial Hall of Fame.

1980 Declared greatest player in history by Professional Basketball Writers Association of America; named to NBA 35th Anniversary All-Time Team.

JOHN STOCKTON

> **"I love John Stockton. He's one of the purest of players. He's a good family man, a good person. I'd admire him even if he wasn't a basketball player."** *John Wooden, legendary UCLA coach.*

Statistics

BORN: *March 26, 1962. Spokane, Wash.*

HEIGHT: *6-1*

WEIGHT: *175*

COLLEGE: *Gonzaga*

PRO TEAMS: *Utah Jazz, 1984-present*

NBA CAREER AVERAGES: *13.3 ppg.; 2.7 rpg; 11.0 apg*

NBA PLAYOFF AVERAGES: *13.6 ppg; 3.3 rpg; 10.2 apg*

TWO OF A KIND: *Stockton's partnership with Karl Malone is legendary around the league.*

His game is a passing fancy, but fancy passing is not at the heart of what makes Utah Jazz point guard John Stockton the NBA's most prolific playmaker of all-time.

Paired with power forward Karl Malone for most of his professional tenure, Stockton has proven to be somewhat of a modern marvel. By appearances, he is rather ordinary, hardly an athletic presence. But his mastery of the simplistic-but-efficient pick-and-roll offense has made him the game's ultimate practitioner of setting up baskets.

"Many people say Magic (Johnson) was a point guard and a better player than John," former Jazz coach and executive Frank Layden said. "But as for a pure point guard, I defy anyone to say there has been anyone better than John Stockton. He's Joe Montana. If you need him to pass it hard, he does it hard. If it needs to be a soft pass, he passes it soft."

Mostly, he passes it. While Stockton possesses a deft outside shot, one with range that extends all the way to the 3-point circle, and while he has possesses a quickness to the basket that belies his unathletic build, he is a passer, first and foremost.

Stockton not only collects assists, he collects them at a staggering pace. Among his NBA records are most assists in a season, most career assists, most seasons with at least 1,000 assists, most times leading the league in assists and highest career assists-per-game average.

"For the most part, his game is predicated on helping the other four players on the floor," Jazz coach Jerry Sloan said. "That's what has made him so great over the years. He makes other people better."

He certainly has done that for Malone, who has reciprocated by making all those shots that keep Stockton's assist total on the rise.

"They're still slicing and dicing you,"

1984 Selected by the Utah Jazz in the first round (16th pick overall) of the 1984 draft.

1988 Matched the NBA Playoffs single-game record with 24 assists against the Lakers in Game 5 of the Western Conference Semifinals.

1991 Closed season with 1,164 assists to set an NBA single-season record. Is one of only three players in NBA history to top 1,000 assists in a season, doing so seven times.

1992 A member of the Dream Team that won the gold medal at the Olympics in Barcelona. Also was a member of the 1996 Dream Team that won gold in Atlanta.

1996 Became the all-time NBA steals leader in a 112-98 victory over the Boston Celtics, breaking Maurice Cheeks' record of 2,310.

1997 Hit the game-winning three-pointer at the buzzer in a 103-100 victory over the Houston Rockets in Game 6 of the 1997 Western

Conference Finals to lift the Jazz to its first NBA Finals.

1998 Scored his 15,000th career point, with 16 points against the Vancouver Grizzlies.

1999 Recorded 13,000th career assist in a 109-93 victory over the Los Angeles Lakers.

2000 Became the first player in NBA history to record 13,500 assists when he passed to Jeff Hornacek for a jumper against the Kings on Feb. 17

former NBA guard Lester Conner said of an act that has played for more than a decade in Salt Lake City. "Pick-and-rolls, with Stockton and Malone."

But Stockton also is not a one-way talent. The NBA's all-time leader in steals? John Stockton. He has proven over the years to be a master at playing the passing lane. And when he does come up with a steal, he immediately heads the other way, confident Malone will be filling the lane for a layup.

About the only thing that is missing for Stockton is an NBA championship. He twice has led the Jazz to the NBA Finals, only to be turned back by Michael Jordan's Chicago Bulls. His 3-pointer against the Houston Rockets in the 1997 Western Conference finals lifted Utah to the first of those two title-series appearances.

Through it all, his humility has remained intact.

"If anyone is ever sitting around the kitchen table talking about my career," he said, "I hope they say they enjoyed watching me play. That's good enough." Unlike so many of today's stars, Stockton has shunned endorsements, prefers to remain outside of the media spotlight, never has pressed for the exposure of playing in a larger city.

Behind the boyish exterior is the will of one of the toughest players in the NBA. Many opponents loathe him because of the fierce back-picks he sets, the way he plays with his elbows up, the not-so-subtle clutching and grabbing he employs when the referees are looking the other way. Some players have called him a cheater, a dirty player, and dangerous rival.

"I've never seen him back down," teammate and friend Malone said. "He takes his, but he always bounces back. He's not afraid to stick his nose in it. Some of us big guys look at some of that and do the same. You can't teach heart."

His list of laurels is lengthy. He was selected in 1996 as one of the 50 Greatest Players in NBA history. He was named to the All-NBA first team twice, to the All-NBA second team six times and to the All-NBA third team twice. He also played in nine consecutive NBA All-Star Games, from 1989 to 1997.

In addition, he was a member of the original Dream Team that won the gold medal at the 1992 Olympics in Barcelona and the 1996 Dream Team that won gold in Atlanta.

In an era of slick passing, one-on-one play and self-serving showmanship, Stockton very much is a throwback to a previous era. He is efficient, intense and respectful of the game's traditions. He also is arguably the greatest pure point guard in NBA history.

COURT VISION: *Even when he does go to the hoop, Stockton will look for a teammate who may be open for a pass.*

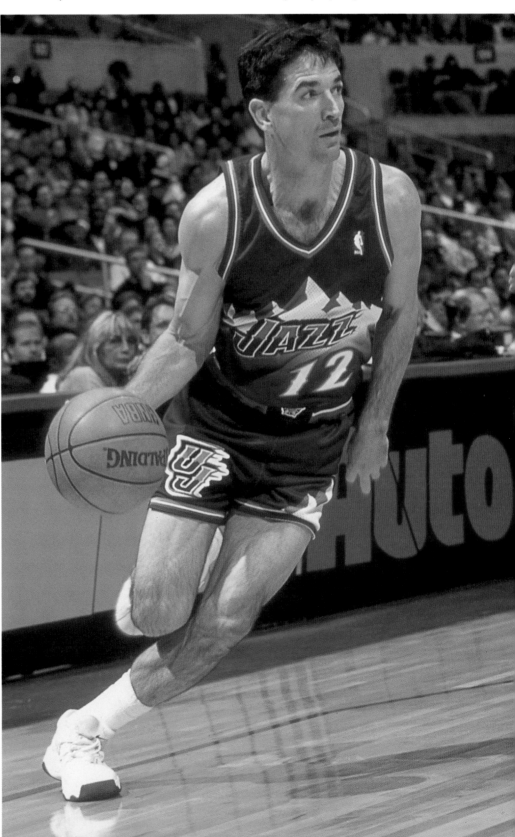

JERRY WEST

"He was a perfectionist. He'd actually be surprised that he would miss an open jump shot."

Fred Schaus, former Lakers coach.

Statistics

BORN: May 28, 1938, at Cheylan, W.Va.
HEIGHT: 6–2
WEIGHT: 185
COLLEGE: West Virginia
PRO TEAM: L. A. Lakers, 1960–74
CAREER AVERAGES:
27.0 ppg; 5.8 rpg; 6.7 apg
PLAYOFF AVERAGES:
29.1 ppg; 5.6 rpg; 6.3 apg

Jerry West came out of the mountains of West Virginia to the glitz and glitter of Los Angeles, armed with a deadly jump shot, quick hands and an indomitable will to succeed. He used those weapons to carve out a Hall of Fame career in a real-life Hollywood script, complete with a frustrating obstacle and a happy ending.

West was not your average, everyday, hillbilly basketball player when he was selected by the Minneapolis Lakers with the second overall pick of the 1960 draft. A 6-foot-2 shooting guard for West Virginia, he was well known for his MVP performance in the 1959 NCAA Tournament and his gold-medal-winning effort for the 1960 U.S. Olympic team. He would join the Lakers for the 1960–61 season, their first on the West Coast.

West, adjusting to the professional game, started off slowly, averaging 17.6 points, 7.7 rebounds and 4.2 assists.

GO WEST: *Jerry West led the Los Angeles Lakers to the greatest heights.*

CAREER HIGHLIGHTS

1959 Led West Virginia to NCAA Tournament finals, where the Mountaineers lost to California, 71–70; earned MVP honors.

1960 Selected by Lakers with second overall pick of NBA draft; joined forces with Oscar Robertson to lead U.S. to gold medal in Rome Olympic Games.

1961 Played in first of 14 NBA All-Star Games.

1962 Set record for NBA guard when he scored 63 points in game against Knicks; finished second pro season

with a 30.8-point average and earned first of 10 All-NBA first- team citations; made first of nine NBA Finals appearances for Lakers.

1965 Finished playoffs averaging 40.6 points per game.

1969 Named NBA Finals MVP, even though Lakers lost to Celtics.

1970 Earned first of four straight All-Defensive team selections.

1972 Named All-Star Game MVP; helped Lakers win first Los Angeles championship.

1974 Retired with 25,192 career points.

1976 Began three-year stint as coach of Lakers.

1979 Elected to Naismith Memorial Hall of Fame.

1980 Named to NBA 35th Anniversary All-Time Team.

1982 Became general manager of the Lakers.

Teaming with Elgin Baylor, he had to restrain his free-lancing game and operate strictly out of the backcourt, providing a Mr. Outside to Baylor's Mr. Inside.

By his second season, West was more comfortable with the role. His average jumped to 30.8 and he collected 7.9 rebounds and 5.4 assists per game. The dynamic Baylor-West combination carried the Lakers to the NBA Finals, where they dropped a seventh-game overtime heartbreaker to Boston. Baylor and West combined for averages of 70.1 points and 24.5 rebounds in the 1962 postseason.

That on-court rapport would continue throughout the 1960s, and so would their frustrating chase of a championship. Seven times the Lakers would reach the Finals from 1962–70, and seven times they would lose. Six of those losses were to the powerful Celtics.

But as Baylor battled ever-worsening knee problems, more of the responsibility fell on West's shoulders—a role he welcomed. By mid-career, the scrappy West was known throughout the NBA as "Mr. Clutch" and one of the game's most well-rounded performers.

"West is the complete basketball player," said Fred Schaus, his coach at West Virginia and for seven seasons in Los Angeles. "He does everything well. He scores points, he rebounds, he plays defense, he sets up the plays. He's a poised leader."

If West had a weakness, it was that he expected to hit every shot, make every pass and win every game. When he didn't, his temper could get in the way.

West made the All-Star team every season of a 14-year career that ended in 1974 and was a four-time member of the NBA All-Defensive first team. He was especially good in the playoffs, where he carried a 29.1-point career mark. In 1965, West exploded for a 40.6-point average.

The happy ending? West averaged 25.8 points for the 1971–72 Lakers, who finally broke the playoff ice and captured the franchise's first Los Angeles championship with a five-game NBA Finals victory over the New York Knicks.

MR CLUTCH: *Jerry West served as the model for the NBA's trademark logo.*

THE GREAT PLAYERS

The NBA'S brightest stars will shine every night. They soar. They fly. They dart. They hang. They slam. And they score from every possible angle, position and contortion. Their elegant feats are the product of athleticism and skill, but their greatness is measured by such qualities as desire, determination, poise and durability.

It has always been that way, from the early days of pass-and-shoot basketball through the evolution of the game into the aerial circus we know today. Great players come in many shapes and sizes and are easily identified. They make the clutch shots, thread the perfect passes, play chest-to-chest defense and control the pace of a game, night after night, season after season, bringing fans back for more.

There's no tried-and-true formula for greatness. Skill-limited players have forged outstanding careers out of the one or two areas of the game they have mastered. Multi-dimensional players have succeeded without ever having mastered a single skill. Some thrive because of their leadership abilities and others dominate because of their intensity and a fierce blue-collar work ethic. Players with limited athletic ability often rank among the game's all-time greats; others with every athletic skill imaginable sometimes cannot overcome the lofty expectations predicted of them.

The following biographies profile two groups of players: those who retired after long careers that set them on a special plane above their peers; and current players who are completing outstanding careers or beginning NBA life with the extraordinary promise of greatness and success. Some of the can't-miss current players will miss and other unheralded performers will take their place.

FAN FAVORITES: *(right) Alonzo Mourning and (opposite page) Jason Kidd and Nick Van Exel (foreground)*

146

A

KAREEM ABDUL-JABBAR

See Legends of the NBA *page 94–95*

SHAREEF ABDUR-RAHIM

BORN: *12-11-76 at Marietta, Ga.*
POSITION: *Forward.*
TEAMS: *Grizzlies, 1996-present.*

One of the top young small forwards in the NBA, Abdur-Rahim finds himself at the wrong place at the wrong time. On an expansion team still going through its growing pains, Abdur-Rahim has been able to excel individually because of scoring skills that have proven effective near the basket and all the way out to the 3-point arc. What he hasn't been able to overcome has been the stigma of playing for one of the worst teams in the NBA. With the Grizzlies lacking a true low-post scoring presence, opponents have been able to double-team Abdur-Rahim and make other Vancouver players beat them. Still, it is only a matter of time before the forward is routinely selected to All-Star teams and begins to earn notice in the balloting for Most Valuable Player. The former standout at the University of California already is the Grizzlies' all-time leading scorer and was a first-team All-Rookie selection in 1997, after he was selected with the third pick in the 1996 draft.

ALVAN ADAMS

BORN: *7–19–54, at Lawrence, Kan.*
POSITION: *Forward/center.*
TEAM: *Suns, 1975–88.*

Adams was an underrated and undersized big man who gave the Phoenix Suns 13 solid NBA seasons. At 6–9 and 220 pounds, Adams was overmatched physically by many centers and was forced to operate in the high post. He did it well, forging a reputation as one of the league's best passing big men while still banging

GRIZZLED GRIZZLY: *Shareef Abdur-Rahim is Vancouver's all-time leading scorer.*

the boards, running the floor and averaging in double figures. The intelligent Adams, who left the University of Oklahoma as a hardship draft pick in 1975, enjoyed a Rookie of the Year debut, averaging 19.0 points, 9.1 rebounds and 5.6 assists while leading the Suns to the NBA Finals. Over his 13 professional seasons, Adams' totals remained amazingly consistent as he changed gears and switched effectively between center and both forward positions. Adams, who played in one All-Star Game, ended his career in 1989 with 13,910 points (14.1 per game), 6,937 rebounds (7.0) and 4,012 assists (4.1).

MICHAEL ADAMS

BORN: *1-19-63 at Hartford, Conn.*
POSITION: *Guard.*
TEAMS: *Kings, 1985-86, Bullets, 1986-87, Nuggets, 1987-91, Bullets, 1991-94, Hornets, 1994-96.*

A story of perseverance who worked his way out of the minor-league Continental Basketball Association into the NBA, Adams emerged as one of the NBA's all-time great 3-point shooters. A player who would pull up and shoot the long ball at almost any time, Adams was at his best with freewheeling offensive teams, such as the Denver Nuggets. With a unique shot-put style to his outside attempts, Adams was able to keep defenders off-balance when it came to defending his shots. An adept playmaker, Adams was at his best when guiding the running game. Although coveted for his outside shooting and penetration abilities, Adams was considered a liability on defense, which is why his value never soared to the level of some lesser-known point guards. Still, he was selected to the All-Star Game in 1992 while with Washington and went to the playoffs five times. At 5 feet 10, Adams stood as one of the premier little men in the game's lore, a player admired for his hustle and determination. Even in his latter years in the league, Adams played at a frenetic pace few younger players were able to match.

LONG DISTANCE: *Michael Adams was known for his speed but he loved to play longball.*

148 MARK AGUIRRE

BORN: *12–10–59, at Chicago, Ill.*
POSITION: *Forward.*
TEAMS: *Mavericks, 1981–89, Pistons, 1989–93, Clippers, 1993–94.*

Aguirre was a multi-talented enigma who posted big numbers and frustrated coaches for 13 NBA seasons. The former DePaul star, the first overall pick of the 1981 draft, formed a love-hate relationship with Dallas coaches Dick Motta and John MacLeod for seven-plus seasons before being traded to Detroit in 1989. The always showy, sometimes moody Aguirre was an explosive small forward. At 6–6, he could burn defenders with a feathery-soft jump shot from long range, he could pull up for the 10-foot power jumper and he could use his burly 235 pounds to slant across the middle or power to the basket. He also was an adept rebounder and passer who averaged better than 20 points for six straight seasons. The three-time All-Star finished his career in 1994 with 18,458 points (20.0) and 4,578 rebounds (5.0).

DANNY AINGE

BORN: *3–17–59, at Eugene, Ore.*
POSITION: *Guard.*
TEAMS: *Celtics, 1981–89, Kings, 1989–90, Trail Blazers, 1990–92, Suns, 1992–95.*

Ainge was a versatile shooting guard who helped the Boston Celtics win two championships and two other teams reach the NBA Finals. Ainge, a former Brigham Young University star who played four seasons of professional baseball, was an outstanding athlete who could drill timely jumpers from 3-point range and play a scrambling, physical defense that frustrated opponents and forced them into temperamental mistakes. He was especially adept at applying pressure to the ball and dropping back to help out when it went to the middle. Ainge began his career in 1981 on the Celtics bench and was a role player for the 1984 champions. He worked his way into the starting lineup by 1985–86, when he averaged 10.7 points and 5.1 assists for another title team. Before retiring in 1995 with 11,964 career

MARKED MAN: *Mark Aguirre frustrated defenders and coaches*

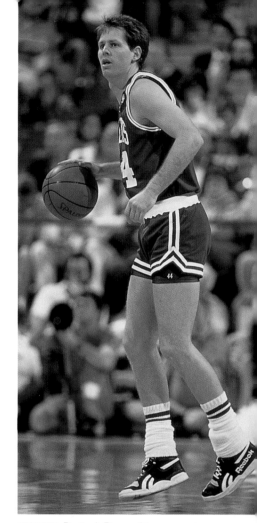

HOME RUN: *Boston's Danny Ainge gave up a baseball career for an NBA title.*

points, Ainge helped Portland and Phoenix to reach the NBA Finals. In 1996–97, he was named head coach of a struggling Suns team and took them to a playoff berth in each of his first three seasons in charge. But he resigned 22 games into the 1999-2000 season, saying he wanted to spend more time with his family. By the end of that season, he was working as a television commentator for TNT.

RAY ALLEN

BORN: *7-20-75 at Merced, Calif.*
POSITION: *Guard*
TEAMS: *Bucks, 1996-present.*

A premier scorer with outside range all the way to the 3-point arc, Allen has been at the heart of the Bucks' revival since he was chosen with the No. 5 selection in the 1996 NBA draft. A crafty offensive player who also is adept at getting into the lane, Allen has

RAY OF HOPE: *Ray Allen has proven to be a quiet assassin*

and dribbling ability to take the ball anywhere he wants and either deliver it to the basket or an open teammate. The 6–1 Anderson was selected by New Jersey with the second overall pick of the 1991 draft after his sophomore season at Georgia Tech. Playing in his own backyard, he started slowly but jumped to the top of his position with averages of 18.8 points and 9.6 assists in a 1993–94 All-Star season. But Anderson was plagued the next year by a wrist injury and accusations that he was dominating the ball and taking bad shots. He was traded to Portland early in 1996 and in 1996–97 he led the Blazers in scoring (17.5) and assists (7.1) while leading the team to a 49–33 record. The slender Anderson, more a penetrator and scorer than a playmaker, found himself on the move again during the 1997–98 season, heading to the Boston Celtics, via Toronto, where under coach Rick Pitino he might get more of an opportunity to showcase his open-court game.

BALL HAWK: *Kenny Anderson is a dangerous man with the ball in his hands.*

been part of a 1-2-3 scoring Bucks punch that also features forward Glenn Robinson and guard Sam Cassell for coach George Karl's team. Respected by his peers for his low-key demeanor, Allen was selected to represent the United States in the 2000 Sydney Olympics, earning his invitation even before the selection committee went for emerging superstar Vince Carter. Initially thought of as a streak scorer, Allen has been able to develop a consistency that has made Milwaukee one of the most feared offensive teams in the NBA. While his defense can be sufficient at times, what has held Allen back on both ends has been Milwaukee's inability to land a premier inside player, which has allowed opponents to place more of a focus on the 6-foot-5 guard.

KENNY ANDERSON

BORN: *10–9–70, at Queens, N.Y.*
POSITION: *Guard.*
TEAMS: *Nets, 1991–96, Hornets, 1996; Trail Blazers, 1996–98, Celtics 1998–present.*

The multi-talented Anderson is a ball-handling magician. He has the quickness

NICK ANDERSON

BORN: *1-20-68 at Chicago, Ill.*
POSITION: *Guard*
TEAMS: *Magic, 1989-99, Kings, 1999-present.*

A prolific inside scorer at the University of Illinois and during the early stages of his career with the Orlando Magic, Anderson has reinvented his game during his NBA tenure. Initially known for his ability to play with a foot in the paint and post-up shorter shooting guards, the 6-foot-6 veteran moved to more of an outside approach when his free-throw shooting began to fail him in a mid-career crisis. Anderson now stands as one of the league's premier 3-point threats, a player who will throw up the long ball no matter the situation on offense. His game certainly is an odd mix, with a greater comfort zone shooting from beyond the 3-point arc than from the much-closer foul line. Where Anderson can make up for his shortcomings is on the defensive end, where his bulk and height make him especially competitive against the league's taller shooting guards. His best moments came in the 1995 playoffs, when he helped lead Orlando to the NBA Finals against the Rockets. That, however, is when his foul shooting betrayed him most.

NATE (TINY) ARCHIBALD

BORN: *9–2–48, at New York, N.Y.*
POSITION: *Guard.*
TEAMS: *Royals/Kings, 1970–76, Nets, 1976–77, Celtics, 1978–83, Bucks, 1983–84.*

Archibald, a lightning-quick point guard out of the University of Texas-El Paso, showcased his triple-threat skills over a 13-year career that produced 16,481 points (18.8), 6,476 assists (7.4), three All-NBA first-team citations and six All-Star Game selections. The 6–1 Archibald was an outstanding passer and long-range shooter, but he was virtually unstoppable when penetrating the middle, either scoring, dishing off for an easy shot or drawing a foul (he led the league in free throws made three times). "Tiny" enjoyed his most impressive season for Kansas City-Omaha in 1972–73, when he won scoring (34.0) and assist (11.4) titles,

becoming the first NBA player to lead the league in those two categories in the same season. With Archibald serving as their floor general, the Boston Celtics led the league in victories three consecutive seasons (1980–82) and won an NBA championship in 1981. He was elected to the Hall of Fame in 1991.

PAUL ARIZIN

BORN: *4–9–28, at Philadelphia, Pa.*
POSITION: *Guard/forward.*
TEAM: *Warriors, 1950–52, 1954–62.*

The 6–4 Arizin was a self-made star who didn't play competitive basketball until his sophomore season at Villanova. Two years later, in 1950, he led the nation with a 25.3 scoring average and was named College Player of the Year. Arizin's scoring prowess served him nicely during a 10-season NBA career that produced 16,266 points, a 22.8-point average, three All-NBA first-team citations and 10 All-Star Game invitations. Arizin, who lost two seasons to military service, was known for his picture-perfect jump shot and ability to carry a team. With Arizin and center Neil Johnston forming a classic inside-outside combination in 1956, Philadelphia won an NBA championship. A year later, Arizin won the second of two scoring titles with a 25.6-point average. "Pitchin'" Paul retired in 1962 and was named to the NBA 25th Anniversary All-Time Team in 1970. He was elected to the Hall of Fame in 1977.

DARRELL ARMSTRONG

BORN: *6-22-68 at Gastonia, N.C.*
POSITION: *Guard*
TEAMS: *Magic, 1994-present.*

Among the greatest stories in perseverance the NBA has witnessed, Darrell Armstrong played just about everywhere before emerging as one of the league's top energy guards in the mid-90s. Among his stops were stints in Spain and Cyprus, as well as just about every minor league

known to modern man. But when the Magic gave him the chance to show what he could do, Armstrong made the most of it. Within five years of joining Orlando, Armstrong won the Sixth Man Award and was named Most Improved Player, with both honors coming in 1999. Energized to the point that he insists on his pregame cocoa and any other form of chocolate he can get his hands on, Armstrong plays a relentless style of defense, often pressuring opposing point guards for all 94 feet. On offense, he can be just as much of a pest, with a lightning-quick ability to pull up and shoot the 3-pointer in transition. He stands among the players NBA point guards fear the most. Through it all, he has remembered his roots and what it took to reach the NBA.

B

VIN BAKER

BORN: 11–23–71, Lake Wales, Fla.
POSITION: Forward/center.
TEAM: Bucks, 1993–97; SuperSonics 1997–present

Baker came out of nowhere in 1993, to claim a spot among the game's top power forwards. That "nowhere" was the tiny college of Hartford where he still attracted enough attention to merit an eighth overall draft pick by the Milwaukee Bucks. The 6–11 Baker has blossomed quickly, establishing the paint as his personal playground where he out-quicks opponents with a variety of spin moves and slide dribbles. Defenders have discovered the hard way that Baker is a warrior who punishes the offensive and defensive boards, goes hard to the basket and sacrifices his body on defense. Baker moved to Seattle in the summer of 1997 in part of a blockbuster three-way trade that took Shawn Kemp to Cleveland. Although his averages fell slightly—from 21.0 points and 10.3 boards per game in '96–97 to 19.2 and 8.0 in '97–98 – his tireless play was applauded around the League. But in the next two seasons, Baker struggled under new coach Paul Westphal. In his first season under Westphal, Baker's averages dipped to 13.8 points and 6.2 rebounds per game. In the 1999-2000 season, they returned to a more typical 16.6 points and 7.7 rebounds per game as Baker tried to battle through some depression. Despite that, he did play in 79 of the Sonics' 82 regular season games and in the first round of the playoffs before Seattle was eliminated by Utah.

LONG-BALL LEGEND: *Dana Barros went two years with at least one 3-pointer per game.*

CHARLES BARKLEY

See Legends of the NBA *page 96–97*

MARVIN BARNES

BORN: *6-27-52 at Detroit, Mich.*
POSITION: *Forward*
TEAMS: *Pistons, 1975-77, Braves, 1977-78, Celtics, 1978-79, Clippers, 1979-80.*

A standout at Providence who first jumped into the American Basketball Association, Barnes was a fierce but skilled power forward who could overwhelm with his strength and his finesse. His best days came in the ABA, where he was named Rookie of the Year in 1975 with the Spirits of St. Louis and also twice was named an All-Star. He then entered the NBA when the two leagues merged, and was selected by the Detroit Pistons in the dispersal draft of ABA players. He was dealt from Detroit to Buffalo the following season, where he upgraded his initial NBA statistics. While he never matched his ABA statistics in the NBA, he was a steady contributor and likely would have had a far longer NBA career if not for a flurry of off-court issues that led teams to consider him a liability. In many ways, the fierce approach that led him to be so successful on the court also led to his downfall. Eventually, he took his game to Europe at the close of his career.

DANA BARROS

BORN: *4-13-67 at Boston, Mass.*
POSITION: *Guard.*
TEAMS: *Sonics, 1989-93, 76ers, 1993-95, Celtics, 1995-2000, Mavericks, 2000, Pistons, 2000-present*

Yet another quick point guard known for his 3-point shooting, Barros established an NBA record when he converted 3-pointers in 89 consecutive games, a streak that began in 1994 and ran through 1996. In the midst of that streak, the 5-foot-11 standout was named the NBA's Most Improved Player while playing for the 76ers in 1995. Barros also led the NBA in 3-point percentage while with the Seattle SuperSonics in 1992. As with many players his size, most of his skills rest on the offensive side of the court, where he is just as adept at taking the ball all the way to the rim as he is at pulling up for quick-release 3-pointers. Barros thought he found the perfect match for his skills in the pressing and running game of the Celtics, when he signed with Boston in 1995 as a free agent, but the turmoil in Boston led to his being lost in the shuffle under coach Rick Pitino.

RICK BARRY

See Legends of the NBA *page 98–99*

ELGIN BAYLOR

See Legends of the NBA *page 100–101*

ZELMO BEATY

BORN: *10-25-39.*
POSITION: *Center.*
TEAMS: *Hawks, 1962-69, Stars, 1970-74, Lakers, 1974-75.*

Although he played in the shadows of other dominant centers of his era, players such as Wilt Chamberlain and Bill Russell, Beaty proved to be a force in his own right during his early NBA tenure with the Hawks. Beaty, in fact, proved such a coveted commodity that he became a significant factor in the bidding war between the NBA and the upstart ABA. Beaty left the Hawks a year after the franchise moved from St. Louis to Atlanta to join the Utah Stars of the ABA. There, he evolved into one of the league's top big men, making a big name for himself in the smaller-but-talented league. Eventually, Beaty would return to the NBA for the close of his career with the Lakers. He was one of several players to appear in both the NBA and ABA all-star games, making three appearances in the ABA's game and two in the NBA's game. He also won an ABA championship while with Utah. Beaty's statistics were slightly better in the ABA, where he spent the prime of his career.

WALT BELLAMY

BORN: *7–24–39, at New Bern, N.C.*
POSITION: *Center.*
TEAMS: *Packers/Zephyrs/Bullets, 1961–65, Knicks, 1965–68, Pistons, 1968–70, Hawks, 1970–74, Jazz, 1974–75.*

Bellamy was an agile 6–11 center who provided serious competition for such contemporaries as Wilt Chamberlain, Bill Russell and a young Kareem Abdul-Jabbar. His Hall of Fame career spanned 14 seasons with five teams and produced 20,941 points (20.1 per game) and 14,241 rebounds (13.7), and his .516 field goal percentage ranked third all-time when he retired in 1975. The Chicago Packers grabbed the former Indiana University star with the first overall pick of the 1961 draft and he rewarded them immediately with averages of 31.6 points and 19 rebounds en route to Rookie of the Year honors.

He averaged well over 20 points for the next four seasons and his rebounding average dipped below double digits only once in his first 12 years. Despite toiling in the massive shadows of Chamberlain and Russell, the steady and consistent Bellamy played in four All-Star Games, but he never hooked up with a championship team. He was elected to the Hall of Fame in 1993.

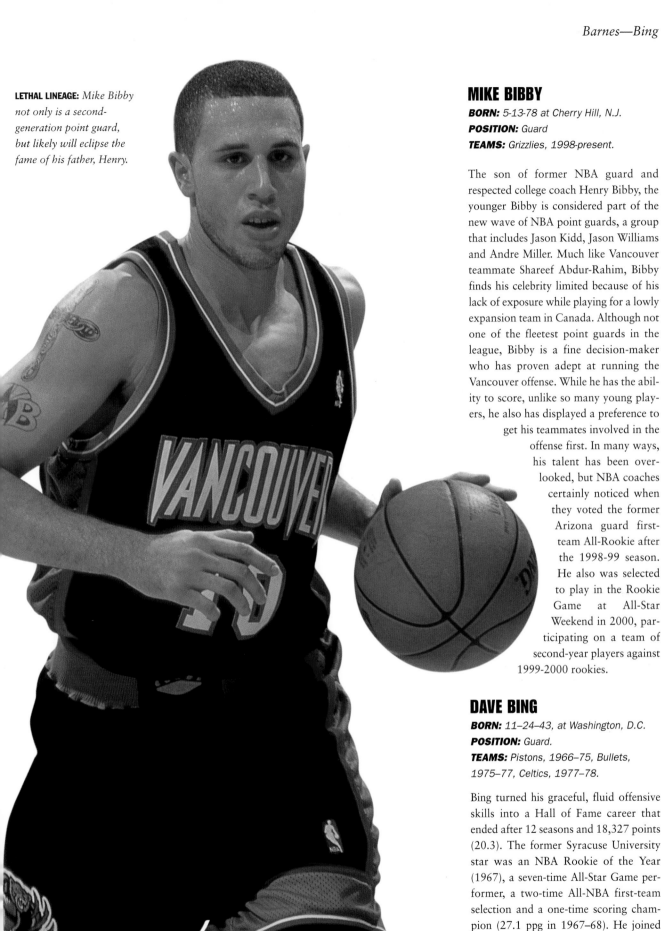

LETHAL LINEAGE: *Mike Bibby not only is a second-generation point guard, but likely will eclipse the fame of his father, Henry.*

MIKE BIBBY

BORN: *5-13-78 at Cherry Hill, N.J.*
POSITION: *Guard*
TEAMS: *Grizzlies, 1998-present.*

The son of former NBA guard and respected college coach Henry Bibby, the younger Bibby is considered part of the new wave of NBA point guards, a group that includes Jason Kidd, Jason Williams and Andre Miller. Much like Vancouver teammate Shareef Abdur-Rahim, Bibby finds his celebrity limited because of his lack of exposure while playing for a lowly expansion team in Canada. Although not one of the fleetest point guards in the league, Bibby is a fine decision-maker who has proven adept at running the Vancouver offense. While he has the ability to score, unlike so many young players, he also has displayed a preference to get his teammates involved in the offense first. In many ways, his talent has been overlooked, but NBA coaches certainly noticed when they voted the former Arizona guard first-team All-Rookie after the 1998-99 season. He also was selected to play in the Rookie Game at All-Star Weekend in 2000, participating on a team of second-year players against 1999-2000 rookies.

DAVE BING

BORN: *11–24–43, at Washington, D.C.*
POSITION: *Guard.*
TEAMS: *Pistons, 1966–75, Bullets, 1975–77, Celtics, 1977–78.*

Bing turned his graceful, fluid offensive skills into a Hall of Fame career that ended after 12 seasons and 18,327 points (20.3). The former Syracuse University star was an NBA Rookie of the Year (1967), a seven-time All-Star Game performer, a two-time All-NBA first-team selection and a one-time scoring champion (27.1 ppg in 1967–68). He joined the Pistons as the second overall draft pick in 1966 and became a classy playmaker for a weak Detroit team. The 6–3

153

OLD PRO: *Wily veteran Rolando Blackman (left) makes a move on a young Reggie Miller.*

Bing averaged 20 points as a rookie—the first of seven 20-point seasons—and claimed his scoring title in a breakthrough second campaign. But he would not play for a team with a winning record until 1970–71, and he would never fulfill his dream of a championship. Bing finished his career with two seasons in Washington and one in Boston. He was elected to the Hall of Fame in 1989.

LARRY BIRD

See Legends of the NBA *page 102–103*

OTIS BIRDSONG

BORN: *12-9-55.*
POSITION: *Guard.*
TEAMS: *Kings, 1977-81, Nets, 1981-88, Celtics, 1989-90.*

A flashy player dating to his days at the University of Houston, Birdsong made his name in the NBA by becoming the league's first million-dollar player. But he was more than that, far more. A stylist, who could bury the jump shot from virtually any spot on the floor, Birdsong was among the preeminent shooting guards

of his era, an era dominated by dazzlers such as David Thompson, George Gervin and Magic Johnson. While he did not have quite the flair of those three, he was nothing short of an offensively gifted player. Although he was buried in small-market Kansas City at the start of his career, he gained needed exposure when he was dealt to the New Jersey Nets. There, playing across the river from the league's largest market, Birdsong drew notice with his consistency for a franchise so desperately seeking an identity. If not for a series of injuries, it is likely there would have been a far more productive career that would have included several All-Star Game appearances.

ROLANDO BLACKMAN

BORN: *2–26–59, at Panama City, Panama.*
POSITION: *Guard.*
TEAMS: *Mavericks, 1981–92, Knicks, 1992–94.*

Blackman, who created defensive mismatches as a 6–6 guard, made good use of that advantage over an outstanding 13-year NBA career. The smooth Blackman, a 1981 draft pick out of Kansas State University, joined a second-year Dallas franchise and helped lead the Mavericks to respectability. From 1983–84 through 1991–92, the consistent Blackman averaged between 18.3 and 22.4 points, 2.7 and 3.8 assists and 3.2 and 4.6 rebounds per game. Blackman was equally deadly when penetrating the lane, posting up a shorter opponent or launching a jump shot from beyond the 3-point line. And he had the quickness to defend opposing point guards. Blackman, a four-time All-Star, teamed with Derek Harper for nine seasons in a first-rate backcourt that helped the Mavericks claim a Midwest Division title and a berth in the 1988 Western Conference finals. Blackman spent his final two seasons with the Knicks before retiring in 1994 with 17,623 career points (18.0 per game) and 2,981 assists (3.0).

MOOKIE BLAYLOCK

BORN: *3–20–67, at Garland, Tex.*
POSITION: *Guard.*
TEAMS: *Nets, 1989–92, Hawks, 1992–1999, Warriors, 1999–present.*

The 6–1 Blaylock is a push-and-pass point guard and one of the better defensive stoppers in the game. The former University of Oklahoma star is highly regarded for his quick hands and a ball-hawking defensive style that has produced more than 200 steals in a season five times and two NBA All-Defensive first-team selections. He's also a capable outside shooter, a fine passer who usually ranks among the league's assist leaders and an instigator of the fast break. Taken by New Jersey in 1989 with the 12th overall pick of the NBA Draft, he settled quickly into the Nets' rotation. But he was traded to Atlanta in 1992 and really blossomed under Hawks Coach Lenny Wilkens. Early in his career, Blaylock was a streaky shooter but he has worked hard to erase that criticism. Although his points per game average fell slightly in '97–98, down from over 17 to 13.2, he led the NBA in steals with an average of 2.61 and earned selection to the All-Defensive second team. He averaged 13.3 points and 2.06 steals the next season, but before the 1999-2000 season, the Hawks traded their all-time steals

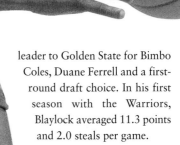

leader to Golden State for Bimbo Coles, Duane Ferrell and a first-round draft choice. In his first season with the Warriors, Blaylock averaged 11.3 points and 2.0 steals per game.

STEAL CURTAIN: *Mookie Blaylock's quick hands make him a threat to steal.*

TYRONE BOGUES

BORN: *1-9-65 at Baltimore, Md.*
POSITION: *Guard.*
TEAMS: *Bullets, 1987-88, Hornets, 1988-97, Warriors, 1997-99, Raptors, 1999-present.*

Among the most unique talents in NBA history, Bogues, at 5 foot 3, has proven that height, alone, is not all it takes to succeed in the NBA. Although short enough that he could dribble through the legs of most of the league's big men, Bogues has emerged not only as a solid ballhandler, with one with of the NBA's best assist-to-turnover ratios of all time, but also as a defender who often pesters bigger point guards into submission. At one point in his career a teammate of 7-foot-7 center Manute Bol, Bogues has emerged as far more than the novelty act he was at the start of his career. Having developed a quality shot, one that extends to 3-point range, Bogues long has been able to score inside from angles that players a foot taller have trouble dealing with. An inspiration for so many, the personable guard is a fan favorite who has provided guidance to many younger teammates.

RON BOONE

BORN: *9–6–46, at Oklahoma City, Okla.*
POSITION: *Guard.*
TEAMS: *Dallas Chaparrals (ABA), 1968–71, Utah Stars (ABA), 1971– 75, St. Louis Spirits (ABA), 1975– 76, Kings, 1976–78, Lakers, 1978– 79, Jazz, 1979–81.*

Boone was a durable all-around shooting guard who set a professional record by playing in 1,041 consecutive games, later eclipsed by A.C. Green's 1,100. The compact 6–2 former Idaho State University star played 660 of them in eight ABA seasons, compiling 12,153 points and an 18.4 average as the league's No. 3 all-time scorer. A member of Utah's 1971 ABA championship team, Boone was a

(Opposite) BIG LITTLE MAN: *At 5-foot-3, Tyrone (Muggsy) Bogues is more than a novelty act; he is a talented playmaker.*

(Right) DOLLAR BILL: *New York's Bill Bradley was on the ball even before he took office.*

physical player with powerful legs and the ability to mix it up with the big boys, but he also possessed a dangerous 20-foot jump shot. Boone, a 1975 ABA All-Star first-teamer, played in Dallas, Utah and St. Louis before signing with the Kansas City Kings after the ABA/NBA merger. He averaged 22.2 points as a 30-year-old NBA rookie and went on to finish his career with the Lakers and Jazz, never missing a game. Boone retired in 1981 with a combined ABA/NBA total of 17,437 points (16.8 per game).

BILL BRADLEY

Born: 7–28–43, at Crystal City, Mo.
Position: Forward.
Team: Knicks, 1967–77.

Bradley's story begins with his decision to spurn more than 70 scholarship offers and pay his own way to Princeton, where he became one of the most celebrated players in college basketball history as well as a Rhodes Scholar. "Dollar Bill" turned the Ivy League into his personal showcase, scoring 2,503 points and averaging 30.2 over his dazzling career. Before joining the Knicks in 1967, the 6–5

Bradley captained the U.S. to the 1964 Olympic gold medal and completed his Rhodes Scholar studies at Oxford in England. Bradley, a thinking-man's player and one of the game's best outside shooters, fit right into a New York Hall of Fame mix—Willis Reed, Dave DeBusschere, Earl Monroe, Walt Frazier—that produced NBA championships in 1970 and '73. He retired in 1977 with a 12.4-point average, but his contributions were measured by intangibles that don't show up on statistical charts. Bradley, who went on to another career as a U.S. Senator from New Jersey, was elected to the Hall of Fame in 1982.

SHAWN BRADLEY

BORN: *3-22-72 at Landstuhl, West Germany.*
POSITION: *Center.*
TEAMS: *76ers, 1993-95, Nets, 1995-96, Mavericks, 1996-present.*

Among the tallest players in the NBA, at 7 feet 6, Bradley is somewhat of an enigma, a big man who would just as soon not have to play inside. Envisioned at the start of his career as a player who

STANDING TALL: *At 7'6", Shawn Bradley has displayed a preference to play on the perimeter.*

could emerge as a front-line center for years to come, Bradley has turned into something far different as his career has evolved. A preeminent shot blocker, Bradley has become almost solely a defensive stopper, a player left to settle into the lane and back up perimeter defenders. Although he displayed promise for developing a wider repertoire on offense, Bradley has mostly been limited to a series of hook and jump shots often taken beyond his range. Still, much like Mark Eaton and Manute Bol, limited shot-blocking big men who preceded him, Bradley will always have a place in the NBA because of his ability to alter shots with his elongated build. Still, for a player considered a future All-Star when he was drafted, that has not turned out to be the case.

ELTON BRAND

BORN: *3-11-79 at Cortland, N.Y.*
POSITION: *Forward.*
TEAMS: *Bulls, 1999-present.*

Few players have been placed in such pressure-packed situations as the one faced by the former Duke star when he was named the No. 1 overall draft pick by the Chicago Bulls in 1999. In essence, Brand became the initial building block for the post-Michael Jordan reconstruction of the franchise. Initially there were doubts, with flashier players such as Steve Francis and Lamar Odom getting off to faster rookie starts elsewhere. But by the middle of his first season, Brand was drawing acclaim from NBA coaches for the way he had learned to dominate the post with his refined inside moves. Considering the Bulls still were in the process of unloading veteran talent when Brand arrived, it made his rookie progress all the more remarkable. While it is doubtful Chicago again can reach the heights it reached with Jordan and Pippen, Brand appears the type of talent who one day just might be mentioned in the same breath. The Bulls were looking for a cornerstone when they drafted Brand. That essentially is exactly what they got.

(Opposite) NOT BRAND X: *Elton Brand arrived as the type of star Chicago needed in the wake of the retirement of Michael Jordan.*

QUIET APPROACH: *Terrell Brandon is never brash, letting his game do all the talking.*

TERRELL BRANDON

BORN: *5-20-70 at Portland, Ore.*
POSITION: *Guard.*
TEAMS: *Cavaliers, 1991-97, Bucks, 1997-98, Timberwolves 1998-present.*

A playmaking point guard who also can get to the basket and hit the open jumper, Brandon at one point in his career with the Cavaliers was considered among the preeminent point guards in the game. In fact, Sports Illustrated, using a rating formula, declared him the best point guard in the NBA. The problem is that Brandon is not the type to display his emotions on the court. That reserved nature has drawn criticism from some, who see all the talent and wonder why there hasn't been more production. That well could be the reason that in just over a year, he was dealt from Cleveland to Milwaukee and then to Minnesota. Nonetheless, Brandon has produced at each of his NBA stops. He helped elevate the Bucks into a playoff team and then was at the heart of the Minnesota attack when the Timberwolves produced their first 50-victory season. He is neither flashy nor spectacular, but he tends to get the job done and limits the turnovers that make so many other point guards liabilities.

FRANK BRIAN

BORN: *7-1-23 at Zachary, La.*
POSITION: *Guard.*
TEAMS: *Packers, 1947-50, Hawks, 1950-51, Pistons, 1951-56.*

Known as "Flash," Brian was a star first in the National Basketball League and then the Basketball Association of America, before those leagues finally gave way to the NBA. Brian led the Anderson Packers to the title of the NBL in 1949 and then averaged a career-high 17.8 points in his first season in the NBA. The majority of his career was spent with Fort Wayne, which he helped lead to the 1955 NBA Finals. Among his backcourt partners was the talented Max Zaslofsky. Brian made the All-Star Game twice in his career, was All-NBA second team twice, All-NBL in 1949 and All-NBL second team in 1948. He appeared in the playoffs in all but one season. He arrived in the pros after playing only one season at Louisiana State, having spent three years in the military. He is listed in the "All-Time Great Players" section of the NBA's official player register, despite playing at a relatively low-profile period for the league.

BILL BRIDGES

BORN: *4-4-39, at Hobbs, N.M.*
POSITION: *Forward.*
TEAMS: *Hawks, 1962-71, 76ers, 1971-72, Lakers, 1972-74, Warriors, 1975.*

Bridges was the basketball equivalent of a football lineman: battling in the trenches, delivering and receiving elbows, getting little recognition. He was an outstanding rebounder, a tenacious defensive stopper and a battler under the basket. Bridges made his NBA debut in 1962–63 for the St. Louis Hawks after spending a season and a half with Kansas City in the short-lived American Basketball League. The 6–6 former University of Kansas star started slowly, averaging 5.3 and 8.5 rebounds off the bench for a team that featured Hall of Famers Bob Pettit and Cliff Hagan. But over the next nine seasons, Bridges never dipped below double figures in either points or rebounds while taking on all of the Hawks' biggest defensive assignments. When he retired in 1975, after short stints with the 76ers, Lakers and Warriors, Bridges had pulled down 11,054 rebounds (11.9), scored 11,012 points (11.9) and played in three All-Star Games.

FRED BROWN

BORN: *8-7-48.*
POSITION: *Guard.*
TEAMS: *Sonics, 1971-84.*

Known as "Downtown" for his long-range shooting expertise, Brown only at the end of his career was rewarded for his long-range proficiency. Although he consistently converted from the distance of the 3-point arc from the start of his tenure in Seattle, Brown did not benefit from the additional point for such accuracy until the NBA added the 3-point shot in 1979. From that point, defenders had no choice but to step out as far as Brown was stationed from the basket. Brown was at the heart of the Sonics' 1979 championship drive. He also made it to the All-Star Game in 1976. Brown not only led the NBA in 3-point shooting the first season the shot was added, but he also helped refine the outside shooting stroke of teammate Vinnie Johnson, who would go on to earn the nickname of the "Microwave" for his scoring ability during two championship seasons with the Detroit Pistons. One of his coaches, legendary Dick Motta, once said of Brown, "His misses are closer than some guys' makes."

KOBE BRYANT

BORN: 23–8–78, at Philadelphia, PA.
POSITION: Guard
TEAM: Lakers, 1996–present

Few players have attracted more hype and attention in the first years of their career than the 6–7 guard who entered the NBA as the 13th pick overall in the 1996 draft. His first year numbers with the Lakers were modest but his style and charisma earned him attention, especially after he won the 1997 Slam Dunk contest during All-Star Weekend. A year later, he became the youngest man ever to start an All-Star Game. At 19 years five months he beat Magic Johnson's record by a full year. The second youngest player ever to appear in an NBA game, Bryant's improvements in his second season were massive. His All-Star appearance was picked upon by the media and turned into a passing of the torch, from Michael Jordan to Kobe, a fact that MJ did not take kindly to as he subsequently outplayed the young Laker in the showcase event. But Bryant showed enough flair and imagination in 1997–98 to suggest that if anyone is able to fill Michael Jordan's legendary boots, it is he. Though he had a good season in 1998-99, he really blossomed when coach Phil Jackson took over the Lakers in the 1999-2000 season. Paired with Shaquille O'Neal, the two reminded many Laker fans of the tandem of Kareem Abdul-Jabbar and Magic Johnson that had brought so much excitement and success to Southern California.

In fact, when O'Neal fouled out and Bryant shrugged off a sprained left ankle

and took over to lead the Lakers to victory over the Indiana Pacers in Game 4 of the NBA Finals, comparisons were made to the rookie Johnson who filled in for the injured Abdul-Jabbar and led the Lakers to the NBA title. Two games later, Bryant had his first NBA title.

C

MARCUS CAMBY

BORN: 3-22-74 at Hartford, Conn.
POSITION: Forward.
TEAMS: Raptors, 1996-98, Knicks, 1998-present.

A college star at Massachusetts who was unable to get untracked during his tenure with expansion Toronto, Camby blossomed as a player when he was traded to New York in 1998 for trusted power forward Charles Oakley. While Camby initially was resented by teammates because his arrival signaled the departure of Oakley, he eventually won over his fellow players with aggressive play off the bench and defensive fervor. With center Patrick Ewing injured during much of Camby's first season with the Knicks, Camby was among the forces who helped deliver New York to the 1999 NBA Finals against the San Antonio Spurs. He was named All-Rookie during his first season in Toronto and received several votes for the Sixth Man Award during his first season with the Knicks. Statistically, Camby's best season might have been in 1997-98, when, while still with Toronto, he led the NBA in blocked shots. With Ewing being traded, Camby figures to be at the core of the rebuilding of the Knicks.

ANTOINE CARR

BORN: 7-23-61 at Oklahoma City, Okla.
POSITION: Forward
TEAMS: Hawks, 1984-89, Kings, 1990-94, Jazz, 1994-98, Rockets, 1998-99, Grizzlies, 1999-2000.

One of several players in the NBA known as "The Big Dog," Carr is an offensively gifted scorer who gets most of his points off effort plays near the basket. Although

he stands 6 feet 9, he tends to play bigger because of his wide build. Part of several high-scoring Hawks teams during the beginning of his NBA career, he later became a valued member of two Utah

JUMP START: *Among Marcus Camby's strengths is his ability to explode to the rim.*

162

Jazz teams that lost to Michael Jordan's Bulls in the NBA Finals. In fact, during the second of those runs to the Finals, Carr had to be talked out of retirement. Although he never made it to the All-Star Game, Carr is a player who almost always helped push his team into the postseason, not bad for a player whose pro career started in the Italian League. Carr could have jumped immediately into the NBA, but elected against signing with the Detroit Pistons after being chosen with the eighth overall selection in the 1983 draft.

THE BIG DOG: *Antoine Carr is known for his dogged determination.*

VINCE CARTER

BORN: *1-26-77 at Daytona Beach, Fla.*
POSITION: *Forward.*
TEAMS: *Raptors, 1998-present.*

Talk about your burdens, Carter already is being projected by some as the Next Michael Jordan, a tag many have been saddled with but few have been able to even come close to deserving. Yet Carter appears to be such a talent, the type of player who not only can score, but score meaningful baskets and do it with flair. Carter basically had his coming-out party during the Slam-Dunk Championship at the 2000 All-Star Weekend. Carter not only won the event, his efforts were so explosive, that many of the NBA's top stars could only look on in awe. In addition, Carter has elevated the play of the expansion Raptors to the point where they made the playoffs for the first time in his second season in the league. While he already has a Rookie of the Year trophy, he has graduated to the level where he also is receiving votes for Most Valuable Player. No, there may never be another Michael Jordan. But in Vince Carter, the NBA has someone who might just come close to the legacy.

BILL CARTWRIGHT

BORN: *7-30-57, at Lodi, Calif.*
POSITION: *Center.*
TEAMS: *Knicks, 1979-88, Bulls, 1988-94, SuperSonics, 1994-95.*

Cartwright was a reliable if unspectacular 7-1 center who played 16 NBA seasons in New York, Chicago and Seattle, helping the Bulls capture consecutive championships in 1991, '92 and '93. The former University of San Francisco star was a combination of power and finesse. If a game called for a physical effort, Cartwright could power his 245 pounds to the basket. If finesse was required, he could pile up points with an accurate turnaround jumper. Cartwright carried more of a scoring load with the Knicks, twice averaging better than 20 points. But he played more of a supporting role for the Bulls, who had plenty of fire-

CENTER FIELD: *Bill Cartwright was a key piece in the Bulls' first three titles.*

power with Michael Jordan and Scottie Pippen. Cartwright, a 1980 All-Star who sat out the 1984–85 and 1985–86 seasons with a stress fracture in his foot, retired in 1995 with 12,713 points (13.2) and 6,102 rebounds (6.3).

SAM CASSELL

BORN: *11-18-69 in Baltimore, Md.*
POSITION: *Guard.*
TEAMS: *Rockets, 1993-96, Suns, 1996, Mavericks, 1997, Nets, 1997-98, Bucks, 1999-present.*

A unique point guard who at times can play as the ultimate distributor and at other times can score with the best of the shooting guards, Cassell has a game that reminds some of Nate Archibald. Like Archibald, Cassell has the knack for putting up big numbers in both points and assists. Cassell demonstrated his savvy from the start, helping guide the Houston Rockets to NBA championships in his first two seasons out of Florida

(Opposite) GOOING UP: *Toronto's Vince Carter electrified fans with his slam dunks during the 2000 All Star Weekend in Oakland*

164

State. Mostly a sparkplug as a sixth man early in his career, Cassell has emerged as a starter so respected that Milwaukee was able to snag him in the three-team deal that landed Stephon Marbury in his place in New Jersey. Teamed with Ray Allen and Glenn Robinson in Milwaukee, Cassell helps form one of the highest-scoring trios in the NBA. While some

contend Cassell shoots too often, the Bucks earned playoff berths in his first two seasons in Milwaukee, after struggling to reach the playoffs before his arrival.

SUDDEN SAM: *Sam Cassell (right) can turn the corner off the dribble, or convert the jumper.*

CEDRIC CEBALLOS

BORN: *8-2-69 in Maui, Hawaii.*
POSITION: *Forward.*
TEAMS: *Suns, 1990-94, Lakers, 1994-96, Suns, 1997-98, Mavericks, 1998-2000, Pistons, 2000-present.*

A point-a-minute type scorer at the start of his career, when he played mostly as a reserve, Ceballos is the type of scorer who gets most of his offense off what are considered "garbage" points, that is scoring that does not necessarily come out of set offense, but instead off of rebounds and fastbreak opportunities. The type of player who can struggle against man-to-man defense, Ceballos is at his best when others are established as primary scorers and he can work on the periphery. The winner of the 1992 Slam Dunk Championship at All-Star Weekend, when he brought down the house with his blindfolded dunk, Ceballos is one of the more athletic players in the league and is a quality rebounder, especially on the offensive end. Whether he can be part of a winner, however, is a question that has dogged him throughout his career. The lack of an outside shot has prevented him from going further as a player.

AL CERVI

BORN: *2–12–17, at Buffalo, N.Y.*
POSITION: *Guard.*
TEAMS: *Buffalo Bisons (NBL), 1937–38, Royals (NBL), 1945–48, Nationals (NBL/NBA), 1948–53.*

Cervi was a scrappy, hustling two-way guard in the professional game's formative years. He began his career with the National Basketball League's Buffalo Bisons in 1937, advancing to the hardcourts from the sandlots of his Buffalo youth. Cervi's career was interrupted by a long stint in the military during World War II, but he joined the NBL's Rochester Royals in 1945 and played three seasons before moving to Syracuse as player-coach. When the Nationals moved to the NBA in 1949–50, Cervi led them to the

NBA Finals. The 5–11 Cervi, an explosive one-on-one performer and an outstanding defender, was considered a master of the three-point play. But more than anything, he was a fiery leader who brought out the best in his teammates and players. After Cervi's 1953 retirement, he went on to coach the Nationals/76ers to 366 victories and the 1955 NBA championship. Cervi was elected to the Hall of Fame in 1984.

WILT CHAMBERLAIN

See Legends of the NBA page 104–105

TOM CHAMBERS

BORN: 6-21-59
at Ogden, Utah.
POSITION: Forward
TEAMS: Clippers, 1981-83, Sonics, 1983-88, Suns, 1988-93, Jazz, 1993-95, Hornets, 1996-97, 76ers, 1997-98.

A big man who could step outside and hit the long-range jumper, Chambers was a cold-blooded scorer throughout an efficient NBA career. A second-team All-NBA selection twice in his career, Chambers also was an All-Star four times. He guided both the Sonics and Suns into the playoffs several times over his career, and his scoring was sought toward the end of the career by the Jazz, as it began its ascension up the standings. More of a rebounder earlier in his career, Chambers began to move his game farther and farther from the basket as his career continued. The lack of physical play cost him some respect, as did a lack of defensive prowess. For a player with his 6-foot-10 build, he was deceptively quick, but also considered somewhat of a selfish scorer. His assist totals never were high and by the end of his career had become miniscule. His most memorable moment may have been when he went for 34 points in the 1987 All-Star Game to be named MVP of the event.

WELL-TRAVELED: *Cedric Ceballos has bounced around the league for 10 years*

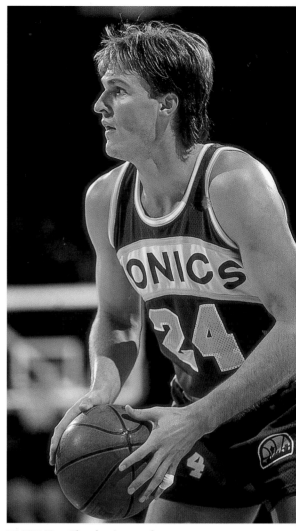

BIG SHOT: *Tom Chambers' game plan was to shoot early and often*

DON CHANEY

BORN: 3-22-46.
POSITION: Guard.
TEAMS: Celtics, 1968-75, Lakers, 1975-77, Celtics 1978-80.

Known as "Duck" and considered one of the best defensive guards of his era, Chaney was a bridge in the Celtic folklore between the Bill Russell Era and the Larry Bird Era, the only player to play alongside both Boston icons. Chaney won two championships with the Celtics early in his career, as a deferential player who knew how to set up his team's stars and then get out of the way and allow them to operate. While Chaney briefly jumped to the St. Louis entry of the ABA, he stayed in the NBA long enough to earn mention on five All-Defensive teams. A standout

player at the University of Houston, Chaney continued his career as coach of the Clippers, Rockets and Pistons before settling in as an assistant with the Knicks, where he was on the sidelines for New York's trip to the 1999 NBA Finals. With a sharp mind for the game, he is considered one of the leading thinkers among assistants, but his friendly nature may have proven too forgiving during his stints as a head coach.

MAURICE CHEEKS

BORN: 9–8–56, at Chicago, Ill.
POSITION: Guard.
TEAMS: 76ers, 1978–89, Spurs, 1989–90, Knicks, 1990–91, Hawks, 1991–92, Nets, 1992–93.

Cheeks, the quiet point guard, was a coach's dream. He wasn't a big scorer, he didn't run up prolific assist numbers and he didn't dazzle fans with fancy ballhandling or passes. But the 6–1 Cheeks was one of the best floor generals of the 1980s. He seldom made turnovers or mistakes, he always got the ball to the right people in the right situations and when defenses sagged on Julius Erving or Moses Malone, he was a dangerous outside shooter. Not surprisingly, Cheeks also was one of the league's best defensive guards— a four-time All-Defensive first-team selection. The former West Texas State star arrived in Philadelphia in 1978 and guided the star-studded 76ers team to seven consecutive seasons of 50-plus wins, three NBA Finals and the 1983 championship. After brief stints in San Antonio, New York, Atlanta and New Jersey, Cheeks retired in 1993 with 15-year totals of 12,195 points (11.1 per game), 7,392 assists (6.7) and 2,310 steals.

ARCHIE CLARK

BORN: 7-15-41.
POSITION: Guard.
TEAMS: Lakers, 1966-68, 76ers, 1968-71, Bullets, 1972-74, Sonics, 1974-75, Pistons, 1975-76.

Despite playing most of his career in the

(Left) **CHEEKY GUARD:** *Maurice Cheeks ran the show for the 76ers in the 1980s.*

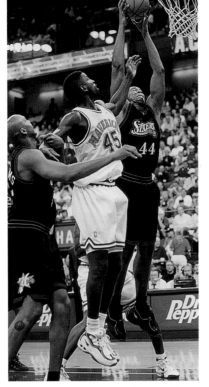

COLEMAN COOLER? *Derrick Coleman (44) can score, but his attitude needs work*

shadows of other great players, Clark earned respect as a classic scorer who could put points on the board when given the opportunity. Despite playing as an understudy to Jerry West with the Lakers and Hal Greer with the 76ers, Clark nonetheless was able to consistently score in double figures for both teams. He went from the Lakers to the 76ers in the trade that delivered Wilt Chamberlain to Los Angeles. Twice named to the All-Star Game, Clark grew into a 20-point scorer later in his career, once he was able to emerge from the shadows of his previous superstar teammates. But in many ways, Clark proved unable to make the most of his career, with injuries and contract disputes preventing him from maximizing his time on the court. Had Clark been featured more often earlier in his career, it is possible he could have reached the heights attained by his former Hall of Fame teammates.

DERRICK COLEMAN

BORN: 6–21–67, at Mobile, Ala.
POSITION: Forward.
TEAMS: Nets, 1990–95, 76ers, 1995–98, Hornets, 1998–present.

Talent-wise, Coleman is a gifted power forward who should be carving out a Hall of Fame career. Psychologically, the Syracuse University product is a 6–10

Cooper, a 6–7 swingman with great quickness and leaping ability, was the defensive genius behind the Los Angeles Lakers' five championships of the 1980s. The lean, 170-pound hardbody was a classic stopper who never backed down from anybody. He could defend the quickest point guard or the 280-pound power forward. While teammates Kareem Abdul-Jabbar, Magic Johnson and James Worthy were taking care of offensive business, Cooper was coming off the bench to work in the trenches and provide inspirational leadership. But the five-time NBA All-Defensive first-team selection could provide other kinds of inspiration as well. Cooper was a good passer and he could nail the 3-pointer with his one-handed set shot. And the Lakers used him on an alley-oop slam that never failed to bring down the house. Cooper, the NBA's 1986–87 Defensive Player of the Year, finished his career in 1990 after 12 Los Angeles seasons and 168 career playoff games.

LARRY COSTELLO

BORN: *7-2-31, at Minoa, N.Y.*
POSITION: *Guard.*
TEAMS: *Warriors, 1954–57, Nationals/76ers, 1957–68.*

Before beginning his successful coaching career, Costello toiled for 13 seasons as a fast-moving point guard for the Philadelphia Warriors and Syracuse Nationals. Costello knew only one speed: fast, and his style was intense, emotional and relentless. The 6–1 Costello, one of the last practitioners of the two-handed set shot, was at his best in a fast-break offense where he could use his speed to blow past helpless defenders and create scoring opportunities. He was a defensive gambler, using his speed to make up for mistakes. Costello, who was picked on the second round of the 1954 draft out of Niagara University, began his career with the Warriors but enjoyed his best years in Syracuse and Philadelphia, where the Nationals moved in 1963. He was a member of the 76ers' powerful 1967 NBA championship team. Costello, a six-time All-Star, retired in 1968 with 8,622 points (12.2 per game) and 3,215 assists (4.6). Three years later, he

coached the Milwaukee Bucks to their first championship.

BOB COUSY

See Legends of the NBA page 106–107

DAVE COWENS

BORN: *10–25–48, at Newport, Ky.*
POSITION: *Center.*
TEAMS: *Celtics, 1970–80, Bucks, 1982–83.*

The 6–9 Cowens, a mobile, undersized center, played with an all-out intensity and aggressive style that helped the Celtics win two NBA championships. The former Florida State star disproved the theory that a center had to play with his back to the basket. Cowens roamed the perimeter sinking soft jumpers, used his superior quickness on drives to the basket and played with a passion that gave him the edge over bigger opponents. He won co-Rookie of the Year honors in 1970–71 and a Most Valuable Player award in 1973. Cowens, a seven-time All-Star Game performer, combined with John Havlicek and Jo Jo White on the Celtics' 1974 and '76 title teams. He served one season (1978–79) as player-coach and finished his career with 13,516 points (17.6) and 10,444 rebounds (13.6). Cowens, who was named to coach the Charlotte Hornets after the 1995–96 deason, was elected to the Hall of Fame in 1991. He lasted seasons with the Hornets before resigning in 1998-99. In 2000, he was named coach of the Golden State Warriors.

TERRY CUMMINGS

BORN: *3-15-61 at Chicago, Ill.*
POSITION: *Forward.*
TEAMS: *Clippers, 1982-84, Bucks, 1984-89, Spurs, 1989-95, Bucks, 1995-96, Sonics, 1996-97, 76ers, 1997, Knicks, 1998, Warriors, 1998-2000.*

From a high-scoring forward at the start of his career to a sage leader in the latter stages, Cummings has undergone a dramatic change in the contributions he has offered. Once a player with more of a self-serving game, the Pentecostal minister has emerged as the type of role player

so coveted by teams. The Rookie of the Year in 1983 out of DePaul, Cummings has been voted first-team, second-team and third-team All-NBA over his career. A diversified scorer with a 6-foot-9 build, Cummings has gone from an outside-shooting slasher to more of a power player in recent years. He also has become quite the pounder inside, a role he was especially adept at when he played for the New York Knicks. Despite his scoring success, Cummings made it to only two All-Star Games, but was at the heart of several playoff campaigns by the Spurs and Bucks.

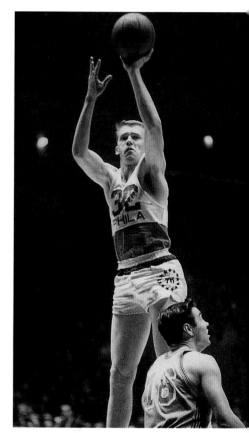

LEAP OF FAITH: *Philadelphia's Billy Cunningham could jump out of the gym.*

BILLY CUNNINGHAM

BORN: *6–3–43, at Brooklyn, N.Y.*
POSITION: *Forward.*
TEAMS: *76ers, 1965–72, 1974–76, Carolina Cougars (ABA), 1972–74.*

Cunningham, a.k.a. "the Kangaroo Kid," was known for his leaping ability and the fiery intensity he brought to the game. A left-handed slasher out of the University of North Carolina, Cunningham vaulted into NBA prominence with a take-no-prisoners style that won the hearts of Philadelphia fans and earned him a prominent place on one of the greatest teams ever assembled. The 1967 76ers, featuring the 6–7 Cunningham, Wilt Chamberlain, Hal Greer and Chet Walker, stormed to 68 victories and ended the Celtics' eight-year championship reign. Cunningham, who also spent two seasons and won an MVP award in the ABA, scored 16,310 professional points and grabbed 7,981 rebounds in an 11-season career that included three All-NBA first-team selections and four NBA All-Star Game appearances. He later coached the 76ers to 454 victories (averaging 57 wins per season) and another championship. Cunningham was elected to the Hall of Fame in 1986.

DELL CURRY

BORN: *6-25-64 at Harrisonburg, Va.*
POSITION: *Guard*
TEAMS: *Jazz, 1986-87, Cavaliers, 1987-88, Hornets, 1988-98, Bucks, 1998-99, Raptors, 1999-present.*

Curry not only is one of the most productive 3-point shooters in NBA history, he also is has one of the quickest releases from beyond the arc, making him especially difficult to cover when he is given any air space beyond the semicircle. A valued contributor, Curry has spent most of his career as a sixth-man, a player who can come off the bench to ignite the offense or mute another team's rally. For such efforts, he was honored with the Sixth Man Award while with Charlotte in 1994. He also led the NBA in 3-point shooting percentage in 1999, making 47.6 percent of his attempts from beyond the arc. A mainstay during the Hornets' expansion years, in recent seasons, Curry has become somewhat of a hired gun. He was brought in by Milwaukee in 1998, when that franchise was on the verge of its first playoff berth in a decade. The next season he was added as a free agent by Toronto, when that team was poised to make what turned into its first appearance in the playoffs.

CURRY'S FAVOR: *There's nothing Dell Curry enjoys more than sinking 3-pointers.*

D

LOUIE DAMPIER

BORN: *11–20–44, at Indianapolis, Ind.*
POSITION: *Guard.*
TEAMS: *Kentucky Colonels (ABA), 1967–76, Spurs, 1976–79.*

Dampier was a hustling, clever, straight-shooting point guard who spent most of his career with the Kentucky Colonels in the ABA. The 6-foot Dampier was living proof that a hard-working little man could thrive in the lofty world of professional basketball. He made a science out of the ABA's 3-point shot, connecting on 794, and he scored more points (13,726), handed out more assists (4,044) and played in more games (728)

WELL TRAVELED: *Adrian Dantley was a scoring machine no matter where he played.*

than any player in the league's nine-year existence. The impressive thing about Dampier was his ability to adjust to his supporting players. In his first three seasons, the former University of Kentucky star averaged better than 20 points per game. When 7–2 Artis Gilmore and high-scoring Dan Issel arrived, he became more of a passer and floor general. Dampier helped the Colonels win the 1975 ABA championship and spent his final three seasons with San Antonio after the 1976 merger. He finished with combined ABA/NBA totals of 15,279 points and 4,687 assists.

BOB DANDRIDGE

BORN: *11–15–47, at Richmond, Va.*
POSITION: *Forward.*
TEAMS: *Bucks, 1969–77, 1981–82, Bullets, 1977–81.*

The hard-working Dandridge was an outstanding do-everything small forward who helped two teams win NBA championships. A slender 6–6, 195-pounder, he was the perfect supporting actor for young Lew Alcindor when the Milwaukee Bucks captured the 1971 title and for Washington big men Elvin Hayes and Wes Unseld when the Bullets won in 1978. He was an accomplished shooter, rebounder, passer and defender—a player who could read the game and do whatever his team might need to win. Most of Dandridge's best work was performed in the trenches—and in the locker room. Dandridge spent his first eight seasons in Milwaukee, averaging better than 18 points and six rebounds seven times. He played for two Washington teams that reached the NBA Finals before closing his career with a 1981–82 return engagement in Milwaukee. The four-time All-Star scored 15,530 points (18.5 per game), grabbed 5,715 rebounds (6.8) and handed out 2,846 assists (3.4).

MEL DANIELS

BORN: *7–20–44, at Detroit, Mich.*
POSITION: *Center.*
TEAMS: *Minnesota Muskies (ABA), 1967–68, Indiana Pacers (ABA), 1968–74, Memphis Sounds (ABA), 1974–75, New York Nets (NBA), 1976–77.*

Daniels was a two-time ABA Most Valuable Player and a key figure on Indiana's 1970, '72 and '73 ABA championship teams. The quiet Daniels was a slender but muscular 6–9 workhorse who possessed a soft fallaway jumper. He averaged better than 20 points three times and won three ABA rebounding titles, never averaging less than 15 boards in any of his first six professional seasons. Daniels provided the blue-collar ethic for a flashy Indiana team that boasted such stars as George McGinnis, Roger Brown and Freddie Lewis. Daniels, a former University of New Mexico star, passed up an offer from the NBA's Cincinnati Royals in 1967 and signed with the Minnesota Muskies, earning Rookie of the Year honors. The seven-time All-Star spent his next six seasons with the Pacers, piling up most of his 11,739 career points (18.7) and 9,494 rebounds (15.1). Daniels spent his final ABA season in Memphis and played 11 NBA games for the New York Nets after the 1976 merger.

ADRIAN DANTLEY

BORN: *2–28–56, at Washington, D.C.*
POSITION: *Guard/forward.*
TEAMS: *Braves, 1976–77, Pacers, 1977, Lakers, 1977–79, Jazz, 1979–86, Pistons, 1986–89, Mavericks, 1989–90, Bucks, 1990–91.*

Dantley was probably the premier one-on-one scoring machine of his era. He played for seven teams over 15 seasons, averaged better than 20 points 11 times and won two scoring titles, with averages of 30.7 and 30.6. Amazingly, the 6–5, 210-pound Dantley, who divided time between small forward and guard, scored most of his points in the paint, defying centers who usually discouraged such activity. Dantley first jumped into the national consciousness in the mid-70s as a scoring phenomenon for Notre Dame and a 1976 Olympic hero. He averaged 20.3 points and 7.6 rebounds in 1976–77 for Buffalo, winning Rookie of the Year honors. But he was traded three times in his first four years before finally settling in Utah. Dantley played seven seasons with the Jazz before career-ending stints with Detroit, Dallas and Milwaukee. The six-time All-Star retired in 1991 with 23,177 points (24.3) and 5,455 rebounds (5.7).

BRAD DAUGHERTY

BORN: *10–19–65, at Black Mountain, N.C.*
Position: Center.
Team: Cavaliers, 1986–94.

Daugherty was a powerful force in Cleveland's middle for seven-plus seasons before major back surgery forced him into retirement. The 7-foot former University of North Carolina star last played in February 1994, averaging 17 points and 10 rebounds. Three years later, Daugherty's No. 43 jersey was raised to rafters of Cleveland's Gund Arena. He was selected by the Cavs with the first overall pick of the 1986 draft and he didn't disappoint, stepping right into the lineup with averages of 15.7 points and 8.1 rebounds. In 1990–91, those averages rose to 21.6 and 10.9 and remained at that level for three straight seasons. Daugherty, not blessed with great jumping ability, relied on fundamentals and a deadly hook shot. The five-time All-Star was also one of the best passing centers in the game and a solid defender. Playing in the shadow of other great centers such as Patrick Ewing, David Robinson and Hakeem Olajuwon, Daugherty retired with 10,389 career points and 19.0 scoring average.

BOB DAVIES

BORN: *1–15–20, at Harrisburg, Pa.*
POSITION: *Guard.*
TEAM: *Royals (NBL/BAA/NBA), 1945–55.*
The 6–1 Davies was the premier playmaker of the early NBA. Content to help teammates carry the scoring load, he was a magician with the ball, performing behind-the-back, over-the-head and through-the-leg maneuvers that astounded conservative fans and players

CENTER PIECE: *Daugherty was a five-time All-Star before a back injury finished his career.*

of his era. After leading Seton Hall University to 43 straight victories from 1939 to '41 and serving in World War II, Davies joined Rochester of the old National Basketball League and remained with the Royals for 10 seasons—seven of them in the BAA/NBA. Davies, who once held the single-game record of 20 assists, led the BAA with 321 in 1948–49 and helped the Royals capture the NBA championship in 1951. He was a four-time All-BAA/ NBA first teamer and played in the league's first four All-Star Games. Davies, who retired in 1955, was elected to the Hall of Fame in 1969 and was selected to the NBA 25th Anniversary All-Time Team a year later.

DALE DAVIS

BORN: *3-25-69 at Toccoa, Ga.*
POSITION: *Forward.*
TEAMS: *Pacers, 1991-2000, Trail Blazers, 2000-present.*

The prototypic complementary player, Davis has been at the heart of the Pacers' defense and rebounding game since he arrived as a first-round pick in 1991 out of Clemson. Although limited in his offensive game, and a low-percentage foul shooter for most of his career, Davis has grown into one of the most respected power forwards in the game for the way he complemented the skills of Indiana scorers Reggie Miller, Rik Smits and Mark Jackson. A tough and durable defender,

HOT HAND: *Walter Davis had an array of offensive skills whenever he got the ball.*

Davis often is matched up against the most talented opposing big man, be hr a center or power forward. His brute strength allows him to keep most big men from getting anywhere near the basket on either end. In recent seasons, Davis has improved his offense to the point where he can hit the short jumper and even provide at least some confidence when he steps to the foul line. For that growth, he was rewarded with a berth in the 2000 All-Star Game. He stands as the Pacers' all-time leading rebounder.

WALTER DAVIS

BORN: 9–9–54, at Pineville, N.C.
POSITION: Guard/forward.
TEAMS: Suns, 1977–88, Nuggets, 1988–91, 1991–92, Trail Blazers, 1991.

The graceful Davis was one of the purest long-range shooters the game has ever produced. At 6–6, the slender 195-pounder was a mismatch waiting to happen. If he played small forward, he was too fast and quick for the bigger opponents who tried to guard him. If he played shooting guard, he could post up smaller defenders. Either way, Davis was an offensive weapon who averaged more than 20 points six times and finished his 15-year career with 19,521—an 18.9 average. Davis, a University of North Carolina star and Olympic gold medal winner (1976), was drafted by Phoenix in 1977 and made an immediate impact, averaging 24.2 points and winning NBA Rookie of the Year honors. He spent 11 years in Phoenix, helping the Suns record four 50-victory seasons and reach the 1984 Western Conference finals. Davis, a six-time All-Star, retired in 1992 after short stints with Denver and Portland.

DARRYL DAWKINS

BORN: 1-11-57.
POSITION: Center
TEAMS: 76ers, 1975-82, Nets, 1982-86, Jazz, 1986, Pistons, 1987-89.

One of the most unique talents to ever play the game, Dawkins was perhaps the most colorful personality in NBA lore. Nicknamed "Chocolate Thunder," Dawkins claimed he was from the planet Lovetron and insisted on giving names to his spectacular dunks. A huge man with unsurpassed brute strength, Dawkins made a habit of shattering backboards with the sheer force of his dunks. Beyond the theatrics, he also was a successful center who helped push the 76ers deep into the playoffs. His abilities around the basket were of all-star level and he was practically impossible to box out when it came to rebounding. While he could have done so much more in his career, it simply was not in Dawkins' nature to take the game too seriously. During the latter stages of his career, it was as if emerging as a personality was more important than emerging as a superstar. Still, he learned the game well enough to move on to a coaching career several years after the end of his playing days.

CHOCOLATE THUNDER: *Darryl Dawkins was never shy when it came to nicknames.*

GOOD D: *Dave DeBusschere was a perfect fit with the New York Knicks.*

DAVE DeBUSSCHERE

BORN: *10–16–40, at Detroit, Mich.*
POSITION: *Forward.*
TEAMS: *Pistons, 1962–68, Knicks, 1968–74.*

DeBusschere's was one of the game's all-time great defensive forwards, but he was no slouch offensively. In 12 NBA seasons with Detroit and New York, he averaged 16.1 points and 11.0 rebounds per game. As a shooter, he was dangerous from inside or out. As a defender, the 6–6 DeBusschere was a physical banger who could take the opposing team's best player out of the game. DeBusschere's talents couldn't help Detroit, which reached the playoffs twice in six seasons. But he was perfect for a Knicks team that rolled to NBA championships in 1970 and '73. A six-time All-Defensive first-team selection, he held several NBA distinctions. At age 24, he was the youngest coach in NBA history (1964–67 with the Pistons). And for four seasons (1962–65), he doubled as a baseball pitcher in the Chicago White Sox organization. DeBusschere was elected to the Hall of Fame in 1982.

THE EYES DON'T HAVE IT: *Vlade Divac takes out a double-team with a no-look pass.*

VLADE DIVAC

BORN: *2-3-68 at Prijepolje, Yugoslavia.*
POSITION: *Center.*
TEAMS: *Lakers, 1989-96, Hornets, 1996-98, Kings, 1998-present.*

One of the first foreign-born big men to find success in the NBA, Divac has succeeded with a finesse game heretofore unseen from NBA big men. Although hardly the classic power-driven center, Divac has been able to carve a niche for himself with a soft shooting touch and deft passing ability. His crafty play is especially suited for high-scoring offenses, which he has been featured in during his time with the Lakers, Hornets and Kings.

Although somewhat defensively deficient, Divac is able to extract his revenge on the offensive end by luring opposing big men into foul trouble with his spin moves and up-and-under shooting. Voted to the NBA's All-Rookie Team in 1990, Divac hardly entered the league as an unpolished neophyte. Before his arrival, he had been a member of Yugoslavia's silver-medal entry at the 1988 Olympics and later would win another silver with the Yugoslavs at the 1996 Games. Given his druthers, Divac would have remained with the Lakers, but he was dealt to Charlotte in the trade that delivered Kobe Bryant to Los Angeles in 1996 and signed with Sacramento as a free agent in 1998.

HIGH WIRE: *Clyde "The Glide" Drexler took a break from his air-obics.*

CLYDE DREXLER

BORN: *6–22–62, at New Orleans, La.*
POSITION: *Guard.*
TEAMS: *Trail Blazers, 1983–95, Rockets, 1995–98.*

Although not most athletic or stylish performer of the Michael Jordan era, the 6–7 Drexler was certainly close. "Clyde the Glide" played on a different level of basketball subspace: slashing to the basket with aerial elegance, hanging majestically in the lane until it was safe to release a soft jumper and popping from long range. But he was most lethal on the break, embarrassing defenders with slick moves and no-look passes. A first round 1983 draft pick, he gave Portland fans 11 exciting seasons, averaging better than 20 points six times with consistent assist and rebound numbers. He led the Trail Blazers to the NBA Finals in 1990 and '92, but his first championship was not until 1995, after a late-season trade to Houston. The eight-time All-Star and 1992 All-NBA first-teamer, was a member of the '92 Olympic team and one of only three players in NBA history to post more than 20,000 points, 6,000

rebounds and 6,000 assists. In 1998 he retired and took over as head basketball coach at the University of Houston where he lasted two seasons.

JOE DUMARS

BORN: *5–24–63, at Shreveport, La.*
POSITION: *Guard.*
TEAM: *Pistons, 1985–99.*

The 6–3 Dumars has been one of the NBA's top shooting guards and classiest acts for more than a decade. Two of his Detroit seasons produced championships (1989 and '90) and another ended in the NBA Finals (1988). Most of Dumars' career was played alongside Isiah Thomas, one of the game's all-time best point guards. Thomas' leadership freed Dumars for the two things he does best: long-range shooting—he has averaged better than 20 points per game in three seasons—and tenacious defense, which earned him four NBA All-Defensive first-team citations during the Pistons' "Bad Boys" era. The 1989 NBA Finals MVP hit a record-tying 10 three-pointers in a 1994 game and earned his sixth All-Star berth in 1997. Now a team-

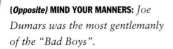

(*Opposite*) **MIND YOUR MANNERS:** *Joe Dumars was the most gentlemanly of the "Bad Boys".*

mate of young superstar Grant Hill, Dumars' leadership was a key ingredient to the Pistons' revival in the middle of the 1990s. Although Dumars retired after the 1998-99 season, he is helping to make sure the Pistons remain a strong team. He is the team's president of basketball operations. As a tribute to this fine gentleman, the NBA named its Sportsmanship Award trophy after him, the only player to have such an honor in his name.

TIM DUNCAN

BORN: *4-25-76 at St. Croix, U.S. Virgin Islands.*
POSITION: *Center.*
TEAMS: *Spurs, 1997-present.*

Expected to be a dominant big man for years to come, Duncan immediately made the Spurs a leading championship contender upon his arrival in San Antonio. By the close of his second year, the Spurs were just that, 1999 NBA titlists. Duncan, paired with veteran Spurs big man David Robinson, helped form one of the great power tandems in NBA lore, proving that the twin-towers approach could succeed after it had failed on so many previous instances. In many ways Duncan is more of a small forward in a center's body, a player with a silky smooth jump shot who has the ballhandling skills to take the ball to the rim from the foul line. Defensively, Duncan also has emerged as a force, his shot blocking causing most smaller players to think twice before entering the lane. Not only was Duncan voted Rookie of the Year in 1998, but he also was named first-team All-NBA that same season. He also was voted second-team All-Defensive his first season in the league and by the close of his second season was first-team All-Defensive. He was selected to play on the U.S. Olympic team for the 2000 Games in Sydney, but a knee injury and surgery late in the season ruled him out.

(*Right*) **SPURRED ON:** *When the going gets rough, the Spurs go to Tim Duncan (right).*

PROFILE IN COURAGE: *The Spurs' Sean Elliott, during the 1999-2000 season, returned to the NBA after a kidney transplant.*

E

MARIO ELIE

BORN: *11-26-63 at New York, N.Y.*
POSITION: *Guard/forward.*
TEAMS: *76ers, 1990, Warriors, 1991-92, Trail Blazers, 1992-93, Rockets, 1993-98, Spurs, 1998-2000, Suns, 2000-present.*

An energy player at both small forward and shooting guard, Elie is the type of emotional leader who has proven the ability to make a good team great. He did that twice in Houston, leading the Rockets to consecutive championships. He then arrived in San Antonio in time for the Spurs' run to the 1999 NBA championship. A player with a unique style, Elie is best from the 3-point arc when shooting a set shot that almost resembles the push shots from previous eras. He often caps off a successful 3-pointer by raising a

(Opposite) **THREE RINGS:** *Mario Elie won two titles in Houston and a third in San Antonio*

finger to his mouth and then into the air, in a sort of "kiss of death" motion. He can also score with various penetration moves to the basket. Among the reasons he is so valued is his ability to play chest-to-chest defense against some of the top small forwards and shooting guards, his grit never questioned by teammates. He also has the type of personality that gets teammates to play harder.

SEAN ELLIOTT

BORN: *2-2-68 at Tucson, Ariz.*
POSITION: *Forward*
TEAMS: *Spurs, 1989-93, Pistons, 1993–94, Spurs, 1994-present.*

At the close of the 1998-99 season, it appeared Sean Elliott's legacy would be as a team leader for San Antonio's first NBA championship team. Little did anyone know at the time that was the least of the story. Instead, it was revealed shortly after the close of the playoffs that Elliott had spent the previous few months playing through kidney failure, in dire need of a transplant. After weeks of waiting for a suitable donor, Elliott found a match in his brother Noel. Shortly thereafter, suc-

cessful transplant surgery was completed. But that was not the end of the story, or the end of Elliott's career. Instead, with full approval of his doctors, Elliott returned to the Spurs at midseason in 2000, and re-emerged as the starting small forward for the playoff-bound Spurs. Along the way, at several of his road stops, Elliott would preach about the need for increased organ donorship. He also would serve as the spokesman for several related foundations.

DALE ELLIS

BORN: *8-6-60 at Marietta, Ga.*
POSITION: *Guard.*
TEAMS: *Mavericks, 1983-86, Sonics, 1986-90, Bucks, 1991-92, Spurs, 1992-94, Nuggets, 1994-97, Sonics, 1997-99, Bucks, 1999-2000, Hornets, 2000, Heat, 2000-present*

A relentless outside shooter, Ellis stands as one of the greatest 3-point threats in NBA history. Unlike some of the game's other top marksman, Ellis remained at a high percentage beyond the 3-point arc despite a high volume of attempts. With a quick release, he could squeeze off shots if defenders were to drop off him by only a foot—or even less. Voted the NBA's Most Improved Player in 1987, he led the NBA in 3-point percentage in 1998, won the league's 3-point shooting contest at All-Star Weekend in 1989, and was voted third-team All-NBA in 1989. Ellis' best years came while with the Seattle SuperSonics. It was with Seattle that he established an NBA record by playing 69 minutes for the Sonics in a five-overtime game against Milwaukee. Ellis could have achieved even more in his career, but ran into differences with coaches when it came to playing time and shot selection.

WAYNE EMBRY

BORN: *3-26-37.*
POSITION: *Forward.*
TEAMS: *Royals, 1958-66, Celtics, 1966-68, Bucks, 1968-69.*

One of the game's first wide bodies, Embry was a big man who was able to muscle his way to the basket. A teammate of such great players as Oscar Robertson and Bill Russell, Embry was able to complement such talents with his rebounding and scoring and overall intensity. The four-time All-Star may have had his most memorable season when he served as Russell's backup in Boston and helped the Celtics to the 1968 championship. Because of his build, Embry was especially adept at setting screens for shooters. It is why so many of his teammates thrived from the perimeter, players such as Robertson and Jack Twyman. Embry's basketball career did not end with his playing days. Instead, he emerged as one of the NBA's top front-office executives, his personnel decisions helping build successful franchises in Milwaukee and Cleveland. In addition to his keen eye for talent, Embry was one of the most personable executives, able to relate the intricacies of front-office management to both fans and the media. He was named to the Hall of Fame in 1999.

ALEX ENGLISH

BORN: *1–5–54, at Columbia, S.C.*
POSITION: *Forward.*
TEAMS: *Bucks, 1976–78, Pacers, 1978–80, Nuggets, 1980–90, Mavericks, 1990–91.*

English was the trigger man for Denver coach Doug Moe's high-powered 1980s offense—a free-lancing style that gave English the opportunity to showcase his uncanny scoring ability. The skinny 6–7 forward, a contradictory combination of graceful glides and awkward contortions, delivered his unorthodox jump shot, arms fully extended over his head, with a flick of his wrist. The shot was virtually unstoppable when he got within 12 feet of the basket. English, a star at the University of South Carolina, was a long-shot second-round draft choice who spent four nondescript seasons with the Bucks and Pacers before being traded to Denver. Over the next decade, he averaged better than 20 points per game nine times, topped 2,000 points in a season eight times and won one scoring title. By his retirement in 1991, English had scored 25,613 points (21.5), grabbed 6,538 rebounds (5.5) and played in eight All-Star Games, numbers that helped to earn him election to the Hall of Fame in 1997.

JULIUS ERVING

See Legends of the NBA *page 108–109*

PATRICK EWING

See Legends of the NBA *page 110–111*

(Left) MOUNTAIN MAN: *Alex English knew how to put the ball in the basket for Denver.*

(Opposite) SUPER SONIC: *Dale Ellis achieve most of his success while playing with the Sonics.*

180

F

DANNY FERRY

BORN: *10-17-66 at Hyattsville, Md.*
POSITION: *Forward.*
TEAMS: *Cavaliers, 1991-2000, Spurs, 2000-present.*

The son of former NBA player and executive Bob Ferry, Danny was a high-scoring forward for some of Duke's legendary teams who had somewhat of an awkward transition to the NBA. Lacking the quickness so essential to play small forward in the NBA and the bulk so critical to play power forward, Ferry found himself caught between positions for most of his career. Even his entry into the NBA proved difficult. Drafted by the Clippers, Ferry refused to play for one of the NBA's worst franchises. Instead, he spent his first professional season in Italy, while a trade was worked out between the Clippers and the Cavaliers. His trade to Cleveland cost the Cavaliers the services of respected guard Ron Harper, and Ferry took the brunt of the criticism. Over his career, however, he proved to be a quality reserve, who could shoot beyond the defensive range of most power forwards and could use his build to score inside against shorter small forwards. Ultimately, he proved to be a valued sixth-man.

SLEEPY FLOYD

BORN: *3-6-60 at Gastonia, N.C.*
POSITION: *Guard*
TEAMS: *Nets, 1982, Warriors, 1983-87, Rockets, 1987-93, Spurs, 1993-94, Nets, 1994-95.*

Although considered a point guard, Floyd was one of the first to play that position but still think shot as often as pass. With a long-armed build, he was known for his daring forays to the basket

SMOOTH SAILING: *Danny Ferry has been able to take his shooting to every edge of the court.*

AWAKE, AWARE: *Don't be fooled by the name, Sleepy Floyd kept opponents on their toes.*

and ability to create shots when they did not appear to be available. One of the truly great streak shooters in the game, Floyd at times could become his team's entire offense during a quarter. He had such a moment on May 10, 1987 in the playoffs for the Warriors against the Lakers, when he set NBA records with 29 points in one quarter and 39 in one half against Los Angeles. Despite his legendary scoring exploits, he made the All-Star Game only once, while with Golden State in 1987. With a wide-eyed approach to the game, Eric entered the NBA with his nickname already in place. The former second-team All-America at Georgetown was the No. 13 pick in the 1982 draft by New Jersey, where he started and finished his career.

CHRIS FORD

BORN: 1-11-49 at Atlantic City, N.J.
POSITION: Forward.
TEAMS: Pistons, 1972-78, Celtics, 1979-82.

Long before he began a lengthy coaching tenure with the Celtics, Bucks and Clippers, Ford was best known for his

CRAZY LIKE A FOX: *Rick Fox has become a perfect role player for the Los Angeles Lakers.*

days as a towel-waving reserve for some of the most energetic Boston teams. But even that does not give Ford the credit he was due at the start of his professional career, when he was a valued contributor for the Detroit Pistons. Ford, throughout his career, was known as a scrappy player, one willing to dive to the floor for a loose ball or give up his body on defense for the benefit of his team. Willing to do all the little things, he emerged as the perfect complement to the Celtics' Big Three of Larry Bird, Robert Parish and Kevin McHale. In 1979, when the NBA followed the lead of the ABA and installed the 3-point shot, Ford became the first NBA player to connect on a 3-point basket. Not only did Ford help the Celtics to one NBA title, but he proved a student of the game, taking the lessons he learned on the court to the sidelines for a respected coaching career.

LARRY FOUST

BORN: 6–24–28, at Painesville, Ohio.
POSITION: Forward/center;
TEAMS: Pistons, 1950–57, Lakers, 1957–60, Hawks, 1960–62.

Foust, one of the best big men in the early NBA, battled the George Mikans, Dolph Schayes and Arnie Risens of his era on even terms as the centerpiece of the Fort Wayne Pistons. Foust, a 6–9, 250-pound giant, entered the professional ranks in 1950 after four outstanding seasons at La Salle University. He made an immediate impact, averaging 13.5 points and 10 rebounds in his rookie season and showing an ability to match up defensively against his fellow big men. Foust was

amazingly consistent, averaging from 12.2 to 17.0 points over his first 10 seasons while topping the 1,000-rebound barrier five times. He also was an eight-time All-Star and an All-NBA first-team selection in 1955. Foust, who helped the Pistons reach the NBA Finals in 1955 and '56, played briefly with Minneapolis and St. Louis before retiring in 1962 with 11,198 points (13.7 per game) and 8,041 rebounds (9.8).

RICK FOX

BORN: 7-24-69 in Toronto, Canada.
POSITION: Forward.
TEAMS: Celtics, 1991-97, Lakers, 1997-present.

A player forced to make the transition between college star and NBA role player, Fox succeeded in the move when he went from the University of North Carolina to the Boston Celtics. Despite the fact that the Celtics already had fallen on hard times upon his arrival, Fox nonetheless was named second-team All-Rookie in 1992. A quality jump shooter who can play scrappy defense, Fox is at his best when used as a complementary-type player, one who feeds off double-teams to hit open shots or goes to the basket when defenses overplay on the perimeter. With Boston struggling during his tenure, he eventually departed to the Lakers as a free agent. Initially he had trouble finding his way, but then emerged to play crucial minutes late in games in place of the more-heralded Glen Rice. With the Lakers led by center Shaquille O'Neal and guard Kobe Bryant, Fox has proven to be exactly the type of role player Los Angeles needs.

STEVE FRANCIS

BORN: *2-21-78 at Silver Spring, Md.*
POSITION: *Guard.*
TEAMS: *Rockets, 1999-present.*

Francis got off to a shaky start in his NBA career, when he refused to play for Vancouver after he was drafted by the Grizzlies with the second selection of the 1999 draft. Saying he did not want to play in Canada, so far from his Maryland home, Francis forced a trade to the Houston Rockets. Francis initially was viewed as a spoiled young star, one who insisted on getting his way. But as he emerged as a rookie, it became clear he was a true prodigy, a player who could change the course of the game on his own with his daring straight-line drives to the basket. A quality floor leader capable of creating his own shot, Francis soon became the focus of the Rockets' offense. With Charles Barkley retiring during Francis' rookie season and Hakeem Olajuwon just a shell of the center he once was, it became apparent in only his first season that Francis was the future of the franchise.

WALT FRAZIER

See Legends of the NBA *page 112–113*

WORLD B. FREE

BORN: *12–9–53, at Atlanta, Ga.*
POSITION: *Guard.*
TEAMS: *76ers, 1975–78, 1986–87, Clippers, 1978–80, Warriors, 1980–82, Cavaliers, 1982–86, Rockets, 1987–88.*

Free, a flashy, fast-shooting 6–3 guard, scored 17,955 points and averaged a lofty 20.3 over a 13-year NBA career that covered five cities. He was instant offense, from his deadly long-range jumper to his creative, whirling, spinning shot repertoire that confounded defenders and brought fans to their feet. But Free, who was drafted by Philadelphia in 1975 out of little Guilford College, had as many detractors as fans. He often was criticized as an undisciplined gunner, a hotdog who would play little defense. Conversely, he

YOUNG GUN: *Steve Francis blasts off for the Houston Rockets every night.*

was praised as a charming man who brought personality and flair to the game. Free, who legally changed his first name from "Lloyd" to "World" in 1981, was all of the above. In retrospect, he was used as a hired gun by struggling teams in search of offensive and box-office help. Free never will be listed among the NBA's great team players, but as a pure offensive force he had few peers.

JOE FULKS

BORN: *10–26–21, at Birmingham, Ky.*
POSITION: *Forward/center.*
TEAMS: *Warriors, 1946–54.*

Fulks is credited as the first player to use a jump shot and he reigned as the early BAA/NBA's scoring sensation. The 6–5 Fulks, nicknamed "Jumpin' Joe," captured scoring championships in his first two Philadelphia seasons, averaging 23.2 points per game in 1946–47 and 22.1 a year later. Both figures were astounding for the period. But there was more to Fulks than just a pretty jump shot. He also was a rugged defensive rebounder and a three-time All-BAA first-team selection. Fulks' all-around play led the Warriors to the BAA's first championship and they advanced to the Finals in 1948 before falling to Baltimore. He finished his eight-year career with a 16.4-point average and his 63-point game in 1949 stood as an NBA record for 10 years. Fulks, who retired in 1954, was named to the NBA 25th Anniversary All-Time Team in 1970, and was elected to the Hall of Fame in 1977.

G

HARRY GALLATIN

BORN: *4–26–27, at Roxana, Ill.*
POSITION: *Forward/center.*
TEAMS: *Knicks, 1948–57, Pistons, 1957–58.*

The 6–6 Gallatin was a workhorse rebounder for a Knicks team that made three consecutive trips to the NBA Finals

in the early 1950s, losing once to Rochester and twice to the powerful Minneapolis Lakers. Never a prolific scorer (13.0 over a 10-year career), he led the NBA in rebounding in 1953– 54 (15.3) and ranked among the league's top 10 rebounders six times. Gallatin was nicknamed "Horse" because of his prolific work on the boards and a durability that allowed him to set a then-NBA record of 682 consecutive games played. The former Missouri State Teachers College star was an All-NBA first-team selection in 1954 and the NBA's Coach of the Year for St. Louis in 1963, five years after his playing career had ended with a final season in Detroit. Gallatin, who was elected to the Hall of Fame in 1990, coached the Knicks in 1965 and '66.

KEVIN GARNETT

BORN: *5-19-76 at Maudlin, S.C.*
POSITION: *Forward.*
TEAMS: *Timberwolves, 1995-present.*

For all the doubts about players making the jump from high school directly to the NBA, without at least some seasoning in the college ranks, Garnett quickly quieted the skeptics upon his arrival in Minnesota in 1995. Having since emerged as one of the premier players in the league, Garnett has proven to be nothing short of a prodigy. Able to learn the NBA game so quickly, Garnett has excelled at virtually every facet of the game, from his shooting to his rebounding to his defensive grace. With such long arms, Garnett has been able to play anywhere from shooting

KEEP AWAY: *Kevin Garnett has passed all the tests the NBA has to offer.*

guard to center. His reach makes his jumpshot practically impossible to defend and the same attribute prevents most opponents from getting off shots in one-on-one situations. Since Garnett's arrival, the Timberwolves have lost talents such as Stephon Marbury and Tom Gugliotta with little in return. Nonetheless, behind Garnett, Minnesota has moved into the elite echelon of teams in the NBA. It only figures to be a matter of time before Garnett receives his first MVP trophy.

GEORGE GERVIN

BORN: *4–27–52, at Detroit, Mich.*
POSITION: *Guard.*
TEAMS: *Virginia Squires (ABA), 1972–74, Spurs (ABA/NBA), 1974–85, Bulls, 1985–86.*

Gervin was one of the great scorers in NBA history. He seemed to glide around the court, delivering the ball to the basket with uncanny accuracy from the most impossible angles and positions. "The Iceman" was always cool and his shot assortment was as clever as his game was explosive. Gervin began his career with the ABA's Virginia Squires after his sophomore season at Eastern Michigan University. But it wasn't until he moved to

the NBA with the Spurs in 1976 that it took off. Gervin averaged more than 20 points nine consecutive seasons and topped 30 twice en route to four scoring titles. When he retired in 1986 after one season in Chicago, Gervin had six 2,000-plus-point seasons, 26,595 combined ABA/NBA points and a 25.1 career average. He also had five All-NBA first-team citations and nine All-Star Game appearances, including a 34-point effort that netted him MVP honors in 1980.

KENDALL GILL

BORN: *5-25-68 at Chicago, Ill.*
POSITION: *Guard/forward.*
TEAMS: *Hornets, 1990-93, Sonics, 1993-95, Hornets, 1995-96, Nets, 1996-present.*

A slashing scorer who has developed his outside stroke over the years, Gill has had trouble finding his niche since being voted third-team All-Rookie in 1990 out of Illinois. After failing to mesh in Charlotte, Gill was traded to Seattle, where he ran into problems with coach George Karl. Gill then was dealt back to the Hornets for guard Hersey Hawkins, but the reunion was short-lived, with Gill soon dealt to New Jersey. It is in New Jersey where Gill has blossomed. One of the league's best players at playing the passing lane, Gill tied an NBA record with 11 steals in an April 3, 1999 game against the Heat. He led the NBA in steals that season, with an average of 2.68 per game.

(Left) ICE MAN: *George Gervin, left, was a brilliant offensive force in San Antonio.*

(Right) ON GUARD: *The net results have been good for Kendall Gill in New Jersey.*

While Gill has the skills to excel, he is caught between being a small forward and a shooting guard. In fact, he has suffered in New Jersey because of the Nets' glut of talent at shooting guard.

ARTIS GILMORE

BORN: *9–21–49, at Chipley, Fla.*
POSITION: *Center.*
TEAMS: *Kentucky Colonels (ABA), 1971–76, Bulls, 1976–82, 1987, Spurs, 1982–87, Celtics, 1988.*

Gilmore, at 7–2 and 265 pounds, was a powerful center whose prolific numbers were overshadowed by contemporary Kareem Abdul-Jabbar. Gilmore was the polar opposite of Abdul-Jabbar—a plodding, no-finesse inside bruiser who dominated with his powerful legs and legendary strength. And whereas Abdul-Jabbar played on six NBA championship teams, Gilmore never got close to a title in 12 NBA seasons with Chicago, San Antonio and Boston. But nobody can deny Gilmore his numbers, which were compiled over a 17-year career in the ABA and NBA: 24,041 points (18.1), 16,330 rebounds (12.3), 11 All-Star Games and one regular-season and playoff MVP (both in the ABA). When Gilmore retired in 1988, he was the NBA's all-time leader in field-goal percentage (.599), a product of his short left-handed hook, delivered for years from point-blank range. Gilmore, who earned just about every ABA honor imaginable in five years with Kentucky, played for the Colonels' 1975 ABA championship team.

TOM GOLA

BORN: *1–13–33, at Philadelphia, Pa.*
POSITION: *Guard/forward.*
TEAMS: *Warriors, 1955–62, Knicks, 1962–66.*

The versatile Gola is one of two men to play on NIT, NCAA and NBA championship teams—and all came in Philadelphia, the city of his birth. The 6–6 Gola, a local high school hero, chose to play collegiate basketball at La Salle and his achievements there took on a storybook aura. En route to becoming college basketball's first four-time All-American, Gola averaged 20.9 points, grabbed an

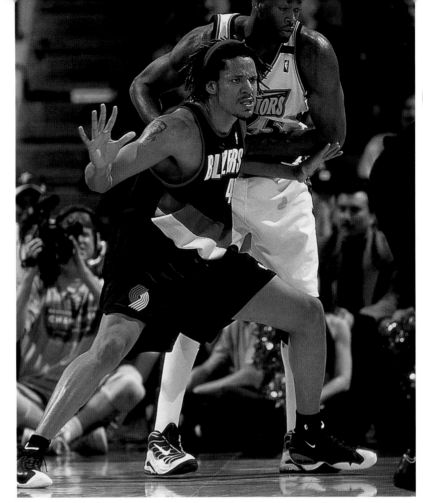

ON FIRE: *Even a bad hair day never stopped Brian Grant (front) from performing on the court.*

NCAA career-record 2,201 rebounds and earned 1955 College Player of the Year honors. He also led La Salle to the 1952 NIT and 1954 NCAA Tournament titles. When Philadelphia grabbed Gola with the first pick of the 1955 NBA draft, the Warriors got a quick, aggressive performer who could score, pass, rebound and play stifling defense. As a rookie, Gola teamed with Neil Johnston and Paul Arizin on the Warriors' 1956 championship team. He played 10 seasons with the Warriors and Knicks and performed in four All-Star Games. Gola was elected to the Hall of Fame in 1975.

GAIL GOODRICH

BORN: *4–23–43, at Los Angeles, Calif.*
POSITION: *Guard.*
TEAMS: *Lakers, 1965–68, 1970–76, Suns, 1968–70, Jazz, 1976–79.*

Goodrich was a versatile little man who could swing effectively between the point and shooting guard positions. The 6–1 lefthander was a phenomenal scorer who always performed in an attacking mode. He would barrel through the lane, pull up for quick jumpers or create his own shots with deft one-on-one moves. Goodrich, also a good long-range shooter, had lightning-quick hands that allowed him to get off impossible shots over bigger defenders. After leading UCLA to NCAA Tournament titles in 1964 and '65, Goodrich spent his first three NBA seasons coming off the Los Angeles Lakers' bench and the next two as point guard for the expansion Phoenix Suns. When he was reacquired by the Lakers, Goodrich became the focal point of the offense, averaging 20 points or better four straight years. The five-time All-Star, a 1974 All-NBA first-teamer who played his final three seasons in New Orleans, retired in 1979 with 19,181 points (18.6 per game) and 4,805 assists (4.7).

BRIAN GRANT

BORN: *3-5-72 at Columbus, Ohio*
POSITION: *Forward.*
TEAMS: *Kings, 1994-97, Trail Blazers, 1997-2000, Heat, 2000-present.*

An energetic forward known for his blond dreadlocks, Grant has emerged as a

GOING FORWARD: *Orlando's Horace Grant keeps his eyes on the prize no matter what he's doing for the Magic.*

premier defender at power forward and a player who can dominate the boards at times. While he has the skills to emerge as a go-to player, with the Trail Blazers he was forced into a secondary role because of the presence of talents such as Rasheed Wallace and Scottie Pippen. What Grant can provide is relentless energy against even the most physical of power forwards. If not for a series of chronic injuries, Grant likely would have been recognized as an All-Star by this point in his career. He was selected first-team All-Rookie when he joined Sacramento out of Xavier in 1994 and his charitable deeds were recognized when he was awarded the J. Walter Kennedy Citizenship Award in 1999. With Portland currently in a win-now mode, with several veterans at the ends of their careers dotting the roster, Grant was traded to Miami in a blockbuster deal that brought Shawn Kemp from Cleveland.

HORACE GRANT

BORN: *7–4–65, at Augusta, Ga.*
POSITION: *Forward.*
TEAMS: *Bulls, 1987–94, Magic, 1994–99, Sonics, 1999-present.*

The 6–10 Grant is a highly respected blue-collar banger who provides the Seattle Supersonics with intensity, leadership, rebounding, interior defense and many of the little things that don't show up in box scores. The proof of Grant's value can be found in his three championship rings, reminders of seven seasons in Chicago where he did much of the trenchwork for the Bulls. After signing with the Orlando Magic as a free agent in 1994, he was asked to take the inside pressure off center Shaquille O'Neal, a job he performed admirably for two seasons before Shaq left for the Lakers. Grant averaged 12.8 points and 9.7 rebounds for an Orlando team that reached the 1995 NBA Finals. Grant, a 1987 first-round draft pick out of Clemson University, complements his offensive work with a tenacious, clawing defense that limits intrusions into the paint. The 1994 All-Star, whose twin brother Harvey played in Washington, has shot 50 percent or better from the field in all of his 10 pro seasons. But that averaged dipped to .459 and .434 in his last two seasons in Orlando and to .444 in his first season in Seattle after the Magic traded him, along with Billy Owens, Dale Ellis, Don MacLean and the draft rights to Duke star Corey Maggette on June 30, 1999. Having Patrick Ewing on board could help to bring his average up again.

A.C. GREEN

BORN: *10-4-63 at Portland, Ore.*
POSITION: *Forward*
TEAMS: *Lakers, 1985–93, Suns, 1993–97, Mavericks, 1997–99, Lakers, 1999–2000.*

The NBA's ultimate iron man, Green holds the streak for most consecutive games played, a streak that reached the 1,100-game mark during the 1999-2000 season. But it is more than longevity that has defined Green's career. A quality defender and rebounder despite his somewhat slight build, Green has gone from the youngster-in-training during the Lakers' championship era to a wily veteran who has turned mentor to many of today's power players. A clean liver who has championed the cause of celibacy, Green returned to the Lakers for the 1999-2000 season and earned his way into the starting lineup. Although he has made only one All-Star Game appearance, he is respected as one of the premier playoff power players and he rarely is guilty of the type of errors that can be so costly in the postseason. Despite his advancing age, retirement does not appear to be in his near-term future. It would not be surprising to see him remain to work with Shaquille O'Neal for years to come.

187

DIRECT CURRENT: *A.C. Green energized the front lines of some of the Los Angeles Lakers' most successful rosters.*

188

HAL GREER

BORN: *6–26–36, at Huntington, W. Va.*
POSITION: *Guard.*
TEAM: *Nationals/76ers, 1958–73.*

Greer's sweet jump shot was a Syracuse and Philadelphia staple for 15 NBA seasons. Through good days and bad, the 6–2 guard provided consistent, durable, athletic play that made him one of the stars of his era. Greer joined the Syracuse Nationals as a second-round 1958 draft pick out of Marshall University and carved out a Hall of Fame career as one of the game's best outside shooters. He had the innate ability to dominate games—an ability that resulted in a career average of 19.2 and eight seasons of 20 or more points per game. Greer also recorded 4,540 career assists and played in 1,122 games—a record when he retired in 1973. But his most memorable season was 1966–67, when he averaged 22.1 points and teamed with Wilt Chamberlain, Billy Cunningham, Chet Walter, Lucious Jackson and Wali Jones on the 76ers team that ended Boston's eight-year championship reign. Greer,

who played in 10 All-Star Games, was elected to the Hall of Fame in 1981.

DARRELL GRIFFITH

BORN: *6–16–58, at Louisville, Ky.*
POSITION: *Guard.*
TEAM: *Jazz, 1980–91.*

Griffith, alias "Dr. Dunkenstein," was a high-flying guard who excited fans with his acrobatic dunks and long-range bombs. From his first game for the University of Louisville through his 10 NBA seasons with the Utah Jazz, the 6–4 Griffith was an electrifying performer who kept fans, players and coaches on the edge of their seats. Griffith was blessed with a 4-foot vertical leap that was neutralized by knee problems. But he still could sky with the best of the game's top players and his outside shot was lethal. His only weakness was a preference for the perimeter game that kept him from using his inside ability. After leading Louisville to the 1980 NCAA Tournament championship and claiming national Player of the Year honors, Griffith averaged 20.6 points for Utah and was named

NBA Rookie of the Year. He never enjoyed that level of success again, but he finished his productive career in 1991 with 12,391 points (16.2).

ERNIE GRUNFELD

BORN: *4-24-55 at New York, N.Y.*
POSITION: *Forward*
TEAMS: *Bucks, 1977-79, Kings, 1979-82, Knicks, 1982-86.*

The co-star of the Ernie and Bernie show at the University of Tennessee along with scoring legend Bernard King, Grunfeld carved out an NBA career for himself behind his gritty play at forward. Although never a high scorer in the NBA, Grunfeld's outside shooting kept defenses honest and he had the type of court savvy to make those around him better. After moving from the Bucks to the Kings, he was reunited with King later in his career with the Knicks. In fact, reunions became common for Grunfeld. Shortly after his playing days with the Knicks, he returned to the team and eventually rose to become general manager. After crafting a team that advanced to the 1999 NBA Finals, Grunfeld took his management skills to Milwaukee, where his NBA career began. There, he also served as general manager. Having twice played as a tandem, Grunfeld and King were inducted together into the New York City Basketball Hall of Fame in 1994.

RICHIE GUERIN

BORN: *5-29-32, at New York, N.Y.*
POSITION: *Guard.*
TEAMS: *Knicks, 1956–63, Hawks, 1963–67, 1968–70.*

Guerin was an intense, up-tempo guard who doubled for five of his 13 NBA seasons as player-coach of the St. Louis/ Atlanta Hawks. Guerin, one of the last two-handed set-shot artists, was most comfortable in the attack mode, using his speed to blow past defenders in his trademark dash to the basket. At 6–4, he was bigger than most guards and quick enough to badger them with his stubborn defense. Guerin, a six-time All-Star, dove

JUMP SHOT: *A four-foot vertical leap made Darrell Griffith a thrilling performer.*

for loose balls, battled for rebounds and sped up the game with his very presence on the court. After four years at Iona College, Guerin played seven-plus seasons for the New York Knicks, averaging better than 20 points four times and twice topping 500 assists. Guerin began doubling as Hawks coach in 1964 and directed the team to 327 victories through 1971–72, two years after his retirement as a player. He finished his career with 14,676 points (17.3) and 4,211 assists (5.0).

TOM GUGLIOTTA

BORN: *12-19-1969 at Huntington Station, N.Y.*
POSITION: *Forward.*
TEAMS: *Bullets, 1992-95, Warriors, 1995, Timberwolves, 1995-98, Suns, 1998-present.*

Known as "Googs," Gugliotta had to toil through several trades early in his career before settling down to become known as one of the most versatile forwards in the league. Despite early success and a first-team All-Rookie nod with the Bullets in 1993, Gugliotta two seasons later was dealt to Golden State for Chris Webber. Before he even unpacked, he then was shipped to Minnesota for Donyell Marshall. It was with the Timberwolves that Gugliotta began to make a name for himself, as a forward able to play a rugged inside style like a power player or a jump-shooting game like a finesse player. His career blossomed when he joined the Suns as a free agent and he earned a berth on the 2000 U.S. entry for the Sydney Olympics, only to have to forfeit that berth due to injury. The two-time All-Star is one of the most gracious players in the league and often has pushed himself to play through injury.

WELL-TRAVELED: *Tom Gugliotta has traversed the NBA map, but has endured nonetheless.*

190

COIN A PHRASE: *Anfernee "Penny" Hardaway would like to return to the form he had in Orlando.*

H

CLIFF HAGAN

BORN: *12–9–31, at Owensboro, Ky.*
POSITION: *Forward.*
TEAMS: *Hawks, 1956–66, Dallas Chaparrals (ABA), 1967–70.*

Hagan will forever be remembered as one of the two forwards traded by the Boston Celtics for the draft rights to Bill Russell. But Hagan forged a Hall of Fame career of his own—elected in 1977—using a deadly hook shot and a natural scoring prowess to amass 14,870 career points in 10 NBA seasons with St. Louis and three more with the ABA's Dallas Chaparrals. The 6–4 Hagan, a high-scoring collegiate star at the University of Kentucky under legendary Coach Adolph Rupp, teamed with Bob Pettit on a Hawks team that won five Western Division titles, captured the 1958 championship and reached the NBA Finals three other times. He averaged 18 points over his NBA career and played in five All-Star Games. The mobile Hagan, who once scored 26 points in a quarter, completed his career in 1970 as player-coach of the Chaparrals.

ANFERNEE HARDAWAY

BORN: *7–18–72, at Memphis, Tenn.*
POSITION: *Guard/forward.*
TEAM: *Magic, 1993–99, Suns, 1999-present.*

The athletic 6–7 point guard lit the fuse in Orlando's offense upon his arrival in 1993. Between 1996 and '97 he matured into a team leader and by the season's end, the Magic had reached the playoffs, and extended the Miami Heat to five games. "Penny" Hardaway has the Jordanesque inside-outside ability to carry an offense, but prefers using his explosive talents to set up opportunities for others. Drafted out of Memphis University after his junior season, he quickly made his presence felt: averaging 16.0 points, 5.4 rebounds and 6.6 assists as an NBA rookie, improving to 20.9, 4.4

and 7.2, respectively, in 1994–95, earning All-NBA first-team honors and helping the Magic reach the NBA Finals. Injuries limited Hardaway to 19 games for the Magic in '97–98 amid suggestions that he was no longer totally commited to playing for Orlando and new coach Chuck Daly. The two lasted one more season together in Orlando before Daly quit and Hardaway was traded to Phoenix for Danny Manning, Pat Garrity and two first-round draft choices. Although injuries limited him to just 60 games in his first season with the Suns, Hardaway averaged 16.9 points, 5.8 rebounds, 5.3 assists and 1.57 steals per game and looked to be well on his way toward re-establishing himself as one of the league's stars.

TIM HARDAWAY

BORN: *9–1–66, at Chicago, Ill.*
POSITION: *Guard.*
TEAM: *Warriors, 1989–96, Heat, 1996–present.*

Before a blown-out knee cost Hardaway one full season and parts of two others, he was penetrating the upper echelon of NBA point guards. When he returned to action in 1994–95, he lacked the explosiveness that made him so difficult to defend. But that returned in 1996–97 when he helped Miami finish 61–21 and earned NBA First Team All-Star honors. Hardaway averaged 20.3 points and 8.6 assists and took the Heat to the Eastern Conference Finals. Although his numbers trailed off slightly a year later (18.9 points and 8.3 assists per game) and Miami disappointed in the play-offs, Hardaway confirmed his status as one of the game's elite with his selection to the US World Championship team. At his best the 6-foot Hardaway, a four time All-Star who was traded to Miami midway through the 1995–96 season, was one of those rare players who could beat you with the shot or the pass and desperately wanted the ball in his hands with the game on the line. But injuries have prevented him from being his best. He averaged 17.4 points and 7.3 assists in the 1998-99 regular season, but hobbled through the playoffs averaging 9.0 points and 6.4 assists as the top-seeded Heat lost to the eighth-seeded New York Knicks in the first round. Still

STILL BURNING: *Tim Hardaway still plays with his usual intensity despite being slowed by injuries.*

more injuries caused him to miss 30 games in the 1999-2000 regular season, but he did average 13.4 points and 7.4 assists. But again, the Heat lost to the Knicks in the playoffs—this time in the second round.

DEREK HARPER

BORN: *10-13-61 at Elberton, Ga.*
POSITION: *Guard.*
TEAMS: *Mavericks, 1983–94, Knicks, 1994–96, Magic, Mavericks, 1996–97, Magic, 1997–98, Lakers, 1998–99.*

Known as perhaps the best player never to be selected for an All-Star Game,

Harper had a dual existence during his NBA career. For a decade, he teamed with Rolando Blackman in Dallas to form one of the most explosive backcourts in the league, the long-standing tandem pushing the Mavericks as far as the Western Conference finals. From there, Harper moved around the league to several teams, used mostly as a defensive force. Tenacious against point guards regardless of their size or quickness, Harper proved a perfect fit for teams with major playoffs designs. Among the league's top 3-point shooters early in his career, Harper had his stroke fail him toward the latter stages of his tenure. He wound up jumping from

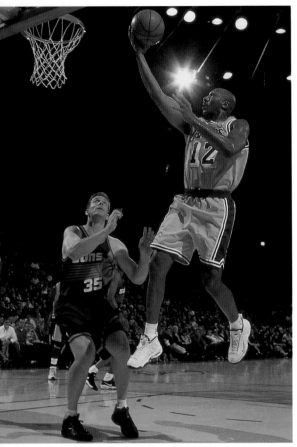

EASY TWO: *Derek Harper's (12) distinguished playing career ended in Los Angeles in 1999.*

team to team at the end of his career, finally deciding to retire rather than accept a trade from the Lakers to the Pistons in 1999. He eventually moved into the Dallas front office in 1999.

RON HARPER

BORN: *1-20-64 at Dayton, Ohio.*
POSITION: *Guard.*
TEAMS: *Cavaliers, 1986-90, Clippers, 1990-94, Bulls, 1994-99, Lakers, 1999-present.*

Like so many players with lengthy careers, Harper has displayed the ability to reinvent his game as his tenure continued. At the start of his career, Harper was a high-flying, acrobatic scorer from the backcourt, whether it was with the Cavaliers or the Clippers. But after a knee injury took much of the hop out of his step, Harper became something far different. By the time he landed in Chicago, Harper was considered more of a defensive guard, one who could hit the 3-pointer, but certainly

not a player who could be at the heart of the offense. Of course, playing alongside Michael Jordan that was not a problem. The result was the second set of three consecutive championships for the Bulls, with Harper filling the role that John Paxson and B.J. Armstrong had filled during Jordan's first three-peat. From there, Harper moved on to the Lakers, serving as the sage backcourt presence alongside Kobe Bryant and Shaquille O'Neal.

CLEM HASKINS

BORN: *7-11-43.*
POSITION: *Guard.*
TEAMS: *Bulls, 1967-70, Suns, 1970-74, Bullets, 1974-76.*

Known at "The Gem," a slashing, quick player with an ability to get to the basket, Haskins first broke into the NBA with the Bulls and broke the 20-point barrier by averaging 20.3 for Chicago in 1969-70. From there he expanded his game with the Suns, using his slashing skills to average in double figures in all three of his seasons in Phoenix. As smart player who could get the ball to an open teammate, his statistics dwindled during the final two seasons of his career, with Washington. But what Haskins had learned in the NBA, he took back to the college ranks, achieving success first at Western Kentucky and then moving on as coach at the University of Minnesota, which he led to a Final Four appearance in the NCAA Tournament, producing NBA quality players, such as Voshon Lenard. Many of today's quick guards are utilizing the same type of slashing moves that had made Haskins successful during extended stretches of his NBA career.

JOHN HAVLICEK

See Legends of the NBA *page 114–115*

CONNIE HAWKINS

BORN: *7-17-42, at Brooklyn, N.Y.*
POSITION: *Forward/center.*
TEAM: *Pittsburgh/Minneapolis Pipers (ABA), 1967-69, Suns, 1969-73, Lakers, 1973-75, Hawks, 1975-76.*

Hawkins, a New York City playground legend, was one of the most spectacular

and flamboyant frequent fliers of the pre-Dr. J era. Although his career was disjointed, Hawkins nevertheless impressed contemporaries with an acrobatic, above-the-rim presence that left fans and fellow players gasping. He left the University of Iowa after his freshman season and enjoyed short stints with the American Basketball League, the Harlem Globetrotters and the American Basketball Association. Hawkins was MVP for the champion Pittsburgh Pipers in the ABA's 1967–68 debut season, when he averaged 26.8 points and 13.5 rebounds. He signed with the NBA's Suns in 1969 and spent four-plus seasons in Phoenix, averaging more than 20 points three times and earning an All-NBA first-team citation in 1970 (24.6 points and 10.4 rebounds per game). The 6–8 "Hawk" played briefly with Los Angeles and Atlanta before retiring in 1976, and he was elected to the Hall of Fame in 1992.

HERSEY HAWKINS

BORN: *6-26-66 at Chicago, Ill.*
POSITION: *Guard*
TEAMS: *76ers, 1988–93, Hornets, 1993–95, Sonics, 1995–99, Bulls, 1999–2000, Hornets, 2000-present.*

A prolific college scorer at Bradley, Hawkins never lived up to those standards when he jumped to the NBA, although he did earn a first-team All-Rookie selection in 1988. Mostly, Hawkins spent his career as a reliable spot-up shooter for post-up players to pass to outside. It was in Seattle where Hawkins made his greatest impact. After Seattle had been ousted in the first round of the playoffs in successive season, Hawkins replaced Kendall Gill in Seattle's backcourt and helped the Sonics advance to the NBA Finals against Michael Jordan and the Bulls. The type of team player who could mesh in any locker room, Hawkins was awarded the J. Walter Kennedy Citizenship Award for his community efforts while with the SuperSonics in 1999. Although he has made only one All-Star Game, Hawkins routinely has been featured in the playoffs, getting to the postseason with the 76ers, Hornets and Sonics. At this point his leadership is the most valuable skill he possesses.

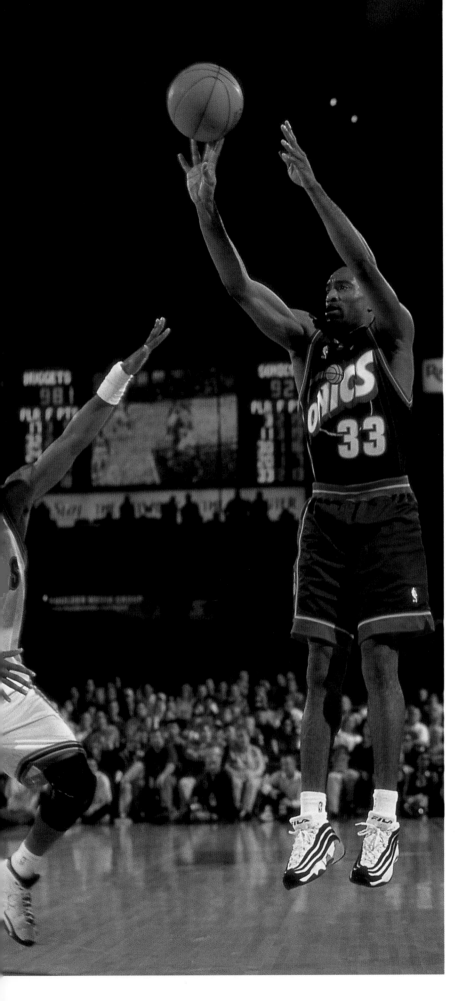

ELVIN HAYES
See Legends of the NBA *page 116–117*

SPENCER HAYWOOD
BORN: *4–22–49, at Silver City, Miss.*
POSITION: *Forward/center.*
TEAMS: *Denver Rockets (ABA), 1969–70, SuperSonics, 1970–75, Knicks, 1975–79, Jazz, 1979, Lakers, 1979–80, Bullets, 1981–83.*

The 6–9 Haywood was a spectacular athlete who is best remembered for a landmark legal battle. He was an explosive leaper who could dominate games offensively and defensively. After his sophomore season at the University of Detroit, Haywood put together an incredible debut season for the ABA's Denver Rockets: He averaged 30 points and 19.5 rebounds per game, and claimed regular-season MVP, All-Star Game MVP and Rookie of the Year honors. But his 1970 jump to Seattle was interrupted by lawsuits that eventually gave NBA teams the right to draft underage college players as "hardship" cases. Haywood averaged better than 20 points in all five of his Sonics seasons, earned All-NBA first-team status twice and played in four All-Star Games before being traded to New York. His NBA career, which lasted seven more seasons before ending in 1983 at Washington, produced 14,592 points (19.2) and 7,038 rebounds (9.3). Haywood was a part-time player on the Lakers' 1980 championship team.

TOM HEINSOHN
BORN: *8–26–34, at Jersey City, N.J.*
POSITION: *Forward.*
TEAM: *Celtics, 1956–65.*

The 6–7 Heinsohn was a vital cog in the Boston Celtics' championship machine of the 1950s and '60s. When the two-time Holy Cross All-American arrived with Bill Russell via the 1956 draft, Boston began the greatest victory parade in team-sports history, a run that produced 11 championships in 13 years. The versatile Heinsohn, who led the star-studded Celtics in scoring from 1960 to '62, earned eight

HAWK'S LANDING: *Hersey Hawkins has spent his career perched on the perimeter.*

JAZZ MAN: *Jeff Hornacek was a star in Utah.*

championship rings in his nine seasons while amassing 12,194 points (18.6), 5,749 rebounds (8.8), six All-Star Game selections and a 1957 nod as NBA Rookie of the Year. Heinsohn, who also enjoyed championship stature as a member of Holy Cross' 1954 NIT title team, later coached the Celtics to 427 regular-season victories and two more titles (1974 and '76). He retired in 1965 with a 19.8 career playoff scoring average (104 games) and was elected to the Hall of Fame in 1986.

GRANT HILL

BORN: *10–5–72, at Dallas, Tex.*
POSITION: *Forward.*
TEAM: *Pistons, 1994–2000, Magic, 2000–present..*

In his 1994–95 co-Rookie of the Year debut with Detroit, Hill was compared often to all-everything Chicago forward Scottie Pippen, in skills as well as poise and court presence. At the end of Hill's third NBA season, he was being compared to Pippen's teammate, Michael Jordan, as one of the game's most complete players on the court and one of the most charismatic off the court. He is at his best when he slashes to the basket, creating shots for teammates as well as

(Opposite) **HILL SIDE:** *Grant Hill ran the show for the Pistons.*

himself. He will drive on anybody and he always finds a way to get the ball to the basket. Hill, the son of former NFL running back Calvin Hill, also led the NBA with 13 triple-doubles in 1996–97, a season in which he was selected NBA first team All-Star. Hill, a five-time All-Star, suffered slightly in a disappointing 1997–98 season for the Pistons, but averages of 21.1 points, 7.7 boards and 6.8 assists per game that season reaffirmed his elite status. His scoring went up to a career-high 25.8 points per game in 1999-2000, but his frustration increased when he was forced out of the playoffs with a fractured ankle. In the off-season, free-agent Hill stunned the Pistons by signing with the Orlando Magic.

TYRONE HILL

BORN: *3-19-68 at Cincinnati, Ohio.*
POSITION: *Forward.*
TEAMS: *Warriors, 1990-93, Cavaliers, 1993-97, Bucks, 1997-99, 76ers, 1999-present.*

A fierce and physical player, Hill led the NBA in fouls in 1992. But that could be expected from a player who goes hard to the basket on every shot, is not afraid about mixing it up inside against bigger opponents and relishes the opportunity to convert a missed attempt by a teammate into an offensive rebound and follow-up basket. Although he lacks the shooting touch to take his game too far from the rim, Hill is an exhaustive worker beneath the boards, often playing through the types of injuries that would sideline other big men. His gritty style earned him an All-Star Game berth in 1995, but what he adds to a team often cannot be listed quantitatively. A player who has been at the heart of the 76ers' tenacious team defense, Hill makes all the right moves on the defensive end, covering up for teammates' mistakes and making sure any opponent who passes through his lane gets a not-so-subtle shove or bump.

JEFF HORNACEK

BORN: *5–3–63, at Elmhurst, Ill.*
POSITION: *Guard.*
TEAMS: *Suns, 1986–92, 76ers, 1992–94, Jazz, 1994–present.*

Hornacek is a heady, fundamentally sound shooting guard who provides the perfect complement to Utah's "Big Two" of Karl Malone and John Stockton. Having the 6-4 former Iowa State U. player on the court with Stockton was like having two point guards at the same time. Hornacek made the extra pass and he was an efficient shooter—50 percent from the floor, 87 percent from the free-throw line and an impressive 40 percent from 3-point range. He once hit a record-tying 11 consecutive 3-pointers. Hornacek also was a gritty defender whose only real deficiencies were rebounding and showmanship. The one-time All-Star was the 46th pick of the 1986 draft after an unspectacular college career and he played six solid seasons in Phoenix, followed by one and a half years in Philadelphia. Traded to Utah in 1994, Hornacek was the team's second leading scorer for the second straight season as he helped the Jazz to its second NBA Finals in as many years. He announced that the 1999-2000 season would be his last, and he went out with a bang, challenging Calvin Murphy's free-throw percentage record of .958 for most of the season before settling for a league-leading .950 (171 of 180.) Every time he stepped to the line, he rubbed his right hand along his jaw as a sign to his children.

ROBERT HORRY

BORN: *8-25-70 at Hartford, Md.*
POSITION: *Forward.*
TEAMS: *Rockets, 1992-96, Suns, 1996, Lakers, 1997-present.*

Not a typical power forward because of his lithe build, Horry has made a career out of drawing opposing big men out of the lane with his 3-point shooting. He proved particularly effective at that at the start of his career with the Rockets, winning NBA titles in Houston in 1994 and '95. An All-Rookie selection when he broke into the NBA in 1993, Horry holds several playoff records for his 3-point shooting and also is in the record book for his seven steals in an NBA Finals game against Orlando in 1995. For most of his career, Horry has been shuffled between the forward positions, considered by some too frail to succeed at power forward and

SILENT APPROACH: *The "H" in his name is silent, but Robert Horry has lots of thunder in his game.*

Wade Houston, the younger of the Houstons was not nearly as effective at the start of his pro career, buried on the end of the bench in Detroit. But even at that stage of Houston's career, NBA scouts could see the potential for greatness. The Knicks certainly did, preparing a free-agent bid that lured Houston out of Detroit. The result has been a Knicks team built around Houston's considerable shooting skills. Houston immediately elevated the Knicks and once Latrell Sprewell was acquired in a trade with the Warriors, New York had one of the most potent backcourts in the NBA. Houston made his All-Star Game debut in 2000, but he is best known for his rim-rattling buzzer-beating shot in the first round of the 1999 playoffs that began New York's run all the way to the NBA Finals. A deadly 3-point shooter, Houston tied an NBA record by converting seven 3-pointers in a half while with the Pistons against Chicago.

JUWAN HOWARD

BORN: *2–7–73, at Chicago, Ill.*
POSITION: *Forward/center.*
TEAM: *Bullets/Wizards, 1994–present*

Howard is a team-oriented workhorse who can swing between the small and power forward positions. He led all rookies in rebounding (8.4 per game) in 1994–95 and followed with a 22.1-point and 8.2-rebound second season. In 1996–97, he helped lead the Bullets to their first post-season in nine years but, as his scoring average dipped to 18.5 a year later, the newly-named Wizards missed out on post-season by a single agonising game. His turnaround jumper is a polished, high-percentage shot. The 6–9, 250-pound Howard was a member of the University of Michigan's "Fab Five" team that lost in the NCAA Tournament championship game in 1992 and '93. His role for the Wolverines was much the same as it is for the Bullets: take high-percentage shots and play hard-nosed defense. Howard is not spectacular, but compensates with gritty trenchwork. The departure of Chris Webber in 1998 and the arrival of Mitch Richmond from the Kings was supposed to rejuvenate the Wizards. But that did not happen. Howard's averages dipped from 18.9 points and 8.1

by others as too slow to compete at small forward. But with his long-armed build, he has succeeded at almost every stop. He likely would still be with the Suns if not for tossing a towel at then-coach Danny Ainge during an argument in the middle of a game. As it turns out, he has emerged as a solid fit for the Shaquille O'Neal Lakers.

ALLAN HOUSTON

BORN: *4-20-71 at Louisville, Ky.*
POSITION: *Guard.*
TEAMS: *Pistons, 1993-96, Knicks, 1996-present.*

A prolific scorer at the University of Tennessee while playing under his father,

HE'S NO.1: *Allen Houston may have the most consistent release in the NBA.*

rebounds per game in 1998-99 to 14.9 and 5.7 in 1999-2000. But the Wizards' struggles were hardly his fault. Since 1996–97, the team has had seven head coaches: Jim Lynam Bob Staak, Bernie Bickerstaff, Jim Brovelli, Gar Heard, Darrell Walker and Leonard Hamilton.

BAILEY HOWELL

Born: 1–20–37, at Middleton, Tenn.
Position: Forward.
Teams: Pistons, 1959–64, Bullets, 1964–66, Celtics, 1966–70, 76ers, 1970–71.

Howell scored 17,770 points (18.7) and grabbed 9,383 rebounds (9.9) over a 12-year career as an NBA overachiever. "I don't have the ability of some of the players in this league," admitted Howell, who more than compensated with a hustle that made him a premier offensive and defensive forward. Howell was a relentless offensive rebounder with a deadly jump shot from the wing. The Mississippi State star started with Detroit in 1959 and played seven seasons with the Pistons and Bullets, averaging over 20 points three

HELP WANTED: *Juwan Howard (left) has faced several road blocks in Washington.*

times with double-digit rebounding totals six straight years. His greatest fame came as part of Boston's 1968 and '69 championship teams, a perfect fit for the leadership and teamwork he brought to the game. Howell, a six-time All-Star, retired in 1971 and was elected to the Hall of Fame in 1997.

LOU HUDSON

BORN: *7–11–44, at Greensboro, N.C.*
POSITION: *Guard/forward.*
TEAMS: *Hawks, 1966–77, Lakers, 1977–79.*

Hudson, known for his sweet jumper and steady influence, was a versatile swing-man for the St. Louis/Atlanta Hawks and Los Angeles Lakers for 13 NBA seasons. The 6–5 Hudson made a career out of mismatches and the perfectly-executed jump shot that earned him the nickname "Sweet Lou." If he played small forward, he was too quick for opposing defenders. If he played shooting guard, he was able to post up smaller opponents. He also had an explosive first step that gave him access to the lane and helped him defend quicker guards. Hudson, a University of Minnesota product, was drafted fourth overall by the Hawks in 1966. He assumed scoring responsibilities with the retirement of Bob Pettit and Cliff Hagan and averaged better than 20 points in

seven of his 11 St. Louis/ Atlanta seasons. When the six-time All-Star retired in 1979 after two seasons in Los Angeles, he had amassed 17,940 career points (20.2 per game) and 3,926 rebounds (4.4).

I

DAN ISSEL

BORN: *10–25–48, at Batavia, Ill.*
POSITION: *Forward/center.*
TEAMS: *Kentucky Colonels (ABA), 1970–75, Nuggets (ABA/NBA), 1975–85.*

What Issel lacked in style and grace he made up for with durability, intensity and a blue-collar work ethic. Nicknamed "Horse," the 6–9, 240-pounder played in 1,218 of a possible 1,242 career games over 15 ABA and NBA seasons. A 33.9-point scorer in his senior year at the University of Kentucky, Issel averaged 29.9 in 1970 for the ABA's Kentucky Colonels, winning co-Rookie of the Year honors and his only career scoring title. After helping the Colonels win the 1975 ABA championship, Issel was traded to Denver and began a successful 10-year run as one of the franchise's most prolific performers. He averaged better than 20 points per game in seven seasons for the Nuggets and completed his career in 1985 with combined ABA/NBA totals of 11,133 rebounds (9.1) and 27,482 points (22.6), which ranks fifth on the all-time scoring list. Issel later coached the Denver Nuggets for three years, and was elected to the Hall of Fame in 1993. After a three-year hiatus, Issel returned as the team's vice president and general manager in 1998 and was behind the bench again for seasons 1999–2000 and 2000–01.

ALLEN IVERSON

BORN: *6-7-75 at Hampton, Va.*
POSITION: *Guard.*
TEAMS: *76ers, 1996-present.*

Known as "The Truth," Iverson has been a prolific scorer since entering the NBA as Rookie of the Year in 1997. While he has not shot at a particularly high percentage, Iverson has the ability to single-handedly take over a game. He was selected first-team All-NBA in 1999, was named All-Rookie when he joined the league, and was MVP of the Rookie Game at All-Star Weekend in 1997. He also has quick hands and set a playoff record with 10 steals against Orlando in 1999. At the heart of Iverson's game is the ability to create shots against virtually any defense and the quickness to blow past almost any defender. In addition to the ability to get to the basket, he has a deadly mid-range jump shot and also is respected for his 3-point shooting. He has made his greatest strides since he has been shifted from point guard to shooting guard, no longer having to worry about getting teammates set up before executing his offense.

J

JIM JACKSON

BORN: *10–14–70, at Toledo, Ohio.*

POSITION: *Guard.*
TEAM: *Mavericks, 1992–97; Nets, 1997; 76ers, 1997–98, Warriors, 1998, Blazers, 1998–99, Hawks 1999–present.*

Jackson, a 6–6, 220-pound shooting guard, has the size, mobility and leadership to rank near the top of his position for years to come. He can produce points inside and out, help on the boards and his passing and defense are still improving. The former Ohio State University star's will to win and floor game rekindle flashes of Oscar Robertson. He appeared to be on his way to that kind of stardom in 1994–95 before an ankle injury broke his third professional season after 51 games, in which he averaged 25.7 points, the fifth-best in the league. Jackson returned a year later to average 19.6 points. In 1996–97, he was sent to New Jersey in a midseason deal, and was then traded to Philadelphia in the offseason.

His career took a couple more interesting turns. Philadelphia traded him to Golden State on Feb. 17, 1998, then he signed as a free agent with Portland the next season. After averaging just 8.4 points per game for the Trail Blazers, he was traded, along with Isaiah Rider, to Atlanta for the 1999-2000 season. Despite painful tendinitis in his knees that required several trips to Canada for special treatment, Jackson played in 79 games for the Hawks, averaging 16.7 points, 5.0 rebounds and 2.9 assists. But with Atlanta stumbling to a 28-54 record, Jackson called it the worst season of his career.

MARK JACKSON

BORN: *4-1-65 at Brooklyn, N.Y.*
POSITION: *Guard.*
TEAMS: *Knicks, 1987–92, Clippers, 1992–94, Pacers, 1994–1996, Nuggets, 1996–97, Pacers, 1997–2000, Raptors, 2000-present.*

(Opposite) NO STOPPING: *Allen Iverson (with ball) has been a true star on the court for the 76ers.*

(Right) ON THE MEND: *Jim Jackson began his NBA journey with the Dallas Mavericks.*

200

A true point guard with a pass-first mentality, Jackson is among the NBA's all-time leaders in assists. He has been at his best when featured with solid shooters, such as is the case in Indiana with Reggie Miller. Although not particularly fleet, Jackson has a knack for getting the ball to the right places at the right times. He has had success with his passing at virtually every stop, although he is not among the elite point guards when it comes to passing the ball ahead on the fast break. With a 3-point set shot that is effective when given time to launch and a variety of push shots in the lane, Jackson also is capable of creating his own offense. He also has an unlikely post-up game for a player at 6-foot-3. In fact, because Jackson would spend so much time attempting to back down shorter point guards, the NBA adopted a rule limiting such attempts to five seconds.

BUDDY JEANNETTE

BORN: *9–15–17, at New Kensington, Pa.*
POSITION: *Guard.*
TEAMS: *Cleveland White Horses (NBL), 1938–39, Detroit Eagles (NBL), 1939–41, Sheboygan Redskins (NBL), 1942–43, Fort Wayne Pistons (NBL), 1943–46, Baltimore Bullets (BAA/NBA), 1947–50.*

Jeannette, a classic playmaker and clutch shooter, was a pioneer of the professional game and one of the premier backcourt players of his era. At 5–11 and 175 pounds, Jeannette made up for his physical limitations with court savvy and a hard-nosed intensity that resulted in four career MVP awards. Three of these came in the old National Basketball League and the other in the American Basketball League, both predecessors of today's NBA. Jeanette's teams also won five league championships, including one that will always be significant in the NBA record books. Jeannette, player-coach of the ABL's Baltimore franchise, was invited to bring his team into the second-year BAA in 1947–48 and the surprising Bullets claimed the championship. Jeannette continued in his role as player-coach for two more seasons and briefly coached the new-edition Baltimore Bullets in the mid-1960s. He was elected to the Hall of Fame in 1994.

POST MAN: *Even though he is only 6–3, posting up is one of Mark Jackson's (left) strengths.*

DENNIS JOHNSON

BORN: *9–18–54, at San Pedro, Calif.*
POSITION: *Guard.*
TEAMS: *SuperSonics, 1976–80, Suns, 1980–83, Celtics, 1983–90.*

Johnson, a solid playmaker and scorer, was the premier defensive point guard of the 1980s and stopper for one Seattle SuperSonics and two Boston Celtics championship teams. He played in-your-face, man-to-man defense that resulted in six selections to the NBA All-Defensive first team. But he also was an outstanding passer and clutch shooter who could post big points totals when defenses sagged off him. Johnson, a second-round 1976 draft choice out of Pepperdine University, was the point man for a Seattle team that reached the NBA Finals in consecutive seasons and defeated Washington for the 1979 championship. Then, after three seasons in Phoenix, he blended perfectly into the talented Celtics team of superstars Larry Bird, Robert Parish and Kevin McHale that reached four NBA finals and captured championships in 1984 and '86. When he retired in 1990, the five-time All-Star had totals of 15,535 points, 5,499 assists, 4,249 rebounds and 1,477 steals. He has returned to the game as an assistant coach with the Clippers.

EDDIE JOHNSON

BORN: *5–1–59, at Chicago, Ill.*
POSITION: *Guard/forward.*
TEAMS: *Kings, 1981–87, Suns 1987–90, SuperSonics, 1990–93, Hornets, 1993–94, Pacers, 1995–96, Rockets 1996–97.*

Johnson built a solid 15-year career as a jump-shooting small forward for six NBA teams. The 6–7 former University of Illinois product was a pure outside shooter at a position that usually demands an inside game. Johnson made up for his inside shortcomings with hard work and a defensive presence that allowed him to extend his career beyond expectations. As a second-round 1981 draft pick, Johnson joined the Kansas City Kings and played sparingly his rookie season. But he blossomed over the next three campaigns, posting averages of 19.8, 21.9 and 22.9, respectively. By the time Johnson reached Phoenix in 1987, he was a solid role player who could come off the bench and provide instant offense. He earned the NBA Sixth Man Award in 1989 as a 21.5 scorer. Johnson, who scored more than 18,000 points, had his last shining moment in the 1997 playoffs, nailing a game-winning three-pointer for Houston over Utah in Game 4 of the Western Conference Finals.

GUS JOHNSON

BORN: *12–13–38, at Akron, Ohio.*
POSITION: *Forward.*
TEAMS: *Bullets, 1963–72, Suns, 1972, Indiana Pacers (ABA), 1972–73.*

Johnson was a flamboyant, acrobatic forward who backed up his showboating with outstanding play. The 6–6, 235-pounder, a legend at the University of Idaho because of his amazing jumping ability, wore a gold star on his front tooth and spent a small fortune on clothing, shoes and jewelry. But over nine seasons with the Baltimore Bullets, the swashbuckling Johnson became a fan favorite who consistently delivered double-digit point and rebounding totals while earning two selections to the NBA All-Defensive first team. Johnson, who reportedly could touch the top of the backboard, played through four knee surgeries before his NBA career ended with a 21-game season in Phoenix. The five-time All-Star signed with the ABA's Indiana Pacers and played a supporting role for the 1973 championship team. He retired with 9,944 NBA points (17.1) and 7,379 rebounds (12.7).

JOHN JOHNSON

BORN: *10-18-47.*
POSITION: *Forward*
TEAMS: *Cavaliers, 1970–73, Trail Blazers, 1973–75, Rockets, 1976–77, Sonics, 1978–82.*

A wonderful complementary player, Johnson found the perfect place for his skills when he was traded to Seattle in time to win an NBA title in 1979 with the Sonics. As part of a talented team that included Lonnie Shelton and Jack Sikma on the front line, Johnson provided enough for the Sonics to get past Wes Unseld and the Washington Bullets in five games in the NBA Finals. While most remember Johnson for that juncture in his

SPLITTING THE D: *Dennis Johnson (3) played during the glory days of the Celtics-Lakers.*

SORE SPOT: *Kevin Johnson's career was hampered by numerous, nagging injuries.*

career, he was a two-time NBA All-Star and averaged in double figures for almost his entire career. In fact, Johnson was far more of a scoring threat earlier in his career, his most prolific scoring seasons coming during the expansion era in Cleveland. About the only time Johnson struggled was a two-season stint with the Rockets, when he twice averaged in single digits. Mostly, he was an across-the-board type of player, who could provide five assists and five rebounds per game in addition to that double-digit scoring.

KEVIN JOHNSON

BORN: 3–4–66, Sacramento, Calif.
POSITION: Guard.
TEAMS: Cavaliers, 1987–88, Suns, 1988–98, 2000.

The 1996–97 season ended with Johnson averaging a team-leading 20.1 points and 9.3 assists for the Suns. But many fans were surprised to learn that while Johnson had shown little signs of slowing down in his 10th NBA season, he had talked of retirement at age 31. Twelve months later, after Johnson had started just 12 games behind Jason Kidd and Rex Chapman, those same fans were probably less surprised when he was released by Phoenix. He had outstanding speed, a solid mid-range jump shot, great court vision and an ability to turn a game with his quickness and fast-break bursts. But the 6–1 former University of California star never played an 82-game NBA season and twice failed to suit up 50 times. Johnson, a 1987 Cleveland draft pick, was traded to Phoenix in 1988. He averaged better than 20 points in his first three full seasons with the Suns and reached double-digit assists in his first four. Johnson's only weakness is lack of durability. Ironically, when Jason Kidd broke his ankle on March 22, 2000, it was Johnson the Suns called out of retirement. He wound up playing six games, averaging 6.7 points and 4.0 assists, before returning to retirement.

LARRY JOHNSON

BORN: 3–14–69, at Tyler, Tex.
POSITION: Forward.
TEAM: Hornets, 1991–96; Knicks, 1996–present.

Johnson is an offensive-minded forward who has been robbed of quickness by serious back injuries. When he joined Charlotte from the University of Nevada-Las Vegas as first overall pick of the 1991 draft, the 6–7 Johnson was a quick 260-pounder who ran circles round power forwards and outmuscled smaller ones. In five seasons with the Hornets he averaged 19.6 points and 9.4 rebounds, twice leading the team to the playoffs. By the end of the 1995–96 season it was apparent that Johnson had lost much of his mobility inside. He was dealt to the Knicks, who needed someone to take the offensive load off center Patrick Ewing. But Johnson, criticized in the media for his lack of offense, sacrificed scoring for team play and defense. Though his stats

slipped to career lows of 12.8 points and 5.2 rebounds, he led the team in field goal percentage at .512 and saw his scoring average rise to 15.5 points per game in 1997–98, helping the Knicks reach the Conference semi-finals. Another rise in 1998–99—to 12.0 points per game in the regular season—followed. Johnson hit a four-point play to beat the Pacers in Game 3 of the Eastern Conference Finals and that propelled the Knicks past the Pacers in six games and into the NBA Finals, where they lost to the San Antonio Spurs. In 1999–2000, however, the Knicks lost to the Pacers in six games in the Eastern Conference Finals.

MAGIC JOHNSON

See Legends of the NBA *page 118–119*

MARQUES JOHNSON

BORN: 2–8–56, at Natchitoches, La.
POSITION: Forward.
TEAMS: Bucks, 1977–84, Clippers, 1984–87, Warriors, 1989–90.

Johnson was an athletic forward who combined equal amounts finesse and power into a solid 11-year NBA career. The 6–7 Johnson, the 1977 College Player of the Year at UCLA, handled the ball like a guard and powered his way to the basket like a big man, often seeming to materialize out of nowhere for spectacular put-back slam dunks. The baseline was his playground, but he worked hard to develop a 20-foot jump shot that made him a complete player. Johnson, a Milwaukee first-round draft pick in 1977, averaged better than 20 points and 6 rebounds in five of his seven Milwaukee seasons and topped 300 assists three times. He also was a solid defensive player and shot-blocker who appeared in five All-Star Games. After leaving the Bucks in 1984, Johnson played three seasons with the Clippers and a 10-game stint with Golden State. Johnson retired with 13,892 points (20.1 per game), 4,817 rebounds (7.0) and 2,502 assists (3.6), but used his broad knowledge of the game to start a career in broadcasting.

(Opposite) KNICK POWER: *Larry Johnson (2) displays his strength in the 2000 playoffs*

THE MICROWAVE: *Vinnie Johnson (right) earned his nickname because of his ability to heat up the scoreboard in a hurry.*

VINNIE JOHNSON

BORN: *9-1-56.*

POSITION: *Guard*

TEAMS: *Sonics, 1979–81, Pistons, 1982–91, Spurs, 1991–92.*

Known as "The Microwave," Johnson was at the heart of the Pistons' back-to-back championships at the start of the '90s. A perfect bench complement to starting Pistons guard Joe Dumars, Johnson would come off the bench in a scoring mode, a contrast to the more-refined approach of Dumars. With an energetic outside release that would prove effective well beyond the 3-point arc, Johnson also could get to the

basket with a series of drives. His thick build enhanced his ability to defend bigger shooting guards and also was perfectly suited for the "Bad Boys" style of approach the Pistons had adopted under center Bill Laimbeer. Without Johnson, it is doubtful Detroit would have won either of its championships. Indeed, the most efficient aspect of those Pistons might have been the bench anchored by Johnson, Dennis Rodman and John Salley. Johnson was successful earlier in his career with Seattle, but not to the level he attained with the Pistons, an organization he left as a free agent to sign with the Spurs.

NEIL JOHNSTON

BORN: *2–4–29, at Chillicothe, Ohio.*

POSITION: *Center.*

TEAM: *Warriors, 1951–59.*

Johnston, who was known for his baseball ability as a college player at Ohio State, became one of the NBA's offensive forces in the early 1950s. Armed with a deadly hook shot that he fired with a sweeping right arm, Johnston won three consecutive scoring titles, led the NBA in field-goal percentage three times and combined with Paul Arizin and Tom Gola on the Warriors' 1956 NBA championship team. Competing successfully as a 6–8 center in the George Mikan era,

Johnston averaged 20 points or better in five of his eight NBA seasons and also captured the 1954–55 rebounding title with a 15.1 average. He was a four-time All-NBA first-teamer, a six-time All-Star Game performer and a 19.4-point career scorer. Johnston's career was cut short in 1959 by a serious knee injury, but he remained as Warriors coach through 1960–61. He was elected to the Hall of Fame in 1990.

BOBBY JONES

BORN: *12–18–51, at Charlotte, N.C.*
POSITION: *Forward.*
TEAMS: *Nuggets (ABA/NBA), 1974–78, 76ers, 1978–86.*

The quiet, modest Jones was every coach's dream. Not only was he the premier defensive forward of the 1970s and '80s, he also was a troubleshooter who provided instant offense. If the 76ers needed points, Jones would go into his scoring mode. If they needed assists, rebounds, blocked shots, steals—it was Jones to the rescue. The 6–9 former North Carolina star could dominate without scoring points. Jones was at his best against the opponents' top scorer. He played two ABA seasons with Denver, two with the Nuggets in the NBA and his final eight with Philadelphia—and he was named to the All-Defensive first team an incredible 10 times. Jones also earned the NBA Sixth Man Award in 1983, the year he helped the 76ers win a championship. On a team that included Julius Erving and Moses Malone, Coach Billy Cunningham often singled out Jones as his MVP. Jones, a four-time All-Star, retired in 1986 with 8,911 points (11.5 per game) and 4,256 rebounds (5.5).

CALDWELL JONES

BORN: *8-4-50 at McGehee, Ark.*
POSITION: *Center.*
TEAMS: *76ers, 1976–82, Rockets, 1982–84, Bulls, 1984–85, Trail Blazers, 1985–89, Spurs, 1989–90.*

One of the league's first great shot-blockers, Jones was a two-time All-Defensive selection in the early '80s and anchored the defenses of five franchises. After starting his career in the ABA, Jones jumped to the 76ers, his defense a key component in some of the franchise's most successful seasons. He spent six seasons in the playoffs with the 76ers, and also was with playoff teams in Chicago, Portland and San Antonio. During his tenure in Philadelphia, the 76ers made it to the NBA Finals three times, although they failed to come away with a championship. Hardly an offensive forward, Jones averaged just 6.2 points over his career. But it was on defense where he made his mark, earning an All-Star berth in the ABA and coaching respect around the NBA. He was a perfect complement in Philadelphia to offensively oriented Darryl Dawkins. Three of his brothers also played professional basketball: Charles Jones, Wilbert Jones and Major Jones.

K.C. JONES

BORN: *5–25–32, at Taylor, Tex.*
POSITION: *Guard.*
TEAM: *Celtics, 1958–67.*

Jones was a dependable playmaker during Boston's dynastic NBA reign and one of the greatest defensive guards ever to put on a uniform. Never an offensive force, Jones more than made up for it with court savvy, a ball-hawking presence and his ability to shut down high-scoring backcourt players like Jerry West and Hal Greer. The 6–1 Jones was a championship machine, playing on two title-winners with Bill Russell at the University of San Francisco, winning a gold medal with the 1956 U.S. Olympic team and capturing eight more championships in nine seasons with the Celtics. He later was assistant coach for two title teams and head coach for two more (with the Celtics in 1984 and '86). Jones compiled a 522–252 coaching mark over 10 seasons, including a 308–102 (.751) record in five Boston campaigns. He was elected to the Hall of Fame in 1989.

SAM JONES

BORN: *6–24–33, at Laurinburg, N.C.*
POSITION: *Guard.*
TEAM: *Celtics, 1957–69.*

Sam was half of Boston's championship-era "Jones Boys," combining with K.C. Jones in a perfectly balanced backcourt.

Sam was the offensive force, K.C. the defensive wizard. Sam joined the Celtics as a first-round 1957 draft pick out of little North Carolina Central College and played a key role in a 12-season run that produced 10 NBA championships for the Celtics. Jones, one of the fastest players in the league, was known for his uncanny long-range bank shot and ability to perform in the clutch. He led the Celtics in scoring three times (including a 25.9 mark in 1964–65) and amassed 15,411 career points, averaging 17.7 per game. Jones also was a playoff force, averaging 18.9 points over 154 games. Jones, who was a five-time All-Star Game performer, was elected to the NBA 25th Anniversary All-Time Team in 1970 and the Hall of Fame in 1983.

MICHAEL JORDAN

See Legends of the NBA *page 120–121*

KEEPING UP WITH THE JONES: *Bobby Jones (right) was a top defender who could score too.*

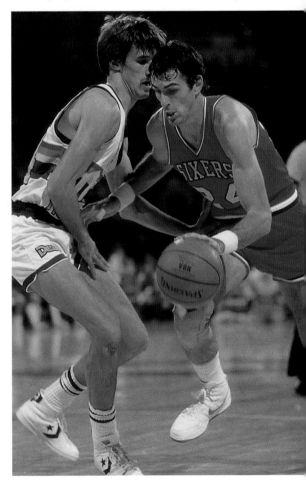

K

SHAWN KEMP

BORN: 11–26–69, at Elkhart, Ind.
POSITION: Forward.
TEAM: SuperSonics, 1989–97, Cavaliers, 1997–2000, Trail Blazers, 2000–present.

Kemp is a highlight-film forward. From his rookie season to his current status as a six-time All-Star, he has steadily improved his game. When Cleveland acquired Kemp from Seattle in 1997 much was expected of him and he did not disappoint, averaging 18 points per game and leading the unfancied Cavs into the playoffs. Not bad for a kid who was

drafted in 1989, aged 20, with no college experience. Kemp struggled through his rookie season before jumping into the Sonics' rotation and averaged 15 points and 8.4 rebounds per game in his second year. The 1995–96 campaign produced his besr averages of 19.6 points and 11.4 rebounds and ended with an NBA Finals loss to Chicago. By the tender age of 28, Kemp had already scored more than 11,500 points and snared over 6,500 rebounds. There was no arguing that he produced for the Cavaliers, despite being forced to play center instead of his natural power-forward position. In 1998-99, he averaged 20.5 points and 9.2 rebounds before missing the last eight games of the season with a foot injury. In 1999-2000, he still led the Cavs, averaging 17.8 points and 8.8 rebounds, but his game had

changed. The high-wire act was a thing of the past with rare exceptions. Instead, he'd become more of a post-up player and a jump shooter.

JOHNNY (RED) KERR

BORN: 8–17–32, at Chicago, Ill.
POSITION: Center.
TEAMS: Nationals/76ers, 1954–65, Bullets, 1965–66.

Kerr was a fun-loving, hard-living center who once held the NBA's ironman streak. Kerr, a happy-go-lucky carouser whose 6–9 body resembled an enlarged Pillsbury Doughboy, more than compensated for his dalliances with spirited play and a willingness to play through injuries. In 11 seasons with Syracuse/Philadelphia and one with Baltimore, the red-headed wonder earned a reputation as the best passing center in the league and a crafty competitor who could beat an opponent with his head as well as his abilities. From his first 1954 game as a Syracuse rookie until November 1965 (his final season), Kerr played in 844 consecutive games, an NBA record that stood for 17 years. He also was part of an NBA championship team in that rookie season and his 12-year career produced 12,480 points (13.8 per game), 10,092 rebounds (11.2) and three All-Star Game appearances. Kerr later coached the Bulls and Suns for four years.

JEROME KERSEY

BORN: 6-26-62 at Clarksville, Va.
POSITION: Forward.
TEAMS: Trail Blazers, 1984-95, Warriors, 1995-96, Lakers, 1996-97, Sonics, 1997-98, Spurs, 1998-2000.

At the heart of two trips to the NBA Finals by the Trail Blazers, Kersey in his prime was one of the NBA's premier high-flying forwards, doing from the small forward spot what many of today's top athletes are accomplishing from the backcourt. On one of the NBA's most well-rounded rosters, he, along with guard Clyde Drexler, provided the flash for a franchise that also had the solid overall skills of guard Terry Porter and power forward Buck Williams. Yet it was not until he moved to the Spurs late in his career that Kersey finally went

BOXED OUT: *Surrounded by youngsters, Shawn Kemp could not lift the Cavs to the next level.*

all the way, part of the San Antonio roster that took the 1999 NBA Finals from the Knicks. Although he never made it to an All-Star Game, his longevity and well-rounded offensive game earned respect from both opponents and teammates. If not for the salary-cap mechanics that so impact the game, he probably would have been a Blazer for life.

JASON KIDD

BORN: *3–23–73, at San Francisco, Calif.*
POSITION: *Guard.*
TEAMS: *Mavericks, 1994–97, Suns, 1997–present.*

Kidd, a second overall draft pick by Dallas after his sophomore season at the University of California, was touted before his 1994–95 rookie season as the best pure point guard to come into the NBA since the Pistons' Isiah Thomas. He lived up to his press clippings, averaging 11.7 points, with 607 assists (7.7) and earning co-Rookie of the Year honors. His second season averages were even more impressive: 16.6 and 9.7. The 6–4 Kidd, who was called "the best passer on the planet" by Bullets General Manager John Nash, is at his best when he penetrates the lane and sets up teammates for easy shots. But defenders who play the pass quickly discover Kidd has a proficient shot arsenal. Midway through his third season, a disgruntled Kidd was sent to Phoenix and helped transform the Suns as he led them into the playoffs two years straight. In 1997–98 he started every game, and finished second in the NBA in assists with 9.1 per game. Although that playoff series ended in first round loss to San Antonio. Kidd was rejuvenated in Phoenix. Despite missing 15 games with injuries, he led the league in assists in 1999-2000, averaging 10.1 a game and keying the Suns' upset of the defending champion San Antonio Spurs in the first-round of the playoffs. But the Suns lost to the Lakers in five games in the Western Conference semifinals. How good has the move to Phoenix been for Kidd? Since his arrival, he's been a two-time All-Star, a two-time All-NBA first-teamer and a two-time All-NBA defender.

FEED THE FLAME: *Jerome Kersey (25) was a key element of the Blazers' powerful teams.*

KIDD STUFF: *Jason Kidd has been a sparkplug for the resurgent Phoenix Suns.*

BERNARD KING

BORN: *12–4–56, at Brooklyn, N.Y.*
POSITION: *Forward.*
TEAMS: *Nets, 1977–79, 1992–93, Jazz, 1979–80, Warriors, 1980–82, Knicks, 1982–87, Bullets, 1987–92.*

King was an explosive scorer and under-rated all-around player who defied odds and revived his career after reconstructive knee surgery. King wandered through New Jersey, Utah and Golden State before finding his niche with the New York Knicks in 1982. The scowling 6–7 forward won over Madison Square Garden fans with his intensity and creative shot-making, an ability fueled by a quick release and explosive first step. Before the injury, King was devastating with his back to the basket, spinning left or right and leading the league with a 32.9 scoring average. After the injury, he was more multi-dimensional, relying less on quickness and power. King returned to full-time action in 1987 with the Bullets and played four more full seasons, averaging better than 20 points in three of them. A two–time All-NBA first-teamer who once enjoyed consecutive 50-point games, he retired in 1993 with 19,655 points (22.5) and 5,060 rebounds (5.8).

KING MAN: *Bernard King was an underrated player.*

TONI KUKOC

BORN: *9-18-68 at Split, Croatia.*
POSITION: *Forward.*
TEAMS: *Bulls, 1993-00, 76ers, 2000-present.*

When Kukoc arrived in Chicago in 1993, he was lauded by Bulls General Manager Jerry Krause as one of the next great talents in the NBA, a player who eventually could take over that mantle when Michael Jordan retired. That only made the pressure tougher on one of the world's great talents. Instead of a smooth transition, it was a difficult one for one of the smoothest players on the international scene. Yet, eventually, Kukoc won over his teammates with the type of all-around game that helped Jordan and company win a second set of three consecutive championships. Although he was not always content in his sixth-man role, Kukoc earned enough respect to win the Sixth Man Award in 1996. Because of Kukoc's success, several other foreign players who had been mulling NBA options decided to follow his lead. In that respect, Kukoc well may have opened the doors to fellow Europeans. Once Jordan left, Kukoc was granted his request for a trade and immediately earned the respect of Allen Iverson when he was dealt to the 76ers.

NO BULL: *Toni Kukoc was one of the last champions to leave the Chicago Bulls.*

CHRISTIAN LAETTNER

BORN: *8-17-69 at Angola, N.Y.*
POSITION: *Forward.*
TEAMS: *Timberwolves, 1992-96, Hawks, 1996-98, Pistons, 1998-2000, Mavericks, 2000-present.*

It wasn't supposed to be this way for Laettner, this difficult a transition to the NBA. So respected was Laettner when he came out of Duke, that he was the lone college player selected to the initial Dream Team that represented the United States at the 1992 Olympics in Barcelona and took home the gold. No sooner was Laettner done with school than he found himself a teammate of Michael Jordan, Larry Bird and Magic Johnson. Yet personality problems became apparent from the start of his NBA career. First Minnesota couldn't wait to unload him to Atlanta. Then the Hawks allowed him to depart as a free agent. For the most part, many of the talents that had made Laettner a success at Duke were still there, including the solid short jumper. But his personality simply was not a good fit at any of his initial NBA stops. By the time he reached Detroit, he was mostly a utility player and little more.

PUT UP YOUR DUKES: *Christian Laettner (left) was a much bigger star in college at Duke than he has been in the NBA.*

BILL LAIMBEER

BORN: 5–19–57, at Boston, Mass.
POSITION: Center.
TEAMS: Cavaliers, 1980–82, Pistons, 1982–94.

Laimbeer was a rough-and-tumble big man who centered the Detroit Pistons' back-to-back championship teams of 1989 and '90. The 6–11 former Notre Dame star often drew accusations of "dirty play." But he never backed down and the Pistons embraced their "Bad Boys" image all the way to the bank. Laimbeer, drafted in 1979 by Cleveland and traded in 1982 to Detroit, was an unusual center who scored most of his points with a soft push shot from the perimeter. Laimbeer could not jump and he was not as athletic as the players he faced, but he got the job done, averaging 12.9 points and 9.7 rebounds over his 14-year career. During his 12 full Detroit seasons, the Pistons won three Central Division titles, topped 50 victories five times and reached the NBA Finals three years in a row. Laimbeer retired after the 1993–94 season.

BOB LANIER

BORN: 9–10–48, at Buffalo, N.Y.
POSITION: Center.
TEAMS: Pistons, 1970–80, Bucks, 1980–84.

Lanier was one of the few NBA centers who could dominate inside and out. At 6–11, he could break down opponents with his short left-handed hook shot, a deft perimeter scoring touch or a defensive presence that forced them away from the middle. Lanier's 19,248 points (20.1) and 9,698 rebounds (10.1) rank among the all-time career totals, but his contributions sometimes are overlooked. When Lanier was in his prime, he played for a weak Detroit team that had to struggle to reach the playoffs. Late in his career, he played for a good Milwaukee team that was overshadowed by Eastern Conference powers Philadelphia and Boston. Still, Lanier played in eight All-Star Games and averaged better than 20 points for

eight consecutive years. After his 1984 retirement, he was honored numerous times for his citizenship and community contributions. Lanier was elected to the Hall of Fame in 1992.

JOE LAPCHICK

BORN: 4–12–1900, at Yonkers, N.Y.
POSITION: Center.
TEAMS: Pre-NBA.

Lapchick was a pioneer of professional basketball and one of the NBA's first great coaches. At 6–5, he was an agile big man equally capable of passing, shooting and controlling the center jump—an important quality in the pre-1937 professional game. Lapchick became most prominent as a member of the mid-1920s Original Celtics, a barnstorming team credited with numerous innovations, particularly in the development of the pivot position (Lapchick's role) as the hub of an offense. As a coach, Lapchick built on those innovations from 1936–47 at St. John's

PIVOTAL: *Joe Lapchick was an NBA pioneer.*

University and for the next nine years with the New York franchise of the BAA/NBA. He coached the Knicks to 326 victories and three NBA Finals before returning to St. John's in 1956. By the time he retired in 1965, Lapchick had coached the Redmen to 334 victories and four NIT championships over 20 seasons. Lapchick was elected to the Hall of Fame in 1966.

FAT LEVER

BORN: 8-18-60 at Pine Bluff, Ark.
POSITION: Guard.
TEAMS: Trail Blazers, 1982-84, Nuggets, 1984-90, Dallas, 1990-94.

One of the great rebounding guards in league history, Lever was an across-the-board statistical whiz. If he wasn't scoring, he was rebounding. If he wasn't passing for assists, he was coming up with steals. His defense was so proficient that he was named second-team All-Defense in 1988 in addition to being named second-team All-NBA in 1987. He appeared in two All-Star Games and likely would have made even more had his teams experienced greater success. To put his rebounding prowess from the backcourt into perspective, consider that when he grabbed 734 rebounds in 1989-90 with Denver, it was a single-season total eclipsed by only three guards in NBA history: Tom Gola, Oscar Robertson and Magic Johnson. Had constant knee injuries not proven so limiting later in his career, he likely would have endured far longer than he did. As for "Fat," the nickname had nothing to do with his superb conditioning, but rather was just a shorter version of his given, Lafayette.

MARKED MAN: *Bill Laimbeer was a big man for the "Bad Boys" in Detroit.*

ON THE BOARD: *Guard Fat Lever (12) had a knack for rebounding and playing defense.*

JIM LOSCUTOFF

BORN: *2-4-30.*
POSITION: *Forward.*
TEAMS: *Celtics, 1955-64.*

At 6-foot-5, Loscutoff hardly was the size of one of today's prototypic bruising forwards. But don't sell him short on that count. There was a reason he carried the nickname "Jungle Jim." A powerful player who helped lead the Celtics to seven NBA titles, Loscutoff ably played in the shadows of such Celtics legends as Bill Russell, Tom Heinsohn, Bob Cousy and Bill Sharman. But that did not mean he was not a prime contributor to Boston's success. A classic role player, he averaged in double figures only once in his career, that in his second season in the league. But he provided enough of the intangibles to keep the chemistry under Red Auerbach flawless. Had the franchise not been so successful, Loscutoff probably could have endured even longer with the league's elite franchise. But because

of that continued parade of talent through the Boston locker room, Loscutoff in effect wound up being pushed aside by John Havlicek and the next wave of Celtics greats. Still, Jungle Jim firmly established a place for himself in Celtics lore.

KEVIN LOUGHERY

BORN: *3-28-40 in Bronx, N.Y.*
POSITION: *Guard.*
TEAMS: *Pistons, 1962-63, Bullets, 1964-71, 76ers, 1972-73.*

"Murph," as he was known because he was forced to sleep on a Murphy bed when he roomed with teammates early in his career, was a feisty guard who never met a shot he did not like. Known for his grit, Loughery anchored the Bullets backcourt for years, even playing alongside the legendary Earl "The Pearl" Monroe. He was a good ballhandler who played with a tenacity of players far taller. For as much as he accomplished during his playing career, he is even better known for the work he did as a coach in the ABA with the New York Nets. As coach of Julius Erving, Loughery led Dr. J to an ABA championship. Just as Erving did with his playing skills, Loughery took his coaching skills to the NBA, working with several teams before finally settling down as a broadcast analyst. He was a favorite of players both as a personable teammate and as a respectful coach.

BOB LOVE

BORN: *12-8-42.*
POSITION: *Forward*
TEAMS: *Royals, 1966-68, Bucks, 1968, Bulls, 1969-76, New York, 1977, Sonics, 1977.*

One of the sweetest shooting forwards in the history of the game, Love was Chicago basketball before there was a Michael Jordan. The lithe forward who went by the moniker "Butterbean," was a smooth player who was featured during the Bulls' early seasons by coach Dick Motta. Until Jordan appeared on the Chicago landscape, no Bull had led the franchise in scoring for as many years as Love, who averaged 20 or more points in six consecutive seasons. Because the Bulls

hardly were winners during his tenure, Love only made it to three All-Star Games. But defenders respected him enough to stay close whenever he got the ball on the perimeter. While he appeared shy and somewhat withdrawn to some, it turned out that a speech impediment had left him reserved, feeling awkward. Years after his playing career, he overcame the impediment and went on to become a praised public speaker, one treated with great affection by Chicago sports fans.

CLYDE LOVELLETTE

BORN: *9-7-29, at Petersburg, Ind.*
POSITION: *Forward/center.*
TEAMS: *Lakers, 1953-57, Royals, 1957-58, Hawks, 1958-62, Celtics, 1962-64.*

Lovellette was big (6-9), physical and capable of putting the ball in the basket. But he enhanced his natural center qualities with a one-handed set shot that allowed him to move outside and create problems for opposing centers. And during a career that included stints alongside George Mikan (Minneapolis) and Bill Russell (Boston), Lovellette often was asked to switch between both forward positions and the middle. No problem. Lovellette had honed his offensive game under Phog Allen at the University of Kansas, where he led the Jayhawks to the 1952 NCAA Tournament championship. He complemented that with an Olympic gold medal (1952) and three NBA championships—1954 with the Lakers and 1963 and '64 with the Celtics. Over 11 seasons with four teams, the versatile Lovellette scored 11,947 points (17.0) and grabbed 6,663 rebounds (9.5). The three-time All-Star retired in 1964 and was elected to the Hall of Fame in 1988.

JERRY LUCAS

BORN: *3-30-40, at Middletown, Ohio.*
POSITION: *Forward/center*
TEAMS: *Royals, 1963-69, Warriors, 1969-71, Knicks, 1971-74.*

From the moment he put on his first uniform at Middletown High School, Lucas was one of the most celebrated players in history. And by the time he was drafted by the NBA's Cincinnati Royals out of

Ohio State in 1962, his resume showed why: two state titles, three appearances in the NCAA Finals, one national championship, two College Player of the Year awards, numerous records and an Olympic gold medal. Lucas, who combined with Oscar Robertson as one of the game's best inside-outside combinations, put his distinctive over-the-shoulder shooting style and aggressiveness to quick work for the Royals, averaging 17.7 points and 17.4 rebounds in a Rookie of the Year debut. Over an 11-year NBA career that included stints in San Francisco and New York, he averaged 17 points and 15.6 rebounds, played in eight All-Star Games and earned three All-NBA first-team citations. Lucas played on his only championship team in 1973, when he helped the Knicks to their second title in four years. He was elected to the Hall of Fame in 1979.

MAURICE LUCAS

BORN: *2-18-52 at Pittsburgh, Pa.*
POSITION: *Forward*
TEAMS: *Trail Blazers, 1976-79, Nets, 1980-81, Knicks, 1981-82, Suns, 1982-85, Lakers, 1985-86, Sonics, 1986-87, Trail Blazers, 1987-88.*

A fierce rebounder and defender, Lucas was among the league's classic enforcers — foul a teammate too hard and it was a safe bet that Lucas was coming after you. In an era before there were flagrant fouls and routine suspensions for hard fouls, there was the type of court justice provided by players such as Lucas. All of that aside, Lucas also was a highly skilled player, one with skills beyond the occasional shove or bump. He was second-team All-NBA in 1978 and second-team All-Defensive that same season. He also was second-team All-NBA in 1979 and was a member of the 1977 NBA Champion Trail Blazers. Lucas began his career in the ABA, where he was an All-Star in the second of his two seasons. He also appeared in four NBA All-Star Games. While players did not necessarily appreciate his style when they were battling, most opponents were respectful of his intensity and dedication.

MUSCLE MAN: *Maurice Lucas was a classic enforcer as well as a talented forward.*

M

ED MACAULEY

BORN: *3–22–28, at St. Louis, Mo.*
POSITION: *Forward/center.*
TEAMS: *Bombers, 1949–50, Celtics, 1950–56, Hawks, 1956–59.*

The 6–8 Macauley was a gifted offensive player who could frustrate bigger defenders with his quickness and gliding moves around the basket. He combined for six seasons with guards Bob Cousy and Bill Sharman in a high-scoring run-and-gun Boston lineup that presaged the 24-second clock. Macauley, a two-time All-American at St. Louis University, will always be remembered as one of the two forwards the Celtics traded for the draft rights to center Bill Russell. But the trade sent him back to St. Louis, where he teamed with Bob Pettit and Cliff Hagan to lead the Hawks to their only NBA championship—a 1958 victory over the Celtics. Macauley, a three-time All-NBA first-team selection and a seven-time All-Star, was player-coach when he retired in 1959 with 11,234 career points (17.5 per game). He coached the Hawks to two Western Division titles. Macauley was elected to the Hall of Fame in 1960.

RICK MAHORN

BORN: *9-21-58 at Hartford, Conn.*
POSITION: *Forward*
TEAMS: *Bullets, 1980-85, Pistons, 1985-89, 76ers, 1989-91, Nets, 1991-96, Pistons, 1996-98, 76ers, 1998-99.*

A bruising and punishing player, Mahorn was a power forward who played with a physical nature that was on the edge of the rules. With the Bullets, at the start of his career, Mahorn teamed with rugged center Jeff Ruland, the two going by the nicknames McFilthy and McNasty, although to this day, no one seems to recall which was which. But Mahorn also was a valued player, helping Detroit win the first of two

(Opposite) BAD BOY: *Rick Mahorn was one of the league's toughest players.*

successive championships in 1989. His style was to bowl over opponents to secure rebounds. His wide posterior made him one of the game's preeminent setters of screens, an ability guards Joe Dumars and Isiah Thomas played so ably off during their time together in Detroit. During the latter stages of his career, Mahorn was valued as a respected locker room presence, kept on rosters at a point far after his skills had severely diminished. As expected, he moved into coaching at the close of his career and appeared on a fast-track toward returning to the NBA in that capacity.

DAN MAJERLE

BORN: *9-9-65 at Traverse City, Mich.*
POSITION: *Guard/forward.*
TEAMS: *Suns, 1988-95, Cavaliers, 1995-96, Heat, 1996-present.*

THUNDER DAN: *Dan Majerle did many things well.*

"Thunder Dan," has recreated himself over his career. At the start of his career, while he was with the Suns, he was a hard-driving physical guard who initially

earned his nickname because of his spectacular dunks. He was fierce, intense, as physical as any backcourt player in the league. But once injuries set in, Majerle moved his game to the perimeter. He not only developed 3-point range, but could set up and convert shots from a good five feet beyond the semicircle. He has led the NBA in 3-point shooting in two seasons, which was a record for such titles when he repeated. He also was selected second-team All-Defensive in 1991 and 1993. An outgoing personality, he has been able to fit in just as easily as a teammate of Charles Barkley in Phoenix as he has under driven Heat coach Pat Riley. Most of all, Majerle has kept the game fun and that passion is visible almost every game.

WHAT'S THE SCORE: *Jeff Malone (right) earned two All-Star berths because of his offensive prowess.*

JEFF MALONE

BORN: *6–28–61, at Mobile, Ala.*
POSITION: *Guard.*
TEAMS: *Bullets, 1983–90, Jazz, 1990–94, 76ers, 1994–96.*

Malone was a catch-and-shoot guard who piled up more than 17,000 points in a 13-year career with Washington, Utah and Philadelphia. The 6–4 shooting guard could provide fast-and-furious offense with an assortment of jump shots that he liked to launch in the 15- to 20-foot range. He was adept at moving without the ball, coming off picks and shooting a soft fadeaway while going either right or left. Malone, who also played solid defense, was selected by the Bullets out of Mississippi State University with the 10th overall pick of the 1983 draft. By his third season, he was a consistent 20-point scorer who would earn two All-Star Game invitations. After seven seasons in Washington, he was traded to Utah and spent three and a half years as an offensive alternative to Jazz teammates Karl Malone and John Stockton. Malone ended his career in January 1996, after an injury-plagued 1994–95 season in Philadelphia.

KARL MALONE

See Legends of the NBA page 122–123

MOSES MALONE

See Legends of the NBA page 124–125

DANNY MANNING

BORN: *5–17–66, at Hattiesburg, Miss.*
POSITION: *Forward.*
TEAMS: *Clippers, 1988–94, Hawks, 1994, Suns, 1994–99, Bucks, 1999–2000, Jazz, 2000–present.*

When healthy, Manning is a mobile 6–10 small forward who knows how to use his size advantage. He has missed considerable time with torn anterior cruciate ligaments in both knees and the injuries have reduced his explosiveness. Late in the 1997–98 regular season he suffered a repeat of the injury, sparking fears over his long-term fitness. Manning was taken by the Los Angeles Clippers with the first overall draft pick of 1988, shortly after he had led the University of Kansas to an NCAA championship. But he was uncomfortable in his go-to offensive role for a weak Clippers team, although he earned two All-Star selections. Manning signed with the Suns as a free-agent in 1994 and stepped into a situation where he could use his team-oriented skills to complement Charles Barkley and Kevin Johnson. The Suns were 36–10 when Manning hurt his left knee, an injury that cost him the rest of that season and part of 1995–96. In 1997–98 he played in 70 games and averaged 13.5 points and a respectable .516 from the field before having his season yet again cruelly curtailed by injury. Although he averaged just 9.1 points in 1998-99, he was able to play in all 50 games in the lockout-shortened season. But the Suns traded Manning and Pat Garrity and two first-round draft choices to Orlando on Aug. 5, 1999. Then the Magic traded Manning and Dale Ellis to the Milwaukee Bucks for Chris Gatling and Armen Gilliam on Aug. 19, 1999. With the Bucks, Manning played in 72 games, averaging just 4.6 points in 16.9 minutes.

PETE MARAVICH

BORN: *6–22–47, at Aliquippa, Pa.*
POSITION: *Guard.*
TEAMS: *Hawks, 1970–74, Jazz, 1974–80, Celtics, 1980.*

"Pistol Pete" will be remembered as the most prolific offensive force in college basketball history and a creative, prime-time performer for 10 pro seasons. When drafted by the Atlanta Hawks out of Louisiana State University in 1970, he owned three national scoring titles and held numerous NCAA offensive records, including career average (44.2) and points (3,667). It wasn't so much that Maravich scored points in bunches, it was how he did it—with the most dazzling repertoire of offensive moves ever assembled. From no-look passes to double-clutching 20-foot jumpers, he played the game creatively and made both fans and players shake their heads. The 6–5 Maravich averaged 23.2 points as an NBA rookie and scored 15,948 points (24.2 per game) over a career that included one scoring title (New Orleans 1976–77), two All-NBA first-team selections and five All-Star Game performances. He was elected to the Hall of Fame in 1987.

STEPHON MARBURY

BORN: *2-20-77 at Brooklyn, N.Y.*
POSITION: *Guard.*
TEAMS: *Timberwolves, 1996-99, Nets, 1999-present.*

An All-Rookie selection in 1997, Marbury appears to be part of a collection of next-wave guards in the NBA, talents such as

NET LOSS: *Stephon Marbury can look forward to enjoying more success in the NBA.*

TURNING IT UP: *Jamal Mashburn's versatility is one reason for the Miami Heat's success.*

Allen Iverson who can be just as spectacular with their scoring as with their passing. The possessor of a cross-over dribble every bit as daunting as the one Tim Hardaway delivered to the league 10 years ago, Marbury is the type of player who can take over a game with his driving ability as well as his outside shooting. Despite playing only one season of college basketball, Marbury matured in a hurry, first helping push Minnesota up the standings and then arriving in New Jersey with the promise of reversing the Nets' struggling fortunes. Marbury's only misstep may have come in 1999, when he demanded a trade from Minnesota, citing the cold weather and small city feel of Minneapolis. That did not sit well with many who saw Marbury and Kevin Garnett making the Wolves an elite team, but the trade certainly helped reinvigorate the Nets.

SLATER MARTIN

BORN: *10–22–25, at Houston, Tex.*
POSITION: *Guard.*
TEAMS: *Lakers, 1949–56, Knicks, 1956, Hawks, 1956–60.*

The 5-10 Martin was a crafty playmaker who provided the steadying influence for five NBA championship teams. Always under control and ever dangerous in the clutch, Martin compensated for his diminutive size with a hard-nosed style that brought out the best in his teammates. After a colorful career at the University of Texas, he joined George Mikan, Jim Pollard and Vern Mikkelsen in Minneapolis and quarterbacked the Lakers to their second consecutive championship in 1950. Three more followed in 1952, '53 and '54 and Martin enjoyed a fifth title in 1958, as a teammate of Bob Pettit, Ed Macauley and Cliff Hagan with the St. Louis Hawks. Statistically, Martin does not raise eyebrows with his 9.8-point and 4.2-assist per game career averages, but numbers don't always tell the story. Martin's success can be measured by NBA championships and his membership in the Hall of Fame. Neither the Lakers nor the Hawks would have been the same without him.

JAMAL MASHBURN

BORN: *11–29–72, at New York, N.Y.*
POSITION: *Forward.*
TEAM: *Mavericks, 1993–97, Heat, 1997–2000, Hornets, 2000–present.*

Mashburn is a talented 6–8 forward who should rank consistently among the league's scoring leaders. But it wasn't until he was traded to Miami in 1996–97 that he learned the meaning of team play. His versatility allows him to fire from 3-point range or challenge the big men inside with a pull-up jumper or a creative slash to the basket. He is explosive, as his 24.1 and 23.4 second- and third-season scoring averages might suggest, and he has worked hard to improve his passing, rebounding and defense. Mashburn declared for the 1993 draft after his junior season at the University of Kentucky and was grabbed by Dallas with the fourth overall pick. He averaged 19.2 points and 4.5 rebounds in 1993–94, earning an NBA All-Rookie first team spot. Mashburn's 1996–97 scoring average slipped to 11.8, as he sacrificed points for victories in coach Pat Riley's team. It rose considerably to 15.1 in a 1997–98 season that was curtailed by injury but was enough to confirm Mashburn has the potential to become one of the league's premier performers. With Tim Hardaway's injuries, Mashburn was called up to take up some of the scoring slack in Miami, where he increased his averaged from 14.8 in 1998–99 to 17.5 in 1999–2000.

BOB McADOO

BORN: *9–25–51, Greensboro, N.C.*
POSITION: *Forward/center.*
TEAMS: *Braves, 1972–76, Knicks, 1976–79, Celtics, 1979, Pistons, 1979–81, Nets, 1981, Lakers, 1981–85, 76ers, 1985–86.*

The 6–9 McAdoo was a sweet-shooting forward who spent his early NBA years winning scoring titles and his later career as a valuable extra on two Lakers championship teams. McAdoo, a University of North Carolina product, was one of the best pure outside shooters the game has ever produced. After winning Rookie of the Year honors in 1973, he exploded into NBA consciousness with consecutive scoring averages of 30.6, 34.5 and 31.1, winning scoring titles each year and a regular-season MVP in 1975. But the Braves' top gun was inexplicably traded to the Knicks in 1976 and he bounced around the league, piling up points and new teams. It wasn't until he reached Los Angeles that he rediscovered success—as a low-scoring role player for the Lakers' 1982 and '85 title teams. McAdoo ended his career in 1986 at Philadelphia with 18,787 points (22.1) and an impressive .503 field-goal percentage. He was elected to the Hall of Fame in 2000 after spending five seasons as an assistant coach to Pat Riley in Miami.

BIG MAC ATTACK: *Bob McAdoo (11) went from Rookie of the Year to NBA champion.*

(Left) XS AND OS: *The X-Files will show Xavier McDaniel was an aggressive scorer.*

XAVIER McDANIEL

Born: 6-4-63 at Columbia, S.C.
Position: Forward.
Teams: Sonics, 1985-90, Suns, 1991, Knicks, 1991-92, Celtics, 1992-95, Nets, 1996-98.

The "X-Man" was as tough as they come, just short of being a thug with his aggressive play, always overtly physical. Although he made it to only to one All-Star Game, in 1988 while with the Sonics, McDaniel was a prolific scorer. He could take his game outside and hit the longest of jumpers, or he could pound inside, often feeding himself off his own offensive rebounds. With a shaven head, he carried a nasty demeanor about himself, and teammates said it wasn't always an act. While his only league accolade was his All-Rookie selection in 1986, teams vied for his presence, knowing he instantly would add toughness to what otherwise might have been passive rosters. During the latter stages of his career, he briefly left the NBA to play in the Greek League. For the most part, he achieved only limited postseason success, advancing deep into the playoffs once with Seattle and once with New York.

ANTONIO McDYESS

BORN: *9-7-74 at Quitman, Miss.*
POSITION: *Forward.*
TEAMS: *Nuggets, 1995-97, Suns, 1997-98, Nuggets, 1998-present.*

Much like his career itself, Antonio McDyess has struggled to find his way. An immense talent who was named first-team All-Rookie in 1995 and third-team All-NBA in 1999, McDyess has the rare mix of finesse in a power player's body. He can score outside, around the rim, pass, block shots and rebound. He would appear to have all the skills to emerge on the level of, say, a Chris

RODNEY McCRAY

BORN: *8-29-61 at Mount Vernon, N.Y.*
POSITION: *Forward.*
TEAMS: *Rockets, 1983-88, Kings, 1988-90, Mavericks, 1990-92, Bulls, 1992-93.*

Although he never received the opportunity to appear in the Olympics, with his United States team in 1980 boycotting the Moscow Games, McCray was rewarded with an NBA championship in 1993 with the Bulls, his final season in the NBA. A fierce defender, McCray was cited for his defensive prowess by being voted first-team

All-Defensive in 1988 and second-team All-Defensive in 1987, both while with the Houston Rockets. With a wide range of skills, McCray could advance the ball like a point guard, convert lengthy shots like a shooting guard, contest defensively against small forwards, and even use his thick build to play against larger power players. While injuries limited McCray during the latter stages of his career, the former Louisville standout was the type of multi-skilled player that so many of today's stars attempt to emulate. His brother, Scooter McCray, also played in the NBA.

(Opposite) GOLDEN NUGGET: *Antonio McDyess (24) shows one of the moves that landed him on the 2000 U.S. Olympic team.*

Webber or Kevin Garnett. Instead, uncertainty has left his career somewhat lagging. Jumping at the opportunity to leave Denver in 1997, McDyess spent one season with Phoenix before he rejoined the Nuggets as a free agent in 1998. While the homecoming may have been important to McDyess, he returned to an inferior team, one where his skills could not be put to their best use. Still, it is only a matter of time before he begins making All-Star Games on a regular basis. Once Denver finds a quality center, his career should blossom.

GEORGE McGINNIS

BORN: *8–12–50, at Indianapolis, Ind.*
POSITION: *Forward.*
TEAMS: *Pacers (ABA/NBA), 1971–75, 1980–82, 76ers, 1975–78, Nuggets, 1978–80.*

McGinnis was a bruising inside force who could beat you with his rebounding or scoring. The 6–8, 235-pound forward, who signed an ABA contract after his sophomore season at Indiana University, literally muscled his way to the top of the offensive charts, throwing in some acrobatic derring-do for good measure. McGinnis' best years were in the ABA, where he won a scoring title, earned one MVP citation and helped the Indiana Pacers to consecutive championships in 1972 and '73. One year before the ABA/NBA merger, McGinnis signed with Philadelphia, where he earned All-

BY GEORGE: *George McGinnis (right) did his best work inside the ABA.*

NBA first-team honors in 1976 and averaged more than 20 points and 10 rebounds for three straight years. He later played for Denver before returning to Indiana to end his career. When the three-time NBA All-Star retired in 1982, he owned combined ABA/NBA totals of 17,009 points (20.2 per game) and 9,233 rebounds (11.0).

DICK McGUIRE

BORN: *1–25–26, at Huntington, N.Y.*
POSITION: *Guard.*
TEAMS: *Knicks, 1949–57, Pistons, 1957–60.*

In the NBA's formative years, McGuire ranked as one of the league's premier point guards. He seldom scored in double figures, but he was a master ball-handler with outstanding court vision. A former star at St. John's, he excelled at penetrating the lane and drawing defenders, leaving a teammate open for one of his slick passes. He led the league with 386 assists as a Knicks rookie in 1949–50 and he averaged 6.3 assists his second season, tying for the league lead. With "Tricky Dick" running the offense, the Knicks reached the NBA Finals in 1951, '52 and '53, losing once to Rochester and twice to Minneapolis. He played eight seasons in New York and three more in Detroit, earning seven All-Star Game selections before retiring in 1960. In 1993, McGuire joined Al McGuire, a former college coach, as the first brother combination in the basketball Hall of Fame.

KEVIN McHALE

BORN: *12–19–57, at Hibbing, Minn.*
POSITION: *Forward/center.*
TEAM: *Celtics, 1980–93.*

McHale spent his early career as a Boston sixth man and the rest as one of the top power forwards in the NBA. The 6–10 former University of Minnesota star had the ability to step off the bench and provide instant offense and defense, a traditional role in Celtics history. But he became even more valuable as a starter alongside Larry Bird and center Robert Parish, providing an all-around consistency that helped Boston win three championships. McHale had exceptionally long arms that allowed him to get off inside shots and an explosive first step to the basket. He was an outstanding

(Opposite) CELTIC PRIDE: *To some, McHale was the best power forward in NBA history.*

rebounder, a three-time All-Defensive first-team stopper and an intimidating, shot-blocking presence in the middle. A seven-time All-Star and a 1987 All-NBA first teamer, McHale averaged better than 20 points five times and ended his career in 1993 with 17,335 (17.9 per game). He also pulled down 7,122 rebounds (7.3). After his retirement, McHale returned to his home state of Minnesota, where he was the Timberwolves' assistant general manager, 1994–95, before being promoted to vice president of basketball operations in 1995.

GEORGE MIKAN

See Legends of the NBA *page 126–127*

VERN MIKKELSEN

BORN: *10–21–28, at Fresno, Calif.*
POSITION: *Forward/center.*
TEAM: *Lakers, 1949–59.*

Mikkelsen, a prototypical power forward at 6–7 and 230 pounds, was one of the cornerstones of the Minneapolis Lakers championship dynasty that also featured center George Mikan, forward Jim Pollard and point guard Slater Martin. Mikkelsen was an intense competitor who did not give up space or rebounds without a serious elbow or two. As a double-figure scorer and rebounder, he was a charter member of one of the greatest frontcourts in basketball history. A six-time All-Star, Mikkelsen used his superior strength and size to muscle his way to totals of 10,063 career points (14.4 per game) and 5,940 rebounds (8.4). Those numbers probably would have been higher in a lineup without the 6–10 Mikan. Mikkelsen, a former star at Hamline University, spent his entire 10-year career with the Lakers and retired in 1959 with four championship rings. He was elected to the Hall of Fame in 1995.

ANDRE MILLER

BORN: *3-19-76 at Los Angeles.*
POSITION: *Guard.*
TEAMS: *Cavaliers, 1999-present.*

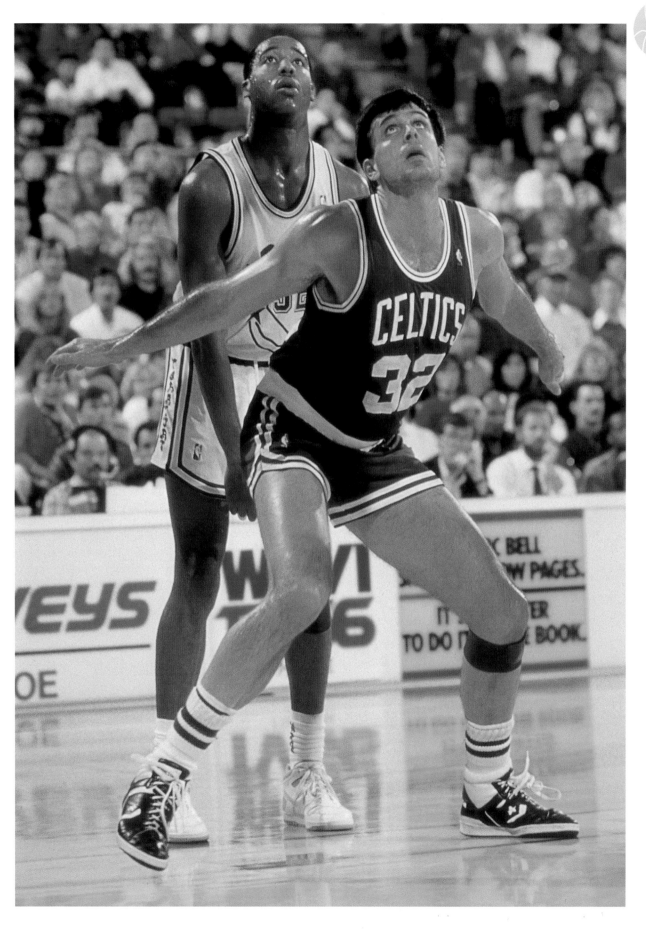

The Cavaliers have a knack for coming up with quality young point guards and they appeared to land another one in the 1999 draft in University of Utah standout Andre Miller. Continuing in the Cavaliers' lineage of Mark Price, Kevin Johnson, Terrell Brandon and Brevin Knight, Miller made an almost flawless transition from the college game to the Cavaliers backcourt. By the middle of his first season, Miller already has supplanted the promising Knight as Cleveland's starting point guard and had been praised by opponents for having a veteran's savvy. One of the few college standouts to spent all four seasons in the NCAA, Miller arrived as a polished player. He can mix a variety or drives and outside shots in his offensive repertoire and has the type of quickness to give the league's veteran guards problems. Although Cleveland has a long way to go to round out its roster, Miller gives the Cavaliers a solid building block at one of the most important positions.

REGGIE MILLER

BORN: *8–24–65, at Riverside, Calif.*
POSITION: *Guard.*
TEAM: *Pacers, 1987–present.*

Miller is a trash-talking, in-your-face shooting guard who owns the fastest gun in the Midwest. His range is well beyond the 3-point line and his confidence is as high as the jump shots he drops through the net. The slender 6–7 Miller won't bang for the rebounds or pile up assists, but, oh, how he can shoot. He has averaged better than 20 points per game six times and most of them come from the perimeter. The former UCLA star, Indiana's 1987 first-round draft pick, is probably the most explosive performer in the game. Once, he scored eight points in 16.4 seconds. In a 1994 playoff game against the Knicks, he

MAKING A POINT: *Andre Miller is another in a long line of fine point guards for the Cavs.*

MILLER TIME: *Reggie Miller is the Pacers' ace.*

erupted for an amazing 25 fourth-quarter points. With the help of 7–4 center Rik Smits, Miller carried the Pacers to within one game of the NBA Finals in 1994 and '95. Miller, a five-time All-Star and 88-percent free-throw shooter, is at his best when a game is on the line. He finally made it to the NBA Finals against the Los Angeles Lakers in 2000, after getting 34 points, five rebounds, four steals and an assist in the Eastern Conference title clinching game in New York, where he so often had burned the Knicks. But the Pacers lost to the Lakers in six games in the Finals.

SIDNEY MONCRIEF

BORN: *9–21–57, at Little Rock, Ark.*
POSITION: *Guard.*
TEAMS: *Bucks, 1979–89, Hawks, 1990–91.*

The silky-smooth Moncrief was a near-perfect blend of offense and defense. He could score 20 points while shutting down a high-scoring opponent—a double talent not many players could claim. The 6–3 Moncrief was the glue for a Milwaukee team that posted seven straight 50-victory seasons, won seven consecutive Midwest and Central Division titles and advanced three times

BUCK SHOT: *Sidney Moncrief was a defensive whiz for the Milwaukee Bucks.*

small-college record 41.5 points as a Winston-Salem State College senior, made a quick impact on the NBA with a 24.3-point average to earn 1968 Rookie of the Year honors. He combined with center Wes Unseld to lead the Bullets into the 1971 NBA Finals and meshed with Walt Frazier in a classy New York backcourt that led the Knicks to the 1973 championship. Monroe, a four-time All-Star who averaged more than 20 points six times, was forced to the sideline in 1980 by a knee injury. He was elected to the Hall of Fame in 1990.

ALONZO MOURNING

BORN: 2–8–70, at Chesapeake, Va.
POSITION: Center.
TEAMS: Hornets, 1992–95, Heat, 1995–present.

Mourning rates among the top five NBA centers. At 6–10, the former Georgetown University star is undersized in his matchups against Patrick Ewing, Shaquille O'Neal, Hakeem Olajuwon and David Robinson, but he battles the boards, blocks

GOOD MOURNING: *Alonzo Mourning kept the Heat on track.*

to the Eastern Conference Finals in the 1980s. Twice he was voted the NBA's Defensive Player of the Year and he was a four-time member of the league's All-Defensive first team. But in each of those four seasons, Moncrief also averaged better than 20 points. His versatility was best illustrated in 1981–82, when he became the first player since Boston's Dave Cowens (in 1975–76) to lead his team in scoring (19.8), rebounding (6.7) and assists (4.8). The former University of Arkansas star retired after one season in Atlanta with 11,931 points (15.6 per game) and 2,793 assists (3.6).

EARL MONROE

BORN: 11–21–44, at Philadelphia, Pa.
POSITION: Guard.
TEAMS: Bullets, 1967–71, Knicks, 1971–80.

The 6–3 Monroe played with a flair that earned him a place among the game's most popular players. "Earl The Pearl" was instant offense, a perpetual fountain of whirling, spinning, double-pumping moves that produced 17,454 points (18.8) and 3,594 assists (3.9) over a 13-year career with the Baltimore Bullets and New York Knicks. Monroe, who had averaged a

shots, moves with agility around the basket and even steps out for an accurate jump shot. Mourning was selected with the second overall pick of the 1992 draft and tabbed as the man who would lead the 4-year-old Hornets out of the expansion wilderness. He was everything he was expected to be: tough and passionate but coachable and averaging 21.0, 21.5 and 21.3 points and 10.3, 10.2 and 9.9 boards during his three years in Charlotte. A contract dispute led to a 1995 trade to Miami, where he averaged 23.2 points and 10.4 rebounds in his first season. In 1996–97 Mourning led Pat Riley's squad to their first Eastern Conference title, and even though his numbers fell off a season later, he finished third in the NBA with a field-goal average of .551 as he averaged 19.2 points and 9.6 boards a game. After leading the league in blocked shots in 1998-99 (3.9) and 1999-2000 (3.7), he was named the NBA's Defensive Player of the Year in each of those seasons. What's more, he was being compared to the great Bill Russell, who revolutionized the concept of defense. Mourning won gold with U.S. team at the 2000 Olympic Games, but was then diagnosed with a kidney ailment and missed the 2000–01 season

CHRIS MULLIN

BORN: *7–30–63, at New York, N.Y.*
POSITION: *Forward.*
TEAM: *Warriors, 1985–97; Pacers, 1997–2000, Warriors, 2000–present.*

Mullin is a high-scoring small forward whose career spans more than a decade with the Golden State Warriors and the Indiana Pacers. The savvy lefthander has won many games with a 3-point shot he hit at 44 percent frequency in '97–98. He is also an excellent passer and free-throw shooter who led the league from the line in his first Pacers season, scoring at a .939 percent rate. Mullin is not a physical player, but will get his rebounds and defends with a nice combination of hard work and instincts. A 1992 All-NBA first-teamer, he came out of St. John's University in 1985 and averaged better than 25 points and 5 rebounds for five straight seasons from

(Opposite) BACK HOME: *Chris Mullin returned to Golden State, where he started in 1985*

STAR POWER: *Gheorghe Muresan (left) had more success in movies than on the NBA court.*

1988–93. Although alcohol rehabilitation and injuries have limited his effectiveness in recent years, Mullin remains one of the game's best pure shooters and most respected performers. The five-time All-Star is a two-time Olympic gold medalist, as an ameteur in 1984 and with the 1992 Dream Team. He made his first trip to the NBA Finals with Pacers in 2000, but his role had declined with the emergence of Jalen Rose. The ideal professional, he took his limited minutes in stride and continued to work as hard as ever.

GHEORGHE MURESAN

BORN: *2-14-71 at Triteni, Romania.*
POSITION: *Center.*
TEAMS: *Bullets, 1993-98, Nets, 1999-2000.*

The star of the film "My Giant," Muresan very much stands as that, a 7-foot-7 Goliath who basically can play a one-man zone. Although foot problems have limited his availability in recent seasons, and while he never was anything close to fleet, just by his mere presence,

228

defense against bigger opponents. Murphy was a five-time 20-point scorer and one of the most deadly free-throw shooters in the game. A 33.1-point scorer over three varsity seasons at Niagara University and one of the legendary players of college basketball history, Murphy was a key player on Houston's 1980–81 team that advanced to the NBA Finals. He finished his career in 1983 with 17,949 points (17.9) and his 4,402 assists still rank as a Rockets record. Murphy was elected to the Hall of Fame in 1993.

DIKEMBE MUTOMBO

BORN: *6–25–66, at Kinshasa, Zaire.*
POSITION: *Center.*
TEAM: *Nuggets, 1991–1996; Hawks, 1996–present.*

Mutombo, a Zaire native, comes from a line of intimidating Georgetown University centers and may rank as the best defender of them all. At 7–2, he is an inside force who in 1997–98 collected a record third award as the NBA's Defensive Player of the Year. He first collected that honor with Denver in 1995 then, after signing as a free-agent with the Hawks, he again won the accolade in 1996–97 after leading his team to a 56––26 record. He is also one of the NBA's best rebounders, grabbing more than 1,000 in two of his first five seasons. Mutombo's weakness is on offense, where he operates mechanically with a shooting range of five feet. His only shots are the dunk and the jump hook. Mutombo arrived in Denver as the fourth overall pick of the 1991 draft and averaged 16.6 points as a rookie. But that average dropped in each of his first four years. By 1998-99, he was down to 10.8 points per game, although he did get 12.2 rebounds a game. In 1999-2000, he scored 11.5 points per game but led the league in rebounding with 14.1 a game. Despite his intimidating presence on the court, Mutombo is a humanitarian off it.

Muresan can force the opposition to change the way it plays offense. Muresan made such strides from the start of his NBA career that he was voted the league's Most Improved Player in 1996 while playing with Washington. However, teams have had a tough time finding a way to utilize him on offense, with his range limited and his inside skills only marginal. The biggest problem simply has been how long it takes him to get from one end of the court to the other. Against fleet centers, such as Alonzo Mourning, it simply is no contest. Still, in a league where Mark Eaton, Manute Bol and Shawn Bradley have

been able to endure, Muresan figures to be around the NBA for a while.

CALVIN MURPHY

BORN: *5–9–48, at Norwalk, Conn.*
POSITION: *Guard.*
TEAM: *Rockets, 1970–83.*

The 5–9 Murphy, the most popular player in Rockets history, zipped around the NBA hardcourts for 13 seasons, dazzling fans with his limitless enthusiasm. What he lacked in size, he made up for with a quickness that allowed him to penetrate, pull out of a sprint for a quick jumper and play aggressive, chest-to-chest

230

N

LARRY NANCE

BORN: *2–12–59, at Anderson, S.C.*
POSITION: *Forward/center.*
TEAMS: *Suns, 1981–88,*
Cavaliers, 1988–94.

Nance was an athletic power forward who created severe matchup problems with his 6–10 height and quickness off the ball. The former Clemson University star was one of the game's great leapers and 1984 winner of the NBA's All- Star Slam-Dunk Championship. That ability made him dangerous on spectacular alley-oop lobs as well as on the offensive and defensive boards. Nance, who could run the floor and defend either centers or small forwards, was a 20th-pick steal for Phoenix in the 1981 draft and rose to prominence after an unspectacular rookie debut. Over the next 11 seasons, he never averaged under 16 points or 8 rebounds while making 54.6 percent of his shots. Over a 13-year career with the Suns and Cavaliers, Nance qualified for three All-Star Games and earned a spot on the 1989 NBA All-Defensive first team. He retired in 1994 with 15,687 points (17.1) and 7,352 rebounds (8.0).

LEAP YEAR: *Larry Nance was known for his incredible leaping ability.*

DON NELSON

BORN: *5-15-40 at Muskegon, Mich.*
POSITION: *Forward.*
TEAMS: *Zephyers, 1962-63, Lakers, 1963-65, Celtics, 1965-73.*

A winner both on the court and the sidelines, Nelson has been successful both as a forward with the NBA-champion Celtics of the Bill Russell Era, and as a coach at stops such as Milwaukee, Golden State and Dallas. A smart player with a most unusual shot-put style of shooting his free throws, Nelson did much of the dirty work for the fabled Celtics, earning his chance to make the team after receiving a tryout invitation from legendary coach Red Auerbach. Although his shot wasn't the prettiest sight to behold, Nelson did lead the league in shooting in 1974-75. In all, he won five championships while with the Celtics. As respected as he was as a player, Nelson's career is defined by the success he has had on the sideline. His innovative techniques, such as using a point forward, have allowed him to succeed despite often playing with undermanned rosters. His players appreciate his coaching style, much of which has to do with having been a player himself.

NORM NIXON

BORN: *10–10–55, at Macon, Ga.*
POSITION: *Guard.*
TEAMS: *Lakers, 1977–83, Clippers, 1983–89.*

Nixon was a pure point guard who played on Los Angeles Lakers' 1980 and '82 championship teams. The 6–2 former Duquesne University star was at his best when running the offense, setting up easy baskets for teammates, leading the fast break and penetrating the lane. But Nixon also was a dangerous shooter, a dimension that set him apart from many other point guards. The popular playmaker, a late 1977 first-round draft pick, enjoyed six solid seasons with the Lakers before a stunning trade sent him to the San Diego Clippers, clearing the way for

CLIP JOINT: *Norm Nixon was a master at running the Los Angeles Lakers' fast break.*

Magic Johnson to operate exclusively at the Lakers' point. Nixon, who played on three Pacific Division winners for the Lakers, spent his final six injury-plagued seasons with a team that never even posted a winning record. He retired after the 1988–89 season with 12,065 points (15.7 per game) and an impressive 6,386 assists (8.3).

DIRK NOWITZKI

BORN: *6-19-78 at Wurzburg, Germany.*

POSITION: *Forward.*

TEAMS: *Mavericks, 1998-present.*

Another of the many foreign players to find success in the NBA in recent seasons, Nowitzki was among the most coveted players in the 1998 draft. In order to get an inside track on the talented forward, several NBA coaches set up covert workouts to view the prospect while he still was playing in the German League in 1997-98. Among the suitors were Boston's Rick Pitino and Dallas' Don Nelson, who eventually landed the intriguing player. While Nowitzki struggled in his rookie season to pick up the pace of the NBA game, by his second season he was receiving consideration for the league's Most Improved Player award. At 6-foot-11, Nowitzki is a small forward who can torment shorter players at the same position with his height. And when opposing teams attempt to play power players against him, Nowitzki has the ability to step outside and launch successful jumpers. Nelson was so intrigued with Nowitzki's ballhandling, he even has used him as a point forward, a position Nelson created originally for Milwaukee's Paul Pressey. Nowitzki averaged just 8.2 points per game in his rookie year. But his points average soared to 17.5 in 1999–2000, when he made 116 of 306 3-pointers (.379).

FOREIGN OBJECT: *Dirk Nowitzki became the latest foreign player to make an impact for coach Don Nelson.*

O

CHARLES OAKLEY

BORN: *12-18-63 at Cleveland, Ohio.*
POSITION: *Forward.*
TEAMS: *Bulls, 1985-88, Knicks, 1988-98, Raptors, 1998-present.*

The soul of the Knicks in the '90s, Oakley is among the game's premier enforcers. While he can score when called upon, and is effective with a set-shot jumper out to 15 feet, his strength rests in his ability to pound the boards and pound opposing power players. Oakley is so respected in his ability to handle the dirty work that teammates complained both times he has been traded in his career. First, Michael Jordan claimed the Bulls blundered when they dealt Oakley to the Knicks for Bill Cartwright. Then several Knicks teammates complained when Oakley was dealt to Toronto for Marcus Camby. Oakley's defensive prowess has been recognized with All-Defensive team selections to the first unit in 1994 and the second unit in 1998. He also was selected for the 1994 All-Star Game. It is rare to find the teammate or former teammate who doesn't rave about the intangibles Oakley offers the team both on the court and inside the locker room.

LAMAR ODOM

BORN: *11-6-79 at Jamaica, N.Y.*
POSITION: *Forward.*
TEAMS: *Clippers, 1999-present.*

Lamar Odom arrived in the NBA as an unknown factor. While he impressed during his brief stay at Rhode Island, he also attempted to pull out of the 1999 NBA draft at the last minute, claiming he wanted to return to college. When that request was denied, Odom wound up missing several draft interviews and the potential first overall selection fell all the way to the No. 4 choice. For the Clippers, that turned out to be a stroke of good

HARD HAT: *Charles Oakley has made a career out of doing all the dirty work.*

luck. While Odom experienced little team success in his first season in the NBA, he displayed a wide range of skills that could place him as a star in the NBA for years to come. Able to handle the ball and play

UP AND OVER: *Will Lamar Odom (jumping) be able to lift the Clippers out of the doldrums?*

as a point forward, Odom has a soft stroke, incredible court vision and the ability to get to the basket. As is the case with so many players who have passed through the Clippers organization, the real challenge could be whether he can continue to endure the losing as he matures as a player.

HAKEEM OLAJUWON
See Legends of the NBA *page 128–129*

SHAQUILLE O'NEAL
See Legends of the NBA *page 130–131*

P

ROBERT PARISH

BORN: *8–30–53, at Shreveport, La.*
POSITION: *Center.*
TEAMS: *Warriors, 1976–80, Celtics, 1980–94, Hornets, 1994–96, Bulls, 1996–97.*

The only 21-year player in NBA history, the 7–1 Parish holds the record for games played and he ranks among the career leaders in many other categories. The former Centenary star has performed his double-decade feat with a workmanlike precision that places him in the company of the game's all-time great centers. There has never been anything flashy about "The Chief," but his career numbers (more than 23,000 points and 14,000 rebounds) and contributions as a member of three Boston championship teams will

CELTIC CHIEF: *Robert Parish (00) was one of the chief reasons for the Celtics' success.*

someday pique the interest of Hall of Fame voters. From his 1976–77 rookie season with Golden State through a 14-year run in Boston and two seasons in Charlotte and one in Chicago, Parish has provided quiet leadership with his solid defense, offensive and defensive rebounding, unselfish passing and deadly high-arcing jumpers that always seem to come at the right moments. A nine-time All-Star, Parish averaged double-digit rebounds 10 times.

GARY PAYTON

BORN: *7–23–68, at Oakland, Calif.*
POSITION: *Guard.*
TEAM: *Sonics, 1990–present.*

Payton, a nice blend of offense and defense, has steadily worked his way into the upper echelon of NBA point guards. Payton quickly established himself as a standout one-on-one defender who could shut down high-scoring guards and set the pace for Seattle's transition attack. But the former Oregon State University star

PAY DAY: *Seattle's Gary Payton (left) is best known for two things: his defense and his trash-talking.*

STILL GOING: *Sam Perkins (14) had a deadly outside shot for a big man.*

makes his shot just about impossible to block at any spot on the court. On the same note, his long arms make him a quality defender both in the post and out on the perimeter. He has had success at just about every stop, whether it was during the Mavericks' initial playoff success, or deep runs into the playoffs with the Lakers, Sonics and Pacers. The 1985 All-Rookie selection set an NBA record in 1997 against Toronto when he converted eight 3-pointers without a miss for Seattle. A member of the gold-medal U.S. Olympic team at the 1984 Games, Perkins has spoken about retirement in recent seasons, but keeps getting lured back by teams desperate for his contributions.

GUN CONTROL: *Chuck Person was known as "The Rifleman" thanks to his quick release.*

entered the NBA in 1990 without an outside shot, giving defenders the option of dropping back into double teams. Payton averaged only 7.2 points as a rookie, but he worked hard on his shot and watched his averages climb steadily each year, to 21.8 in 1996–97. With defenders now forced to respect him outside, Payton uses his quickness to create shots and passes off the dribble and his assist totals are always respectable. Nicknamed "The Glove" for his tight defense, he is a six-time All-Star and seven-time All-Defensive first team selection and was the NBA's defensive player of the year in 1995-96. The king of trash talk, Payton can back up whatever he says. After the Sonics traded

Shawn Kemp, Payton carried his team, averaging career highs in points (24.2) and assists (8.9) in 1999–2000.

SAM PERKINS

BORN: *6-14-61 at Brooklyn, N.Y.*
POSITION: *Center.*
TEAMS: *Mavericks, 1984-90, Lakers, 1990-93, Sonics, 1993-98, Pacers, 1998-present.*

Perkins is a lot of things at 6-foot-9, but a true center is not one of them. Instead, Perkins is just as likely to be found at the 3-point circle as he is in the paint. One of the game's premier shooting big men, Perkins has an overhead release that

CHUCK PERSON

BORN: *6-27-64 at Brantley, Ala.*
POSITION: *Forward.*
TEAMS: *Pacers, 1986-92, Timberwolves, 1992-94, Spurs, 1994-98, Hornets, 1998-99, Sonics, 1999-2000, Lakers 2000.*

Nicknamed "The Rifleman," Person is a gunner who could shoot from any spot on the floor at any time, and more than likely make a high percentage of those shots. One of the game's elite 3-point shooters, Person has not stopped shooting since being named Rookie of the Year in 1987 and making the All-Rookie team that same season. While he has not appeared in an All-Star Game, his shooting has been coveted for more than a decade. Even when back injuries began to limit his playing time, he still had the ability to come off the bench late in games and knock down crucial 3-point baskets. In addition to pulling the trigger with his shots, Person also established his legend as one of the game's great trash talkers, trading words during the course of games with many of the sport's superstars. While his career has been on the decline in recent seasons, his brother Wesley Person remains a respected shooting guard with the Cleveland Cavaliers.

BOB PETTIT

See Legends of the NBA *page 132–133*

ANDY PHILLIP

BORN: *3–7–22, at Granite City, Ill.*
POSITION: *Guard.*
TEAMS: *Stags (BAA/NBA), 1947– 50, Warriors, 1950–53, Pistons, 1953–56, Celtics, 1956–58.*

Phillip ranked alongside Slater Martin, Bob Cousy and Dick McGuire as one of the premier passing guards of the early years of the NBA. He had quick hands and a peripheral vision that allowed him to spot passing lanes and thread the ball to spots other guards would never consider. The 6–2 Phillip, a member of the University of Illinois' "Whiz Kids" of the early 1940s, began his 11-year BAA/NBA career with the Chicago Stags and enjoyed later stints with Philadelphia, Fort Wayne and Boston. A five-time All-Star Game performer, Phillip holds the distinction of being the first NBA player to record more than 500 assists in a single season (1951–52). When Boston Coach Red Auerbach needed a playmaker for a title run in 1956, he talked Phillip out of retirement and he helped the Celtics win their first championship. Phillip, who finished his outstanding career in 1958 with 3,759 assists (5.4 per game), was elected to the Hall of Fame in 1961.

RICKY PIERCE

BORN: *8-19-59 at Dallas, Texas.*
POSITION: *Guard*
TEAMS: *Pistons, 1982-83, Clippers, 1983-84, Bucks, 1984-90, Sonics, 1991-94, Warriors, 1994-95, Pacers, 1995-96, Nuggets, 1996-97, Hornets, 1997, Bucks, 1997-98.*

A relentless scorer who knew just about every NBA trick when it came to getting points on the board, Pierce has scored in just about every situation with, seemingly, just about every team in the NBA. A high-percentage shooter for someone who attempts so many outside jumpers, Pierce was instant-offense personified during his career. Some of his greatest moments came when he played off the bench, injecting life into the offense as soon as he entered. That trait allowed him to be voted the Sixth Man Award in 1987 and 1990 while with the Bucks. Later in his career, he bounced from team to team, almost as a hired gun for scoring-depleted rosters. He made only one appearance in the All-Star Game, in 1991 while with Milwaukee, but throughout his career was one of the most respected scorers in the league. A classic mid-range shooter, he never forced his attempts from the 3-point arc.

DRIVE TIME: *Ricky Pierce made his mark with eight teams in 16 years.*

STILL WAITING: *Scottie Pippen hoped the Blazers would be as successful as the Bulls.*

SCOTTIE PIPPEN

BORN: *9–25–65, at Hamburg, Ark.*
POSITION: *Guard/forward.*
TEAM: *Bulls, 1987–98, Rockets, 1998–99, Trailblazers, 1999–present.*

Scottie Pippen, a 1987 first-round draft pick, was a part of the two-headed monster that ruled professional basketball in Chicago. The former Central Arkansas star, like teammate Michael Jordan, is an athletic force who gave the Bulls a powerful presence on both ends of the court. If you like offense, Pippen can provide it with a soft outside jumper, a pull-up runner or a spectacular dunk. If you prefer defense, he can go chest-to-chest with anybody in the game. The 6–7 swingman is a three-time All-NBA first-team selection and a seven-time NBA All-Defensive first-teamer. But more importantly, he was a valuable cog on Chicago's six championship teams of the 1990s. To illustrate Pippen's all-around abilities, consider 1994–95: He led the Bulls in scoring (21.4), rebounding (8.1), assists (5.2), steals (2.94), blocks (1.13) and minutes (38.2). The seven-time All-Star was in the 1992 and 1996 Olympic Dream Teams. But after helping the Bulls to their sixth championship in 1997-98, Pippen struggled to find the same sort of success after the Bulls disbanded. He was traded to Houston, joining Charles Barkley and Hakeem Olajuwon in what was supposed to launch the Rockets into the NBA Finals. But they lost in the first round, Pippen criticized Barkley's work habits and wound up being traded to Portland. He did lead the Blazers into the Western Conference Finals against the Los Angeles Lakers, but the Lakers prevailed in seven games.

JIM POLLARD

BORN: *7–9–22, at Oakland, Calif.*
POSITION: *Forward.*
TEAM: *Lakers (NBL/NBA), 1948–55.*

Pollard, a 6–5 leaper, was the perfect complement to George Mikan and Vern Mikkelsen in a vaunted Minneapolis Lakers frontcourt that otherwise lacked finesse and athleticism. Pollard was a deadly outside shooter who could bang inside and perform dazzling aerial displays. The "Kangaroo Kid" began his professional career in the American Basketball League before joining Mikan and the newly formed Lakers in the National Basketball League. The Lakers rolled to an NBL championship in 1948 and followed with BAA/NBA titles in 1949, '50, '52, '53 and '54. The Minneapolis frontcourt, with point guard Slater Martin directing traffic, was simply unstoppable and Pollard was a major factor. When Pollard retired in 1955, he had scored 6,522 points (13.1) and played in four All-Star Games. Pollard, an All-NBA first-team selection in 1950, was elected to the Hall of Fame in 1977 He also coached at the college, ABA and NBA levels.

KEVIN PORTER

BORN: *4–17–50, at Chicago, Ill.*
POSITION: *Guard.*
TEAMS: *Bullets, 1972–75, 1979–83, Pistons, 1975–77, 1978–79, Nets, 1978.*

Porter was a classic NBA point guard who used his outstanding quickness and clever passing to set up teammates for easy baskets. Porter, who played his college ball at St. Francis of Pennsylvania, worked with a cockiness that made him an unpopular figure among NBA opponents. But he was a master at the fast break and teammates had to constantly beware of pinpoint passes seemingly coming from nowhere. The ever-scowling Porter began his career in Baltimore and blossomed into a big-time assist man. In 1974–75, he averaged 8.0 and a year later he raised that average to 10.2 in Detroit. In 1978–79, he became the NBA's first 1,000-assist man and also averaged a career-high 15.4 points. Porter, who spent his first three seasons with the Bullets and returned to Washington for his last three, retired in 1983 with 7,645 points (11.6) and 5,314 assists (8.1).

FOLLOW THE LEADER: *Terry Porter brought veteran leadership to three teams.*

TERRY PORTER

BORN: *4-8-63 at Milwaukee, Wis.*
POSITION: *Guard.*
TEAMS: *Trail Blazers, 1985-95, Timberwolves, 1995-98, Heat, 1998-99, Spurs, 1999-present.*

A player who has beaten the odds almost his entire career, Porter emerged from small-school Wisconsin-Stevens Point to first earn a place at the 1984 Olympic basketball trials and then move on to a respected career with the Trail Blazers. The heart of a Portland team that twice made it to the NBA Finals, Porter ably set up teammates Clyde Drexler and Jerome Kersey for nearly a decade. He then moved on to a second stage of his career, when his veteran savvy was used in a reserve role to help tutor younger players in Minnesota, Miami and San Antonio. Despite playing well into his late 30s, Porter remains one of the best-conditioned players in the NBA, capable of putting up the same type of numbers he did when he was in his 20s. He remains a player capable of taking and making clutch shots. In addition to making two All-Star Games, he was voted the J. Walter Kennedy Citizenship Award for community service in 1993 while with Portland.

MARK PRICE

BORN: *2-15-64, at Bartlesville, Okla.*
POSITION: *Guard.*
TEAMS: *Cavaliers, 1986–95, Bullets, 1995–96, Warriors, 1996–97; Magic, 1997–99.*

Price is living, proof there is still a place for the little man in the NBA. The 6-foot former Georgia Tech point guard thrived for a decade, mystifying critics who said he was too slow, too small and too deliberate for a high-level game. Price, a second-round 1986 pick by Dallas, was acquired by Cleveland in a draft-day trade that helped turn the Cavaliers into an Eastern Conference power. Through hard work and gritty determination, he developed into a first-class floor general, a nice combination of shooter, penetrator and defender who can step up his game at critical moments. One of the best 3-point marksmen in the league, Price also was a

PRICE IS RIGHT: *Mark Price played in Cleveland during the Cavaliers' glory days.*

career 90-percent free-throw shooter who ranked consistently among the assist leaders. The two-time Long Distance Shootout champion and four-time All-Star was plagued by injuries after 1995, a factor in his trades to Washington, Golden State and Orlando, where he played 63 games, including 33 starts, in 1997–98. After being waived by the Magic in June, 1998, he retired as a player, but returned to his alma mater to become an assistant to Bobby Cremins at Georgia Tech.

240

R

FRANK RAMSEY

BORN: *7–13–31, at Corydon, Ky.*
POSITION: *Guard.*
TEAM: *Celtics, 1954–64.*

Ramsey carved a Hall of Fame career out of his nine seasons as a substitute guard for the powerful Boston Celtics. Never a starter, the 6–3 Ramsey had the ability to come off the bench in pressure situations and ignite an offense, a trump card Celtics Coach Red Auerbach played to perfection. Time after time, the heady and steady Ramsey came through in the clutch, never complaining about playing time and earning the respect of apprecia-tive Boston fans. Ramsey, a former star under Adolph Rupp at the University of Kentucky, was rewarded with seven championship rings as he piled up 8,378 points (13.4) and a surprising 3,410 rebounds (5.5). His averages in 98 post-season games were mirror images of the regular season. Ramsey, who played through 1964 without ever performing in an All-Star Game, was elected to the Hall of Fame in 1981.

WILLIS REED

BORN: *6–25–42, at Hico, La.*
POSITION: *Center.*
TEAM: *Knicks, 1964–74.*

Reed was the physical and inspirational leader of a Knicks team that captured championships in 1970 and '73. The hard-working center, who suffered a series of knee injuries, scored 12,183 points (18.7 per game) and grabbed 8,414 rebounds (12.9) over a 10–year career that ended in 1974. The 6–10, 240-pound Reed, a former Grambling State University star, earned Rookie of the Year honors in 1964–65 while bat-tling tenaciously against the likes of Wilt Chamberlain and Bill Russell. His physi-cal presence was complemented by an ability to move outside for a soft left-handed jump shot. Reed was at his best in 1969–70, when he became the first player

WAR GAMES: *Willis Reed (left) won NBA Championships with the Knicks in 1970 and '73.*

to earn All-Star Game, regular-season and NBA Finals MVP citations in the same season while leading the Knicks to their first championship. Injuries destroyed his 1971–72 season, but he returned to ignite another title run in 1972–73. Reed, a seven-time All-Star, was elected to the Hall of Fame in 1981.

BRYANT REEVES

BORN: *6-8-73 at Fort Smith, Ark.*
POSITION: *Center.*
TEAMS: *Grizzlies, 1995-present.*

Known as "Big Country," Reeves is among the bulkiest centers in today's NBA, which has its advantages and also presents its negatives. Because of his build, Reeves is able to clog the lane by himself, preventing opposing players from gaining easy entry to the rim. The downside is that Reeves is one of the most immobile big men in the game, with quicker opposing centers able to almost walk around him on the way to the basket. A player who has cultivated a decent offensive game from limited basketball roots, Reeves is capable of posting consistent 20-point games when featured in the offense. However, for a player of his size, he does not exactly put up the type of rebounding and blocked-shot totals that the Grizzlies might have expected. Offseason condi-tioning also has been a problem, with

Reeves continually reporting to training camp well above his playing weight. Still, he was voted second-team All-Rookie in 1996 and opposing coaches respect his offensive game enough to often send a double-team into the lane.

GLEN RICE

BORN: *5–28–67, at Flint, Mich.*
POSITION: *Guard/forward.*
TEAMS: *Heat, 1989–95, Hornets, 1995–98, Lakers, 1998–2000, Knicks, 2000–present.*

Rice is one of the game's pure outside shooters. When the 6–8 small forward goes into his zone, he can produce points in bunches from any place and angle on the court. Rice, whose long-range bombing helped the University of Michigan win the 1989 NCAA Tournament championship, was drafted by the Miami Heat with the fourth overall pick of the 1989 draft. He averaged 13.6 points as a rookie and jumped his average to 22.3 two years later, when he also grabbed 5.0 rebounds per game. Rice was the focus of the struggling Heat's offense for six seasons before a 1995 trade sent him to Charlotte, where he averaged 21.6 points in his first season. In 1996–97 his 26.8 average was the league's

TITLE TIME: *The Lakers traded Glen Rice to New York weeks after winning the NBA title.*

BIG COUNTRY: *Bryant Reeves was supposed to be a cornerstone for the expansion Grizzlies.*

third-best and he earned All-Star Game MVP honors after scoring 26 points in 25 minutes. Critics have labelled Rice a one-dimensional shooter, but he has worked hard to develop a floor game and improve his defensive play, a fact that earned him a deserved third All-Star appearance in 1998. In the 1998-99 season, he was traded to the Los Angeles Lakers for Eddie Jones and Elden Campbell. He averaged 17.5 points per game that season. But his averaged dropped to 15.9 in his second season, when coach Phil Jackson arrived with his triangle offense. Rice did not take kindly to becoming the third option behind Shaquille O'Neal and Kobe Bryant, and he was often the subject of trade rumors. An uneasy peace followed, and the team made it to the NBA Finals, where Rice—and his wife—spoke out about his diminished role. But after the Lakers beat the Pacers in six games to win the title, Rice said he'd like to remain in L.A. However, he was traded to the New York Knicks in the off-season.

242

MITCH RICHMOND

BORN: *6–30–65, at Fort Lauderdale, Fla.*
POSITION: *Guard.*
TEAMS: *Warriors, 1988–91, Kings, 1991–98; Wizards, 1998–present*

A well-rounded shooting guard who carried the scoring load for the Sacramento Kings, this 6–5 former Kansas State University star can fire from 3-point range, drive the lane, finish the fast break and post up smaller guards. Richmond, the fifth overall pick of the 1988 draft, averaged 22 points and 5.9 rebounds in 1988–89 en route to Rookie of the Year honors. Over his first nine seasons, his scoring average never dipped below 21.9—including a career best in 1996–97—putting him in select NBA

RICH HISTORY:
Mitch Richmond was was slowed by injuries late in his career but he remained a respected veteran.

company. Richmond spent three seasons with Golden State before a 1991 trade brought him to lowly Sacramento. Although he remained a reliable performer, Richmond was unable to bring about the hoped-for improvement in the Kings' fortunes and, in 1998 after much trade speculation, was sent to the Washington Wizards, with Otis Thorpe, in exchange for Chris Webber. One highlight of Richmond's career was the 1995 All-Star Game, when he came off the bench for the West and scored 23 points, earning MVP honors. He has been unable to duplicate feats like that in Washington, where he averaged 19.7 points in 1998–99 and 17.4 in 1999–2000, when injuries forced him to miss eight games. Still he remained a key figure in Washington.

ISAIAH RIDER

BORN: *3-12-71 at Oakland, Calif.*
POSITION: *Guard*
TEAMS: *Timberwolves, 1993-96, Trail Blazers, 1996-99, Hawks, 1999-2000, Lakers, 2000-present.*

Talk about your enigmas. Few players in the league and very few guards in the league possess the types of talents that Rider possesses. He can score from the perimeter with ease. He can get to the rim either with his quickness or through his strength. He can create scoring opportunities when they seemingly aren't there. He is the type of shooting guard that every team covets. Yet, despite all of that, he also is a shooting guard that three teams could not wait to get rid of and one that seemingly is unable to stick with a team for an appreciable period of time. For Rider, it all comes down to personality problems. He is habitually late to practices. He has trouble getting along with coaches and players. He insists on being the focus of the offense, but many times does not display the leadership necessary for such a role. While Rider figures to remain in the NBA for years to come, it also figures to be a tenuous ride. So much talent. Such little payoff. It is what has defined his career to this point.

DOC RIVERS

BORN: *12-13-61 at Chicago, Ill.*
POSITION: *Guard*
TEAMS: *Hawks, 1983-91, Clippers, 1991-92, Knicks, 1992-94, Spurs, 1995-96.*

One of the most cerebral and likable players in NBA lore, Rivers only recently took the step from player to coach. As with his play on the court, Rivers experienced immediate success on the sidelines with the Orlando Magic. Rivers went through several incarnations during his playing days. With Atlanta, he was part of a fast-paced offense, feeding the scoring skills of Dominique Wilkins, Kevin Willis, Tree Rollins, John Battle, Cliff Levingston, and, of course, himself. The Hawks were a treat to watch, even if they did not experience great playoff success. From there, Rivers evolved into more of a playmaker and defensive presence during his tenures

ROUGH RIDE: *Isaiah Rider's act got old in Atlanta, just as it had in Minnesota and Portland.*

with the Clippers, Knicks and Spurs. He was among the best in the league at drawing charging violations, with opponents continually accusing him of "flopping," which, truth be told, often was the case. He made only one All-Star Game appearance over his career, but still stands as the Hawks' all-time leader in assists.

ALVIN ROBERTSON

BORN: *7–22-62, at Barberton, Ohio.*
POSITION: *Guard.*
TEAMS: *Spurs, 1984–89, Bucks, 1989–93, Pistons, 1993, Raptors, 1995–96.*

Robertson was a do-everything big guard for over a decade. The 6–4 former University of Arkansas star was a hard-working offensive and defensive player who made his mark on the game. In his prime, Robertson was a double-digit scorer, a hard-nosed rebounder and an outstanding passer, whether in a half-court game or on the break. He also was a two-time All-Defensive first-teamer who topped 200 steals in a season six times. Robertson, a first-round 1984 draft pick by San Antonio, played five seasons

BREAKING DOWN: *Alvin Robertson did a little bit of everything in his years with San Antonio.*

with the Spurs, averaging better than 17 points four times and posting consistent rebounding and assist totals. He spent the next three seasons in Milwaukee before splitting 1992–93 with the Bucks and Pistons. A four-time All-Star and 10,000-point scorer, Robertson sat out the 1993–94 and 1994–95 seasons with back problems, resurfacing in 1995–96 with the Raptors.

OSCAR ROBERTSON

See Legends of the NBA *page 134–135*

CLIFF ROBINSON

BORN: *12-16-66 at Buffalo, N.Y.*
POSITION: *Forward.*
TEAMS: *Trail Blazers, 1989-97, Suns, 1997-present.*

Nicknamed "Uncle Cliffy" during Portland's two runs to the NBA Finals and known for his ubiquitous headbands, Robinson is a big man who can take his game all the way out to the 3-point arc and find success. While he was forced into playing more of a power role earlier in his career, he has thrived when allowed to play a perimeter role. With his 6-10 build, he is able to shoot over smaller forwards with ease and also can play a more efficient game than when he is inserted in a pivot role. While personality questions left him as a second round pick out of the University of Connecticut in 1989, he quickly evolved into one of the game's top young players. He proved especially efficient off the bench in Portland, behind veteran talents such as Kevin Duckworth and Buck Williams. He was voted the Sixth Man Award in 1993 while with the Trail Blazers, but all the while expressed a preference to one day emerge as a starter. When that opportunity was presented in free agency, he quickly jumped at the chance to join the Phoenix Suns, where he has revived his career.

DAVID ROBINSON

BORN: *8–6–65, at Key West, Fla.*
POSITION: *Center.*
TEAM: *Spurs, 1987–present.*

Robinson, the NBA's 1994–95 MVP, is the perfect center. He can score, pass, shoot free throws, run the floor and guard with a Bill Russell-like intensity. His 18-foot jumper is deadly and his shot-blocking defense stifling. The Spurs were so taken with the 7–1 U.S. Naval Academy senior that they drafted him with the first overall pick of '87 and waited two years while he fulfilled his military commitment. "The Admiral" blossomed quickly, averaging 24.3 points and 12.0 rebounds en route to 1989–90 Rookie of the Year honors. After leading the league in scoring in 1993–94 (29.8), his average dipped below 23 for the first time in 1997–98 (to a team-leading 21.6) as rookie Tim Duncan took some of the offensive load off Robinson's shoulders. Robinson, a left-hander who averaged an

(Opposite) BANDING TOGETHER: *Cliff Robinson (center) was a fan favorite in Portland.*

ADMIRAL SAILS: *David Robinson (50) overcame numerous injuries to help the Spurs win a title.*

season, Robinson was drafted with the first overall pick and forged a 21.9 rookie average while grabbing 6.4 rebounds per game. He averaged 20.2 points in a solid second season before the departure of his young frontcourt partner Vin Baker to the SuperSonics placed even more of an offensive burden on his young shoulders. Robinson responded by raising his scoring average to 23.4 points per game and improved his field shooting average by five points, to .470. Although the Bucks improved slightly to 36 wins, it was, unfortunately, still not good enough to make the playoffs. That changed in 1998–99, when new coach George Karl led the Bucks back into the post-season. Robinson averaged 18.4 points in the regular season and 20.7 in the playoffs, though the Bucks were swept by the Indiana Pacers in the first round. Robinson averaged 20.9 points the next season, as the Bucks returned to the playoffs. This time they extended the series to five games, only to fall again to the Pacers.

GUY RODGERS

BORN: *9–1–35, at Philadelphia, Pa.*
POSITION: *Guard.*
TEAMS: *Warriors, 1958–66, Bulls, 1966–67, Royals, 1967, Bucks, 1968–70.*

Rodgers, a left-handed version of NBA idol Bob Cousy, was a flashy point guard with great passing and ball-handling

FLASH AND DASH: *Left-hander Guy Rodgers was a flashy point guard for the Warriors.*

NBA-leading 4.49 blocks in 1992, is a four-time All-NBA and All-Defensive first-teamer and 1992 Defensive Player of the Year. A member of the 1992 gold medal-winning Olympic Dream Team, injuries limited him to just six games in the 1996–97 season. He came back strong in 1997-98, averaging 21.6 points and 10.6 rebounds in 73 games. Then, with Duncan's emergence, Robinson took a step back, averaging just 15.8 points and 10.0 rebounds in 1998-99. But his unselfishness was rewarded when the Spurs beat the New York Knicks to win their first NBA championship. Despite Robinson averaging 17.8 points and 9.6 rebounds, the Spurs were unable to repeat

in 1999-2000. Without an injured Duncan, they lost in the first round to the Phoenix Suns.

GLENN ROBINSON

BORN: *1–10–73, at Gary, Ind.*
POSITION: *Forward.*
TEAM: *Bucks, 1994–present.*

Milwaukee's "Big Dog" will be a big offensive force for years to come. The 6–7 small forward is an explosive scoring machine, both at the basket and from 3-point range. He entered the NBA in 1994 following a spectacular three-year college career at Purdue. After a national-best 30.3-point scoring average in his junior

skills. He was at his best when running the fast break for the Philadelphia/San Francisco Warriors. But he also was the creative force who found ways to get the ball low to scoring machine Wilt Chamberlain, his Warriors teammate for five-plus seasons. The 6-foot Rodgers was drafted out of Temple University in 1958, and quickly unveiled his bag of tricks—behind-the-back dribbles, no-look passes and dazzling scoop shots—that made him an instant fan favorite. Three times he averaged double figures in assists, leading the league twice, and he once recorded 28 in a single game, tying Cousy's then-NBA record. Rodgers, a four-time All-Star, spent eight of his 12 seasons with the Warriors and retired in 1970 after short stints in Cincinnati, Chicago and Milwaukee. He finished with career totals

FLOWER POWER: *Jalen Rose (right) has blossomed since he arrived at Indiana.*

of 10,415 points (11.7 per game) and 6,917 assists (7.8).

DENNIS RODMAN

See Legends of the NBA *page 136–137*

JALEN ROSE

BORN: *1-30-73 at Detroit, Mich.*
POSITION: *Guard/forward.*
TEAMS: *Nuggets, 1994-96,*
Pacers, 1996-present.

A classic case of a "tweener," Rose for years at the start of his career was limited by coaches who insisted on defining him as a small forward. While that is a position he has played with great success in recent years, Rose is far more than just that. An efficient ballhandler, Rose has expanded his game in recent seasons when such shackles have been removed and he has been allowed to play as any-

thing from a point guard to a shooting guard to a small forward. He finally has found himself in Indiana, where he continues to evolve into the Pacers' most reliable offensive threat, assuming that mantle from perennial All-Star Reggie Miller. With a deft outside shot and a lanky build that allows him to maneuver with ease around the basket, Rose has become one of the league's consummate shot-makers. His growth likely will have him as the cornerstone of Indiana's rebuilding project, as veterans such as Miller, Rik Smits and Mark Jackson are replaced by younger talents such as Travis Best, Al Harrington and Jonathan Bender. Of the famed Fab Five freshman at Michigan, Rose and Chris Webber have gone the farthest with their skills.

BILL RUSSELL

See Legends of the NBA *page 138–139*

S

DOLPH SCHAYES

BORN: 5-19-28, at New York, N.Y.
POSITION: Forward/center.
TEAMS: Nationals, 1949-63, Warriors, 1963-64.

The durable Schayes was one of the more athletic players of the early NBA and one of its most consistent performers. The former New York University star played 15 NBA seasons, all but one for Syracuse, and retired with a then-record 1,059 games played, 706 consecutively from 1952 to '61. Over his long career, Schayes opened up defenses with his ability to hit long-range set shots and penetrate to the basket. He also dominated the boards, posting 11 straight double-digit rebounding seasons and leading the league in 1950-51 (16.4). Schayes, a deadly free throw shooter, led the Nationals to the NBA Finals in 1950 and '54 and their only championship in 1955. A six-time All-NBA first-team selection and a 12-time All-Star, Schayes finished his career in 1964 with 19,247 points (18.2) and 11,256 rebounds (10.6). He was named to the NBA 25th Anniversary All-Time Team in 1970 and elected to the Hall of Fame in 1972.

DETLEF SCHREMPF

BORN: 1-21-63, at Leverkusen, Germany.
POSITION: Forward.
TEAMS: Mavericks, 1985-89, Pacers, 1989-93, SuperSonics, 1993-99, Trailblazers, 1999-2000.

Schrempf, a German native and a four-year star at the University of Washington, developed into one of the NBA's better all-around players. Schrempf is the complete offensive package, a 6-10 small or power forward who could pass, shoot, rebound and play defense. He was an unselfish player who made the most of his opportunities. Schrempf was a model of consistency since 1987, averaging between 14.8 and 19.1 points, while posting an excellent .514 (93 of 181) shooting percentage

TRIPLE THREAT *Detlef Schrempf was all-around threat in Dallas, Indiana, Seattle and Portland.*

from three-point range in 1991-92. Schrempf was selected by Dallas with the eighth pick of the 1985 draft and was used sparingly by the Mavericks. He didn't blossom until a 1989 trade to the Pacers increased his minutes and he really stepped up after Seattle acquired him in 1993. Schrempf, a two-time NBA Sixth Man Award winner with Indiana, suffered a succession of injuries, but still went past

15,000 career points. After six seasons in Seattle, Schrempf signed as a free agent with the Portland Trail Blazers for the 1999-2000 season. Used primarily as a backup, he averaged 7.5 points, 4.3 rebounds and 2.6 assists per game and did help Portland advance to the Western Conference Finals against the Los Angeles Lakers, but the Blazers lost in seven games. Schrempf retired after the season.

BYRON SCOTT

BORN: *3–28–61, at Ogden, Utah.*
POSITION: *Guard.*
TEAMS: *Lakers, 1983–93, Pacers, 1993–95, Grizzlies, 1995–96, Lakers, 1996–97.*

The 6–4 Scott spent most of his 10 Los Angeles seasons providing outside firepower as a complement to Magic Johnson's penetrating dish-off game. It was a perfect match for the former Arizona State University star, whose catch-and-shoot talent requires a point guard who can push the ball to the basket and draw away defenders. Scott was drafted by the Los Angeles Clippers in 1983 and his draft rights were traded to the Lakers, who watched him blossom in a solid rookie season. From 1984 through 1992, Scott's scoring average ranged from 14.5 points to 21.7. In 1985, he led the league in 3-point shooting with a .433 percentage and he helped the Lakers win championships in 1985, '87 and '88. Scott spent two years with Indiana and one with the expansion Grizzlies, before returning to the Lakers in 1996 to backup Eddie Jones at off guard. He saw enough action to surpass 15,000 points. In 1997-98, Scott played for Pananthinaikos in Greece before retiring as a player. He became head coach of the New Jersey Nets in 2000.

BILL SHARMAN

BORN: *5–25–26, at Abilene, Tex.*
POSITION: *Guard.*
TEAMS: *Capitols, 1950–51, Celtics, 1951–61.*

Sharman teamed with Bob Cousy for 10 years in one of the great backcourts of basketball history. Cousy provided the flash and glitter, while Sharman was the straight shooter for a Boston Celtics team that introduced the run-and-gun offense. Sharman, who starred at the University of Southern California, spent one year with the Washington Capitols before moving into Boston's backcourt of the future. While Cousy was dazzling fans and opponents with no-look passes and fancy drib-

OH, SHOOT: *Byron Scott's outside shooting complemented Magic Johnson's inside game.*

bling, Sharman was scoring in double figures and doing the little things that don't show up in the box scores. He was named All-NBA first team four times and played in eight All-Star Games, winning MVP honors in 1955. Sharman finished his career in 1961 with 12,665 points (17.8 per game) after playing on four championship teams as a charter member of the Celtics' 13-year basketball dynasty. He was named to the NBA 25th Anniversary All-Time Team in 1970 and elected into the Hall of Fame in 1975.

JUMPING JACK: *Jack Sikma (43) was another center who was adept at shooting from the outside.*

JACK SIKMA

BORN: *11–14–55, at Kankakee, Ill.*
POSITION: *Forward/center.*
TEAMS: *SuperSonics, 1977–86, Bucks, 1986–91.*

The 7-foot Sikma was an outstanding all-around center and the most popular player in Seattle's NBA history. Drafted out of little Illinois Wesleyan University in 1977, Sikma spent nine of his 14 seasons in Seattle, leading the SuperSonics to NBA Finals appearances in his first two campaigns and a 1979 championship. Sikma was a 250-pounder who thrived offensively inside the lane with an ugly, overhead jumper that was virtually unstoppable and a short hook. He was an aggressive rebounder who averaged in double figures eight times and a coachable, tireless worker who steadily improved his game, both offensively and defensively. The seven-time All-Star was traded to the Bucks in 1986, and spent his final five seasons in Milwaukee without an appreciable drop in production. Sikma retired in 1991 with 17,287 points (15.6) and 10,816 rebounds (9.8).

PAUL SILAS

BORN: *7–12–43, at Prescott, Ariz.*
POSITION: *Forward.*
TEAMS: *Hawks, 1964–69, Suns, 1969–72, Celtics, 1972–76, Nuggets, 1976–77, SuperSonics, 1977–80.*

Silas, a physical 6–7 battler, built a 16-year career around his ability to grab rebounds and play intense, chest-to-chest defense. Never a headline or attention grabber, Silas valiantly performed behind-the-scenes trenchwork for three NBA champions. The former Creighton University star was drafted by the St. Louis Hawks in 1964, but it wasn't until a 1969 trade to Phoenix that he blossomed into a valuable role player. Over the next seven seasons, Silas averaged better than 11 rebounds per game and he anchored Boston's 1974 and '76 title teams as Dave Cowens, John Havlicek and Jo Jo White garnered the headlines. When Seattle acquired an aging Silas in 1977, the Sonics made consecutive NBA Finals appearances, winning a championship in 1979. Silas, a two-time All-Defensive first-team selection, retired in 1980 with only a 9.4 scoring average, but his 12,357 rebounds (9.9) rank among the all-time leaders.

JERRY SLOAN

BORN: *3–28–42, at McLeansboro, Ill.*
POSITION: *Guard/forward.*
TEAMS: *Bullets, 1965–66, Bulls, 1966–76.*

The hard-nosed Sloan was the guts of a Chicago Bulls team that advanced to the

Western Conference Finals twice in the mid-1970s. The 6–5 Sloan, an Evansville University product, was an intense, in-your-face defensive stopper who frustrated opponents with a rugged physical presence that drew charges of "dirty play." But the only thing dirty about Sloan was his uniform after games in which he bumped bodies under the basket, hit the floor after taking charges and dove relentlessly into every ball scramble on the court. He was emotional, he was dedicated and he knew only one speed—full throttle. Sloan played one season for Baltimore before joining the Bulls in the 1966 expansion draft. He spent the next 10 seasons averaging 14 points and 7.4 rebounds while claiming four NBA All-Defensive first-team citations. After retiring in 1976, Sloan took his intensity to the bench as a successful coach for the Bulls and the current-edition Utah Jazz.

JOE SMITH

BORN: *7–26–75, at Norfolk, Va.*
POSITION: *Forward.*
TEAM: *Warriors, 1995–98, 76ers, 1998, Timberwolves, 1998–present.*

The hard-working Smith will climb the NBA talent ladder quickly. He entered the league in the 1995 draft at age 19 and quickly displayed the talents that could help him become one of the game's top swing forwards. Smith, who was grabbed by the Warriors with the draft's first overall pick after his sophomore season at Maryland, showed agility around the basket while averaging 15.3 and 18.7 points in his first two seasons. He can use either hand and his shooting range goes to 18 feet. Smith also will run the court, battle on both backboards—averaging 8.7 and 8.5 rebounds in his first two seasons—and his interior defense will improve because he is coachable. Smith, who averaged 20.8 points and 10.6 rebounds as a college sophomore, shows great effort every time he steps on the court. That's why the Philadelphia 76ers were so eager to get him in a trade for Clarence Weatherspoon and Jim Jackson on Feb. 17, 1998. But after averaging just 14.6 points that season, Smith signed as a free agent with the Minnesota Timberwolves before the 1998-99 season. There, he averaged 13.7 points

THROWN TO THE WOLVES: *Joe Smith has found greater success with Minnesota's Timberwolves.*

in his first season and 9.9 in his second and became a key part of the Wolves' attack.

RANDY SMITH

BORN: *12-12-48.*
POSITION: *Guard*
TEAMS: *Braves, 1971-78, Clippers, 1978-79, Cavaliers, 1979-81, Knicks, 1981-82, Clippers, 1982-83, Hawks, 1983.*

The NBA does not list Smith among its "all-time greatest players" in that section in its official player register. And that is a shame, because in a game defined by endurance, few have been able to endure as well as the feisty, fleet and quick ball-handler. For 10 consecutive seasons, Smith appeared in each of his teams' 82 games,

an NBA record for consistency that stood until forward A.C. Green recently surpassed that stretch. But Smith was not only a player who showed up on a nightly basis, he also was one of the fastest, if not the all-time fastest, guard in league history. He could outrun multiple opponents on the way to the basket in transition. And it wasn't only fleet feet that allowed him to endure. With two of the fastest hands in the business, Smith was one of the great steals artists. Smith twice appeared in the All-Star Game and even took home the Most Valuable Player trophy from his second appearance. He was a scorer, who could defend and a defender who could quickly turn the tables with one of his steals. But, mostly, he endured.

NO POINT: *Steve Smith (right) has thrived since his move from point guard to shooting guard.*

RIK SMITS

BORN: *8–23–66, at Eindhoven, Holland.*
POSITION: *Center.*
TEAM: *Pacers, 1988–2000.*

Smits was not your typical 7–4 center. He possessed good shooting range for a big man and his career .500-plus field-goal percentage was among the best in the league. Because he had size, agility and a soft-shooting touch. Smits, who was born and raised in Holland, was selected by Indiana with the second overall pick of the 1988 draft after four seasons at Marist College. He earned a spot on the NBA All-Rookie first team in 1988–89. Smits became as a top-line center, capable of matching up with any of the game's best pivot men. He averaged a career best 18.5 points in 1995–96 but it was 1997–98, when his average fell to 16.7, that demonstrated he was reaching the pinnacle of his career. Foot problems hobbled him for the next several seasons, and in 1999–2000 his averaged dipped to 12.9 points and 5.1 rebounds. Still, the

FOOT SOLDIER: *Injuries to both feet limited the effectiveness of 7–4 Rik Smits.*

STEVE SMITH

BORN: *3-31-69 at Highland Park, Mich.*
POSITION: *Guard*
TEAMS: *Heat, 1991–94, Hawks, 1994–99, Trail Blazers, 1999–present.*

A classic spot-up jumper shooter, Smith was much more at the start of his NBA career, when he also could use his famed hesitation dribble to also get to the basket with ease. But knee troubles began to limit his game during his tenure with the Heat, when he underwent two operations. From that point, he was mostly content to spot up near the 3-point arc and bury the long jumper. His game began to blossom when he accepted the fact that he was more of a shooting guard than a point guard. It was a difficult adjustment at first, when Smith insisted he wanted to following in the footsteps of another famed Michigan State alum, Magic Johnson. But once he moved to shooting guard, Smith thrived. He formed a potent tandem in Atlanta for several years playing alongside Mookie Blaylock and he continued his success when he was dealt to Portland to play alongside Damon Stoudamire. Among the streakiest shooters in the league, Smith at times could dominate his team's offense for an entire quarter, yet at other times could go through a game without hitting more than one or two shots.

CHOKE HOLD: *Despite his many talents on the court, Latrell Sprewell (8) is best remembered for his off-court behavior.*

Pacers advanced to NBA Finals, where Smits faced the Lakers' powerful center Shaquille O'Neal. In order to keep him out of foul trouble, Pacers coach Larry Bird usually did not have Smits guard O'Neal on defense, but he did take advantage of Smits' outside shooting on offense, which pulled O'Neal away from the basket. The Pacers wound up losing to the Lakers in six games.

LATRELL SPREWELL

BORN: *9–8–70, at Milwaukee, Wis.*
POSITON: *Guard.*
TEAM: *Warriors, 1992–98; Knicks, 1998–present.*

Sprewell can score, pass and play pressure defense. Sadly, he will be remembered more for his off-court problems than his on-court talent. Sprewell was involved in an ugly fight with Golden State coach P.J. Carlesimo, an act that earned him headlines around the world and sparked a national debate about the modern professional athlete. He was initially banned by the NBA for one year, a suspension that was reduced on appeal. The other side of Sprewell is the ability that earned him a 1994 All-NBA citation and three trips to the All-Star Game. Perhaps having played in only one post-season series in his first six years was the main cause of Sprewell's questionable attitude. His finest season came in 1996–97 when he established career highs with 24.2 points and 6.3 assists per game. Sprewell possesses a special talent for creating shots, especially off the dribble, but it also results in a lower shooting percentage. An iron man on the court, Sprewell has averaged more than 40 minutes a game in four seasons. After Golden State traded him to New York before the 1998-99 season, Sprewell got back on track. He was the Knicks' second leading scorer in the regular season and led them in the playoffs by averaging 20.4 points per game. New York advanced to the NBA Finals but lost to the San Antonio Spurs in five games. In 1999-2000, he averaged 18.6 points, 4.3 rebounds, 4.0 assists and 1.3 steals per game during the regular season. But in the playoffs, New York lost to Indiana in six games in the Eastern Conference Finals.

JERRY STACKHOUSE

BORN: *11–5–74, at Kinston, N.C.*
POSITION: *Guard/forward.*
TEAM: *76ers, 1995–97, Pistons 1997–present.*

Stackhouse was followed by the Michael Jordan spotlight through two college seasons at North Carolina and his rookie

STACKING UP: *Jerry Stackhouse (front) has taken over as the Pistons' main sparkplug.*

campaign with the Philadelphia 76ers. As an acrobatic shooting guard who played at Jordan's alma mater, the comparisons were natural. And Stackhouse lived up to early billing with a solid rookie performance that produced 19.2 points per game. Stackhouse plays with an intensity that convinced Detroit to trade for his services after he had played 22 games for the 76ers in the 1997–98 season. He is explosive to the basket, his outside jump shot is improving and he can score in bunches. His scoring average rose to 20.7 in his second season before dipping to a cumulative 15.7 in the year of his trade. Part of the reason behind his departure from Philadelphia was a displeasure at having to share the ball with Rookie of the Year Allen Iverson. Of course, in Detroit he had to learn to play with Grant Hill, which took some time. In his first season, he averaged 14.5 points and often complained about how he was being used. But in his second season, he blossomed and averaged a career-best 23.6 points per game while receiving serious consideration for the league's Most Improved Player Award.

JOHN STARKS

BORN: *8-10-65 at Tulsa, Okla.*
POSITION: *Guard.*
TEAMS: *Warriors, 1988–89, Knicks, 1989–98, Warriors, 1998–99, Bulls, 2000, Jazz, 2000–present.*

Among the streakiest and feistiest players in recent memory, Starks was the spirit of Knicks basketball during much of the Patrick Ewing era. He could dominate a game with his outside shooting or his intense defense. He also could hurt his team's chances with his overly emotional play and awkward shot attempts. But he was respected as a teammate for the way he played each game as if it meant something. He led the Knicks to the NBA Finals in 1994, only to shoot the Knicks out of the title series against Houston with his wayward marksmanship. Nonetheless, New York would not have had nearly the success it did if he was not in place. During his tenure in New York, he won the Sixth Man Award in 1997 and also was named second-team All-Defensive in 1993. He also was selected for the 1994 All-Star Game. His Knicks career ended when he was dealt to Golden State in the trade that landed guard Latrell Sprewell and effectively began the next era of Knicks basketball.

JOHN STOCKTON

See Legends of the NBA *page 140–141*

MAURICE STOKES

BORN: *6-17-33.*
POSITION: *Forward*
TEAMS: *Royals, 1955-58.*

Stokes was headed toward what appeared to be a Hall of Fame career when he broke into the NBA in 1955 with Rochester. A remarkable rebounder, Stokes averaged 16.3, 17.4 and 18.1 rebounds in his three seasons, numbers that would

STARK PLUG: *John Starks took his high-energy game to the Utaz Jazz in 2000.*

have placed him at the top of the charts had his career been allowed to run a natural course. He also was a prolific scorer, averaging 16.8, 15.6 and 16.9 points during those three seasons. All the while, Stokes also was a team player, averaging at least 4.6 assists in each of his three seasons. But that's when tragedy robbed the sport of one of its potentially greatest talents. Apparently, during a game against the Lakers, a seemingly innocent mishap led to a brain injury that would incapacitate Stokes. He began feeling ill on the return flight from that game and was left paralyzed and bed-ridden. Twelve years after the incident, Stokes died from apparent complications, one of the most tragic losses in the game's history. Through it all, teammate Jack Twyman remained at his side.

DAMON STOUDAMIRE

BORN: *9-3-73 at Portland, Ore.*
POSITION: *Guard.*
TEAMS: *Raptors, 1995-98, Trail Blazers, 1998-present.*

Another former University of Arizona point guard who has found success in the NBA, Stoudamire helped carry the Raptors through the franchise's infancy. He still stands as that team's all-time leader in scoring and assists. He was successful from the start of his career, named Rookie of the Year in 1995 despite his team's deplorable finish in the standings and also was named first-team All-Rookie that season. The stakes were raised when he was dealt to Portland, a team with significant playoff hopes. While Stoudamire has experienced success with the Blazers, his shoot-first mentality has not always sat well with teammates. In fact, during his early trips to the postseason with Portland, he often would be yanked late in games in favor of the veteran savvy of Greg Anthony. Still, Stoudamire is considered one of the top young point guards in the game and even

FLOOR GENERAL: *Damon Stoudamire runs the show for the star-studded Portland Trail Blazers.*

with Portland's star-studded roster still is a player who all too often finds the ball in his hands when a critical shot is needed.

ROD STRICKLAND

BORN: *7-11-66 at Bronx, N.Y.*
POSITION: *Guard*
TEAMS: *Knicks, 1988-90, Spurs, 1990-92, Trail Blazers, 1992-96, Wizards, 1996-present.*

Another of the game's great enigmas, Strickland is among the most talented point guards in the NBA, a player who can approach 20 assists or 20 points and also put himself regularly in range of a triple-double with his rebounding. Yet,

seemingly at every stop there have been problems. He did not want to play in San Antonio and his actions on the court made that apparent. He never maximized his abilities while with Portland, and was dealt from there to Washington. And with the Wizards, he often would show up late for practices and games and at other times disappear even while on the court. The shame is that few players possess the skills of Strickland and with any discipline he likely would have made the All-Star Game several times by now, instead of still be awaiting his first invitation. His is respected enough to have made second-team All-NBA in 1998 and second-team All-Rookie in 1989.

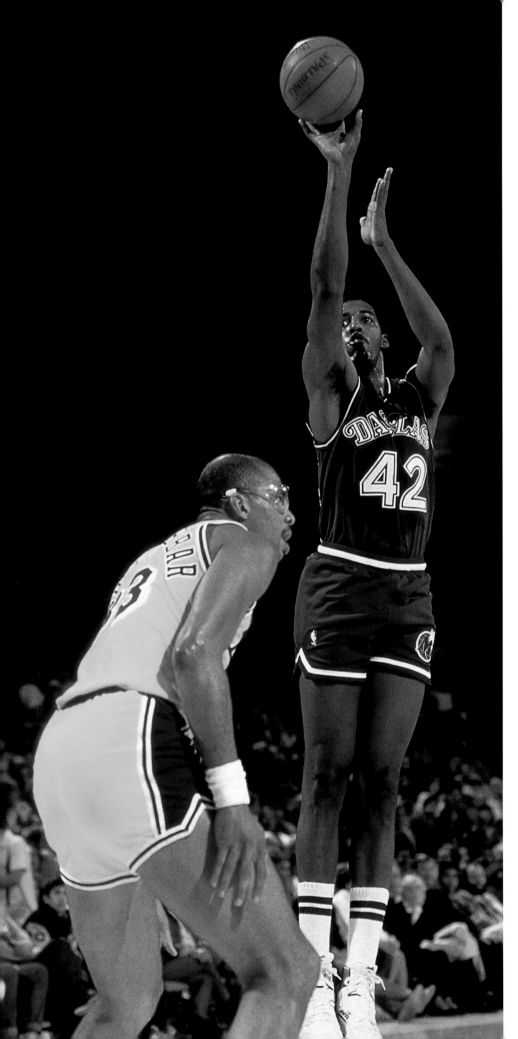

T

ROY TARPLEY

BORN: *11-28-64 at New York, N.Y.*
POSITION: *Forward.*
TEAMS: *Mavericks, 1986-91.*

Few players can make as convincing case about the dangers of drug abuse than Tarpley, a player who seemingly had it all at the start of his career with the Mavericks. This was a player, who, at 6-foot-11, displayed the skills of a center, power forward and small forward. He could play outside or bang inside. Named to the All-Rookie team in 1987, he later would win the Sixth Man Award in 1988. He appeared on the fast track to unlimited success, the Mavericks one of the NBA's most promising franchises with him in the lineup. And then it all ended abruptly. One of the few players to so violate the NBA's drug rules that he was suspended permanently, Tarpley was forced to seek basketball refuge overseas. There was talk of NBA comebacks, but Tarpley never was able to pull his personal life together. It is a shame, because his skills were amazing. He was a rebounder, a scorer and a defender, with long arms that made him a nuisance.

REGGIE THEUS

BORN: *10–13–57, at Inglewood, Calif.*
POSITION: *Guard.*
TEAMS: *Bulls, 1978–84, Kings, 1984–88, Hawks, 1988–89, Magic, 1989–90, Nets, 1990–91.*

The 6–7 Theus was an offensive-minded point guard who might have been better off as a shooting guard—a position that would have better utilized his long-range shooting and inside scoring capabilities. But he played most of his 13-year career with Chicago and Kansas City/Sacramento teams that needed him to be a play-maker—a role he filled reluctantly at first. But as Theus matured into a less point-

NO COMEBACK: *Drug problems cut short the promising career of Roy Tarpley (right).*

time leader in points, steals and assists, made his NBA debut in 1981, after leading Indiana University to an NCAA Tournament championship in his sophomore season. Thomas set a then-NBA record in 1984–85 with 1,123 assists (13.9) and he currently ranks fourth on the all-time list. Since his playing days, Thomas has been active in basketball administration. From 1994-97, he was a vice president and part owner of the Toronto Raptors. Thomas also became the majority owner of the Continental Basketball Association in 1999–2000, but

sold it when he became coach of the Indiana Pacers. He was elected to the Hall of Fame in 2000.

DAVID THOMPSON

BORN: 7–13–54, at Shelby, N.C.
POSITION: Guard/forward.
TEAMS: Nuggets (ABA/NBA), 1975–82, SuperSonics, 1982–84.

Thompson, one of the most athletically gifted players the game has ever produced, struggled through a controversial career that was short-circuited by sub-

RUNNIN' REBEL: *The run-and-gun style suited Reggie Theus since his days at UNLV.*

conscious team leader, his assist totals rose and his game took on a new dimension. Theus was most comfortable in a running-style offense, the kind he played for three run-and-gun seasons at the University of Nevada Las Vegas. He could be acrobatic at times and his shooting range was somewhere beyond the sidelines. Theus, a two-time All-Star, retired in 1991, after one-season stays in Atlanta, Orlando and New Jersey. He left with 19,015 points (18.5) and 6,453 assists (6.3).

ISIAH THOMAS

BORN: 4–30–61, at Chicago, Ill.
POSITION: Guard.
TEAM: Pistons, 1981–94.

Thomas, the ultimate point guard, treated the basketball court as his personal playground for 13 amazing seasons in Detroit. He penetrated, he passed, he shot, he cajoled and he led the Pistons to consecutive championships in 1989 and '90. By the time he was finished, in 1994 the lightning-quick, 6–1 Thomas had scored 18,822 points (19.2), handed out 9,061 assists (9.3) and appeared in 11 All-Star Games, winning MVP honors in two of them. He was a three-time All-NBA first-team selection and MVP of the 1990 NBA Finals, when he averaged 27.6 points and 7.0 assists in a scintillating performance. Thomas, the Pistons' all-

MAN IN CHARGE: *When Detroit dominated the NBA, Isiah Thomas (11) was its undisputed leader.*

258

stance abuse and personal problems. Thompson, who used his 44-inch vertical leap to skywalk North Carolina State University to the 1974 NCAA Tournament championship, burst upon the ABA scene in 1975 as one of the most heralded players in history. He didn't disappoint, thrilling Denver fans with above-the-rim acrobatics that produced averages of 26 points and 6.3 rebounds and the ABA's Rookie of the Year award. The amazing Thompson could score from anywhere with his smooth jump shot or dazzling aerial explosions. After the 1976 merger, the 6–5 Thompson brought his high-wire act to the NBA, averaging better than 21 points per game in five consecutive seasons and earning two All-NBA first-team berths. But his career quickly unraveled amid rumors of drug problems and he played only three more seasons, one with the Nuggets and two with the SuperSonics. The four-time NBA All-Star finished with a combined ABA/NBA total of 13,422 points (22.7).

NATE THURMOND

BORN: *7–25–41, at Akron, Ohio.*
POSITION: *Center.*
TEAMS: *Warriors, 1963–74, Bulls, 1974–75, Cavaliers, 1975–77.*

The 6–11 Thurmond was the perfect blend of offense and defense. He was physical around the basket, whether claiming rebounds or blocking shots, and he was smooth from the perimeter, where he could hit a soft jumper or feed a cutting teammate. The former Bowling Green State star was drafted by San Francisco in 1963 and played power forward because Wilt Chamberlain was dominating the middle. But the Warriors thought so highly of Thurmond, they traded Chamberlain in 1965. Over a 14-year career that included short stints with Chicago and Cleveland, Thurmond averaged 15 points (14,437) and 15 rebounds (14,464) per game. He also was a two-time All-Defensive first-teamer and a seven-time All-Star. The best illustration of Thurmond's versatility is that he was the first player to record a quadruple-double—22 points, 14 rebounds, 13 assists and 12 blocked shots in a 1974 game. He was elected to the Hall of Fame in 1984.

WAYMAN TISDALE

BORN: *6-9-64 at Tulsa, Okla.*
POSITION: *Forward.*
TEAMS: *Pacers , 1985-89, Kings, 1989-94, Suns, 1994-97.*

A college star at Oklahoma with an array of inside scoring skills, Tisdale brought his low-post game to the NBA and delivered with aplomb. He was a unique talent who would play in an area where most big men would succeed with brute force. Instead, Tisdale mastered a series of spins and fakes that allowed him to score without all the bumping and bruising employed by so many other players of his stature. A member of the gold-medal winning U.S. Olympic team at the 1984 Games, Tisdale did not garner any awards or All-Star berths during his NBA career, but was a respected scorer who twice averaged more than 20 points. His

KEEPING PACE: *Wayman Tisdale's low-post game included a variety of spins and fakes.*

best years came while playing in Indiana. Later in his career, injuries began to limit his play, to the point where he only was a shell of himself by the time he retired. Quitting was not as difficult for Tisdale as some others. Instead, he quickly assumed full-time interest in his passion for making music.

GARY TRENT

BORN: *9-22-74 at Columbus, Ohio*
POSITION: *Forward.*
TEAMS: *Trail Blazers, 1995-98, Raptors, 1998, Mavericks, 1998-present.*

And undersized power player, Trent has succeed in the NBA in much the same way he had succeeded as a college star at Ohio University — with a downright nasty approach to the game. Although his 6-foot-8 build leaves him somewhat undersized to play in a power role, Trent long has overcome such hurdles. In college, he played with such force in the Mid-America Conference that he was known as the Shaq of the MAC, a comparison to leviathan Lakers center Shaquille O'Neal. Buried on the bench during the early stages of his career in Portland, Trent flourished when he signed with the Dallas Mavericks as a free agent. On a team that features lithe 7-foot-6 center Shawn Bradley, Trent has been able to provide much-needed bulk to the lineup. While most of Trent's points come from near the basket, he is skilled enough to take the ball out on the floor to succeed. He also can be a fierce rebounder.

JACK TWYMAN

BORN: *5–11–34, at Pittsburgh, Pa.*
POSITION: *Guard/forward.*
TEAM: *Royals, 1955–66.*

Twyman will be remembered as one of the best pure-shooting forwards in the 1950s and '60s. The 6–6 University of Cincinnati product, who spent his entire 11-year professional career with the Royals—first in Rochester then in Cincinnati—averaged 31.2 points in 1959–60 and topped the 25-point barrier three times. By the time he brought the curtain down on his career in 1966, Twyman had scored 15,840 points (19.2 per game) and grabbed 5,424 rebounds (6.6). Twyman, who played in

TOUGH GUY: *Despite being undersized, Gary Trent more than makes up for it with his attitude.*

six All-Star Games, was most comfortable from the corner, where he punished sagging defenses. But he also could score inside and he formed a lethal offensive combination with Cincinnati teammates Oscar Robertson and Jerry Lucas for three exciting seasons. Twyman's efforts off-court in humanitarian activities were also well-known, especially his long-time legal guardianship of former teammate Maurice Stokes, who was paralyzed in a 1958 game and passed away 12 years later. Twyman was elected to the Hall of Fame in 1982.

260

U

WES UNSELD

BORN: *3–14–46, at Louisville, Ky.*
POSITION: *Center.*
TEAM: *Bullets, 1968–81.*

The 6–7, 245-pound Unseld was an enforcer-like center who ruled the boards and helped the Bullets reach four NBA Finals during the 1970s. Never a prolific scorer, Unseld made up for it with his leadership, intensity and unflagging dedication to rebounding. The physical

Unseld, a two-time Louisville All-American, was especially adept at pulling down missed shots and triggering the fast break with strong outlet passes. Over his 13 NBA seasons, all spent with the Bullets, he grabbed 13,769 rebounds (14.0) and scored 10,624 points (10.8). Unseld had a memorable debut season in 1968–69 at Baltimore, becoming only the second NBA player to be named Rookie of the Year and MVP in the same season. Over the next decade, Unseld's Bullets would win seven Central and Atlantic Division titles, four Eastern Conference titles and one championship (1978). The five-time All-Star, who later coached the Bullets for seven seasons, was elected to the Hall of Fame in 1988.

V

NICK VAN EXEL

BORN: *11–27–71, at Kenosha, Wis.*
POSITION: *Guard.*
TEAM: *Lakers, 1993–98, Nuggets, 1998–present.*

Van Exel is a point guard with an attitude. He's so arrogant and aggressive his Los Angeles Lakers teammates didn't dare take their eyes off the ball. The 6–1 left-hander has averaged more than 400 3-point shots a season in his career, connecting on over one-

POINT OF ATTACK: *Nick Van Exel (left) plays the point with attitude, whether in Los Angeles or Denver.*

third of them, but he's just as likely to explode to the basket with lightning-quick dashes. In his 1993–94 rookie season, most of those dashes ended up with him taking a shot. But since then, he has dished off more and raised his assists average to a career-high 8.5 in 1996–97. Van Exel's career numbers of 15.2 points and 7.5 assists per game might just be the tip of the iceberg and his maturing style of play was rewarded in 1998 with his first selection to the All-Star Game. He was a 1993 second-round steal for the Lakers, who ignored reports of attitude problems at the University of Cincinnati. But the Lakers weren't so enamored with him that they weren't willing to part with him. They traded him to Denver in 1998 for Tony Battie and the draft rights to Tyronn Lue. With the Nuggets, the headstrong Van Exel averaged 16.5 points and 7.4 assists in 1998–99 and 16.1 points and 9.0 assists in 1999–2000.

KEITH VAN HORN

BORN: *10-23-75 at Fullerton, Calif.*
POSITION: *Forward.*
TEAMS: *Nets, 1997-present.*

A combination small forward and power forward, Van Horn initially had to fend off comparisons to former Celtics legend Larry Bird. While Van Horn has a feathery outside touch and, like Bird, can take the ball to the basket despite apparently lacking quickness, he in many respects is more of an athlete than Bird. A dynamic jumper, Van Horn torments defenders with his array of scoring capabilities. Put a small forward on him and he will continue to post up and launch turnaround jumpers. Put a power player on him and he will take his game to the 3-point arc and either launch jumpers or beat his man to the basket. While his defense is lacking, there are enough other skills to overcome such a shortcoming. In addition to his scoring, passing and rebounding also are strong suits of the former University of Utah star. He was named first-team All-Rookie in 1998 and likely soon will find himself in a regular rotation at the All-Star Game. In many ways, he is a star the Nets could build around for years to come.

NET RESULT: *Keith Van Horn brings many skills to the Nets, but New Jersey still struggles.*

KIKI VANDEWEGHE

BORN: *8–1–58, at Wiesbaden, West Germany.*
POSITION: *Forward.*
TEAMS: *Nuggets, 1980–84, Trail Blazers, 1984–89, Knicks, 1989–92, Clippers, 1992–93.*

Vandeweghe was an offensive-minded small forward who thrived in Denver Coach Doug Moe's run-and-gun attack of the early 1980s. The 6–8 former UCLA star knew one speed—fast forward—and he never stopped running in a 13-year NBA career that produced 15,980 points and an impressive 19.7 per game average. Vandeweghe, the son of former NBA guard Ernie Vandeweghe, was not blessed with great speed or leaping ability. But he possessed a first-step quickness that allowed him to blow past defenders with either hand and a quick release that permitted him to get off shots in heavy traffic. His shoulder fake threw defenders off balance and his 20-foot jumper was soft and accurate. Vandeweghe averaged better than 20 points seven times, including a 26.9 mark for Portland in 1986–87, when he led the NBA in 3-point shooting (48.1 percent). The two-time All-Star retired in 1993, after short stints with the Knicks and Clippers.

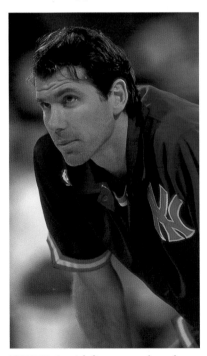

FOOT STEP: *A quick first step made up for the deficiencies in Kiki Vandeweghe's game.*

262

W

ANTOINE WALKER

BORN: *8-12-76 at Chicago, Ill.*
POSITION: *Forward.*
TEAMS: *Celtics, 1996-present.*

Yet another perplexing personality, Walker is part of the new breed of players who enter the NBA way too cocky. Yes, he is good, very good. But all too often Walker tends to think he is better than he is. A remarkable ballhandler for a player of his size, Walker can score from almost anywhere on the court. He just as easily can knock down the 3-pointer as score off an offensive rebound. But many opponents loathe a style that tends to draw attention to himself. Indeed, if there is one word most often used to describe Walker, it is immaturity. It is why, despite talents that led Walker to being named first-team All-Rookie in 1997, the Celtics spent the next few seasons seeking possible trade options. Despite the off-court concerns, Walker is unlike many other talents in the league. He is at his best with a series of finesse moves around the basket, but also must be honored for his ability to hit the jumper. He also has the athleticism to play the pressing defense style that was employed when he first joined the Celtics.

CHET WALKER

BORN: *2–22–40, at Benton Harbor, Mich.*
POSITION: *Guard/forward.*
TEAMS: *Nationals/76ers, 1962–69, Bulls, 1969–75.*

"Chet The Jet" was one of the best one-on-one players the game has produced. The 6–6 former Bradley University star had an incredible knack for creating shots, pumping two or three times while in the air and either making the basket or drawing a foul that he usually turned into two points. Because of those instinctive offensive abilities and a natural 20-foot jump shot, Walker was the late-game go-to man for the Philadelphia 76ers and Chicago Bulls over a 13-year NBA career that produced 18,831 points (18.2) and 7,314 rebounds (7.1). Walker was a key figure for the 76ers' 1966–67 championship team that won a regular-season-record 68 games and ended the Boston Celtics' eight-year title reign. He averaged 19.3 points and 8.1 rebounds for a squad that included Wilt Chamberlain, Billy Cunningham and Hal Greer. Walker played in seven All-Star Games and averaged 18.2 points over 13 postseason appearances.

RASHEED WALLACE

BORN: *9-17-74 at Philadelphia, Pa.*
POSITION: *Forward.*
TEAMS: *Bullets, 1995-96, Trail Blazers, 1996-97.*

A fierce talent who sometimes allows that intensity to get the best of him, Wallace stands among the most athletic big men in the game. To complement dunks so dynamic that opponents tend to clear out of the way when he comes into the lane, Wallace also has the skills to step out and hit the long jumper. He also plays defense with a fervor, his shot-blocking capabilities a key to his team's defensive sets. There is, however, a dark side. Wallace has yet to demonstrate an ability to get his temper under control. During the 1999-2000 season, he set an NBA record for technical fouls in a season. His temper

NO BACKING DOWN: *Antoine Walker has proven he can score from anywhere on the court.*

is to the point that the Trail Blazers almost have to plan that he will be ejected from a certain number of games every season. Still, that is part of the tradeoff with Wallace. He plays hard, he competes hard, and he all too often can be too hotheaded. But with the skills he brings to the court, he remains a valued asset.

BILL WALTON

BORN: *11–5–52, at La Mesa, Calif.*
POSITION: *Center.*
TEAMS: *Trail Blazers, 1974–79, Clippers, 1979–85, Celtics, 1985–87.*

Walton will be best remembered for his brilliant college career at UCLA. The 6–11 center could do everything: score, rebound, defend, block shots and trigger the fast break. Only a series of foot and knee injuries kept the big redhead from joining Wilt Chamberlain and Bill Russell on the list of all-time great professional pivot men. Even though he lost four full seasons and numerous partial seasons to injuries, Walton still ranked among the best. In 1976–77, he averaged 18.6 points and 13.2 rebounds while leading Portland to its first NBA championship. A year later, Walton averaged 18.9 points, 14.4 rebounds, 5.0 assists and 2.5 blocks en route to regular-season MVP honors. He managed only one more healthy season— 1985–86, when he came off Boston's bench and helped the Celtics win a championship. Walton was elected to the Hall of Fame in 1993.

BOBBY WANZER

BORN: *6–4–21, at New York, N.Y.*
POSITION: *Guard.*
TEAM: *Royals, 1948–57.*

Wanzer was one of the best shooting guards of his era and a perfect backcourt mate for Bob Davies in Rochester. But the 6-foot former Seton Hall star was more than a proficient point scorer. Wanzer handled the ball, passed and played chest-to-chest defense, never giving less than 100 percent effort. Wanzer, Davies and big man Arnie Risen were an NBA force in the early 1950s, winning one championship (1951) and challenging for numerous others. But the Royals were blocked by the Minneapolis Lakers, who won five

FIERY TEMPER: *Portland's Rasheed Wallace admits his temper sometimes gets the better of him.*

264

titles in six seasons. Wanzer, a five-time All-Star, was the first free-throw shooter to average better than 90 percent for a season (90.4 in 1951–52) and he topped 80 percent for his career. Wanzer, who retired in 1957 with 6,924 points, was Rochester player-coach in 1955–56 and 1956–57 and coach only in 1957–58. He was elected to the Hall of Fame in 1987.

SPUD WEBB

BORN: *7-13-63 at Dallas, Texas.*
POSITION: *Guard.*
TEAMS: *Hawks, 1985-91, Kings, 1991-95, Hawks, 1995, Timberwolves, 1996.*

At 5-foot-7, Webb proved that height often is just a state of mind when it comes to NBA talent. What Webb accomplished in his NBA career at his diminutive stature was nothing short of remarkable. Despite his lack of height, he was able to regularly take the ball to the basket, pass over the tops of taller defenders, and somehow hold his own on the defensive end against bigger point guards. Perhaps his greatest statement came during the

TALL ORDER: *Despite being 5-7, Spud Webb was the NBA's 1986 Slam Dunk Champion.*

ON THE BLOCK: *Chris Webber (right) counts defense and shot-blocking among his many talents.*

All-Star Weekend in 1986. That is when Webb not only entered the Slam-Dunk Championship on All-Star Saturday, but won the event. Think about that—in a league of 7-foot giants, it was a 5-7 player who took the league's annual dunking competition. And yes, he dunked on the same regulation basket as the other competitors. While he never played in an All-Star Game itself, Webb was respected as a quality point guard as much for his abilities as for what he had been able to overcome. For that reason, he was a huge fan favorite.

CHRIS WEBBER

BORN: *3–1–73, at Detroit, Mich.*
POSITION: *Forward.*
TEAMS: *Warriors, 1993–94; Wizards, 1994–98; Kings, 1998–present.*

Webber is a do-everything power forward with triple-double potential. The 6–10 former University of Michigan star has extraordinary ballhandling ability for a big man and the inside skills to produce a lot of points. Webber is not a strong outside shooter, but there's no reason for him to wander beyond 18 feet. The only thing standing between him and stardom is a questionable attitude that already has forced two trades. Webber was drafted by Orlando with the first overall pick in 1993 and the Magic traded him immediately to Golden State for Anfernee Hardaway and a package of future draft picks. He averaged 17.5 points and 9.1 rebounds in 1993–94 and won Rookie of the Year honors, but constant bickering with Coach Don Nelson finally forced a trade to the Bullets. Maturing in a talented frontcourt with former Michigan teammate Juwan Howard, Webber averaged 20.1 points and 10.3 rebounds in 1996–97 to help Washington to reach the playoffs for the time in nine seasons. Although his scoring average rose to 21.9, 1997–98 was a disappointing campaign for Webber and the Wizards and the close of the season saw him traded to Sacramento in exchange for Otis Thorpe and Mitch Richmond. It proved to be exactly what Webber and the Kings needed. Although initially disappointed with the move, Webber eventually warmed to the idea and wound up leading the league in rebounding, averaging 13.0 a game, and helping the Kings into the playoffs, where they lost a thrilling five-game first-round series to the Utah Jazz. He and the Kings came back strong again the next season, when Webber averaged a career-high 24.5 points per game to go with 10.5 rebounds per game.

JERRY WEST

See Legends of the NBA *page 142–143*

PAUL WESTPHAL

BORN: *11-30-50 at Torrance, Calif.*
POSITION: *Guard.*
TEAMS: *Celtics, 1972-75, Suns, 1975-80, Sonics, 1980-81, Knicks, 1981-83, Suns, 1983-84.*

Long before he became a successful coach with the Phoenix Suns, Westphal was a dynamic shooting guard for the Celtics, Suns, Sonics and Knicks. A creative shooting guard, Westphal could charge his way to the basket, seemingly fall out of shooting position, yet find a way to get the ball into the basket. He was acknowledged for his success by being named first-team All-NBA in 1977, 1979 and 1980 and also was second-team All-NBA in 1978. He went to the All-Star game as both a member of the Suns and the Sonics. And for working his way back from injury, he was named Comeback Player of the Year in 1983 while with the Knicks. Known for his easy-going nature as a player, Westphal then slid into a coaching role with the Suns and guided Phoenix to the 1993 NBA Finals in his first season as a head coach. He later moved on to become coach of the Seattle SuperSonics.

JO JO WHITE

BORN: *11–16–46, at St. Louis, Mo.*
POSITION: *Guard.*
TEAMS: *Celtics, 1969–79, Warriors, 1979–80, Kings, 1980–81.*

White was the cool point guard who led Boston to five straight Atlantic Division titles and two championships in the 1970s. The 6–3 White, a think-and-react floor general who could provide equal parts offense and defense, performed his duties quietly and efficiently while flashier teammates like Dave Cowens and John Havlicek garnered recognition. He seldom tried to perform beyond his capabilities and he never tried to draw attention, something that finally came because of his reliability in the clutch. The former University of Kansas star was a fine outside shooter who averaged 17.2 points over his 12-year career, but he also was a fine passer who could open up and tighten the Celtics' offense with crafty change-of-pace maneuvers. White was at his best in the 1976 postseason, when he averaged 22.7 points and 5.4 assists and claimed NBA Finals MVP honors. The seven-time All-Star retired in 1981, after short stints with Golden State and Kansas City.

LENNY WILKENS

BORN: *10–28–37, at Brooklyn, N.Y.*
POSITION: *Guard.*
TEAMS: *Hawks, 1960–68, SuperSonics, 1968–72, Cavaliers, 1972–74, Trail Blazers, 1974–75.*

Wilkens will always be remembered as the winningest coach in NBA history, but his playing career also was Hall of Fame-caliber. He was an outstanding point guard who scored 17,772 points (16.5) and handed out 7,211 assists (6.7) over 15 seasons with four teams. Wilkens, who made his first national impact with Providence

WHITE FLAME: *Jo Jo White gave the Boston Celtics offense and defense as needed.*

College, was a first-round 1960 draft pick of the St. Louis Hawks and he went on to average double-digit points in each of his first 14 seasons. He also played in nine All-Star Games, claiming the MVP award in 1971. It was during a four-year stay in Seattle that Wilkens got his first taste of coaching, directing the Sonics from 1969 to '72 as player-coach. He did same thing for a year at Portland before retiring in 1975 to devote full time to coaching. The 6–1 Wilkens, who played in 1,077 regular-season games, was elected to the Hall of Fame in 1988.

JAMAAL WILKES

BORN: *5-2-53.*
POSITION: *Forward.*
TEAMS: *Warriors, 1974-77, Lakers, 1977-85, Clippers 1985-86.*

A three-time All-Star, Wilkes was known for one of the NBA's softest shooting strokes, a player with such an awkward release that it made his shot on of the hardest in the league to block. He was a cornerstone of several successful Lakers teams. Wilkes won the first of four cham-

pionship rings while a teammate of Rick Barry with the Golden State Warriors. He then signed as a free agent with the Lakers and went on to win three more championships, teaming with Magic Johnson and Kareem Abdul-Jabbar. Eventually, he would give way at small forward in the Lakers dynasty to James Worthy. He was a different player than Worthy, a player whose game was so smooth that he earned the nickname "Silk." He began his career as Keith Wilkes, winning two collegiate championships at UCLA, and then changed his name during the course of his career. In addition to his scoring, Wilkes also was noted for his defense, twice earning nomination to second-team All-Defensive.

DOMINIQUE WILKINS

BORN: *1–12–60, at Paris, France.*
POSITION: *Forward.*
TEAMS: *Hawks, 1982–94, Clippers, 1994, Celtics, 1994–95, Spurs, 1996–97, Magic, 1998–99.*

Wilkins was a high-scoring, high-soaring forward who has played above NBA rims

for 15 seasons, interrupted by two one-year stints in Europe. The acrobatic 6–8 shotmaker could produce points from anywhere on the court and did it with stylish flair. Wilkins left the University of Georgia after his junior season and became one of the most prolific scorers in NBA history over the next 11-plus seasons in Atlanta. From 1983–84 to '93–94, Wilkins never averaged less than 20 points or 6 rebounds and he captured a scoring title in 1985–86 with a 30.3 mark. With Wilkins leading the charge, the Hawks thrived on the court, but they never had the accessory talent to advance deep into the playoffs. Wilkins is a nine-time All-Star, 1986 All-NBA first-teamer and two-time winner of the All-Star Slam Dunk Championship. He returned to the NBA in 1996–97 after a season in Greece to lead the Spurs in scoring at 18.2. He played with Italy's TeamSystem Bologna in 1997-98 before attempting one last fling in the NBA. He signed as a free agent with Orlando for the 1998-99 season but averaged just 5.0 points before being waived after the season. Still, his 26,668 points rank him eighth all-time in scoring in the league.

BUCK WILLIAMS

BORN: *3–8–60, at Rocky Mount, N.C.*
POSITION: *Forward.*
TEAMS: *Nets, 1981–89, Trail Blazers, 1989–96, Knicks, 1996–98.*

Williams was a power forward who carved a 17-year career out of rebounding and defense. The 6–8, 225-pound tireless worker earned two All-Defensive first-team selections. He averaged better than 12 rebounds per game over his first six seasons with New Jersey, and helped Portland reach the NBA Finals in two of his first three seasons after a 1989 trade to the Trail Blazers. Williams, who left the University of Maryland after his junior season, was selected by New Jersey with the third overall pick of the 1981 draft. He earned the 1981–82 Rookie of the Year honors with averages of 15.5 points and 12.3 rebounds. Those numbers did not vary much over the years as Williams settled into his role as one of the league's most consistent performers. He joined the Knicks in 1996 and fin-

HAWK TALK: *Dominique Wilkins was often referred to as "The Human Highlight Film."*

BUCKING THE ODDS: *Buck Williams (52) was known as much for his consistency as his longevity.*

JASON WILLIAMS

BORN: *11-18-75 at Belle, W.Va.*
POSITION: *Guard*
TEAMS: *Kings, 1998-present.*

Jason Williams entered the NBA out of the University of Florida as a first-round pick in 1998 as something the league had never seen. A player who seemingly did everything with flash, although often out of control, it was as if he was playing at 45 rpm while the rest of the league was playing at 33 rpm. His impact immediately lifted the lowly Kings to an upper echelon in the NBA and put Sacramento back into the playoffs. His passes would come from any angle and at any time. His play immediately lifted the play of teammate Chris Webber and meshed wonderfully with the passing skills of center Vlade Divac. The trouble was Williams also was just as liable to shoot from any spot on the floor at any time, a trait that does not blend well with playoff basketball. For his panache, Williams was voted first-team All-Rookie in 1999. By his

TAKE A PASS: *Jason Williams never met a pass he didn't like as the Kings' floor general.*

ished the 1997–98 season with 1,307 games played (fourth all time) and more than 16,500 points and 13,000 rebounds.

GUS WILLIAMS

BORN: *10–10–53, at Mount Vernon, N.Y.*
POSITION: *Guard.*
TEAMS: *Warriors, 1975–77, SuperSonics, 1977–84, Bullets, 1984–86, Hawks, 1986–87.*

Williams was described by contemporaries as the best open-court player in the game. The 6–2 blur was devastating on the fast break, where he could knife between defenders for a basket, whip a no-look pass to a streaking teammate or stop and pop a long-range jumper. The former University of Southern California star, who played his first two seasons with the Golden State Warriors before finding his niche with Seattle in 1977–78, formed an outstanding backcourt combination with defensive-minded point man Dennis Johnson. With their guards pulling a heavy load and Jack Sikma manning the middle, the SuperSonics powered their way to the 1978 NBA Finals and captured their first championship in 1979. But Williams enjoyed his best season in 1981–82, when he averaged 23.4 points and 6.9 assists while earning All-NBA first-team honors. When the two-time All-Star ended his career in 1987, after short stays in Washington and Atlanta, he had piled up 14,093 points (17.1) and 4,597 assists (5.6).

second season, some of the luster had been lost, his game all too often viewed as out of control. Still, since Pete Maravich the league had seen nothing like what Williams had delivered.

JAYSON WILLIAMS

BORN: *2-22-68 at Ritter, S.C.*
POSITION: *Forward/center.*
TEAMS: *76ers, 1990–92, Nets, 1992–2000.*

Among the hardest working men in the NBA, Williams was also one of the most personable. Just as likely to offer a joke as to fight you for an offensive rebound, Williams in many ways replaced now-retired Charles Barkley as the goodwill ambassador of the NBA. Still, the wit and charm should not minimize what Williams, when healthy, was able to accomplish on the court. Despite his undersized build for a center, Williams attacked the glass with a passion. He attempted to control every carom and had put himself at a Dennis Rodman level when it came to rebounding. However, knee and foot troubles sidetracked Williams' career, forcing him to retire in 2000. He tried valiantly to make it back during the 1999–2000 season, as his team fell out of playoff contention, but sustained too many setbacks to endure. All the while, his book, full of his amusing anecdotes, rose to the top of many best-seller lists. In the New York media market, he was a perfect fit.

JOHN WILLIAMSON

BORN: *11-10-52.*
POSITION: *Guard*
TEAMS: *Nets, 1973-76, Pacers, 1977, Nets, 1977-79, Bullets, 1980-81.*

"Super John" was a dynamic offensive force, one of the greatest players in the ABA and a player who teamed with Julius Erving to make the Nets the marquee franchise of the ABA until the league was dissolved. While Williamson was also a standout in the NBA, it was in the free-wheeling ABA where he was most able to express himself. His high-kicking jump shot, which resembled him climbing stairs, often left him wide open in the lane. A burly player, he was able to bull his way to the basket and stop opposing players on the defensive end. Williamson would go on to win two ABA championships before moving to the NBA. If not for injuries and other personal problems, he likely would have emerged as an NBA All-Star. Instead, his career continued to fade. He eventually would revitalize his game and take his scoring skills to Europe, where he would play for another decade after his NBA career was over.

PUNCH LINE: *Jayson Williams was a terror on the basketball court and a comedian off it.*

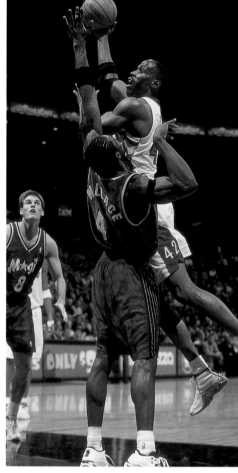

UP AND AWAY: *The baby hook shot has been a favorite weapon in Kevin Willis' arsenal.*

KEVIN WILLIS

BORN: *9-6-62 at Los Angeles, Calif.*
POSITION: *Forward.*
TEAMS: *Hawks, 1984-94, Heat, 1994-96, Warriors, 1996, Rockets, 1996-98, Raptors, 1998-present*

A high-scoring power forward with an almost unstoppable baby hook shot, Willis started his career on a dynamic Atlanta team that also featured the high-flying scoring attempts of forward Dominique Wilkins. With both players attempting to dominate the offense, it often became a war of wills to see who could get a shot off first. Willis certainly is not shy when it comes to scoring, considered "a black hole," a player who once the ball goes into the paint, it rarely comes out without a shot being lofted. That said, Willis commanded double-team defense throughout his career because of his ability to score seemingly at will near the basket. He also could be a proficient rebounder when so motivated. Defense, however, at times was a struggle. Unusually short arms limited Willis in his low-post defense and he often needed help from teammate to guard the NBA's better low-post scorers. His lone All-Star Game appearance came in 1992 with the Hawks.

JAMES WORTHY

BORN: 2–27–61, at Gastonia, N.C.
POSITION: Forward.
TEAM: Lakers, 1982–94.

Worthy was the quiet enforcer for the Los Angeles Lakers' 1980s championship machine. Because he was overshadowed by Kareem Abdul-Jabbar and Magic Johnson most of his 12-year career, the 6–9 Worthy toiled in relative obscurity as one of the best small forwards in the NBA. He was one of the quickest big men the game has ever produced, which explained his explosive power drives through the lane or along the baseline. Worthy also could bury the outside

jumper and play the kind of chest-to-chest defense that produces championships. The former North Carolina star, who helped the Tar Heels win the 1982 NCAA Tournament, played on three championship teams for the Lakers and four more that lost in the Finals. He averaged 22.0 points, 7.4 rebounds and 4.4 assists in the 1988 Finals, claiming MVP honors. The seven-time All-Star retired in 1994 with 16,320 points (17.6)—not bad for a team's third-option star.

GEORGE YARDLEY

BORN: 11–23–28, at Hollywood, Calif.

POSITION: Forward.
TEAMS: Pistons, 1953–59, Nationals, 1959–60.

Yardley, a.k.a. "The Bird," was an early NBA scoring machine for the Fort Wayne Pistons and Syracuse Nationals. The 6–5 Yardley was an unlikely looking basketball star who stood out because of a prematurely balding head, knobby elbows and knees and a loping run that made him look like an ostrich tip-toeing through a minefield. But there was nothing amusing to NBA defenders about his ability to put the ball in the basket. Yardley could score from anywhere on the court, which he did at a 19.2-point clip through his seven-year career, and he was an aggressive rebounder, twice averaging in double figures. He had an instinctive knack for being in the right spot at the right time. Yardley, a six-time All-Star, won a scoring title in 1957–58 when he averaged 27.8 and became the first player to top 2,000 points in a season. Yardley finished his career in 1960, after a short stay at Syracuse.

HAVING A BALL: *James Worthy didn't get much publicity with the Lakers—just Championship rings.*

MAX ZASLOFSKY

BORN: 12–7–25, at Brooklyn, N.Y.
POSITION: Guard/forward.
TEAMS: Stags, 1946–50, Knicks, 1950–53, Bullets, 1953, Hawks, 1953, Pistons, 1953–56.

Zaslofsky was one of the most feared outside shooters in a BAA/NBA career that lasted from 1946 to '56. The former St. John's star could score with a two-hand set or a running one-hand jumper, shots he got away with one of the quickest releases in the game. His cat-like quickness made him a dangerous defender and he was known for his diving, ball-hawking intensity. Zaslofsky averaged 21.0 and 20.6 points over the 1947–48 and 1948–49 seasons for the Chicago Stags, impressive totals for the period. Not surprisingly, he was an All-BAA first-team selection in each of his first three seasons. But it wasn't until the Stags franchise folded in 1950 that Zaslofsky enjoyed the team success he longed for. He led the Knicks and Pistons to the 1951, '52, '53 and '55 NBA Finals, but couldn't quite get a championship ring. Zaslofsky retired in 1956 with 7,990 points (14.8).

THE GREAT COACHES

He's an architect, strategist, motivator, screamer and father confessor. He cracks the whip one day, holds hands and consoles shattered egos the next.

A coach is the glue that binds a team's individual parts into a unit. But most of all, he is a teacher who provides young and impressionable players with a framework for winning.

Winning is the ultimate goal for any coach, but how he accomplishes that end is open to interpretation. Red Auerbach, the master builder of the Boston Celtics dynasty, was a volatile personality, aggressive and passionate at practice as well as during games. John Kundla, who coached the Minneapolis Lakers to five championships, was a quiet, calm sideline presence. Don Nelson was a basketball version of Dr. Jekyll and Mr. Hyde, a ferocious bulldog during games, a patient teacher during practice. Jack Ramsay was the ultimate teacher, Billy Cunningham the ultimate motivator.

For every coach, style is simply a means to an end—winning. So are the more mundane qualities he must possess: evaluation of talent, framing that talent within the proper system, communicating with players, handling adversity and executing game strategy.

He must also be an amateur psychologist and philosopher. Phil Jackson's unique brand of Zen Buddhism and Native American mysticism helped lead a potentially explosive mix that included Michael Jordan, Scottie Pippen and Dennis Rodman to six NBA titles in eight years.

While often different in style and approach, every good coach has one common denominator: a commitment to defense. Few championships have been won—and few coaches have survived—without it. Scoring comes and goes. Defense remains.

Red Auerbach	**Phil Jackson**	**Adolph Rupp**
The master of Boston	The power of Zen	Wildcat legend
Billy Cunningham	**John Kundla**	**Dean Smith**
Driven by passion	The NBA's first dynasty	Dignity in victory or defeat
Chuck Daly	**Don Nelson**	**Pat Summitt**
Detroit spinner	Still looking for a title	Setting new standards
Rod Holzman	**Jack Ramsey**	**Lenny Wilkens**
Respect for team play	The ultimate teacher	Double Hall of Famer
Hank Iba	**Pat Riley**	**John Wooden**
Casting a giant shadow	More than a sharp suit	Teaching teams to win

COUNT TO ZEN : *The multi-faceted Phil Jackson helped unite the Bulls as a team.*

RED AUERBACH

Architect of the Boston Celtics' dynasty

SEEING RED: *Red Auerbach put together the greatest dynasty in the NBA history.*

His name weaves through the NBA history books like a road through the countryside. Arnold (Red) Auerbach has dominated the game from his early days as coach and master builder of the Boston Celtics dynasty, to his current status as evaluator of talent, advisor and elder statesman of basketball's most storied and successful franchise.

The always volatile Auerbach can trace his coaching roots back to 1946, the year the Basketball Association of America began play as the forerunner to the NBA. A brash, self-assured 29-year-old, Auerbach guided the Washington Capitols to a 49–11 first-year record and the Eastern Division championship.

Two more seasons in Washington produced another division title and one year with the Tri-Cities Blackhawks set the stage for a more permanent move. When Auerbach took the Celtics reins in 1950, he immediately began pouring the foundation for a basketball dynasty.

In retrospect, Auerbach's genius was in his vision. He wanted a slicker, faster offense with racehorse guards who could get out on the fast break and a dominating center who could feed them the ball. Ball-handling magician Bob Cousy arrived in 1950 and off-guard Bill Sharman a year later. The dominating center, Bill Russell, was acquired in 1956 at a stiff draft-day price—high-scoring forwards Cliff Hagan and Ed Macauley, two future Hall of Famers.

With the pieces in place and a steady stream of supporting players (Tom Heinsohn, Sam Jones, K.C. Jones, John Havlicek, Tom Sanders, Don Nelson) parading through Boston Garden, the cigar-chomping Auerbach concentrated on coaching the powerhouse he had assembled. And from 1957 through 1966, the Celtics won nine Eastern Division titles and nine NBA championships—including a team sports-record eight in a row. The only miss came in 1958, when the Celtics lost to St. Louis in the NBA Finals.

FACTS & FIGURES

Personal	Born: September 20, 1917, at Brooklyn, N.Y.
Teams	Capitols, 1946–49, Blackhawks, 1949–50, Celtics, 1950–66
NBA Coach of the Year	1965
NBA Finals Appearances	1957, 1958, 1959, 1960, 1961, 1962, 1963, 1964, 1965, 1966
NBA Championships	1957, 1959, 1960, 1961, 1962, 1963, 1964, 1965, 1966

Coaching Record	G	W	L	Pct.
Regular Season	1,417	938	479	.662
Playoffs	168	99	69	.589

Auerbach's sideline presence was anything but passive. He was aggressive, demanding and ready to explode at a moment's notice. Referees were an easy target and his sharp tongue irritated and provoked thin-skinned opponents. He fought for every call, every break, and he pushed his players to the limit, espousing the principles of teamwork and breakneck defense.

The players understood and readily accepted Auerbach's passion for winning and his devotion to the game.

"I've never known anybody who has played under Red Auerbach who didn't like him," Russell once said. "Of course, I've never known anybody who has

"I've never known anybody who has played under Red Auerbach who didn't like him."
Bill Russell

played against him who did like him."

Auerbach stepped down after the 1966 championship and turned the team over to Russell, who directed the Celtics to titles in 1968 and '69. Auerbach finished his outstanding career with a 938–479 regular-season record, a 99–69

LIGHTING UP: *Red Auerbach's victory cigars begame a symbol of the Celtics' success: nine NBA titles from 1957–66.*

playoff mark and one Coach of the Year citation (1965). His 938 wins stood as an NBA milestone until 1995.

True to his nature, Auerbach did not submit to a passive retirement. He served in various front-office capacities and continued building teams that claimed five more titles in the 1970s and '80s. Auerbach was named NBA Executive of the Year in 1980, the same year he was selected by the Professional Basketball Writers Association as the "Greatest Coach in the History of the NBA."

BILLY CUNNINGHAM

The legend of Billy C

SHORT AND SWEET: *Billy Cunningham had a .698 winning percentage as a coach.*

"He has gone from being a real student of the game and coaching the way a player might do it, to one who is making the moves and organizing the club."
Julius Erving

Billy Cunningham coached only eight NBA seasons and he spent all of them with the Philadelphia 76ers—the team he represented for nine years as a player. He never tore down and rebuilt rosters, he never rescued forlorn franchises and he never jumped from team to team in search of more money and a longer career.

Cunningham's short tenure casts him as a misfit among the game's all-time great coaches, but his 454–196 career record yielded a .698 winning percentage, the third-best mark in NBA history; his .629 playoff winning percentage ranks third all-time; he reached the 300- and 400-victory plateaus faster than any coach except Pat Riley; and his teams won one championship (1983) and lost in the NBA Finals twice (1980 and '82).

Cunningham was not your typical Xs-and-Os coach. His sideline demeanor was much like his playing style: foot-stomping, emotional and intense. He battled referees, chastised malingering players and demanded hustle and a commitment to defense—qualities he never lacked as a jumping-jack forward who averaged more than 20 points and 10 rebounds over a career that also included two ABA seasons. The Brooklyn native—a first-round draft choice out of North Carolina in 1965—averaged 18.5 points, 7.3 rebounds and 2.5 assists as the 76ers won the 1967 NBA title. That was the kind of

FACTS & FIGURES

Personal	Born: June 3, 1943, at Brooklyn, N.Y.			
Teams	76ers, 1977–85			
Coach of the Year	None			
NBA Finals Appearances	1980, 1982, 1983			
NBA Championships	1983			
Coaching Record	G	W	L	Pct.
Regular Season	650	454	196	.698
Playoffs	105	66	39	.629

effort and success he expected when he reutrned as a coach 10 years later, five years after retiring as a player.

Critics point out that he inherited a loaded roster with Julius (Dr. J) Erving, George McGinnis and Doug Collins when he left the broadcast booth in 1977 to replace Gene Shue. But Cunningham coaxed the 76ers into maximum effort that produced three Atlantic Division titles and at least 52 victories in seven of his eight seasons. And he did it while learning on the job.

"He's as good as any coach in the league," Erving said in 1982. "He's not a totalitarian kind of coach, but he's quite good."

McGinnis was more succinct. "If I had to give a one-word description of Billy," he said, "it would be 'intense.'"

Cunningham, a key player for the 76ers' 1967 championship team, carried that intensity over to a team that battled the Boston Celtics for Eastern Conference supremacy in the 1980s. Dr. J remained as its heart and soul through Cunningham's coaching regime, but McGinnis, Collins and Darryl Dawkins gave way to Maurice Cheeks, Andrew Toney and Bobby Jones.

The 76ers won their battles against Boston in 1980 and '82, but they lost both NBA Finals wars to Western Conference power Los Angeles. It wasn't until the arrival of 6-foot-11 center Moses Malone, immediately following the second loss to the Lakers, that Cunningham and the 76ers could claim a championship, which was punctuated by a shocking four-game Finals sweep of the Lakers. He lasted two more seasons, winning 110 games. After taking the 76ers to the 1985 Eastern Conference finals (a loss to the Celtics) he retired, saying he needed time off and the players needed to hear a new voice.

Cunningham has never returned to the sideline, although he did resurface in 1987, as the driving force behind a successful effort to get an expansion franchise for the city of Miami. He remained as a part-owner from 1987–95. The following year, he was named one of the 50 greatest players in the history of the NBA.

EYE OF THE STORM: *Billy C. was composed during a 1984 game against Denver.*

CHUCK DALY

Better Late than Never for Daly, Pistons

For a man who didn't even land his first NBA head coaching job until age 51, Chuck Daly traveled a long road very fast. In 14 whirlwind seasons, he piled up 638 victories, a .593 winning percentage, two NBA championships and an Olympic gold medal as coach of the greatest basketball team ever assembled.

Daly's meandering career stretched through eight seasons as a high school coach and six more as an assistant at Duke University. His first contact with the national spotlight came in 1969, when he became head coach at Boston College and he raised eyebrows from 1971 to '77 when he coached an overachieving University of Pennsylvania team to four Ivy League titles and four NCAA Tournament berths.

When Daly took a job as assistant to Philadelphia coach Billy Cunningham in 1978, it appeared to be a brief diversion from the college basketball wars. But Daly helped Cunningham carve out two division titles in four-plus seasons and when the Cleveland Cavaliers came calling in 1981, he jumped at the chance for an NBA head job—a decision he would regret.

The Cleveland organization was in shambles, thanks to the wheeling and dealing of owner Ted Stepien. Daly's first NBA test ended in disaster—he was fired with a 9–32 record at midseason and spent the next season as a broadcaster.

When Detroit beckoned in 1983, Daly was better prepared. The Pistons, who had not qualified for postseason play in six seasons, compiled a 49–33 record and earned the first of nine consecutive playoff berths under Daly.

The 1980s were exciting for long-suffering Detroit fans. The new coach began assembling a talented lineup around point guard Isiah Thomas and 6-foot-11 center Bill Laimbeer. Shooting guard Joe Dumars came aboard in 1985 and high-scoring Adrian Dantley arrived a year later. Vinnie Johnson, Mark Aguirre, John Salley, Dennis Rodman and James Edwards filled out a championship-caliber roster.

Daly molded the Pistons into a defensive machine that bumped, bruised and pounded opponents into physical and mental mistakes. His players embraced the philosophy. "He's a player's coach," Laimbeer said. "He realizes it's a player's game, not a coach's game. A coach's job is to guide the team to get it in position to win and that's what he does."

With Thomas, Dantley and Dumars handling the scoring load, Detroit's "Bad Boys" posted five consecutive 50-win seasons, won three straight Central Division titles and reached the NBA Finals in 1988, '89 and '90. With consecutive title-series victories over Los Angeles (1989) and Portland (1990), the Pistons became only the second repeat

FACTS & FIGURES

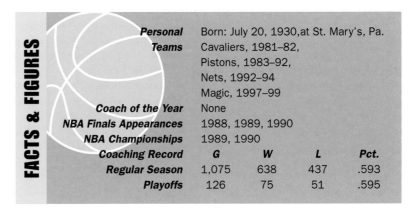

Personal	Born: July 20, 1930, at St. Mary's, Pa.
Teams	Cavaliers, 1981–82,
	Pistons, 1983–92,
	Nets, 1992–94,
	Magic, 1997–99
Coach of the Year	None
NBA Finals Appearances	1988, 1989, 1990
NBA Championships	1989, 1990

Coaching Record	G	W	L	Pct.
Regular Season	1,075	638	437	.593
Playoffs	126	75	51	.595

"He's a player's coach. He realizes it's a player's game, not a coach's game."
Bill Laimbeer, *former Detroit center*

MOTOR CITY MAGIC: *Always dapper, Chuck Daly made his biggest splash with Detroit.*

A DALY OCCURRENCE: *With the exception of Cleveland, Chuck Daly has had success at each of his stops in the NBA.*

NBA champions in more than two decades.

Daly took his defense-first philosophy to New Jersey in 1992, guiding the Nets to their first winning record (43–39) since 1984–85. After another winning season, he retired with a 564–379 regular-season mark and a .607 playoff winning percentage.

Daly will also be remembered as the man who coached the original Dream Team that stormed through the 1992 Olympic Games at Barcelona. The greatest team ever assembled featured Michael Jordan, Magic Johnson, Charles Barkley, Larry Bird and numerous other superstars. And, of course, one of the greatest coaches— Chuck Daly.

Then in June 1997 at the age of 67, and after a three-year absence from coaching, Daly signed to become the head coach of the Orlando Magic. Although his stint in Orlando was a relatively short one, it was productive nonetheless.

His first team finished 41–41. But in the lockout-shortened 1998–99 season, the Magic surprised everyone by running off to a 33–17 record and trying for the Eastern Conference title with Miami and Indiana.

The balloon burst in the playoffs, however, when the Magic was ousted by the Philadelphia 76ers in four games in the first round.

Daly resigned as coach shortly afterward, and it looked as if he might settle into retirement. But after the 1999–2000 season, he was hired by the Vancouver Grizzlies as a senior adviser.

Someone always needs his expertise.

RED HOLZMAN

New York, New York

For 18 years, Red Holzman worked his coaching magic in cities around the National Basketball Association. He pushed, he cajoled and he introduced his players to the principles of teamwork and defense. And when he was finished, he stepped proudly off the court with 696 career victories and a .547 playoff winning percentage that ranked among the best in history.

But for all of his accomplishments, Holzman will always be remembered for one magical season and one beautifully sculptured team that lifted New York to the top of the professional basketball world. The 1969–70 Knicks not only captured the heart of the Big Apple, they did it with a presence, a strut that gave them status among the NBA's all-time great teams.

Holzman became head coach of New York in 1967, a decade after completing four years as coach of the Hawks. The Knicks, still looking for their first NBA championship in their 22nd season, were stumbling under Dick McGuire when Holzman took the reins and guided them to a 28–17 finish. The team jumped to 54 victories in 1968–69, a portent of things to come.

The 1969–70 Knicks were a perfect blend of Holzman's philosophies. Willis Reed, a 6-foot-10 bulldog, manned the middle, Bill Bradley and Dave DeBusschere controlled the wings and Dick Barnett and Walt Frazier dominated the backcourt. The Knicks could play up-tempo or half court, they were

RED HOT: *Red Holzman let the New York Knicks to the pinnacle of success.*

smart, they could shoot and they played outstanding defense. Frazier, one of the best defensive guards ever to play the game, was the Knicks' go-to scorer.

With Holzman dictating the team's pace from his familiar sideline crouch, the Knicks rolled to a 60–22 record, an Eastern Division title and playoff victories over Baltimore and Milwaukee. They culminated their special season and brought bedlam to Madison Square Garden with a seven-game NBA Finals victory over the Los Angeles Lakers.

> ### "His contribution to the game helped revive respect for team play and, in particular, team defense."
> *U.S. Senator Bill Bradley, former Knicks forward*

Holzman, a former player with a Rochester Royals team that passed through the NBL, BAA and NBA in the 1940s and '50s, was the toast of New York. And he didn't stop there. The 1970–71 Knicks won another division title, the 1971–72 team advanced to the NBA Finals before losing to the Lakers and the 1972–73 Knicks returned to the championship circle with a five-game triumph over the Lakers. Reed, Bradley, DeBusschere, Frazier and newcomers Earl Monroe and Jerry Lucas never deviated from Holzman's winning credo: "If you play good, hard defense, the offense will take care of itself."

Although there were to be no more championships under Holzman, the New York fans remained fiercely loyal to the man who had brought the Knicks their only two NBA successes. He would remain a familiar figure on the Knicks' sideline until 1982, when he retired at age 62. His New York success was recognized later by the Basketball Writers Association of America, which voted him NBA Coach of the Decade for the 1970s.

Holzman, the man and the coach, probably was captured best by the words of Bradley, who went on to greater fame as a United States Senator and presidential candidate: "His contribution to the game helped revive respect for team play and, in particular, team defense," Bradley said.

(Opposite) **OFFICIAL PROTEST** *Red Holzman expected a lot from himself, and referees.*

FACTS & FIGURES

Personal	Born: August 10, 1920, Brooklyn,			
N.Y. Teams	Hawks, 1953–57,			
	Knicks, 1967–77, 1978–82			
Coach of the Year	1970			
NBA Finals Appearances	1970, 1972, 1973			
NBA Championships	1970, 1973			
Coaching Record	G	W	L	Pct.
Regular Season	1,300	696	604	.535
Playoffs	106	58	48	.547

HANK IBA

Turning "country boys" into champions

He preached a slowdown game, because that is what he believed produced the most efficient offensive results.

He employed a big man in the middle, because the rules were too favorable at the time not to take advantage of the type of stature other coaches shunned.

He was one of the great early legends of the sidelines, whose success compares to any coach of any generation.

As Indiana's Bob Knight so eloquently put it, "Of all the shadows that cast over the game of basketball, his was the biggest."

Few could argue that categorization of Hank Iba.

Iba won 767 games in 41 seasons and led Oklahoma State—then called

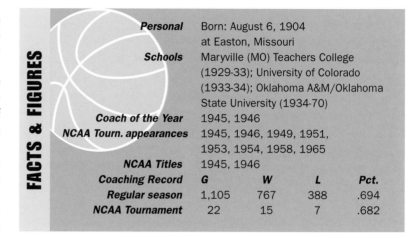

FACTS & FIGURES				
Personal	Born: August 6, 1904 at Easton, Missouri			
Schools	Maryville (MO) Teachers College (1929-33); University of Colorado (1933-34); Oklahoma A&M/Oklahoma State University (1934-70)			
Coach of the Year	1945, 1946			
NCAA Tourn. appearances	1945, 1946, 1949, 1951, 1953, 1954, 1958, 1965			
NCAA Titles	1945, 1946			
Coaching Record	G	W	L	Pct.
Regular season	1,105	767	388	.694
NCAA Tournament	22	15	7	.682

Oklahoma A&M—to national championships in 1945 and '46 behind the play of 7-foot center Bob Kurland.

Iba was so respected, he rarely had to get involved in the recruiting game.

Much like John Wooden and Adolph Rupp, players vied for the honor of playing for him.

"He felt he was a teacher," Kurland said. "If people wanted to play the game of basketball, they would come to him. And they did."

Like Rupp, Iba would take home-state talent and school it on the college level.

"I realize it takes talent to coach skilled kids," said Jack Hartman, a former Iba player who later achieved significant coaching success at Kansas State. "But Mr. Iba could take a lot of Oklahoma country boys and take them as far as they could possibly go, and make them compete with the very best."

He would coach the collegiate game until 1970, following the game from its roots to its greatest heights.

"He began his career with coaches like Phog Allen and Adolph Rupp and finished with Dean Smith and Bobby Knight and all the people recognized what he had given to the game," said Eddie Sutton, who was among those to follow Iba as coach at Oklahoma State. "They all admired the class that he brought to the game."

Iba's legacy was that seven of his former players would coach teams into the NCAA Tournament, among them Hartman, Sutton and Don Haskins.

SUSTAINED BRILLIANCE: *Iba was a force on the collegiate sidelines for almost 50 years.*

"He inspired such confidence," Sutton said, "that there was never any question in my mind that his philosophy offered the best opportunity to be successful. The things he gave us are as valid today."

The Iba trademarks were offensive weaves and low scores. He also was a defensive pioneer, designing a "swinging gate" approach that involved a team concept in a man-on-man scheme, a style still emulated today.

"We ran our offense with set plays," Iba said. "There was no freelance. We'd run the set, and reset and run it again."

Iba's Aggies became the first team to win consecutive NCAA titles (1945 and 1946). Oklahoma A&M also won 14 Midwestern Valley titles during his tenure.

In many ways he was a players' coach.

"One thing Iba told us early in the scheme of things, and this was the great thing about him," Kurland said, "he said, 'You guys are going to have all the wins. I'm going to take all the losses — but we'll do it my way.'"

And they did. With goaltending legal at the time, that meant Kurland guarding the basket as much as his man.

"We had complete confidence in what he told us," Kurland would later say. "There was never a deviation from the strategy and the style and the tactics that he developed."

"The things he gave us are as valid today."
Eddie Sutton, Oklahoma State

On the international front, Iba coached the U.S. Olympic team three times. His teams won gold medals in 1964 and '68, only to lose the gold-medal game to the Soviet Union in 1972 in Munich in one of the most controversial finishes in the history of the game.

That such a wonderful legacy could have been so tainted was too much for

ANY TIME, ANY PLACE: *Iba has coached all over, including Madison Square Garden.*

Knight, who asked Iba to serve as a special assistant coach at the 1984 Olympics and speak to the team each day at practice. After winning the gold medal, the players honored Iba by carrying him on their shoulders around the court.

"There weren't many of us who knew what was going on that didn't have tears in our eyes," Bill Wall, an executive with USA Basketball, said of that moment of vindication for Iba. "Maybe some of those kids didn't know who he was, but each of them had just spent a month with him."

That, alone, spoke volumes of the Iba legacy, that a coach who began his career on the sidelines in 1929 could, more than 50 years later, still deliver a passion about the game to players born more than 30 years after he already had begun to teach the sport. To this day, many of Iba's precepts are still followed.

282

PHIL JACKSON

Chicago's Free Spirit

ZEN MASTER: *Phil Jackson was the perfect coach for Jordan and the Bulls.*

"He has a great feel for the game, a great feel for people and he has a knack for keeping everybody happy."
Red Holzman,
former New York Knicks coach

N othing about Phil Jackson's early career suggested basketball life beyond his playing years. As a 1960s and '70s forward for the New York Knicks, Jackson was a gangly, 6-foot-8 NBA hippie, with long hair, beard and a free spirit.

But everybody should have suspected there was more to the man than met the eye. Especially when he parlayed an awkward lefthanded jumper and an ugly hook shot into a 12-year playing career. Jackson survived the NBA because he understood that he could make up for his shortcomings with hard work and defense.

"He's a very, very intelligent guy, about basketball and about other things," said Red Holzman, who coached Jackson when he played for the Knicks. "He has a great feel for the game, a great feel for people and he has a knack for keeping everybody happy."

Those qualities became very important in 1989, when Jackson, who had spent five seasons coaching in the

Continental Basketball Association and two as a Chicago assistant under Doug Collins, was hired to guide a Bulls team that seemingly had everything, starting with Michael Jordan and Scottie Pippen, one of the greatest one-two punches in the history of the game.

As a rookie coach, Jackson installed a triangle offense, which would require Jordan to play within a team-oriented system. The three-time scoring champion resisted briefly, but finally embraced Jackson's philosophies as the victories began piling up. The Bulls won 55 games and Jordan won another scoring title in Jackson's first season, setting the stage for the most dominant title run in a quarter of a century.

The 1990–91 Bulls were a study in precision. Jackson relaxed team rules, gave his players a freer rein and asked only that they act like professionals and dedicate themselves to winning. During the games, he seldom raised his voice and never lost his cool.

There really wasn't much reason to. With a lineup featuring Jordan, Pippen, Horace Grant and John Paxson, the Bulls rolled to 61 victories, a Central Division title and an NBA Finals date with Los Angeles. The Bulls capped the season by winning Chicago's first-ever championship with a five-game romp past the Lakers.

In 1991–92, Chicago was even more dominating. The Bulls posted a franchise-record 67 victories, repeated as division champs and defeated Portland in a six-game Finals. The following season, the Bulls made it three straight championships with another six-game Finals victory, this time over Phoenix.

FACTS & FIGURES

Personal	Born: September 17, 1945, at Deer Lodge, Mont.			
Teams	Bulls, 1989–1998, Lakers, 1999-present			
NBA Coach of the Year	None			
NBA Finals Appearances	1991, 1992, 1993, 1996, 1997, 1998, 2000			
NBA Championships	1991, 1992, 1993, 1996, 1997, 1998, 2000			
Coaching Record	G	W	L	Pct.
Regular Season	820	612	208	.746
Playoffs	178	126	49	.720

They became the first team to win three consecutive titles since the Celtics of 1964–66.

But Jackson's best coaching jobs came in 1993–94, when he led a Jordanless team to 55 victories, and 1995–96, when he guided the Bulls, with Jordan, to an unprecedented 72–10 regular-season record, a 15–3 playoff run and the franchise's fourth championship in six years. Chicago defeated Seattle in a six-game NBA Finals.

A year later Jackson led the Bulls to a 69–13 record and their fifth title of the decade by defeating the Utah Jazz in six games in the Finals. In a 1997–98 season that Jackson insisted was his last, the same opponents were again vanquished in six games as the Bulls made it six championships in eight years. In nine years in Chicago, Jackson had averaged over 60 wins and compiled a .738 winning percentage, the highest in league history.

After Chicago's sixth championship, Jackson resigned, which led to the eventual dismantling of the Bulls.

He took a year off to enjoy some of his many and varied other interests away from basketball, but when he indicated a willingness to return, he was wooed by any team with an opening—and some that offered to make openings where there were none.

He eventually settled with the Los Angeles Lakers, who immediately returned to the lofty perch they had held in the 1980s.

Jackson proved to be the coach who got Shaquille O'Neal to reach his potential, and the Lakers finished the 1999-2000 season with a league-best 67-15 record and went on to defeat the Indiana Pacers in six games in the NBA Finals.

Jackson is the 22nd coach to take his team to the NBA Finals in his first season as coach of the team and the 10th to win a title. Jackson is also the seventh coach to take more than one team to the NBA Finals. Alex Hannum holds the league record with three (St. Louis Hawks, San Francisco Warriors and Philadelphia 76ers.)

MASTER MOTIVATOR: *The former New York Knick knew how to get his point across.*

JOHN KUNDLA

Johnny on the spot for the Minneapolis Lakers

George Mikan looms over the Minneapolis Lakers record book like a massive redwood. At 6-foot-10 and 245 pounds, the powerful and relentless Mikan brutalized smaller opponents as the centerpiece for the first dynasty in National Basketball Association history.

But lost in the shadow of Mikan's accomplishments are several outstanding players—Jim Pollard, Vern Mikkelsen and Slater Martin—and the man who choreographed Mikan's NBA career. John Kundla was the guiding force for a Lakers team that won five NBA championships in six seasons and gave the NBA its first appearance in the national spotlight.

Kundla was an up-and-coming coach at St. Thomas College in Minnesota when the Lakers were organized to compete in the 1947–48 National Basketball League. Young, bright and articulate, the 31-year-old Kundla was the perfect choice for a young team that would require patience and a steady hand.

But before the first season opened, Kundla and Minneapolis got a giant surprise—literally. With the disbanding of the Chicago Gears franchise, players rights were distributed around the league and Mikan was awarded the Lakers.

The Mikan–Kundla combination proved lethal. The Lakers rolled to a first-year NBL championship, then jumped to the two-year-old Basketball Association of America and won another. They made it three straight in 1949–50 when the BAA officially

DEAR JOHN: *John Kundla was blessed with a weapon in 6–10 center George Mikan.*

became the NBA. After missing out in 1950–51, the Lakers came back and rattled off three more championships, giving them five NBA titles in six years.

Kundla, a perfectionist, pushed his players to the limit of their skills while remaining in the background. "The players do the work; they should get the publicity," he told one reporter in the midst of the Lakers' championship run.

But not everybody bought into that modesty. "Kundla has devised one of the finest series of plays (cuts and blocks) I've ever seen to make full use of George Mikan," noted New York Knicks coach

"Kundla has devised one of the finest series of plays I've ever seen to make full use of George Mikan."
Joe Lapchick, former New York Knicks coach

Joe Lapchick in the 1952–53 season.

Lapchick was referring to Minneapolis' innovative motion offense, which Kundla redesigned when the league widened the foul lane from 6 to 12 feet, attempting to minimize Mikan's growing dominance by getting him away from the basket. But instead of neutralizing Mikan's power game, the maneuvering opened up the lane for Kundla's streamlined cutting-and-passing attack.

First he experimented with a double pivot, with players cutting to the basket in intricate and confusing weaves. Then he positioned Mikan high and created room for his adept passing and elbow-clearing drives to the basket. Shortly after the wider lane was introduced, Mikan exploded for a 61-point game.

But Kundla preached more than power offense. In three of their first four NBA seasons, the Lakers led the league in fewest points allowed. Even after Mikan's 1954 retirement, the Lakers remained an NBA force because of their commitment on the defensive end.

Kundla coached the Lakers through 1958–59, a season that culminated with another visit to the NBA Finals. This time, however, the Lakers, featuring rookie Elgin Baylor, lost to the rising Boston Celtics. Kundla, who left the team with a 423–302 career mark and a lofty .632 playoff winning percentage, coached nine more seasons at the University of Minnesota.

(Opposite) BENCH COACH: *John Kundla had a .632 winning percentage in the playoffs.*

FACTS & FIGURES

Personal	Born: July 3, 1916, at Star Junction, Pa.			
Teams	Lakers, 1948–59			
Coach of the Year	None			
NBA Finals Appearances	1949, 1950, 1952, 1953, 1954, 1959			
NBA Championships	1949, 1950, 1952, 1953, 1954			
Coaching Record	G	W	L	Pct.
Regular Season	725	423	302	.583
Playoffs	95	60	35	.632

DON NELSON

The Basketball Guru Longs For an NBA Title

STILL WAITING: *Don Nelson is looking forward to his first NBA title as a coach.*

Everything about his sideline demeanor belied the real Don Nelson. He paced, bounded, yelled instructions to players and complained to officials. His complaints often were vociferous enough to draw technicals and his temperament in defeat was not congenial.

But away from the court or during practice, Nelson became a teacher, a basketball guru who molded young minds and bodies into the ways of the NBA. He was patient, he treated players and fans with respect and he built winners.

"He's the perfect coach," Philadelphia Coach John Lucas once said. "You know he cares about you by the way he deals with you." Lucas played two seasons under Nelson at Milwaukee.

Nelson "dealt" with players for almost two decades after finishing his outstanding 14-year playing career in 1976 with the Boston Celtics. In 11 seasons with the Bucks, seven with the Golden State Warriors and part of one with the New York Knicks, he compiled 851 coaching victories, won seven division titles and delivered nine seasons of 50 or more wins.

The only thing missing from Nelson's coaching resume is an NBA championship, an honor he enjoyed five times as a Boston player. "What burns inside of me is that ... I've never won a title as

a coach," he said when he took the Knicks job in 1995. "It's something I would like to do before I hang up my sneakers."

That dream died quickly as a veteran New York team refused to buy into Nelson's up-tempo offensive philosophy, forcing a midseason parting of the

FACTS & FIGURES

Personal	Born: May 15, 1940, at Muskegon, Mich.			
Teams	Bucks, 1976–87, Warriors, 1988–95,			
	Knicks, 1995–96, Mavericks			
	1997–present			
Coach of the Year	1983, 1985, 1992			
NBA Finals Appearances	None			
NBA Championships	None			
Coaching Record	G	W	L	Pct.
Regular Season	1,628	907	721	.557
Playoffs	112	51	61	.455

ways. Nelson resurfaced in the NBA a year later, not on the bench but in the front office as General Manager of the Dallas Mavericks.

It came as no surprise to anyone who knew "Nellie" that 16 games into the 1997–98 season he took over the position of Head Coach with the ailing franchise.

Nelson's coaching career began in 1976 when he was invited to become Larry Costello's Milwaukee assistant. Costello unexpectedly resigned in the 1976–77 season, and Nelson was thrust into the spotlight. Nelson "worked on two very simple priorities: Teach good defense and run like hell on offense."

That philosophy served him well as his Bucks, featuring Sidney Moncrief, Marques Johnson and Junior Bridgeman, rolled to 540 victories and seven consecutive Central Division titles in 11 seasons. Unable to get the Bucks past the conference finals, Nelson moved to Golden State as the team's

"He's the perfect coach. You know he cares about you by the way he deals with you."
John Lucas, a former NBA coach and Milwaukee player

executive vice president in 1987 and took the coaching reins in 1988–89. The Warriors perked up under his direction and compiled a 277–260 record over seven seasons.

One of the highlights of Nelson's West Coast stay was a 1994 trip to the Toronto World Championships as coach of Dream Team II. Nelson and the U.S. came away with a gold medal.

Nelson holds two NBA distinctions that say a lot about his love for the game and his ability to motivate players: He appeared in more games (more than 2,800) as a player and head coach than anybody except Lenny Wilkens and with Pat Riley he earned a record three

INTENSE: *Nelson's fiery coaching style did not go over with the Knicks.*

Coach of the Year citations.

Despite his best efforts, however, none of those came in his first seasons with the Mavericks. In fact, his winning percentage of .242 in his first season there was the worst of his career. Dallas showed slight improvement the next season, finishing 19–31 (.380). But the breakthrough really occurred in

1999–2000, when the Mavericks put together a strong finish over the last couple months of the season to end 40–42, finishing a surprising fourth in the Midwest Division.

Although Nelson had been expected to pass the reigns on to his son, Donn, the elder Nelson agreed to stay on the bench for a few more seasons.

JACK RAMSAY

The ultimate teacher

"Victories are produced by a team. Defeats, I take personally, because it means I didn't get my job done."

Jack Ramsay

There was no big secret to Jack Ramsay's success. Ramsay was the ultimate teacher, an education Ph.D. who conducted his classes in National Basketball Association arenas around the country. As a coach for four teams over 21 seasons, he taught basic skills, shaped character and gave his players a chance to succeed.

"Teaching," Ramsay once said, "is something that has been rewarding to me. Victories are produced by a team. Defeats, I take personally, because it means I didn't get my job done."

When Ramsay retired in November 1988, his resume suggested a job well done: an 864–783 record, 16 playoff appearances, 14 winning records, one NBA championship and a .525 winning percentage. He still ranks in the top five of most major all-time coaching categories and his record doesn't even include the 234 victories he compiled as coach at his alma mater, St. Joseph's College.

It was during his 11 seasons at St. Joseph's that Ramsay earned his Ph.D. and determined his life course. Unable to

shake the basketball bug that had bitten him during his years as a college coach and educator, he left St. Joseph's in 1966 to become general manager of the Philadelphia 76ers and found himself back on the sidelines two years later, coaching the team to a 55–27 record and second-place finish in the NBA's Eastern Division.

He would not leave the sidelines again for 20 years. After another three seasons in Philadelphia, Ramsay took over the 2-year-old Buffalo Braves in 1972–73 and suffered through a 21–61 disaster. But with Bob McAdoo scoring points and Randy Smith directing the offense, Ramsay's Braves posted their first winning record in 1973–74 and earned the first of three playoff berths—the only three in franchise history until the relocated Los Angeles Clippers qualified in 1991–92.

But Ramsay's real genius would not be displayed until 1976–77, when he took the helm of the 6-year-old Portland Trail Blazers, another franchise that had never experienced a winning season or qualified for the playoffs. With a healthy Bill Walton at center and burly Maurice Lucas at forward, Ramsay's Blazers recorded a 49–33 record and won 14 of 19 playoff games en route to one of the great Cinderella championships in NBA history. Ironically, the Blazers beat the 76ers in a six-game Finals.

Portland followed that success with a 58–24 record and reached the playoffs in nine of Ramsay's 10 seasons there. But there would be no more serious cham-

pionship runs. In 1986, Ramsay headed for Indianapolis and a new challenge—a team that had not won more than 26 games in four years and had made one postseason appearance in the last 10.

The 1986–87 Pacers perked up under Ramsay, recording a 41–41 record and reaching the playoffs. But in 1988–89, when Indiana got off to an 0–7 start, the 63-year-old Ramsay resigned, citing lack of enjoyment and concern about not getting the job done.

"All I can say is that he is a great basketball coach," said Bob Whitsitt, SuperSonics President at the time of Ramsay's resignation. "He has done a lot of good for the game. His record speaks for itself."

(Opposite) TAKE A KNEE: *Ramsay's greatest success came with the Portland Trail Blazers' 1976–77 Championship run.*

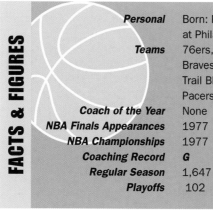

DR. JACK: *Jack Ramsay's Ph.D. in education led to his nickname.*

FACTS & FIGURES

Personal	Born: February 21, 1925, at Philadelphia, Pa.			
Teams	76ers, 1968–72, Braves, 1972–76, Trail Blazers, 1976–86, Pacers, 1986–88			
Coach of the Year	None			
NBA Finals Appearances	1977			
NBA Championships	1977			
Coaching Record	G	W	L	Pct.
Regular Season	1,647	864	783	.525
Playoffs	102	44	58	.431

PAT RILEY

The Fire Burns Deep

> **"As the team (the Los Angeles Lakers) continued to win, it was taken for granted."**
>
> *Pat Riley*

He sits on the sideline, gazing distantly through the frenzied action on the court. His hair is always perfectly coiffed and his expensive suit partially covers his shiny shoes. Pat Riley is at work, a calm presence amid the NBA storm.

Calm, at least, on the surface. But those who have played or worked for Riley know different. The inner fire burns intensely and his demands for organization and perfection are obsessive, explaining one of the most amazing coaching records ever compiled.

Over 18 seasons, Riley's teams have a winning percentage of .697 —the best among NBA coaches with at least 10 years on the job. Riley has coached and won more playoff games than any other NBA boss and his Lakers teams won four NBA championships and reached the NBA Finals on three other occasions. He made an eighth NBA Finals appearance in 1994 with the Knicks. Riley's 1999 regular-season victories place him second on the all-time list and he could challenge Lenny Wilkens' all-time record before he is done.

Ironically, Riley did not have coaching ambitions in 1976, when he finished a nine-year playing career in Phoenix. He was in the broadcast booth three years later when Lakers coach Jack McKinney suffered severe head injuries in a bicycle accident was replaced by Paul Westhead. Westhead invited Riley to be his assistant. When Westhead butted heads two years later with team owner Jerry Buss and star player Magic

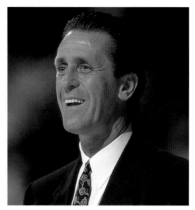

WILL TO WIN: *Pat Riley's intensity is legendary throughout the NBA.*

Johnson, Riley took over and guided the Lakers to the 1982 championship.

"When I got the head coaching job in 1981, I was looked at as a lucky guy who just walked into a situation where I had talented players," Riley said. "As the team continued to win, it was taken for granted. Now, everything's gone beyond my imagination."

Blessed with a lineup that included Johnson at the point, Kareem Abdul-Jabbar at center and James Worthy at forward, Riley opened up the Lakers' offense and the team cruised through the 1980s. Riley led the Lakers to nine straight Pacific Division titles and a record four consecutive 60-victory seasons, winning three more championships in six NBA Finals visits.

Riley left Los Angeles after the 1989–90 season for a television job with NBC, but he returned to the court in 1991 as coach of the New York

Knicks—an underachieving team in need of a philosophy and direction.

Riley provided both, molding a physical team around Patrick Ewing, his intimidating center. While the Lakers ran opponents off the court with their "Showtime" offense, the Knicks bullied, bumped and bruised them with a physical defense that kept scores under triple figures. Riley's Knicks were criticized for being a throwback to the boring game of yester-year, but they won three Atlantic Division titles and reached the NBA Finals in 1994, losing to Houston in seven games.

Riley moved to Miami in 1995 as coach and team president. In his first year he acquired Alonzo Mourning to build his team around, and also point guard Tim Hardaway. In his second season, Riley led the team to the Division title, took them to the Eastern Conference finals and was named NBA Coach of the Year again. Although the 1997–98 season ended in a first round playoff loss to the Knicks, he added another Atlantic title Division to his name.

The Knicks proved to be his nemesis. Despite two more Atlantic Division titles (the Heat tied with the Magic for that honor in 1998-99), Riley's Heat could not get past the Knicks in the playoffs.

In 1998-99, the eighth-seeded Knicks shocked the top-seeded Heat in five games in the first round. In 1999-2000, it was the second round, but the outcome was still the same—a loss to the Knicks in seven games.

The two teams developed a heated rivalry that erupted into violence on more than one occasion. But each time it was the Knicks—not the Heat—who found a way to regroup and advance.

(Opposite) **HEATING UP:** *Pat Riley has tried to get Miami fired up in the playoffs.*

FACTS & FIGURES

Personal	Born: March 20, 1945, at Rome, N.Y.			
Teams	Lakers, 1981–90, Knicks, 1991–95, Heat, 1995–present			
Coach of the Year	1990, 1993, 1997			
NBA Finals Appearances	1982, 1983, 1984, 1985, 1987, 1988, 1989, 1994			
NBA Championships	1982, 1985, 1987, 1988			
Coaching Record	**G**	**W**	**L**	**Pct.**
Regular Season	1,301	914	387	.703
Playoffs	237	147	90	.620

ADOLPH RUPP

The South Shall Rise

"His presence will last forever, in Kentucky and nationally."

Cliff Hagan, NBA player and Kentucky All-American

BARON OF BLUEGRASS: *Adolph Rupp is the father of Kentucky basketball.*

FACTS & FIGURES				
Personal	Born: September 2, 1901 at Halstead, Kansas			
Schools	University of Kentucky (1930-72)			
Coach of the Year	1949, 1950, 1959, 1966			
Coach of the Year	1990, 1993, 1997			
NCAA Tourn. appearances	1942, 1945, 1948, 1949, 1951, 1952, 1955, 1956, 1957, 1958, 1959, 1961, 1962, 1964, 1966, 1968, 1969, 1970, 1971, 1972			
NCAA Titles	1948, 1949, 1951, 1958.			
Coaching Record	G	W	L	Pct.
Regular Season	1,065	875	190	.822
Playoffs	48	30	18	.625

When Adolph Rupp arrived as coach at the University of Kentucky in 1930, he delivered what previously had been considered a city game to the South. He introduced the fast break, was a master at offensive efficiency and won 876 games.

"He was one of the soundest coaches basketball has ever seen," said famed UCLA coach John Wooden. "He didn't use a lot of fanciness and flair. He didn't need to."

When the great coaches are considered, Rupp holds the same esteemed rank for his offensive genius as many credit Hank Iba for his defensive precepts.

Once Rupp made his mark, Kentucky was about more than thoroughbred racing. It was about a statewide passion for basketball.

"He should be credited with basketball's growth, not just in the South but all over the country in the 1940s and '50s," said Cliff Hagan, a former Kentucky All-America. "Every time you see a basketball goal on a barn or kids in a playground, you have to credit Coach Rupp. His presence will last forever, in Kentucky and nationally."

Rupp's legacy is such that Wildcats supporters routinely make pilgrimages to his gravesite at Lexington Cemetery.

"They always ask directions to Rupp's grave—the coaches and their players who weren't even born when Coach Rupp died," said Mark Durbin, a cemetery official. "You see fathers bringing their sons here. Old fans, young fans. Adolph Rupp will never be forgotten, not in Kentucky."

Understand, the legacy is the man, the man is the legacy. His gravestone reads: "U.S. Basketball Coach 42 years; Olympic Coach 1948; Four NCAA Championships; National Basketball Hall of Fame."

Rupp was many things. He could be gruff, taciturn, perhaps overly driven. He was a brown suit, white shirt and brown tie. He was stubborn, not using a black player until adding center Tom Payne in 1969, three seasons before his retirement.

"Coach Rupp was very demanding, but his players always held him in high esteem, always thought he was the best coach on the bench," Hagan said, "always felt they were the best-prepared, best-conditioned team."

Nicknamed the "Baron of Bluegrass," Rupp fielded more than 80 percent of his players from the school's home state. Like many of today's passionate coaches, Rupp preached relentless man-to-man defense and an aggressive running game on offense.

One of Rupp's first great teams was the unit that in the 1947–48 and 1948–49 seasons won 68 of 73 games. The first of those two teams was known as the "Fabulous Five" and won an NCAA title. The second might have, as well, had an ugly gambling scandal not tainted that season. Rupp, though, stressed the integrity of his program.

"Nobody would give me credit for this," he said of his recruiting, "but the first thing I look at is that academic record. If you're taking a poor student, you're wasting your time. Next you would like to have size. Then you would like to have speed."

He also stressed principles of leadership. Rupp learned his lessons well, having played for the legendary Phog Allen at Kansas.

"It's getting five men and teaching them how to play together," he said, "and giving them the pattern to play by and practicing that pattern over and over until they know how to meet any situation, with a good coach sitting on the bench to remind them now and then."

Through that guidance, 24 of Rupp's players earned All-American honors, while seven captured Olympic gold medals and 28 played professionally. And like Dean Smith at North Carolina, who eventually would pass Rupp atop college basketball's all-time coaching victory list, Rupp's school would eventually play its games in his namesake facility, Rupp Arena.

Rupp's best team may have been the 1953–54 Wildcats, of which St. Louis coach Ed Hickey said, "They're the sweetest-operating team to watch that I've ever seen." The irony is that Kentucky was not allowed to field a team the previous season, because of rules infractions. From inactivity, Kentucky rolled to a 25–0 record. The leaders of that team included Hagan, Frank Ramsey and Lou Tsioropoulos.

"We were coming back with that great Kentucky tradition," Ramsey said.

Rupp's team, however, was unable to compete for the national championship that year because of player-eligibility issues.

Rupp was forced into that retirement, turning 70, the mandatory retirement age in Kentucky, after the 1972 season.

When Rupp passed away on December 10, 1977, a day of mourning was proclaimed in Kentucky. Even in death, he remains larger than life among Kentucky fans.

OLD SCHOOL: *Adolph Rupp was an old-fashioned, demanding coach.*

293

DEAN SMITH

Character and Dignity Defined the Man

He graduated his players. He reacted to the losses (as rare as they were) with the same dignity he reacted to the victories.

His teams played by the rules, played fair and played for national championships with great regularity. Dean Smith is more than the winningest coach in major college basketball. He stood as the beacon of everything that is right in the sport.

Of Smith's ability to not only become the winningest coach, but also to record each of those victories at the same institution, legendary Indiana coach Bob Knight noted, "It's indicative of a guy that, number one, really knows how to coach, and, number two, decided from day one things are going to be done the absolute right way."

By nature, college coaches are competitive. They recruit against each other, they scheme against each other, they often vie for the same jobs. Yet until his retirement, Smith stood beyond reproach, that respected, that appreciated.

Times, of course, were not always easy. The first six trips to the Final Four ended with a single championship. And Smith certainly could have an ornery

BE PREPARED: *Dean Smith's coaching style prepared players for the NBA—and life.*

side. He worked the games, his players, sometimes opposing players hard. When it came to efficiency, Smith never lost focus.

Not only did Smith win, but he won in the fiercely competitive Atlantic Coast Conference, against the likes of Duke, Maryland, Virginia, North Carolina State, schools with their own basketball glory.

But Smith's rosters were loaded. He not only coached Michael Jordan, James Worthy and Sam Perkins, he coached the three as teammates. Some of his other rosters were nearly as talented. And he wasn't afraid of youth, the way some stodgy coaches can grow.

"One of the pet peeves I have is that, seniors through freshmen, I play the best team. I'd be foolish not to," Smith admitted. "If the freshman's best, then he plays. Off the court, or at practice chasing loose balls, those are the things we do with freshmen."

While much is made of Smith being the only person able to keep Jordan from scoring, the other side is that he sent a remarkably polished player into the NBA, one who already was capable of greatness.

"Coach taught me the game, when to apply speed, how to use your quickness, when to use that first step, or how to apply certain skills in certain situations," Jordan said. "I gained all that knowledge so that when I got to the pros, it was just a matter of applying the information. Dean Smith gave me the knowledge to score 37 points a game and that's something people don't understand."

Smith was inducted into the Basketball Hall of Fame in 1983 and was inducted into the North Carolina Sports Hall of Fame in 1981.

"No coach can win championships without talent," legendary UCLA coach John Wooden once said. "But not all coaches who have talent win championships. I think Dean is the best teacher of basketball that I have observed."

So did most NBA coaches during Smith's tenure.

"We always look for players from North Carolina," says Miami Heat coach Pat Riley. "If we could draft players every year from North Carolina, we'd do it. You know they know how to play. The players are so

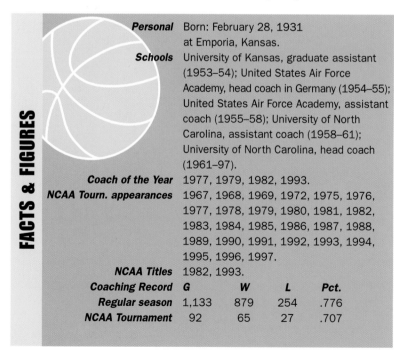

FACTS & FIGURES

Personal	Born: February 28, 1931 at Emporia, Kansas.			
Schools	University of Kansas, graduate assistant (1953–54); United States Air Force Academy, head coach in Germany (1954–55); United States Air Force Academy, assistant coach (1955–58); University of North Carolina, assistant coach (1958–61); University of North Carolina, head coach (1961–97).			
Coach of the Year	1977, 1979, 1982, 1993.			
NCAA Tourn. appearances	1967, 1968, 1969, 1972, 1975, 1976, 1977, 1978, 1979, 1980, 1981, 1982, 1983, 1984, 1985, 1986, 1987, 1988, 1989, 1990, 1991, 1992, 1993, 1994, 1995, 1996, 1997.			
NCAA Titles	1982, 1993.			
Coaching Record	G	W	L	Pct.
Regular season	1,133	879	254	.776
NCAA Tournament	92	65	27	.707

NET RESULTS: *It took Smith nearly three decades in coaching to win his first title, but less than a decade for the second to arrive.*

full of character. I have a lot of respect for Coach Smith."

In addition to his collegiate success, Smith guided the United States to a gold medal at the 1976 Montreal Olympics, making Smith one of only three coaches in history to win titles at the NCAA Tournament, NIT and Olympics, joining Knight and California's Pete Newell.

Smith's innovations were many, but most of all he was flexible. He could stall you into submission with his four-corners offense, or he could attack. He would play straight-up man-to-man defense or he would innovate by double-teaming off the pick-and-roll.

"Dean is one of the most organized and brilliant minds that I've ever met in basketball," said former Georgetown coach John Thompson.

Indeed, he has taught well. Among his former players or aides who have gone on to successful coaching careers are Larry Brown, Roy Williams and Bill Guthridge.

Smith is also the author of Basketball: *Multiple Offenses and Defenses*, which has been translated into several foreign languages and is the best-selling techni-cal basketball book in history.

So beloved was Smith at North Carolina that his legacy is the Dean E. Smith Center. The facility, better known as the Dean Dome, is where the Tar Heels play their homes games.

"Dean Smith gave me the knowledge to score 37 points a game."
Michael Jordan, NBA legend.

PAT SUMMITT

Unqualified Success is a Hallmark at Tennessee

More than 800 victories. More than 26 seasons at the same institution. A regular place at the NCAA Tournament and a realistic opportunity at another national championship ever year her team takes to the court.

There is a reason Pat Summitt is viewed as the finest coach in women's basketball and among the greatest collegiate coaches, regardless of gender.

When it comes to winning, few programs can match what Summitt has

FACTS & FIGURES

Personal	Born: June 14, 1952 at Henrietta, Tenn.
Schools	University of Tennessee (1974–present).
Coach of the Year	1983, 1987, 1989, 1994, 1995, 1998.
NCAA Tourn. Appearances	1982, 1983, 1984, 1985, 1986, 1987, 1988, 1989, 1990, 1991, 1992, 1993, 1994, 1995, 1996, 1997, 1998, 1999,2000.
NCAA Titles	1987, 1989, 1991, 1996, 1997, 1998.

Coaching Record	G	W	L	Pct.
Regular Season	878	728	150	.829
NCAA Tournament	82	69	13	.841

VICTORIOUS VISAGE: *Tennessee's Pat Summitt has won all the honors a coach can win.*

accomplished at the University of Tennessee.

When Summitt was inducted in June 1999 into the Women's Basketball Hall of Fame it was as if the institution had been conceived as a prelude to her arrival.

Summitt not only has elevated the Tennessee program with her excellence, she has elevated the women's game. Beyond presenting Tennessee with a third consecutive national championship in 1998, she delivered a book to the best-sellers list, *Reach for the Summit*,

> ## "She's an icon. The only people you can compare her to are John Wooden and Dean Smith."
>
> *Jane Albright, Wisconsin coach.*

and became the first female coach to grace the cover of *Sports Illustrated*.

In the 1990s alone, Summitt delivered four NCAA titles (1991, 1996, 1997 and 1998) to the Knoxville campus. She also got her Lady Vols to the 2000 title game, only to be subdued by Connecticut.

Her coup de grace might have been in 1998, when she not only guided Tennessee to a 39–0 championship finish, but did so with an average victory margin of 30.1 points.

Summitt was the youngest coach in the nation to reach 300 victories (34 years old), 400 victories (37 years old), 500 victories (41 years old), and 600 victories (44 years old).

In all of college basketball, Summitt trails only UCLA's legendary coach John Wooden for the most NCAA titles. Wooden recorded 10 in 29 years. Summitt has won six in 26.

Already, there have been more NCAA Tournament victories for Summitt than for Wooden or Bob Knight, two mainstays of the men's tournament. Despite that success, or perhaps because of it, Summitt remains committed to the women's game.

"My commitment is to women and women's basketball," she said. ``We've had a lot of tough growing pains and we've had to clear a lot of hurdles. I'm all about promoting the women's game. I love men's basketball. And I think I could do it. I'm probably the type of person who would tell you, 'Sure, I could do it.' But what I really want is to continue to help grow our sport and make a difference for young women so they can go out and feel they're prepared for life when they leave this program."

Respected Connecticut women's coach Geno Auriemma said Summitt would succeed on any level, with any gender player.

"For Pat," he said, "getting the respect of a men's team wouldn't be difficult at all. Pat's really good at what she does. She would command the respect of anyone she coached."

Indeed, while maternal off the court, and an overwhelming success at getting her players to leave with their degrees, on the court Summitt is an autocrat. Her players work hard and for long hours. Her voice resonates across the court. There is a Bob Knight-like intensity to her demeanor.

"She's an icon," said Wisconsin coach Jane Albright, a former graduate assistant under Summitt. "She's the single biggest ambassador for this game, and if she ever leaves, it will never be the same. The only people you can compare her to are John Wooden and Dean Smith. No one else has had her kind of impact on the game."

On the international level, Summitt won an Olympic silver medal as a player in 1976. As a coach in international

PASSIONATE LEADERSHIP: *Pat Summitt is committed to promoting women's basketball.*

competition, she brought home the first U.S. gold medal in women's basketball at the 1984 Games.

The accompanying honors have been many. In 1990 she was enshrined in the Women's Sports Foundation Hall of Fame. In 1996, she was inducted into the National Association for Sport and Physical Education's Hall of Fame. In 1997, she was honored at a White House luncheon given by First Lady Hillary Clinton recognizing the "25 Most Influential Working Mothers" as selected by *Working Mother* magazine.

Understand, Summitt is a legend in Tennessee, where there have been plenty of successful men's college teams, as well as a pro football team that made it all the way to the 2000 Super Bowl in Atlanta. Gregg Williams, defensive coordinator for those Tennessee Titans, counts himself among Summitt's fans.

"She's able to make everyone around her a better person and really a better player," he said. ``That's the true mark of a great coach and that is being able to effect change no matter what level they're at."

Out of the Shadows and Into the Spotlight

LENNY WILKENS

He's the NBA's quiet man, always under control and never speaking without careful consideration. Nothing about him is spectacular, demonstrative or exciting. And for the better part of two decades, Lenny Wilkens has been lost in the shadows of the game's most dominant personalities, unwilling to dramatize his case as professional basketball's most underrated coach.

But that changed on January 6, 1995, when Wilkens was thrust into the spotlight by the enormity of his own accomplishment. When his Atlanta Hawks posted a 112–90 victory over Washington, Wilkens earned his 939th career victory and moved past the legendary Red Auerbach into first place on the all-time list.

Wilkens' victory total stood at 1,179 entering the 1999–2000 season and he has only just turned 63. The passion is still there, the ability to motivate and communicate with players is still intact and the competitive instincts are still strong, suggesting the victory record could climb out of sight.

"Lenny is always under control," said Chuck Daly, coach of the 1989 and '90 Detroit championship teams and a long-time admirer. "His teams are always prepared and his players trust him. He is one of the great coaches of our time."

When Wilkens, a skinny point guard, began an outstanding 15-year playing career with the Hawks in 1960, he never

QUIET APPROACH: *Lenny Wilkens shuns the spotlight despite all his success.*

dreamed of extending that career to the sideline. But coaches and management took note of his cool, intelligent, unselfish and mistake-free playing style, qualities that would push him into his career calling. From 1969–72, Wilkens served as player-coach for the expansion Seattle SuperSonics and in 1974–75 he performed the same role for Portland. Those seasons were merely warmups for the long road into the record books.

Wilkens returned to Seattle in 1977 and coached the Sonics for eight seasons, producing six winning records, three

50-victory campaigns and two NBA Finals appearances. The 1978 Sonics, featuring Gus Williams, Jack Sikma and Dennis Johnson, lost the Bullets in seven games, but the 1979 team beat Washington in five. The championship would be the first and last on Wilkens' resume.

Wilkens moved to Cleveland in 1986 and undertook a major rebuilding job for a demoralized organization. In his third season, the Cavs posted a franchise-record 57 victories and the team qualified for the playoffs in five of his seven years. The 1991–92 team, featuring Brad Daugherty, Mark Price and Larry Nance, won 57 games and reached the Eastern Conference finals, losing to eventual champion Chicago.

As in Seattle and Cleveland, Wilkens brought instant credibility to the Hawks when he took the reins in 1993. In his first year, his team won a franchise-tying record of 57 games and won the Central Division title.

"He is one of the great coaches of our time."
Chuck Daly, NBA Championship-winning coach

"Lenny transformed one of the worst defensive teams in the league into one of the best," said Hawks President Stan Kasten.

In 1996, he coached Dream Team III to a gold medal in the 1996 Atlanta Olympic Games. He followed that up by leading the Hawks to consecutive 50-win seasons, although he could not advance Atlanta beyond a second round playoff loss to Chicago in 1997.

Little did he know that would soon seem like the good old days. In 1998, the Hawks failed to get by the Charlotte Hornets in the first round. In 1999, the Hawks beat the Detroit Pistons in the first round before being swept by New

FACTS & FIGURES

Personal	Born: October 28, 1937, at Brooklyn, N.Y.			
Teams	SuperSonics, 1969–72, 1977–85, Trail Blazers, 1974–76, Cavaliers, 1986–93, Hawks, 1993–2000, Raptors, 2000–present			
Coach of the Year	1994			
NBA Finals Appearances	1978, 1979			
NBA Championships	1979			
Coaching Record	G	W	L	Pct.
Regular Season	2,160	1,179	981	.546
Playoffs	157	72	85	.459

York, 4-0, in the second round.

From that point on, it was a nightmare. Eager to try to change their fortunes, the Hawks traded Steve Smith to Portland for Jim Jackson and the troubled Isaiah Rider. It was a disaster from the start. As had been the case in Rider's previous two stops in Minnesota and Portland, his off-court behavior became a total distraction until the Hawks were forced to take the drastic step of cutting him in the middle of the season.

But by that time, Atlanta was on its way to a 28-54 record, and the .341 winning percentage was the lowest in Wilkens' stellar career. He wound up resigning under pressure, but was hired by the Toronto Raptors a short time later.

A NEW LEAF: *Lenny Wilkens prepares for a fresh start in Canada with the Raptors.*

300

JOHN WOODEN

The Wizard of Westwood

LISTEN AND LEARN: *Winning was a way of life at UCLA when John Wooden was the coach.*

To fully appreciate John Wooden is to have had to wait until he departed UCLA. Only then was it obvious that a coaching legend, and not a program alone, could guarantee such enduring success.

When Wooden was winning championships at the Los Angeles-area school at such a remarkable pace in the 1960s and '70s, it was almost accepted that everything UCLA was golden.

Yet no sooner did the Wizard of Westwood depart, than the magic ceased, the victories became harder to come by, the domination not nearly as dramatic.

It wasn't the uniforms, the recruiting, the lure of Los Angeles, it was Wooden, who, it safely now can be said, established a dynasty that never will be matched, 10 championships in 12 seasons, including seven in a row.

While Wooden would concentrate his recruiting focus on the fertile courts of Southern California, the nation's elite often contacted him, asking for an opportunity to be part of the tradition.

"He had a mystique about him," long-time college coach Bill Foster, formerly of Clemson and Miami, said. "Kids were kind of in awe of him. When he called, it was unbelievable and kids were overwhelmed."

Wooden was a three-time All-America at Purdue, one who made the Basketball Hall of Fame as a player in 1960, 12 years before he was re-enshrined as a coach.

In his 27 seasons at UCLA, Wooden compiled a 620–147 record. He coached 24 first-team All-Americas, including

FACTS & FIGURES

Personal	Born: October 14, 1910 at Martinsville, Indiana.
Schools	Indiana State University (1946-48); UCLA (1948-75).
Coach of the Year	1964, 1967, 1969, 1970, 1972, 1973.
NCAA Tourn. appearances	1950, 1952, 1956, 1962, 1963, 1964, 1965, 1967, 1968, 1969, 1970, 1971, 1972, 1973, 1974, 1975.
NCAA Titles	1964, 1965, 1967, 1968, 1969, 1970, 1971, 1972, 1973, 1975.

Coaching Record	G	W	L	Pct.
Regular Season	826	664	162	.804
Playoffs	57	47	10	.825

legendary big men Lew Alcindor (who later changed his name to Kareem Abdul-Jabbar) and Bill Walton. It was with Walton aboard that Wooden's Bruins won an NCAA-record 88 consecutive games.

Wooden worked in a self- deprecating manner.

"I am not a strategic coach," he said. "I am a practice coach."

His teams were fundamentally sound. What often is overlooked is that for 15 years Wooden coached in virtually obscurity at UCLA. It wasn't until his 1963–64 championship team that there was a taste of what was to come. That dynamic lineup featured such future NBA stars as Gail Goodrich, Walt Hazzard and Keith Erickson.

"In retrospect, it was a team that epitomized Wooden's brilliance," Hazzard would later say. "He took the strengths of his individual players and adjusted his system to maximize those abilities."

It was during that stage of the Wooden legacy that UCLA's press grew to become one of the nation's most feared defensive alignments. For more than a decade, the Bruins' pressure would force opponents into submission.

From that first title season, Wooden would go on to recruit Alcindor and Walton — and everything changed.

Wooden's relationship with Walton was especially unique.

"Bill was a rebel," Wooden said. "Of course, during Bill's playing days, it was probably a little more rebellious time."

Forward Larry Farmer, who later would return to UCLA as a coach, said Wooden would allow freedoms, to a limit.

"He treated us all the same when we were on the basketball court," Farmer said. "He had us in great shape, and we were fundamentally sound players. I

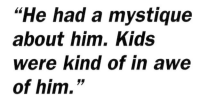

301

"He had a mystique about him. Kids were kind of in awe of him."
Bill Foster, veteran college coach

guess the combination of all those things, and the fact that he was a great teacher, led to his incredible win streaks that I don't think will be matched in any sport."

Under Wooden, the Bruins set records with four perfect 30–0 seasons, those 88 consecutive victories, 38 consecutive NCAA tournament victories and a staggering 20 conference championships.

Wooden first learned about basketball when he was at age 8, in 1918, just 27 years after the invention of the game. With a pair of his mother's hose stuffed with rags as a ball, Wooden began his basketball education by shooting at a tomato basket his father had nailed to a wall in their barn.

The 1932 College Player of the Year, Wooden studied the game at Purdue under Hall of Fame coach Ward "Piggy" Lambert. Following coaching stints at two high schools, Wooden took over as coach at Indiana State, where he recorded a 44-15 record over two seasons. In 1948, he took over at UCLA.

Wooden centered his coaching philosophy around sets of threes. There were forwards, guards, centers. The actions were shoot, drive, pass. The elements on the court were ball, you, man. To prepare there was conditioning, skill, teamwork.

Among those who benefited from Wooden's wisdom were noted players such as Hazzard, Goodrich, Alcindor, Lucius Allen, Mike Warren, Sidney Wicks, Curtis Rowe, Henry Bibby, Walton, Keith Wilkes, Richard Washington and Dave Meyers.

Wooden is one of only two people enshrined in the Basketball Hall of Fame as both a player and a coach. To this day, long since retired as a coach, Wooden remains a popular speaker and interview subject, always willing to share his expertise with a new generation of fans.

HE'S A CLASSIC: *John Wooden at the 1999 John Wooden Classic in Anaheim, Calif.*

THE NBA'S SECOND SEASON

302

It happens every spring. The NBA's regular-season preliminaries come to a merciful end, 16 teams move into a more competitive dimension and re-energized players intensify their chase for basketball's Holy Grail.

It's called the "Second Season," but many who compete consider the playoffs the "Only Season." The first 82 games are the appetizer; the 15 to 26 it might take to win a championship are the main course and dessert.

The NBA's 29 teams spend the six-month regular season fighting for one of the 16 playoff berths, jockeying for home-court advantage and trying to make their journey through the postseason maze as easy as possible. The regular season does have its perks—division championships, scoring titles, awards—but nothing has meaning until the first postseason elbow is delivered—and received.

How, who, where and when

The NBA's playoff format is a logical succession that begins with the eight most suc-

cessful regular-season teams from the Eastern and Western Conferences qualifying for postseason play. They are seeded one through eight, with the two division winners getting the top positions and the rest of the teams lining up according to their record. The first seed pairs off against the eighth, second against seventh, third against sixth, and fourth against fifth in first-round best-of-five series. The higher ranked teams always benefit from home-court advantage. In the first round they are home in games one, two and, if necessary, five.

A slightly different format is used in the Conference semi-finals and finals. The first-round winners advance to the best-of-seven semi-final series and the winners to the Conference finals. The format for home-court advantage in these series is 2–2–1–1–1; Conference semi-finalists with the best

regular-season record—not division winners—host games one, two, and if necessary, five and seven.

The Eastern and Western Conference champions battle in the NBA Finals for supremacy. The title series is set up in a 2–3–2 format with the better regular-season team hosting games one, two, six and seven at home, if the series goes the full distance.

The following pages offer a year-by-year glimpse of the NBA Finals and the coronation of each season's champion.

(Opposite) FAMILIAR POSE: *Chicago's Michael Jordan clutches the 1997 NBA Championship trophy.*

(Below) THE FINALS TIP: *Hakeem Olajuwon (Houston, left) and Shaquille O'Neal (Orlando, right) in the 1995 NBA Finals.*

304 NBA FINALS 1947–2000

YEAR	WINNER	HEAD COACH	SERIES	LOSER	HEAD COACH
1947	Philadelphia Warriors	Eddie Gottlieb	4–1	Chicago Stags	Harold Olsen
1948	Baltimore Bullets	Buddy Jeannette	4–2	Philadelphia Warriors	Eddie Gottlieb
1949	Minneapolis Lakers	John Kundla	4–2	Washington Capitols	Red Auerbach
1950	Minneapolis Lakers	John Kundla	4–2	Syracuse Nationals	Al Cervi
1951	Rochester Royals	Les Harrison	4–3	New York Knicks	Joe Lapchick
1952	Minneapolis Lakers	John Kundla	4–3	New York Knicks	Joe Lapchick
1953	Minneapolis Lakers	John Kundla	4–1	New York Knicks	Joe Lapchick
1954	Minneapolis Lakers	John Kundla	4–3	Syracuse Nationals	Al Cervi
1955	Syracuse Nationals	Al Cervi	4–3	Fort Wayne Pistons	Charley Eckman
1956	Philadelphia Warriors	George Senesky	4–1	Fort Wayne Pistons	Charley Eckman
1957	Boston Celtics	Red Auerbach	4–3	St. Louis Hawks	Alex Hannum
1958	St. Louis Hawks	Alex Hannum	4–2	Boston Celtics	Red Auerbach
1959	Boston Celtics	Red Auerbach	4–0	Minneapolis Lakers	John Kundla
1960	Boston Celtics	Red Auerbach	4–3	St. Louis Hawks	Ed Macauley
1961	Boston Celtics	Red Auerbach	4–1	St. Louis Hawks	Paul Seymour
1962	Boston Celtics	Red Auerbach	4–3	Los Angeles Lakers	Fred Schaus
1963	Boston Celtics	Red Auerbach	4–2	Los Angeles Lakers	Fred Schaus
1964	Boston Celtics	Red Auerbach	4–1	San Francisco Warriors	Alex Hannum
1965	Boston Celtics	Red Auerbach	4–1	Los Angeles Lakers	Fred Schaus
1966	Boston Celtics	Red Auerbach	4–3	Los Angeles Lakers	Fred Schaus
1967	Philadelphia 76ers	Alex Hannum	4–2	San Francisco Warriors	Bill Sharman
1968	Boston Celtics	Bill Russell	4–2	Los Angeles Lakers	B. van Breda Kolff
1969	Boston Celtics	Bill Russell	4–3	Los Angeles Lakers	B. van Breda Kolff
1970	New York Knicks	Red Holzman	4–3	Los Angeles Lakers	Joe Mullaney
1971	Milwaukee Bucks	Larry Costello	4–0	Baltimore Bullets	Gene Shue
1972	Los Angeles Lakers	Bill Sharman	4–1	New York Knicks	Red Holzman
1973	New York Knicks	Red Holzman	4–1	Los Angeles Lakers	Bill Sharman
1974	Boston Celtics	Tommy Heinsohn	4–3	Milwaukee Bucks	Larry Costello
1975	Golden State Warriors	Al Attles	4–0	Washington Bullets	K.C. Jones
1976	Boston Celtics	Tommy Heinsohn	4–2	Phoenix Suns	John MacLeod
1977	Portland Trail Blazers	Jack Ramsay	4–2	Philadelphia 76ers	Gene Shue
1978	Washington Bullets	Dick Motta	4–3	Seattle Supersonics	Lenny Wilkens
1979	Seattle Supersonics	Lenny Wilkens	4–1	Washington Bullets	Dick Motta
1980	Los Angeles Lakers	Paul Westhead	4–2	Philadelphia 76ers	Billy Cunningham
1981	Boston Celtics	Bill Fitch	4–2	Houston Rockets	Del Harris
1982	Los Angeles Lakers	Pat Riley	4–2	Philadelphia 76ers	Billy Cunningham
1983	Philadelphia 76ers	Billy Cunningham	4–0	Los Angeles Lakers	Pat Riley
1984	Boston Celtics	K.C. Jones	4–3	Los Angeles Lakers	Pat Riley
1985	Los Angeles Lakers	Pat Riley	4–2	Boston Celtics	K.C. Jones
1986	Boston Celtics	K.C. Jones	4–2	Houston Rockets	Bill Fitch
1987	Los Angeles Lakers	Pat Riley	4–2	Boston Celtics	K.C. Jones
1988	Los Angeles Lakers	Pat Riley	4–3	Detroit Pistons	Chuck Daly
1989	Detroit Pistons	Chuck Daly	4–0	Los Angeles Lakers	Pat Riley
1990	Detroit Pistons	Chuck Daly	4–1	Portland Trail Blazers	Rick Adelman
1991	Chicago Bulls	Phil Jackson	4–1	Los Angeles Lakers	Mike Dunleavy
1992	Chicago Bulls	Phil Jackson	4–2	Portland Trail Blazers	Rick Adelman
1993	Chicago Bulls	Phil Jackson	4–2	Phoenix Suns	Paul Westphal
1994	Houston Rockets	Rudy Tomjanovich	4–3	New York Knicks	Pat Riley
1995	Houston Rockets	Rudy Tomjanovich	4–0	Orlando Magic	Brian Hill
1996	Chicago Bulls	Phil Jackson	4–2	Seattle SuperSonics	George Karl
1997	Chicago Bulls	Phil Jackson	4–2	Utah Jazz	Jerry Sloan
1998	Chicago Bulls	Phil Jackson	4–2	Utah Jazz	Jerry Sloan
1999	San Antonio Spurs	Gregg Popovich	4–1	New York Knicks	Jeff Van Gundy
2000	Los Angeles Lakers	Phil Jackson	4–2	Indiana Pacers	Larry Bird

Warriors surprise Stags behind no ordinary Joe

1947 NBA FINALS

Philadelphia	84	Chicago	71	at Philadelphia
Philadelphia	85	Chicago	74	at Philadelphia
Philadelphia	75	Chicago	72	at Chicago
Chicago	74	Philadelphia	73	at Chicago
Philadelphia	83	Chicago	80	at Philadelphia

Like a newborn colt taking its first uneasy steps, the Basketball Association of America tottered through its first professional season, groping for steadying hands and the hope of firmer footing just around the corner.

Nothing had come easy in its debut campaign and every decision had been made with uncertainty and bottom-line accountability. But every team official understood one basic fact: The league needed appealing events and players—and it needed them fast.

So it was not without some measure of satisfaction that the Philadelphia Warriors, a team that had staggered through much of the season before meshing over the final month, reached the league's first championship series. The Warriors, owned and coached by Eddie Gottlieb, had the league's most marketable star, a high-scoring Kentucky hillbilly named Joe Fulks.

Jumpin' Joe was the man who popularized the jump shot, a scoring maneuver he executed from unusual angles while leaning, running or standing alone on the perimeter. Fulks was an offensive marvel to the conservative Eastern basketball fans and he averaged a league-best 23.2 points in 1946–47, an unsightly total in the pre-shot clock game.

Fulks was at his best during the BAA's first playoff season, and the Warriors' drive to a championship was enhanced by an awkward system that did not benefit the league's best regular-season teams. Philadelphia had finished 14 games behind

the Eastern Division-champion Washington Capitols, who were coached by young Red Auerbach. But BAA officials set up a strange format that matched division winners, second-place finishers and third-place teams in the opening round. Auerbach's Capitols were upset by Western Division champion Chicago while the Warriors defeated the St. Louis Bombers and New York Knickerbockers to advance to the Finals.

And the Warriors got an additional break when scheduling problems at Chicago Stadium forced the first game of the final series to be played at a packed Philadelphia Arena, where Fulks unleashed a 37-point shooting blitz that buried the Stags, 84–71. Fans and reporters marveled at one of the greatest shooting exhibitions ever staged.

Fulks was quiet in Game 2 at Philadelphia, but the Warriors still claimed an 85–74 victory and a 2–0 series advantage, thanks to Howie Dallmar (18 points) and center Art Hillhouse, who scored 7 of his team's final 10 points.

By the time the series shifted to Chicago, the Warriors were riding an unstoppable wave of momentum—and Fulks was doing the driving. Jumpin' Joe fired in 26 points in

Game 3 as the Warriors held off a frantic Chicago rally in a 75–72 decision.

The Stags delayed elimination in Game 4 on the combined 38-point scoring of Max Zaslofsky and Don Carlson in a 74–73 victory, but the Warriors rode Fulks' 34-point explosion to a title-clinching 83–80 Game 5 victory before the home fans at Philadelphia.

The BAA had its first champion, its first superstar and its first Cinderella in a memorable NBA Finals upset.

JUMPIN' JOE: *Joe Fulks dominated the finals with his jump shot.*

306 1948

The Bullets join the Big Time

The Baltimore Bullets were a late, late addition to the Basketball Association of America—a team taken from the regional American Basketball League to fill out the BAA lineup when four of the circuit's 11 charter franchises folded after one season.

But the Bullets were more than an afterthought in the young league's second postseason. Led by player/coach Buddy Jeannette, they tied for second in the Western Division and zipped past Chicago in a semifinal playoff. When the defending-champion Warriors posted a 71–60 victory in the championship series opener and stormed to a 41–20 halftime lead in Game 2, it appeared Cinderella was about to lose her glass sneaker.

Not so. Recoveries from 21-point deficits in the pre-shot clock era were inconceivable, but that's exactly what the Bullets did. They pulled within 48–40 at the end of three quarters, forged ahead late in the game and secured victory on Paul Hoffman's tip-in with four seconds remaining. The 66–63 victory, the biggest comeback in NBA Finals history, gave the Bullets the momentum they needed.

When the series returned to Baltimore, they scored 72–70 and 78–75 victories.

The Warriors recovered for a 91–82 Game 5 triumph at Philadelphia, but the Bullets closed out the shocking series with an 88–73 blowout at Baltimore.

The "minor leaguers" were BAA champions and no one was foolish enough to overlook them again.

FIRED UP: *A late addition to the league, the Bullets rallied for the championship.*

1948 NBA FINALS

Philadelphia	71	Baltimore	60	at Philadelphia
Baltimore	66	Philadelphia	63	at Philadelphia
Baltimore	72	Philadelphia	70	at Baltimore
Baltimore	78	Philadelphia	75	at Baltimore
Philadelphia	91	Baltimore	82	at Philadelphia
Baltimore	88	Philadelphia	73	at Baltimore

1949

A Dynasty takes Shape

The Minneapolis championship reign opened as the Lakers rode the broad shoulders of 6–10 center George Mikan to a 44–16 regular-season record, playoff sweeps of Chicago and Rochester and a six-game NBA Finals victory over Red Auerbach's Washington Capitols.

The Lakers, one of four National Basketball League teams to jump to the BAA, captured the first three games against Washington. The opener, an 88–84 thriller that featured Mikan's 42-point outburst, was not decided until Don Carlson broke an 84–84 deadlock with two last-minute free throws.

The Capitols worked hard to keep the ball away from Mikan in Game 2 and he scored only 10 points, but Carlson poured in 16 and Herm Schaefer added 13 in a 76–62 Lakers' romp. Mikan rebounded for 35 points in Game 3 at Washington, and the Lakers rolled to a 94–74 victory.

The Lakers' 3–0 advantage was fortunate because Mikan hit the floor hard during the Capitols' 83–71 Game 4 victory, breaking his wrist. But playing with a cast, the Minneapolis big man scored 22 points in a 74–66 loss before keying the Lakers' title-clinching 77–56 victory at Minneapolis.

Mikan, the regular-season scoring champion with a 28.3 average, finished the playoffs with 303 points (30.3).

GEORGE THE FIRST: *George Mikan was the Lakers' main man throughout the finals.*

1949 NBA FINALS

Minneapolis	88	Washington	84	at Minneapolis
Minneapolis	76	Washington	62	at Minneapolis
Minneapolis	94	Washington	74	at Washington
Washington	83	Minneapolis	71	at Washington
Washington	74	Minneapolis	66	at Washington
Minneapolis	77	Washington	56	at Minneapolis

308 # 1950

Another Title for Minneapolis, by George

1950 NBA FINALS

Minneapolis	68	Syracuse	66	at Syracuse
Syracuse	91	Minneapolis	85	at Syracuse
Minneapolis	91	Syracuse	77	at St. Paul
Minneapolis	77	Syracuse	69	at St. Paul
Syracuse	83	Minneapolis	76	at Syracuse
Minneapolis	110	Syracuse	95	at Minneapolis

The Minneapolis Lakers, with rookies Slater Martin (guard), Tiger Harrison (guard) and Vern Mikkelsen (power forward) bolstering a starting lineup that already featured Jim Pollard and George Mikan, squared off against the Syracuse Nationals and Dolph Schayes in the NBA Finals.

This marked a new era in the league, as six teams from the National Basketball League joined 11 teams from the Basketball Association to form the 17-team NBA.

The league was divided into the Eastern, Central and Western Divisions, with the top four teams in each division making the crowded playoffs.

The Nationals had forged the best regular-season record (51–13) in the bulky 17-team "National Basketball Association," but they were no match for Minneapolis in the title series.

John Kundla's Lakers won the opener at Syracuse, 68–66, on Harrison's 40-foot set shot and claimed Games 3 and 4 with 14 and 8-point victories before their home fans.

The Nationals' only breakthroughs came on their home court—91–85 and 83–76 decisions in Games 2 and 5. In both victories, Syracuse guard Paul Seymour held Pollard to low point totals, leaving Mikan to handle the offensive load. He scored 60 points in the two losses.

Seymour's defense had no impact on Game 6 as Mikan's 40-point explosion carried the Lakers to a 110–95 title-clinching, fight-filled victory at Minneapolis Auditorium.

The powerful Mikan averaged 32.2 points in the six games as the Lakers became the first team to win consecutive BAA/NBA championships.

EASY BASKET: *Vern Mikkelsen played a key role as a rookie for the Lakers.*

New York, New York, it's a wonderful State

An all-New York NBA Finals that pitted Rochester against the upstart Knicks developed into the first seven-game battle in league history. Amazingly, the Knicks, third-place Eastern Division finishers during the regular season, almost triumphed after losing the first three games. New York was led by Larry Gallatin, who averaged 12.8 points in the regular season and helped the Knicks down Boston and Syracuse in the playoffs.

The Royals, who had advanced to the Finals by beating the injury-plagued Minneapolis Lakers in the Western Division finals, handled the Knicks with 92–65, 99–84 and 78–71 series-opening victories behind the inspired play of center Arnie Risen and guard Bob Davies. The 6–9 Risen dominated inside, scoring 27 points in the Game 3 victory at New York's Armory.

But just as quickly as the Knicks had fallen into their deep hole they pulled themselves out. They blew a 17-point lead in Game 4 but managed to pull out a 79–73 victory. Then they rode the combined 50-point scoring of Connie Simmons and Max Zaslofsky to a 92–89 upset at Rochester. Zaslofsky's 23-point Game 6 outburst carried the Knicks to an 80–73 series-tying triumph at New York.

The Knicks fell behind by 14 points early in the finale at Rochester, but they rallied in the second half and edged in front, 74–72, with two minutes remaining. The game was tied 75–75 with less than a minute to play when Davies delivered the killing blows—a pair of free throws. Jack Coleman's last second layup clinched the Royals' 79–75 victory. Risen led Rochester scorers with 24 points and Davies added 20.

STAR GUARD: *Bob Davies delivered in the clutch with two crucial free throws in Game 7.*

1951 NBA FINALS

Rochester	92	New York	65	at Rochester
Rochester	99	New York	84	at Rochester
Rochester	78	New York	71	at New York
New York	79	Rochester	73	at New York
New York	92	Rochester	89	at Rochester
New York	80	Rochester	73	at New York
Rochester	79	New York	75	at Rochester

310 1952

Return of the King lets Lakers to regain Throne

The Minneapolis Lakers, who had fallen in the 1951 playoffs when George Mikan broke a bone in his ankle, returned to the NBA throne—but not without a seven-game scare from the Knicks.

Mikan averaged 23.8 points and as the Lakers finished second in the Western Division but beat Rochester 3-1 to reach the Finals.

New York advanced to the Finals for the second straight season after finishing third in the NBA's Eastern Division. But unlike 1951, when they lost the first three games to Rochester, the Knicks took the Lakers to overtime in an 83–79 opening game loss at St. Paul and pulled off an 80–72 second-game upset as they held Mikan to 18 points and Jim Pollard to 13.

The Lakers stormed back for an 82–77 victory at New York, but they suffered a double loss in Game 4—the Knicks held Mikan to 11 points in a 90–89 overtime victory, but Pollard, a 34-point scorer in the opener, was sidelined with a back injury.

It didn't seem to matter as Mikan and Vern Mikkelsen each scored 32 points in a 102–89 Game 5 rout, but the Knicks bounced back for a third time with a 76–68 sixth-game triumph that knotted the series at 3–3.

As usual, the Lakers' fortunes were tied to Mikan's coattails and the big center came through in the decisive seventh game. He scored 22 points and grabbed 19 rebounds as Minneapolis clinched its third championship in four years.

Pollard came off the injured list and provided a clinching spark in the Lakers' 82–65 victory. He scored all 10 of his points in the fourth quarter.

HE'S BACK: *Jim Pollard returned from a back injury to help the Lakers win again.*

1952 NBA FINALS

Minneapolis	83	New York	79 (OT)	at St. Paul
New York	80	Minneapolis	72	at St. Paul
Minneapolis	82	New York	77	at New York
New York	90	Minneapolis	89 (OT)	at New York
Minneapolis	102	New York	89	at St. Paul
New York	76	Minneapolis	68	at New York
Minneapolis	82	New York	65	at Minneapolis

1953

Four out of five for Mikan and his Lakers

It was a 1952 rematch and for the first time the NBA Finals featured division champions. New York was making its third straight title-series appearance and the Lakers were making their fourth in five years. But Minneapolis had won in each of its Finals; the Knicks had lost their previous two.

The New Yorkers served notice they had every intention of changing that when they marched into Minneapolis, scored 30 points in an impressive fourth quarter and walked away with a surprising 96–88 opening victory.

Minneapolis stormed back for a 47–30 halftime lead in Game 2, but the Knicks

BALL BOY: *As usual, George Mikan (99) had the ball in the Lakers' lineup.*

staged a frantic rally that tied the game and turned it into a late free throw-shooting contest. The Lakers finally prevailed, 73–71.

Under a new playoff format, the next three games would be played at New York—and this series was decided there. The Lakers claimed their fourth title in five years with a Big Apple sweep that featured 90–75, 71–69 and 91–84 victories.

Game 4 was decided by Whitey Skoog's two last-minute baskets, and Game 5 was secured by George Mikan's late three-point play after the Lakers had almost frittered away a 20-point lead.

1953 NBA FINALS

New York	96	Minneapolis	88	at Minneapolis
Minneapolis	73	New York	71	at Minneapolis
Minneapolis	90	New York	75	at New York
Minneapolis	71	New York	69	at New York
Minneapolis	91	New York	84	at New York

1954

Lakers win again as Mikan Era ends

When the NBA's 1953–54 season opened, Minneapolis forward Jim Pollard was 31 and center George Mikan was closing in on 30. Pollard's athletic skills were deteriorating and Mikan's powerful body was showing the ravages of physically relentless defenders. A dynasty was showing signs of decay.

That first NBA dynasty would crumble after the 1954 playoff season when the 6–10, 245-pound Mikan announced the end of his outstanding career. The Lakers star retired a body that had endured two broken legs, broken bones in its feet, wrist, nose, thumb and fingers and cuts and slashes that required more than 150 stitches.

But Mikan was not the injured party when his final title series opened at Minneapolis. The Syracuse Nationals had emerged from a bruising round-robin Eastern Division playoff battle against New York and Boston, paying a heavy price. Star forward Dolph Schayes entered the Finals with a broken wrist, guard Paul Seymour had a broken thumb and forward Earl Lloyd had a broken hand. Then guard George King suffered a broken wrist in Game 2 of the Finals when Mikan tried to block his shot.

It only figured that the Nationals, who had tied for second place in the Eastern Division during the regular season, would provide easy prey for the Lakers' third consecutive championship and fifth in six seasons. But Syracuse had shown plenty of

FINAL SHOT: *This marked the last time George Mikan lined up with the Lakers.*

heart in the experimental round-robin preliminary and it showed plenty more against the Lakers.

Minneapolis claimed first blood in the opener when backup center Clyde Lovellette, filling in for the foul-plagued Mikan, scored 16 points and the Lakers' defense held the injured Schayes and Lloyd to a combined three points in a 79–68 victory. But the Lakers' mystique took a serious blow in a Game 2 thriller that ended on a 40-foot Seymour set shot that produced a 62–60 Syracuse victory with seven seconds remaining. The playoff loss was the first for the Lakers at Minneapolis Auditorium in seven seasons.

But with Schayes and Lloyd still playing at half speed and King sitting out, Mikan took control of Game 3—a 30-point, 15-

rebound performance in which he connected on 11 of 18 shots. The 81–67 victory at Syracuse was a lesson in power basketball, with Mikan, Vern Mikkelsen and Lovellette throwing their weight and elbows, while Slater Martin directed traffic from the perimeter.

The Nationals, however, refused to back down and evened the series four nights later with an 80–69 victory, keyed by Seymour's 25-point effort. But again they paid a price, this time losing guard Billy Gabor to a knee injury.

The Lakers reasserted their inside dominance during an 84–73 victory in Game 5 at Syracuse, but the Nationals stunned them again at Minneapolis, 65–63, when unlikely hero Jim Neal, a backup center, connected on a 25-foot, buzzer-beating shot.

Syracuse's magic finally ran out. With Pollard scoring 22 points, the Lakers grabbed a big Game 7 lead and cruised to a title-clinching 87–80 triumph, despite an heroic 18-point effort by the cast-hindered Schayes.

The Lakers were kings for one last glorious season.

1954 NBA FINALS

Minneapolis	79	Syracuse	68	at Minneapolis
Syracuse	62	Minneapolis	60	at Minneapolis
Minneapolis	81	Syracuse	67	at Syracuse
Syracuse	80	Minneapolis	69	at Syracuse
Minneapolis	84	Syracuse	73	at Syracuse
Syracuse	65	Minneapolis	63	at Minneapolis
Minneapolis	87	Syracuse	80	at Minneapolis

1955

A clockwork Victory for wound-up Nationals

With Minneapolis weakened by the retirement of George Mikan and Syracuse Owner Danny Biasone's shot-clock innovation speeding up a foul-plagued game, the NBA opened a faster-paced era. Ironically, Biasone's Nationals benefited from both developments and engaged Fort Wayne in an exciting seven-game Finals.

Play opened at Syracuse and the Nationals rolled to a quick 2–0 advantage

with 86–82 and 87–84 victories. Red Rocha sparked the Game 1 win with 19 points and hit a clinching 25-foot set shot in the final seconds of Game 2.

But the tide turned quickly when the Nationals traveled to Indianapolis, the Pistons' post-season home because of scheduling problems at Fort Wayne. The Pistons, led by Mel Hutchins' 22 points, won the third game 96–89 and evened the series with a 109–102 verdict, despite

28-points from Dolph Schayes. Frank Brian hit two late free throws to give the Pistons a 74–71 Game 5 victory and a 3–2 series edge.

But Syracuse wouldn't die. The Nationals survived George Yardley's 31 points and pulled even with a 109–104 victory—their 27th consecutive triumph over the Pistons at Syracuse. No. 28 would come in Game 7.

Syracuse had to wipe out a 17-point Fort Wayne lead in the finale and survive a late-game scare. The clincher in the Nationals' 92–91 victory wasn't delivered until 12 seconds remained when George King sank a tiebreaking free throw.

King, who finished with 15 points, was one of seven Syracuse scorers in double figures. Larry Foust led the Pistons with 24.

TEAMING UP: *Syracuse coach Al Cervi (center) kept the NBA trophy close at hand.*

1955 NBA FINALS

Syracuse	86	Fort Wayne	82	at Syracuse
Syracuse	87	Fort Wayne	84	at Syracuse
Fort Wayne	96	Syracuse	89	at Indianapolis
Fort Wayne	109	Syracuse	102	at Indianapolis
Fort Wayne	74	Syracuse	71	at Indianpolis
Syracuse	109	Fort Wayne	104	at Syracuse
Syracuse	92	Fort Wayne	91	at Syracuse

314 **1956**

The Philadelphia Story stars Johnston, Arizin

The NBA's first decade ended just like it started—with the Philadelphia Warriors sitting atop the basketball world. The Warriors, featuring the high-scoring tandem of center Neil Johnston and forward Paul Arizin, cruised to the league's best record (45–27), defeated Syracuse in an Eastern Division playoff and eased past Fort Wayne in a five-game NBA Finals. Arizin had been second in the league in scoring with 24.2 points per game, while Johnston led the league by making 499 of 1,092 shots—a .457 shooting percentage.

The Pistons, making their second consecutive Finals appearance, were no match for the Warriors, even with high-scoring George Yardley firing from all over the court. And that became clear in the Philadelphia opener when the Warriors fell behind by 15, rallied behind the inspired play of reserve forward Ernie Beck (23 points) and scored a 98–94 victory.

The Pistons battled back in Game 2 for an 84–83 win, the decisive points coming on two of Yardley's 30 points. But that was Fort Wayne's last hurrah.

Arizin and Johnston combined for 47 points in Philadelphia's 100–96 Game 3 victory, and Arizin was unstoppable in Game 4, contributing 30 points in the Warriors' 107–105 triumph.

The Game 5 clincher was decided by a late third-quarter Philadelphia rush that broke open a 64–60 battle. Fort Wayne never got closer than seven points the rest of the way and the Warriors coasted to their 99–88 victory. Joe Graboski scored 29 points and Arizin added 26 for Philadelphia, more than offsetting Yardley's 30-point effort.

The Warriors, winners of the BAA's first title in 1947, were champions for a second time.

BY HOOK OR BY CROOK: *Philly's Neil Johnston puts up a hook shot in the finals.*

1956 NBA FINALS

Philadelphia	98	Fort Wayne	94	at Philadelphia
Fort Wayne	84	Philadelphia	83	at Fort Wayne
Philadelphia	100	Fort Wayne	96	at Philadelphia
Philadelphia	107	Fort Wayne	105	at Fort Wayne
Philadelphia	99	Fort Wayne	88	at Philadelphia

Here come the Celtics, look out below

Two first-timers matched up in the NBA Finals—the first of four dramatic meetings over five years. And the intensity was illustrated by two 125–123 double-overtime thrillers—St. Louis' Game 1 victory and Boston's Game 7 clincher.

The opener, which featured a 37-point performance by St. Louis' Bob Pettit and a 36-point effort by Boston's Bill Sharman, was decided in the second extra period when Jack Coleman hit a long jumper. But the Celtics held Pettit to 11 points in the second game and rolled to a 119–99 triumph.

When the series moved to St. Louis, the teams traded victories with St. Louis winning 100–98 on Pettit's last-second jumper and Boston responding with a 123–118 victory keyed by Bob Cousy's 31 points. The Celtics took a 3–2 series edge with a 124–109 victory at Boston

FIRST OF MANY: *For the Celtics the 1957 season was the start of glorious run.*

Garden and the Hawks fought back at St. Louis when Cliff Hagan tipped in a last-second shot for a 96–94 win.

Game 7 was a classic. Cousy and Sharman shot a combined 5 for 40, but rookies Bill Russell and Tom Heinsohn picked up the slack with a combined 56 points and 55 rebounds. The game was not decided until the second overtime when Jim Loscutoff hit a clinching free throw and the Hawks just missed on a desperate last-second tip attempt. The game ended when St. Louis player/ coach Alex Hannum threw a half-court pass off the Hawks' backboard to Pettit, who missed the point-blank tip.

The Celtics' 13-year championship run was underway.

1957 NBA FINALS

St. Louis	125	Boston	123 (2 OT)	at Boston
Boston	119	St. Louis	99	at Boston
St. Louis	100	Boston	98	at St. Louis
Boston	123	St. Louis	118	at St. Louis
Boston	124	St. Louis	109	at Boston
St. Louis	96	Boston	94	at St. Louis
Boston	125	St. Louis	123 (2 OT)	at Boston

316 1958

Pettit roars, Hawks soar past outmanned Celtics

It was basketball's version of a heavy-weight boxing championship rematch: the power-packed St. Louis Hawks against the jab-and-run Boston Celtics. Bob Pettit, Cliff Hagan, Ed Macauley and Slater Martin versus Bill Russell, Bob Cousy, Tom Heinsohn, Bill Sharman and newcomer Sam Jones.

The Celtics, laying the foundation for the championship mystique that would engulf the NBA for more than a decade, had scored a 1957 seven-game decision that produced the franchise's first title. The Hawks, who were looking for a little mystique of their own behind the high-scoring tandem of Pettit (24.6 points per game) and Hagan (19.9), were hoping for a quick 1958 knockout.

It wasn't quick, but it was decisive. The series matched the early pattern of 1957 as the Hawks marched into Boston Garden and pulled off a 104–102 first-game upset and the embarrassed Celtics recovered with style in a 136–112 Game 2 rout. Little did anybody realize that Game 3, at St. Louis' Kiel Auditorium,

1958 NBA FINALS				
St. Louis	104	Boston	102	at Boston
Boston	136	St. Louis	112	at Boston
St. Louis	111	Boston	108	at St. Louis
Boston	109	St. Louis	98	at St. Louis
St. Louis	102	Boston	100	at Boston
St. Louis	110	Boston	109	at St. Louis

would provide the series turning point—by accident.

The Hawks won the game, 111–108, but the Celtics lost the series when the 6–10 Russell tore ankle ligaments, an injury that put pressure on Heinsohn and aging Arnie Risen to stop St. Louis' powerful frontcourt.

Russell tried to play with a heavily taped ankle, but without him in top form, Boston was overmatched. Still, the Hawks had to work for every inch of their championship journey.

Boston Coach Red Auerbach used the Russell injury to inspire his team in a sur-prising 109–98 Game 4 victory. But the Hawks struck back for a 102–100 fifth-game triumph that set up Boston for the knockout punch.

Game 6 ranks among the great games in NBA Finals history and most of the dramatics were provided by Pettit, St. Louis' classy power forward. As 10,218 fans howled their approval at Kiel Auditorium, Pettit scored 50 points, single-handedly held off a late Boston rally and delivered St. Louis its only NBA title.

The 110–109 sixth-game victory began taking shape when the Hawks surged ahead 95–93 on a Pettit field goal with 6:16 remaining. Three times the Celtics pulled to within a point and three times Pettit answered with a critical basket. His final two-pointer gave the Hawks a 110–107 lead with 16 seconds to play and Sharman's uncontested layup determined the final margin.

After Martin dribbled away the final seconds, the St. Louis players lifted Pettit onto their shoulders and carried him around the floor. Pettit, who connected on 19 of 34 field goals and 12 of 19 free throws, scored 19 of St. Louis' final 21 points. His 50 points were a record for a regulation playoff game and he finished the series with a 29.3 average.

Sharman scored 26 points in the finale and Heinsohn added 23.

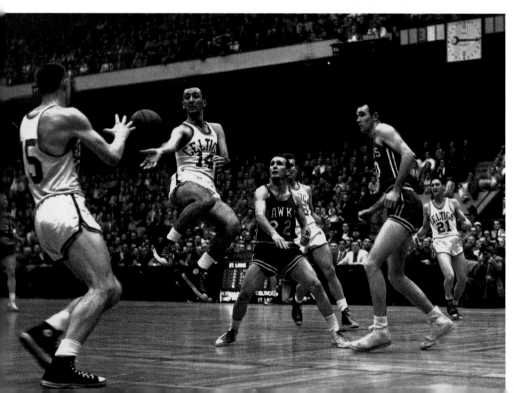

PASSING FANCY: *Bob Cousy (14) passes to Tom Heinsohn in the 1958 NBA Finals.*

1959

A Finals first: Celtics sweep the Lakers

BALL HUNT: *The Lakers' Vern Mikkelsen (left) and Boston's Frank Ramsey fight for possession.*

1959 NBA FINALS

Boston	118	Minneapolis	115	at Boston
Boston	128	Minneapolis	108	at Boston
Boston	123	Minneapolis	110	at St. Paul
Boston	118	Minneapolis	113	at Minneapolis

A funny thing happened on the way to another Boston–St. Louis NBA Finals masterpiece. The Hawks, who had finished 16 games ahead of the 33–39 Lakers in the Western Division, were upset by surprising Minneapolis in a six-game division finals series.

Boston versus Minneapolis was a masterpiece only in the eyes of championship-hungry Celtics fans. Boston had defeated the Lakers 18 consecutive times over two seasons and had buried them 173–139 in a late February meeting that set numerous NBA point-scoring records. To say that the Lakers were overmatched, even with rookie scoring sensation Elgin Baylor, was an understatement.

The series opened in Boston and the Celtics rolled to 118–115 and 128–108 victories. When the action moved to Minneapolis, the Celtics continued their domination with a 123–110 triumph that set Minneapolis up for the kill.

Game 4, a 118–113 Boston clincher, belonged to the Celtics trio of Bill Sharman (29 points), Frank Ramsey (24) and Tom Heinsohn (23).

The game, like the series, was a testimony to Boston's front-line talent and depth. How overpowering were the Celtics?

They scored 487 points (at an average of 121.8 per game), an NBA Finals record for a four-game series. Center Bill Russell intimidated Minneapolis shooters and averaged an amazing 29.5 rebounds, grabbing 30 in three straight outings. Guard Bob Cousy, who handed out 19 assists in Boston's Game 3 rout, averaged 12.8 for the series.

The championship was Boston's second in three seasons and the four-game sweep was the first in NBA Finals history. Although the average margin of victory was 10.25 points, two of the games (the first—118–115— and the last—118–113) were won by five points or fewer.

318 # 1960

Firing on all Cylinders, Boston tops St. Louis again

1960 NBA FINALS

Boston	**140**	St. Louis	**122**	at Boston
St. Louis	**113**	Boston	**103**	at Boston
Boston	**102**	St. Louis	**86**	at St. Louis
St. Louis	**106**	Boston	**96**	at St. Louis
Boston	**127**	St. Louis	**102**	at Boston
St. Louis	**105**	Boston	**102**	at St. Louis
Boston	**122**	St. Louis	**103**	at Boston

Boston's burgeoning juggernaut rolled to an NBA-record of 59 regular-season victories en route to a championship series rematch with St. Louis. And true to past Celtics–Hawks encounters, this one went the distance.

The teams traded early punches. The Celtics earned a 140–122 Game 1 victory at Boston and a 102–86 Game 3 win at St. Louis behind the backcourt play of Bob Cousy, Bill Sharman and Frank Ramsey and the inside domination of Bill Russell. The Hawks countered with 113–103 and 106–96 road and home victories behind the three-pronged frontcourt attack of Bob Pettit, Cliff Hagan and Clyde Lovellette, who had combined to average 71.7 points per game during the regular season.

The Celtics regained the advantage with a 127–102 Game 5 rout at Boston, but the Hawks knotted the series with a 105–102 win at St. Louis. Boston's hopes for a second consecutive championship would be decided in a seventh game at Boston Garden.

It was no contest. Russell scored 22 points and grabbed 35 rebounds, sixth man Ramsey amassed 24 and 13, Tom Heinsohn had 22 and 8, and Cousy scored 19 points and handed out 14 assists in a 122–103 Boston victory. The championship machine was in full gear.

GIVING CHASE: *John McCarthy (left) grabs the ball in front of Boston's Bob Cousy.*

Balancing Act brings Boston a third straight Title

TO THE HOLE: *Boston's Tom Heinsohn (15) is put under pressure by Woody Sauldsberry.*

The Boston team that swept to 57 regular-season victories and advanced to its fifth straight NBA Finals featured dominating center Bill Russell and had six players who averaged 15 or more points per game—Tom Heinsohn (21.3), Bob Cousy (18.1), Russell (16.9), Bill Sharman (16.0), Frank Ramsey (15.1) and Sam Jones (15.0).

That balance was too much for a frontcourt-heavy St. Louis team that went down quietly in its fourth NBA Finals appearance in five years—the last for Hall of Fame forward Bob Pettit.

The Celtics demonstrated their dominance in a 129–95 Game 1 rout that would stand for 17 years as the NBA Finals record for the largest margin of

victory. Russell grabbed 31 rebounds en route to a series average of 28.5.

St. Louis forward Cliff Hagan exploded for 40 points in Game 2, and Pettit matched that total in Game 4, but the Celtics still pulled off 116–108 and 119–104 victories. The Hawks' only triumph came in a 124–120 Game 3 thriller at the Kiel Auditorium in St. Louis.

Russell was at his ferocious best in the Celtics' 121–112 Game 5 clincher at Boston Garden. He grabbed 38 rebounds and intimidated St. Louis shooters with his inside defense. Boston's third straight championship was accomplished with an impressive 121-point average.

1961 NBA FINALS

Boston	129	St. Louis	95	at Boston
Boston	116	St. Louis	108	at Boston
St. Louis	124	Boston	120	at St. Louis
Boston	119	St. Louis	104	at St. Louis
Boston	121	St. Louis	112	at Boston

1962

Lakers' shot at Destiny comes up inches short

TITLE TIME: *Boston Celtics players celebrate their fourth consecutive NBA title.*

In the minds of Los Angeles basketball fans, it always will be remembered as "The Shot."

Game 7 of the NBA Finals. Score tied 100–100. Lakers' ball with five seconds remaining. A dream about to crumble at Boston Garden in mid-dynasty.

For Los Angeles fans, this was the opportunity for their Lakers to ascend to the NBA throne in just their second season after moving from Minneapolis. They were young, they were talented and they were blessed with one of the greatest superstar tandems in league history—forward Elgin Baylor and guard Jerry West.

For Boston fans, this was the opportunity for their Celtics to do something no other professional basketball team—and few other sports teams—had ever accomplished: four consecutive championships. Red Auerbach's Celtics were experienced, they were deep and they were poised.

The crucial five seconds unfolded with Hot Rod Hundley dribbling near the top of the key, looking for the well-defended Baylor and West. He settled for Frank Selvy, who was open on the baseline, about eight feet from the basket. Selvy, a hero only moments earlier when he scored two baskets to tie the score, launched his potential winner and watched it bounce short off the rim.

"I would trade all my points for that last basket," a dejected Selvy told reporters after the game.

Given a reprieve, the Celtics stormed back in overtime for a dramatic 110–107 victory. Sam Jones keyed the charge, scoring 5 of his 27 points, and sixth man Frank Ramsey punctuated the effort with 23 points. But, more important, the Boston title streak was intact.

Nothing about this championship was easy. The Celtics, who had cruised through the regular season with 60 victories, won the opener at Boston Garden, 122–108, but the Lakers evened matters the next day when West scored 40 points in a 129–122 verdict and took a 2–1 edge two nights later in a thriller at Los Angeles.

The Lakers' 117–115 Game 3 triumph, which was decided at the final buzzer when West stole a Boston inbounds pass and dribbled in uncontested for a layup, sent the record crowd of 15,180 at the Los Angeles Sports Arena into a frenzy. But if the Celtics felt the jolt of that last-second heartbreaker, they did not show it during a methodical 115–103 Game 4 victory that knotted the series.

The stage was set for Baylor, who confounded the double-teaming Celtics and a full house at Boston Garden with a 61-point, 22-rebound Game 5 performance that keyed a 126–121 Lakers victory. Baylor's 61 points still stand as an NBA Finals record.

But just when it appeared the Celtics were staggering, the Boston mystique took over. Defying the law of averages, the Celtics stunned another sellout Sports Arena crowd and knotted the series with a 119–105 victory, setting up the seventh-game drama.

The Celtics posted their title-clinching victory despite another big performance by Baylor—41 points. Boston center Bill Russell countered that with an NBA Finals-record 40 rebounds.

1962 NBA FINALS

Boston	122	Los Angeles	108	at Boston	
Los Angeles	129	Boston	122	at Boston	
Los Angeles	117	Boston	115	at Los Angeles	
Boston	115	Los Angeles	103	at Los Angeles	
Los Angeles	126	Boston	121	at Boston	
Boston	119	Los Angeles	105	at Los Angeles	
Boston	110	Los Angeles	107 (OT)	at Boston	

Boston wins one for "The Cooz" to make it five

1963 NBA FINALS

Boston	117	Los Angeles	114	at Boston
Boston	113	Los Angeles	106	at Boston
Los Angeles	119	Boston	99	at Los Angeles
Boston	108	Los Angeles	105	at Los Angeles
Los Angeles	126	Boston	119	at Boston
Boston	112	Los Angeles	109	at Los Angeles

The Celtics had survived a 1962 scare and Coach Red Auerbach was looking for the inspiration that might carry them to a fifth consecutive championship. He got it when veteran guard Bob Cousy announced he would retire after the season.

Winning one for the "Cooz" became the battle cry as the Celtics rolled to 58 regular-season victories, advanced through a difficult seven-game divisional playoff series against Cincinnati and settled in for a rematch with the Los Angeles Lakers. Auerbach's job became even easier when the Celtics opened with 117–114 and 113–106 victories at Boston Garden.

The Lakers revived briefly in Game 3 at Los Angeles, posting a 119–99 decision behind Jerry West's 42-point outburst. But Boston moved within a game of another title two days later with a 108–105 victory.

Los Angeles got 43 points from Elgin Baylor and 32 from West and staved off elimination in a 126–119 Game 5 win at Boston. But the Lakers were just delaying the inevitable.

John Havlicek scored 11 straight points as Boston built a 14-point halftime lead in Game 6 and Tom Heinsohn secured the victory with four late free throws that closed out his 22-point effort.

Fittingly, Cousy, who scored 18 points and overcame a fourth- quarter ankle injury, dribbled away the final seconds of Boston's 112–109 title-securing victory.

West (32) and Baylor (28) combined for 60 points in the Lakers' losing cause.

But it was Cousy who was the emotional star of the series. He averaged 14.1 points, 2.5 rebounds and 8.9 assists per game in the playoffs that season. He retired as the Celtics' all-time leader in assists with 6,945—a record that still stands.

CLOSE QUARTERS: *Boston's Bill Russell (6) and Tom Heinsohn battle for the ball with the Lakers' Elgin Baylor in Los Angeles.*

1964

Six and counting as Boston keeps the Streak alive

The Celtics, playing their first season without inspirational leader Bob Cousy, took the best shot of another would-be champion. But, like all challengers before them, the San Francisco Warriors and high-scoring Wilt Chamberlain were unable to derail Boston's title express.

Bill Russell vs. Chamberlain took center stage in an intriguing battle that fell short of expectations. The 7–1 Chamberlain did have his spectacular moments—38 rebounds in Game 4, 30 points in Game 5—but the victory clearly went to Russell and another title, the record sixth in a row, to the Celtics.

Russell was a defensive animal as Boston took quick control of the series with 108–96 and 124–101 victories at Boston Garden. A 115–91 thrashing in Game 3 when the series moved to San Francisco proved to be only a temporary setback for the Celtics, who rebounded for a 98–95 win behind the 25-point scoring of Tom Heinsohn and a 23-point effort by Sam Jones. The Celtics were poised for the kill as the series moved back to Boston.

Russell held Chamberlain scoreless in the first six minutes of Game 5 and Heinsohn, Sam Jones and Frank Ramsey combined for 55 points in the 105–99 clincher. When Russell secured victory with an emphatic last-minute jam, exuberant fans rushed the court, hoisting triumphant Boston players and Coach Red Auerbach on their shoulders.

The Celtics' six straight titles have never been matched by any major professional sports team. In the National Hockey League, the Montreal Canadiens claimed a record five consecutive Stanley Cups and in baseball the New York Yankees won five World Series in a row. No National Football League team has ever managed to win more than three consecutive championships and no new dynasty is on the horizon.

TAKING HIS SHOT: *Wilt Chamberlain (13) shoots over Bill Russell (6) in Game 2 at the Garden.*

1964 NBA FINALS

Boston	108	San Francisco	96	at Boston
Boston	124	San Francisco	101	at Boston
San Francisco	115	Boston	91	at San Francisco
Boston	98	San Francisco	95	at San Francisco
Boston	105	San Francisco	99	at Boston

Seven and Counting as the Lakers fall again

GOOD D: *Los Angeles' Leroy Ellis (left) rejects the shot from Boston's Tom Sanders.*

After the Celtics escaped a seven-game division finals upset bid by Philadelphia, they braced for a title-series meeting with old rival Los Angeles. But Boston's pursuit of a seventh straight championship lacked drama, thanks to a knee injury suffered by Elgin Baylor in a playoff game.

With only Jerry West to carry the Lakers' offensive banner, the Celtics rolled off quick 142–110 and 129–123 victories at Boston Garden. Boston defensive wizard K.C. Jones "held" West to 26 points in the opener, far below the prolific 40.6 average he would compile in the series.

West scored 43 points and 6–10 LeRoy Ellis added 29 as the Lakers recovered for a 126–105 Game 3 victory at Los Angeles. But a 37-point performance by Sam Jones propelled to Celtics to a 112–99 triumph that pushed them to within a game of another title.

The Celtics didn't waste time finishing off the overmatched Lakers. With Bill Russell controlling the boards (30 rebounds), the Celtics ran off 20 unanswered fourth-quarter points and coasted to a 129–96 clincher.

1965 NBA FINALS

Boston	142	Los Angeles	110	at Boston
Boston	129	Los Angeles	123	at Boston
Los Angeles	126	Boston	105	at Los Angeles
Boston	112	Los Angeles	99	at Los Angeles
Boston	129	Los Angeles	96	at Boston

324 1966

The Lakers see red as the Celtics win again

The announcement came like a bolt of lightning. Arnold (Red) Auerbach, the 48-year-old cigar-chomping architect of Boston's NBA championship dynasty, was retiring after the 1966 playoffs. But that wasn't all. Auerbach also announced that 10-year center Bill Russell would become player/ coach—the first black coach in NBA history.

True to Auerbach's nature, the timing of the announcement served a more subtle purpose. His Celtics had just lost a 133–129 overtime game to Los Angeles in the opener of the NBA Finals and the wily veteran needed something to spark an aging team in its pursuit of an eighth straight title.

As usual, Auerbach's psychological ploy worked. With the Lakers' Game 1 success (Jerry West scored 41 points, Elgin Baylor 36) obscured by Boston's changing of the guard, the Celtics exploded behind Russell, John Havlicek and Sam Jones

for consecutive 129–109, 120–106 and 122–117 victories—the second and third at the Los Angeles Sports Arena. Boston won Game 4 despite West's 45-point performance.

But just when it appeared Auerbach had successfully orchestrated his grand finale, the Lakers struck back. Baylor, who was still fighting the effects of a serious 1965 knee injury, kept them alive in Game 5 with a 41-point outburst that produced a 121–117 victory at Boston Garden. Then

Los Angeles evened the count at Los Angeles with a 123–115 victory that featured Gail Goodrich's 28-point effort. The series returned to Boston Garden for another seventh-game classic.

It appeared the Celtics were going to win easily when they bolted to a big early lead and Baylor was held to two first-half points. They led by 19 two minutes into the third quarter when the Lakers began chipping away. West, who scored a game-high 36 points, led the comeback that pulled Los Angeles to within six points with 25 seconds remaining.

Auerbach, as had been his trademark for 16 Boston seasons, lit his cigar, signaling victory to the 13,909 Garden fans. But in this case, his confidence was ill-advised. The Lakers pulled within two points with four seconds remaining and Auerbach had to sweat a little before the clock finally ran out on the 95–93 victory.

Fittingly, the key figure in Boston's Game 7 triumph was Russell, who scored 25 points, grabbed 32 rebounds and then officially took the coaching baton from Auerbach. Sam Jones added 22 points and Tom Sanders and Don Nelson combined to hold Baylor to 18 points.

Auerbach finished his coaching career in fine style—eight consecutive championships, nine in 10 seasons and nine Eastern Division titles.

1966 NBA FINALS					
Los Angeles	133	Boston	129 (OT)		at Boston
Boston	129	Los Angeles	109		at Boston
Boston	120	Los Angeles	106		at Los Angeles
Boston	122	Los Angeles	117		at Los Angeles
Los Angeles	121	Boston	117		at Boston
Los Angeles	123	Boston	115		at Los Angeles
Boston	95	Los Angeles	93		at Boston

HOOK SHOT: *The Celtics' Bill Russell (6) shoots over the Lakers' Leroy Ellis (25) .*

Chamberlain, 76ers end Boston's Title reign

For the first seven seasons of his prolific career, Wilt Chamberlain was an offensive machine. He won seven scoring titles, led the NBA in rebounding five times, averaged an incredible 50.4 points for an entire season and never fell below 33.5 points or 22.3 rebounds in any campaign. The numbers, like his powerful 7-foot-1 body, were intimidating.

But something was missing. Over those seven seasons, a Chamberlain team never won a championship. The 1963–64 San Francisco Warriors reached the NBA Finals, but they were shackled by the Boston Celtics in five games. While Boston center Bill Russell collected championship rings, Chamberlain collected critics who labeled him a "me-first" prodigy.

But the sniping stopped in 1966–67, as did the Celtics' relentless title machine. Chamberlain, at the urging of Coach Alex Hannum, put less emphasis on offense, defended with Russell-like intensity and became the middle man for one of the most talented lineups ever assembled.

This Philadelphia 76ers outfit was no ordinary team. Joining Chamberlain in an All-Star cast were forwards Billy Cunningham, Chet Walker and Lucious Jackson and guards Hal Greer, Wali Jones and Larry Costello. Six 76ers averaged in double figures, led by Chamberlain (24.1) and Greer (22.1), and Wilt led the league with a phenomenal .683 shooting percentage while finishing third with 7.8 assists per game.

This well-balanced attack averaged 125.2 points, played stifling defense and rolled to an unprecedented 68–13 record, easily winning the Eastern Division title over a Boston team that won 60 times. But the ultimate test was passed in the division finals when the 76ers blew past the Celtics in a five-game storm, ending Boston's eight-year championship reign.

The last order of business was an NBA Finals matchup with San Francisco, a team that featured high-scoring Rick Barry, 6–11 center Nate Thurmond and guard Jeff Mullins. But Philadelphia's biggest opponent after Boston was complacency.

That became apparent in the title-series opener when the 76ers built a 19-point first-half lead, frittered it away in the final minutes and were forced into overtime on Mullins' two late free throws. They finally prevailed, 141–135, as Greer finished with 32 points, Jones 30, Cunningham 26 and Walker 23—more than countering Barry's 37.

Game 2 was all 76ers as Chamberlain grabbed 38 rebounds and Greer connected for 30 points in a 126–95 rout. But the Warriors bounced back in a 130–124 third-game explosion set off by Barry's 55 points and Thurmond's 27 boards.

Philadelphia all but settled the issue with a 122–108 Game 4 decision as Greer scored 38 and Walker 33. And after the Warriors had claimed a 117–109 fifth-game verdict, the 76ers closed out their first championship the next day with a 125–122 victory at San Francisco.

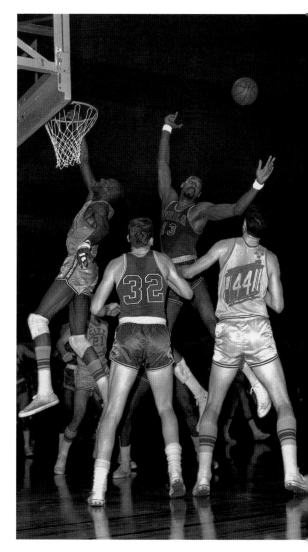

ABOVE THE RIM: *Wilt Chamberlain (13) reaches for the ball against San Francisco.*

Chamberlain, fittingly, was a Game 6 hero and he did it with rebounding and defense. All six of his blocked shots and 8 of his 23 rebounds came in the final quarter when he shared the spotlight with Cunningham, who scored 13 straight points.

It was a sweet victory for Chamberlain—and exoneration—for the NBA's top gun.

1967 NBA FINALS

Philadelphia	141	San Francisco	135 (OT)	at Philadelphia
Philadelphia	126	San Francisco	95	at Philadelphia
San Francisco	130	Philadelphia	124	at San Francisco
Philadelphia	122	San Francisco	108	at San Francisco
San Francisco	117	Philadelphia	109	at Philadelphia
Philadelphia	125	San Francisco	122	at San Francisco

326 1968

Boston Baked Revenge brings another Title

The Philadelphia 76ers, who had dethroned the Boston Celtics in 1967, returned to the top of the 1967–68 Eastern Division standings with 62 victories and cruised to a 3–1 edge in a division finals rematch. But in a dramatic turnaround sparked by the fierce determination of player/coach Bill Russell, Boston shocked the 76ers by winning the next three games and advanced to its 11th NBA Finals in 12 years—and its sixth against the Lakers.

The Celtics held the high-scoring tandem of Elgin Baylor and Jerry West to a combined 18-of-55 shooting in the first game and claimed a 107–101 victory, but the Lakers answered with a 123–113 Game 2 win at Boston Garden.

The alternating victory pattern continued in Los Angeles with Boston

1968 NBA FINALS					
Boston	107	Los Angeles	101	at Boston
Los Angeles	123	Boston	113	at Boston
Boston	127	Los Angeles	119	at Los Angeles
Los Angeles	118	Boston	105	at Los Angeles
Boston	120	Los Angeles	117 (OT)	at Boston
Boston	124	Los Angeles	109	at Los Angeles

winning, 127–119, and the Lakers responding, 118–105, behind West's 38 points. The series returned to Boston for the pivotal fifth game.

The Celtics bounded to a 19-point first-half lead, but a frantic rally pulled the Lakers close and last-minute baskets by West (35 points) and Baylor forced overtime. The Celtics, who got 31 points from John Havlicek and 26 from Don

Nelson, finally prevailed, 120–117.

Buoyed by that success, Boston wrapped up another championship two days later at Los Angeles when Havlicek scored 40 points and Bailey Howell added 30 in a 124–109 victory.

ROLLING THUNDER: *It looks more like bowling as Boston's Bailey Howell (front) passes to John Havlicek (17).*

1969

One last Fling for Bill Russell and the Celtics

With player/coach Bill Russell fighting age and leg problems in his final season, the Boston Celtics had slipped to fourth place in the Eastern Division. Only pride had carried them through three playoff rounds, setting up a seventh NBA Finals battle with the Lakers.

The Lakers, who had been bolstered by the addition of center Wilt Chamberlain, finally had reason for optimism. Veteran guard Jerry West made that clear in the Finals opener when he scored 53 points, handed out 10 assists and personally delivered a 120–118 Los Angeles message.

West fired another 41 points at the Celtics in Game 2, but John Havlicek countered with 43. The verdict was decided by Lakers forward Elgin Baylor, who scored his team's final 12 points in a 118–112 victory.

Havlicek scored 34 as the Celtics broke through for a Game 3 victory, 111–105, and they pulled even two days later when

Sam Jones hit an off-balance 18-foot jumper that bounced around the rim as the final buzzer sounded, finally falling through for an 89–88 victory. West scored 39 points as Los Angeles pulled back in front with a 117–104 win, but the Celtics forced a seventh game with a 99–90 decision at Boston.

With thousands of balloons positioned in the rafters of the Los Angeles Forum in anticipation of a Lakers championship,

IN A TRAP: *Boston's John Havlicek has the ball but is surrounded by Lakers defenders.*

the Celtics took a 17-point lead into the fourth quarter. With Chamberlain sitting the final 5½ minutes with a knee injury and West frantically carrying a team on his shoulders (42 points, 13 rebounds, 12 assists), the Celtics barely held on for a 108–106 title-clinching victory to complete one of the most memorable runs in history.

1969 NBA FINALS

Los Angeles	120	Boston	118	at Los Angeles
Los Angeles	118	Boston	112	at Los Angeles
Boston	111	Los Angeles	105	at Boston
Boston	89	Los Angeles	88	at Boston
Los Angeles	117	Boston	104	at Los Angeles
Boston	99	Los Angeles	90	at Boston
Boston	108	Los Angeles	106	at Los Angeles

MVP: Jerry West, Los Angeles

328 1970

New Era begins as Reed leads the Knicks to Title

The roar from the Madison Square Garden crowd was deafening. All eyes focused on a lone figure hobbling out of the shadows. The New York Knicks stopped their warmups and watched with admiration. The Los Angeles Lakers stopped and scrutinized the monumental challenge the basketball gods had thrown into their path.

Without a word, with no sign of emotion, Willis Reed stepped onto the court and gave New York its first NBA championship. Never mind the seventh-game victory that would be needed to confirm it. The game was over before it started. Reed, his leg heavily bandaged because of a muscle tear he had suffered in Game 5, already had given his teammates everything they would need to win.

The 6-foot-10 center didn't even contest the opening jump against Los Angeles center Wilt Chamberlain, but he did contest everything else Chamberlain tried to do. And the crowd roared again when Reed scored New York's first two

NOT MUCH ON: *Jerry West has few options with Nate Bowman (17) applying pressure.*

baskets. For a full half, Reed gave it everything he had, finishing with four points, three rebounds and respectable defense against Chamberlain.

Emotionally charged, the Knicks were unbeatable. With guard Walt Frazier scoring 36 points, handing out 19 assists and playing his usual stifling defense, the Knicks rolled to a 61–37 halftime lead and powered to a 113–99 title-clinching victory. Reed capped a marvelous season in which he recorded an unprecedented regular-season, All-Star Game and NBA Finals MVP sweep.

Reed was merely one cog in New York's 1970 title machine. The big left-hander, who could confound less mobile centers with his ability to move outside, was the centerpiece in a lineup that included forwards Bill Bradley and Dave DeBusschere and guards Dick Barnett and Frazier. The lineup was short on stars but long on teamwork and defense—Coach Red Holzman's trademark.

The Knicks started their title run with a league-best 60 victories and advanced through the playoffs with only a second-round scare. The Knicks entered the title series as three-time NBA Finals losers; the Lakers, featuring aging Jerry West, Elgin Baylor and Chamberlain, had lost seven straight Finals—all to the Boston Celtics.

New York drew first blood when Reed, moving his game to the perimeter to counter Chamberlain, scored 37 points and grabbed 16 rebounds in a 124–112 victory. The Lakers answered as West scored 34 points and hit a pair of free throws that decided a 105–103 win.

The victory-trading pattern continued. The Lakers forced a Game 3 overtime when West hit a 60-foot basket as time expired, but the Knicks came back to claim a 111–108 victory behind Reed's 38 points and 17 rebounds. Game 4 also went into overtime before the Lakers prevailed, 121–115, behind West's 37 points and 18 assists.

Game 5 long will be remembered for Reed's injury and the Knicks' inspiring play without him en route to their 107–100 victory. Reed crumpled to the floor on a first-quarter drive, writhing in pain. The Knicks trailed 25–15 as their center was helped to the sideline and the Madison Square Garden crowd fell into a stunned silence. But that changed quickly as the Knicks scratched and clawed their way back into the game, forced 19 second-half Los Angeles turnovers and posted their shocking victory.

But there was nothing inspiring about Game 6 as Chamberlain, unimpeded with Reed on the sideline, scored 45 points and grabbed 17 rebounds in a 135–113 rout, setting the stage for Reed's heroics in Game 7.

1970 NBA FINALS

New York	124	Los Angeles	112	at New York
Los Angeles	105	New York	103	at New York
New York	111	Los Angeles	108 (OT)	at Los Angeles
Los Angeles	121	New York	115 (OT)	at Los Angeles
New York	107	Los Angeles	100	at New York
Los Angeles	135	New York	113	at Los Angeles
New York	113	Los Angeles	99	at New York

MVP: Willis Reed, New York

Young Bucks grow Horns in Championship Season

1971 NBA FINALS					
Milwaukee	98	Baltimore	88	at Milwaukee	
Milwaukee	102	Baltimore	83	at Baltimore	
Milwaukee	107	Baltimore	99	at Milwaukee	
Milwaukee	118	Baltimore	106	at Baltimore	

MVP: Lew Alcindor, Milwaukee

He was the perfect blend of basketball talents. Oscar Robertson could thread the perfect pass, grab the clutch rebound, hit the outside shot, penetrate to the basket and play defense against smaller guards or bigger forwards.

When the basketball gods drew up a blueprint for the perfect player, they used a Big O. And from the moment Robertson entered the NBA as a three-time NCAA scoring champion from the University of Cincinnati, nobody doubted the incredible impact he would have on the game. He scored almost at will. He set assist records and challenged the league's giants for rebounds. He turned the Cincinnati Royals into an instant winner.

But one important line was missing from Robertson's resume. He was never a champion, from his collegiate days with Cincinnati through his 10-year professional career with the Royals. When he was traded to the 3-year-old Milwaukee Bucks in 1970, Robertson looked at his new assignment with a sense of purpose.

The 1970–71 Bucks were unlike any expansion team in league history. The 1969 draft had yielded a 7-foot-2 prize and the normal building process was pushed into fast forward. Lew Alcindor, who had led UCLA to three straight NCAA titles and an 88–2 three-year record, was the ticket to quick success and Robertson was asked to become a guiding force.

He took the challenge seriously. Robertson ran the show, sacrificing shots to get teammates more involved, scolding when he thought somebody needed a push and cajoling when he thought somebody needed a tender nudge. Coach Larry Costello encouraged his veteran star and young players like Alcindor, forwards Bobby Dandridge and Greg Smith and guard Lucius Allen thrived.

Operating with mechanical precision, the Bucks began rolling off victory after victory, including an NBA-record 20 straight at one point. When the season ended, the Bucks were 66–16 and Alcindor was league scoring champion (31.7) and MVP. The Bucks rolled through two quick playoff series before squaring off against Eastern Conference-champion Baltimore in the NBA Finals.

The banged-up Bullets were no match for the healthy Bucks. Alcindor, who later converted to the Islamic faith and changed his name to Kareem Abdul-Jabbar, dominated 245-pound Wes Unseld, who was playing on a badly sprained ankle. Robertson was too much for Earl Monroe, who was fighting pulled muscles. And Baltimore forward Gus Johnson, battling knee problems, played in only two games.

Alcindor fired in 31 points and the Bucks opened the final series with a 98–88 victory at Milwaukee. Robertson sparked a 102–83 second-game rout at Baltimore by scoring 22 points and holding Monroe to 11. When the series returned to Milwaukee, Dandridge scored 29 points in a 107–99 victory and the Bucks pulled to within a game of the second sweep in Finals history.

The series ended in fitting fashion with Robertson, Milwaukee's father figure, pouring in 30 points in a 118–106 clincher. The Big O finally had a ring and the NBA had a three-year-old champion.

LEGENDS CLASH: *Lakers' Wilt Chamberlain tries to stop the Bucks' Lew Alcindor (with ball) in the Western Conference finals.*

330 # 1972

Dominating Lakers end West Coast frustration

DEFENSIVE PRESSURE: *New York's Walt Frazier faces a posse of Lakers including Jim McMillian (center) and Jerry West (right).*

Jerry West's first 11 professional seasons were bittersweet. His Lakers pairing with Elgin Baylor had been fruitful, his reputation as one of the game's great shooters had spread far and wide and the road to the NBA championship had passed consistently through Los Angeles.

And that was the source of his frustration. The road passed through Los Angeles—and on to Boston and New York. Seven times West had played in the NBA Finals and seven times he had experienced defeat. Four times West's Lakers had fallen in excruciating seventh games. His personal Finals ledger was phenomenal; his team's was much less.

So it was with some suspicion that West viewed the incredible 1971–72 season as it unfolded. He relinquished some of his scoring responsibilities to

backcourt mate Gail Goodrich for more of a point guard role. Baylor, his knees no longer able to withstand the rigors of playing in the NBA, retired after playing nine games. Center Wilt Chamberlain was 35 years old. West was 33.

The day Baylor announced his retirement, the Lakers won a game. They also won their next game, the one after that and 30 more over a two-month span. When defending-champion Milwaukee handed the Lakers a 120–104 setback on January 9, they ended an incredible 33-game winning streak—the longest ever compiled by a professional sports team.

The loss left Los Angeles at 39–3 and the Lakers went on to post an unprecedented 69–13 record. The table was set for the city's first championship and the Lakers passed a big test with a six-game

conference finals victory over the Milwaukee Bucks, who sported a 63–19 regular-season mark. The last challenge would come from the Knicks, who had posted a seven-game Finals victory over the Lakers in 1970.

The 1970 Knicks had received inspired play from center Willis Reed, who could not play in this series because of aching knees.

So it was all the more shocking when Jerry Lucas scored 26 points, Bill Bradley connected on 11 of 12 field-goal attempts and the Knicks won the Finals opener 114–92—at Los Angeles.

Happy Hairston, known for his rugged rebounding, gave the Lakers a Game 2 spark when he scored 12 second-half points and Los Angeles evened the series with a 106–92 victory. Then the Lakers took control of the series and bolted to a 2–1 edge with a 107–96 triumph at New York.

Game 4 brought back memories of 1970—in reverse. This time it was Chamberlain (not Reed) who fell to the floor in the first quarter, severely spraining his wrist. But Chamberlain refused to leave the game and blocked several key shots in overtime, helping the Lakers to a key 116–111 victory. Chamberlain's inspiration was complemented by the relentless scoring of Goodrich and West.

The Knicks got another dose of their own 1970 medicine in Game 5 when Chamberlain, his aching wrist numbed by painkillers, incited the Los Angeles crowd with a heroic 24-point, 29-rebound performance. The 114–100 victory gave the Lakers their long-awaited championship and the best combined regular season/ playoff record in league history—81 victories, 16 defeats.

For West, it ended more than a decade of frustration.

1972 NBA FINALS

New York	114	Los Angeles	92	at Los Angeles
Los Angeles	106	New York	92	at Los Angeles
Los Angeles	107	New York	96	at New York
Los Angeles	116	New York	111 (OT)	at New York
Los Angeles	114	New York	100	at Los Angeles

MVP: Wilt Chamberlain, Los Angeles

In the Knick of Time, New York wakes up

1973 NBA FINALS

Los Angeles	115	New York	112	at Los Angeles
New York	99	Los Angeles	95	at Los Angeles
New York	87	Los Angeles	83	at New York
New York	103	Los Angeles	98	at New York
New York	102	Los Angeles	93	at Los Angeles

MVP: Willis Reed, New York

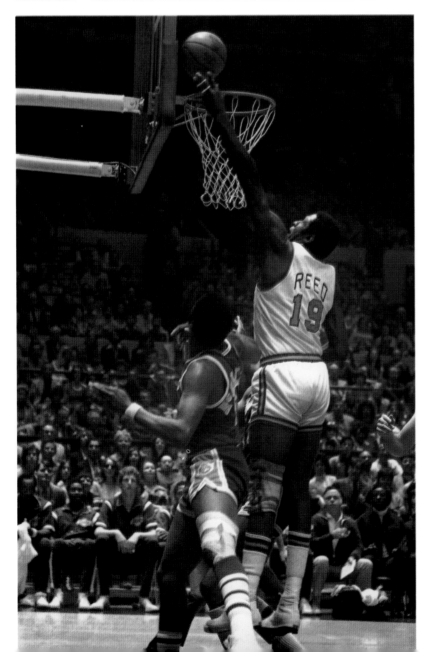

The Knicks versus the Lakers—it was beginning to sound like a broken record. The Knicks had defeated Los Angeles in 1970, giving New York its first NBA championship. The Lakers had returned the favor in 1972, giving Los Angeles its long-awaited first title. The rubber match, featuring two aging teams, followed a different script.

The Lakers took quick advantage of the tired Knicks, who had only one day of rest between their seventh-game conference finals victory over Boston and the title-series opener in Los Angeles. When New York stumbled out of the blocks, the Lakers rolled up a 20-point lead en route to a 115–112 victory.

But the fatigue so evident in Game 1 was lost in a second-game defensive haze. New York guards Walt Frazier and Earl Monroe turned up the pressure on Jerry West and Gail Goodrich and a limping Willis Reed combined with Jerry Lucas to stop Wilt Chamberlain inside, sparking a 99–95 series-knotting triumph. The biggest offensive blow was delivered by backup Phil Jackson, who came off the Knicks bench to score 17 points.

Games 3, 4 and 5 were more of the same—a stifling New York defense that held Chamberlain to 22 total field goals and refused to let Los Angeles top 100 points.

Reed sparked the 87–83 Game 3 victory at New York's Madison Square Garden with 22 points and Dave DeBusschere exploded for 33 points two nights later in a 103–98 triumph. Five Knicks reached double figures in a 102–93 Game 5 triumph that completed the five-game blitz.

As a testament to that Knicks team's strength, six players, Frazier, Monroe, Reed, DeBusschere, Dick Barnett and Bill Bradley, would have their numbers retired.

KNICK HERO: *An aging Willis Reed (19) was still too much for the Lakers to handle.*

332 # 1974

Return of the King sees Boston rule again

The script for Game 7 was simple: The Boston Celtics, making their first NBA Finals appearance since 1969, had to find an answer for Milwaukee's Kareem Abdul-Jabbar—the NBA's ultimate team against its ultimate player.

But a funny thing happened on the way to a championship. Boston's David dropped the Bucks' Goliath with a spec-

tacular 28-point, 14-rebound performance and the Celtics claimed their 12th championship in 18 years with a 102–87 victory at Milwaukee.

Boston's David had the last name of Cowens. The 6–9 center combined with John Havlicek (16 points) in a late Celtics surge that broke open a 71–68 battle. Boston defenders spent the game sagging on Abdul-Jabbar, who finished with 26

NOT SO FAST: *The Bucks swept Chicago in the Conference Finals but fell to Boston.*

points—below his 32.5 series average.

The series was a tug of war that pitted the scoring punch of Abdul-Jabbar against the more balanced attack of Havlicek, Cowens and Jo Jo White. Boston won Games 1 and 5 at Milwaukee and the third contest at Boston Garden. The Bucks countered with victories in Games 2 and 4 and forced Game 7 with a 102–101 victory at Boston in a thriller that went to double-overtime.

Milwaukee took a two-point lead into the final seconds of Game 6, but Boston tied at 86–86, when Havlicek hit a long jumper. The first overtime ended when Havlicek missed a jumper over Abdul-Jabbar, grabbed his own rebound and converted, forcing a second extra session. Abdul-Jabbar ended the game with a buzzer-beating skyhook, giving the Bucks a series-extending victory.

1974 NBA FINALS

Boston	98	Milwaukee	83	at Milwaukee
Milwaukee	105	Boston	96 (OT)	at Milwaukee
Boston	95	Milwaukee	83	at Boston
Milwaukee	97	Boston	89	at Boston
Boston	96	Milwaukee	87	at Milwaukee
Milwaukee	102	Boston	101 (2 OT)	at Boston
Boston	102	Milwaukee	87	at Milwaukee

MVP: John Havlicek, Boston

The little Team that could pulls off huge Upset

1975 NBA FINALS

Golden State	101	Washington	95	at Washington
Golden State	92	Washington	91	at San Francisco
Golden State	109	Washington	101	at San Francisco
Golden State	96	Washington	95	at Washington

MVP: Rick Barry, Golden State

It was not surprising that the 1975 post-season produced the third NBA Finals sweep in league history. But it was a major shock to see the broom being wielded by the unheralded Golden State Warriors instead of the powerful Washington Bullets.

If Golden State's victory wasn't the greatest upset in NBA Finals history, it was close. And Al Attles' overachievers—48-game winners during the regular season—performed their little miracle with pressure defense, fierce hustle and the machine gun-like firepower of star forward Rick Barry.

The series opened at the Capital Centre in Washington and the Warriors quickly set the series tone. They jumped to a 14-point halftime lead, held off the Bullets down the stretch and rode the play of backup guard Phil Smith (20 points) to a 101–95 victory. Barry's jumper with 38 seconds remaining secured the outcome.

Games 2 and 3 were played in San Francisco because of scheduling conflicts and Golden State took quick advantage. Barry scored 36 points in a tense 92–91 second-game victory, and 38 in a 109–101 triumph that gave the Warriors a shocking 3–0 advantage.

Game 4 at Washington was typical Warriors. They trailed by 14 points early and 8 in the final five minutes but wiped away both deficits before clinching a 96–95 victory. Barry was high scorer with 20, but Butch Beard scored his team's final seven points.

Golden State's unsung hero was rookie Jamaal Wilkes, who held high-scoring Washington forward Elvin Hayes to 44 points in the series. Wilkes was later named Rookie of the Year, while Barry was the Most Valuable Player in the Championship Series.

GOLDEN DREAM: *Elvin Hayes (11) tries to stop Golden State's Jamaal Wilkes (41).*

334 1976

Celtics make Suns set in Game that will never die

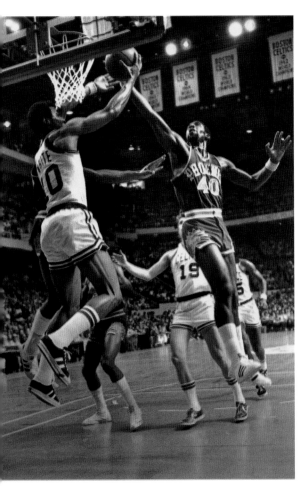

For the young and ambitious Phoenix Suns, Game 5 of the NBA Finals offered a ticket to immortality—the opportunity for a basketball frog to turn into a prince. For the aging and experienced Boston Celtics, Game 5 offered a different kind of challenge—the opportunity for a last championship hurrah before reconstructive surgery.

Both teams had scratched and clawed their way to a pair of victories, the Celtics winning Games 1 and 2 at Boston Garden and the Suns holding serve in the third and fourth contests at Phoenix. The time was right for both teams to seize the moment in a fifth-game classic that became an indelible entry in NBA lore.

There was nothing classic about the opening minutes of Game 5 as the Celtics raced to a 32–12 lead and entered the intermission with a 15-point advantage. But the Suns, inspired by the halftime pleadings of Coach John MacLeod, stepped up their defensive pressure, got the ball to guard Paul Westphal and center Alvan Adams, and crawled back into the game.

The dramatics started at the end of regulation when the Suns forced a 95–95 tie and both teams blew opportunities to win at the free throw line. Curtis Perry missed a pair of foul shots for Phoenix; John Havlicek missed two for Boston.

When the first overtime ended, the game was knotted at 101–101, and Phoenix coaches were arguing vehemently that they should be awarded a technical foul because Boston forward Paul Silas had tried to call an illegal timeout in the waning seconds. The referees chose to ignore Silas' miscall.

The second overtime was even more controversial. The Celtics held a three-point lead with 15 seconds remaining and chants of "We're No. 1" filled Boston Garden. But the chants died quickly when Dick Van Arsdale cut the lead to one and Perry connected off a Westphal steal, giving the Suns a shocking 110–109 advantage.

With four seconds left, Havlicek raced upcourt and banked in a dramatic 18-foot shot, putting the Celtics back on top as ecstatic fans raced onto the court. Mayhem prevailed as players were swarmed, fights broke out and trash was thrown while the referees tried to restore order. A single second remained on the clock.

After a long delay, the fans were pushed to the edges of the court and the Suns called an illegal timeout, taking an intentional technical foul that Boston's Jo Jo White, a 33-point scorer, hit for a two-point lead. But Phoenix now got the ball at halfcourt and inbounded it to Garfield Heard, who fired up a 25-foot miracle jumper that swished through the net. Another overtime.

With fans now in an ugly mood and harassing Phoenix players from close quarters, the game proceeded and took still another turn. Several Boston players had fouled out and seldom-used 6–6 forward Glenn McDonald stepped into the spotlight. He scored six overtime points, the final two giving the Celtics a dramatic 128–126 win. The greatest game in Finals history was over—finally.

Demoralized, the Suns lost an anticlimactic sixth game at Phoenix, 87–80. Charlie Scott scored 25 points for the winning Celtics, who procured their 13th championship in 20 years and second in three seasons.

1976 NBA FINALS

Boston	98	Phoenix	87		at Boston
Boston	105	Phoenix	90		at Boston
Phoenix	105	Boston	98		at Phoenix
Phoenix	109	Boston	107		at Phoenix
Boston	128	Phoenix	126 (3 OT)		at Boston
Boston	87	Phoenix	80		at Phoenix

MVP: Jo Jo White, Boston

Blazing to a Title, Portland gets a glass Slipper

The 1977 NBA Finals produced another Cinderella champion—a Portland expansion franchise competing in its seventh season. And it produced a title-series first—a team coming back to win four straight games after losing the first two.

The prospects for a Portland championship appeared bleak when the Philadelphia 76ers rode the combined 63-point scoring of Julius Erving and Doug Collins to a 107–101 Game 1 victory and stormed to a 107–89 second-game rout that was marred by a late brawl.

But when the series moved to Portland three days later, the only brawling was done by the riled-up Trail Blazers, who stepped up the pace, defended tenaciously and rolled to a 129–107 momentum-reversing victory. Power forward Maurice Lucas and center Bill Walton bullied the 76ers for a combined 47 points and 30 rebounds.

It was more of the same in Game 4 as Walton dominated the middle and Lucas powered his way for easy baskets. The 130–98 victory sent the series back to Philadelphia with a sense of inevitability.

The 76ers got 37 points from Dr. J in Game 5, but the Blazers continued to dominate behind Walton (24 rebounds), Lucas (20 points, 13 rebounds) and Bobby Gross (25 points). The 110–104 victory touched off a wave of Blazermania that engrossed the city of Portland.

The Game 6 finale at Portland was both entertaining and tense right down to the final buzzer. The Blazers express appeared to be chugging relentlessly toward victory with a 12-point lead and only six minutes to play, but success seldom comes easily.

Philadelphia refused to die and cut the deficit to three with 51 seconds remaining. Lucas hit a Portland free throw, but a George McGinnis basket cut the lead to two. The 76ers regained possession in the final seconds and Erving, Lloyd Free and McGinnis missed potential game-tying jumpers before time expired on Portland's 109–107 victory.

Walton, appropriately, put the finishing touches on the championship with 20 points, 23 rebounds, an NBA Finals record 8 blocked shots and 7 assists in the title-clincher. Gross added 24 points. Erving scored 40 points in a losing cause.

1977 NBA FINALS					
Philadelphia	107	Portland	101	at Philadelphia
Philadelphia	107	Portland	89	at Philadelphia
Portland	129	Philadelphia	107	at Portland
Portland	130	Philadelphia	98	at Portland
Portland	110	Philadelphia	104	at Philadelphia
Portland	109	Philadelphia	107	at Portland

MVP: Bill Walton, Portland

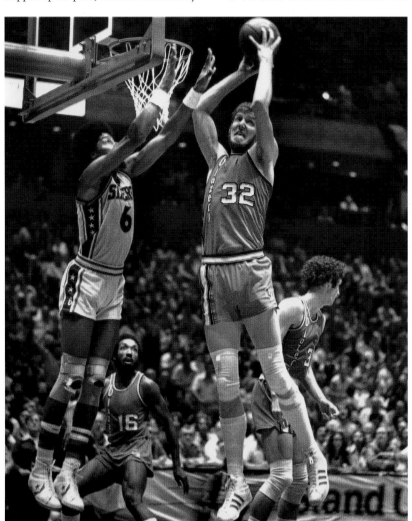

PAYING THE BILLS: *Portland's Bill Walton (32) dominated Julius Erving (6) and the 76ers'.*

1978

Bullets are Road Warriors in winning first Title

In a continuation of its rags-to-riches script, the 1978 NBA Finals featured two underdog teams looking for their first championships. Washington had finished the regular season as the third-best team in the East and Seattle had advanced through the playoffs after compiling the fourth-best mark in the West. What the series lacked in marquee appeal, it made up for with drama and intensity.

The SuperSonics grabbed the early momentum with a 106–102 Game 1 victory at Seattle and a tense 93–92 third-game win at Washington. The Bullets had their backs against the wall when they tipped off for a Game 4 showdown at Seattle's Kingdome—a game that was witnessed by an NBA Finals record crowd of 39,547.

Guard Dennis Johnson gave Seattle fans a 33-point performance and the Sonics held a 15-point advantage late in the third period. But the Bullets raced back, finally taking a 106–104 lead on a Bob Dandridge three-point play. Seattle tied again on Fred Brown's long jumper, forcing overtime.

The extra period belonged to Bullets guard Charles Johnson and Washington went on to claim a series-squaring 120–116 triumph. Home advantage was decisive in games 5 and 6, though Seattle struggled more in their 98–94 victory than Washington did in taking the latter game 117–82. It set up Game 7, which was played at Seattle Coliseum, where the Sonics had won 22 consecutive games.

That streak would end. Charles Johnson and Dandridge scored 19 points apiece and center Wes Unseld hit two critical free throws as the Bullets clinched with a 105–99 win. Washington became only the third NBA Finals team to win a seventh game on the road.

TURNING THE CORNER: *Seattle's John Johnson can't stop the Bullets' Bob Dandridge.*

1978 NBA FINALS

Seattle	106	Washington	102	at Seattle
Washington	106	Seattle	98	at Washington
Seattle	93	Washington	92	at Washington
Washington	120	Seattle	116 (OT)	at Seattle
Seattle	98	Washington	94	at Seattle
Washington	117	Seattle	82	at Washington
Washington	105	Seattle	99	at Seattle

MVP: Wes Unseld, Washington

1979 337

Dodging more Bullets, Seattle wins the Rematch

By the time Washington and Seattle squared off in an NBA Finals rematch, they had discarded their Cinderella labels. The Bullets had begun defense of their 1978 crown with an Atlantic Division title and the SuperSonics, winners in the Pacific Division, had outspoken designs on removing the Bullets from their throne.

This battle pitted Washington's outstanding frontcourt of Elvin Hayes, Bob

1979 NBA FINALS					
Washington	99	Seattle	97	at Washington
Seattle	92	Washington	82	at Washington
Seattle	105	Washington	95	at Seattle
Seattle	114	Washington	112 (OT)	at Seattle
Seattle	97	Washington	93	at Washington

MVP: Dennis Johnson, Seattle

Dandridge and Wes Unseld against Seattle's classy backcourt of Dennis Johnson, Gus Williams and Fred Brown. And the big guys drew first blood with a series-opening 99–97 victory on Larry Wright's two free throws after time had expired.

But the little guys ruled the rest of the way as Seattle raced to four straight victories and its first championship. Game 2 was a 92–82 momentum-grabber at Washington and Game 3 was a 105–95 celebration at the massive Kingdome, where 35,928 Seattle fans basked in a coronation-like atmosphere. Williams scored 31 points and the defensive-minded Johnson added 17.

The Bullets showed life in Game 4 when they forced an overtime on Unseld's layup, but the Sonics recovered for a 114–112 victory. Williams and Johnson, who scored more than half of Seattle's points in the series, combined for 68 in this game and center Jack Sikma added 20 with 17 rebounds.

Seattle finished its impressive title run in Washington with a 97–93 victory that was sealed by Brown's four late baskets. Williams wound up leading the the Sonics in scoring in each of the five games, averaging 29.0 points per game.

VICTORY TIME: *The Sonics' Gus Williams runs down the clock to close out Game 5 and Seattle's first NBA Championship.*

338 **1980**

Magic saves the Day for inspired Lakers

The news was disconcerting for Los Angeles Lakers fans. Center Kareem Abdul-Jabbar, a scoring machine through the first five games of the NBA Finals, would not be available for Game 6 at Philadelphia's Spectrum because of a severely sprained ankle.

Suddenly the 76ers' 3–2 deficit didn't seem so ominous. The powerful Lakers with a 7-foot-2 hole in their middle were not so daunting and proper strategy seemed obvious: Try not to get embarrassed in Game 6 and return home to Los Angeles for the clincher, hopefully with Abdul-Jabbar in the lineup.

But somebody forgot to tell the Lakers to lay down. And nobody envisioned the powerful Magic spell Coach Paul

1980 NBA FINALS					
Los Angeles	109	Philadelphia	102	at Los Angeles
Philadelphia	107	Los Angeles	104	at Los Angeles
Los Angeles	111	Philadelphia	101	at Philadelphia
Philadelphia	105	Los Angeles	102	at Philadelphia
Los Angeles	108	Philadelphia	103	at Los Angeles
Los Angeles	123	Philadelphia	107	at Philadelphia

MVP: Magic Johnson, Los Angeles

Westhead would cast over his young team. Magic, as in Earvin (Magic) Johnson, the 6–9 rookie with an effervescent smile and the amazing ability to play any position on the court—including, as everybody would quickly discover, center.

Johnson's teammates understood the mesmerizing control he could exhibit on a basketball court—his no-look passes, court sense, clever penetrations to the basket and ability to quarterback the fast break. They had watched him dominate opponents as a point guard, a small forward and a power forward, averaging 18 points, 7.7 rebounds and 7.3 assists over the regular season. But when Westhead announced that the 20-year-old former Michigan State star would fill in at center for the stricken Abdul-Jabbar, even his closest friends shook their heads in disbelief.

For the record, Magic lost the center jump to 6–11 Darryl Dawkins. But that's just about the only thing he lost in a game viewed by a captivated national television audience. Johnson bounced, boxed out, shot, defended and charmed the nation while scoring 42 points, grabbing 15 rebounds and handing out 7 assists in an unfamiliar position against players three inches taller.

MAGIC MOMENT: *Magic Johnson (32) is closely guarded by the 76ers' Lionel Hollins.*

With the 37-point help of Jamaal Wilkes, who keyed a third-quarter surge that enabled the Lakers to pull away, Johnson dominated the 76ers and Los Angeles closed out its second West Coast championship with a 123–107 victory.

Before Johnson's "Show-time" rescue, the series had belonged to Abdul-Jabbar. The Lakers' big man scored 33 points, grabbed 14 rebounds and blocked six shots in a 109–102 Game 1 victory at the Los Angeles Forum and he scored 38 points in Game 2, 33 in Game 3 and 40 in Game 5—before and after he sprained his ankle.

And the Lakers needed every one of those points against the stubborn 76ers. Dawkins, Julius Erving and Maurice Cheeks combined for 71 points in Philadelphia's 107–104 Game 2 victory. And after the Lakers had pulled back in front with a 111–101 Game 3 win, the 76ers answered 105–102 as Dawkins scored 26 and Erving 23.

The Lakers held a two-point third-quarter lead in Game 5 when Abdul-Jabbar sprained his ankle and retired to the locker room. He returned early in the fourth quarter, scored 14 invaluable points down the stretch and converted a three-point play that secured a 108–103 victory.

Then, like millions of fans, he watched an extraordinary Game 6 on television—probably, like everybody else, in disbelief.

Back in the Spotlight, the Celtics win Title No. 14

The Boston Celtics, out of the spotlight since 1976, claimed the franchise's 14th championship with a six-game triumph over the Houston Rockets. The Celtics survived despite a five-game scoring slump by second-year forward Larry Bird.

Bird struggled through most of Game 1 at Boston Garden, but still came up with the key play in a 98–95 victory. It came late in the fourth quarter when Bird launched a long jump shot, realized immediately it was off target and darted inside for the rebound. He grabbed the ball before it hit the floor near the baseline, switched it to his left hand as he was falling out of bounds and swished a 15-footer. It was one of the greatest shots in the history of the NBA Finals.

Down but hardly out, the Rockets fought back in Game 2 for a 92–90 victory behind the 31 points of center Moses Malone. But the Celtics answered with a stifling defensive effort that keyed a 94–71 masterpiece at Houston. The Rockets held Bird to eight points for the second straight game and evened the series one day later with a 91–86 win.

The momentum turned in Game 5 and it wasn't Bird making the big plays. Cedric Maxwell exploded for 28 points and 15 rebounds in a 109–80 romp that set the Rockets up for the kill.

The Game 6 clincher marked the offensive rejuvenation of Bird, who scored 27 points and hit his only series 3-point basket in the stretch run of a 102–91 victory.

Even though it was not one of Bird's most memorable playoff performances, he did average 21.9 points, 14 rebounds and 6.1 assists per game throughout the playoffs. It more than justified his selection to the All-NBA First Team in just his second season in the league.

FLIGHT TIME: *The Celtics' Larry Bird scores with an easy layup against the Rockets.*

1981 NBA FINALS

Boston	98	Houston	95	at Boston
Houston	92	Boston	90	at Boston
Boston	94	Houston	71	at Houston
Houston	91	Boston	86	at Houston
Boston	109	Houston	80	at Boston
Boston	102	Houston	91	at Houston

MVP: Cedric Maxwell, Boston

340

1982

Showtime: Another L.A. Hit lifts Lakers over 76ers

The Los Angeles Lakers returned their "Showtime" attack to center stage and captured their second championship in three seasons—another six-game decision over Philadelphia. But this series lacked the Game 6 dramatics of 1980 as the Lakers won three of the first four contests and wrapped up their third West Coast title before a full house at the Los Angeles Forum.

When the Lakers put together a 40–9 second-half blitz that wiped out a 15-point Game 1 deficit en route to a 124–117 victory, it seemed like business as usual. Los Angeles had used its devastating fast break and tenacious zone-trap defense to roll past Phoenix and San Antonio in unprecedented playoff sweeps. The first-game NBA Finals victory was their ninth in a row.

That streak ended three days later when the 76ers, behind Julius Erving's 24 points and 16 rebounds, ran off a 110–94 victory at Philadelphia. But the Lakers rolled off consecutive wins at the Forum and put the 76ers' hopes on the critical list.

Point guard Norm Nixon keyed the 129–108 third-game victory with 29 points, offsetting a 36-point outburst by Philadelphia guard Andrew Toney. Magic Johnson and Jamaal Wilkes both scored 24 points and Kareem Abdul-Jabbar added another 22 in the Lakers' 111–101 Game 4 triumph.

The 76ers staved off elimination thanks to the strong Game 5 play of Darryl Dawkins. The center held Abdul-Jabbar to a shocking six points and scored 20 himself in a 135–102 romp.

But the Lakers rebounded emphatically in Game 6. Wilkes scored 27 and Johnson performed a "13 triple"—13 points, 13 rebounds and 13 assists—in Los Angeles' 114–104 championship clincher.

NO ROOM: *Jamaal Wilkes (52) is covered by Darryl Dawkins (53) and Julius Erving (6).*

1982 NBA FINALS

Los Angeles	124	Philadelphia	117	at Philadelphia
Philadelphia	110	Los Angeles	94	at Philadelphia
Los Angeles	129	Philadelphia	108	at Los Angeles
Los Angeles	111	Philadelphia	101	at Los Angeles
Philadelphia	135	Los Angeles	102	at Philadelphia
Los Angeles	114	Philadelphia	104	at Los Angeles

MVP: Magic Johnson, Los Angeles

1983

Moses finds Promised Land, leads Sixers to Title

The 76ers, three times a bridesmaid since their lone Philadelphia championship in 1967, finally broke through—and they did it in style against an old nemesis. The 76ers recorded the fourth sweep in NBA Finals history, defeating the same Los Angeles Lakers who had handed them Finals losses in 1980 and 1982, and they completed the postseason with an unprecedented 12–1 record.

Amazingly, Philadelphia won each game after trailing at the half and the 76ers did it behind the inside/out domination of center Moses Malone, guard Andrew Toney and forward Julius Erving. Malone, who had been acquired in an offseason trade to firm up the team's soft middle, averaged 25.8 points and tenaciously pounded the boards, outrebounding Lakers center Kareem Abdul-Jabbar 72–30. Toney averaged 22 points and Erving 19.

The injury-plagued Lakers entered the series without forward James Worthy and with point guard Norm Nixon and backup forward Bob McAdoo at less than full strength. And their vulnerability quickly became evident.

Malone set the tone for the series when he scored 27 points and grabbed 18 rebounds in a 113–107 opening victory at Philadelphia. And he finished in style, scoring 24 points and pulling down 23 rebounds in the 115–108 title-clincher at the Los Angeles Forum. In between, the

ONE-ON-ONE: *The 76ers' Moses Malone (2) is is guarded by the Lakers' Kurt Rambis.*

76ers recorded a 103–93 victory at Philadelphia's Spectrum and a 111–94 triumph at the Forum.

Final statistics suggest Philadelphia saved its best for last. The 76ers won the series in the four fourth quarters, when they outscored the Lakers 124–79.

1983 NBA FINALS

Philadelphia	**113**	Los Angeles	107	at Philadelphia
Philadelphia	**103**	Los Angeles	93	at Philadelphia
Philadelphia	**111**	Los Angeles	94	at Los Angeles
Philadelphia	**115**	Los Angeles	108	at Los Angeles

MVP: Moses Malone, Philadelphia

342 1984

A Long-Awaited Rematch

The Boston Celtics continued their NBA Finals mastery over the Los Angeles Lakers in a bitter seven-game battle that pitted Larry Bird against Magic Johnson for the first time. The Celtics had recorded seven Finals victories over the Lakers from 1959–69, and the renewal of that rivalry after 15 years was memorable.

The teams split the first four games, Los Angeles posting lopsided 115–109 and 137–104 victories and Boston answering

with two overtime thrillers the Lakers probably should have won.

The Game 2 overtime was forced when Celtics guard Gerald Henderson stole a James Worthy pass in the final seconds and converted a game-tying layup. Boston won, 124–121, on a Scott Wedman jumper. Game 4 was pushed into overtime when Johnson missed a pair of late free throws and Boston went on to win 129–125.

With the series tied at 2–2, the Celtics

CROWD CONTROL: *Celtics fans storm onto the court to celebrate Boston's 15th NBA title while Robert Parish (00) and Kareem Abdul-Jabbar are still playing.*

really turned up the heat in Game 5—literally. The contest was played in a sweltering 98 degrees at Boston Garden and the Lakers wilted as Bird soared. While overheated fans swooned in the stands and the Lakers gulped down oxygen on the sideline, Bird connected on 15 of 20 field-goal attempts, scored 34 points and sparked a memorable 121–103 victory.

The Lakers recovered in the cool of the L.A. Forum for a 119–108 win behind Kareem Abdul-Jabbar's 30 points, but the balanced Celtics were too much in Game 7. Cedric Maxwell finished with 24 points and 8 assists, Bird had 20 points and 12 rebounds and defensive-minded Dennis Johnson scored 22 points in a 111–102 victory. The Celtics were champions for a 15th time.

1984 NBA FINALS

Los Angeles	115	Boston	109	at Boston
Boston	124	Los Angeles	121 (OT)	at Boston
Los Angeles	137	Boston	104	at Los Angeles
Boston	129	Los Angeles	125 (OT)	at Los Angeles
Boston	121	Los Angeles	103	at Boston
Los Angeles	119	Boston	108	at Los Angeles
Boston	111	Los Angeles	102	at Boston

MVP: Larry Bird, Boston

1985 343

Sweet Revenge: Lakers End Long Celtics Hex

The Boston Celtics had taken great delight in their 1984 NBA Finals victory over the Lakers—maybe a little too much. Their comments were arrogant, their attitude was cavalier and their post-series shots were stinging and sarcastic.

Los Angeles players had not forgotten M. L. Carr entering Boston Garden before Game 7 wearing goggles, in a mocking imitation of the Lakers center Kareem Abdul-Jabbar; or Cedric Maxwell's choke signal to James Worthy as he prepared to shoot a free throw late in Game 4; or Larry Bird's insinuations that Magic Johnson's inept play had helped the Celtics win; or Kevin McHale's joking reference to "Tragic Johnson."

And the Lakers were well aware of the franchise's inability to beat the Celtics in the NBA Finals: eight tries, eight failures. Never had a coach entered a championship series with more motivational weapons than Lakers Coach Pat Riley in 1985—and never has a team responded in a more negative fashion: Celtics 148, Lakers 114.

The Memorial Day Massacre, coming off the bitter 1984 loss, was humiliating and hard to believe. Abdul-Jabbar, 38 years old, looked every bit his age as he tried to keep up with Boston center Robert Parish. The "Showtime" running game was slowed to a crawl and the final spread probably could have been even bigger.

On the Boston side, Scott Wedman hit all 11 of his shots and guard Danny Ainge shared the spotlight. Everything the Celtics did worked and the game ended with Coach K.C. Jones in a suspicious mood.

And rightly so. In retrospect, Game 1 might have been the best thing that could have happened to the Lakers. Embarrassed and determined to make the pain go away, they got 30 points, 17 rebounds and 8 assists from Abdul-Jabbar and 22 points from Michael Cooper en route to a 109–102 victory at Boston. Game 3 at

Los Angeles was a 136–111 Lakers blowout, sparked by Worthy's 29 points.

The Celtics, down but not out, responded in Game 4 with a 107–105 victory that was decided by Dennis Johnson's buzzer-beating jump shot. With the fifth game scheduled for the Forum under the league's new 2–3–2 format, the Lakers revved up their Showtime engines for a big finish.

Worthy, Abdul-Jabbar and Magic combined forces in a 120–111 victory that put the Lakers within a game of their fourth West Coast championship. Abdul-Jabbar scored 36 points, Worthy added 33 and Johnson scored 26 while handing out 17 assists.

Game 6 was a Lakers' landmark. Not only did they defeat the Celtics for the first time, they did it on the parquet floor of Boston Garden where the Celtics had never lost a title-clinching game. The 111–100 victory was posted behind the firepower of Abdul-Jabbar (29 points), Worthy (28) and Johnson (a 14–10–14 triple-double).

Abdul-Jabbar was named the MVP of the series. But perhaps the most valuable lesson to come out of the championship was the knowledge that the Lakers could beat their old nemesis the Celtics, helping L.A. to turn a corner in its development.

HAVING A BALL: *The Lakers' Kareem Abdul-Jabbar holds the MVP trophy aloft.*

1985 NBA FINALS

Boston	148	Los Angeles	114	at Boston
Los Angeles	109	Boston	102	at Boston
Los Angeles	136	Boston	111	at Los Angeles
Boston	107	Los Angeles	105	at Los Angeles
Los Angeles	120	Boston	111	at Los Angeles
Los Angeles	111	Boston	100	at Boston

MVP: Kareem Abdul-Jabbar, Los Angeles

344 1986

Celtics blast Rockets thanks to Bird and Parish

Boston Coach K.C. Jones had the perfect solution for the problems posed by Houston's Twin Towers. He simply let his Bird fly over, under and around the imposing Ralph Sampson and Hakeem Olajuwon in a six-game NBA Finals that produced the Celtics' 16th championship.

With Larry Bird and center Robert Parish in top form, the 7–4 Sampson and 7-foot Olajuwon did not pose a serious problem for the Celtics. Bird averaged 24 points, 9.7 rebounds, 9.5 assists and 2.7 steals as Boston duplicated its six-game 1981 victory over Houston. This NBA title meant that the Celtics matched Los Angeles as a three-time champion in the 1980s.

The Celtics rolled to an easy 112–100 victory in Game 1 at Boston Garden as Parish scored 23 points, Bird and Kevin McHale accounted for 21 each, and Bird handed out 13 assists, more than compensating for Olajuwon's 33 points. Bird's 31-point effort keyed Boston's 117–95 second-game rout.

But any thoughts of a sweep dissolved quickly in Houston when Sampson exploded for 24 points and 22 rebounds and the Rockets held off a late Boston charge for a 106–104 win. The Celtics regained control, however, when Bird and backup center Bill Walton hit key last-minute baskets that produced a 106–103 Game 4 triumph.

Ahead 3–1, the Celtics dropped a 111–96 decision in Houston when Olajuwon scored 32 points, grabbed 14 rebounds and blocked 8 shots.

But they wrapped up the series in Game 6 in Boston, 114–97, behind Bird's triple-double: 29 points, 11 rebounds and 12 assists.

CHIEF CONTRIBUTION: *The Celtics' Robert Parish dunks during Boston's 106–103 defeat of the Houston Rockets in Game 4.*

1986 NBA FINALS

Boston	112	Houston	100	at Boston
Boston	117	Houston	95	at Boston
Houston	106	Boston	104	at Houston
Boston	106	Houston	103	at Houston
Houston	111	Boston	96	at Houston
Boston	114	Houston	97	at Boston

MVP: Larry Bird, Boston

1987

Settling an old Score, the Lakers take the Title

In the rubber match of a bitter 1980s rivalry, the Lakers prevailed in a six-game NBA Finals romp over the Celtics. Magic Johnson did most of the damage, but he got plenty of help from Kareem Abdul-Jabbar, James Worthy, Michael Cooper and the rest of the Lakers cast.

The tone was set at the Los Angeles Forum where the fast-breaking Lakers pounded out 126–113 and 141–122 victories. Worthy scored 33 points in the

1987 NBA FINALS

Los Angeles	126	Boston	113	at Los Angeles
Los Angeles	141	Boston	122	at Los Angeles
Boston	109	Los Angeles	103	at Boston
Los Angeles	107	Boston	106	at Boston
Boston	123	Los Angeles	108	at Boston
Los Angeles	106	Boston	93	at Los Angeles

MVP: Magic Johnson, Los Angeles

opener and Magic totaled 51 points and 33 assists in the two games. The wounded Celtics returned to Boston Garden looking for a dose of that old championship pride.

They found some in Game 3, a 109–103 face-saving victory. Larry Bird scored 30 points and Dennis Johnson added 26. But their fate would not be determined until the waning seconds of Game 4.

The Celtics appeared headed for a series-evening victory as time ticked away in another classic Lakers-Celtics battle. Bird's 3-point basket had given them a 106–104 lead with 12 seconds remaining, but an Abdul-Jabbar free throw cut the margin to one. When Abdul-Jabbar missed the second free throw, Boston's Kevin McHale grabbed the rebound, but lost the ball out of bounds. Johnson delivered a championship-crushing blow when he connected on a "junior, junior skyhook" as time expired.

Boston held serve one more time at Boston Garden 123–108, but the Lakers wrapped things up at the Forum as Abdul-Jabbar (32 points) and Johnson (19 assists) keyed a 106–93 victory.

It was another classic match-up in the storied Lakers- Celtics history.

THREE'S A CROWD: *Robert Parish (with ball) is surrounded by Lakers everywhere he looks: Kareem Abdul-Jabbar (33), James Worthy (42) and Magic Johnson (32)*

346

1988

Lakers fight off "Bad Boys," fulfill Guarantee

Not long after Los Angeles' 1987 championship-clinching victory over Boston, somebody asked Coach Pat Riley if the Lakers could become the first team to win back-to-back titles since the Celtics of 1968 and 1969. "Not only can the Lakers win again," Riley responded, "I'll guarantee it."

With those bold words, Riley set the tone for the 1987–88 season. The Lakers, with 40-year-old Kareem Abdul-Jabbar still manning the middle, were talented enough to pull off Riley's prediction, but like all wanna-be repeat champions before them, they would have to overcome many obstacles: complacency, injuries, hungry challengers and, of course, Lady Luck.

The luck factor was minimized during a 62–20 regular season that insured the Lakers of home-court advantage throughout the playoffs. That was fortunate because they were extended to seventh games at the Los Angeles Forum by conference rivals Utah and Dallas during an exhausting postseason run.

Not surprisingly, that seven-game pattern continued in a rough-and-tumble NBA Finals against Detroit's Pistons—the "Bad Boys" of the Eastern Conference. The Pistons, a rising NBA power, featured the super backcourt of Isiah Thomas and Joe Dumars and a confrontational frontcourt with bruisers Bill Laimbeer, Rick Mahorn, John Salley, Dennis Rodman and James Edwards. Frontcourt scoring was provided by the slashing Adrian Dantley.

Any thoughts that the glitzy Lakers would run right past the defensive-minded Pistons were discarded during an eye-opening first game at the Forum. After best friends Thomas and Magic Johnson exchanged center-court kisses before tipoff, Dantley connected on 14 of 16 field-goal attempts and Detroit defenders pushed the Lakers all over the court in a 105–93 victory.

The Lakers, facing a must-win Game 2

L.A. CONFIDENT: *Byron Scott hit a critical basket late in Game 6.*

on their home court, showed heart with a 108–96 win as James Worthy scored 26 points. Game 3 was played before 39,188 Detroit fans at the Pontiac Silverdome and Los Angeles escaped with a 99–86 victory.

The Pistons did not make another misstep before their home fans. Dantley scored 27 points in a 111–86 Game 4 victory and 25 two nights later in a 104–94 win that gave Detroit a 3–2 series advantage. Game 5 was played before a crowd of 41,732, the largest in NBA Finals history.

Game 6 at the L.A. Forum was the series classic. With his team trailing 56–48 early in the third quarter, Thomas went on a scoring spree that almost delivered Detroit its first NBA championship. He scored the next 14 points, suffered a severely sprained ankle that forced him to the sideline for half a minute and still finished the period with 11-of-13 shooting for 25 points—an NBA Finals one-quarter record. The Pistons rode that momentum into the final minute carrying a 102–99 edge.

But the Lakers responded in championship fashion. Byron Scott's basket cut the deficit to one point and two Abdul-Jabbar free throws with 14 seconds remaining decided the Lakers' 103–102 victory. Thomas finished with 43 points and 8 assists.

Having cut the heart out of Detroit's title hopes, Los Angeles closed out the series with a 108–105 victory that featured Worthy's first career triple-double (36 points, 16 rebounds, 10 assists).

The Lakers were champions for a fifth time in the 1980s—this time guaranteed.

1988 NBA FINALS

Detroit	105	Los Angeles	93	at Los Angeles
Los Angeles	108	Detroit	96	at Los Angeles
Los Angeles	99	Detroit	86	at Detroit
Detroit	111	Los Angeles	86	at Detroit
Detroit	104	Los Angeles	94	at Detroit
Los Angeles	103	Detroit	102	at Los Angeles
Los Angeles	108	Detroit	105	at Los Angeles

MVP: James Worthy, Los Angeles

A changing of the Guard leaves Pistons on top

MAIN MAN: *Isiah Thomas directed the "Bad Boy" offense.*

En route to their first championship, Detroit's "Bad Boys" had won 63 regular-season games and generated dislike around the league for their brutish style. But the Pistons laughed at critics all the way through an easy playoff run and a shocking Finals sweep that closed out 42-year-old Lakers center Kareem Abdul-Jabbar's outstanding career and snapped the Los Angeles championship streak at two. The Lakers had won five of the last nine NBA titles.

Detroit's victory was decided by its rugged frontcourt and the scoring of guards Isiah Thomas, Joe Dumars and Vinnie Johnson, who combined for 65 points in a 109–97 Game 1 victory at Detroit.

Game 2 was more competitive, but the Lakers' fate was sealed when Magic Johnson pulled a hamstring in the third quarter, an injury that was to restrict him the rest of the way. The Lakers, already playing without injured Byron Scott, scored just 13 fourth-quarter points and fell 108–105 as Dumars connected for 33.

Dumars continued his hot shooting with 31 points in Game 3 (21 in the third quarter) and Detroit moved ahead 3–0 with a 114–110 victory. That set the stage for only the fifth sweep in NBA Finals history.

The Pistons fell behind by 16 points early in the second quarter of Game 4. But they chipped away at the deficit and got a fourth-quarter boost from backup center James Edwards, who scored all 13 of his points in the period. Dumars finished with 23 in the 105–97 title-clinching victory.

The series ended with the Los Angeles Forum crowd chanting, "Kareem, Kareem, Kareem" as the Pistons hugged and celebrated on the court.

While the 1988 Detroit Pistons were losing a championship to Los Angeles in a bitter seven-game NBA Finals, they were learning a valuable lesson—how to win. They did a little teaching of their own when they squared off with the aging Lakers in a 1989 rematch, a battle that ended 40 years of franchise frustration dating back to their early life as the Fort Wayne Pistons.

1989 NBA FINALS

Detroit	109	Los Angeles	97	at Detroit
Detroit	108	Los Angeles	105	at Detroit
Detroit	114	Los Angeles	110	at Los Angeles
Detroit	105	Los Angeles	97	at Los Angeles

MVP: Joe Dumars, Detroit

348

1990

Detroit's little Big Man

O ne season after breaking their 40-year championship jinx, the Detroit Pistons became only the third franchise to win consecutive titles. The five-game victory over the Portland Trail Blazers was signed, sealed and delivered by point guard Isiah Thomas, who averaged 27.6 points and made a number of big plays just when it appeared that the Pistons were down and out.

Thomas sent a message in Game 1. The Blazers held a 90–80 lead with seven minutes remaining and appeared to be coasting when he suddenly stepped up. With Thomas leading the charge, the Pistons pulled closer and closer, finally forcing a 94–94 tie en route to a 105–99 victory. Thomas finished with 33 points, including 10 in a row down the stretch.

Portland fought back in Game 2 with a 106–105 overtime victory that was decided on Clyde Drexler's two free throws. But the Pistons shocked the Blazers by winning the next three games at Portland—a place where they had not won since 1974.

Joe Dumars keyed the 121–106 Game 3 triumph with 33 points and the three guards—Dumars, Thomas and Vinnie Johnson—combined for 78 points in a 112–109 fourth-game win. The Thomas-Johnson combo clicked again in a

shocking Game 5 clincher.

The Blazers, on the verge of forcing a sixth game, carried a 90–83 lead into the final two minutes. But Johnson suddenly caught fire, Portland went cold and Detroit scored nine straight points in a shocking conclusion to a 92–90 victory. Thomas, who scored 29 points, set up Johnson's 15-foot winner with 0.7 seconds remaining after a Portland turn-over. The basket capped a marvelous 15-point final quarter for Johnson, who scored seven of the final nine.

The Detroit guards wound up outscoring the Portland guards in the five-game series, 304-252. Detroit's bench finished with 125 points and 73 rebounds.

MVP: *Isiah Thomas scored when he needed to and passed when he didn't.*

1990 NBA FINALS

Detroit	105	Portland	99	at Detroit
Portland	106	Detroit	105 (OT)	at Detroit
Detroit	121	Portland	106	at Portland
Detroit	112	Portland	109	at Portland
Detroit	92	Portland	90	at Portland

MVP: Isiah Thomas, Detroit

1991

Bulls end 25-year drought with victory over Lakers

The Chicago Bulls ended a quarter century of frustration when Scottie Pippen, Michael Jordan and John Paxson combined for 82 points in a 108–101 Game 5 victory over Los Angeles and clinched the franchise's first NBA championship.

The Bulls, who lost the NBA Finals opener at Chicago Stadium when the Lakers' Sam Perkins hit a three-point shot with 14 seconds remaining, completed their four-game comeback blitz at the Los Angeles Forum and ended their playoff run with a 15–2 record. The Bulls simply smothered the Lakers defensively while Jordan, Pippen and Paxson glistened in the offensive spotlight.

Jordan collected 30 points and 10 assists in the clincher and finished the series with a 31.2-point average. Pippen upstaged his teammate with a 32-point, 13-rebound, 7-assist, 5-steal effort in the finale. But the Lakers' real thorn was Paxson, who hit 29 of his final 42 NBA Finals shots. The hot-shooting guard scored 20 Game 5 points, eight in a key fourth-quarter Chicago run that decided the game.

After losing the opener despite Jordan's 36-point effort, the Bulls bounced back for a 107–86 second-game rout and claimed Game 3 in overtime, 104–96. A Jordan jump shot tied the game with 3.4 seconds left in regulation and he scored six points in the extra period. Game 4 was a 97–82 mismatch.

The Bulls, who held the Lakers to a record-low 458 points, could not stop Magic Johnson, who averaged 18.6 points and 12.4 assists in a losing cause. But Johnson couldn't do it alone.

The Lakers played the finale without injured starters James Worthy and Byron Scott.

REJECTED: *L.A.'s Sam Perkins(left) is foiled by Chicago's Scottie Pippen (right).*

1991 NBA FINALS

Los Angeles	93	Chicago	91	at Chicago
Chicago	107	Los Angeles	86	at Chicago
Chicago	104	Los Angeles	96 (OT)	at Los Angeles
Chicago	97	Los Angeles	82	at Los Angeles
Chicago	108	Los Angeles	101	at Los Angeles

MVP: Michael Jordan, Chicago

350 # 1992

Bulls give an Encore as Jordan leads the Way

It took the Chicago Bulls 25 years to win their first NBA championship, but just one year to win a second. It was the Michael Jordan show as the Bulls posted a 97–93 Game 6 victory over the Portland Trail Blazers and became only the fourth NBA franchise to claim consecutive titles.

Jordan, who averaged 35.8 points and claimed his unprecedented second straight MVP award, scored 33 in the finale and combined with Scottie Pippen (26) to score the Bulls' final 19 points. The Trail Blazers held a seemingly safe 79–64 lead entering the final period but were outscored, 14–2, in the opening minutes.

The amazing comeback climaxed a series in which the Bulls seemed to toy with fate. After Jordan sparked a 122–89 opening-game romp with an NBA Finals-record 35-point first half, the Blazers showed a little comeback spark of their own. They wiped out Chicago's 10-point fourth-quarter Game 2 lead with a 15–5 spurt and won the game in overtime, 115–104. Clyde Drexler scored 26 points for Portland, but guard Danny Ainge provided the victory spark by scoring nine points in the extra period.

The teams split the next two games, Chicago winning 94–84 at Portland and losing 93–88 when the Trail Blazers scored 19 of the game's final 27 points. But Jordan came to the rescue with a 46-point effort in the fifth game that sparked a 119–106 victory and set the stage for the dramatic Chicago finale.

Only the Minneapolis (1940s and '50s) and Los Angeles Lakers (1987–88), the Boston Celtics (1960s) and Detroit Pistons (1989–90) had won consecutive championships before the Bulls.

None of those teams however, relied as heavily on one player as the Bulls did in Jordan.

IS IT A BIRD? *Michael Jordan lit up the finals with many of his patented slam dunks.*

1992 NBA FINALS

Chicago	122	Portland	89	at Chicago
Portland	115	Chicago	104 (OT)	at Chicago
Chicago	94	Portland	84	at Portland
Portland	93	Chicago	88	at Portland
Chicago	119	Portland	106	at Portland
Chicago	97	Portland	93	at Chicago

MVP: Michael Jordan, Chicago

1993 · 351

Three Titles are a Charm for Jordan-Powered Bulls

The "three-peat" talk started shortly after Chicago's 1992 NBA Finals victory over Portland. Everybody agreed: The Bulls, fueled by the incredible Michael Jordan, were capable of winning a third consecutive championship. It hadn't happened for 27 years, but nothing, it seemed, was beyond Jordan's extensive reach.

And virtually everything in his career had come in such multiples. Seven scoring titles; three regular-season MVPs; two NBA Finals MVPs; seven All-NBA first-team citations; six All-NBA Defensive first-team selections; three steals titles. The "three-peat" fantasy provided a noble challenge for the basketball player who had everything.

The idea began gathering momentum when the Bulls won their third straight Central Division title, advanced unscathed through the first two rounds of the playoffs and recovered from a 2–0 deficit to defeat the New York Knicks in the Eastern Conference finals. The only remaining obstacle was a Phoenix team featuring Charles Barkley, Dan Majerle and Kevin Johnson—a team that had posted a league-best 62 wins.

The Suns' championship hopes took a severe blow when the Bulls charged into America West Arena and grabbed 100–92 and 111–108 series-opening victories. Chicago pulled away in the fourth quarter of the opener when Jordan scored 14 of

his 31 points. Jordan (42 points, 12 rebounds) and Barkley (42, 13) offset each other in Game 2, but the Bulls got 26 points from Horace Grant and a triple-double from Scottie Pippen.

Game 3 at Chicago Stadium was a 3-hour, 20-minute marathon that matched the longest game in NBA Finals history—three overtimes. A three-point play by Horace Grant tied the game at 103, forcing the first extra session, and the teams battled fiercely before Phoenix finally prevailed, 129–121. Barkley, Johnson and Majerle (six 3-pointers) combined for 77 points, more than offsetting the combined 70 of Jordan (44) and Pippen (26).

Game 4 was a case of too much Jordan, who exploded for 55 points and keyed a 111–105 victory. But Johnson and Richard Dumas scored 25 points apiece and the Suns broke serve again in Game 5 with a 108–98 win that sent the series back to Phoenix.

The Bulls, their backs planted firmly against the wall, built an 87–79 lead through three quarters of Game 6 but suddenly went ice cold—a drought that produced a record-low 12 fourth-quarter points. They were blanked for six minutes as Phoenix raced to a shocking 98–94 lead.

But Jordan cut the deficit to two with less than a minute to play and the Bulls got

UNBELIEVA-BULL: *Michael Jordan seemingly scored at will against the Suns.*

the ball back in the final seconds. The pass went low to Grant, who flipped it out to John Paxson unattended beyond the 3-point line. Paxson drilled the championship-winning shot with 3.9 seconds remaining.

1993 NBA FINALS

Chicago	100	Phoenix	92	at Phoenix
Chicago	111	Phoenix	108	at Phoenix
Phoenix	129	Chicago	121 (3 OT)	at Chicago
Chicago	111	Phoenix	105	at Chicago
Phoenix	108	Chicago	98	at Chicago
Chicago	99	Phoenix	98	at Phoenix

MVP: Michael Jordan, Chicago

352

1994

Rockets dismantle Knicks with tough Defense

SCORING MACHINE: *Hakeem Olajuwon played like a dream for the Rockets.*

1994 NBA FINALS

Houston	85	New York	78	at Houston
New York	91	Houston	83	at Houston
Houston	93	New York	89	at New York
New York	91	Houston	82	at New York
New York	91	Houston	84	at New York
Houston	86	New York	84	at Houston
Houston	90	New York	84	at Houston

MVP: Hakeem Olajuwon, Houston

I t wasn't pretty, but the Houston Rockets showed what it takes to win a championship: defense, defense and more defense—and a large dose of Hakeem Olajuwon.

The Rockets' seven-game victory over the Knicks was a titanic defensive struggle in which the winners scored a seven-game record-low 603 points—New York totaled 608. Neither team broke 100 during the series and no game was decided by more than nine. In the end, Olajuwon won his battle with New York's Patrick Ewing and they won the first championship in franchise history.

The 7-foot Olajuwon scored 28 points and grabbed 10 rebounds as the Rockets won the opener at Houston, 85–78. But the Knicks bounced back for a 91–83 Game 2 victory and the next two games followed script, the Rockets winning the New York opener and the Knicks prevailing in Game 4.

But the Knicks broke pattern in Game 5 at Madison Square Garden when Ewing scored 25 points and grabbed 12 rebounds and John Starks added 19 points in a 91–84 victory that put the Knicks on the brink of their first title since 1973. But that was not to be.

Returning to Houston, the Rockets rode Olajuwon's 30-point, 10-rebound effort to an 86–84 victory. The outcome was not decided until Olajuwon blocked Starks' three-point attempt with two seconds remaining. Starks scored 16 of his 27 points in the fourth quarter.

Olajuwon, who averaged 26.9 points, took center stage in the 90–84 finale, scoring 25 points and grabbing 10 rebounds. Vernon Maxwell broke out of his series-long slump to score 21.

But it was Maxwell's defense that made the difference as he held the Knicks' Starks to just eight points as missed all 11 three-pointers he tried.

A Dream come true

1995 NBA FINALS

Houston	**120**	Orlando	**118 (OT)**	at Orlando
Houston	**117**	Orlando	**106**	at Orlando
Houston	**106**	Orlando	**103**	at Houston
Houston	**113**	Orlando	**101**	at Houston

MVP: Hakeem Olajuwon, Houston

LIKE A DREAM: *The repeat was sweet for Olajuwon and the Rockets.*

The Houston Rockets shot down critics with a surprising sweep of the Orlando Magic and joined the growing list of repeat title winners.

The Rockets rode the inspired play of Hakeem Olajuwon, who had averages of 32.8 points, 11.5 rebounds and 5.5 assists per game. His counterpart, Shaquille O'Neal, averaged 28 points and 12.5 rebounds but Olajuwon's teammates won the long-distance war. The teams attempted 210 3-pointers, a record for a four-game series.

The turning point might have occurred in a wild first game as the Magic did a late disappearing act before their home fans. The Magic had a 20-point first-half lead, led 110–107 in the final moments of regulation and lost a golden opportunity to secure victory when Nick Anderson missed four free throws in the final 10 seconds. Houston's Kenny Smith buried a dramatic 3-point shot with 1.6 seconds left to force overtime and the Rockets finally won, 120–118, when Olajuwon tipped in a missed shot as time expired.

Olajuwon scored 34 points and backup guard Sam Cassell fired in 31 as Houston completed its surprising Orlando sweep with a 117–106 victory. Game 3 at Houston, a 106–103 Rockets win, was decided by Robert Horry's 3-point bomb with 14.1 seconds showing on the clock.

The Rockets joined the Celtics, Lakers, Pistons and Bulls as repeat champions with a 113–101 win in the finale.

1996

Chicago delivers crowning blow to 87–13 season

The Chicago Bulls, putting an exclamation point behind their claim as the greatest single-season team ever assembled, closed out their fourth championship in six years with a six-game NBA Finals victory over Seattle and brought their final 1995–96 ledger to 87–13.

The centerpiece for the Bulls was Michael Jordan, who earned his record eighth NBA scoring title, his fourth regular-season and NBA Finals MVP awards.

Jordan scored 28 points, Scottie Pippen 21 and Toni Kukoc 18 as the Bulls got a jump on the Sonics with a 107–90 victory at the United Center.

The Sonics, 64-game regular-season winners, stepped up their game and made a late run that fell just short in Chicago's 92–88 victory. Jordan scored 29 points, but Chicago's difference might have been Rodman, who grabbed 20 rebounds, 11 in the third quarter.

The Bulls blew away the Sonics in Game 3. But any thoughts of a Finals sweep dissolved in Game 4, a Seattle victory with Shawn Kemp scoring 25. Re-energized and buoyed by their Game 4 effort, the Sonics won Game 5, too, 89–78.

But Seattle was only delaying the inevitable. Chicago's 87–75 series-ending victory contained all the elements of success that had carried the Bulls through the regular season—intense, stifling defense, a combined 39 points from Jordan and Pippen and nine points and 19 rebounds from Rodman.

TAG TEAM: *Michael Jordan (right) and Scottie Pippen (left) were dominant.*

1996 NBA FINALS

Chicago	107	Seattle	90	at Chicago
Chicago	92	Seattle	88	at Chicago
Chicago	108	Seattle	86	at Seattle
Seattle	107	Chicago	86	at Seattle
Seattle	89	Chicago	78	at Seattle
Chicago	87	Seattle	75	at Chicago

MVP: Michael Jordan, Chicago

1997

Vulnera-Bulls make it five Titles in seven seasons

1997 NBA FINALS

Chicago	84	Utah	82	at Chicago
Chicago	97	Utah	85	at Chicago
Utah	104	Chicago	93	at Utah
Utah	78	Chicago	73	at Utah
Chicago	90	Utah	88	at Utah
Chicago	90	Utah	86	at Chicago

MVP: Michael Jordan, Chicago

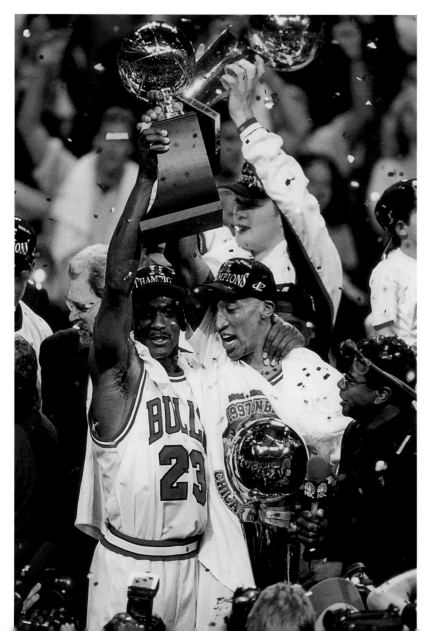

Throw away the last few seconds of Games 1 and 6, and the Utah Jazz may have claimed their first championship. But because the ball was in Michael Jordan's hands in the waning moments of both those contests, the Chicago Bulls were able to snatch their fifth NBA crown in seven seasons.

In the opener, Karl Malone missed two free throws with 9.2 seconds remaining and the score tied at 82–82. Jordan then nailed an 18-footer for a game winning basket. Utah's weakest effort of the Finals came in Game 2, when they fell behind, closed the deficit in the fourth quarter, but were blown away down the stretch.

The series moved to Salt Lake City, where the Jazz had compiled a 38–3 home record during the regular season. As the noise at the Delta Center reached plane-decibel proportions, Malone bounced back, scoring 37 points as the Jazz won 104–91.

The Bulls' 90–88 Game 5 victory was the high point of the series. Jordan scored 17 second-quarter points, to trim Utah's early 16-point lead to 53–49 at the half. The game lay in the balance until Jordan hit a three-pointer with 25 seconds left, to give the Bulls an 88–85 lead.

Utah led for most of the first three quarters of Game 6, but Jordan (39 points) again brought the Bulls back. With the game tied, Jordan—double-teamed—spotted Steve Kerr open, and he drilled a 16-footer with five seconds remaining.

But it was more than just another clutch play for Jordan. It may have been one of the most incredible performances of his career, given that he was sick before the game and the Bulls weren't sure he would be able to play.

TWO OF A KIND: *Jordan (left) and Pippen (right) celebrate another championship.*

356 # 1998

The end of the Road? Jordan's last Hurrah

DONE DEAL: *Michael Jordan sinks a dramatic "last second" jumper in Game 6.*

1998 NBA FINALS

Utah	88	Chicago	85 (OT)	at Utah
Chicago	93	Utah	88	at Utah
Chicago	96	Utah	54	at Chicago
Chicago	86	Utah	82	at Chicago
Utah	83	Chicago	81	at Chicago
Chicago	87	Utah	86	at Utah

MVP: Michael Jordan, Chicago

It may have been the end of an era for the Chicago Bulls as Michael Jordan lifted yet another Championship and yet another Finals MVP award after a decisive Game 6 win in Salt Lake City. But, if it was, what a way to end that dynasty.

They faced a Utah team fresh from a ten-day lay-off following their morale-boosting four-game sweep of the fancied LA Lakers in the Western Conference Finals.

When the Jazz won the first game, despite not playing up to their own high standards, it looked as though the Bulls' critics would finally see the Jordan empire crumble. They had reckoned, of course, without Jordan and his ever-improving supporting cast. But with Karl Malone and John Stockton struggling in Game 2, Jordan scored 37 points in a five-point Bulls win.

Game 3 saw a rampant Bulls tear the heart out of the Jazz back at the United Center. The win was the largest in playoff history. But the Jazz of the Malone-Stockton era are nothing if not persistent, and Game 4 was close-run, the Jazz having improved substantially, but the Bulls took it 86–82 with Scottie Pippen in stunning form.

In Game 5, Malone finally got the better of his Bulls defenders—scoring 39 points. The Finals returned to Salt Lake City intriguingly poised. The outcome was not decided until the final 20 when Jordan stole the ball from Malone and drove up court before wrong-footing his defender and hitting the winning jump shot with 5.2 seconds to play. The basket took Jordan's game total in the 87–86 win to 45 and his series average to 33.5 and had his grateful coach, Phil Jackson, paying the ultimate accolade.

"I don't know if anyone could have written a scenario as dramatic as this. It was just an awesome thing. How many times does he have to show us that he is a real life hero?"

Twin Towers terrorize New York

SPURRED ON TO VICTORY: *Tim Duncan led the Spurs in both victory and celebration.*

A year after the fact, Lakers coach Phil Jackson chided the San Antonio Spurs about winning "the asterisk" championship in 1999.

The insinuation was that because the 1998–99 season had been reduced from 82 games to 50 by the NBA's first work stoppage, the championship was somewhat devalued.

Try telling that to David Robinson, the long-suffering Spurs center, who had gone nine brilliant seasons before securing his first championship ring.

If anything, the Spurs' title deserved an asterisk because Eastern Conference champion New York had to play the title series in the absence of injured center Patrick Ewing.

But the bottom line was there was no alteration to the playoff schedule, even with the postseason pushed deeper into the spring because of the lockout. It still took 15 victories to produce a champion, and the Spurs steamrolled their way through the competition.

In the first round, there was a 3–1 thrashing of the Minnesota Timberwolves in a best-of-5 series. That was followed by successive 4–0 sweeps of the Los Angeles Lakers and Portland Trail Blazers.

EMBRACEABLE TWO: *Spurs center David Robinson hugs teammate Malik Rose.*

And in the NBA Finals, the Knicks simply had no answer for the Twin Towers presence of Robinson and Tim Duncan.

The Spurs pummeled the Knicks in the first two games of the Finals, Duncan going for a combined 58 points in those two. After New York won on its home court to draw within 2–1 in the best-of-7 series, Duncan went for 28 points and Robinson for 17 rebounds as the Spurs won Game 4 96–89. The series drew to a close on a decisive jumper by Spurs point guard Avery Johnson with 47 seconds to play in Game 5.

1999 NBA FINALS

San Antonio	89	New York	77	at San Antonio
San Antonio	80	New York	67	at San Antonio
New York	89	San Antonio	81	at New York
San Antonio	96	New York	89	at New York
San Antonio	78	New York	77	at New York

MVP: Tim Duncan, San Antonio

358

2000

Shaq and Kobe revive Showtime in Los Angeles

RARE MOMENT: *Reggie Miller scores without Shaq defending the rim, a very rare sight in the finals.*

2000 NBA FINALS

L.A. Lakers	104	Indiana	87	at Los Angeles
L.A. Lakers	111	Indiana	104	at Los Angeles
Indiana	100	L.A. Lakers	91	at Indianapolis
L.A. Lakers	120	Indiana	118 (OT)	at Indianapolis
Indiana	120	L.A. Lakers	87	at Indianapolis
L.A. Lakers	116	Indiana	11	at Los Angeles

MVP: Shaquille O'Neal, Los Angeles

The 2000 NBA Finals were as much a coronation of the Los Angeles Lakers as a championship competition.

While the Indiana Pacers fought gamely in what coach Larry Bird said would be his final stand on the sidelines, the subplots for the Lakers seemingly overwhelmed the series itself.

For hulking center Shaquille O'Neal, this was vindication at the highest level, the opportunity to show he was capable of carrying a team on his leviathan shoulders.

For youthful guard Kobe Bryant, this was the ultimate stage to prove that he may yet live up to the comparisons to the game's ultimate player, Michael Jordan.

And for sage coach Phil Jackson, this was a moment to prove that he was capable of guiding a team to the ultimate prize without Jordan in his arsenal, as he emerged as the victorious coach in the Finals for the seventh time in 10 seasons.

Lost in the shuffle was heroic play by Pacers shooting guard Reggie Miller, breakthrough performances by Pacers small forward Jalen Rose, and a nation-wide introduction to Indiana's throwback arena, the nostalgia-riddled Conseco Fieldhouse.

The series was compelling, with Game 4's overtime classic one of the gripping competitions in championship-round history.

Most of all, though, the two weeks were about the dominance of O'Neal, of how one 330-pound Goliath refused to be slayed by the Eastern Conference's deepest roster.

In being named Most Valuable Player of the Finals, O'Neal joined Jordan and Willis Reed as the only players to be named MVP of the All-Star Game, regular season and Finals in the same year. O'Neal averaged 38 points and 16.6 rebounds in the six games against Indiana.

(Opposite) SHAQ ATTACK: *The Pacers could not stop Shaquille O'Neal in the 2000 finals.*

THE NBA ALL-STAR GAME

See Michael slam. See Charles jam. Watch Larry shoot and Magic pass. In its most basic element, its simplest form, the NBA All-Star Weekend is a spectacular parade of one-name basketball superstars who strut their most creative stuff for adoring fans and a growing global audience.

The Greatest Show Off Earth

It is Michael Jordan winning the 1987 Slam-Dunk Championship with a magnificent leap from the free-throw line. It is Larry Nance's 1984 two-ball, windmill slam and Cedric Ceballos' 1992 "Hocus-Pocus" blindfolded jam. It is Larry Bird firing in a stream of 3-point baskets in rapid-fire succession to win the first AT&T Long Distance Shootout. It is Craig Hodges connecting on a crowd-silencing 19 straight 3-pointers en route to the second of a record-tying three consecutive Shootout titles.

And, of course, it's the All-Star Game, which remains the cornerstone of what is now a weekend-long extravaganza that promotes the individual creativity players are asked to harness during regular-season play. For one game every year, the best of the NBA's best are allowed to use their sweetest one-on-one moves, throw their most dazzling no-look passes, test their hang time both inside and outside the paint and perform their most artistic slams.

It is a prime-time basketball show that has gained status as one of the year's most popular sports attractions.

In the Beginning

When NBA Public Relations Director Haskell Cohen proposed his idea for an NBA All-Star Game, he was sitting in the league office on the 80th floor of New York's Empire State Building. It was an appropriate setting for a lofty idea.

But lofty was in the eye of the beholder. Even though the 1950 NBA was in desperate need of respect and publicity, President Maurice Podoloff and the bottom-line conscious league owners were skeptical that such a game would draw enough interest and worried that a public relations flop would do more harm than good.

Fortunately for the NBA, Boston Owner Walter Brown did not accept their misgivings. Not only did he disagree, he enthusiastically embraced the idea of a midseason classic that would rival the success of baseball's All-Star Game. Brown was so sure the game would provide a boost to the NBA's image that he offered Boston Garden as a free venue and said he would pay all expenses and incur any losses.

Thanks to Brown's perseverance, the NBA unveiled its All-Star Game on March 2, 1951, before 10,094 fans at Boston Garden. The Eastern Conference, featuring the offensive-minded starting lineup of Joe Fulks, Dolph Schayes, Ed Macauley, Bob Cousy and Andy Phillip, rolled to an easy 111–94 victory over the George Mikan-led Western Conference. The game was an unqualified success and Brown's status as a basketball visionary was insured.

High-Rising Fortunes

The early All-Star Game was a marvelous showcase for the prime NBA talent that went unnoticed by a large segment of the sports-viewing public. The game attracted television interest that helped boost the NBA's image, but it lacked the glitz and glitter that would lift it into worldwide prominence in the 1980s and '90s. Players were selected and brought in for the one-night show and sent back to their appointed cities to resume the regular-season grind. In the 1950s and '60s NBA, many underpaid players viewed the classic as an unnecessary extension of an already too-long season.

"It's true that most players were pretty blasé when they were first selected," conceded former Celtics Coach Red Auerbach, an 11-time coach of the Eastern Conference Stars. "They like to make you think they don't care. But once they walk inside that arena on the night of the game, see the size of the crowd and feel the electricity, their whole attitude changes.

"One thing about the great ones: They've got that tremendous pride. All you have to do is wake up that competitive instinct and they're ready to go."

For three decades, that pride and competitive instinct were enough to make the All-Star Game a successful midseason fixture. The Wilt Chamberlains, Oscar Robertsons, Elgin Baylors, Bob Pettits and Bill Russells could be counted on to provide an exciting and memorable show. But when the NBA enjoyed an incredible popularity explosion in the early 1980s, its All-Star classic developed a personality of its own.

A major chunk of that personality is provided by players who now are eager to compete in a status-enhancing hoopfest that begins on Thursday and continues to entertain throngs of fans and television

(Opposite) RARE AIR: *Michael Jordan wins the 1988 slam dunk contest at Chicago Stadium.*

362 viewers through the crowning of an MVP following the Sunday All-Star Game.

The growth and blossoming of All-Star Weekend in the 1980s mirrored the explosion of professional basketball as a worldwide phenomenon, taking root with the addition of fan-friendly events that would build to the main course.

Slams, Bombs and Other Things

The rise of the All-Star Game to super-event status started in 1984, when marketing-conscious David Stern took the reins as NBA Commissioner and introduced All-Star Saturday. As a preliminary to the Sunday game, players were brought in to compete in a crowd-pleasing slam-dunk competition and two teams of former NBA stars competed in the Legends Classic, which has since been replaced by a Rookie All-Star Game.

The competitions were an immediate success. Phoenix forward Larry Nance rose into prominence with the whirling jam that gave him an exciting victory over the 76ers' Julius Erving in 1984 and Atlanta's Dominique Wilkins won the second competition a year later. The 1986 festivities included the popular 3-point-shooting contest that was dominated by Boston's Bird for the first three years.

Buoyed by those successes and ever mindful of the unconquered worlds that lay at its fingertips, the NBA continued an All-Star expansion that would transcend

HAPPY DAYS: *Magic Johnson (center) enjoyed the NBA's 50th Anniversary celebration in '97.*

anything baseball, football or any other sport had to offer. In 1990, the NBA added a Friday night "Stay in School Celebration" that offered All-Star city students an appetizing dose of NBA stars, musical and television performers and other entertainers. Since 1993, the All-Star Weekend has started on Thursday, thanks to the Jam Session hoop festival that offers four days of interactive booths, exhibits and 3-on-3 competitions in a theme park-like atmosphere.

So, just how popular has this All-Star basketball frenzy become? Consider: The All-Star Game has been played before crowds of 44,735 (Houston's

Astrodome), 43,146 (Indianapolis' Hoosier Dome) and 34,275 (Seattle's Kingdome); the 1998 game was viewed by more than 600 million people in 196 countries around the world and covered by about 1,400 American and foreign journalists and reporters.

In an attempt to freshen the format, the NBA introduced a new event, the 2Ball—a shooting competition that paired NBA stars with women from the WNBA—in place of a Slam Dunk contest.

The All-Star Game has become fan-friendly in every sense. Starting lineups are selected by fans and the contest is rotated among the 28 NBA cities. Coaches, who select the reserves to fill out their rosters, are determined by the teams with the best conference records at the three-month stage of the season.

All-time All-Stars

It was an All-Star Game for the ages. When the NBA turned 50 in 1997, the league celebrated its first half-century with an incredible extravaganza during the All-Star Game in Cleveland's Gund Arena, where the top 50 players in history were honored.

It was a fan's dream, a living, breathing Who's Who of basketball. When they were introduced at halftime of the game, amid fireworks and popping flashbulbs that turned the darkened arena bright as day, there was an extended roar from the crowd that somehow managed to

A Little Bit of Heaven

In the big, bigger, biggest world of the NBA, the 1986 All-Star show was stolen by two of the game's littlest warriors—Atlanta's 5-foot-7 Spud Webb and Detroit's 6–1 point guard Isiah Thomas.

Webb became the media darling during the All-Star Saturday festivities when he outpointed seven other players in the Slam-Dunk competition. Performing before family and friends in his hometown of Dallas, Webb gave away 10 inches to his shortest rival and walked away with the trophy.

With the crowd at Reunion Arena giving him rousing support, Webb started the competition with a twisting, reverse dunk that was slammed so hard it bounced off his head and back through the basket cylinder. He also performed two 360-degree jams and finished with a put-back dunk that he slammed home after bouncing the ball off the floor and backboard.

"It gives hope to everybody under 5–11 that you can play," marveled West Coach Pat Riley. Thomas took center stage for the East team the next day with a 30-point, 10-assist, 5-steal effort that earned him a second All-Star MVP honor. Thomas scored 12 of his points in the fourth quarter when the East pulled away for a 139–132 victory.

Here are some All-Star facts worth noting:

● Kareem Abdul-Jabbar played in a record 18 All-Star Games and scored a record 251 points (13.9 per game). But Michael Jordan (21.9) and Oscar Robertson (20.5) were more prolific All-Star scorers.

● Former St. Louis great Bob Pettit earned a record four MVP citations, one more than Robertson. One came in 1962, when the ever-intense Hawks forward grabbed a record 27 rebounds and added 25 points for good measure.

● Wilt Chamberlain set the All-Star single-game record with 42 points in that same 1962 classic, two points better than Jordan managed in 1988 while playing in front of his home Chicago fans. Both Chamberlain and Jordan connected on 17 of 23 shots.

● Larry Bird, fittingly, scored the first 3-point basket in All-Star history with 1:40 left in a 1980 overtime period.

● Utah's John Stockton and Karl Malone became the first teammates to share an MVP award after leading the West to an overtime victory in 1993.

cheer in spite of the lumps in everyone's throats and a goodly share of tears as well.

After a memorable video presentation of highlights on the scoreboard to the song, "Unforgettable," the guards were introduced first, a decision that meant Michael Jordan started off the proceedings. Undoubtedly there was more than just symbolism in having Jordan introduced as No. 1.

Cleveland fans were able to forget for a moment the fact that Jordan had been such a thorn in their sides for years, and they greeted him with a deafening salute that never waned throughout the 24-minute proceedings.

CLASH OF THE TITANS: *Kareem Abdul-Jabbar (top) shoots over Wilt Chamberlain in '72.*

Well, except when Karl Malone was introduced. In an odd and embarrassing quirk, fans actually booed Malone as he was honored as one of the NBA's top 50 players. Fans were responding to some remarks the veteran power forward made in the days leading up to the game—remarks that were misunderstood.

A dedicated family man, Malone has often remarked he'd rather have some time off with his family to rest and relax during the All-Star break. He reiterated those sentiments before the game at Cleveland, but he added that he was planning to skip his post-game shower in order to leave the city as quickly as possible after the game. Unfortunately, while he was not really criticizing Cleveland—and in fact is a huge fan of the Cleveland Indians baseball team—fans took exception to his remarks and booed him mercilessly, an odd reaction in the midst of the joyous festivities.

Still, the ceremonies—and the noise— continued until 72-year-old George Mikan, arguably the league's first star, was gently helped onto the platform by Celtics great Bill Russell. From Jordan to Mikan. How fitting. How fantastic.

In between Jordan, Malone, Russell and Mikan, the following players also were honored: Kareem Abdul-Jabbar, Nate Archibald, Paul Arizin, Charles Barkley, Rick Barry, Elgin Baylor, Dave Bing, Larry Bird, Wilt Chamberlain, Bob Cousy, Dave Cowens, Billy Cunningham, Dave DeBusschere, Clyde Drexler, Julius Erving, Patrick Ewing, Walt Frazier, George Gervin, Hal Greer, John Havlicek, Elvin Hayes, Magic Johnson, Sam Jones, Jerry Lucas, Moses Malone, Kevin McHale, Earl Monroe, Hakeem Olajuwon, Robert Parish, Bob Pettit, Scottie Pippen, Willis Reed, Oscar Robertson, David Robinson, Dolph Schayes, Bill Sharman, John Stockton, Isiah Thomas, Nate Thurmond, Wes Unseld, Bill Walton, Lenny Wilkens and James Worthy. Shaquille O'Neal and Jerry West did not attend the proceedings. The late Pete Maravich was represented by his sons, Jaeson and Josh.

Because the 50 greatest players were selected by a committee of basketball experts, naturally there was some controversy about several players who were left out, such as Bob McAdoo, Dennis Rodman and Dominique Wilkins.

But for the players selected, it was a once-in-a-lifetime experience, and they all realized it.

"That is a privilege," Jordan said of being in the company of the 50 greatest players. "If I get a chance, I'd like to say thank you to all of them because the roads they paved for myself and the other ones that are here ... without their dedication and their love for the game, quite naturally, we wouldn't be here. So they deserve a lot of credit for the success on the NBA."

Added Barkley, "This is better than the (1992 Olympic) Dream Team because this is history. That's a walking basketball encyclopedia right there."

The young stars of the league, good enough to be named All-Stars but not

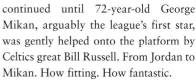

STOCK ANSWER: *Utah's John Stockton was honored as one of the NBA's 50 greatest.*

COMING IN TO LAND: *The Lakers' Kobe Bryant won the 1997 slam dunk contest in Cleveland.*

Added Glen Rice, " I think most of the guys were in awe." Of course, that happens at almost every All-Star Game, when the very best players in the league compete with their peers. There's no doubt they try and impress each other as much as the crowd.

But there was an air of reverence at the 1997 All-Star Game. Even the All-Stars were asking for autographs. On this weekend, they realized the NBA was bigger than any of them individually and that basketball was the real star of the show.

The Slam Dunk story

The Slam Dunk contest was deader than a doornail after 1997.

Yes, Kobe Bryant, then a rookie with the Los Angeles Lakers, won the event by putting the ball between his legs, slamming it through and then flexing in front of the All-Stars who were seated on the bench in front of him in Gund Arena in Cleveland.

But overall the competition left little to be desired. It was as if athletes simply had run out of ways to impress the judges and the fans. Cleveland's Bob Sura had the crowd behind him, which gave him a big adrenaline rush. But his first start was called back because the television cameras weren't ready. That seemed to take everything out of him and he missed his first dunk.

The tone for the evening was set. There were plenty of other ill-advised attempts before Bryant's winner. In the finals, for instance, Michael Finley of the Dallas Mavericks tried to do a cartwheel and dunk. He also tried to slam two balls, but he managed to throw down only one.

Of the cartwheel, he said, "I have a lot of respect for the U.S. gymnastics team right now. In practice, I did the cartwheel perfect. In the heat of the moment, my knees kind of buckled."

It was a far cry from the early days of the Slam Dunk contest. When Julius Erving took off from the foul line to dunk and win the first Slam Dunk title in the American Basketball Association back in 1976 in Denver, Woody Paige of the *Denver Post* wrote, "Someday, I'll set my grandchild on my knee and say, 'Kid, your old granddaddy was there that night

quite in the legends category, also appreciated their surroundings.

"It's great," said Tim Hardaway. "Wilt Chamberlain, those guys, what can I say? It's great being in the same room, the same hotel, being around those guys. It's great to be around them because they built it for us."

Added Grant Hill, "It's an honor to be here when they are honoring the 50 greatest players."

So inspired were those taking part in

the weekend that East coach Doug Collins allowed his team the unprecedented privilege of watching the half-time festivities on television in the locker room.

"Great players love greatness, no matter what the era or when it occurred," Collins said. "All of our players were riveted to the TV."

Said Terrell Brandon, "To see every player nominated for that, it was just a great, great atmosphere."

when the ABA put on the gawldangest show these tired old eyes have ever witnessed. If you shut your eyes and open your ears, I'm gonna tell you all about it. That was the night Dr. J sucked all the air out of the building as he went up, and everyone's ears popped. Jimmy Naismith would have loved it, I tell you. Mercy me."

Erving tried that dunk in the NBA Slam Dunk contest the next year. But he lost to Larry Nance, who dunked two balls.

Players were having trouble dunking even one in 1997. As a result of that lackluster competition, the league called a timeout for the contest, opting to replace it for the 1998 game in New York with the Nestle Crunch All-Star 2Ball competition, a shooting game featuring an NBA star paired with a WNBA star.

The lockout in 1998–99 canceled the All-Star Game scheduled for Philadelphia. But the league brought back the Slam Dunk contest for the 2000 All-Star Game in Oakland, and Vince Carter of the Toronto Raptors made it look like a very good decision, electrifying the crowd on All-Star Saturday in the Oakland Arena.

Even before the competition started, there was a buzz in the building. Carter had often been compared to fellow North Carolina alum Michael Jordan, a two-time Slam Dunk champion. Carter's seemingly endless array of dunks were regularly featured on the nightly sports highlight segments, which was no doubt responsible for him being the No. 1 vote-getter in the 2000 All-Star Game, with 1,911,973 votes from the fans.

In addition, in an effort to liven up the proceedings, the new rules allowed the dunker to have an assistant pass him a ball, thus opening up a whole new range of possibilities.

As it turned out, all anybody needed to liven up the evening was Carter.

His program included a 360, a windmill and a between the legs tomahawk. On another dunk, he momentarily hung from the rim by his right elbow.

The clincher was his third dunk in the first round, when he took a low pass from his cousin and fellow contestant Tracy McGrady, wrapped it between his legs and slammed it. That brought judge Isiah

AIR CANADA: *Toronto's Vince Carter was a popular 2000 Slam Dunk champion at Oakland.*

Thomas leaping over the scorer's table and sent Carter in front of the television cameras to mouth, "It's over."

All-Stars like Shaquille O'Neal and Kevin Garnett rocked back and forth on the bench in amazement.

Finally, Paige had something to write about again—especially after Carter informed the media that he made up the dunks as he went along.

And despite the fact that he started out Sunday's All-Star Game by slamming a pass from Allen Iverson, Carter, who first dunked in seventh grade, told reporters he wanted to be known as more than a dunk artist.

"Dunkers come and go," he told *Sports Illustrated*. "You can go down to the playground and find a bunch of guys who can do fancy dunks. The great players excel at all aspects of the game. That's what I want to be."

How his game and his career progress have yet to be seen. But one thing already is for sure. He single-handedly revived the Slam Dunk competition.

Tea for 2Ball

There's a new game in town. After introducing 2Ball as a replacement for the Slam Dunk contest in 1998, the NBA has been promoting the two-person shooting game around the world from the U.S. to Asia, from Europe to Central America.

It's fairly uncomplicated. Played on a halfcourt, two players alternate shots from six locations on the court. Points are awarded for degree of difficulty and bonus points are awarded for making shots from each of the spots. There are three categories of competition—boys, girls and coed—with three age groups within each—9–11, 12–14 and 15–17.

Each NBA team sponsors a local competition, with winners advancing to area, city and national championships. The national finals are contested at an NBA arena during the NBA playoffs and are televised on Nickelodeon.

In the first All-Star Saturday competition in New York, Clyde Drexler of the Houston Rockets and Cynthia Cooper of the Houston Comets won the event. The lockout cancelled the 1999 game, but Jeff Hornacek of the Utah Jazz and Natalie Williams of the Utah Starzz won the 2000 matchup, beating Jason Kidd of the Phoenix Suns and Jennifer Gillom of the Phoenix Mercury.

According to Hornacek, one of the league's best shooters who also claimed the AT&T Shootout that weekend, 2Ball is not as easy as it appears.

"That's the first time I did the 2Ball," he said after the competition. "Natalie and I kind of went over it one day for about 15 minutes. We thought we had to take a shot from every spot, and we practiced twice like that. The third round, someone told us you can shoot from wherever you want, just so you alternate it. We had a little strategy for there. Yesterday we talked about it and changed it up a little more."

The two alternated shots from opposite baselines.

"I think we liked our strategy," Williams said. "He was a great partner. I wanted to hold my end up, and luckily I did."

The Shootout

In the Wild West days in the United States, shootouts featured cowboys on horses or the sheriff and his posse against some evil gunslingers. In the Roaring Twenties, there were shootouts between gangsters and government agents.

In the NBA, contestants bring those same sorts of mentalities to the annual AT&T Shootout, which determines the best 3-point shooter in the league —at least on that given day.

Although the contest has proven to be every bit as exciting and popular as the Slam Dunk contest, NBA commissioner David Stern had to be convinced to incorporate it into the All-Star festivities.

In 1986, Rick Welts, who would become an executive vice president and chief marketing officer of the league, proposed adding the shootout after seeing it in the Continental Basketball Association.

Stern was doubtful.

"I said it was ridiculous, it would never do," Stern said. "Rick said, 'Could we try it, please?' I said, 'Yes, but I'll always blame you for it.'"

There was no need for that.

"About two players into the (1986) competition, I knew we'd be all right," recalled Welts, who had some doubt himself. "One of those players was Larry Bird. The thing I forgot to figure in was the skill of the NBA players. Most of their shots went in. In the CBA, most of them didn't."

As it turned out, the NBA shooters were every bit as arrogant about their skills as the slam dunkers. Legend has it that three-time champion Bird once walked into the locker room, looked around at his fellow competitors and asked, "Which one of you is playing for second?"

As they watched field-goal percentages and scoring averages decline year after year, basketball purists often lamented the state of shooting in the league. But as long as defenses double-team the post and clog up the middle, there will always be a need for the shooters to draw them away from the basket and keep them honest. This contest was for them.

In the AT&T Shootout, there are five stations positioned around the 3-point

Slam-Dunk Championship/2Ball Competition

The 2Ball Competition replaced the Slam-Dunk in 1998. No All-Star Weekend in 1999.

Year	Player	Team	Height
1984	Larry Nance	Phoenix	6–10
1985	Dominique Wilkins	Atlanta	6–8
1986	Spud Webb	Atlanta	5–7
1987	Michael Jordan	Chicago	6–6
1988	Michael Jordan	Chicago	6–6
1989	Kenny Walker	New York	6–8
1990	Dominique Wilkins	Atlanta	6–8
1991	Dee Brown	Boston	6–1
1992	Cedric Ceballos	Phoenix	6–7
1993	Harold Miner	Miami	6–5
1994	Isaiah Rider	Minnesota	6–5
1995	Harold Miner	Miami	6–5
1996	Brent Barry	L.A. Clippers	6–6
1997	Kobe Bryant	L.A. Lakers	6–7
1998	Not held		
2000	Vince Carter	Toronto Raptors	6–6

2Ball Competition

1998	Cynthia Cooper/Clyde Drexler	Houston Comets/Rockets
2000	Natalie Williams/Jeff Hornacek	Utah Starzz /Utah Jazz

line. A ball rack is located at each station and holds five balls—four brown balls and one multicolored ball. Each participant has a minute to shoot the balls. Each brown ball is worth one point and each multicolored ball is worth two. But the multicolored ball can be shot only after the four brown balls at each spot. Each round is scored separately.

In previous years, two competitors shot at once in the preliminary rounds. But the rules were changed for the 2000 Shootout, and contestants shot one at a time.

Utah's Jeff Hornacek, who had announced the 1999–2000 season was going to be his last, successfully defended his title by scoring 13 points in the final round, beating Dallas' Dirk Nowitzki and Milwaukee's Ray Allen.

"For a lot of guys, it was the first time," Hornacek said of his fellow competitors. "The first time out is a tough time to do it. So I had a little experience going for me."

LONG SHOT: *Jeff Hornacek won again in 2000.*

The 36-year-old veteran also knew enough to pace himself. "Guys were coming off saying, 'Boy, I was tired by midway through'," Hornacek said. "You don't realize that the first 10 shots of that are pretty easy. You have energy. Then you do get tired and you have to adjust a little bit. I tried not to warm up a whole lot. At my age, I need to save all the energy I could."

The AT&T Long Distance Shootout

The following players have won the NBA's 3-point shooting competition, which became a regular All-Star Saturday feature in 1986:

Year	Player	Team	Position
1986	Larry Bird	Boston	forward
1987	Larry Bird	Boston	forward
1988	Larry Bird	Boston	forward
1989	Dale Ellis	Seattle	guard/forward
1990	Craig Hodges	Chicago	guard
1991	Craig Hodges	Chicago	guard
1992	Craig Hodges	Chicago	guard
1993	Mark Price	Cleveland	guard
1994	Mark Price	Cleveland	guard
1995	Glen Rice	Miami	forward
1996	Tim Legler	Washington	guard
1997	Steve Kerr	Chicago	guard
1998	Jeff Hornacek	Utah	guard
1999	*All-Star Weekend not held: No Long Distance Shootout*		
2000	Jeff Hornacek	Utah	guard

And another thing

The third mainstay of the NBA's All-Star Weekend has undergone several transformations.

Originally, the league presented the Schick Legends Classic from 1984 through 1993, which featured All-Stars from years gone by competing as hard as their aching backs and creaky knees would let them.

While fans seemed to love seeing the old-timers hobbling around, the games often suffered and the players definitely did—with injuries mounting along with the players' ages.

So in 1994, the league went the other way and introduced the Schick Rookie Game, featuring the most promising young stars of the future.

The first game was a classic shootout between Orlando's Penny Hardaway and Golden State's Chris Webber. There was a classic storyline as well. In 1993, Orlando had used the No. 1 pick in the draft to take Webber out of the University of Michigan and then traded him to Golden State for Hardaway, from Memphis State, who'd been the No. 5 pick in the draft.

In the end, Webber scored 18 points on nine of 13 field goals to lead his Phenoms to a 74-68 victory over the Sensations, who were led by Hardaway with 22 points.

Things were going along swimmingly until 1999, when the lockout canceled the All-Star Game that had been scheduled for Philadelphia. To make up for the lost opportunities for the rookie class of '99, the league decided to feature the first-year players against the second-year players in what then became known as the Schick Rookie Challenge during the 2000 All-Star Saturday in the Oakland Arena.

Surprisingly, it was the rookies who prevailed, 92–81, in overtime. They were led by most valuable player (and later co-rookie of the year with Houston's Steve Francis) Elton Brand of Chicago, who finished with 14 points and 21 rebounds, and Cleveland's Andre Miller, who led all scorers with 21 points but got booed when he refused to dunk, opting for layups instead.

Boston's Paul Pierce led the second-year players with 18 points, but the play of the game may have come from Sacramento's Jason Williams, who passed the ball off his elbow and back to Denver's Raef LaFrentz for a layup.

Still, the rookies prevailed in the new format, which the league vowed to continue in an effort to promote even more youngsters.

"I think we had a lot to prove," Brand said. "This was for bragging rights during the season."

There are two things fans can depend on when the star-studded lineups take the court: The game will be wide open with lots of points and it will be filled with razzle-dazzle and free-wheeling offense. And, of course, the cream usually will rise to the top.

East-West All-Star Games

March 2, 1951, at Boston, East 111, West 94

Celtics forward Ed Macauley rewarded 10,094 Boston Garden fans with a 20-point, 6-rebound performance that earned him MVP honors in the first All-Star classic. Macauley, who received 19-point support from the Warriors' Joe Fulks, also excelled defensively, holding Lakers center George Mikan to four field goals and 12 points. Indianapolis' Alex Groza led the West with 17 points.

February 11, 1952, at Boston, East 108, West 91

A 16–3 East run, in the final five minutes, settled a contest that was dominated by two players—the Warriors' Paul Arizin (26 points, 6 rebounds) and Lakers center George Mikan (26 points, 15 boards). Arizin, who hit 9 of 13 field-goal attempts and all eight of his free throws, earned MVP honors.

January 13, 1953, at Fort Wayne, West 79, East 75

Rochester guard Bob Davies scored eight of his nine points in the final quarter to help the West hold on for its first All-Star victory. But the real damage was inflicted by 6–10 Lakers center George Mikan, who earned MVP honors with a 22-point, 16-rebound effort. It was the lowest-scoring game in All-Star history.

January 21, 1954, at New York, East 98, West 93 (OT)

Celtics guard Bob Cousy scored 10 of his 20 points in the first All-Star overtime period and the East thrilled 16,487 Madison Square Garden fans with its third victory in four years. The West, which got 23 points from Lakers forward Jim Pollard, forced the extra period on two last-second George Mikan free throws.

January 18, 1955, at New York, East 100, West 91

The Boston backcourt of Bob Cousy and Bill Sharman combined for 35 points as the East recovered from a third-quarter deficit in a game that featured 20 lead changes. MVP Sharman scored 10 of his 15 points in the decisive final period as the East won for the fourth time in five years.

January 24, 1956, at Rochester, West 108, East 94

St. Louis forward Bob Pettit scored 20 points and sparked a 41-point third-quarter explosion that carried the West to its second All-Star victory. Pettit, the game's MVP, also grabbed 24 rebounds, keying the West's whopping 79–53 rebounding advantage. Rochester's Maurice Stokes thrilled the home crowd with 10 points and 16 rebounds.

January 15, 1957, at Boston, East 109, West 97

Warriors center Neil Johnston scored 15 of his 19 points in the third quarter and Boston guard Bob Cousy earned his second MVP award with a 10-point, 7-assist effort. But the play of the game was provided by Celtics guard Bill Sharman, who connected on a 70-foot, buzzer-beating bomb just before halftime.

January 21, 1958, at St. Louis, East 130, West 118

Philadelphia's Paul Arizin scored 24 points and Boston's Bob Cousy added 20 points and 10 assists to key the East victory. But Bob Pettit put on a show for his hometown fans with a monster 28-point, 26-rebound effort that gave him the distinction of becoming the first member of a losing team to capture MVP honors.

January 23, 1959, at Detroit, West 124, East 108

Co-MVPs Bob Pettit (St. Louis) and Elgin Baylor (Minneapolis) combined for 49 points and 27 rebounds and the West pulled away in the final period for its third All-Star victory. Pettit finished with 25 points and 16 rebounds while Baylor, an NBA rookie, totaled 24 and 11.

WESTERN EXPOSURE: *The Lakers' George Mikan was the star of the 1953 West team.*

Added fellow rookie Lamar Odom of the Los Angeles Clippers, "It was raining in Oakland all weekend, but I think today there was a lot of sunshine in the gym. It was just a great, great atmosphere, and I was happy to be a part of it."

Down Memory Lane

Over the years, the All-Star Game has produced a little of everything: five overtimes, a 70-foot, halftime-buzzer-beating bomb, an 87-point half, a last-second 20-foot game-winner and a player coming out of retirement to claim MVP honors.

370

January 22, 1960, at Philadelphia, East 125, West 115

Rookie Philadelphia center Wilt Chamberlain delighted the hometown fans with a 23-point, 25-rebound MVP effort as the East coasted to its seventh victory in 10 classics. Tom Gola, Chamberlain's teammate at Philadelphia, helped preserve the victory with three third-quarter steals and four straight fourth-quarter baskets.

January 17, 1961, at Syracuse, West 153, East 131

Cincinnati rookie guard Oscar Robertson scored 23 points and handed out an All-Star record 14 assists as the West exploded to a 47–19 first-quarter lead and never looked back. Robertson claimed MVP honors over West teammate Bob Pettit (St. Louis), who set an All-Star record with 29 points. Five players topped 20 points in the game.

January 16, 1962, at St. Louis, West 150, East 130

The West won its second straight All-Star Game, despite a record 42-point effort by the East's Wilt Chamberlain. Hawks forward Bob Pettit claimed his fourth All-Star MVP with 25 points and a record 27 rebounds, but he got plenty of help from Elgin Baylor (32 points), Oscar Robertson (26 points, 13 assists) and Walt Bellamy (23 points, 17 rebounds).

January 16, 1963, at Los Angeles, East 115, West 108

Boston center Bill Russell scored 19 points, pulled down 24 rebounds and outdueled West big man Wilt Chamberlain in the first All-Star Game to be staged on the West Coast. Russell, the game's MVP, got 21-point support from Cincinnati guard Oscar Robertson while St. Louis' Bob Pettit led the West with 25 points.

January 14, 1964, at Boston, East 111, West 107

A contest that was threatened by a potential players' strike was decided by the

HELPING HAND: *Elgin Baylor scored 32 points in the 1962 All-Star Game at St. Louis.*

double-barreled combination of East guard Oscar Robertson (Cincinnati) and center Bill Russell (Boston). Robertson, the game's MVP, scored 26 points, grabbed 14 rebounds and handed out 8 assists. Russell scored 13 points and pulled down 21 rebounds.

January 13, 1965, at St. Louis, East 124, West 123

The East squandered most of a 16-point fourth-quarter lead but held on behind the efforts of two Cincinnati stars. Oscar Robertson scored a game-high 28 points and Jerry Lucas grabbed MVP honors with 25 points and 10 rebounds. Baltimore's Gus Johnson led West scorers with 25 points.

January 11, 1966, at Cincinnati, East 137, West 94

Cincinnati guard Adrian Smith, the least heralded of the talented All-Star contingent, delighted his home fans with a 24-point outburst that keyed the East's easy victory and earned him an MVP trophy. The outcome was never in doubt

as the East raced to a 63–36 halftime advantage and coasted to its 11th All-Star victory. The 43-point winning margin was the biggest in the history of the game.

January 10, 1967, at San Francisco, West 135, East 120

Forward Rick Barry, playing on his home court, connected on 16 of 27 field-goal attempts and scored 38 points to help the West end its four-game All-Star losing streak. Barry's MVP effort got plenty of support from Detroit forward Dave DeBusschere (22 points) and Lakers forward Elgin Baylor (20).

January 23, 1968, at New York, East 144, West 124

Philadelphia guard Hal Greer connected on all eight of his field-goal attempts, scored 21 points and led the East to an easy victory before an All-Star record crowd of 18,422 at Madison Square Garden. Greer, the game's MVP, scored 19 of his points in a third-quarter run that helped the East pull away. East guard John Havlicek (Boston) led all scorers with 26 points.

January 14, 1969, at Baltimore, East 123, West 112

Cincinnati guard Oscar Robertson claimed his third MVP trophy with a 24-point performance that helped the East to its 13th All-Star victory. The East grabbed a 16-point first-quarter advantage but needed a 37-point final period to nail down the triumph. Earl Monroe, playing on his home court, added 21 points for the East.

January 20, 1970, at Philadelphia, East 142, West 135

The West staged a frantic, record-setting 50-point fourth-quarter rally, but it was too little too late to salvage victory in the 20th All-Star Game. New York's Willis Reed earned MVP honors with 21 points and 11 rebounds, but San Diego's Elvin Hayes took game honors with 24 points and 15 boards.

January 12, 1971, at San Diego, West 108, East 107

Young Milwaukee center Lew Alcindor completed a three-point play with 48 seconds remaining to lift the West to an exciting one-point victory. Alcindor finished with 19 points, but Seattle guard Lenny Wilkens claimed MVP honors by sinking 8 of 11 field-goal attempts, scoring 21 points and sparking a late 14–1 surge that made victory possible.

January 18, 1972, at Los Angeles, West 112, East 110

Lakers guard Jerry West, playing on his home court, brought a sudden end to the most exciting game in All-Star history when he sank a running 20-foot jumper as time expired. West, the game's MVP, scored 13 points and was one of seven West players to score in the 10- to 13-point range.

January 23, 1973, at Chicago, East 104, West 84

Boston center Dave Cowens scored 15 points and grabbed 13 rebounds in the East's easy victory at Chicago Stadium. Cowens, the game's MVP, sparked a third-quarter 19–6 run that broke a 57–57 tie. Kansas City-Omaha guard Nate Archibald finished with a game-high 17 points for the West.

January 15, 1974, at Seattle, West 134, East 123

West reserves Bob Lanier (Detroit) and Spencer Haywood (Seattle) combined to make 21 of 32 field-goal attempts, score 47 points and pull down 21 rebounds in a convincing West victory. The West raced to a 25-point first-half lead and was never threatened. Lanier took MVP honors with 24 points and 10 rebounds in 26 minutes.

January 14, 1975, at Phoenix, East 108, West 102

In a game dominated by opposing guards Walt Frazier (Knicks) and Nate Archibald (Kings), the East prevailed for its 16th All-Star victory. Frazier made 10 of 17 field-goal attempts and scored 30 points en route to MVP honors. Archibald sank 10 of 15 shots and led the West with 27 points.

February 3, 1976, at Philadelphia, East 123, West 109

Washington guard Dave Bing scored all of his 16 points after intermission as the East overcame a five-point halftime deficit and won easily. Bing earned MVP honors, but Bob McAdoo (Buffalo) scored 22 points and Dave Cowens (Boston) pulled down 16 rebounds for the East. The game was played in Philadelphia as part of the city's Bicentennial celebration.

February 13, 1977, at Milwaukee, West 125, East 124

Phoenix guard Paul Westphal made a pair of baskets and a key steal in the closing minutes to preserve the West's one-point victory. Westphal finished with 20 points, but game scoring honors were claimed by East stars New York's Bob McAdoo and Philadelphia's Julius Erving, who finished with 30 apiece. Erving became the second player from a losing team to win MVP honors.

February 5, 1978, at Atlanta, East 133, West 125

The East, sparked by hot-shooting Buffalo guard Randy Smith, staged a frantic 41–25 fourth-quarter rally that secured a come-from-behind victory. Smith connected on 30- and 40-foot bombs to end the first and second quarters, hit 11 of 14 shots and scored a game-high 27 points en route to MVP honors.

February 4, 1979, at Detroit, West 134, East 129

The West, in danger of blowing an 80–58 halftime lead, held off a furious East rally to claim victory before a record All-Star crowd of 31,745 at Detroit's Pontiac Silverdome. David Thompson of Denver earned MVP honors with 25 points, but Philadelphia's Julius Erving (29 points) and San Antonio's George Gervin (26) sparked the comeback effort that came up just short.

February 4, 1980, at Landover, East 144, West 136 (OT)

Boston rookie Larry Bird sank the first All-Star 3-point field goal with 1:40 left in overtime, breaking a 136–136 tie and sending the East on to victory. Houston's Moses Malone contributed to the triumph with five overtime points, but East teammate George Gervin (San Antonio) claimed MVP honors with a game-high 34.

February 1, 1981, at Cleveland, East 123, West 120

Boston playmaker Nate Archibald scored nine points, handed out nine assists and short-circuited a West comeback with his excellent late-game ballhandling to claim MVP honors. Seattle guard Paul Westphal (19 points) and Phoenix guard Dennis Johnson (19) led a spirited West comeback from a 113–99 deficit.

January 31, 1982, at East Rutherford, East 120, West 118

Larry Bird scored 12 of his 19 points in the final 6½ minutes to claim MVP honors and Boston teammate Robert Parish scored a team-high 21 as the East won for the third consecutive year. Bird and Parish were a combined 16 of 24 from the field while Seattle's Gus Williams scored a game-high 22 for the West. Magic Johnson added 16 points and 7 assists for the West.

February 13, 1983, at Los Angeles, East 132, West 123

High-flying Philadelphia forward Julius Erving scored a game-high 25 points and the East rolled to its fourth straight All-Star victory. The East needed Erving's

MVP performance to overcome the double-edged heroics from Los Angeles Lakers stars, Earvin "Magic" Johnson (a record 16 assists) and Kareem Abdul-Jabbar (9-of-12 shooting, 20 points).

January 29, 1984, at Denver, East 154, West 145 (OT)

Detroit guard Isiah Thomas scored all 21 of his points after intermission as the East overcame a 14-point halftime deficit for its fifth straight All-Star victory and its 23rd overall in 34 midseason classics. The third overtime classic featured a 34-point explosion by Philadelphia's Julius Erving and a record-setting 22-assist performance by Los Angeles point guard Magic Johnson.

February 10, 1985, at Indianapolis, West 140, East 129

The West snapped its five-game All-Star losing streak as 7–4 Houston center Ralph Sampson claimed MVP honors with 24 points and 10 rebounds. San Antonio's George Gervin chipped in 23 points and Lakers guard Magic Johnson thrilled the record All-Star crowd of 43,146 at the Hoosier Dome with 21 points and 15 assists.

February 9, 1986, at Dallas, East 139, West 132

Detroit point guard Isiah Thomas claimed his second MVP award in three years with an outstanding 30-point, 10-assist, 5-steal performance. The West team held a two-point lead after three quarters, but Thomas and Boston's Larry Bird, a 23-point scorer, were too much down the stretch.

February 8, 1987, at Seattle, West 154, East 149 (OT)

Dallas guard Rolando Blackman successful attempted a pair of free throws after regulation time had expired to force overtime and the West went on to record its second All-Star victory in three years. Seattle forward Tom Chambers, a late addition to the West squad, scored 34 points to claim MVP honors while Blackman added 29.

SAMPSON STARS: *1985 MVP Ralph Sampson (50) challenges Julius Erving above the net.*

GLASSY EYED: *Kareem Abdul-Jabbar puts up a shot in the 1988 All-Star Game as he becomes the event's all-time leading scorer.*

February 7, 1988, at Chicago, East 138, West 133

Bulls guard Michael Jordan gave Chicago fans a highlight-film performance, scoring 16 of his game-high 40 points in the final 5:51 to secure a victory for the East. Jordan, who also grabbed 8 rebounds and made 4 steals, stole the spotlight from the West's Kareem Abdul-Jabbar (Los Angeles Lakers), who registered 10 points and became the highest scoring player in All-Star Game history.

February 12, 1989, at Houston, West 143, East 134

The West's victory in the 39th All-Star classic was delivered by Utah's "Mailman," Karl Malone, who scored 28 points and pulled down 9 rebounds. But Malone got plenty of help from elsewhere. Seattle's Dale Ellis provided 27 points and Jazz teammate John Stockton handed out 17 assists. The game was played before a record All-Star crowd of 44,735 at Houston's Astrodome.

February 11, 1990, at Miami, East 130, West 113

The East squad shot 54.3 percent and had seven scorers reach double figures as it posted an easy victory in the 40th All-Star Game. But Los Angeles Lakers point guard Magic Johnson, who scored 22 points and grabbed 6 rebounds, became only the third player from a losing team to capture the MVP award. The triumph lifted the East's overall All-Star advantage to 26–14.

February 10, 1991, at Charlotte, East 116, West 114

The 41st classic was the Michael and Charles show. The Bulls' Michael Jordan scored 26 points, but Philadelphia's Charles Barkley earned the MVP award with a crowd-pleasing 17-point, 22-rebound performance. Five players scored in double figures for a balanced West team, but it fell just short in its attempt to come back from a nine-point halftime deficit.

February 9, 1992, at Orlando, West 153, East 113

Magic Johnson came out of retirement to put on a dazzling performance in the West's easy victory. Johnson connected on 9 of 12 field-goal attempts, made all three of his 3-point shots, scored 25 points, handed out 9 assists and grabbed 5 rebounds to earn the MVP award. Portland guard Clyde Drexler added 22 points for the West.

MOST VALUABLE: *Magic Johnson scores two of his 22 points in his 1990 MVP performance.*

DYNAMIC DUO: *Seattle teammates Gary Payton (left) and Shawn Kemp have a serious discussion during the 1997 All Star Game in Cleveland.*

February 21, 1993, at Salt Lake City, West 135, East 132 (OT)

The West captured the NBA's fifth All-Star overtime game behind the 1–2 Utah punch of forward Karl Malone and point guard John Stockton. Malone scored 28 points and pulled down 10 rebounds while Stockton distributed 15 assists. Malone and Stockton became only the second duo to share All-Star MVP honors.

February 13, 1994, at Minneapolis, East 127, West 118

The East rebounded from consecutive losses behind the 29-point effort of Chicago's Scottie Pippen. Pippen, who punctuated his MVP performance with five 3-point baskets and 11 rebounds, received 20-point support from East teammates Patrick Ewing (Knicks) and Mark Price (Cavaliers).

February 12, 1995, at Phoenix, West 139, East 112

Mitch Richmond, Sacramento guard and the game's MVP, came off the bench to hit 10 of 13 shots, score a game-high 23 points and lead the West to an easy victory. Utah's Karl Malone scored 13 of his 15 points in a 41-point second-quarter explosion that gave the West a lead it never relinquished.

February 11, 1996, at San Antonio, East 129, West 118

Chicago's Michael Jordan scored 10 of his 20 points in a third-quarter explosion that carried the East to a double-digit lead and set the tone for an easy victory. Jordan, who claimed his second MVP award in his first All-Star appearance since 1993, got 25-point, 10-rebound support from Orlando center Shaquille O'Neal.

February 9, 1997, at Cleveland, East 132, West 120

Miami's Glen Rice scored a record 20 points in one quarter and Chicago's Michael Jordan recorded the first triple double (14 points, 11 rebounds, 11 assists) in All-Star Game history as the East overcame a 23-point deficit before cruising to victory. Rice, who led all scorers with 26 points and won MVP honors, hit four consecutive three-pointers as the East went on a 21–3 run to steal the game in the third quarter. The East was also aided by 19 points and 12 rebounds from Milwaukee's Vin Baker. Golden State's Latrell Sprewell led the West in scoring with 19 points.

February 8, 1998, at New York, East 135, West 114

The Game at Madison Square Garden was supposed to see Michael Jordan pass the symbolic torch of NBA supremacy to Kobe Bryant. Unfortunately someone forgot to tell Michael who scored 23 points, dished out 8 assists, had 6 rebounds and 3 steals in 32 minutes of a dominant East display. He took his third All-Star MVP award and assured rookie coach Larry Bird got off to a winning start. Bryant's performance was more than respectable (18 points, 6 rebounds, 1 assist, 2 steals) as he led the West, but there was no doubt who was still the greatest All-Star of them all.

February. 14, 1999 at Philadelphia

This year's game was a casualty of the lockout by NBA owners. Instead of being ready for their midseason break, players were still working to get the kinks out after not starting the season until February 5, 1999. NBA commissioner David Stern announced that the 2002 All-Star Game would be held in Philadelphia to compensate for the one lost in 1999.

February. 13, 2000 at Oakland, West 137, East 126

Co-MVPs Shaquille O'Neal and Tim Duncan helped the West lead for all but three minutes of the game. The East used a 15–4 run to pull into a 91–91 tie with 2:08 left in the third quarter. The score was still tied at 97–97 before a layup by Chris Webber gave the West a 99–97 edge as the third-quarter buzzer sounded.

The West took control of the game with an 8–0 run early in the fourth quarter. Michael Finley made a 3-pointer and a layup, while Gary Payton added three free throws after being fouled on a 3-point attempt to push the West's lead to 109–99. The closest the East got after that was eight points. Behind O'Neal, Duncan, David Robinson and Kevin Garnett, the West outscored the East in the paint, 86–54.

"It's a battle of size versus quickness, and just on this given day, size won," said Duncan, who finished with 24 points and 14 rebounds.

O'Neal added 22 points, nine rebounds and three blocked shots.

TWO INTO ONE: *Tim Duncan (left) and Shaquille O'Neal shared the 2000 All-Star Game MVP award.*

THE NBA DRAFT

Philosophically, theoretically and fundamentally, nothing about the NBA Draft has changed over the last 50 years. Cosmetically, physically and socially, almost everything about the Draft is different.

The search for parity

In its purest form, the NBA Draft remains what it always has been: an opportunity for weaker teams to get the first shots at the best available college and amateur players in the league's perennial quest for parity. Since July 1, 1947—the humble beginning of the annual selection process—teams have taken turns picking players in inverse order of their previous season's position in the final standings, theoretically closing the gap between top and bottom.

In its most flamboyant form, the draft has turned into a media monster, a prime-time extravaganza that has graduated from the smoky back rooms of anonymity to the noisy fan-filled arenas of today's NBA. Television cameras capture the pomp and circumstance of a frill-covered proceeding that includes center-stage introductions, draft-pick interviews and the intrigue of watching team officials try to change the direction of long-suffering franchises.

Simply stated, the NBA Draft is a case study in short-term evolution. It's a phenomenon, a fascinating example of how an embryonic process can get from there to here.

Calling All Czars

The early NBA was almost an after-thought for the sports-conscious American. Baseball, college football and boxing captured the daily headlines and even professional football, still groping for recognition and respect, received more attention. Not surprisingly, the annual NBA Draft was nothing more than an agate listing on the back pages of NBA-city newspapers.

For obvious reasons, the league conducted its draft in quiet anonymity, making a conference call from its New York headquarters to team representatives who made their selections in the comfort of their own offices. For most teams, the process was a guessing game. Few franchises had the money for full-time scouts, some didn't even have assistant coaches and talent often was evaluated by word-of-mouth reports and newspaper accounts of college games.

Typical of the period was Boston Coach Red Auerbach's discovery and acquisition of center Bill Russell, who would eventually lead the Celtics to 11 NBA championships in 13 seasons in a brilliant Hall of Fame career. Auerbach's fascination with the 6-10 University of San Francisco star was born from his need for a rebounder and defender to center his fast-paced attack. He had never seen him play.

"I had to have somebody who could get me the ball," Auerbach said. "Bill

DONE DEAL *Paul Arizin (left) signs with the Warriors after leaving Villanova in 1950.*

(Reinhart) said Russell was the greatest defensive player and greatest rebounder he'd ever seen."

Reinhart, Auerbach's former George Washington University coach, was right. And Auerbach trusted his judgement so much that he swung a 1956 draft-day

FIND THE HANDLE: *Lefthander Guy Rodgers was drafted by Philadelphia out of Temple in 1958.*

TWIN TOWERS: *Centers Akeem Olajuwon (left) and Ralph Sampson were coin-flip first selections by Houston in 1984 and '83 respectively.*

trade with St. Louis, giving up Ed Macauley and Cliff Hagan, two future Hall of Famers.

Auerbach also demonstrated the value of another early-draft rule in 1956, when he grabbed Holy Cross forward Tom Heinsohn, another important piece to his championship puzzle, with a territorial pick. The rule permitted any team, in an attempt to boost box-office appeal, to precede the regular draft by selecting a player from a college in its immediate geographic area. Any team using a territorial pick would forfeit its first-round selection.

Before the territorial rule was dropped after the 1965 draft, such all-time stars as Vern Mikkelsen (Lakers), Macauley (Bombers), Heinsohn (Celtics), Paul Arizin (Warriors), Guy Rodgers

(Warriors), Oscar Robertson (Royals) and Jerry Lucas (Royals) had entered the league as territorial picks. Wilt Chamberlain became territorial property of the Warriors in 1959, even though he played his college ball at Kansas University. The Warriors were granted permission to sign him because he was born and raised in Philadelphia.

With the 1965 demise of the territorial rule, the NBA began tinkering with other methods of insuring parity—and integrity.

Heads or Tails

As scouting procedures and communication became more sophisticated and teams became more aware of the impact the draft could have on their roster, the process began undergoing changes—and the movement toward national recognition

inched forward.

From 1966 through 1984, the league determined its first and second overall picks through an annual coin flip, a process designed to protect the system from teams intentionally losing end-of-season games to enhance their draft position. The teams with the worst records from the Eastern and Western conferences "flipped" for No. 1 status, an important consideration in years when one player stood out as a franchise-turning prospect.

Such was the case in 1969, when the one-year-old Milwaukee Bucks won the flip over the Phoenix Suns and drafted UCLA center Lew Alcindor, who led them to a 1971 championship. In 1979, the Los Angeles Lakers beat out Chicago for the chance to draft Magic Johnson and in 1984, the Houston Rockets grabbed Hakeem Olajuwon, leaving Portland with second choice Sam Bowie. The third pick of that 1984 Draft belong to Chicago, and the Bulls took Michael Jordan.

The NBA further distanced its teams from the possibility of late-season maneuvering with the 1985 institution of a draft lottery, which threw the names of its seven non-playoff qualifiers into a hat and drew lots for first-round positioning. The New York Knicks won the first lottery and they drafted Georgetown center Patrick Ewing.

The league refined its lottery process in 1990, heavily weighting its drawing in favor of the teams with the worst records.

With 11 teams competing in the drawing because of expansion, the weakest team was given 11 lots, the second-worst team received 10 lots, and so on. In 1994, the lottery system was weighted even more in favor of the weaker teams.

From No-Show to Showtime

But the NBA Draft's most dramatic advance has been in packaging, mirroring the global explosion of the game itself. From the back-room, conference-call atmosphere of the early years, the draft has become a media-hyped, well-choreographed show that entertains thousands of fans in huge arenas as well as international television audiences.

With the proliferation of the college game, the scouting of star players, postseason all-star tournaments, pre-draft camps, cable television and other sources of information, rabid fans and "draftniks" are almost as knowledgeable about today's players and team needs as the teams themselves. But still the draft retains a mystique and charm, thanks to the unpredictability of a process that encourages draft-day trades and maneuvering that is guaranteed to distort everybody's best-laid plans.

That mystique was reflected by the league's 1992 decision to move the draft out of New York and turn it into a veritable traveling show. Now it hops from city to city every June, attracting huge crowds and more and more publicity. A record throng of 21,268 attended the 1995 show at Toronto's SkyDome—the first draft held outside the United States.

The modern selection process is like a major party, complete with cheers and jeers from fans and the presence of high draft picks who revel in the opportunity to be showcased in front of a huge audience. Teams that make bad judgements or come unprepared risk international humiliation.

Two other important developments have helped to shape the draft. A 1971 court decision supported Spencer Haywood's right to become eligible for the draft before his college eligibility had expired, opening the door for future players to leave school early. Now underclassmen can declare themselves available for the draft simply by sending written notice to the league office. Such stars as Magic Johnson, Isiah Thomas, Michael Jordan, James Worthy, Dominique Wilkins, Hakeem Olajuwon and Karl Malone have all successfully made the jump, but many others have tried and failed. A record 10 underclassmen were chosen in the first round of the 1995 draft.

One of the most obvious differences between then and now is the length of the draft. Early drafts had no limit and the 1960 process extended a record 21 rounds. But in 1974, the league restricted its draft to 10 rounds and it was subsequently reduced to seven in 1985, to three in 1988, and to the present two rounds in 1989.

DOUBLE TEAM: *Akeem Olajuwon (left) and Ralph Sampson led Houston to the 1986 Finals.*

On the Flip of a Coin

The NBA began using a coin flip in 1966 to determine its first and second draft positions. The following chart illustrates the annual winners and losers:

Year	Winner	Selection	Loser	Selection
1966	Knicks	Cazzie Russell	Pistons	Dave Bing
1967	Pistons	Jimmy Walker	Bullets	Earl Monroe
1968	Rockets	Elvin Hayes	Bullets	Wes Unseld
1969	Bucks	Lew Alcindor	Suns	Neal Walk
1970	Pistons	Bob Lanier	Rockets	Rudy Tomjanovich
1971	Cavaliers	Austin Carr	Trail Blazers	Sidney Wicks
1972	Trail Blazers	LaRue Martin	Braves	Bob McAdoo
1973	76ers	Doug Collins	Cavaliers	Jim Brewer
1974	Trail Blazers	Bill Walton	76ers	Marvin Barnes
1975	Hawks	David Thompson	Lakers	Dave Meyers
1976	Rockets	John Lucas	Bulls	Scott May
1977	Bucks	Kent Benson	Kings	Otis Birdsong
1978	Trail Blazers	Mychal Thompson	Kings	Phil Ford
1979	Lakers	Magic Johnson	Bulls	David Greenwood
1980	Warriors	J.B. Carroll	Jazz	Darrell Griffith
1981	Mavericks	Mark Aguirre	Pistons	Isiah Thomas
1982	Lakers	James Worthy	Clippers	Terry Cummings
1983	Rockets	Ralph Sampson	Pacers	Steve Stipanovich
1984	Rockets	Hakeem Olajuwon	Trail Blazers	Sam Bowie

The lottery

When Magic Johnson and Kareem Abdul-Jabbar were leading the Los Angeles Lakers to four NBA titles in the 1980s under the watchful eye of coach Pat Riley, their act was known as "Showtime."

Now that description could apply to the NBA's draft lottery as well. The league has taken what essentially could be a press release and turned into high drama. Conducted at the NBA Entertainment headquarters in Seacaucus, New Jersey, just outside New York City, it's basketball's version of an off (way off) Broadway production.

The lottery was created in 1984, the year before Georgetown's Patrick Ewing was scheduled to graduate from college. In order to prevent teams from losing games in order to get a shot at Ewing in 1985, the board of governors instituted a lottery to determine the draft order for all the teams that failed to make the playoffs. (Prior to 1985, the teams with the worst record in each conference flipped a coin to determine which team would draft first.)

In 1986, the rules were changed so that the lottery determined the top three spots in the draft, with the remainder of the teams drafting in inverse order of their records. In other words, under the new system, the team with the worst record in the league can draft no worse than fourth.

In 1989, the league adopted a weighted system in an attempt to give the worst teams a better chance at winning the lottery. Then in 1993, after Orlando won

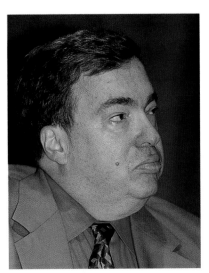

NO BULL: *Chicago Bulls General Manager Jerry Krause builty a basketball dynasty.*

its second straight lottery with a 41-41 record that was almost good enough to make the playoffs, the league further increased the chances of the worst teams by drawing combinations of numbers for the lottery. Prior to the drawing, combinations are assigned to the lottery teams based on their order of finish in the regular season.

This increased the chances of the worst team in the league obtaining the first pick from 16.7 percent to 25 percent.

With nervous team officials clutching good-luck charms while sitting before the television cameras during halftime of an NBA playoff game, the drawing is conducted off camera in front of another set of good-luck-charm-armed team officials and representatives of the Ernst & Young accounting firm, none of whom are allowed to leave the room until the results have been announced on national television.

After the drawing, cards with team logos on them are placed in envelops marked 1 through 13. Those are brought on stage, where commissioner David Stern or deputy commissioner Russ Granik opens them in reverse order— from 13 to 1. Neither the league officials nor the team officials has any idea what will happen ahead of time—at least not until a team doesn't appear in the expected order. Even then, no one is sure of the order of the top three teams or which one will win the No. 1 pick.

That assured the sort of genuine emotion shown by Philadelphia president Pat Croce, who jumped up and delivered high fives upon winning the lottery in 1996, and by Chicago vice president Jerry Krause, who opted for a more subdued fist-pumping after winning in 1999.

The weighted system did not help the Vancouver Grizzlies or Los Angeles Clippers that year. They both had worse records than the Bulls. Naturally, that prompted some griping.

Still, the league holds fast to the system, and most observers don't expect that to change in spite of the fact that with so much tinkering the drawing is almost back to the original idea of the worst team picking first.

"I doubt if they'll ever go back to that," said Cleveland Cavaliers general manager Jim Paxson.

The camps

For more than 20 years, pre-draft camps have helped NBA executives familiarize themselves with prospective draft choices.

According to Cleveland Cavaliers president Wayne Embry, the pre-draft circuit used to be almost a month-long junket from the East Coast of the United States all the way to Hawaii for the Aloha Classic.

"Back in those days it was a treat to go to Hawaii, so all the best players were invited there and we followed them," Embry said.

Actually, the executives started out in Portsmouth, Virginia, where players not quite in the top echelon were invited to perform before general managers and scouts. From there, there was a one-day stop in Las Vegas for the Pizza Hut Classic all-star game and then it was on to Hawaii.

Eventually, the Las Vegas game was dropped altogether. The Aloha Classic moved first to Orlando and then to Phoenix, where it has been renamed the Desert Classic.

In addition, the NBA now runs its own pre-draft camp in Chicago in early June, when everyone who's anyone in the NBA (and who isn't involved in the NBA Finals) gathers chiefly to evaluate talent but also to network and gossip. The camp is run by Marty Blake, a colorful character and former general manager who discovered Scottie Pippen in just this kind of setting.

In these days of satellite dishes and videotapes, one might question why scouts still need to see potential players so often. But, as Embry explained, "It's good to see them out of their college systems. Sometimes playing within a different system, you can get fooled."

It has become commonplace for the best players in the country _ those projected as certain first-round draft choices _ to skip all these workouts entirely. Agents and advisors have convinced them that they can only hurt their draft position by playing _ or that they can hurt themselves, period. Some of these players will work out for the scouts by themselves in Chicago, or teams will bring in potential draft choices to

work them out and interview them

With all this, how can a team make a mistake?

"That's a good question," Embry said, laughing. "Sometimes you think a player will get better, but you don't know how long it will take. Sometimes they get the money and retire after two years—but they don't tell you. Sometimes they get hurt. But sometimes they make us look good."

The new rules

When the NBA and the NBA Players Association signed their new collective bargaining agreement in 1999, it meant there were some changes in store for first-round draft choices.

Wage scales were nothing new. For years, players' contracts had been determined by their draft position. But, originally, the scales were for three years. The new collective bargaining agreement gave teams an option for a fourth year. If a team wants to exercise the option, it must do so before October 31 following the player's second season.

The change was put into effect because teams were concerned that after they worked with a young player for three seasons the player could leave for another team just as he was beginning to come into his own.

Here are two other draft rules according to the current collective bargaining agreement:

Section 5: Application to players with remaining intercollegiate eligibility.

(a) A person residing within the U.S. whose high school class has graduated shall become eligible to be selected in an NBA draft if he renounces his intercollegiate basketball eligibility by written notice to the NBA at least 45 days prior to such draft. If such person is selected in such draft by a team, the following rules apply:

(i) Subject to Section 5(b) below, if the player does not thereafter play intercollegiate basketball, then the team that drafted him shall, during the period from the date of such draft to the date of the draft in which the player would, absent renunciation of intercollegiate eligibility, first have been eligible to be selected, be the only team with which the player may negotiate or sign a player contract,

provided that such team makes a required tender to the player each year. For purposes hereof, the draft in which such player would, absent renunciation of such intercollegiate eligibility, first have been eligible to be selected, will be deemed the "subsequent draft" as to the player, and the rules applicable to a player who has been drafted in a subsequent draft will apply. If the player, having been selected in a draft for which he was eligible by virtue of renunciation of intercollegiate eligibility, has not signed a player contract with the team that drafted him in such draft following a required tender by that team and is now drafted in the subsequent draft (as defined in the previous sentence) he shall become a rookie free agent.

(ii) If the player does thereafter play intercollegiate basketball, then the team that drafted him shall retain the exclusive NBA rights to negotiate with and sign the player for the period ending one year from the date of draft in which the player would, absent renunciation of intercollegiate eligibility, first have been eligible to be selected, provided that such team makes a required tender to the player each year. For purposes hereof, the draft in which such player would, absent renunciation of intercollegiate eligibility, first have been eligible to be selected, will be deemed the "initial draft" to that player. The next NBA draft shall be deemed the "subsequent draft" as to that player, and the rules applicable to a player who has been drafted in a subsequent draft will apply.

(b) A person residing within the U.S. whose high school class has graduated, who is not eligible to be selected in an NBA draft, and who signs a player contract with a professional basketball team not in the NBA, shall thereupon become eligible to be selected in the next NBA draft, and if so selected, shall be treated as though he were a player referred to in Section 4 above. For purposes of this subsection, a "professional basketball team" shall mean any team in any country that pays money or compensation of any kind (in excess of a stipend for living expenses) to a basketball player for rendering such services to such team.

Odds and Ends – Strange Draft Facts

● The ABA signing war claimed a major NBA casualty in 1975, when the Atlanta Hawks selected North Carolina State's David Thompson and Morgan State's Marvin Webster with the first and third overall picks of the draft—and lost both. Thompson and Webster signed with the ABA's Denver Nuggets.

● Prior to 1967, no NBA team had ever signed a player before the draft. But both Detroit and Baltimore, which owned the first and second overall picks, entered the selection process with contracts already signed, sealed and delivered. The Pistons announced the signing of Providence's Jimmy Walker the day before the draft and the Bullets said they had signed Winston-Salem State star Earl Monroe when they made their choice.

● To say that the 1979 draft was conducted in a state of confusion is an understatement. Only eight of the 22 franchises selected in their fixed positions and 14 first-round choices were peddled back and forth 21 times. Six teams did not make first-round picks.

● The shocker of the 1987 draft was Washington's first-round pick (12th overall) of 5-foot-3 point guard Tyrone (Muggsy) Bogues, who went on to a nice career with the Charlotte Hornets.

● The NBA conducted 19 coin flips to determine the No. 1 and No. 2 draft positions, and eight times the coin flip loser landed the league's Rookie of the Year. Lew Alcindor (1969) and Ralph Sampson (1983) were No. 1s who attained top-rookie status. But award winners Dave Bing (Detroit, 1966), Earl Monroe (Baltimore, 1967), Wes Unseld (Baltimore, 1968), Sidney Wicks (Portland, 1971), Bob McAdoo (Buffalo, 1972), Phil Ford (Kansas City, 1978), Darrell Griffith (Utah, 1980) and Terry Cummings (San Diego, 1982) were all No. 2s. Bing, Monroe and Unseld also are Hall of Famers.

● More and more underclassmen have made themselves eligible for the draft, and a record 17 were selected in the 1996 draft, including Allen Iverson, the No. 1 pick overall. Other underclassmen selected included Marcus Camby, Shareef Abdur-Rahim, Stephon Marbury and Ray Allen. Conversely, in the 1999 draft, not a single underclassmen was taken in the second round.

● Duke University became the first college to have four players taken in the first round of an NBA draft. In 1999, Elton Brand was taken by Chicago, Trajan Langdon was taken by Cleveland, Corey Maggette was taken by Seattle and traded to Orlando and William Avery was taken by Minnesota.

FOUR ON THE FLOOR: *Trajan Langdon was one of four Duke University players to be first round picks in the 1999 NBA Draft; the Cavs selected him.*

Slipping Through the Net

Many players have enjoyed (or are enjoying) highly successful careers despite not being drafted in the first round. Here are some examples:

Player	Year Drafted	Round	Overall Pick	Team
Jack Twyman	1955	2nd	10th	Royals
K.C. Jones	1956	2nd		Celtics
Hal Greer	1958	2nd	14th	Nationals
Doug Moe	1961	2nd	22nd	Packers
Chet Walker	1962	2nd	14th	Nationals
Willis Reed	1964	2nd	10th	Knicks
Paul Silas	1964	2nd	12th	Hawks
Ron Boone	1968	11th	147th	Suns
Nate Archibald	1970	2nd	19th	Royals
Dan Issel	1970	8th	122nd	Pistons
Calvin Murphy	1970	2nd	18th	Rockets
George Gervin	1974	3rd	40th	Suns
World B. Free	1975	2nd	23rd	76ers
Alex English	1976	2nd	23rd	Bucks
Dennis Johnson	1976	2nd	29th	SuperSonics
Maurice Cheeks	1978	2nd	36th	76ers
Bill Laimbeer	1979	3rd	65th	Cavaliers
Danny Ainge	1981	2nd	31st	Celtics
Eddie Johnson	1981	2nd	29th	Kings
Spud Webb	1985	4th	87th	Pistons
Jeff Hornacek	1986	2nd	46th	Suns
Dennis Rodman	1986	2nd	27th	Pistons
Cedric Ceballos	1990	2nd	48th	Suns
Nick Van Exel	1993	2nd	37th	Lakers

Section 6. Application to foreign players.

(a) For purposes to this section, a "foreign player" shall mean any person residing outside the U.S. who participates in the game of basketball as an amateur or as a professional.

(b) A foreign player is eligible to be selected in an NBA draft held during the calendar year in which such player has his 22nd birthday. Any foreign player who is older than 22 and who has not selected in the NBA draft held during the calendar year of his 22nd birthday is a rookie free agent.

(c) Notwithstanding subsection (b) above, a foreign player who is at least 18 years old and who has not exercised intercollegiate basketball eligibility in the U.S. shall become eligible to be selected in an NBA draft held prior to the calendar year in which he has his 22nd birthday if he expresses his desire to become eligible to be selected in the next NBA draft by

written notice to the NBA at least 45 days prior to such draft.

(d) A foreign player who exercises intercollegiate basketball eligibility in the U.S. during the season prior to an NBA draft shall be subject to the rules regarding completion or renunciation of collegiate eligibility, as set forth in Section 5 above.

Draft guru

Chris Monter's not too sure about that "draftnik" label.

"I don't think I've ever been called that," he said. "I prefer draft analyst. Some people say 'draft expert,' but I think that makes it sound like you should know everything."

Monter knows plenty, which is why he's one of the more thorough and respected men in the business of predicting the NBA draft.

His interest in sports goes back to his childhood in Alliance, Ohio.

"I was better at knowing the game than playing the game," he admits.

He was one of those kids who would diagram plays on the covers of his notebooks. Long before fantasy leagues became all the rage, he and a friend would draft teams and then argue over who had a better lineup. When he was 16, his family moved to Lakeville, Minnesota, and his love of sports moved with him. In fact, one of the reasons he went to Mankato State University was because it was where the National Football League's Minnesota Vikings trained, and he thought he could make some good contacts.

Basketball was his real love, though, and his goal was to become an NBA scout, despite the fact that most scouts are former coaches or players or relatives of former coaches and players. He sent his resume to every team, and he was hired by the Detroit Pistons ... in sales.

Once in Detroit, he got to know the player personnel people, who advised him he might want to get his masters in sports administration. He decided on Western Illinois, but he kept busy doing freelance writing work. One of his assignments was to write about former University of Minnesota star Willie Burton, who was attending the pre-draft camps in anticipation of the 1989 draft.

When Burton headed for the camp in Orlando (which has since moved to Phoenix), Monter thought he'd have a chance to meet "draftnik" Don Leaventhal. Much to Monter's surprise, Leaventhal told him he didn't attend the pre-draft camps before making his predictions.

Once he got to talking to some of the scouts at the camps, Monter saw an opening.

He started his draft newsletter in 1990 with about 40 subscribers. Ten years later, he has 1,200 subscribers and a website: www.monterdraftnews.com.

Patching Up Those First-Round Cracks

The young man sits nervously, watching the show unfold amid the cheers and jeers of thousands of fans in one of 29 NBA arenas. One name is called, then another and another. Each announcement sends a cold shiver down his spine as he waits. Finally, his name is called. He makes the triumphant strut to center stage to be greeted by NBA Commissioner David

Stern. At that moment, a lifetime's dream is fulfilled. This is followed by interviews, pats on the back, questions and, finally, the inevitable self doubts as the young man realizes the difficult tasks that face him as a first-round draft pick.

That scenario unfolds 29 times every year on a special June day. Television cameras and reporters deliver the moment to viewers and readers worldwide. By the time he steps on that stage, the young man has been tested, analyzed, questioned, prodded and pressured for months by teams that cannot afford a first-round mistake.

It's getting harder and harder for that to happen. Team officials are armed with dossiers and film on hundreds of college players they have spent many hours and thousands of dollars evaluating for months, if not years. They have gleaned additional information from postseason all-star tournaments, pre-draft camps and interviews that give them a strong feel for personality and attitude, as well as players' desire to perform in their city.

Today's sophisticated, computerized, high-tech scouting methods are light years removed from the word-of-mouth, one-quick-look, take-a-chance draft techniques of yesteryear. But there were fewer rosters to stock in the early NBA and the elite talents were always easy to spot, even if teams were not blessed with large scouting staffs.

Still, in any era, there are players who manage to slip through the first-round cracks. Sometimes the key to success can be found in the second or third rounds—usually the blue-collar players who make up for talent deficiencies with hard work and dedication.

The Waiting Game

Those who believe good things come to those who wait can find two solid examples in the NBA Draft. Master Celtics architect Red Auerbach was roundly criticized in 1978, when he used Boston's first-round pick (sixth overall) on Indiana State forward Larry Bird, a junior-eligible selection who already had announced he would stay in school for his senior year. The Celtics, who were coming off a 32–50 season and needed immediate help, would have to struggle through another campaign without any. But Auerbach and the Celtics persevered during a 29–53 1978–79 season. And when Bird arrived, Auerbach came away looking like a genius. Bird led Boston to a 61–21 first-year record, eight Atlantic Division titles in his first nine seasons and three NBA championships in the 1980s.

The San Antonio Spurs took a similar gamble in 1987 when they selected 7–1 Navy center David Robinson with the first overall pick—even though Robinson would have to fulfill two years of military duty before he could play. The Spurs suffered through 31–51 and 21–61 seasons while waiting for Robinson, who quickly turned them into Midwest Division champions. With Robinson, the 1995 league MVP, in the post, San Antonio won division titles in three of his first six seasons and posted 62-, 56-, 55- and 55-victory records.

How important would Lew Alcindor have been to the health and well-being of the ABA? Perhaps the answer can be found in the NBA Draft.

The NBA was so worried the ABA would pick off the biggest player plum in many years that it conducted the first two rounds of its 1969 selection process (29 picks) over the telephone a month ahead of its final 18 rounds. That allowed the Milwaukee Bucks time to pursue Alcindor (later Kareem Abdul-Jabbar) while other

WAITING GAME: *Boston's Larry Bird was selected sixth in the 1978 NBA Draft, but did not play until a year later.*

CANDY MAN: *Michael Olowokandi of the Clippers was the first player taken in 1998.*

NBA teams raced to sign the rest of the year's best players. The Bucks, of course, signed Alcindor, ruining the ABA's chance for a major off-court victory.

The expansion Orlando Magic got rich quick and exposed a major flaw in the draft lottery system in 1992 and '93 when they walked away with consecutive No. 1 overall picks that produced center Shaquille O'Neal and swingman Anfernee Hardaway.

There was nothing strange about the Magic's 1991–92 season, which produced a 21–61 third-year record and seventh place in the Atlantic Division. That losing record was a winning formula in the draft lottery, which gave the Magic the first overall pick and franchise center O'Neal.

With O'Neal in 1992–93, the Magic improved to 41–41, and just missed qualifying for the playoffs. That earned them a 1-in-66 shot at another No. 1 pick in the weighted lottery—and they won again.

The embarrassed NBA re-weighted its lottery system, making it very unlikely—but not impossible—that such a situation will ever occur again.

By 1998, the extent to which the NBA had become "internationalized" was illustrated by the fact that two foreign players were selected in the first nine picks. Michael Olowokandi, born in

It's a Lottery

The NBA began its draft lottery system in 1985, with seven non-playoff qualifiers gaining first-round position through a lottery system. The following chart traces the history of the lottery with the order of teams selecting and their first picks:

Year	Team	Player	Year	Team	Player	Year	Team	Player
1985	New York	Patrick Ewing	1992	Orlando	Shaquille O'Neal	1997	San Antonio	Tim Duncan
	Indiana	Wayman Tisdale		Charlotte	Alonzo Mourning		Philadelphia	Keith Van Horn
	L.A. Clippers	Benoit Benjamin		Minnesota	Christian Laettner		Boston	Chauncey Billups
	Seattle	Xavier McDaniel		Dallas	Jimmy Jackson		Vancouver	Antonio Daniels
	Atlanta	Jon Koncak		Denver	LaPhonso Ellis		Denver	Tony Battie
	Sacramento	Joe Kleine		Washington	Tom Gugliotta		Boston	Ron Mercer
	Golden State	Chris Mullin		Sacramento	Walt Williams		New Jersey	Tim Thomas
				Milwaukee	Todd Day		Golden State	Adonal Foyle
1986	Cleveland	Brad Daugherty		Philadelphia	Clarence		Toronto	Tracy McGrady
	Boston	Len Bias			Weatherspoon		Milwaukee	Danny Fortson
	Golden State	Chris Washburn		Atlanta	Adam Keefe		Sacramento	Olivier Saint-Jean
	Indiana	Chuck Person		Houston	Robert Horry		Indiana	Austin Croshere
	New York	Kenny Walker					Cleveland	Derek Anderson
	Phoenix	William Bedford	1993	Orlando	Chris Webber			
	Dallas	Roy Tarpley		Philadelphia	Shawn Bradley	1998	L.A. Clippers	Michael
				Golden State	Anfernee Hardaway			Olowokandi
1987	San Antonio	David Robinson		Dallas	Jamal Mashburn		Vancouver	Mike Bibby
	Phoenix	Armon Gilliam		Minnesota	J.R. Rider		Denver	Raef LaFrentz
	New Jersey	Dennis Hopson		Washington	Calbert Cheaney		Toronto	Antawn Jamison
	L.A. Clippers	Reggie Williams		Sacramento	Bobby Hurley		Golden State	Vince Carter
	Seattle	Scottie Pippen		Milwaukee	Vin Baker		Dallas	Robert Traylor
	Sacramento	Kenny Smith		Denver	Rodney Rogers		Sacramento	Jason Williams
	Cleveland	Kevin Johnson		Detroit	Lindsey Hunter		Philadelphia	Larry Hughes
				Detroit	Allan Houston		Milwaukee	Dirk Nowitzki
1988	L.A. Clippers	Danny Manning					Boston	Paul Pierce
	Indiana	Rik Smits	1994	Milwaukee	Glenn Robinson		Detroit	Bonzi Wells
	Philadelphia	Charles Smith		Dallas	Jason Kidd		Orlando	Mike Doleac
	New Jersey	Chris Morris		Detroit	Grant Hill		Orlando	Keon Clark
	Golden State	Mitch Richmond		Minnesota	Donyell Marshall			
	L.A. Clippers	Hersey Hawkins		Washington	Juwan Howard	1999	Chicago	Elton Brand
	Phoenix	Tim Perry		Philadelphia	Sharone Wright		Vancouver	Steve Francis
				L.A. Clippers	Lamond Murray		Charlotte	Baron Davis
1989	Sacramento	Pervis Ellison		Sacramento	Brian Grant		L.A. Clippers	Lamar Odom
	L.A. Clippers	Danny Ferry		Boston	Eric Montross		Toronto	Jonathan Bender
	San Antonio	Sean Elliott		L.A. Lakers	Eddie Jones		Minnesota	Wally Szczerbiak
	Miami	Glen Rice		Seattle	Carlos Rogers		Washington	Richard Hamilton
	Charlotte	J.R. Reid					Cleveland	Andre Miller
	Chicago	Stacey King	1995	Golden State	Joe Smith		Phoenix	Shawn Marion
	Indiana	George McCloud		L.A. Clippers	Antonio McDyess		Atlanta	Jason Terry
	Dallas	Randy White		Philadelphia	Jerry Stackhouse		Cleveland	Trajan Langdon
	Washington	Tom Hammonds		Washington	Rasheed Wallace		Toronto	Aleksandar
				Minnesota	Kevin Garnett			Radojevic
1990	New Jersey	Derrick Coleman		Vancouver	Bryant Reeves		Seattle	Corey Maggette
	Seattle	Gary Payton		Toronto	Damon Stoudamire			
	Denver	Chris Jackson		Portland	Shawn Respert	2000	New Jersey	Kenyon Martin
	Orlando	Dennis Scott		New Jersey	Ed O'Bannon		Vancouver	Stromile Swift
	Charlotte	Kendall Gill		Miami	Kurt Thomas		L.A. Clippers	Darius Miles
	Minnesota	Felton Spencer		Milwaukee	Gary Trent		Chicago	Marcus Fizer
	Sacramento	Lionel Simmons		Dallas	Cherokee Parks		Orlando	Mike Miller
	L.A. Clippers	Bo Kimble		Sacramento	Corliss Williamson		Atlanta	DerMarr Johnson
	Miami	Willie Burton					Chicago	Chris Mihm
	Atlanta	Rumeal Robinson	1996	Philadelphia	Allen Iverson		Cleveland	Jamal Crawford
	Golden State	Tyrone Hill		Toronto	Marcus Camby		Houston	Joel Przybilla
				Vancouver	Shareef Abdur-		Orlando	Keyon Dooling
1991	Charlotte	Larry Johnson			Rahim		Boston	Jerome Moiso
	New Jersey	Kenny Anderson		Milwaukee	Stephon Marbury		Dallas	Etan Thomas
	Sacramento	Billy Owens		Minnesota	Ray Allen		Orlando	Courtney
	Denver	Dikembe Mutombo		Boston	Antoine Walker			Alexander
	Miami	Steve Smith		L.A. Clippers	Lorenzen Wright			
	Dallas	Doug Smith		New Jersey	Kerry Kittles			
	Minnesota	Luc Longley		Dallas	Samaki Walker			
	Denver	Mark Macon		Indiana	Erick Dampier			
	Atlanta	Stacey Augmon		Golden State	Todd Fuller			
	Orlando	Brian Williams		Cleveland	Vitaly Potapenko			
	Cleveland	Terrell Brandon		Charlotte	Kobe Bryant			

FIRST PLACE: *University of Cincinnati star Kenyon Martin's name was called first.*

Nigeria, was first overall with Germany's Dirk Nowitzki taken ninth. The pair were just two of a record-equalling six non-Americans taken in the first round.

From the mouths of babes

It's the day they've been waiting for all of their lives. Not their wedding day. Not graduation. Draft day.

The Class of 2000 was every bit as excited as all those who have gone before and all those who will follow.

Asked how much he was looking forward to the draft, Cincinnati's Kenyon Martin said, "It's a major point in your life when you are in a position like this. It's like a stepping stone. I can't wait to see where I am going."

Iowa State's Marcus Fizer said the draft process was much like the recruiting process high school players go through before selecting a college.

"It's a lot alike," he said. "I just try to, when it's all over with, just be the same person I have always been. I just sit at home and watch TV and relax. I don't go out to a lot of parties. I try to keep my mind focused on the task at hand. I try to realize what I did to get to this point and not change anything about that."

Naturally, the young players try to prepare themselves for what lies ahead by asking others what to expect.

"I talked to a lot of NBA guys who said that there is a big transition from playing 35 to 40 games to playing 80-plus games," said Michigan State's Morris Peterson. "You have to be prepared physically and mentally. NBA guys say every rookie hits a little wall. It's a time when they get tired. So I want to be prepared for that. I have been working out every day."

Added Florida's Mike Miller of the advice he received about going pro, "It's a different lifestyle. You've got to know what to do with your time. You have a lot of free time and that's what gets a lot of these guys in trouble. I think with where I've grown up and how I've grown up, I'll do a good job of spending my time wisely. It's a lot of hard work and it's going to be a transitional phase that most of us are not used to. We're going to have to deal with that, too."

But first they have to make it through Draft Day, and there's enough pressure there to prepare them for anything.

SIXTH SENSE: *Mike Miller (left) meets NBA Commissioner David Stern on Draft Day.*

THE ARENAS OF THE NBA

There's no place like home, whether it be in Kansas or the NBA. The great basketball venues, past and present, provide a nostalgic mix of charm, inspiration, fan appeal and glorious memories.

OLD SCHOOL: *The Celtics' Boston Garden was one of the NBA's most storied arenas.*

The Storied Arenas

BOSTON GARDEN
Mystique, Memories and Championships

It was dank, musty, smelly, dark and either uncomfortably cold or swelteringly hot, depending on the time of year and the weather outside. It housed rats the size of rabbits, cockroaches the size of rats and memories bigger than all the oversized vermin combined. The fans who worshipped there were loud, raucous, belligerent, obnoxious and borderline fanatical.

Boston Garden was not your typical high-tech, see-and-be-seen, follow-the-bouncing cheerleader arena. It was a no-nonsense, blue-collar architectural dinosaur that changed little from its 1928 opening to its 1995 last hurrah. Sports-hardened New England hockey and basketball fans did not go there to socialize. They took their teams seriously and supported them with enthusiasm and loyalty.

That's just as well because the Garden was as hard on them as it was the opposing players who tried to ignore and penetrate its mystique. There was no air-conditioning to defend against the oppressive summer heat; there was minimal heat to fend off the bitterly cold winter temperatures; the slatted wooden mustard-yellow seats were hard and uncomfortable and some were positioned behind huge support pillars; there was no instant replay, no high-tech scoreboard, no scantily-clad dancing girls, no courtside celebrities. For sports events, Boston Garden was all business.

The Garden was born in a pre-Depression boom as a hockey facility and remained true to that calling for 68 years. It was first and foremost home of the Bruins, but the NBA's Celtics, co-tenants since 1946, gave the building a championship aura the Bruins could not. The green-and-white clad Celtics, coached by the colorful and very Irish Red Auerbach, ran their distinctive parquet floor in black high-top sneakers, winning championship after championship and the begrudging support of skeptical hockey fans. When the Garden ended its reign as dean of U.S. sports arenas after the 1994-95 season, it did so with 16 Celtics and five Bruins championship banners hanging majestically from its rafters.

The banners and the teams were passed on to Boston's new 18,600-seat FleetCenter before the 1995–96 hockey and basketball seasons, but the aura and the memories—the heart and soul of the Boston Garden mystique—were retired with the rats and roaches. They survive only in the telling and retelling of stories by those who were there and the NBA records that confirm the invincibility of the team that gave the building respect and personality.

ROSE IN BLOOM: *Portland's Rose Garden.*

PORTLAND
MEMORIAL COLISEUM
MEMORIAL COLISEUM
PORTLAND
BLAZERS
BLAZERS
PORTLAND City of Roses

Some of the Garden's subtle images are of opposing players and referees getting blasted by ice cold water in the middle of a shower; or showered visitors trying to dry themselves with already damp towels; or complaints of tiny, hole-in-the-wall dressing rooms with roaches running rampant and little heat; or dead spots on the parquet floor that the Celtics used to great advantage—or the belligerent Boston fans positioned precariously close to the court and in balconies overhanging the floor. But the basketball images are more vivid:

● Auerbach lighting up a cigar in the final minute of a game, signaling official confirmation of another Celtics victory.

● Bill Russell versus Wilt Chamberlain.

● Excited fans storming onto the floor to celebrate one of Boston's 11 NBA championships in a 13-year span from 1957–69.

● The Celtics versus Jerry West, Elgin Baylor and the Lakers in the NBA Finals.

● John Havlicek running…and running…and running…and running some more.

● Bob Cousy making another no-look, behind-the-back pass to a surprised teammate.

● Sam Jones connecting on a 20-foot bank shot.

● Frank Ramsey, Havlicek, Don Nelson, Larry Siegfried, Kevin McHale—all successful Celtics "Sixth Men."

●The Celtics versus Magic Johnson, Kareem Abdul-Jabbar, James Worthy and the Lakers in the NBA Finals.

●Larry Bird firing in a 3-point jumper.

For those who prefer the incredible games, performances and plays that graced the Celtics' parquet, there's plenty to choose from. A good starting point is Game 7 of the 1957 NBA Finals—a 125–123 double-overtime victory over the St. Louis Hawks that produced Boston's first championship and started a winning legacy that would gain legendary status. That game ended on an incredible note when the Hawks' Alex Hannum made a half-court pass to Bob Pettit—off the backboard—and Pettit, apparently surprised that such a maneuver could

work, missed the point-blank, game-tying tip-in.

Another Boston championship was the product of a missed shot. The Lakers, six-time NBA Finals losers to Boston in the 1960s, lost a golden opportunity to interrupt the Celtics' eight-year title run in Game 7 of the 1962 Finals when Frank Selvy missed a last-second, wide-open 10-foot jumper in regulation play. Given a reprieve, the Celtics posted a 110–107 victory in overtime.

One of the most famous Boston victories was recorded three years later in Game 7 of the Eastern Conference finals when Havlicek preserved a 110–109 victory over Philadelphia with a last-second steal. Long-time Boston announcer Johnny Most immortalized the moment with his classic radio call: "Havlicek stole the ball." The words were delivered with such force and urgency by Most's distinctive voice that the game became an immediate classic.

Perhaps more significant in the Celtics' long success story was the off-balance 18-foot leaner that Sam Jones threw toward the basket with time running out in Game 4 of the 1969 Finals. As the buzzer sounded, the ball rolled tantalizingly around the rim before falling through. The 89–88 victory over the Lakers propelled the Celtics to their final title of the "Bill Russell era."

The Celtics really turned up the heat for Game 5 of the 1984 NBA Finals in another Garden classic. With temperatures rising over 100 degrees outside, Boston Garden thermostats reached a sweltering 98 as both players and fans battled heat exhaustion and dehydration. As the Lakers gulped oxygen on their sideline and dozens of fans swooned in the stands, a seemingly refreshed Bird soared for 34 points in a 121–103 victory.

The NBA's first All-Star Game was played at Boston Garden in 1951 and Chicago's Michael Jordan dented the Celtics for a playoff-record 63 points in a 1986 double-overtime thriller, but most long-time Celtics watchers insist that Game 5 of the 1976 NBA Finals was the greatest game in Garden history—maybe the greatest basketball game ever.

That 128–126 triple-overtime win over Phoenix was full of dramatic turning

points and plays, none more memorable than the 22-foot game-tying desperation heave by the Suns' Garfield Heard at the end of the second overtime. Heard's miraculous shot was delivered off a Phoenix inbounds pass with one second remaining on the clock and Boston fans ringing the court, ready to storm the floor for a victory celebration. It set off a fan melee that held up play for several minutes and it set up the third-overtime heroics of Boston reserve Glenn McDonald. The loss demoralized the exhausted Suns and the Celtics went on to easily claim another championship.

The personalities (P.R. man Howie McHugh, organist John Kiley, trainer Buddy LeRoux, former owners Walter Brown, Marvin Kratter and Paul Gaston, Auerbach), the decaying building, the players, the banners, the parquet floor and even the rats—they all were part of a Boston Garden atmosphere that stretched above and beyond the worlds of hockey and basketball.

In its long, glorious history, the Garden played host to political rallies, religious revivals, ice shows, concerts, circuses, rodeos, poultry shows, home shows, conventions and various sports events— bicycle races, wrestling, Roller Derby, lacrosse, tractor pulls, boxing and even indoor baseball. It truly was a building for all seasons, but none more special than the one that ran from November to May or June—the time required for each of the Celtics' 16 championships.

When Boston Garden played host to its final basketball game in 1995, the Celtics had posted an incredible 1,291–424 home record there. The moss-covered building with one elevator and 10 bathrooms quietly gave way to the modern FleetCenter with its seven elevators, 13 escalators, 34 bathrooms, 104 luxury boxes and numerous other conveniences never experienced before by the hard-core, no-nonsense Boston sports fans.

It was a familiar transition. Boston Garden was neither the first nor last of the NBA's storied arenas to give way to the recent obsession for modernistic, space-aged facilities with all the conveniences of home. The following profiles describe some of the most engaging structures, both past and present.

BULL PEN: *Rowdy old Chicago Stadium hosted the Bulls' first three NBA Championships and also the NFL Bears' 1932 championship game.*

CHICAGO STADIUM
Loud, Proud and Rowdy

The old barn on Madison Street closed its doors after the 1993–94 season with a combination of sadness and relief.

Like Boston Garden, 65-year-old Chicago Stadium had become dirty, dingy and decayed, a former state-of-the-art facility that had fought valiantly against the ravages of time. Right up to the end, its dedicated fans were the loudest and rowdiest in sports and the old building still could generate the emotion and electricity that influence championships. But everyone agreed: it was time to go.

So the once-venerable Stadium was turned into a parking lot and the NHL's Blackhawks and NBA's Bulls moved into the 21,711-seat United Center, with its more than 200 luxury suites and high-tech, fill-every-need conveniences. It took less than a minute inside the new building to see that sports, Chicago-style, could never be quite the same.

Chicago Stadium was built in the pre-Depression boom (1929) as a hockey arena and fans had to ease into professional basketball after the expansion Bulls became tenants in 1967. While hockey, basketball and boxing have provided the main entertainment, the old barn could never be called one or two-dimensional. In its 65 years, Chicago Stadium hosted political conventions (Franklin D. Roosevelt coined his "New Deal" slogan there), rodeos, circuses, ice shows, concerts, jitterbug contests and sports events ranging from bicycle races and roller derby to indoor track and soccer.

It also will be remembered as the site of the first indoor professional football game—an NFL championship-deciding contest that was hastily staged on a makeshift 80-yard imported-dirt field because of a driving Chicago snowstorm. The Bears won that historic 1932 title, 9–0, over the Portsmouth Spartans.

Part of the Stadium's enduring charm was the trademark Barton Organ that kept the building rocking, rolling and swaying through good times and bad. The organ's pipes, which would have measured more than a city block if laid end to end, were built into the foundation of the building and thus couldn't be moved to the United Center. The ear-pounding organ provided the background music for many of the building's most dramatic moments.

The best recent memories were provided by the Bulls—most of them since the 1984 arrival of Michael Jordan. Not only did Jordan mesmerize Chicago fans with his high-flying artistry and phenomenal scoring, he led the Bulls to three consecutive NBA titles from 1991–93—the first "three-peat" since the 1960s Celtics won eight championships in a row.

Bulls announcer Red Kerr, a veteran of Chicago Stadium as a player and coach, fondly recalled his favorite moment—the Bulls' championship ring ceremony after their second title—for the Chicago Tribune: "One of the great thrills was to see the players come back up out of the bowels of the stadium. It was fantastic. I've heard the Stadium is loud, but after everyone else was on the floor and there was only one more, the announcer said, 'And now, the greatest basketball player this planet will ever see …' Nobody heard it, but they all knew Michael was the only guy not out there. That was the loudest the Stadium has ever been."

Perhaps the most fitting epitaph was offered by Bulls Coach Phil Jackson before the Stadium's final hurrah in 1994.

"You get a wonderful feeling in this building," he said. "Boston Garden or other places like that aren't even close to this place. The noise, closeness to the playing floor, the connection among the fans in each section with the players all contribute to the warmness, the heartiness of the place."

390

MADISON SQUARE GARDEN
The Granddaddy of All Sports Arenas

Madison Square Garden cannot claim distinction as America's oldest existing arena, but it has survived in name for more than a century in the sports capital of North America. Four Madison Square Gardens have existed on three different sites since 1879, offering New York patrons every kind of entertainment venue imaginable.

Madison Square Garden I and II were constructed on the same site at Madison Square bordering 26th Street and Madison Avenue. The first building was demolished in 1890 and replaced by a bigger, better Garden that endured until 1925.

MADISON SQUARE GARDEN III

Indoor sports as we know it today took its New York foothold in 1925 when promoter Tex Rickard oversaw the construction of an 18,000-seat arena at 49th Street and Eighth Avenue. Rickard's principal attraction was the NHL's Rangers, but it didn't take long for the new Garden to be recognized as America's premier recreational showplace.

The Rangers and boxing ruled the professional sports venue in the early years, but the Garden soon became known as the "Mecca of Basketball" under the expert direction of Ned Irish, another outstanding promoter. Irish became well known for his college basketball double-headers and he was the primary moving force behind the prestigious National Invitation Tournament, an annual Garden event that overshadowed the up-and-coming NCAA Tournament in the late 1930s and '40s.

Professional basketball took its place in the Garden showcase when the Basketball Association of America, the predecessor to the NBA, was formed in 1946. The Knickerbockers' presence in the country's No. 1 sports market helped legitimize the NBA during its painful early years and, although the Knicks never won an NBA championship in the building, they grew into one of the game's venerable franchises while playing there. And the league itself grew in stature.

THE GARDEN: *Madison Square Garden lives up to the claim, "The World's Most Famous Arena."*

MADISON SQUARE GARDEN IV

When New York officials bill the current Garden as "The World's Most Famous Arena," it's hard to argue the point.

Opened in 1968 as a huge multi-purpose complex, Garden IV featured a circular cable-suspended roof that covered a 19,000-seat arena, 5,000-seat Felt Forum, the 48-lane Bowling Center, a 500-seat cinema, the Hall of Fame Club, the National Art Museum of Sport, a 50,000-square-foot Exposition Rotunda and a 29-story office building with a pedestrian mall.

The new Garden, located between 31st and 33rd Streets and Seventh and Eighth Avenues on Manhattan's West Side, cost $43 million and opened for business when Bob Hope and Bing Crosby hosted a USO salute. The Knicks played their first basketball game there three days later—appropriately, on Valentine's Day.

It was love at fourth site for the up-and-coming Knicks, who captured their first NBA championship in 1970 when they defeated the Lakers in a memorable NBA Finals Game 7 at the Garden. The Knicks added another title in 1973.

Almost three decades of memories have flooded through the hallowed building—Ali vs. Frazier, the Rangers ending 54 years of Stanley Cup frustration, Hope and Crosby, Frank Sinatra, the Rolling Stones, Elvis Presley, Michael Jackson, Elton John, Luciano Pavarotti, Billy Joel, Bruce Springsteen, Barbra Streisand, political conventions and famous personalities ranging from future U.S. presidents and a Pope to the Harlem Globetrotters and the Muppets.

And through its more than a quarter of a century, the Garden has moved steadily forward with state-of-the-art scoreboards, in- stant replay equipment, numerous renovations, dramatic facility updates and even an upscale surge of clientele.

In its bid to keep up with the Los Angeles Forum of the '80s, the Madison Square Garden of the '90s even boasts its own celebrity row, featuring such high-profile fans as Spike Lee, Woody Allen, Dustin Hoffman, Donald Trump and special guests like Madonna and Arnold Schwarzenegger.

THE GREAT WESTERN FORUM
Glitz, Glamour and Showtime

Basketball, Los Angeles-style, is more than a game. It's an event, a social experience and a theatrical production, expertly wrapped in Hollywood glitz and complete with celebrities, dancing girls and high-tech scoreboards and replay screens.

NBA images of the Forum include actors Jack Nicholson and Dyan Cannon at courtside, the "Showtime" Lakers, Magic and Kareem, the Laker Girls and, of course, the championships—one in 1972 and six in 32 glorious years. From its grand opening in December 1967 to the Lakers' move to The Staples Center in 1999, the Forum and its upscale patrons changed the ambience of professional basketball.

When Jack Kent Cooke, then owner of the Lakers and NHL Kings, built his Forum at an unbelievable cost of $16 million, he envisioned a social atmosphere that would contrast the fan intensity of such facilities as Boston Garden and New York's Madison Square Garden. His $16 million cost would dwarf the $5 million of Philadelphia's new Spectrum and it would give L.A. fans such luxuries as fully upholstered, extra-wide, theater-style seats set in rows with plenty of legroom.

Cooke billed the Forum as a modern-day version of the Colosseum of Ancient Rome and newcomers gawked at the 80 support columns that stood 57 feet high and weighed 55 tons. Cooke outfitted male ushers in togas, usherettes in short pants and his Lakers in purple and gold uniforms. He realigned courtside seating, charging hefty fees for season tickets that were snapped up by celebrity fans like Nicholson and Walter Matthau.

The building remained the "Forum" through the 1979 sale of the building and its teams to Jerry Buss and all of the Lakers' six championships. It was changed to "The Great Western Forum" in 1988 as part of a major advertising agreement.

Everything about the Forum was upscale, clean and fast, from its celebrity patronage and 17,505 theater-friendly basketball seats to the Lakers' run-and-gun style. The Forum will be best recalled as the home of the "Showtime" Lakers featuring Magic Johnson, Kareem Abdul-Jabbar and James Worthy. But it also played host to more than 200 events per year and showcased some of sports' greatest athletes and the entertainment world's top performers. And in 1984, the Forum served as the basketball venue for the Los Angeles Olympic Games.

MEMORIAL COLISEUM
Everything's Coming Up Roses

When the Trail Blazers ended their stay in the 35-year-old Coliseum in May 1995 with a 117–109 playoff loss to Phoenix, they also completed a string of 810 straight sellouts—the longest string in the NBA.

The sellout string was both good and bad. It certainly proved that Portland fans were loyal to their only professional sports franchise. But it also was a reflection of the arena's 12,888 seating capacity—the smallest in the NBA. The last Coliseum game that was not sold out was April 5, 1977, when 12,359 showed up to see the Blazers play Detroit.

Unlike many of the players who fretted about life away from Chicago Stadium and Boston Garden when those arenas were abandoned, Portland welcomed the 1995 move into the 21,500-seat Rose Garden. Coliseum facilities were cramped, warmup jackets often were required for winter practices and power outages were not uncommon. And players often complained that fans were so quiet during games you could hear a sneaker drop.

That wasn't always the case. Portland fans were as noisy as any in the league during the early years and they helped the Blazers through their unlikely 1977 championship run. But there was virtually no turnover in season tickets as the years passed and the Coliseum crowd got old. The fans also grew mellow and serene, a generational characteristic that didn't sit well with the young players.

In the 25 years of Trail Blazers basketball, the Coliseum hosted three NBA Finals, a college basket-ball Final Four, Dream Team exhibitions and the first NBA game attended by a U.S. chief executive. President Gerald Ford dropped in for a 1974 contest against Buffalo.

The Rose Garden joined the growing list of glitzy new arenas before the 1995–96 season, a trend that's likely to continue.

THE PHILADELPHIA SPECTRUM
A $5-Million Fortress

The Spectrum, which joined the growing list of defunct sports facilities at the end of the 1995–96 seasons, was part of a late 1960s arena blitz that also produced the Los Angeles Forum and the fourth edition of New York's Madison Square Garden. But whereas the vast Garden complex was constructed at a cost of $43 million and the Forum was built for $16 million, the Spectrum came in at $5 million.

The Wilt Chamberlain and Hal Greer-led 76ers, coming off a 1966–67 championship season, played their first game in the new building on October 18, 1967, and posted an impressive 103–87 victory over the Los Angeles Lakers. They went on to win 62 games and advanced to the Western Conference finals before losing a tough seven-game series to Boston.

Over the building's 29 years, the 76ers won five more division titles, advanced to four NBA Finals and won one more championship. The NHL's Flyers added to the legacy with Stanley Cup championships in 1974 and '75.

The 1982–83 76ers, coached by former star Billy Cunningham and featuring Julius Erving, Moses Malone, Maurice Cheeks, Andrew Toney and Bobby Jones, gave the Spectrum its greatest basketball memory by posting 65 regular-season wins and a 12–1 playoff run that ended with a Finals sweep of the Lakers. Fittingly, players from that team were honored guests when the 76ers played their last game there in April 1996.

"This homecourt became a fortress for us," Dr. J told a crowd of 18,168 during halftime ceremonies of the basketball finale. "The other teams felt that we were running downhill and they were running uphill. If the walls could talk, they would have some great stories to tell."

Some of them not so positive. The great 76ers teams of the 1980s were countered by some not-so-great teams of the 1970s and 1990s. The 1972–73 Sixers struggled through a 9–73 season—the worst record in NBA history. The 1995–96 Sixers struggled to 18–64, the NBA-record sixth consecutive season in which they had lost more games than the previous year. But the Sixers finished with an impressive 745–402 record at the Spectrum.

392 The Arenas

Some are newer than others. Some are bigger than others. Some are louder than others. But virtually all of the 29 arenas that house NBA teams are state-of-the-art facilities full of amenities for the comfort and enjoyment of the fans.

Just like coaches and players, each building has a unique personality, based on the area of the country and the history of the team. Long after the retirement of Michael Jordan, for instance, the Bulls still used the same sort of video introduction at the beginning of every game in the United Center, and when that music started, there was no mistaking your whereabouts.

Each team, each building, strives to evoke the same sort of memory. Despite the fortunes of the squads from year to year, team officials want every visit to be a fun one. More than anything, of course, they want the fans to come back year after year.

ATLANTA

ARENA: *Philips Arena*
CAPACITY: *20,000*
OPENED: *1999*

The Hawks like to brag that their landmark building is revolutionary, unlike any other sports facility in the world. Famed architects HOK and Arquitetonica created a dramatic exterior and a main entry that touches the CNN Center atrium and features 400 yards of food and entertainment, open 365 days a year. It includes mementos from the demolished Omni, the former home of the Hawks.

The seating also is revolutionary, with all 96 suites stacked on one side. About 60 percent of the other seats are located in the lowest level and the first row of the upper level is six rows closer and lower than any other recent comparable arena.

The Thrashers of the NHL also play at Philips Arena, named after the electronics giant.

BOSTON

ARENA: *FleetCenter*
CAPACITY: *18,624*
OPENED: *1995*

The Celtics were able to move all their championship banners and most of their famous parquet floor into the FleetCenter, but they have not been able to duplicate their successes of the unique mystique of the Boston Garden.

But how close was the new facility to the old one? Only nine inches separated the FleetCenter from the back of the Garden—at least until it was demolished.

The $160-million, 755,000-square-foot facility is air-conditioned, however, which gives it a huge edge over the old Boston Garden, and it offers views of the Inner Harbor, which is much more attractive than the old view of Causeway Street.

The Bruins of the NHL also play in the FleetCenter, which is also host to the Beanpot college hockey tournament and the Blazers lacrosse team.

NEW DIGS: *The FleetCenter became the new home of the Boston Celtics in 1995; they brought all their championship banners with them.*

CHARLOTTE

ARENA: *Charlotte Coliseum*
CAPACITY: *23,799*
OPENED: *1988*

The home of the Hornets is nicknamed "The Hive." A humming sound, like the buzzing of a hornet, often plays loudly over the public-address system, especially if the opponents are mounting a comeback. The interior is done in shades of teal to match the uniforms. The exterior walls are split-faced masonry, precast concrete and glass with aluminum doors. Forty-four diamond-shaped windows are 22 feet high to provide natural light and minimize the scale of the 465,000-square-foot building.

The Crown Club, located one level below the main concourse, has increased from 7,000 square feet to 14,000 and can be divided into five rooms for private parties. It can seat up to 450 people for dinner and hold up to 1,000 for receptions. The WNBA's Sting also play in this building.

UNITED FRONT: *The United Center rocked with atmosphere when the Bulls were winning.*

CHICAGO

ARENA: *United Center*
CAPACITY: *21,711*
OPENED: *1994*

According to the Bulls press guide, the $175 million, 960,000-square foot United Center, required 3,500 tons of steel (enough to build 28 life-sized replicas of the Statue of Liberty) and 41,000 cubic yards of concrete. The scoreboard is as tall as a two story building (20 feet), weighs nearly as much as 26 cars and displays 17,500 different lights. There are 1,850 doors, 6,500 parking spaces, eight escalators, nine elevators and 50 public restrooms.

When the Bulls were winning, it tied Madison Square Garden for the best atmosphere in the league, but that has changed in recent years.

The Blackhawks of the National Hockey League also play in the building.

CLEVELAND

ARENA: *Gund Arena*
CAPACITY: *20,592*
OPENED: *1994*

Gund Arena and Jacobs Field, home of the Indians American League baseball team, helped revive the Cleveland downtown and are the cornerstones of a downtown area known as Gateway, which includes residential areas as well as hotels, restaurants and other business and retail outlets.

Special features of the arena include an upstairs practice court, the unique artwork found surrounding the building, as well as two restaurants inside. Gordon's Sports Bar, named for owner Gordon Gund, offers casual dining as well as the Cleveland Legends Wall of Fame. Bridges, named for the scenic view it offers of many of the city's landmark bridges, offers more formal dining before, during and after games.

The building also is home to the WNBA Rockers and the minor-league hockey Lumberjacks.

394

FAMILY REUNION: *Dallas' Reunion Center is home to the Maverick and the NHL's Stars.*

DALLAS

ARENA: *Reunion Arena*
CAPACITY: *18,042*
OPENED: *1980*

Reunion Arena is one of the oldest arenas in the league and one of the few without luxury boxes. Its most recent renovations were completed in 1993, when all the seats were replaced, new glass railings were installed in the upper level and the press facilities were expanded. The scoreboard was added in 1990. The building also is home to the Stars of the NHL and the Sidekicks indoor soccer team.

The 2000–01 is slated to be the last at Reunion Arena as the Mavericks are slated to move to the new American Airlines Center in downtown Dallas in the fall of 2001.

DENVER

ARENA: *Pepsi Center*
CAPACITY: *19,300*
OPENED: *1999*

Located just on the edge of downtown, the $160,000 arena was built with private funds. It sits on 52 acres; the 675,000-square-foot arena itself takes up 45. It is surrounded by 718 trees, 1,806 shrubs, 1,006 groundcover plants and seven waterscape ponds making it a parklike setting.

The Avalanche of the National Hockey League also play here.

DETROIT

ARENA: *The Palace of Auburn Hills*
CAPACITY: *22,076*
OPENED: *1988*

There was no doubt the building was a success as soon as it opened. Not only did the Pistons win their first of back-to-back NBA championships, but it also earned kudos from two entertainment trade publications when it was named

ROCKY MOUNTAIN HIGH: *The Pepsi Center houses the Denver Nuggets and is located on the edge of the city's Downtown area.*

PALATIAL ESTATE: *Detroit's home is truly a palace and the Palace of Auburn Hills is where the Pistons were crowned NBA kings in 1989 and '90.*

GOLDEN GLOW: *The Arena in Oakland is home the Golden State Warriors and hosted the 2000 All-Star Weekend.*

"New Venue of the Year" by Performance and "Best New Concert Venue" by Pollstar. Since then, it was been named "Arena of the Year" seven times by Performance and twice by Pollstar.

The 570,000-square-foot facility has undergone more than $42 million in improvements to maintain its reputation. Its air-conditioning system is powerful enough to cool 500 single-family homes or turn one million gallons of water into ice.

The building also is home to the minor-league hockey Vipers and the WNBA Shock.

GOLDEN STATE

ARENA: *The Arena in Oakland*
CAPACITY: *19,596*
OPENED: *1997*

The new arena, which is adjacent to the Oakland Coliseum, home of the Oakland A's American League baseball team and Oakland Raiders of the National Football League, opened in November, 1997 on the site of the old Coliseum Arena, which had been demolished in August, 1996.

The new building is 106 feet tall with a 70-foot high glass exterior that is 1,418 feet long and contains 3,072 panes of glass.

HOUSTON

ARENA: *Compaq Center*
CAPACITY: *16,285*
OPENED: *1975*

Formerly named The Summit, the home of the Rockets sits on a seven-acre site about four miles from downtown. Another of the league's oldest buildings, the first game was played on November 2, 1975, when Houston beat Milwaukee, 104–89. Through the 1999–2000 season, the Rockets had compiled a 56–36 mark at home during the playoffs, winning NBA championships in 1994 and 1995.

In addition, Compaq Center is home to the Comets of the WNBA, who won the first three WNBA championships behind Cynthia Cooper.

INDIANA

ARENA: *Conseco Fieldhouse*
CAPACITY: *18,500*
OPENED: *1999*

See pages 401–2.

LOS ANGELES CLIPPERS

ARENA: *Staples Center*
CAPACITY: *19,282*
OPENED: *1999*

One of the busiest buildings in the NBA, the Staples Center serves as the home to the Clippers and Lakers, as well as the Kings of the National Hockey League and the Avengers of the Arena Football League.

It was designed for the fans of Los Angeles, who are used to the ultimate in entertainment. The arena includes 1,200 television monitors as part of a specially designed $1.5 million Bose facility sound system that includes 675 speakers outside the seating area. There also is a $2 million lighting package.

Along the five concourses are 23 refreshment stands, featuring a variety of dining choices, including the City View Grill, an outdoor-dining experience with a spectacular view of the downtown skyline. There also is a FOX Sports Sky Box, a 300-seat sports bar open daily.

On game days, the staff will reach 1,200 people as the center strives to provide an experience second-to-none.

LOS ANGELES LAKERS

ARENA: *Staples Center*
CAPACITY: *19,282*
OPENED: *1999*
See preceding.

MIAMI

ARENA: *AmericanAirlines Arena*
CAPACITY: *19,600*
OPENED: *1999*

The arena opened with a bang. Gloria Estafan headlined a concert on New Year's Eve 1999 as the world welcomed the new millennium.

DOUBLE DIP: *The Lakers and Clippers both call the Staples Center in Los Angeles home.*

This, truly, is one of the most unique buildings in the league, featuring seats in blazing yellow, orange and red and a scoreboard hanging on what appears to be a huge, silver dandelion. Located on a 14.63-acre sight along Biscayne Bay, the 680,000-square-foot building has a pedestrian bridge to the Bayside Market Place as well as a small boat access.

Inside the arena, which also is the home for the WNBA Sol, is the Club Chivas Regal Restaurant/Lounge with a wine bar and a view of the court, five outdoor balconies and an outdoor plaza with a Bacardi Bar and view of the bay.

LAYOVER: *The AmericanAirlines Arena in Miami has access for cars and small boats.*

398

MILWAUKEE

ARENA: *Bradley Center*
CAPACITY: *18,717*
OPENED: *1988*

Located across the street from the old Milwaukee Arena that had been the Bucks' home since their inception, the $91 million building was a gift to the city from Jane Pettit and her former husband, Lloyd, in honor of Mrs. Pettit's father, Harry Lynde Bradley. Bradley was one of the founders of the Allen-Bradley Co., a national manufacturer of electrical controls, whose headquarters were in Milwaukee. Allen-Bradley Co. is now a subsidiary of Rockwell International.

Pettit's minor league hockey team, the Admirals, also play in the building, as does the basketball team from Marquette University.

The building takes up an entire city block and rises to a height of 13 stories. The exterior is polished and flame-treated South Dakota granite, with the same red-and-pink granite used in the columns in the glass-enclosed 60-foot atrium on the front of the building. The seating area consists of three levels instead of the usual two.

Although the building was just seven years old, a new scoreboard was installed in 1995. A new court was put in before the 1998-99 season and a new renovation plan was put into place at the turn of the century to add amenities to the seating area, lobbies and concourses and exterior.

MINNESOTA

ARENA: *Target Center*
CAPACITY: *19,006*
OPENED: *1990*

The building is located on the western edge of Minneapolis' downtown business district and in the heart of the warehouse bar, restaurant and entertainment district.

Comfort is a major factor. The building boasts the highest restroom-to-patron ratio in the industry. There is one restroom unit for every 45 persons, with 60 percent of the facilities dedicated to women. Most buildings offer one unit for every 172 patrons. The seats also are an inch to two inches wider than industry regulations. It was the first arena in the country to be smoke-free.

There is a full-service health club and a separate restaurant. The arena has one of only two movable floors in the U.S. and it includes ice-making capabilities. It can be raised or lowered five feet in 25 minutes to ensure excellent viewing and tailored sightlines for each event.

BUCKING THE ODDS: *Milwaukee's Bradley Center is being improved almost every year.*

NEW JERSEY

ARENA: *Continental Airlines Arena*
CAPACITY: *20,049*
OPENED: *1981*

The arena is located in the heart of New Jersey's sports facilities, adjacent to the Meadowlands horse racing track and football stadium, where the National Football League's New York Giants and Jets play. Although there has been talk of a move to downtown Newark, the Nets refurbished their existing facility in an effort to prove their commitment to success.

NEW YORK

ARENA: *Madison Square Garden*
CAPACITY: *19,763*
OPENED: *1968*

See accompanying story.

ORLANDO

ARENA: *TD Waterhouse Centre*
CAPACITY: *17,248*
OPENED: *1989*

Another busy building, the arena also is home to the WNBA's Miracle, the minor-league hockey Solar Bears, and the Arena Football League Predators.

Aesthetically pleasing, the uniquely-constructed arena features curved walls made of 49,000 glass blocks, four corner nodes covered in imported red lilies, shiny terrazzo floors and beautifully landscaped grounds in Florida-style arrangements with a huge fountain. It was voted Arena of the Year in 1991 and nominated on two other occasions.

It is one of six facilities owned and operated by the City of Orlando under the name of "The Orlando Centroplex." The other five facilities include the Bob Carr Performing Arts Centre, the Orlando Expo Centre, Tinker Field, Ben White Raceway and The Florida Citrus Bowl.

PHILADELPHIA

ARENA: *First Union Center*
CAPACITY: *20,444*
OPENED: *1996*

The $210 million arena has five seating areas, two public and three private. There are 30 concession stands on the public

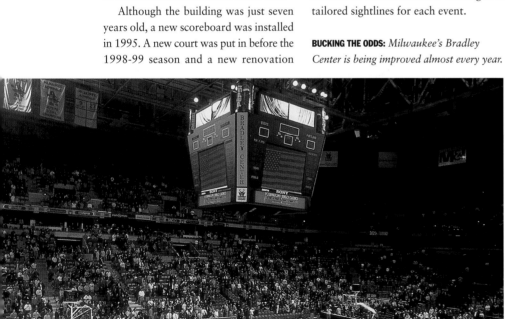

CENTRE STAGE: *The Orlando Magic cast their spells in the TD Waterhouse Centre, part of the Orlando Centroplex.*

levels, including the only in-arena microbrewery in the league—the Red Bell Brewery and Pub—and the only in-arena cigar club —the Holt's Cigar Club.

The First Union Center joins the First Union Spectrum in forming a unique sports entertainment complex with two major arenas side-by-side.

Martha Snider was the design coordinator for all aspects of the arena, including architecture, interior design, graphic design, staff uniforms and artwork. She commissioned Martha Madigan to create a large public sculpture—AElements—for the atrium of the building. The sculpture consists of eight digital photographic images suspended between 9 ft x 4 ft sheets of starphire crystal glass that cascade from the ceiling supported by a steel armature. It takes the form of a rising spiral, symbolizing the eternal perfection found in nature. Each glass panel is a translucent image of a figure in action representing a variety of athletes and performers.

The arena also was the first to combine memorabilia displays with interactive tough-screen video kiosks.

The building also is home to the Flyers of the National Hockey League and the lacrosse Wings.

PHOENIX

ARENA: *America West Arena*
CAPACITY: *19,023*
OPENED: *1992*

The $90-million, one-million-square foot arena is owned by the city of Phoenix. When it opened, it was voted the best place to play by NBA insiders. It was voted "Best New Concert Venue" by Pollstar Magazine and "New Venue of the Year" by Performance Magazine.

Named for Phoenix's hometown airline, this building is also home to the Coyotes of the National Hockey League, the Mercury of the WNBA, the Rattlers of the Arena Football League, the Phoenix Suns Athletic Club, SRO Communications in-house advertising and public relations firm and ProDine food service.

PORTLAND

ARENA: *The Rose Garden*
CAPACITY: *19,980*
OPENED: *1995*

The Oregon Arena Corp., a sister company of Trail Blazers Inc., was created in 1991 to develop a new arena for Portland. It now oversees and manages the Rose Quarter, 32 acres just across the Willamette River from downtown Portland that includes the Rose Garden arena, the Memorial Coliseum, the Rose Quarter Commons and the One Center Court office complex.

In its first two years, the Rose Garden was nominated for the "Arena of the Year" award from Pollstar magazine, was named "Prime Site" by Facilities Magazine and was one of five finalists for the Country Music Association's "Venue of the Year" award. It finished the 1996 calendar year as the second highest top-grossing arena in the country among 20,000-seat or more arenas as rated in Performance magazine.

A software program developed by the Trail Blazers in conjunction with owner Paul Allen's Asymetrix Corp. treats Rose Garden fans to in-game entertainment and is used in other arenas and stadiums as well. The Blazers were one of the first teams to provide fans with up-to-date statistics and invited fans to tune into postgame press conferences via the Internet.

SACRAMENTO

ARENA: *Arco Arena*
CAPACITY: *17,317*
OPENED: *1988*

Home of some of the loudest fans in the NBA, Arco Arena was sold out for an

NBA-leading 497 consecutive sellouts over the 13 seasons from 1985–86 to 1997–98. The 442,000-square foot, $40 million facility was built without taxpayer dollars. Although the 3,900 trees and 8,000 shrubs on the 105-acre parcel give a rural feel to the area, it is only about 15 minutes outside downtown Sacramento and 90 minutes from the San Francisco Bay Area.

The building also is home to the Monarchs of the WNBA and the Knights of the World Indoor Soccer League, who have averaged 6,000 fans a game in each of the first seven seasons.

SAN ANTONIO

ARENA: *Alamodome*
CAPACITY: *20,557 (for basketball)*
OPENED: *1993*

This building is unlike any other stadium in the world because of its design and versatility. It has a cable-suspended roof, a retractable seating system, a flexible floor grid system, formal entries and large food court areas.

Following an NBA-record opening night crowd of 36,523 that saw the Spurs beat the Golden State Warriors, 95–90, on November 5, 1993, more than five million fans visited in the next six seasons.

The building can be configured from 5,000 for small conventions to 65,000 for major football games, like the Sylvania Alamo Bowl.

The total cost of the building was $186 million raised by a half-cent sales tax that was in effect from 1989–94.

SEATTLE

ARENA: *Key Arena*
CAPACITY: *17,072*
OPENED: *1995*

The building is owned and operated by the City of Seattle and sits on the campus of The Seattle Center, a 74-acre entertainment complex located on the north side of downtown Seattle. The biggest feature of the complex is the Space Needle, the city's landmark built for the 1960 World's Fair.

Construction began on June 16, 1994, and the doors opened on October 26, 1995. The Sonics played their first game against the Lakers and celebrated the new building by playing host to the Chicago Bulls in the NBA Finals at the end of the season, eventually losing in six games.

The city chipped in $74.5 million and the Sonics $20 million. It was the first publicly financed arena supported by earned income from the building.

The 129,000 square foot facility is a 360-foot square that is 135 feet high.

TORONTO

ARENA: *Air Canada Centre*
CAPACITY: *19,800*
OPENED: *1999*

The $265 million downtown facility features 152 luxury suites and 40 Platinum lounges, unique to North America. It boasts a Sony JumboTron, the first 16-foot by 9-foot LED board in Canada, as well as 650 Sony televisions throughout and a Bose sound system. All the seats are fully upholstered. There are five restaurants, including Lord Stanley's Mug brewpub, the Original Six Bar and Grill sports bar, the Air Canada Club, the Platinum Club and the Hot Stove Club. The Raptors' practice court also is located in the facility.

One of the unique aspects of the building, which is also home to the Maple

O CANADA: *The Toronto Raptors play in the Air Canada Centre along with the Maple Leafs of the National Hockey League*

GRIZZLIES' DEN: *General Motors Place is the home of the Vancouver Grizzlies.*

Leafs of the National Hockey League, is the artwork of people on the facades between levels.

UTAH

ARENA: *Delta Center*
CAPACITY: *19,911*
OPENED: *1991*

This arena is one of the loudest in the NBA, and it's only partly because the Bear mascot arrives on a motorcycle. The Utah fans are among the rowdiest in the league. Many a reporter donned ear plugs during the NBA Finals between the Chicago Bulls and Utah Jazz in 1997 and 1998.

Located on the west edge of downtown, the $66 million building, home to the figure skating competition in the 2002 Winter Olympics, is 743,000 square feet, 136 feet high and sits on 10 acres. There are 56 luxury suites, four sky suites and numerous hospitality and multi-purpose rooms.

VANCOUVER

ARENA: *General Motors Place*
CAPACITY: *19,193*
OPENED: *1995*

Another of the league's state-of-the-art arenas, the downtown facility features a Bose sound system and OrcaVision, an eight-sided video scoreboard featuring Mitsubishi DiamondVision Mark IV video boards and four Whiteway matrix

boards, as well as skilled, in-house production, lighting and rigging crews and broadcasting capabilities. Superior sightlines and comfortable seating also are features.

The Canucks of the National Hockey League also play here.

WASHINGTON

ARENA: *MCI Center*
CAPACITY: *20,674*
OPENED: *1997*

With premium seating for 2,500 and 110 luxury suites that start just 19 rows from the floor, fans feel as if they're right on top of the action. But many of the amenities here are outside the arena.

Located in the heart of the nation's capital and surrounded by art and history museums, the MCI National Sports Gallery features memorabilia and interactive displays of American sports throughout the years. The American Sportscasters Association Hall of Fame and Museum, featuring such broadcasting greats as Harry Caray, Jim McKay and Curt Gowdy, is part of the Sports Gallery.

There's the Capital Club fine dining restaurant, as well as a Discovery Channel store and a Modell's Sporting Goods store.

The building also houses the Capitals of the National Hockey League, the Mystics of the WNBA and the Georgetown University men's basketball games.

Back to the future

Who was it who sang, "Everything old is new again?"

Was he from Indiana?

That would explain the adoration Indiana fans have not only for the sport of basketball but for the shrine they've erected to house it in the city of Indianapolis.

Conseco Fieldhouse, home of the NBA's Pacers, opened for the 1999-2000 season to rave reviews from coaches, players, team executives, fans—in short, anyone who has entered the doors of the $183 million downtown facility. What Baltimore's Camden Yards is to baseball, Conseco Fieldhouse is to basketball.

"This place is just the ultimate," said Larry Bird, the Hall of Famer and Indiana native who coached the Pacers in their first season in the building, which is named after an insurance and investment firm. Remember Bird played for the Boston Celtics in Boston Garden, often viewed as the quintessential basketball arena—despite the rats.

"The best of the new facilities, bar none," said Quinn Buckner, a former Pacer—and Celtic—player who is now a broadcaster.

"This is the best one I've seen ... This ought to be the model," said Seattle coach Paul Westphal. "A lot of buildings are nice because they're new. This is nice because they put a lot of thought into it."

Said Pacers veteran Chris Mullin, "It's magnificent. It's geared totally toward basketball—not a hockey/basketball place. That's a big advantage. It's got a tight feel. It doesn't feel as big as it is. It's like a good, broken-in gym."

That's exactly what the architects from Ellerbe Beckett had in mind. They researched the history of the fieldhouses in Indiana, including the first one in the nation located in Newberry, Indiana. They created a one-of-a-kind palace but managed to recreate the feeling of Butler University's Hinkle Fieldhouse, which was featured in the classic sports movie, "Hoosiers."

Project manager John Hilkene worked on Cleveland's Gund Arena and Washington's MCI Center, but they are totally different from Conseco Fieldhouse.

"I think people will be amazed when

they see it," he said. "You're transported back in time."

Indeed, after spending a couple of hours inside, it feels as if you should head right to the malt shop on the way home and listen to a couple of Frank Sinatra ditties on the juke box.

Everything is completely retro. From the signage to the brick interior walls to the glass exterior walls to the lighting to the scoreboard and the seats, it's a total throwback. In a very real sense, the Pacers are returning to their roots. When they joined the American Basketball Association in 1967 (the ABA merged with the NBA in 1976), they played in The Coliseum at the Indiana State Fairgrounds.

Conseco takes all the best from such venues and improves upon it.

"Unbelievable," said Pacer star Reggie Miller. "Absolutely unbelievable. Far beyond my expectations. You feel like you should be wearing Chuck Taylors in this place."

The popular old tennis shoes that were the only choice for young players years ago would be right at home. In fact, there probably are a pair or two among the many, many prominent displays of memorabilia from Indiana's basketball history. Those, too, add to the nostalgia of the building.

Before every game, a video on the scoreboard begins with a family sitting in front of an old console radio and evolves into a modern day highlight film. The video ends with the following words printed on the scoreboard: "In 49 states it's just basketball. But this is Indiana."

Pacers president Donnie Walsh is a New Yorker who played at North Carolina. He knows the state has a special connection with the sport.

"All these little towns have their own gymnasiums," he told the New York Times. "You might have 10,000 people in the town, but the guy holds 12,000 and it is sold out every game. This is part of their culture."

Now, too, is Conseco Fieldhouse. Everybody who considers themselves basketball fans will have to make a pilgrimage to the sport's newest mecca. It will not disappoint.

From the moment fans come through the entrance, which resembles a train station and is patterned after the original Madison Square Garden, they are transported to another simpler time. That's not to say the building doesn't have all the modern conveniences. In addition to wider aisles, corridors and seats, there are 54 concession stands, 71 restrooms, a "barber shop" that offers face painting and the Home Court Gift Shop, which has on display a basketball that is 18 feet in diameter and weighs 3,860 pounds. It took 820 hours to construct, including the hand carving of 6,870 dimples on the surface of the ball. And, yes, the whole place is air-conditioned.

There are five major sponsor pavilions —the Indianapolis Star newspaper, the Indianapolis Motor Speedway, Clarian Health, American Trans Air and The Finish Line—and each of their displays stays true to the retro concept. The Speedway pavilion, complete with old race car, is not to be missed.

Amid all these bells and whistles, the basketball wasn't too bad either.

In their first season in the new building, the Pacers won the Central Division and finished the season with a 36–5 record at Conseco, tying the Los Angeles Lakers for best home record in the league. How much did the Pacers enjoy their new digs? Their statistics in every major category were better at home than on the road. While that's the norm for most teams, the differences for the Pacers were significant in a couple of categories. For instance, they averaged 104 points per game in Conseco and just 98.6 on the road. They shot 47.2 percent from the field at home and 44.6 away from home.

Maybe their opponents were just too busy enjoying the view. Now that would be a homecourt advantage.

Of course, the homecourt advantage really is based on the support of the fans, and the Pacer supporters are among the loudest and most enthusiastic in the league. They have a team and a building to be proud of, and they're not shy about saying so.

Said Pacers general manager David Kahn of the fabulous facility, "People are certain to be blown away, no ifs, ands or buts. I'm convinced, after seeing them all, that this one will stand on its own as the best in the business. I really believe that. I think that everybody in the NBA and everybody who is a basketball fan will be talking about this building for years to come."

Home sweet dome

When the demolition crew blew the Seattle Kingdome to kingdom come on March 26, 2000, it was no great loss to the world of basketball.

As it turns out, playing basketball in a dome wasn't a very good idea in the first place. But basketball became a part of the package deal when massive, domed, multi-purpose facilities were all the rage in the 1970s.

The excitement over the Astrodome— "the eighth wonder of the world"—that made its debut in Houston in 1965 provided the momentum for massive, enclosed stadiums in Seattle, Minneapolis, Montreal, Detroit and New Orleans, among others.

In theory, the dome is magnificent. No rainouts. No cold feet. No sunburns. Year-round usage. Big enough for football games and boat shows and rock concerts. Easily downsized for baseball and soccer. Easily downsized even more for basketball. Plenty of parking. Permanent bars and restaurants and offices. And, oh, so impressive.

In reality, bigger isn't always better. The domed stadium was a jack of all trades, master of none. While it was capable of housing all sports, it was ideal for none.

Sight lines are different for every sport, as are traditions. So the recent trend is for facilities built to cater to each individual sport with an eye toward nostalgia.

Baseball facilities are being built to look like the ballparks that were built at the start of the last century, with the players, the fans and the real grass subject to rain and sunshine. Football facilities are being built to accommodate the game, the players and the folks who can afford luxury boxes on the 50-yard-line. And basketball is going back to the buildings that bring fans close enough to the court to hear the ball thump and the sneakers squeak.

KEY FACTOR: *Seattle's basketball fans love their Key Arena more than the now-demolished Kingdome even if there are many fewer seats.*

Back when the Kingdome was built, in 1976, architects were trying to keep up with the Texans.

As soon as the Kingdome was finished, it was the home of the Seattle Seahawks of the National Football League. The Seattle Mariners major league baseball team moved in for the 1977 season. And the Supersonics of the National Basketball Association opened its 1978–79 season in the dome. But while football and baseball stayed to the end, the Sonics were out after 1985.

Not that the Kingdome hurt the franchise any. The Sonics were calling the Kingdome home when they won the NBA title in June of 1979. And fans did go there to see the Sonics play. The largest crowd to see a basketball game in the Kingdome was the crowd of 39,457 that gathered for the game the Supersonics lost to the Washington Bullets in the NBA playoffs on May 30, 1978.

Still, the Sonics couldn't wait to get into the Key Arena, an entertainment complex on the north side of downtown Seattle. The Key Arena is built specifically for basketball, with stands ringing the court and providing the up-close-and-personal feel the game should have.

In fact, all but one NBA team that has had to play in a dome has left for cozier surroundings.

The San Antonio Spurs are the only NBA team currently playing in a dome, and they are clamoring to get out. Like other domes, the Alamodome in San Antonio is good for first impressions and mindboggling numbers, but not much good for basketball.

The Spurs started the 1993–94 season in the Alamodome before an NBA opening night record crowd of 36,523. With a popular and successful team on the court, the Spurs have been able to maintain good average attendance despite the cavernous site. And the Spurs were calling the Alamodome home when they won the NBA title in 1999.

But the Alamodome experience is not a hoop fan's dream.

An expansive parking lot extends for acres around the building, making for a hike even before a fan can get inside and begin the trek on miles of ramps to get to seats that seem to be a county away from the hardwood court. Even courtside seats have a disconnected feel because they are all moveable chairs and stands.

There just is no way to give the Alamodome the same feel for the tradition of the game that exists in Madison Square Garden or existed in Boston Garden.

The Alamodome lends itself more to tractor pulls, demolition derbies and ice shows than it does to any mainstream

sport, although it comes closer to feeling like a football facility.

The Alamodome was built with the promise that it would lure an NFL football team to South Texas. That never did come to pass, although it did manage to lure an annual college bowl game.

The massive space can be rearranged into several configurations ranging from a 5,000-seat plan for small conventions to a 65,000-seat plan for football. It has been used for Dallas Cowboys exhibition games and pro hockey exhibition games.

But it is best-suited for hosting Mick Jagger and the Rolling Stones. So the Spurs are looking to move.

In all likelihood, their stay in the dome will be a relatively short one, although it will be one of the longer ones. Most NBA teams that have played in domes were just passing through.

The Minnesota Timberwolves played in the Metrodome their first year, 1989, while waiting for their arena to be built in downtown Minneapolis. Despite attracting the third-largest crowd for a regular-season game, 49,551, in their final game at the Metrodome to claim the league's single-season attendance record at 1,072,572, the Wolves happily opened the 1990–91 season in the much cozier Target Center.

The Jazz played in the cavernous New Orleans Superdome until becoming the

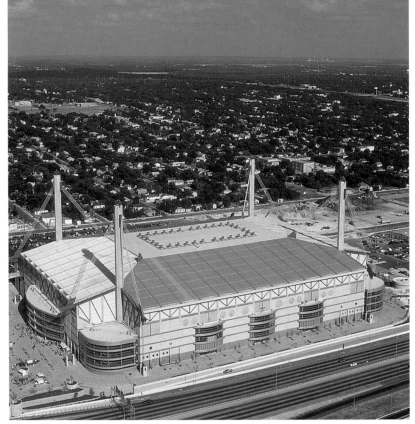

REMEMBER THE ALAMO: *The San Antonio Spurs play in the Alamodome, but want to move.*

Utah Jazz and moving to Salt Lake City. Despite the fact that the team's nickname is totally inappropriate for its surroundings, the Delta Center has become one of the loudest arenas in the league.

When Toronto was granted an NBA franchise it was with the plan to build a 22,500-seat basketball arena in Toronto. It was necessary, though, for the Raptors to play in the Skydome their first two seasons and part of a third until the Air Canada Centre was ready.

Again, despite the disappointing atmosphere and the difficulty of promoting basketball in a traditional hockey hotbed, the team was able to draw. The Raptors set a season-high for attendance in 1995–96 when 36,131 showed up to see the Raptors beat the first-place Chicago Bulls on March 24, 1996.

When the Atlanta Hawks lost the Omni after the 1996–97 season, they had to split time between Georgia Tech and the Georgia Dome in 1997–98. The Hawks, too, managed to maintain strong attendance while playing in a too-big venue and set the single-game record by attracting 62,046 for a game against the Chicago Bulls on March 27, 1998. The Georgia Dome is home to the Atlanta Falcons of the National Football League and had its biggest moments as host to the

Super Bowl in 1994 and the Olympic basketball and gymnastics competitions in the 1996 Olympic Games.

But the Hawks had no intention of playing there any longer than they had to. They were in their new Philips Arena for the start of the 1999 season.

The suite life

The game gets underway while some guests are still selecting appetizers from a chafing dish and others are finishing salads or baked chicken or pasta on the plush sofa in front of the big screen TV. Only a few of the guests have stepped through the glass doors out onto the balcony to watch the tipoff live.

Most of the arena seats on the overhang of this luxury suite remain empty as the Cleveland Cavaliers play basketball and the party progresses. It's the same for most of the neighboring suites. Well-dressed, well-behaved ladies and gentleman eat, drink, chat and keep a casual eye on the action.

Caterers slip into the suite to take away the remains of the meal before wheeling in the dessert cart.

The thoughtful host, a representative of the corporation that pays for this luxury suite in Gund Arena in Cleveland, has provided a selection of hot dogs that will

stay in a warming tray throughout the game. It wouldn't be fitting for a guest who felt the urge for a traditional game treat to have to step out into the concourse among the throngs of fans scurrying for restrooms and standing in line at concession stands.

There is no need for occupants of suites to mingle with the public. Not when the suite has a refrigerator stocked with soft drinks, beer and wine; not with caterers taking care of the meal and the snacks; not with the private restroom.

There are similar suites—and more opulent ones—in basketball arenas throughout the country as well as in the football and baseball facilities. The new Browns Stadium just a few blocks away on the shores of Lake Erie has expansive, beautifully appointed (and heated) suites to keep the most fortunate football fans out of the blustery winds. And next door to Gund Arena, in Jacobs Field, equally impressive suites provide the Cleveland Indians' elite fans an ideal—if not necessarily traditional—baseball experience.

Andy Zimbalist, an economics professor at Smith College who has testified before Congress on the subject of sports marketing, has called the trends toward club seats and luxury suits a "gentrification" of the audience.

Architects are busy with new designs for new buildings that allow for more and more of these special spaces, including the less impressive but still quite expensive "club seats" in VIP areas with preferred parking and exclusive clubs and restaurants.

The forerunner of the luxury suite was the owners' box, usually next to the pressbox in baseball and football facilities. In years past, minority owners and city leaders and corporate sponsors and TV executives were invited to watch the game with the owner.

But as corporate money and corporate sponsorship has become a major player in the economy of sports franchises, more and more private boxes are needed. Especially for corporations paying millions of dollars to put their names on the facility.

Basketball is following the lead of football and baseball when it comes to corporate naming and corporate signage.

Even colleges are cashing in on corporate sponsorship and naming—and even colleges are providing luxury suites for sponsors and million dollar-donors.

There will be no more classic old arenas named Boston Garden or Madison Square Garden. In Atlanta, the new basketball site is called Philips Arena. In Toronto, it's Air Canada Centre. In Miami, it's the AmericanAirlines Arena. In Chicago, the United Center. In Los Angeles, Staples Center.

In the Atlanta Hawks' new Philips Arena, all 96 private suites are located on one side of the court. In selling the new configuration to the public, the Hawks stressed that this allowed for seats on the other side of the arena to be closer and lower than seats in other arenas. But it also allows owners of suites and club seats to have "a dedicated entry, lounge and restaurant."

In other words, no contact with the masses.

And the Philips Arena even one-ups its own 96 private suites with 10 courtside suites that will provide, the Hawks' press guide says, "never-before-seen-views from private suites."

When the Air Canada Centre opened boasting 22,500 seats for basketball, it was noted that 1,140 of those seats were within luxury suites.

Even the monstrous Alamodome the San Antonio Spurs are trying to hard to flee, a structure obviously built with masses of people in mind, has 32 luxury suites. But that's not enough to put the Spurs' ledgers over the top. With a winning team and great attendance the Spurs still lost $2 million in 1998–99 because the hulking Alamodome doesn't produce enough cash flow—which means it isn't built to cater to wealthy and corporate clients.

Luxury boxes are the driving force behind the building frenzy throughout the sports world. When teams label their facilities built within the last 20 years "obsolete," they aren't referring to sight-lines, satellite hookups or a lack of handicapped accessibility ramps. They are saying that the old designs won't allow for enough of the profitable suits to keep up with escalating player salaries.

And new arenas can be built at such a brisk clip because of the corporate money.

The spin that keeps the "gentrification" of attending sports events from turning the average citizen off is the storyline that corporate naming and luxury suites will allow a community to hold on to a beloved franchise without having to use taxpayer money to build or update facilities.

That's largely true. While there is a salary cap, there seems to be no cap on what corporations and the very wealthy will pay for the best access to the games.

Think maybe the luxury accommodations, as great as they are, still don't rival the kind of on-the-court seats Jack Nicholson and Dyann Cannon have for Lakers games? Well, before the Miami Heat played its first game in its new AmericanAirlines Arena, the team had sold six "star boxes." These new-approach, top-end luxury areas went for $500,000 each. The suite is actually located under the arena, with a private entry to courtside seats. Four courtside seats are included each package.

These half-a-million-dollar deals weren't hard to sell. The Heat originally planned four such suites but had to build six.

That's a quick, additional $1 million a year for eight high-end seats in the arena. How many high-up seats have to be sold to make that much profit?

Prices at some other arenas are not so far behind. Luxury boxes in Staples Center in Los Angeles and Madison Square Garden in New York go for $300,000 each.

STAR POWER: *AmericanAirlines Arena has six "Star Boxes" for VIPs at $500,000 each.*

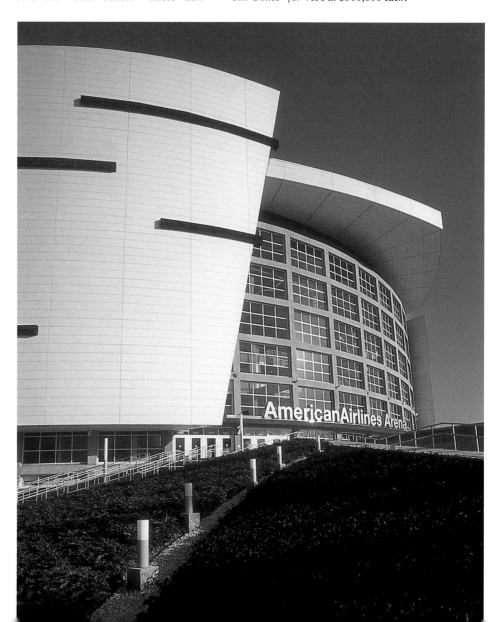

OLYMPIC GAMES

It has become a case of being careful for what you wish for. With the world's basketball powers intent on seeing the best at the Olympics, the Dream Team concept was born on April 7, 1989. Three years later, the rest of the planet marveled as Magic, Jordan and Bird offered a performance for the ages. The gap has since closed at the Games, but the awe remains.

The disappointment was relative. Nobody was prepared to say that the United States was not still the dominant basketball power on the planet.

But chinks in the armor had begun to surface. The disappointment of the 1972 Olympics and the Soviets' apparent theft of the Olympic gold, coupled with another loss at the Games, this time in 1988 to the Soviet Union in Seoul, set in motion the process that would deliver the greatest players on earth to the globe's premier athletic competition.

Entering the 1992 Barcelona Olympics, the United States, birthplace of Dr. James Naismith's game, had not won a major international men's basketball competition since the 1986 World Championships. The United States had finished second in the 1987 Pan American Games, third in the 1988 Olympics, second in the 1989 Goodwill Games, third in the 1990 World Championships and third in the 1991 Pan American Games.

For a nation that had not lost in its first 63 Olympic games, this simply was not

(Above) **KG IN SYDNEY:** *Kevin Garnett was among the latest group of NBA stars to win gold.*

(Opposite) **TAKING FLIGHT:** *Larry Bird took his dead-eye shooting form to the 1992 Games.*

good enough. And, apparently, neither were the units it had stocked with premier collegiate and amateur athletes.

On April 7, 1989, the face of Olympic basketball forever changed. On that date, at a World Congress called for by FIBA, the governing body of international

408 basketball, delegates voted 59–13 in favor of "open competition."

Interestingly, the United States cast its vote against the proposal, perhaps to appear modest, perhaps in recognition of what would follow.

Thus, came the birth of the Dream Team, arguably the greatest collection of basketball players ever to wear the same uniform at the same time. The 1992 U.S. Olympic team was not merely a collection of players headed to the Basketball Hall of Fame in Springfield, Massachusetts; these were players deserving of their own wing.

In many ways, perhaps it was fitting that the Olympics had waited for this moment to accept NBA players. Pro basketball was at the height of its popularity. The NBA had become a worldwide spectacle.

It was what the world wanted, what the NBA, with its insatiable marketing hunger, was more than willing to provide.

Michael Jordan. Magic Johnson. Larry Bird. An argument could be made they are the game's three greatest players, or, at the least, three most influential forces.

Karl Malone and Charles Barkley, two players who defined the power-forward position.

Patrick Ewing and David Robinson, quintessential big men.

John Stockton, Chris Mullin and Clyde Drexler, pro's pros.

Scottie Pippen, the ultimate in versatility.

And Duke forward Christian Laettner, for those who insisted one amateur be part of the transition.

Initially, there was a backlash from the purists, even though professionals long had dotted the rosters of other nations'

Olympic teams. The move also was seen as a vehicle to quash any notion of competition.

"It's a ridiculous idea," Robinson said of the thought that the United States was acting arrogantly in so loading its roster. "Other countries who dominate sports never want to let up."

At a time when foreign cars dotted American highways, when American players played in foreign-produced footwear, when technology was imported from the Orient instead of developed at home, Jordan saw it as time for the American game to return to American fame.

"We're going over there to regain the pride and dignity of U.S. basketball," Jordan said of the eve of the trip to the Barcelona Games. "Some way, even if it's just basketball, we can at least show the world that we can take control of some-

PURE MAGIC: *Magic Johnson delivered his blend of joy and skill to the first U.S Dream Team on its march to the 1992 Olympic gold medal.*

thing. If it's an overkill, it's an overkill."

Said Bird, "I'm sure we will have some good tests along the way."

Seen as aloof by some, the U.S. players had taken to heart their nation's semifinal loss and silver-medal finish in the 1988 Games in Seoul.

"I was watching on TV when Russia beat our guys and they lifted up the coach like they had beaten America's best," Malone said of a victory that instead was produced over a team comprised solely of collegians, many of whom would go on to only marginal NBA careers. "That kind of pissed me off."

The Americans were determined to not only win, but to dominate.

"I fail to see why the USA has less right than any other country to put its best foot forward," said Dave Gavitt, then president of USA Basketball. "We shouldn't be ashamed, defensive or embarrassed in any way."

The world was braced for what would follow.

"We, of course, know the U.S. will win everything for the time being," said FIBA General Secretary Boris Stankovic. "But we also think that the only way others can improve is by playing against the best."

The Dream Team won its first game 116-48 against Angola.

"Our aim was to lose by less than 45 points," was the verdict of Angola coach Victorino Cunha.

Later there was a 127–83 victory over Brazil.

"The only thing we were hoping for," Brazil coach Jose Medalha said, "was to lose by the minimum number of points possible. You can't hope for anything else when playing against the USA."

The pattern would continue.

USA 122, Spain 81. Spanish guard admitted Jose Biriukov, "It was like a dream come true."

USA 127, Lithuania 76. Lithuanian forward Arturas Karnisovas said, "They are my heroes. I even brought my camera along to take pictures of them."

Having experienced the NBA first hand, as a guard with the Golden State Warriors, Lithuania's Sarunas Marciulionis explained, "They're too good for the rest of the world."

By the numbers, this was not necessarily the most efficient Olympic team the United States had produced. The 1964 entry had limited opponents to 29.2-percent shooting; this team 36.5 percent. The 1956 team had won by an average margin of 53.5 points; this team by 43.8. But out of 320 minutes of competition at those Barcelona Games, the Dream Team led for a staggering 306 minutes, 54 seconds.

For those who had thought the international community had closed the gap in Olympic competition, this ultimate collage of basketball talent painted a stark reality.

"All you can do is hope to play a close game with the U.S. and count it as a moral victory," said German center Hansi Gnad. "Any everybody knows that moral victories don't count in the Olympics."

But medals do, which is why competition remained fierce, even as the Dream Team dominated.

"The gold medal is already gone for these Olympics," Croatia coach Peter Skansi said at the outset of the 1984 Games. "Everybody else will play for two medals—the silver and the bronze."

Yet if the gold was a given, it was a bauble that truly was cherished.

"This is possibly the most important thing in my life," Magic Johnson said, having emerged from retirement to compete with the Dream Team. "I've never been in such an important event. We'll never see another team this good."

In the end, there only was awe.

"That is as close as you can get to the perfect basketball team," said Cuba coach Miguels Calderon Gomez.

Or, as Canada center Bill Wennington, a fellow NBA player, would say, "The world will end before the U.S. is beaten."

In assessing his team's place in history, 1992 Olympic coach Chuck Daly, who had guided the Detroit Pistons to two NBA titles, was not thinking about Armageddon, just posterity.

"You will see a team of professionals in the Olympics again," he correctly predicted. "But I don't think you'll see another team quite like this. This was a majestic team."

In retrospect, Daly would say the toughest competition for the Dream Team

DREAM FULFILLED: *Hakeem Olajuwon gained his U.S. citizenship in time for Atlanta.*

came before the Olympics, when the squad gathered to practice in Monte Carlo. One intrasquad scrimmage had grown so fierce, that when it ended in a tie, Daly refused to allow it to continue, worried an injury might be the result.

"A lot of people thought we were 12 stars who wouldn't be able to play together," Johnson said. "Obviously, they were wrong."

One more time

Dream Team I begot Dream Team II, with similar results.

This time the mix was less top-heavy on legends, with a balance between stars present and NBA stars future.

Back from the first Dream Team for the 1996 Atlanta Olympics were

410

Stockton, Malone, Robinson, Pippen, Barkley and Robinson. But with Bird retired, Johnson out of the game and Jordan opting to let the next generation have the limelight, fresh faces such as Penny Hardaway, Grant Hill, Reggie Miller, Shaquille O'Neal, Gary Payton, Mitch Richmond and recently naturalized Hakeem Olajuwon were granted roster spots.

Just as its predecessor did, Dream Team II swept through the Olympics, easily capturing gold.

Led by coach Lenny Wilkens, and with the homecourt advantage, the NBA's legends attracted an average crowd of 32,263 for their games at the Georgia Dome.

Robinson paced the initial victory, his 18 points and seven rebounds guiding the United States to a 96–68 victory over Argentina.

In the next game, it was Malone's turn, as his 12 points paced a balanced attack in an 87–54 victory over Angola.

Barkley then proved up to the sup-

TWO THE HARDAWAY: *Penny Hardaway was part of the next generation at the '96 games.*

posed challenge from Lithuania, with 18 points and five rebounds in a 104–82 victory.

Pippen then would go for 24 points as the Americans steamrolled China 133–70. The points were the most ever for a U.S. Olympic team.

Richmond, getting revenge for his bronze-medal in 1988, followed by scoring 16 points as the United States concluded the opening round with a 102–71 victory over Croatia.

In the quarterfinals, former Orlando Magic teammates Hardaway and O'Neal combined for 25 points as the United States blitzed Brazil 98–75.

In the semifinals, Barkley went for 24 points and 11 rebounds, as Australia was vanquished 101–73.

Finally, in the gold-medal game, before 34,600, Yugoslavia was handed its lone loss of the Games, the 95–69 result allowing the United States to again savor gold. That game, however, at least provided a challenge, with the Americans ahead only 51–50 with 14:03 to play.

"We won the gold medal and that is what matters," a satisfied Malone said of the tighter-than-expected nature of the title game.

Robinson, who had been a member of the humbled '88 U.S. team, paced the victors with 28 points.

"We were a little bit tight in the first and I could tell we needed a spark," Robinson said, "and I just tried to come off the bench and give us that."

The most emotional moment during the championship game may have come when Muhammad Ali was given a gold medal to replace the one he no longer had from his 1960 Olympic boxing victory. IOC President Juan Antonio Samaranch made the presentation at midcourt.

What the relative closeness of the title game showed was how the world methodically was catching up.

"It's just that this has been a very grueling month, mentally and physically," Barkley admitted of his second go-round with a Dream Team.

Indeed, the opposition displayed far more of a willingness to fight back than

against the original Dream Team.

In the opening minutes of the championship game, Malone threw Yugoslavia's Vlade Divac to the floor, Yugoslavia's Sasha Danilovic and the Americans' Payton had to be separated and Yugoslavia's Zarko Paspalj was forced to leave with a wound. And in the Americans' game before that, Australian Andrew Vlahov got into shoving matches with Pippen and Malone, with Malone drawing a technical foul.

For Dream Team II coach Wilkens it truly was a dream. Not only was he an Olympic coach, but he got to coach in the same city where he was guiding the NBA's Atlanta Hawks.

"I'd like to keep these players here with me and have the home crowd cheering for us like this," he said.

Set in stone

With overwhelming results, on-court success and little off-court criticism of the dominance, the Dream Team approach has become a way of life, the star-studded NBA rosters also employed for both the 1994 World Championships in Canada and the 1999 Tournament of the Americas in Puerto Rico.

How in demand are the NBA's best? In 1998, another Dream Team was expected to represent the United States at the World Championships in Greece. Sellout crowds had been anticipated in Athens for the Americans' appearances. But when labor problems shut down the NBA, the elite players who were selected to participate in the event boycotted the World Championships. The result was that the attendance plummeted.

While USA Basketball has attempted to retire the Dream Team moniker—the second Dream Team no match for the original, all others paling in comparison —the NBA's elite apparently will remain a fixture at major international competitions for years to come.

For the 2000 Sydney Games, two players with previous Dream Team experience, Payton and Hill, both of whom played at the 1996 Atlanta Games, headed the All-Star cast. Also on the 2000 U.S. team were guard Ray Allen, forward Vin Baker, forward Vince Carter, center Tim Duncan, forward Kevin Garnett,

COMMON GOAL: *The Olympics have provided NBA regular-season foes the opportunity, such as in 2000, to share some rare camaraderie.*

guard Tim Hardaway, guard Allan Houston, guard Jason Kidd, center Alonzo Mourning and guard Steve Smith. Forward Tom Gugliotta also was selected, but was unable to participate because of a knee injury.

Over the years, the criteria for the selection of these elite teams of NBA stars has evolved. Because of several ugly incidents at the 1994 World Championship in Toronto, it was decided that poise, as much as polish, would be factored into the selection process.

"We weren't thrilled with what happened," Warren Brown, executive director of USA Basketball, which oversees the selection process for international competitions, said of the U.S. representation

at those 1994 World Championships.

Stressed NBA Vice President Rod Thorn, who headed the U.S. selection committee for the 2000 Olympics, "The 1994 team … didn't act well as a group. We didn't win well. You want to win with some grace. You want to show the best aspects of your sport—and we didn't win gracefully. I think if they could have done it again, a lot of them wouldn't have done some of the things that they did."

While some initially believed that NBA players would tire of the extensive travel in addition to the 82-game schedule and league playoffs, the competition has remained fierce to represent the United States.

As Mourning said upon his selection

to the third U.S. Olympic team to be comprised of NBA players, "Being named to the Olympic team is a quite a thrill, having grown up watching the Olympics and now being able to participate is something I'll cherish for a lifetime. I'll be able to tell my grandkids that their grandfather was an Olympian."

Wilkens said with so many of the world's best national teams featuring professionals, there can be no turning back from the use of NBA players.

"We have some outstanding college players, but they won't beat the Croatians, the Lithuanians, the Yugoslavians," he said. "They're all pro players." Instead the NBA pros are 3-for-3 against the world.

412

1936
BERLIN

Basketball had been contested at the Olympics only as a demonstration sport in 1904, 1924 and 1928, otherwise not even part of the Games. In 1935, the International Olympic Committee formally recognized the International Basketball Federation. That paved the way for the sport to be adopted for the 1936 Berlin Games as a full-scale medal competition.

The initial Olympic competition was held outdoors, on a tennis courts composed of clay and sand, a clearly unsuitable combination, as it turned out, when the championship game was contested in a driving rain. The result was conditions that made it practically impossible to dribble.

Through it all, the United States endured to defeat Canada 19–8.

For the Americans, the very rules of the initial competition came as a shock. Only upon the team's arrival in Europe did it learn that rosters would be limited to seven players and that those taller than 6-foot-2 would be banned. While the United States was able to get the height limitation dropped (it featured four players 6–3 or taller), it was less successful with the roster limitation.

The result was that only the seven players who competed in the championship game were allowed to claim gold medals, even though the United States had alternated dual seven-player teams throughout the competition.

Ironically, the start of the Americans' 63-game Olympic winning streak would come by the forfeit score of 2–0, when the Spanish team failed to present itself, as the result of the Spanish civil war. Some Olympic record books continue to list the Americans' winning streak at 62 games, discounting that forfeit victory.

It was, to say the least, an odd debut.

1948
LONDON

With war-torn Europe limited in its ability to field competitive teams in the first post-war Games, five of the eight teams that advanced to the quarterfinals hailed from the Americas.

This certainly was not the most memorable moment for basketball competition in the Games. Twice in these Games, Iraq lost by 100 points, on the way to an 0–7 finish. Ireland would average only 17 points, on the way to an 0–6 record. A British referee was knocked unconscious during a game between Chile and Iraq. And in a truly bizarre moment, a Chinese player managed to dribble the ball—and himself—through the legs of 7-foot U.S. center Bob Kurland to score a basket.

After a 59–57 escape against Argentina in the preliminaries, the United States cruised to the gold medal.

PERFECT MIX: *The 1948 champions were made up of players from the Phillips 66ers and the University of Kentucky.*

The United States entry was mostly comprised of players from the Phillips 66ers, winners of the 1948 national AAU title, and the 1948 college champs, the University of Kentucky. In fact, throughout most of the '48 Games, players from those teams played almost solely in units, rotated in shifts.

1952
HELSINKI

The most intense rivalry in all of Olympic basketball began to take shape when the Soviet Union, in the midst of the Cold War, elected to send its first athletes to the Games since 1912.

Indeed, the Cold War nearly turned into an Olympic freeze out.

Routed 86–58 by the United States during the preliminary round, the Soviets immediately went into a stall when the teams met in the gold-medal game.

Ten minutes into the title game, the United States led 4–3. At halftime, the Americans were up 17–15. The Soviets would pull ahead briefly in the second half before the Americans began to not only give themselves some breathing room, but actually settled into their own stall. The turnabout did not sit well with the Soviets, with one of their players reduced to sitting on the court in protest, until his coach ordered him to rise. The United States won 36–25.

Once again, the United States shuttled in entire separate units, this time made up of players from two distinct amateur teams, the AAU Peoria Caterpillars and the University of Kansas.

MAN IN THE MIDDLE: *Bob Kurland stood tallest in the 1952 Games, just as he had throughout his collegiate career.*

With the sports still in its inception internationally, these Games featured moments such as when France was reduced to three eligible players because of fouls and when the feisty Uruguay team belittled a referee for almost five minutes before realizing a call actually had gone in its favor.

Uruguay, in fact, would brawl its way through the competition, injuring three Soviet players in one game and getting involved in a brawl with Argentina that would turn into a 25-person melee. The end of that game with Argentina would result in only three players from Uruguay and four from Argentina remaining eligible.

1956
MELBOURNE

In a defining moment for the integration of the United States effort, black players Bill Russell, a center, and K.C. Jones, a guard, both from the University of San Francisco, would lead the Americans.

Russell's dedication to the Olympic effort was such that he delayed his entry to the NBA to compete, with the reversed seasons in Australia leading the summer Games to be contested during what were the winter months in the northern hemisphere.

The United States proved even more dominant than in the Dream Team Era. The Americans averaged nearly 100 points, eclipsed that total four times, and won by an average of 53.5 points.

Russell set the tone immediately, scoring 20 points in an opening 98–40 victory over Japan.

In the next two games, Thailand was dismissed 101–29, and the Philippines were mauled 121–53. The Soviets then were routed 85–55 and Uruguay was drilled 101–38.

An 89–55 victory over the Soviets delivered the gold medal.

The U.S. Olympic team wasn't even done then. It returned to the United States to win a college tournament that December that featured San Francisco, Loyola and Santa Clara.

The Olympic experience did not take the edge off Russell's game. He appeared in 48 of the Boston Celtics' 72 games during the 1956–57 season, as Boston won the NBA championship.

1960
ROME

Until the Dream Team arrived in 1994, the 1960 U.S. entry was considered the most talented to grace the Olympics.

With a backcourt of Jerry West and Oscar Robertson and with frontcourt

(*Opposite*) **COMMITMENT:** *Bill Russell put off his pro career in order to lead the U.S. to gold.*

STANDING TALLEST: *Again, in 1960, the U.S. were by far the dominant team at the Games.*

players such as Jerry Lucas and John Havlicek, the Games served as a preview for future inductions into the Basketball Hall of Fame.

The United States won every game by at least 24 points, and averaged 101.8 per game. Ten players from Pete Newell's roster would go on to play in the NBA.

As an example of the dominance, against Yugoslavia in the semifinals, the

Americans took a 32–1 lead on the way to a 104–42 victory.

Against the loathed Soviets, also in the semifinal round, the Americans would have little trouble with 7-foot-3, 320-pound center Jan Kruminsh, rolling to an 81–57 victory.

With Lucas scoring 25 points, the Americans routed Brazil 90–63 for the gold medal.

1964
TOKYO

In a battle of unbeatens in the gold-medal game, the United States and the Soviet Union both entered with 8–0 records. The Soviets moved to a 16–13 lead, but that came at the cost of early foul trouble to star Alexander Petrov. By halftime, the Americans were ahead 39–31 and used a dynamic fastbreak to roll to a 73–59 victory. Luke Jackson led the Americans with 17 points, with future U.S. Presidential candidate Bill Bradley adding 10.

Despite the eventual dominance, there was initial concern about the United States' ability to compete, with talk of a potential boycott of all black American athletes during those racially charged times. The boycott never materialized, fortunately leaving the Americans with the services of Joe Caldwell, Jim Barnes and Jackson.

About the only factor to take attention off the Americans during the competition was that the Peruvians, dismissed 60–45 by the United States, featured four Duarte brothers on their Olympic team.

1968
MEXICO CITY

There were concerns about the United States' undefeated Olympic status entering these games.

The U.S. team that had toured Europe prior to the games had gone only 1–3 against both the Soviets and Yugoslavs.

Among those who did not compete for what could have been a far stronger U.S. entry were centers Elvin Hayes and Lew Alcindor (later Kareem Abdul-Jabbar). Hayes was ineligible because of a pro contract he had signed and Alcindor had cited his collegiate studies and support for a proposed boycott of the Games by black American athletes.

These proved to be treacherous Games for the United States.

JUMPING JOE: *At the '64 Games, it was easy to see how Joe Caldwell got his nickname.*

418

After squeezing to a 61–56 victory over Puerto Rico, the United States led only 32–29 at halftime of the championship game against Yugoslavia.

But that was when the United States staged one of the most furious displays of strength in Olympic lore. Led by Kansas guard Jo Jo White and junior-college standout Spencer Haywood, the Americans stormed back with a 22–3 blitz to make the 65–50 outcome elementary. The effort was so appreciated that the Mexican crowd, which had come out in support of the underdog Yugoslavs, turned their allegiance to the Americans during the rally. Haywood finished with 21 points, with White adding 14.

For Haywood, it was a worldwide coming out. At 19, he stood, at the time, as the youngest player to make a U.S. Olympic roster. During the competition, Haywood shot a remarkable 71.9 percent, giving a hint of what he later would deliver to the University of Detroit and then the ABA and NBA.

ATTACKING THE GLASS: *In '68, Spencer Haywood (8) made more than 70 percent of his shots.*

1972
MUNICH

What was scheduled as late-night theater in Munich turned into a horror show for the United States, in perhaps the most disputed outcome of any sporting event ever.

The United States breezed through much of the early competition, the only challenging test a 61–54 victory over Brazil in the preliminary round.

In the semifinal round, a 68–38 victory over Italy set up the gold-medal game against the Soviets.

The United States entered that title game still unbeaten in Olympic competition. The game began at 11:45 p.m. local time on a Sunday night to accommodate television interests in the United States.

The Soviets jumped to a 7–0 lead and were ahead 26–21 at halftime. With 12:18 to play, with the Soviets ahead 38–34, it got ugly. Dwight Jones, the United States' leading scorer and rebounder, and Soviet reserve Dvorni Edeshko ejected for scuffling.

From there, the United States trimmed its deficit to 49–48 on a jump shot by forward Jim Forbes with 40 seconds remaining. The Soviets worked the clock down to 10 seconds, but an attempt by center Aleksander Belov was blocked by U.S. forward Tom McMillen, a future U.S. Congressman, and guard Doug Collins, the future NBA coach of the Chicago Bulls and Detroit Pistons, intercepted a pass attempt from center Belov, who gained control of the blocked shot.

From there, insanity reigned.

Collins drove to the basket, only to be fouled intentionally with three seconds to play by Sako Sakandelidze. Groggy, Collins regained his senses enough to make both free throws to give the United States a 50–49 lead, even though the second free throw was taken while the timing horn seemingly was inadvertently sounded.

The Soviets immediately inbounded after Collins' foul shots and failed to score.

Game over? Not quite.

An official apparently had signaled a

stop to play, with the horn for a Soviet timeout, during Collins' second free-throw attempt.

The Soviets insisted they had called for time.

With the officials ruling the Soviets should be able to again inbound, a Soviet pass wound up off line as time seemingly again expired.

Game over? Not quite.

For some reason, when the clock was reset, it was reset for 50 seconds instead of three.

That's when R. William Jones, Secretary General of FIBA, ordered the clock again reset, even though he lacked the Olympic clout to order such a replay.

What followed was as wild as the timing irregularities. As a long pass was hoisted to Belov, U.S defenders Kevin Joyce and Jim Forbes appeared in position to thwart a potential scoring attempt. But as Belov caught the pass, the Soviet center sent the two defenders sprawling. Belov proceeded to score the deciding points in what ultimately was listed as a 51–50 Soviet victory.

Even that final play was suspect. For example, for an unknown reason, McMillen, who was defending the passer, inexplicable was warned by the referee to allow more room. Televisions replays also showed the pass came with a foot on the baseline, which could have been ruled a violation, returning possession to the United States. With none of the officials speaking English, there was little recourse.

The United States immediately filed a protest, which was denied four hours later by a five-man Jury of Appeals, which voted 3–2 to allow the final score to stand. Judges from Hungary, Cuba and Poland voted in the affirmative, in a sign of Eastern-bloc solidarity, while judges from Italy and Puerto Rico sided with the United States.

The Soviets ascended the medal platform for their gold medals, with the United States boycotting the presentations, its players to this day refusing to accept the silver medals.

The ultimate insult was delivered when, while signing the official protest, U.S. coach Henry Iba was victimized by a pickpocket, who emptied $370 from his trousers.

1976
MONTREAL

Without getting an opportunity to play the Soviets, the United States avenged what stood as its lone Olympic loss with a 7–0 sweep to the gold.

But there was yet another harrowing moment for the United States. In its second game, Butch Lee, a New Yorker who was overlooked for an invitation to the U.S. Olympic trials, suited up for Puerto Rico and nearly sparked an upset with his 35 points, before the United States held on for a 95–94 victory. With eight seconds to play and the United States ahead 93–92, Lee was called for a charging foul on a possession that could have delivered the victory for the U.S. commonwealth. Lee finished 15-of-18 from the field.

Yugoslavia then delivered a break to the Americans, upsetting the Soviets 89–84 in the semifinals. The United States then defeated the Yugoslavs 95–74 for the gold medal.

1980
MOSCOW

In the first of consecutive competitions tainted by international politics, the United States and many Western-bloc nations boycotted the Games because of the Soviet invasion of Afghanistan.

Argentina, Canada, China, Mexico and Puerto Rico, which also had qualified for the basketball competition, also were part of the boycott.

At the Games, Yugoslavia upstaged the Soviet Union on its home soil, rolling to a 9–0 record and the gold. The Soviets, at 7–2, could manage only the bronze, behind silver-medal Italy. The Soviets' losses came 87–85 to Italy and 101–91 to Yugoslavia in overtime.

The competition was diluted to the point that last-place India lost its seven games by an average score of 66–116.

CLOSELY CONTESTED: *The 1972 Games ended in disappointment for the U.S. team.*

Having selected an Olympic team, one that featured such future NBA legends as Isiah Thomas, Mark Aguirre and Buck Williams, the United States competed in a series of exhibitions on American soil against various teams comprised of NBA players. The Olympians won all but one of the five competitions.

1984
LOS ANGELES

This time many of the Soviet-bloc nations boycotted, in protest of U.S. foreign policy. But with the powerful Yugoslavs, the defending Olympic champions, attending, there still was true competition.

With the sport being contested for the first time in the Games' history in the home nation of the birthplace of basketball, both the U.S. men's and women's teams would roll to gold, marking the first such double.

With players such as Michael Jordan, Patrick Ewing and Chris Mullin, players who all would reunite on the first Dream Team, the United States steamrolled the competition, its closest game a 78–67 victory over West Germany.

While Yugoslavia likely would have given the United States its toughest competition, the two teams never met, with the Yugoslavs upset 74–61 by Spain in the semifinals.

The United States secured the gold with a 96–65 victory over Spain.

Jordan, just beginning to establish his legend, led the United States with a 17.1-point scoring average.

1988
SEOUL

After years of waiting, the United States finally caught up to the Soviets in Olympic competition, in a game that ultimately would change the way the Americans selected their rosters.

Having struggled in its second game, defeating Canada 76–70, the United States nonetheless arrived in the semifinals 6–0 to face the Soviets.

The United States trailed 47–37 at halftime, twice closed within two early in the second half, but then fell behind 69–60. The United States later would draw within three points, but ultimately fell 82–76.

In the gold-medal game, the Soviets faced a Yugoslav team that had defeated it 92–79 in early pool play. But in the championship game, the Soviets prevailed 76–63.

The United States exited with the bronze medal with a 78–49 victory over Australia.

As the result of the worst finish by the United States in Olympic basketball history, consideration immediately was given to allowing NBA players to compete in future Olympiads.

Indeed, professional players from other countries long had participated in the competition, including Brazil's Oscar Schmidt, who averaged an incredible 42.3 points in the 1988 Games.

In fact, once such allowances for NBA players were approved, several players from 1988 Olympic rosters jumped to the NBA, including Alexander Volkov, Sarunas Marciulionis and Arvydas Sabonis from the Soviet entry; Drazen Petrovic, Toni Kukoc, Zarko Paspalj, Stojan Vrankovic, Vlade Divac and Dino Radja from the Yugoslav entry; and Luc Longley, Andrew Gaze and Mark Bradtke from the Australian entry that placed fourth.

Four years later, the Dream Team era would begin.

(Opposite) MJ HAS ARRIVED: *Michael Jordan's Olympic debut came at Los Angeles in 1984.*

Olympics 1972 injustice

The 1972 Munich Games were about far more than an injustice on the basketball court. The Olympic community still grieves for the 11 Israeli athletes taken hostage and murdered by Arab terrorists.

In that respect, what happened to the United States against the Soviet Union in the gold-medal game is trivial in comparison.

But the bitterness still lingers.

Twice the Americans thought they had defeated the Soviets. Twice they celebrated as time seemingly expired. But each time they were called back for more.

A timeout was called, the officials initially insisted of a failed final-seconds bid by the Soviets to overcome a one-point deficit. The timing mechanism was off, was the reason another replay was ordered. And, finally, the Soviets, on an equally questionable sequence, stole into the night for a 51–50 victory.

Not only did the Americans refuse to take the medal stand at the conclusion of the competition, but, to this day, those unclaimed silver medals remain stored in a vault, the U.S. players refusing to accept the consolation baubles.

"You think you won, then they tell you lost," said former American forward Tom McMillen, who later served in the U.S. Congress. "It was the lowest point of my life." Things happened there you wouldn't expect in a high school game, let alone the Olympics."

Said U.S. coach Henry Iba, "Our players left not knowing whether we had won or not."

Iba would be invited back to the Olympics in 1984 by U.S. coach and longtime friend Bob Knight to work with the gold-medal winning U.S. team in Los Angeles. But his thoughts remained with those 1972 U.S. Olympians.

"The boys decided not to take the silver medals, and I still think we did the right thing," he said.

It was, after all, never about the silver.

"Somewhere in the Soviet Union there's a gold medal I should have," guard Kenny Davis said nearly two decades later.

The loss may well have set the stage for the emergence of the Dream Team concept, with American professionals sent to the Olympics, leaving little to chance.

"If we had sent our professional like they did," McMillen said of the 1972 Games, "it would have been over in the first five minutes."

INTERNATIONAL BASKETBALL

Created by a Canadian and played by athletes all over the world, basketball truly is an international endeavor. The NBA's growth as a global phenomenon is reflected in the diversity of its team's rosters. From Alaska to Zurich, basketball brings the world closer.

SHINING STAR: *The Houston Rockets' Hakeem Olajuwon, originally from Nigeria but now a U.S. Citizen, with the NBA trophy.*

From its inception, basketball was an international game. Its inventor, after all, was Dr. James Naismith, a Canadian teaching at Springfield College in Massachusetts. And long before Britain's John Amaechi or France's Tariq Abdul-Wahad or Australia's Luc Longley, there was an international element in the National Basketball Association. International players were part of the league from Day One. Literally.

In the very first game of the brand new Basketball Association of America, the forerunner of the NBA, Hank Arcado Biasatti, an Italian Canadian, took the court in the hallowed Maple Leaf Gardens for the Toronto Huskies in a 68–66 loss to the New York Knicks on November 1, 1946.

By the turn of the century, there were 37 international players from 22 different countries on NBA rosters as basketball was threatening to overtake soccer as the most popular game in the world. The league had played host to its first Cuban—Lazaro Borrell of the Seattle Supersonics—and its first Mexican—Horacio Llamas of the Phoenix Suns, as well as its first player from Belize (Vancouver's Milt Palacio) and the

Grenadines (Golden State's Adonal Foyle.)

But first there was Biasatti. Along with giveaways like nylon stockings and tons of coal, the Huskies thought a Canadian player would convince hockey fans—who occasionally yelled, "Check 'em" during games—to give basketball a look.

A 6-foot forward from Windsor and Assumption College (now the University of Windsor), Biasatti, 21, was a promising baseball player who played first base for

(Opposite) FOREIGN POLICY: *Charles Oakley (right) does a celebration chest-bash with former teammate, Jamaican-born Patrick Ewing*

the Toronto Maple Leafs of the International League. Born in Italy and raised in Windsor, he was one of three Canadians in the Huskies' first training camp. (Harry Mayzel of Toronto and Pat Sheehan of Newfoundland were the others, although Newfoundland did not actually become part of Canada until later.) Biasatti and Windsor's Gino Sovran, another Assumption College player, were the only Canadians to play with the Huskies that season. It was quite a change from the college game.

"There seems to be more bodily contact in the pro game than in amateur," Biasatti told Toronto reporters. "And, of course, it's much faster."

Biasatti was so aggressive defensively that he got into a fight with teammate Charlie Hoefer during training camp. But coach Ed Sadowski liked his style.

"He's a rugged, hard working little man," Sadowski told The Telegram newspaper. "And with a left hand that is beautiful. He can't figure out the stop-and-go move that is very important in our style of play. But I'm spending a lot of time with him, and I think the Toronto fans will see a greatly improved player over his performances last year with Assumption College."

Huskies fans didn't see much of Biasatti, however. Though he received a $1,000 signing bonus for agreeing to a contract that paid him $800 a month, he scored just six points in six games before being released in December.

Throughout the years, other Canadians have made their way to the NBA—Bill Wennington and, more recently, Rick Fox, Todd MacCulloch and Steve Nash, just to name a few. But they entered the league in the traditional way for most international players—

DET RELIEF: *Germany's Detlef Schrempf played for many NBA teams.*

by attending U.S. colleges and then being selected in the college draft. That was the course taken by Jamaica's Patrick Ewing, who attended high school in Massachusetts and went to Georgetown University, Holland's Rik Smits, who attended Marist, Nigeria's Hakeem Olajuwon, who attended the University of Houston, the Congo's Dikembe Mutombo, who attended Georgetown University, Germany's Detlef Schrempf, who attended the University of Washington, and Australia's Luc Longley, who attended the University of New Mexico.

But by the end of the 20th century, basketball had become so popular and so advanced all over the world that international players were coming into the NBA straight from the international leagues. Most NBA teams had international scouts, and several key sports agents were specializing in foreign-born players.

Herb Rudoy, a Chicago-based agent, represents Portland's Arvydas Sabonis and Cleveland's Zydrunas Ilgauskas and many other international players, as well as American stars.

"The big change is that the Russians, Serbs and Croats are MTV babies and no longer the typical Iron Curtain non-athletes of the 1960's and 70's," Rudoy said. "They are athletic and completely comfortable with the NBA and the lifestyle in the United States."

Not all of the international players grew up with the game of basketball. Olajuwon, for instance, was a handball and soccer player, one reason scouts believed his footwork was so tremendous. Nash played hockey, lacrosse and soccer. In fact, his father, John, played professional soccer in England and South Africa, where Steve was born. Lithuanian Sarunas Marciulionis was an

(Opposite) AN ACE: *Sarunas Marciulionis (Lithuania) was a tennis star, too.*

TREND SETTER: *Hawks' president Stan Kasten realized the potential of the international leagues.*

The next summer, the Atlanta Hawks became the first NBA team to visit the former Soviet Union. The trip was the brainchild of Hawks president Stan Kasten, one of the first NBA executives to realize the potential of the international talent pool.

How he came to that realization is an interesting story in itself. After Kasten graduated from Columbia Law School in 1976, he treated himself to a tour of Major League Baseball parks, and he met Atlanta Braves (and Turner Broadcasting System) owner Ted Turner at a game in St. Louis. The two hit it off, and shortly afterward Kasten went to work for Turner, eventually becoming president of the Hawks and vice president for sports teams at TBS. It was through his work in that capacity that he was exposed to international basketball competition, and he made sure the Hawks took full advantage of his knowledge.

"We were pioneers," said Mike Fratello, who coached the Hawks from 1983–90 and the Cleveland Cavaliers from 1993–99. "Stan Kasten had really great foresight. Stan was very perceptive in understanding there was a lot of talent in other countries we needed to start paying attention to."

Fratello coached the Hawks on that summer tour against the Soviets in 1988, and one of the highlights of the trip was his preparation of a big Italian feast for the entire traveling party. That helped bridge the gap between what the NBA entourage was used to and all the new experiences they found abroad.

On the court, though, everything went as expected. The Hawks stars shined. One of the stops was in Vilnius, Lithuania, where a 13-year-old Ilgauskas sat spellbound with his father. At that time, he had no idea that he'd become a first-round draft choice eight years later. Instead, he marveled over the high wire act of Atlanta's Dominique Wilkins and dreamed about his own basketball future.

A few months later, at the Summer Olympics in Seoul, those same Soviets won the gold medal, the Yugoslavians took the silver and the U.S. collegians earned the bronze.

The common perception is that the outrage over losing the gold medal fueled

accomplished tennis player.

But increasingly, international players grew up with the game of basketball. In 1999, the NBA Finals were broadcast to 205 countries in 41 languages. By the year 2000, the NBA had sponsored clinics and tournaments in every part of the world and had set up offices in Paris, London, Barcelona, Hong Kong, Melbourne, Tokyo, Taipei and Mexico City. NBA teams regularly play exhibition games in Mexico City and throughout Europe as part of the McDonald's Opens, and for several years, the league has scheduled regular season opening games in Tokyo.

The first McDonald's Open was held in Milwaukee in 1987, but the groundwork was laid three years earlier when NBA commissioner David Stern met to open a dialogue with Boris Stankovic,

Secretary General of The Federation Internationale de Basketball, or FIBA, the world governing body for basketball. Both organizations would benefit greatly by working together.

At the first McDonald's Open, the Milwaukee Bucks played host to Tracer Milan and the Soviet National Team, featuring a flashy point guard named Marciulionis. The Bucks beat both teams and won the tournament, but the competition was more important than the outcome.

Marciulionis said, "We got our butts kicked. But that was a good lesson. There was a direction in which to go."

Little did he know, that direction was west—across the Atlantic Ocean—and much sooner than he could possibly have imagined.

the U.S. push to make professionals eligible for the Olympics. In truth, the proposal had been introduced and narrowly defeated several years earlier. Its time finally came on April 8, 1989, when FIBA voted to eliminate the distinction between amateurs and professionals, making all players eligible for FIBA competitions, including the Olympics.

Thus, the Dream Team was born. Magic Johnson, Larry Bird, Michael Jordan, Charles Barkley and the rest of the NBA All-Stars all together on one team that stormed through the 1992 Summer Olympic Games in Barcelona.

But the ruling also allowed players from around the world to play in the NBA without jeopardizing their eligibility for their Olympic teams. And it didn't take long for them to take advantage of this new opportunity.

For the 1989–90 season, Marciulionis, who represented Lithuania following the break-up of the Soviet Union, joined the Golden State Warriors. Drazen Petrovic, a Croatian, joined the Portland Trail Blazers. Zarko Paspalj, of Montenegro, joined the San Antonio Spurs. Alexander Volkov, a Russian, joined the Hawks.

They had varying degrees of success and lengths of stay.

Marciulionis averaged 12.1 points as a rookie and increased that to 18.9 points his third season and 17.4 his fourth. He was traded to Seattle, Sacramento and Denver before retiring after the 1996–97 season.

Petrovic averaged 7.6 points as a rookie with Portland before being traded to New Jersey. He averaged 22.3 points in his fourth season and was on the verge of becoming a full-fledged star before he died in a car crash in the summer of 1993.

Paspalj lasted just one season with the Spurs, averaging 2.6 points in 28 games.

Volkov played two seasons with the Hawks, increasing his average from 5.0 points to 8.6 points per game.

That may not have been exactly what Kasten envisioned, but at least it was a step in the right direction. The Hawks' first two ventures into the international basketball world never got that far.

In 1970, the Hawks drafted Italian star Dino Meneghin in the 11th round. He never played in the league.

FROM RUSSIA WITH LOVE: *Alexander Volkov of Russia played with the Atlanta Hawks.*

Then in 1985, the Hawks picked 20-year-old Sabonis, a Lithuanian who was one of the stars for the U.S.S.R. team, in the fourth round. That selection eventually was voided because Sabonis had not reached his 21st birthday.

But the Hawks were just getting warmed up, thanks to scout Richard Kaner. Kaner started out helping place U.S. players on teams overseas, but as his knowledge of the various international teams and leagues grew, he couldn't help but notice players he thought could make it in the NBA.

HOLD OUT: *Arvydas Sabonis never did play for Atlanta after being drafted.*

"He was right on the money," Fratello said of Kaner, who still works for the Hawks. "He had those guys down cold as to who could play and who couldn't."

When Sabonis didn't sign with the Hawks, they lost his rights—although the rules were changed the next season and teams retained the rights of players they drafted even when they didn't sign. So when the Portland Trail Blazers drafted Sabonis in the first round in 1986, they were able to keep his rights until he finally decided to come to the NBA for the 1995–96 season.

Nonetheless, the Hawks persisted. In 1986, they drafted Italian Augusto Binelli in the second round and the U.S.S.R.'s Volkov and Valery Tikhonenko in the sixth and seventh rounds, respectively. In 1987, they drafted China's Song Tao in the third round, Greece's Theo

FAR FROM HOME: *Georgi Glouchkov, from Bulgaria, played just one season in the NBA.*

Christodoulou in the fourth round, Spain's Jose-Antonio Montero in the fifth round, Italy's Ricardo Morandoti in the sixth round and Yugoslavia's Franjo Arapovic in the seventh round. In 1988, they took Argentina's Jorge Gonzalez in the third round.

Not all of the players came to the U.S, and only Volkov actually played in the NBA. But it made for some interesting communication during practices and the summer leagues. Fratello took it all in stride.

"I'm Italian, I talk with my hands anyway," he said. "They just followed what I said with my hands."

The Phoenix Suns had discovered some of the same problems three years earlier when they signed Georgi Nikolov Glouchkov of Bulgaria, making him the first player from behind the Iron Curtain to join the league in 1985-86.

Glouchkov lasted only one season in the league. He was not the first nor the last player from overseas to find the transition a difficult one. All sorts of reasons play into an athlete's decision to leave his or her homeland and play in another culture. Some find it easier to do so than others.

"There are plenty of things that are different than in Europe," said Toni Kukoc of the Philadelphia 76ers. "You have to adjust your lifestyle. This is my sixth year in the United States, so I think that I'm pretty well adjusted."

Said Cleveland's 7-foot-3 Ilgauskas, "The hardest thing is to blend in. You come in without your family. You have cultural differences, language difference. People look at you a little differently."

There are adjustments on the court as well.

"You always play the same game, but the NBA game has more talent," Kukoc said. "The players are readier to play. You have to travel more. You really have to be ready for the games."

Kukoc, from Croatia, and Vlade Divac, from Serbia, played together on the Yugoslavian team that won the silver medal in the 1988 Olympic Games. Of all the international players to come to the NBA without attending college, they have had two of the longest and most distinguished careers.

Divac arrived first, taken with the 26th pick of the 1989 NBA Draft by the Los Angeles Lakers. He spent seven successful seasons in Los Angeles. His highest scoring average came in his sixth season, when he scored 16.0 points per game. After the next season, he was traded to the Charlotte Hornets for the rights to Kobe Bryant. He played two seasons in Charlotte before signing as a free agent with the Sacramento Kings before the 1998–99 season.

But his fans back home never lost track of him.

"Every time my team plays on TV, they show the game in my hometown," he told the *Chicago Tribune*. "They show the game live. So when our game starts at 8 p.m., it's two in the morning there. But they are awake to watch the game. I call my dad and I say, 'Dad, I played pretty good.' And he says, 'I know, I watched the game.' That's amazing. I am from a village in the middle of nowhere, a village of about 25,000 people. It just shows you that basketball's not really an American game, but an international game."

Kukoc, known as "The Croatian Sensation" after playing all five positions on his team, was selected with the 29th pick in the 1990 NBA Draft by the Chicago Bulls. He spent the 1990–91 season playing in Yugoslavia and then played in Italy the next two seasons before finally joining the Bulls for the 1993–94 season. Three seasons later, he won the first of three straight NBA championships and won the league's Sixth Man Award as well—quite an accomplishment for a player who was used to being the star of his team.

With the retirement of Michael Jordan after that third title and the subsequent dismantling of the Bulls, Kukoc played another season and a half in Chicago

PHILADELPHIA FREEDOM: *Toni Kukoc of Croatia now plays with the 76ers.*

430

before being traded to the Philadelphia 76ers in February, 2000.

While international stars have come and gone from the NBA, U.S. players also have made the trek overseas to play in leagues from Japan to Turkey, from Australia to Europe. It is not unusual, in fact, for teams to recommend to their young and physically immature draft choices that they travel overseas and play for a year or two to gain invaluable experience.

But some big-name players have played overseas, as well.

Joe Barry Carroll played in Milan, as did Bob McAdoo.

Danny Ferry, whose father, Bob, played in the league for 10 years and then became vice president/general manager of the Washington Bullets for 17 years, was the second pick in the 1989 NBA draft by the Los Angeles Clippers. Before the draft, he and his agent, David Falk, had informed the Clippers that Ferry would not play for them. But the Clippers decided they couldn't pass on the All-American from Duke who'd won the Naismith Award his senior year and was a finalist for the Wooden Award.

Ferry carried through on his promise and opted to play for the Il Messaggero team in Rome for the 1989–90 season. He averaged 22 points and six rebounds a game that season, returning to the U.S. only after the Clippers traded his rights, along with Reggie Williams, to the Cleveland Cavaliers for Ron Harper and the Cavs' first-round draft choices in 1990 and 1992 and their second-round pick in 1991.

"I'm glad I went," said Ferry, whose Italian perks included a five-story, 13th-century piazza, complete with maids, and a BMW. "It was a good experience."

Brian Shaw was another American who played with Ferry in Rome. The next season he returned to the U.S. and played for the Boston Celtics.

Minnesota's Sam Mitchell played in France from 1987–89, and he and his wife, Anita, totally immersed themselves in French culture—speaking French at home and becoming experts on French wine.

Coaches, too, have traveled overseas to gain experience and knowledge of their craft. Fratello was one to make friends wherever he appeared, and many coaches from around the world made their way to Cleveland to take in a few of his practices.

Milwaukee coach George Karl spent two seasons as the coach of Real Madrid in the Spanish League.

Dallas assistant coach Donn Nelson, son of head coach Don Nelson, struck up a friendship with Marciulionis when the two were together at Golden State and, as a result, served as an assistant coach on the Lithuanian Olympic team, which won bronze medals in the 1992 and 1996 Olympics and a silver medal in the 1995 European Championships. Nelson had spearheaded the signing of Marciulionis—who became the first player from the former Soviet Union to do so—and he was the only American coach to participate in a Soviet National training camp.

In March of 1998, Nelson was an assistant coach for a team of international stars during the Nike Hoop Summit in

OWNER OPERATED: *L.A.'s Kobe Bryant is co-owner of Olimpia Milano in Italy.*

WRIGHT STUFF: *Vitaly Potapenko (right), of the Ukraine, first played basketball in the U.S. at college, starring for Wright State University.*

San Antonio, and the Mavericks played host to the top U.S. and international high school players the week before the Summit. That summer Nelson also led a series on Nike clinics through China.

Bryant, the young star of the Los Angeles Lakers, took his international involvement one step further—actually buying part of a team overseas. He owns 50 percent of the Olimpia Milano of the International Professional Basketball League. The team, which has won 25 Italian championships, was founded in 1936 and plays in the 12,000-seat Assago Forum. It has an international reputation with fans as passionate as those of the Lakers or Celtics.

For Bryant, the purchase brought him back to his roots. He grew up in Italy while his father, Joe, was playing basketball there.

"I loved growing up in Italy and have always had a special place in my heart for the country and its people," Bryant explained. "In fact, Italian is a second language for everyone in our family. My involvement with Olimpia Milano fulfills my desire to reconnect with Italy, while also providing business opportunities in basketball.

"I'm looking forward to helping Olimpia Milano continue delivering a premier level of professional basketball to European sports fans. I'm also interested in helping my corporate partners leverage my relationship with Olimpia Milano to grow their businesses around the world."

Joe Bryant will serve as the team's vice president and Kobe plans to spend part of his off-season in Milan to make appearances and work with his corporate partners.

"We are thrilled to welcome Kobe as our partner," said Pasquale Caputo, who owns the other 50 percent of the team. "We have come to know him as a very intelligent, mature person who has a deep respect and knowledge of basketball management, and a passion for Italy, its people and this team. I am confident he and his father will make a valuable contribution for many years to come."

By the turn of the century, the level of play and scouting internationally had risen to such a level that players from overseas were being taken with high draft choices. Teams were no longer taking chances on foreign players. They were selecting them as key building blocks for their teams.

In 1996, for instance, the Cleveland Cavaliers selected Ukranian Vitaly Potapenko, the "Ukraine Train," from Wright State with the No. 12 pick in the draft. They took Ilgauskas at No. 20.

The two were polar opposites on the court. The 6–10, 285-pound Potapenko was a bull, strong enough to hold his own against anyone in the post and tough enough to take on anyone who challenged him. The 7–3, 260-pound Ilgauskas was lanky and lithe, with a flair for the flashy pass, not unlike his idol, Sabonis. Alas, foot problems sidelined him for four of five seasons. In the middle, though, he wowed the fans in Cleveland and around the NBA, averaging 13.9 points and 8.8 rebounds.

Ilgauskas was named most valuable player in the Schick Rookie Game during All-Star Weekend and made the all-rookie first team. For years, callers on hold at the Cavaliers office heard the radio replay of Ilgauskas stripping the ball from Washington point guard Rod Strickland, dribbling the length of the court and wrapping the ball around his waist before slamming it through the basket.

The strengths of those two should dispel the notion that European players are highly skilled offensively but somewhat lacking defensively.

"I think that's overrated," Ilgauskas said. "Basketball is the same game. Some teams in the NBA don't play any defense.

Some teams in Europe play good defense. It depends where you go. Usually the guys from Europe are playing a good level of basketball over there. If the guy is talented over there and gets a chance—some of the guys don't get a chance to show what they can do.

"You can't put all the players together and say they can't play defense or aren't physical enough. When you look at Vitaly, he's probably the strongest guy in the NBA. And they say Europeans aren't physical. You can't put everybody at the same level. You've got to look at each person individually."

Selected even higher than Potapenko and Ilgauskas, Germany's Dirk Nowitzki was taken ninth in the 1998 draft by the Milwaukee Bucks. He was immediately traded to Dallas for the rights to Robert Traylor. The Mavericks had loved Nowitzki ever since they saw him perform during that Hoop Summit.

An ambidextrous shooter who actually took part in the Long Distance Shootout during the 2000 All-Star Weekend in Oakland, Nowitzki was destined to be an athlete. His parents were both elite athletes. His father, Joerg, played handball and his mother, Helga, starred for the German women's national team. His older sister, Silke, plays first-league basketball in Wurzburg.

Given the increasing respect given to international players—men and women—both Dirk and Silke could someday find themselves in the Basketball Hall of Fame in Springfield, Massachusetts, the ultimate validation for a basketball player.

According to curator Mike Brooslin, there have been international displays in the Hall of Fame since that first McDonald's Open. Much of the hall's international collection is on display in its Olympic section, but there is a separate display of international items, including a subsection on European women's pro ball, which was one of the few professional avenues open to women before the NBA created the WNBA. According to Brooslin, a much larger non-Olympic display is planned for the new Hall of Fame, scheduled to open in 2002.

AT THE SUMMIT: *Dirk Nowitzki of Germany was acquired by the Dallas Mavericks.*

That expansion, as much as anything, confirms the widespread popularity and respect for international basketball.

"We've always had international exhibits," said Brooslin, who put together and expanded the Olympic display in 1994, with funding provided by FIBA. "But I wasn't happy with what we had. It deserved a little more than what we had. So starting with the 1992 Olympics, we really started actively collecting. I, personally, would love to do more.

"The rest of the world really looks at things like the world championships and the European games and leagues. Visitors from the U.S. pay more attention to the Olympics."

Brooslin's commitment to broadening the hall's notion of international basketball was rewarded when some visitors from Brazil were thrilled to find displays including Brazilian stars Oscar Schmidt and Hortencia.

"Wow," they said to Brooslin.

Internationals stars have been wowing crowds in their homelands for years. It's only in the past decade that their skills really are being appreciated in the NBA and worldwide, thanks to the league's far-reaching communications network.

Children from Longley's Australia to Olajuwon's Nigeria to Biasatti's Canada are growing up surrounded by basketball, and there is hardly a playground in the world that hasn't amused a youngster with a ball and a hoop and an empty afternoon. Sometimes it's nothing more than a patch of dirt or sand with a 10-foot high goal. But the dream it fosters is much loftier.

International players

The international flavor of the NBA goes way beyond the sushi in Toronto, the bratwurst in Milwaukee or the pizza in Chicago.

Players have come from all over the globe with different backgrounds, different styles, different likes and dislikes. Most have been successful in their homelands and have had varying degrees of success upon arriving in the NBA.

Their coaches and teammates try to help them adjust to a new culture, while they try to hold on and share memories from home. Some transitions are easier than others, but everyone is better off for having made the attempt.

And while living in a new place, the international players never forget what's going on at home.

Here is a look at some interesting aspects of some of the top international athletes to play in the NBA.

JOHN AMAECHI

Orlando Magic

Although he was born in Boston, Mass., Amaechi was raised in Manchester, England, then attended high school in Toledo, Ohio, and college at Penn State. He was a rugby star before he ever picked up a basketball. He graduated 11th in his class in high school, earned a degree in psychology from Penn State and is enrolled in a doctoral program focusing on child clinical psychology.

A 6–10, 270-pound center, he started his NBA career as a rookie free agent with the Cleveland Cavaliers in the 1995–96 season, but he averaged just 12.8 minutes, 2.8 points and 1.9 rebounds with the Cavs.

"Even I wouldn't have played me in Cleveland," the self-deprecating Amaechi said of his time with the Cavs.

After knocking around for three seasons overseas, where he played with the Sheffield Sharks in England, Italy's Kinder Bologna and Panathinaikos of Greece, he returned to training camp with the Orlando Magic, worked his way into the starting lineup and became a candidate for the NBA's 1999–2000 Most Improved Player Award.

He was the first player from Great Britain to play in the NBA.

TARIQ ABDUL-WAHAD

Denver Nuggets

Born Olivier Saint-Jean in Maisons Alfort, France, and raised in Paris, the Nuggets' 6-foot-6, 223-pound shooting guard embraced the Islamic religion in 1996 and changed his name in 1997. His first name, Tariq, means "morning star" and his last name, Abdul-Wahad, means "servant of the one God." His mother, George Goudet, played pro basketball in France and taught her son to play while she was coaching youth basketball. Abdul-Wahad speaks fluent French, Spanish and English and enjoys spending time with family, studying religion and visiting museums. An art history major at San Jose State, he started taking youth groups to art museums in Denver after he was traded there from Orlando in the middle of the 1999–2000 season. A first-round draft choice of the Sacramento Kings in 1997, he was traded to Orlando before the 1999 season.

Despite the fact that surgery on his left wrist ended his season prematurely, he continued to be active in the Denver community and also announced a plan to bring 20 of France's top players to a developmental camp in the United States.

"This is a skills camp for French players that will help them get better and expose them to the States," Abdul-Wahad told the Denver Post. "It is going to be fun, and it's something that I have always thought about. I've wanted to do something that helps me give back."

He was the first French-born player to play in the NBA.

LAZARO BORRELL

Seattle Supersonics

A rookie free agent with the Sonics in the 1999–2000 season, the 6-foot-8, 220-

SUPERSONIC: *Seattle's Lazaro Borrell was the first Cuban in the NBA.*

pound forward was the first Cuban player to play in the NBA.

In 1998–99, he averaged 20.8 points for Obras Sanitarias in the Argentina Basketball League, where he was named "Best Foreign Player" and was selected to the all-league second team. He averaged 21.3 points and 10.3 rebounds per game in three games for Cuba in the Pre-Olympic qualifying tournament in Puerto Rico in July, 1999. During that tournament, he defected from the Cuban team.

No matter where he's playing, though, he still loves salsa music and his favorite foods are avocados and plantains.

VLADE DIVAC

Sacramento Kings

The 7-foot-1, 260-pound center from Kraljevo, Yugoslavia, has had a long and productive career since being drafted by the Los Angeles Lakers in the first round of the 1989 NBA draft. He played seven seasons in Los Angeles, which no doubt

434

helped him land parts in the movies *Eddie*, *Driving Me Crazy*, and *Space Jam*, as well as television roles in *Coach*, *Good Sports* and *Married with Children*. He also appeared on the talk shows *Larry King Live* and *The Tonight Show*.

He was traded to Charlotte and after two seasons signed with Sacramento as a free agent.

But it is really in his home country that he has become a hero. He'd always been a star there. His 1989 marriage to his wife, Snezana, was attended by more than 1,000 people and was televised nationally.

But those were in better times. As the war has waged, Divac has lost friends and relatives. But he believes those who are blessed with wealth and comfortable lifestyles must give back to those less fortunate. Thus, he has lobbied in California for passage of a school bond bill needed to repair schools.

He has served as the NBA's international representative for its anti-drug program, and after adopting an orphan (infant daughter) and being appalled by the living conditions at institutions back in Serbia, has spent countless hours touring California orphanages to help find a better way. He is planning to meet with officials throughout Eastern and Central Europe in an attempt to introduce them to the methods and procedures followed in Western Countries.

With Divac's special affinity for young, impoverished children, he also founded a Group7 foundation that raises funds for children impacted by the war in the Balkans, regardless of race, religion or ethnic origin, organized a three-city exhibition tour of Serbia and Montenegro last summer with members of the Yugoslav national, raising $500,000 that was spent on clothing and other bare necessities for youngsters, organized a toy drive in Sacramento that collected 10,000 gifts that were shipped to Serbia for Christmas

QUICK AS A FOX: *Canada's Rick Fox has been a key figure for the Los Angeles Lakers.*

and donated proceeds from his three-week basketball camp this summer in Sacramento to the Group7 fund.

As a result, he was named the winner of the 2000 J. Walker Kennedy Citizenship Award presented by the Professional Basketball Writers of America.

RICK FOX

Los Angeles Lakers

Ulrich Alexander Fox was born in Toronto and moved to the Bahamas with his parents, Ulrich and Dianne, when he was 2 years old. He majored in Radio, Television and Motion Pictures at North Carolina, but he couldn't possibly have known how handy that would come in later.

A defensive star who never missed a game in his four years at North Carolina, he was a first round selection of the Boston Celtics in 1991, the 24th player taken overall. He played six years in Boston, where as a rookie he had the pleasure of being on the same team as Larry Bird, Kevin McHale and Robert Parish. After representing Canada in the 1994 World Championships in Toronto, he later signed with the Lakers as a free agent in 1997, in part to pursue his interests in the entertainment field.

As it turned out, though, he is not the most well-known figure in his household.

His wife is singer/actress Vanessa L. Williams. The two were married in September, 1999.

ADONAL FOYLE

Golden State Warriors

The slender 6–10, 250-pound forward grew up on the small island of Canouan, Grenadines. He did not play organized basketball until he was 16, but he caught on fast enough to play collegiately at Colgate, where he became the NCAA's all-time leader in blocked shots. He also made the All-Academic team with a 3.47 in history. He also enjoys soccer, tennis and track and field and lists the National Football League's Philadelphia Eagles as his favorite football team. Taken by Golden State with the eighth pick in the 1997 NBA draft, he is the commissioner of the Afterschool Drug Free Basketball

FOYLED AGAIN: *Adonal Foyle (Grenadines) played his college ball at Colgate.*

MY GIANT: *Gheorghe Muresan of Romania played for the Bullets before joining the Nets.*

League, which serves more than 2,000 youths in the San Francisco area. An avid reader who once wrote a diary for one of the Bay Area newspapers, he also frequently reads aloud to students in local libraries and in the City of Oakland's reading program.

GHEORGHE MURESAN
New Jersey Nets

The 7-foot-7 Romanian is the tallest player ever to play in the NBA. He wears a size 20 shoe and has a 7-foot 10-inch wingspan. Drafted by Washington in the second round of the 1993 draft, the 30th player taken overall, the center played his first four seasons with Washington, leading the NBA in field-goal percentage at .604 in the 1996–97 season. He sat out

most of the next two seasons with injuries, including a stretched tendon in his ankle and a compressed nerve in his back. He signed as a free agent with New Jersey on May 3, 1999.

For all the attention he has drawn in the NBA, his biggest role may have been off the court, where he starred with Billy Crystal in the movie, *My Giant.*

DIKEMBE MUTOMBO
Atlanta Hawks

A five-time All-Star and three-time Defensive Player of the Year, the 7-foot-2 Mutombo, who spent his first five NBA seasons in Denver, recently was voted the International Player of the Decade (1990's) in a NBA.com poll.

Born in Kinshasa, Zaire (Congo),

his full name is Dikembe Mutombo Mpolondo Mukamba Jean Jacque Wamutombo. He speaks English, French, Portuguese, Spanish and five African dialects and earned a bachelor's degree in linguistics and diplomacy from Georgetown University, after which he became a first-round draft choice of the Nuggets in 1991, the fourth player taken overall.

In addition to serving as a vice-president of the NBA Players Association, funding the Zaire women's basketball team in the 1996 Olympics and touring Africa as a spokesman for CARE, Mutombo developed the Dikembe Mutombo Foundation to provide humanitarian assistance to his homeland.

In an effort to build a 300-bed hospital in his hometown, he has explored all avenues for funding. During the 1999–2000 season, he appeared on the American news program "60 Minutes," which generated a great deal of interest, including a phone call from Barbara Bush, the wife of former U.S. president George Bush. Also, during the Hawks' trip to Seattle, Mutombo met with Microsoft tycoon Bill Gates.

"They gave $750 million to a foundation, so they are very generous," Mutombo said. "But the thing that is so good for us is that you have to get an invitation to go see them. You can't call up and say, 'Hello, I would like you to give me some money for my charity.' If they don't want to see you then you don't talk to them … It was an honor that they called and said they would like to see me."

For his many charitable activities, Mutombo was nominated for the 1999 J. Walter Kennedy Citizenship Award presented by the Professional Basketball Writers Association.

HAKEEM OLAJUWON
Houston Rockets

Born in Nigeria, his last name translates into "always being on top" and, indeed, he led the Rockets to the top of the NBA when they won back-to-back championships in 1994 and 1995. The 7-foot, 255-pound center was named the most

(Opposite) BOARD MEETING: *Dikembe Mutombo (Congo) is a rebounding force in Atlanta.*

valuable player in each of those championship rounds. Not bad for an athlete who started out playing soccer and handball and didn't pick up a basketball until age 15. As a 17-year-old, he played for Nigeria in the All-African Games. He earned a scholarship to the University of Houston, where he starred on the high-flying team nicknamed "Phi Slama Jama."

The No. 1 pick in the 1984 NBA draft, he has spent his entire career with the Rockets. He became a U.S. citizen in 1993, representing the U.S. at the 1996 Olympic Games in Atlanta. His parents, who owned a cement business, are retired and still live in Lagos.

MICHAEL OLOWOKANDI

Los Angeles Clippers

Of all the international players in the NBA, the arrival of this 7-foot, 269-pound center may be as unorthodox as they come. The first player taken in the 1998 NBA draft, Olowokandi, whose father, Ezekial, is a Nigerian diplomat, was born in Nigeria but was raised in England. On his 20th birthday, as a student at Brunel University in Uxbridge, Middlesex, England, he opened a library copy of the Peterson Guide to American Colleges and Universities and his gaze landed on Pacific.

He phoned the Pacific basketball office to ask if his credits would transfer. When he happened to mention he was a 7-footer, assistant basketball coach Tony Marcopolos must have thought he'd won the lottery. Of course, Olowokandi didn't point out that he'd only played basketball recreationally until he transferred. The fact that he'd participated in track and field, cricket and rugby and held Great Britain high school records in the long jump and high jump really was of no consequence.

But he wound up with the most blocked shots in school history as well as the highest career field goal percentage—.591—and was named the Big West Conference Player of the Year as a senior. He also earned a degree in economics and set the school non-football bench press record of 350 pounds.

(Opposite) **DREAM MACHINE:** *Hakeem Olajuwon (Nigeria) has been a huge star in Houston.*

DRAZEN PETROVIC

Willis Reed remembers the phone call as if it were yesterday.

"I didn't believe it," said the Hall of Famer who is senior vice president of the New Jersey Nets. "I just thought there was a breakdown (in the translation.) It just didn't happen."

What happened on June 7, 1993, rocked Reed and the Nets to the core. Drazen Petrovic, the popular 28-year-old Croatian who'd led the team in scoring the previous season, had been killed when the car in which he was riding slammed into a truck on a rain-slicked German autobahn.

"He was a special person," said Reed softly, his voice thickening with emotion at the memory. "I think he had an impact on a lot of people's lives and the New Jersey Nets organization and the basketball world, the NBA and internationally. It was a great loss, a great loss.

"It was a great blow to the franchise. Drazen Petrovic had won the hearts of everyone in this organization, all the workers, everyone here, the ownership and our fans."

The 6-foot-5, 208-pound shooting guard made his mark on the basketball world long before playing in the NBA. Born in Sibenik, Croatia, a town of 80,000 on the Adriatic Sea, he was playing first division basketball with the Sibenka team by the time he was 15. He moved on to the Cibona team in Zagreb, where he led the squad to one national championship, three National Cups, two European Club Championships and one European Winners Cup Championship and once scored an incredible 112 points in a league game.

In 1988–89, he led Real Madrid to the European Winners Cup and Spanish Cup Championships. In 1989, he was a member of the European National Championship winning team, and in 1990 he led the National Team to a gold medal at the World Championships in Argentina. He won three Olympic medals, including a silver in 1992, when the Croatians finished second to the U.S. Dream team in Barcelona. He was voted European player of the year in 1986, 1989, 1992 and 1993, more than any other player in history.

The Portland Trail Blazers picked him in the third round of the 1986 draft, but he didn't come to the United States until 1989. After riding the bench for his first season and averaging just 7.6 points, the Blazers gave in to his wish to be traded and sent him to New Jersey in the middle of the next season.

He'd been averaging 4.4 points that season with Portland. He tripled that to average 12.4 with New Jersey and, in the meantime, he impressed everyone with his talent and work ethic.

"There are players who you really like in basketball," Reed said. "There are guys you enjoy watching play. I remember when I was growing up, for example, when I first started watching basketball, I would always watch the Celtics, and I would watch Bill Russell. He was my idol. After I got to the NBA, I loved to watch Earl Monroe play, and Oscar Robertson and Elgin Baylor. Through the years, I loved to see Julius Erving play, and Larry Bird. It was the same thing with Drazen Petrovic. He was such a dedicated, hard-working player.

"His enthusiasm was infectious. I used to watch him play. He would stand out on the perimeter, and if he missed that shot, you'd say, 'I can't believe it.' He didn't miss that shot. That was a rare thing to see him wide open and miss a shot. He was dedicated. He worked to become a great offensive player.

"There's a funny story (former Nets coach) Chuck Daly tells about him. They'd go on the road and have a pre-game shootaround about noon, go back to the hotel and guys would eat and rest. Chuck found out Drazen was coming back to the hotel and then doing another workout in the workout facilities in the hotel. Chuck asked him, 'What are you doing?' He told Chuck he wanted to be in the best shape, he wanted to be the best player, he wanted to be the best foreign player who ever played. Chuck told him, 'Drazen, you don't need to do all this. You are a great player. You need to save (your energy) for the game.' That just shows how dedicated and what a hard worker he was. I think that, too, was infectious for the rest of the players on the team."

Petrovic, nicknamed "Petro," really began to bloom with the Nets, further

439

developing the feistiness that so endeared him to teammates and fans. In his first full season with the team, 1991–92, he averaged 20.6 points per game, shooting 50.8 percent from the floor, 80.8 percent from the line and an amazing 44.4 percent from 3-point range. He increased all of those the next season, averaging 22.3 points per game, shooting 51.8 percent overall, 87 percent from the line and 44.9 percent from 3-point range. As a result, he was named to the All-NBA third team, placing him among the top 15 players in the league.

Likewise, the Nets' fortunes were improving. They won 26 games in his first season, 40 the next season and 43 in his third, making the playoffs the last two years. With a nucleus of Petrovic, Derrick Coleman and Kenny Anderson, the Nets looked like a team to be reckoned with for years to come.

"I have often wondered what would have happened," Reed admitted. "I think about what a difference he would have made in the fate of this franchise, where it was going at that point at the end of the season before it happened, what would have happened had he lived. We were going through all this stuff with negotiations. We wanted to re-sign him. I told him, 'We want you here.' At that point, he had become a leader on the team. After he died, the whole disposition of the team … well, it just didn't work out.

"You just don't know. You know you had three good players. With Drazen providing the leadership, Kenny liked playing with him and Derrick was doing a great job. Chuck (Daly) was doing a great job, so we had great coaching. We had a lot of good things going on, and the loss of one player can really change a

franchise. It changed our destiny."

Petrovic was a free agent at the time of his death, and he was not happy with how negotiations were going. He had threatened to return to Europe, where he knew he'd be appreciated.

But Reed was confident everything would have worked out with the Nets, who retired his number in 1994.

"He was going to be an All-Star player. That's what he wanted to be. He wanted to be the first great foreign player. It was there. He was going to be an All-Star. It was just a matter of time. As third team NBA, he was already an All-Star. There was no way he would not have been an All-Star the next season.

"We wanted to give him a four-year deal. He wanted a three-year deal and he wanted to go back to Europe. I told him we'd do a three-year deal, but I figured we'd get him to stay longer. When you play that long, you want to stay. He could still go two years later and go back to Europe and play.

"I remember us trying to sign him. I knew we were going to sign him because I said, 'Drazen, tell you what. When we finish this contract, the only guy playing the No. 2 position who will make more money than you will be Michael Jordan.' He liked that."

Other than his contract situation, the thing that most troubled him was the war in his homeland. One summer he took a few days off from his strenuous training regime. He said he was going to Florida to visit his brother. In fact, he returned home to visit family and friends.

"I'm playing basketball, and my friends are getting killed," he said.

Another friend he lost was Vlade Divac. The two had played together before the war, but afterward that was not possible.

"I saw how much the war in Croatia affected his life," Reed recalled. "He and Divac had a great relationship, but being Croatian and Serb, there was a lost friendship. You could see a lot of times how he was troubled by the whole process."

His death did nothing to bring the two sides together. It was only a momentary

NET GAIN: *Drazen Petrovic (Croatia) was a star in Europe before he shone in the U.S.*

SUN SPOT: *Georgi Glouchkov's career in Phoenix and the NBA was a short lived.*

interruption in the carnage. But Reed said the funeral in Croatia was incredible.

"I went to the funeral with Chris Dudley and Chris Morris," said Reed, who also attended the memorial service at the Croatian church Petrovic attended in Manhattan. "It was very difficult. It was almost like it was my son. I had that much feeling for the young man."

That feeling was widespread.

"You would have thought the head of state passed," Reed said. "It was tremendous in terms of the number of people and how large the ceremony was. He was this great symbol, an icon of what all the kids want to be and what all the parents wanted their sons to accomplish. This little guy came from this little country and he comes to the NBA and makes the all-NBA third team. It was amazing.

"We were lucky enough to get him. He came here and he was this great jewel of a player and a great person. His mom and dad used to come and his brother. We knew the family. They were part of the New Jersey Nets. Even today, we have the Drazen Petrovic scholarship. It's been good because it's going to help some Croatian kids. But I would have loved to see him play until he was retired."

In an effort to keep Petrovic's memory alive, the Nets established the Drazen Petrovic Memorial Scholarship, which provides a $5,000 stipend to Croatian-American students studying in the U.S. at accredited colleges. The scholarship is awarded to a deserving student who exhibits the same work ethic and will to succeed that made Petrovic such an intense competitor and unique symbol of

Croatian spirit and pride.

In addition, the championship trophy in the McDonald's Open is now named for Petrovic.

Little things, to be sure, but big enough to bring him back in spirit.

Of course, it seems as if he's never too far from Reed's mind anyway.

When Charlotte's Bobby Phills was killed in a car crash in January, 2000, the memories of Petrovic came rushing back. And recently, Reed said he was at a function in New York and met a woman who was a New York Knicks fan and whose mother was from Croatia. He sent the mother a prayer card from Petrovic's funeral seven years ago.

"It just doesn't seem like it's been that long," said Reed, who still hasn't fully recovered. "Anybody in this organization who was here during that time loved him. He was such a nice person, very courteous, the ideal kid. He was like everybody's son or brother."

GEORGI GLOUCHKOV

Georgi Glouchkov certainly was not the first international player in the NBA when he joined the Phoenix Suns in 1985. That honor belonged to Hank Biasatti, a Canadian who played with the Toronto Huskies in the first game of the Basketball Association of America, the forerunner to the NBA.

But Glouchkov, a Bulgarian who had studied economics at the university in Varna, was the first in the new wave of European players to join the league, four years before the FIBA ruling that opened the doors for NBA players to take part in the Olympics, which, in turn, allowed international players to play in the NBA without jeopardizing their Olympic status.

Glouchkov, a 6-foot-8, 235-pound center, was born on Jan. 10, 1960, in Triavna, a small city in central Bulgaria on the slopes of the Balkan mountains. He played eight years with the Bulgarian National Team, and he was named the Player of the Year in Bulgaria in 1984 and 1985. In addition, in 1984 he was named the top center in the Balkans, which at the time encompassed Yugoslavia, Romania, Turkey, Greece and Bulgaria.

Dick Percudani, a Suns scout and former coach in the Italian League, spotted Glouchkov at the European championship after the 1984–85 season and convinced the Suns to take him in the seventh round of the 1985 NBA Draft.

Then Jerry Colangelo, the Suns general manager, had to convince the Bulgarians to let Glouchkov come to the NBA. At first, they would agree only to let him try out with the Suns, although they did postpone three games in order to facilitate the audition. So he arrived on September 23, accompanied by his coach, Simeon Nanev Varchev, and by an international basketball referee, Stefko Stanev Stoev, who also served as an interpreter.

His performance spoke loud and clear. In two pre-season games, he had 28 points, 15 rebounds and two blocked shots.

Glouchkov returned to Bulgaria on Oct. 6, and Colangelo followed, finally getting the Bulgarians to allow Glouchkov to sign for a two-year guaranteed contract, plus a player transfer fee. In addition, the Suns agreed to help the Bulgarian team set up a tour of the U.S., as well as an exchange program that would allow promising young Bulgarian players to participate in American camps. The Suns also agreed to hold some clinics in Bulgaria.

After all that, it took several weeks for Glouchkov to return. Before his October 31 arrival, the Suns public relations department kicked into high gear, providing reporters with an exhaustive amount of information on Bulgaria, including maps as well as historical and geographical data. There also was a list of common basketball phrases in Bulgarian. Layup, for instance, was translated as "shut pod kosha."

Although Glouchkov also enrolled in a Berlitz language course, when he returned to the Suns, he was accompanied by Bozhidar "Bo" Takev, 65, a former Bulgarian national team player and coach an honorary lifetime member of FIBA who was acting as an interpreter and chaperone. Takev was designated an "assistant trainer" for the Suns, so he could sit on the bench and help with translation.

That didn't always work out too well, though, according to John MacLeod, coach of the Suns at the time.

"Bo was hard of hearing, so by the time I'd repeat what I needed him to interpret for Georgi during a timeout,

we'd have to be back on the floor," MacLeod said.

Despite those problems, Glouchkov and Takev seemed to enjoy their time in the United States. Through Takev, Glouchkov made the following observations, although he declined to talk about politics:

On the U.S. and Bulgaria, "My country is a small country and the United States is a huge country, so they are difficult to compare. I have lived here too short a time to be able to give a comprehensive answer … This is not my first visit to the United States. So far, I have not seen anything that would give me 'culture shock'. "

On food, "I like any kind of food as long as it is cooked well and is tasteful. So far, I've had American, Chinese and Mexican, and I've enjoyed them all."

On his NBA contract and money, "Basketball is the most important thing for me now. I really want to become a good basketball player. Money is a natural consequence of that."

On MacLeod, "He seems to be a very good coach. He makes good explanations of the game and of the plays."

On the Suns, "They are very fine people, and they have helped me a lot They are very nice guys. We attempt to have conversations in English and I can understand a great deal."

On communications "Yes, it is a problem. If I knew the language, not only could I listen, but I could also ask questions and learn faster. I understand much of what the team does, but I have difficulty with very specific things, which can't be demonstrated on the court."

Little wonder then that although Glouchkov wound up averaging 4.9 points and 3.3 rebounds in 49 games with Phoenix, when he showed up the next season 25 pounds lighter, the Suns sent him back to Europe.

It would be four more years before the influx of European players, most of whom had longer stays than Glouchkov.

OSCAR SCHMIDT

It was, Oscar Schmidt said, the time of his life.

Schmidt, the retired Brazilian star, was speaking of the 1987 Pan American Games, where he scored 46 points, 35 in

the second half, as the Brazilians upset David Robinson, Danny Manning and the Americans, 120–115, to win the gold medal.

At first the crowd in Market Square Arena in Indianapolis was stunned. But as the fans watched Schmidt and the rest of the Brazilian team hugging and rolling around the court in celebration, they began to applaud an outstanding performance. Later, Schmidt recalled, the team got a standing ovation as it walked into a restaurant.

"This was unbelievable," Schmidt told *Sports Illustrated*. "The whole scene, how can I say it? This was what we dream."

A dream. That's how most observers described Schmidt's shot. After recording three of the top four scoring games in Olympic history and becoming the all-time leading Olympic scorer with 1,040 points through the 1996 Summer Games in Atlanta—his fifth Olympiad, also a record—Schmidt retired, but not before earning a place as one of the greatest basketball players ever—probably the best player never to play in the NBA.

Not that he didn't have his chances. The New Jersey Nets had drafted him and tried to sign him during the 1980s. But they couldn't come close to matching the salary he was getting in Italy, so he returned to play overseas, saying he never regretted the decision.

"I know my limitations, my defects," he told *Sports Illustrated*. "But I could never play only 10 minutes a game. NBA is great if you are a star. But if not, you get moved around. My friend (Georgi) Glouchkov played a year with Phoenix. He tells me bad stories about NBA. The guards no like him, so they don't pass him ball. I would no like that. I could no stand that."

The Nets were sure he would have been a star.

"I'm convinced Oscar could have been our backup small forward for a year and then moved into the starting lineup," Al Menedez, then the Nets' player personnel director, told *Sports Illustrated*. "People who say he isn't tough enough should watch him in the Italian league. You try to hurt this guy and you'll be in a fight. He gets up and keeps on firing. And that long-range shot? I'll put him up there with

MISSING IN ACTION: *Brazil's Oscar Schmidt is probably the best player never to play in the NBA.*

the (Larry) Birds, the (Rick) Barrys, the Sudden Sam Smiths, anybody. He's in the top 10 shooters I've ever seen in my life."

Schmidt was born in Natal on the north coast. His father was a track star, his mother a volleyball player. The family moved to the capital, Brasilia, but in order to further his basketball career, Schmidt soon moved to Sao Paulo. He was cut from the national team at 17. But two years later, switched from center to forward, he made the national team and was 20 when he first played in the world championships in Manila in 1978. He made the all-tournament team.

But his teammates weren't always happy with his trigger-happy mentality, and there was often internal bickering and jealousy. So while Schmidt continued to play on the national team in international competitions, he moved to Italy to play professionally in 1982.

Though he enjoyed a comfortable life and became an international star, the victory in the Pan American Games seemed to push Schmidt and his sport into a new stratosphere. In the following year, the

Brazilian leagues added 20 more teams and attendance rose 30 percent. All the qualifying games for the 1998 Olympics were televised, and Schmidt, with his chisled profile and spikey brush haircut, was sought after for all sorts of commercial endorsements. Everybody clamored for Oscar, who wore his first name—not the more traditional last name—on the back of his jersey.

"This was the victory of the generation," he told *Sports Illustrated*. "Everybody loves me. It is great. It is beautiful."

Alas, the Brazilians were not able to duplicate their success in the Olympics. Though Schmidt averaged 42.3 points per game, Brazil was unable to win even the bronze medal in either the 1988 Olympics in Seoul or the 1996 Olympics in Atlanta.

He became a media darling in Atlanta, where reporters paid him homage.

"He is the Grand Old Man of international basketball," wrote Bill Lyon in the *Philadelphia Inquirer*. "A better long-range jump shooter has never lived. Including Larry Bird."

But Schmidt admitted his skills were declining at the age of 38.

"I can still shoot, maybe better than I ever have," he said. "Of course, I don't have the same quickness as before, or the same jump. But I live for the game, and I can still play it."

Indeed, the fans who came to watch could not have cared less that his teammates often had to set screens to free him up for those beautiful jumpers. He was still something to see.

"We still enjoy watching him play," U.S. coach Lenny Wilkens said after Schmidt scored 26 points in the Americans' 98–75 victory in Atlanta. "He has been a fabulous player over his career."

Said Australia's Andrew Gaze, after Schmidt scored 24 points in a 109–101 double overtime loss to Australia in the 1996 Games, "He shoots shots and you don't know where they came from. You wonder how any man could have absolutely no conscience like that with some of the shots he takes. But he hits them."

Added Australian Scott Fisher, "He must have been frightening 10 or 12 years ago. That U.S. Pan Am team he beat single-handedly. There must be some guys that still have nightmares about that."

For Schmidt, though, it was a dream, one that he never had again.

"I would change my whole (scoring) record for a bronze medal," he said after his last Olympics in Atlanta. "I have never won an Olympic medal, and it is what I have always wanted. It has always been my dream."

So frustrated was he in his pursuit of that dream that he lashed out after the overtime loss to the Australians, when he went 2 for 12 in the second half, showing that, in fact, he was human and not quite the player he once had been.

"I wanted to play a fair game and that was not fair," he said. "Never in my life have I played 50 minutes in a hard, aggressive game and not gotten a single foul shot. I feel like I have offended someone here and I do not understand."

Some time later, Schmidt recanted.

"These are my last Olympic Games," he said. "I'm not happy with our game. But I'm very happy that I'm still here."

THE WNBA

444

Perhaps Washington Mystics forward Nikki McCray summed it up best when she noted, "This is an incredible time for women's sports." For women's basketball, it has never been better. From the WNBA to the women's college game to international leagues, this is a sport whose time has come.

(Left) **JUST PERFECT:** *UConn, with Rebecca Lobo (left) and Vickie Johnson, went 35–0.*

(Opposite) **LONG STRETCH:** *The Comets' Tina Thompson (7) outjumps Mercury's Michelle Griffiths (12) in the 1998 WNBA Finals.*

The birth of the Women's National Basketball Association was a well-planned conception. In the summer of 1997, the timing was right.

● The American Basketball Council reported that girls basketball had become the fastest-growing sport in America; from 1987 to 1997 the number of females participating increasing from 11 million to 13.7 million.

● Attendance at women's college games in the United States had quadrupled.

● The 1993 NCAA Women's Final Four had produced the event's first sellout, putting it par with the men's annual ticket chase. In the process, a guard from Texas Tech had scored 44 points in the title game to draw comparisons to Michael Jordan. That player, Sheryl Swoopes, soon would become one of the first players to sign with the WNBA—and the first active player in a major American league to deliver a child during the course of a season.

● The University of Connecticut had produced a 35–0 championship season that had allowed center Rebecca Lobo to emerge as a national figure, one whose fame had eclipsed many of the stars from the men's collegiate game.

● And 25 years after the enactment of Title IX of the U.S. Civil Rights Act

CAPITAL GAIN: *Nikki McCray has been a huge success in Washington.*

required equal opportunity in U.S. schools for female athletic participation, a generation of participants and followers had been cultivated.

For years, followers of women professional athletes in the United States had to turn their interests toward individual sports, such as golf and tennis. There was no forum for the release of the passion that only truly can be manifested for a team sport.

If there was a specific catalyst for the WNBA's emergence and success it was the gold-medal effort by the American women at the 1996 Atlanta Olympics. With the appearance of the second Dream Team of NBA stars putting the focus on the sport, the women's team seized the opportunity to share the spotlight.

In effect, those Summer Olympics brought world-class women's basketball to America—and the WNBA wasn't about to let it go.

"We knew that in order for the league to survive, the key (was) we had to do well in the Olympics," said Olympian Ruthie Bolton-Holifield, who would go on to become a mainstay with the WNBA's Sacramento franchise. "We couldn't go there and win a medal. We had to go there and win the gold."

By the start of the WNBA's third season, any fears of trying to do too much too soon had been allayed.

"This is an incredible time for women's sports, and it's going to get even better," said Washington Mystics forward Nikki McCray. "Women's sports and women's basketball have exploded with opportunity in the past five years."

From outset, the WNBA was a league of committed partners.

Van Chancellor. the coach of the Houston Comets said, "We're gonna do anything necessary to make this league go, because we're out of a job if it doesn't." His commitment contributed to league championships for his team in each of the league's first three seasons.

While the NBA's approach to the league is that of a step-sister, the players understand the need for the marketing might of the premier basketball organization, with the entire WNBA owned collectively by the 29 NBA team owners.

"The thing about women's basketball," Lobo acknowledged, "is if you can get people to watch it, they like it. The NBA is good at getting people to watch."

Ultimately, the lack of such backing did in the rival women's American Basketball League after only 2½ seasons of head-to-head competition.

Left to compete in smaller markets, the ABL took an opposite approach to the NBA, spending the majority of its funding on player salaries instead of marketing. The players who opted for the ABL's first-year average contracts of $80,000 soon learned that the WNBA first-year maximum of $50,000 might have been the more prudent choice.

Economics aside, Gary Cavalli, founder of the ABL, knew he was on to something, that the time had come for major-league women's professional basketball in the United States.

"This is the right thing to do at the right time," he said of the two leagues opening for business in 1997. "There has been an acceptance of the evolution of women as role models in our society. A lot of people see women's basketball as a movement, a cause."

Rival league-founder Val Ackerman was equally committed.

"We hoped to attract a fan base than included families, women and the core basketball fan who might be in withdrawal after the NBA season," the WNBA's first and only president said after the league's inaugural season. "We guessed right about who we'd attract, but we underestimated their number."

The concerns of playing in NBA-sized arenas quickly faded. With first-year crowds averaging 9,804, the stands at WNBA games often appeared as full as for some games of the parent NBA. Unlike with the NBA and its corporate base, these were fans who purchased tickets and used them.

Among those fans were the types of faces who attract other faces. From model Tyra Banks, to filmmaker Spike Lee, to actors Jimmy Smits, Gregory Hines, Arsenio Hall and Billy Baldwin, and actresses Penny Marshall and Rosie O'Donnell, WNBA games became places to see and be seen.

NBA players also flocked to the games, not as much because of the common ownership umbrella, but because they, too, had little girls who wanted to dream what only sons heretofore had been able to dream. Going into its third season, the WNBA featured an audience that was 70 percent female.

To put the initial interest in perspective, league merchandisers quickly found themselves well short on their projected orders for team memorabilia.

A STEP AHEAD: *Cynthia Cooper retired after the 2000 season, and a fourth Comets title.*

"The fans found out they could reach out and touch the players," Ackerman said, "and they touched back. It's safe to say we've been a success everywhere."

The league also struck a moral cord with it fans.

Unlike the NBA, which was seen as rocking the cradle, luring players not only out of college early, but even drafting them straight out of high school, the WNBA opened with a rule that required a player to have completed her collegiate eligibility or be 21. What the WNBA was assuring itself of were players who would be refined not only on the court but also

as ambassadors for the sport.

With so many players having been forced into near exile by the lack of a suitable U.S. professional league for so many years, the WNBA opened with a veteran talent base, many players already schooled in professional etiquette through world tours.

Houston Comets guard Cynthia Cooper, for example, spent a decade playing in Spain and Italy after helping guide the University of Southern California to consecutive national championships. The accidental tourist returned home with a flourish, being named WNBA Most

448

Valuable Player in each of the league's first two seasons.

New York Liberty guard Teresa Weatherspoon had to endure a similar detour. After leading collegiate powerhouse Louisiana Tech to the 1988 NCAA title, Weatherspoon was forced to take her game to Russia for two years and Italy for six.

"There are a lot of (international) players who are playing over here," Phoenix Mercury coach and former basketball legend Cheryl Miller said, "and for a long time it was the reverse. We were always the ones going overseas and finding out where the action was."

With the WNBA, the players knew what they had, what they had to hold onto.

"The WNBA has given us an opportunity to succeed and show the American public that women can play basketball," Lobo said.

In return, the NBA connections gave the world's greatest women's players a taste of the NBA life, with players that first season hailing from Brazil, Germany, Russia, New Zealand, Great Britain, France, Japan, Democratic Republic of Congo, Czech Republic, Yugoslavia, Italy, Poland, China and Australia.

"There's no comparison between this and Europe and even home," said Australian backcourt sensation Michele Timms, among the first imports to join the WNBA. "It's really, really efficient."

To a degree.

While NBA teams travel by luxurious private aircraft, WNBA teams must travel by commercial carriers, forced to the same lines and into the same cramped seats as business travelers.

In addition, only before the league's third season was a wide-ranging collective-bargaining agreement hammered out. The league top stars, through personal-services contracts with the WNBA, still earn no more than about $250,000—or roughly what an NBA superstar such as Alonzo Mourning or Shaquille O'Neal can earn for two nights' work.

Yet while several foreigners have thrived in the WNBA, American players are relieved just to have a league at home.

As with American men who go overseas to play professional basketball, the expectations elsewhere for U.S. female

HAPPY HOMECOMING: *The WNBA gave Teresa Weatherspoon the opportunity to return home.*

expatriates was that they would dominate.

"When Americans play overseas, we're expected to play 40 minutes, take all the shots, and be the hero," said Sacramento's Bolton-Holifield.

Renee Brown, the WNBA's director of player personnel, said the league rightfully should be considered part of a homecoming for the players.

"It's important because it gives women a great opportunity to continue their basketball careers professionally by playing in the States in front of their family and friends," she said.

Brown said she was overwhelmed by just how many wanted in at the league's inception.

"I heard from people who dreamed of playing pro and maybe hadn't played in 10 years and maybe had four kids," she said in "A Celebration," the book that

commemorated the WNBA's first season. "Thousands of phone calls from players, husbands of players, uncles, fathers, the mayor of the town. From every walk of life. Not only Americans. From Israel to Hungary to Germany to China, all wanting to be part of the WNBA. Fathers about daughters, doctors about patients, bosses calling about their secretaries. These things actually happened. Boyfriends calling about their girlfriends, husbands about wives, kids about moms."

Just as it was appreciated by prospective players, the WNBA was appreciative of its place in the American sports scheme. Ackerman said a summer schedule was the only schedule considered. Unlike the ABL, which failed with its winter fare, Ackerman never sought to take on the men's game or the college game head-to-head.

But Ackerman, as dynamic a management force as the NBA has produced since Commissioner David Stern, nonetheless vows a goal for the WNBA "to become the fifth major-league." However, moving up to the level of the National Football League, National Hockey League, Major League Baseball or NBA could be another issue altogether.

The WNBA already has succeeded where the NBA, NHL and NFL won out too—by eliminating the competition.

With the folding of the ABL before the WNBA's third season, Ackerman's league was able to add such talented former ABL stars as Jennifer Azzi, Natalie Williams, Yolanda Griffith, DeLisha Milton, Crystal Robinson, Edna Campbell and Chasity Melvin.

The opportunities afforded today's female players are not lost on those who did not have such an attractive alternative during their formative years.

Nancy Lieberman-Cline, among the finest collegians to grace the hardwood, played in a men's summer league, the United States Basketball Association, and for the Washington Generals, the foils for the comedic Harlem Globetrotters, as a means of continuing her career.

When the WNBA arrived, even at age 38, participating was an opportunity that Lieberman-Cline could not bypass. Her best days clearly behind her, she then settled in as coach of the Detroit Shock.

"This is a wonderful time to be a girl," she said. "There are more opportunities for us, and people are taking us seriously."

How seriously?

For years, legendary UCLA coach John Wooden preached the virtues of women's basketball, of how a game played below the rim required far more skill, teamwork, brought the game back to its roots. Fundamentally, Wooden insisted, the women's game was basketball while the men's game had turned too much into "basket-brawl."

And if one was to doubt the love for the game on the distaff side, consider the passion of the Liberty's Weatherspoon.

Upon arriving in New York, back in the States to do what she loves most, she

ANOTHER CHANCE: *Nancy-Lieberman-Cline has played in men's and women's leagues.*

Kim Perrot

WNBA President Val Ackerman would eulogize her as "as a woman of great heart and indomitable courage, who refused to be daunted by any challenge. She has been an inspiration to countless people within and outside the basketball community."

Houston Comets guard Kim Perrot was all that. A point guard for the only champion the WNBA had known in its first two seasons, Perrot was struck down by cancer as her teammates were on the way to winning a third title in the summer of 1999.

From its inception, the WNBA had been almost life affirming. These were mothers opening new horizons for daughters. This was Sheryl Swoopes, as much a portrait in grace as an expectant mom during the first WNBA season as she would be on the court in ensuing seasons for these same Comets.

It is why the courage of Kim Perrot and her loss hit the league so hard.

At just 5 feet 5 and 130 pounds, Perrot had made the team through an open tryout. Like so many, she had toiled around the world—with stops in France, Israel, Germany, and Sweden—waiting for an opportunity to come home. The native of Lafayette, Louisiana, relished every moment on the court.

"I knew the Good Lord blessed me with so much talent and I have a message," she said during the first of her two seasons with the Comets. "That message is to all the young athletes, whether short, tall, lightweight, heavyweight, whatever it is, if you put your mind to it in sports, you can do it."

She did it. Houston embraced her. The league embraced her. There was devastation when she passed at the age of 32. The Comets would dedicate their third consecutive championship in her honor.

"She took this city and this team by storm, and she stole our hearts in the process," said Leslie Alexander, owner of the Comets and NBA's Houston Rockets. "Kim Perrot was an amazing person with an extraordinary personality."

She also proved to be an extraordinary teammate.

"Losing Kim was very hard for me," Comets forward Tin Thompson said. "She was one of my favorite people, not just in the Comets' organization, but in the world. It was really tough. But Kim left us with a lot of great things and I've taken them and applied them to my own life. I've become a better leader because of the positive way she led our team."

ENDURING INSPIRATION: *The late Kim Perrot.*

filled her hotel suite with basketballs.

"I never know what time of night I might wake up and want to shoot one in the air," she said, "just to keep myself close to the game at all times."

The history

What was born on that summer afternoon in 1997 owed its legacy to what transpired nearly 100 years earlier at Smith College, Massachusetts, in 1893, when gymnastics instructor Senda Berensen adapted James Naismith's basketball rules for women.

Interestingly, Berensen preached against intercollegiate play, with the belief at the time that women were too fragile for such strenuous competitions, and she did not allow players to jab at the ball in what was considered unladylike play. Also, men were not allowed to attend the competitions at Smith, to prevent them from seeing the bloomers worn by the players.

In fact, early women's competitions were staged as social affairs, often followed by the serving of elaborate meals.

Among the initial women to partake in the sport was Maude Sherman, who later would marry Dr. Naismith.

Dr. Naismith noted of his first encounter with women playing his game, "The girls appeared at the gymnasium, some with tennis shoes, but the majority with street shoes. None of them changed from their street clothes, costumes which were not made for freedom of movement. I shall never forget the sight that they presented in their long trailing dress with leg-of-mutton sleeves, and in several cases with the hint of a bustle."

Three years after Berensen adopted her rules, Clara Gregory Baer, a physical-education instructor at Sophia Newcomb College in New Orleans introduced a women's game at her school and on March 13, 1895 published *Basquette*, the first set of known rules for women's basketball competition.

Ironically, the version of the game Baer designed was by accident. Her game did not allow players to leave designated thirds of the court. The belief is she misinterpreted the markings Dr. Naismith had placed on his diagram for the men's game. Those markings were intended to show shot lines—not limitations players could not traverse. Yet, for more than a

half-century, women were not permitted to run the entire court, with only a selected few allowed to stand in scoring position. Even after the error was discovered, the rules remained intact, with an early rule book noting, "It has been found that a number of girls who play without division lines have developed a hyperthrophy of the heart."

Just over a year later, with guidelines in place, the first women's intercollegiate game was contested on April 4, 1896 at Armory Hall in San Francisco between Stanford and the University of California. Despite the stride forward, the result showed just how far the game still had to go—Stanford won 2–1.

At the turn of the last century, in 1901, Berensen edited *Basket Ball for Women* In 1903, the length of the women's game was shortened from 20-minute halves to 15-minute halves.

Still hardly anything that resembled today's women's game, in 1905 women's basketball featured nine players per team, with 11 officials overseeing play. That same year, the National Women's Basketball Committee was formed under

the oversight of the American Physical Education Association.

Guidance, however, still was limited. In 1916, for example, coaching only was allowed at halftime.

The rules remained under revision through the 1910s, with Dr. J. Anna Norris culminating such efforts with the publication of the *Official Basket Ball Guide for Women* in 1919.

In 1924, the women's game received a significant boost when the International Women's Sports Federation was formed, staged its own Olympics, and included women's basketball in the competition.

By 1925, 37 states were staging girls' basketball tournaments. And in 1926, the Amateur Athletic Union sponsored the first-ever women's basketball national championship. That event was staged using men's rules.

In 1936, the All American Red Heads Team was formed, and competed against men's teams using men's rules.

Meanwhile, women's rules continued to be modified. In 1938, the women's game was down to six players per team, with the court divided into halves instead

Previous women's leagues

Before the WNBA entrenched itself as the world's premier women's basketball league, 13 American women's leagues had been launched—and failed—in the previous 23 years.

In previous incarnations of U.S. women's leagues, the focus was not always on the game.

In 1991, the Liberty Basketball Association was founded with the basket nearly a foot lower than regulation and player uniforms that were of a somewhat higher cut—form-fitting "unitards"—leaving little to the imagination.

Before that, there was an attempt with the Women's Basketball League in the early 1980s, an operation on such a shoestring budget that games were played at aging ice-skating arenas.

But the American Basketball League, founded in 1997, was different. Playing a winter schedule, and therefore with a head start against the WNBA's inau-

gural season, the ABL quickly locked up the world's best female players, offered greater salaries and featured a lengthier schedule more in tune with men's pro basketball leagues.

Yet even with such marquee names as Kara Wolters, Kate Starbird, Katrina McClain, Dawn Staley and Teresa Edwards, the lack of exposure eventually did in the league within 2½ seasons, its top stars eventually siphoned away by the WNBA and its advanced marketing.

While the WNBA waited for NBA teams to vacate their arenas in the summer months, the ABL dared to go head-to-head with the NBA and college basketball.

"We feel that women's basketball is a great sport that deserves to stand on a stage of its own during the traditional basketball season," ABL founder Gary Cavalli said of an approach that ultimately met the same fate as previous women's leagues.

of the three thirds that had been the case previously.

International exposure continued in 1953, when the U.S. women won the gold medal at the World Championships.

The modern era for women's basketball effectively then began in 1971, when a five-player, fullcourt game was adopted as the universal playing system. At that time, a 30-second shot clock also was introduced.

A huge step forward then came in 1976, when women's basketball debuted at the Montreal Summer Olympics. At 18, Nancy Lieberman becomes the youngest U.S. basketball player to win a medal when the United States earned the silver.

Two years later, on December 9, 1978, the first game of the Women's Professional Basketball League was staged between the Chicago Hustle and the Milwaukee Does. The eight-team league would last three seasons.

Ann Meyers, a forward at UCLA, furthered the movement when, on August 30, 1978, she signed a one-year, $50,000 contract with the NBA's Indiana Pacers on a tryout basis. She did not make the team, with sexist undercurrents accompanying her departure.

In 1982, the two rival U.S. women's collegiate basketball associations staged rival championship games. The first NCAA title went to Louisiana Tech, which defeated Cheyney State 76–62 on March 28 in Norfolk, Virginia. Meanwhile, on that same date, Rutgers defeated Texas 83–77 to win the final AIAW title.

The international success for the Americans that began with a 1982 victory over the vaunted Soviet Union continued in 1984 when the United States captured the gold medal at the Los Angeles Summer Games. That same year, three founders of the women's game—Berenson, Bertha Teague and Margaret Wade—were inducted into the Basketball Hall of Fame in Springfield, Massachusetts, the first women to be so honored.

In 1985, another woman made it to the pros, this time former University of Kansas guard Lynette Woodard, who became the first woman to play for the barnstorming Harlem Globetrotters.

The WNBA ball

So how did the WNBA select its unique oatmeal-and-orange undersized ball?

It spray-painted 16 balls a variety of colors and then tested the barely dried spheres in a variety of maneuvers at famed Madison Square Garden in New York in the winter of 1997, as cameras clicked away.

With photogenic qualities the key for a league that would survive based on its television appeal, contestant No. 8 was deemed the most alluring.

But that did not mean the league was off to a rolling start. The paint was so fresh that streaks were left on the hardwood, with the NBA's New York Knicks about to take the court shortly thereafter.

The ball is 28.5 inches in circumference, about one inch smaller than the NBA's regulation ball.

WNBA rules

The WNBA game consists of a 30-second shot clock—similar to the college game, but six seconds longer per possession than in the NBA—a 19-foot, 9-inch 3-point shooting semicircle and two 20-minutes halves.

For the most part, the rules closely resemble those of the college game, with the WNBA games 20 percent shorter than the NBA's 48-minute test. Another difference between the WNBA and NBA is that zone defenses are allowed, which has made for an easier transition for players who have returned home from overseas leagues, which also allow zone defenses.

Also, WNBA teams feature 11-player rosters, as opposed to the 12-player rosters allowed by NBA teams.

As is the case with the NBA, WNBA rules continue to evolve, taking into account the increasing speed and strength of today's players.

Already, the WNBA has moved from single-game elimination playoff rounds to multi-game series more closely resembling the NBA format.

Also in 1985, the NCAA adopted a smaller women's ball, one that is 28½ inches in circumference, weighing from 18 to 20 ounces.

Lieberman, at 28, continued as a trendsetter in 1986, when she became the first woman to compete in a men's league by playing for the Springfield Fame of the United States Basketball League, a summer tryout league for NBA prospects.

With the women proving to be as efficient with the outside shot as their male counterparts, the 3-point shot was adopted by the NCAA in 1987. That same year, Lieberman signed on with the Washington Generals, the team that serves as the basketball foils for the comedic Harlem Globetrotters.

A second consecutive gold medal for the Americans followed at the 1988 Seoul Summer Olympics.

Yet another breakthrough came in 1990, when Bernadette Locke became the first female assistant for a major men's college program, when she was hired by coach Rick Pitino at the University of Kentucky.

Another women's league, the Liberty Basketball Association was launched in 1991. It hardly was a step forward, with it skin-tight one-piece uniforms, shorter court and lower basket. The effort folded after one game.

A year later came the demise of the small-scale Women's Basketball Association.

The amateur success, however, took a small step back, with the Americans taking only the bronze medal at the 1992 Barcelona Summer Games.

Further recognition was about to be realized when, in 1994, plans were announced for the Women's Basketball Hall of Fame in Knoxville, Tennessee, home of the potent University of Tennessee women's collegiate program.

The best U.S. players, still lacking a substantive professional option in their home country, then were pulled together in 1995, as a means of spreading the gospel of the women's game. This USA Basketball Women's National Team completed its world tour at 52–0, culminating the effort with the gold medal at the 1996 Atlanta Summer Games.

Within a year, the WNBA was born.

Dreams unfulfilled

The WNBA boasts the greatest female players of its generation. But the arrival of the league came too late to make the type of all-time boasts the NBA can offer.

Among the legends who were ahead of their time were Carol Blazejowski, Anne Donovan, Meyers, Miller, Lusia Harris Stewart and Ora Washington.

Blazejowski may be the greatest U.S. player never to appear in an Olympics. Having produced a 52-point game in venerable Madison Square Garden during her time at Montclair State in New Jersey, she purposely stayed away from professional competition following her collegiate career so as to not jeopardize her amateur standing at a time when professionalism still was a foreign concept at the Games. But when the United States boycotted the 1980 Summer Games in Moscow, her Olympic dream died with the boycott. She went on to serve as general manager and vice president of the WNBA's New York Liberty.

Donovan, a dominant player at Old Dominion, played in three Olympics (1980, '84, and '88) before retiring to become a collegiate coach. She then served as coach of the ABL's Philadelphia Rage.

Meyers was the first four-time women's basketball All-America while at UCLA and earned a silver medal as a member of the 1976 U.S. Olympic Team. She also broke ground when she signed on for a tryout with the NBA's Indiana Pacers, only to be quickly released early in training camp.

"The attitude about women and sports was not as accepting as it is today," said Meyers, whose brother David had a distinguished NBA career.

Meyers became the first woman to have her uniform displayed at the Basketball Hall of Fame.

Miller led the United States in scoring, rebounding, assists and steals during the 1984 Los Angeles Olympic Games, where the U.S. women's team earned its first-ever gold medal. In high school, Miller became the first male or female to be named All-America four straight years and was a four-time All-American at the University of Southern California. She became the first athlete—male or female—to have her jersey retired at USC.

As Miller's brother, NBA shooting star Reggie, once put it, "Cheryl could dunk, she could pass like Magic (Johnson) and she could shoot like Larry (Bird). No question. No woman would have been able to stop her."

Harris Stewart is best known for having scored the first-ever basket in Olympic women's basketball history in 1976 in Montreal. In 1977, she was drafted in the seventh round by the NBA's New Orleans Jazz but declined the offer, leaving it to Meyers to break that ground. She did play three years for the Houston Angels of Women's Basketball League, a low-budget operation with few similarities to today's major-league WNBA.

Washington well may have been the first great woman's professional. She played 18 years with the Philadelphia Hustle, an all-black barnstorming team in the 1920s, 1930s and 1940s. Legend has it that in nine years, the Hustle only lost six times, the six losses to men's all-black teams playing men's rules. Washington also was an accomplished tennis star, held back by segregationist policies that limited her opportunities in that venue.

WEARING THE PANTS: *Cheryl Miller continues to make her coaching mark in the WNBA.*

The pioneer pro

Then there is Lieberman-Cline, (her married name) who arrived in the WNBA at age 38, her best days behind her, but with enough passion for the game to make sure she would be there for the start of a new era.

The youngest member of the 1976 U.S. Olympic team at 18, Lieberman-Cline displayed a determination to play professionally, playing in every U.S. professional women's league other than the ABL.

She played the early 1980's with the Women's Basketball League's Dallas Diamonds, the mid 1980's with the Women's American Basketball Association's Dallas entry, then became the first woman to play in a men's professional league when she joined the Springfield, Massachusetts, entry of the United States Basketball League, a summer circuit for male players with NBA aspirations. She returned to that men's league in 1987 to play for the Long Island (New York) Knights.

From there, she joined the Washington Generals, the foils for the comedic Harlem Globetrotters. That union produced another union. While with the Generals, a teammate was former minor-league standout Tim Cline. The two were married a year later.

And when the WNBA debuted in 1997, she was on the roster of the Phoenix Mercury, participating in 25 games.

Her dream of playing for a major-league women's league accomplished, the former 15-year-old member of the U.S. national team left the game as a player, to serve as coach and general manager of the WNBA's Detroit Shock. In her first year as Shock coach and general manager, Lieberman-Cline led Detroit to a 17–13 record, that .567 winning percentage the highest by an expansion team in American major-league sports.

Her passion for sports was so embedded, Lieberman-Cline became personal trainer for women's tennis star Martina Navratilova in 1981 and remained in the position for three years

"I am proud of where women's basketball is today, at the professional and collegiate levels," she expressed. "It has taken years for women to be able to play a game that we love with people in the stands and watching us on TV, with all of the trappings that have been afforded men's professional sports. Since I was 10 years old, no sport has every been inside of me the way basketball is."

Lieberman-Cline's accomplishments were duly noted when she was named No. 44 on *Sports Illustrated*'s list of the Top 100 Female Athletes of the 20th Century.

NEXT STEP: *Lieberman-Cline made the logical progression from player to coach.*

"It's an honor for people to think of me as one of the great athletes of all time," she said upon receiving the honor. "I played because I loved, and I still love, what I do. You never really know your place in history until something like this happens."

Having seen it all in the evolution of women's basketball, Lieberman-Cline always was able to participate in perhaps, the most dynamic era of the sport.

"I played from the '60s through the '90s. In the '70s, my favorite player to play against was Ann Meyers because she always made me better. We would have wars. She's four years older than I am, and it was apparent to me that we'd go at it every day in practice," Lieberman-Cline said on one of the internet chat sessions that have been so instrumental in advancing the WNBA. "In the '80s, I really enjoyed playing against Lynette Woodard. She was an incredible athlete and I looked forward to those encounters. In the '90s, Cynthia Cooper. She's certainly one of the all-time greatest players that I've ever seen, male or female."

The modern era

The first WNBA players were signed on October 23, 1996, 18 months after the NBA Board of Governors had approved the concept of a women's league. The first two players to sign were Swoopes and Lobo. Shortly thereafter, Bolton-Holifield, Lisa Leslie, Cooper and Timms (the league's first international player) were added.

"It was important to have stars," Ackerman said.

Eight teams were announced for the league's first season, with the Eastern Conference featuring the Charlotte Sting, the Cleveland Rockers, the Houston Comets and New York Liberty, and the Western Conference featuring the Los Angeles Sparks, the Phoenix Mercury, the Sacramento Monarchs and the Utah Starzz.

From the logos to the nicknames, a symmetry was created. The Comets joined the NBA's Rockets in Houston. The Mercury attempted to rise with the NBA's Suns in Phoenix. Sacramento had its Kings of the NBA, so now it would add its Monarchs. As the double-z

LUCKY 7: *Tina Thompson has been a mainstay on the Comets dynasty that has won four titles.*

approach of the Jazz was maintained with Utah's WNBA entry.

On January 16, 1997, the first 16 WNBA players were assigned to teams and a month later two of what the league would term "elite players" were added to each of the franchises.

From that point, the WNBA settled into an annual draft structure similar to that of the NBA. Tina Thompson, a forward, was the first selection of the inaugural WNBA draft in 1997, going to Houston. The first choice in the 1998 roster allocation was Margo Dydek, a

7-foot-2 center from Poland who went to the Starzz. And in 1999, Tennessee star Chamique Holdsclaw arrived in Washington with the expansion Mystics as the top overall selection.

From its modest eight-team roots, the WNBA continued a prudent expansion program that left it with 16 franchises for the start of its fourth season. Washington and the Detroit Shock were added in 1998. In 1999, the league added the Minnesota Lynx and the Orlando Miracle. And for the 2000 season, the new entries were the Miami Sol, the

456 Indiana Fever, the Portland Fire and the Seattle Storm.

With merchandizing critical to the league's success, everything from team logos to the league logo received close scrutiny. The red, white, blue league logo—"Logo Woman" as the league calls it—was selected from about 50 designs. It is similar to the NBA logo that features of a silhouette that is strikingly similar to the shooting form of Los Angeles Lakers legend Jerry West.

As the league increased in size, the schedule also expanded. The inaugural 1997 season featured a 28-game schedule. In 1998 that increased to 30 games and the schedule leveled off at 33 games for the 1999 season. Because of the potential for conflict with the NBA, it is not likely the WNBA ever would approach the NBA's 82-game schedule. As it is, the start of the WNBA season conflicts with the NBA playoffs.

With the growth in teams and schedule came an accompanying growth in revenues. On April 29, 1999 that led to a benefits-rich working agreement with the players, making the WNBA the first league in women's team sports with its own collective-bargaining agreement. As with its NBA counterparts, WNBA play-ers encountered initial opposition from the league on several points. But, unlike with the NBA, the players understood it was not worth risking a season, as the NBA nearly did in 1998, when a lockout cut the schedule from 82 games to 50.

The inaugural NBA season tipped-off on June 21, 1997, when the Liberty played the Sparks in the Great Western Forum in Inglewood, Calif., the same facility that had hosted such Lakers legends as West, Johnson, Kareem Abdul-Jabbar, Magic Johnson and coach Pat Riley. A crowd of 14,284 watched as Sparks guard Penny Toler scored the first basket in WNBA history. The Liberty won 67–57, spoiling the debut for the home fans.

From that point, attendance grew to 1 million, a milestone accomplished on August 22, 1997, by factoring in the crowd for a Mercury home game at America West Arena in Phoenix.

Overall, the league averaged 9,669 tickets sold in its first season and then eclipsed the 10,000 average per game in its second season.

Keeping its fans connected, the league also developed its own web site, WNBA.COM, a sister component to the NBA's highly successful, NBA.COM.

In another move to more closely resemble its male counterpart, the league staged its first All-Star Game on July 14, 1999 at famed Madison Square Garden, home of the NBA's New York Knicks. The game drew a sellout crowd of 18,649. The West, led by game Most Valuable Player Lisa Leslie of the Sparks, defeated the East 79–61. The Western Conference hosted it first All-Star Game on July 17, 2000, when it was played at America West Arena, home of the Mercury and NBA Phoenix Suns.

The WNBA also reached out beyond the court. It initiated WNBA Be Active, a grassroots program that targets boys and girls ages 11 to 14 with the goal of encouraging them to be physically active. The league also devoted its means to the WNBA Breast Health Initiative, which is a partnership with the National Alliance of Breast Cancer Organizations, to draw attention to the issue of breast cancer and the importance of early detection through the 3-Point Play for Good Breast Health—clinical breast exam, self-exam and mammography.

The faces

Black, white, male or female, it is the faces that make the game.

The face of the WNBA is a melange of personalities, ones fans can relate to, admire, marvel at and be appreciative of. Perhaps the most compelling story is that of Cooper, Most Valuable Player of the WNBA for the league's first two seasons. The Comets guard proved to be more than just a leader on the court for Houston. Not only did Cooper uproot her family from the dangerous streets of Watts, outside of Los Angeles, but also spent two years tending to her ailing mother, Mary Cobbs, before she succumbed to cancer. Cooper then shifted her caring and warmth to teammate Kim Perrot, who would succumb to cancer in the midst of the Comets' third consecutive run to a championship in the league's third season.

Her coach, Chancellor, called Cooper, "the most unique human being I've ever been around."

In her 1999 autobiography, *She Got*

GUIDING FORCE: *Van Chancellor has been the only coach the Comets have known.*

Game, Cooper wrote of her struggles as a youth, of realizing that basketball would be her ticket out of the ghetto. It was that persistence that allowed her to endure 11 seasons overseas before the WNBA allowed her dream to be realized closer to home, in her mid 30s about to seize the opportunity to become the best player among the best collection of women's talent ever assembled.

Cooper has embraced the WNBA as much as the league has embraced its most unlikely first star.

"We play under the rim, but we play hard," she said.

To appreciate the worldwide respect Cooper has garnered, consider that in a poll by the Italian basketball magazine *Superbasket*, Cooper was voted the world's greatest female player. Of course, Cooper led the Italian League in scoring eight times in 10 seasons and also was the leading scorer in the 1996 European Cup, her final season overseas, when she averaged a staggering 37.5 points in Italy.

Cooper was prevented from a three-peat of MVP honors when Sacramento Monarchs forward Yolanda Griffith took the award in the WNBA's third season.

Griffith played two seasons in the ABL before its demise and had spent three seasons in Germany after leaving Florida Atlantic University.

Like so many of the WNBA's pioneers, it was a difficult road to the top, with Griffith forced to repossess cars while attending junior college in Florida.

In her first season in the WNBA, Griffith did not just excel, she dominated.

Griffith not only led the WNBA in rebounding and steals immediately after moving over from the ABL, but also finished second in the WNBA in 1999 in scoring and field-goal percentage, arguably the most dominant season of any player in the WNBA's first three years.

For Cooper and Griffith, the WNBA experience provided a mid-life revival, at least in basketball years. For Holdsclaw, the WNBA represented a seamless transition to pro basketball, the same seamless experience collegiate men have been afforded for decades by the NBA.

TOTAL TENACITY: *Yolanda Griffith stands as one of the best defenders in the WNBA.*

A 6-foot-2 guard, Holdsclaw entered the WNBA in 1999 as perhaps the most prized rookie in the league's first three seasons. From the women's basketball factory at the University of Tennessee, she emerged as the hope for the fledgling Washington Mystics.

"She's the whole package," Miller said. "If there's one kid over the last 10 years that I could honestly say, 'Now that kid reminds me of me,' it's Holdsclaw."

With the combination of athleticism and charisma that had defined the career of Michael Jordan and his male impersonators, Holdsclaw has displayed an uncanny ability to be like Mike. No sooner had Jordan realized they shared the same shoe size, than Jordan recommended they share the same shoes. A lucrative endorsement contract for Holdsclaw with Nike followed shortly thereafter.

Further, Holdsclaw made her entrance into the WNBA with the same agent as NBA stars Grant Hill and Tim Duncan and shares a friendship with NFL quarterback Peyton Manning, a fellow Tennessee alum.

"She's our future," Cynthia Cooper admitted. "Chamique is the future of women's basketball."

To the founding footsoldiers, the greatest reward would be creating continued rewards for emerging women's talent. "Hopefully, they'll be a league in 15 or 20 years and we'll be seen as the pioneers," Lobo said.

Rebecca Lobo, the former college star who was riddled by injuries at the start of her WNBA career, set her goals high from the start of her career.

"In basketball I looked up to Larry Bird as a kid," she said. "I thought he did the most amazing things on the basketball court."

A pioneer from the time she scored 100 points in high school—in the first half, alone—to her jaunts down runways as a fashion mode, Los Angeles Sparks center Lisa Leslie quickly became the face of the WNBA, an athlete as at home in *Vogue* as *Sports Illustrated*, the perfect marketing mix of lipstick and length.

THE NEW BREED: *Clamique Holdsclaw arrived as a part of the next generation.*

"Pick any superlative you want," former WNBA and NBA coach Frank Layden said. "Lisa is a streamliner. She was absolutely built to play this game."

The mix of runways and running made Leslie among the WNBA's first millionaires. She could be ferocious on the court, yet at the same time feminine, tall yet only a Size 6.

SHINING STAR: *Lisa Leslie (right) has been a model player on and off the court.*

"I wish she'd been around when I was a kid," said actress Whoopi Goldberg.

For Leslie, the ultimate goal was success, but not necessarily basketball success. Growing up, there was no WNBA, no option for the American women's player who wanted to continue the pursuit of the game but also remain stateside. That served as the impetus to succeed elsewhere, to keep the options open. It is why she now can seamlessly slide between a day on the court to a guest shot on a situation comedy.

Everything has become big in Leslie's life, including her representation by Los Angeles super-agent Leonard Armato, the same agent who represents Los Angeles' other beacon of success, Lakers center Shaquille O'Neal.

"It just feels great to be a part of history," she said.

While winning has become the driving force in Leslie's life, it is not something she harps on. She has trouble recalling where she placed her gold medal from the 1996 Olympics, but remembers the 35

points she scored in the competition against Japan, a U.S. Olympic record.

She also is cognizant of the duality of her life.

"I wear lipstick and fingernail polish 90 percent of the day," she said.

For many in the league, the public life is all new. No longer are they strangers in strange lands, forced overseas by the lack of a significant American alternative.

The opportunity has been gratifying and challenging.

"It was kind of like we were instant superstars and there was no one before us to make a path," said Thompson, a key to the Comet's three consecutive championships at the WNBA's inception. "It was like, 'What do we do next?' I believe all the women in the WNBA are great role models. It's a constant now because we're in the spotlight. It's turned out to be a great thing because we have great women who have responded to the challenge."

The dynasty

The odds of the WNBA bursting from the gate with a bona-fide dynasty were minimal. The mix was too diverse, the veterans and the rookies, the imports and the former exports who finally had the opportunity to come home, teams thrown together only weeks before the start of an adventure that no one was certain would lead to success.

Yet somehow, from the start, one

460

All American Red Heads

Before there was the WNBA, before there were those minor-level women's leagues, before a schoolgirl could dream of financing her college education by playing basketball, there were the All American Red Heads.

They played the American game. And yes, they are were redheads.

A team, and sometimes a group of teams, of elite women's players, the troupe toured the world from 1936 to 1973, winning at least 100 games a year. A year before the ensemble's demise, these female globetrotters claimed a 558–84 record—with each of those games against men's teams.

While players came and went, red hair—genuine, through a bottle or with a wig—remained as much a requisite as the ability to compete and entertain.

In honor of their contribution to the women's game, several former members were invited to lay bricks at the ground-breaking of the Women's Basketball Hall of Fame in Knoxville, Tennessee.

WNBA team was able to exceed all expectations. At a time when Michael Jordan was putting the final touches on the Chicago Bulls' NBA dynasty, with a two-pack of three consecutive championship seasons, the Houston Comets were emerging as the WNBA's elite.

Behind the play of Cooper, Swoopes and Thompson, the Comets won the league's first two titles.

Chancellor still was not impressed.

"You have to win about three more championships to be considered a dynasty," he said.

So what did the Comets do the following seasons? Win another title. And another. Four-for-four, excellence that at least invited comparisons to the NBA legacies of the Celtics, Lakers and Bulls.

"We've got the three best players and they play very hard-nosed," Chancellor said when asked about the secret to his success. "They just play extremely hard and do a great job. They love to play every night and want to beat everybody."

FOUR PLAY: *Cynthia Cooper celebrates another Houston Comets title.*

Chancellor, after three title seasons, realized what he had was special, much the same way Red Auerbach relished his Celtics dynasty, Pat Riley his Lakers years and Phil Jackson his Bulls tenure.

Once, when a neophyte fan requested an autograph, the girl asked, "You coach Sheryl, don't you?" Replied Chancellor, "Yeah, I've been fortunate."

So, for that matter, was the WNBA.

It knew it had marquee players at its inception, most tested for years in international play. It knew it had the brawn of the NBA as its driving marketing force.

But it did not know if it had a signature franchise.

That's when the Comets started winning and winning and winning.

"What we have is the greatest will to win I've ever seen," Chancellor said.

Cooper exulted after the third championship.

"Right now you don't want to point the finger and say how great you are," she said. "You just want to experience the awesome feeling of winning the championship first of all, but also winning three in a row."

Comets forward Janeth Arcain summed up the experience.

"The first season, no one knew each other at first, we just had to learn how to play together," she told the league's official web site, WNBA.com. "That time was great. The second season, we just played hard and believed in ourselves. The third time, we got so much press because we had won two championships, there was more pressure to win, but we did. We played so well together, did our job."

The boss

If the legacy of NBA Commissioner David Stern is of the dynamo who delivered pro basketball to a world market, then the legacy of Ackerman is the nurturing force behind the emergence of women's pro basketball on an NBA-like scale.

As president of the WNBA, Ackerman has provided the type of guidance and leadership that had made Stern a beacon among commissioners of American professional sports.

Ackerman's basketball roots run deep.

Awarded only half a scholarship to the University of Virginia, typical of an era when men already were enjoying full rides, Ackerman was a four-year starter and two-time Academic All-American. Her leadership skills also became apparent early, as she became the first player in program history to be named captain as a sophomore, to also repeat the honor for her final two seasons.

She was so respected in the program that she kindled a friendship with legendary Virginia center and future NBA All-Star Ralph Sampson, who playfully would palm Ackerman's head when the two would cross paths at the gym.

Without a viable alternative closer to home, she then played one season in France before returning stateside to earn a law degree.

"We represent an opportunity for a career that wasn't there before," she said. "When my college days were over, I played overseas. Now, that opportunity is here."

She soon turned her combined basketball and legal acumen into a position as an assistant to Stern, himself a lawyer, in 1990 and soon was running the NBA's business affairs.

By the middle of the decade,

THE BOSS: *Val Ackerman has overseen the WNBA's growth into a respected league.*

Ackerman was spearheading the effort to organize an elite women's team that would play an extended tour around the country and then represent the United States in the 1996 Atlanta Olympics.

That '96 Olympic effort would not only produce gold for the Americans, but increase the fortunes for what would grow into the WNBA.

"I feel like I was in the right place at the right time," Ackerman said. "I feel like I have the perfect job. My job is made even more special by the fact that I have daughters, and the WNBA shows the growing opportunities that are available to women."

Stern takes almost a patriarchal pride in Ackerman's accomplishments.

"She has the perfect background in terms of having played the game, the legal background, a winning personality and an iron will," he said.

It is why she approaches the job more as a passion than an obligation.

"I feel sort of a combination of 'I can't believe it,' and 'It's all finally happening in my lifetime,'" she said. "There's definitely a sense of satisfaction that comes from being part of an effort that creates new opportunities and to be involved with something that I've got so much personal investment in. Women's sports have been part of my life, all my life."

Among Ackerman's most notable achievements was the drafting of the first

collective-bargaining agreement for an American women's league.

With the drafting of the agreement, for the 1999 season, salaries for veteran players doubled from $15,000 to $30,000 and were to escalate over the terms of the deal to $32,500 in 2000, $35,000 in 2001, and $40,000 in 2002.

A separate minimum base salary for rookie players also was established, starting at $25,000 in 1999 and increasing to $26,500 in 2000, $28,000 in 2001, and $30,000 in 2002.

Beyond the base salaries, a variety of salary bonuses remained in place for team accomplishments and personal successes.

In addition, steps were taken to enhance future success for the league's players, including apprenticeships with companies such as national sponsors of the league and tuition reimbursement for players to attend graduate school in the offseason while they're under contract.

"I feel very lucky I'm in the position I'm in," Ackerman said.

The male appeal

From its logo to its marketing to its core audience, the WNBA is a full-court female experience.

But on the sideline, the league has been able to mesh the uniqueness of the women's game to the strategies and pro precepts that had made the NBA so successful.

462

So, often when players head into one locker room after a game, coaches head into another.

Such has been the case for former NBA coaches Layden, Richie Adubato and Ron Rothstein, all of whom have made the jump to the WNBA.

Adubato, who has coached the Orlando Magic, Dallas Mavericks, Detroit Pistons of the NBA, was skeptical at first of taking over as bench leader of the New York Liberty. But his time on the sideline proved to be refreshing and provided a few revelations along the way.

"I got positive vibes from every single one," Adubato said of previous male coaches to work the women's game. "They said the women loved to be coached and they work hard."

They worked hard enough for

Adubato to get him to the championship series in his first season on the bench, before the Comets closed out their third consecutive championship in 1999.

"The women want to learn to get better," Adubato said. "They let you coach. There's a lot of coaching, because few players can take over a game with natural ability, like they do in the NBA. They pass the ball so much. They're so unselfish I actually have to tell them, 'Please, shoot it.' "

T.R. Dunn, a former NBA player and assistant coach, said the transition to becoming coach of the Charlotte Sting hardly was a transition at all. Basketball, he said, simply is basketball.

THE OTHER SIDE: *Richie Adubato made the switch from the NBA to the WNBA.*

Hall of Fame

Twenty-six pioneers of women's basketball were selected for the first class to the Women's Basketball Hall of Fame in Knoxville, Tennessee. The 26 won election in 1998 and were enshrined in 1999:

● Lidia Alexeeva: A member of the Soviet National team in the 1950 who coached the Soviets to gold medals in the 1976 and 1980 Olympics. She also was involved with 14 European Championships and 17 Soviet National Championships.

● Senda Berensen: Considered the "mother of women's basketball," she authored and developed the first basketball guide for women while at Smith College in Massachusetts.

● Carol Blazejowski: A proficient college scorer and winner of the Wade Trophy for collegiate basketball excellence at Montclair State in New Jersey, she went on to become general manage of the New York Liberty of the WNBA.

● Joanne Bracker: A leading coach in women's collegiate basketball who compiled a .758 winning percentage during a 28-year coaching career at Midland Lutheran College in Fremont, Nebraska.

● Walter Byers: The director of the NCAA collegiate ruling body during the

period when it stepped to the forefront as an all-encompassing governing body for men's and women's athletics. During his tenure with the NCAA, the women's Final Four grew into one of the premier American sporting events.

● Jody Conradt: The winningest coach in women's collegiate history, with much of that success accomplished at the University of Texas.

● Joan Crawford: A 13-time AAU All-American. Was named Most Valuable Player at the 1963 and 1964 AAU National Tournament and won gold medals at the 1959 and 1963 Pan American Games.

● Denise Curry: A two-time Olympian and three-time All-American at UCLA.

● Anne Donovan: A three-time Olympian from 1980 to 1988 who was a driving force for the heralded Old Dominion collegiate program.

● Carol Eckman: Established the first National Invitational Women's Intercollegiate Basketball Tournament in 1969. Referred to as the "Mother of National Collegiate Championships."

● Betty Jo Graber: Established one of the first women's basketball programs in the Southwest at Weatherford College in Texas.

● Lusia Harris Stewart: A three-time

All-American at Delta State University in Mississippi. She scored the first points in Olympic women's basketball as a member of the 1976 U.S. team in Montreal.

● John Head: Coached women's basketball 17 for seasons at Nashville Business College in Tennessee, compiling a 689–95 record. Coached the American women to titles at the World Championships in 1953 and 1957.

● Nancy Lieberman-Cline: The only two-time winner of the Wade Trophy, the former Old Dominion University star became the youngest basketball player in Olympic history to win a medal, a silver at the age of 18 in 1976. She then became a WNBA player and later coach and general manager of the league's Detroit Shock.

● Darlene May: Became the first female to officiate an Olympic women's basketball game, during the 1984 Games in Los Angeles.

● Ann Meyers: A four-time All-American at UCLA who was the first woman to receive a full athletic scholarship to the school. She later received a tryout with the NBA Indiana Pacers and went on to become a respected television analyst for men's and women's college games.

"I think the best advice you can get at any level of basketball is 'never stop working to improve your game,' " he said. "Lots of players are good at one thing, and they think they can get by doing just one thing. But to truly reach your potential as an athlete, you have to work on the parts of the game that don't come easy to you."

Michael Cooper, a member of the legendary Lakers teams coached by Riley, also made the shift to the WNBA bench, guiding the Los Angeles Sparks. He previously had served as an assistant coach to Magic Johnson with the Lakers.

So why the WNBA?

"Being around players that want to play the game with passion, dignity and the love of being out there," he said. "That was one thing I missed when I was coaching with the Lakers—you get kind of jaded with all that money flying around. The players in the WNBA still have that human side to them—they play the game not for the dollars, but because they love the game and I love being around that."

The future

Ackerman plans to go slow despite the league's remarkably quick start.

By the close of its second season, the WNBA had surpassed all attendance goals, "especially when you consider it took the NBA 29 seasons to average over 10,000 spectators, and we did it in two."

When discussing the direction of her league, Ackerman often finds herself speaking of the women's sports movement as a whole.

"I think we have been a trailblazer in terms of creating an unprecedented level of awareness for women's basketball through our television contracts. We have made a lot of progress, and we're mindful of the impact we've had on other sports."

And while the league is American by design, affording the opportunity for its players to come home, it has become international in scope. By the start of its third season, the WNBA was televised in 125 countries, broadcast in 18 languages. The oatmeal-and-orange ball could be seen from Ghana to Lithuania to Uruguay.

"We want to make our league one that stands out internationally," Ackerman said upon its inception.

And while the arena audience is 70 percent female and 30 percent male, the

FAME GAME: *Cheryl Miller was a Hall of Fame player before her coaching days.*

● Cheryl Miller: The sister of noted NBA guard Reggie Miller led the University of Southern California to a 112–20 record, including back-to-back NCAA championships in 1983 and 1984. She then served as floor leader for the U.S. entry that won the Olympic gold in 1984. An analyst for NBA telecasts, she also serves as coach and general manager of the WNBA's Phoenix Mercury.

● Billie Moore: The first coach of a U.S. Olympic women's basketball team, serving in Montreal in 1976. Coached UCLA (1978) and Cal State-Fullerton (1970) to women's collegiate championships.

● Sinja Park: Recognized as the premier women's player in Asia for more than a decade. Served as the administrator for both the 1979 FIBA World Championships and the 1988 Seoul Olympics.

● Harley Redin: Recorded an impressive 431–66 record in 18 years with victories in each of her first 76 games as women's coach at Wayland Baptist College in Plainview, Texas.

● Uljanna Semjonova: The 7-foot center helped the Soviet Union win two Olympic gold medals and played for the national team for more than two decades. Participated in 11 European Championships and three World Championships.

● Jim Smiddy: Recorded the most victories in U.S. girls high school basketball history, finishing a 45-year career with 1,217 wins and only 206 losses while guiding two high schools in Tennessee.

● Pat Head Summit: Coached the U.S. to its first women's Olympic gold medal in 1984 and led the University of Tennessee to six NCAA championships.

● Bertha Teague: Coached the girls' team at Byng High School in Oklahoma from 1926 to 1969, compiling a record of 1,152–115.

● Margaret Wade: The Wade Trophy presented to the outstanding women's collegiate player is named in her honor for her contributions in the development of the game. Won championships as coach at the collegiate and high school levels in Mississippi.

● Nera White: A 15-time AAU All-American from 1955 to 1969, she was selected the Most Valuable Player at the AAU national tournament 10 times.

Selection criteria: Voting was based on various factors that included moral character, integrity, sportsmanship, record of performance, ability, national or international recognition, and contributions to the game of women's basketball. Contributions were evaluated on the significance of their accomplishments to women's basketball whether on a voluntary basis or performing the duties of a salaried position.

THE OTHER LEAGUE: *Teresa Edwards was one of many women pros who opted to play in the now-defunct ABL, in her case with the Rage.*

television audience is 50–50, with a strong percentage of non-adult viewers.

To those who have blazed the path, the game is just beginning.

"It's important that our sport continue to grow," U.S. Olympian Teresa Edwards said. "The powers-at-be have to understand this is important to a lot of women and little girls dribbling a basketball in their driveways today and watching Olympic and WNBA games. The American public really has to accept the female athlete and respect the fact that we are all professional just like they do football, baseball and men's basketball."

Having been part of every previous incarnation of women's professional basketball in the United States, Lieberman-Cline understands this remains the infancy of women's basketball as a major-league enterprise.

"We're still a new business and we're growing," she said. "We're trying to maintain the blueprint … Certainly Val and David Stern have the vision for where they want the league to go internally. We're all pieces to the puzzle, each individual franchise, each player, coach, people within the organizations."

The opportunity is there, as is the technology.

"I think the Internet in women's sports is the next frontier," Lieberman-Cline said, "this will give us tremendous exposure and visibility and play to our strength as consumers."

Building a passion remain the key

"I think that is the next thing that must happen," said University of Connecticut coach Geno Auriemma, one of the most accomplished women's coaches of all time. "Men spend a lot of time watching sports on television, and I think men will spend a lot of time watching women's sports on television; but, I think women will have to spend that same time and interest in order to … build a broader fan base."

The internet, television, a collective-bargaining agreement. All will continue to evolve.

But with a league in place, perhaps Leslie put it best at the WNBA's inception when she said, "It gives little girls the opportunity to look at us as role models."

Cheryl Swoopes

At first Cheryl Swoopes did not know what to expect. Here a league was attempting to promote the female Michael Jordan and the female Michael Jordan would miss the start of the WNBA's inaugural season due to an unplanned pregnancy.

TROPHY CAREER: *Yet more hardware.*

"I just thought, 'All my sponsors, they're not going to want me anymore,' " said the first player signed to a WNBA contract.

Instead it was just what they wanted, a women who was walking in their shoes, being a mother and a professional at the same time.

The arrival of Jordan—yes, as in you-know-who—humanized the entire league. During one game, Swoopes breast-fed the newborn during halftime.

Swoopes quickly became an inspiration to those who returned from the maternity ward to the workplace.

"She had a baby," said actress and WNBA fanatic Rosie O'Donnell, "and six weeks later she was back on the court looking fierce."

Baby Jordan's mother had one-upped Air Jordan.

"Welcome Back Mom" a banner read upon her return in 1997, 43 days after delivery.

In one of her first games back from maternity leave, Swoopes scored 18

NEW LIFE: *Sheryl Swoopes has delivered on and off the court for the Comets.*

points in a 76–56 Houston victory over the Utah Starzz.

"I've been waiting for the moment," she said.

When the WNBA decided to stage its inaugural All-Star Game in 1999, Swoopes received more votes in the fan balloting than any other player.

"I feel like I've come a long way," she said of the honor that annually had gone to Michael Jordan for the NBA's All-Star Game. "And the thing is, there were a lot of people who had doubts ...

after having my child, that I would be able to come back, not only to play, but to be in the shape I was in before—and to be the old Sheryl Swoopes."

By her third season, the Houston Comets forward was just that, finishing as runner-up to Sacramento forward Yolanda Griffith in the balloting for WNBA Most Valuable Player.

"I tell people she might be our first mom-player," WNBA President Val Ackerman said, "but I'm sure she won't be the last."

COLLEGE BASKETBALL

Long before the National Basketball Association and its professional-league predecessors established a foothold in the national sporting consciousness, the collegiate game, with its rabid student following and the loyal alumni support, was providing the sport with the widespread forum it needed to compete with American mainstays such as baseball and football.

The birth of big-time college basketball well may have come on December 19, 1934, with a doubleheader at famed Madison Square Garden in New York that saw New York University defeat Notre Dame 25–18 and Westminster College of Pennsylvania defeat St. John's of New York 37–33.

Amid a difficult economic climate, 16,188 turned out for the event organized by noted basketball promoter and journalist Ned Irish.

Two years later, the Garden would host another of the great precursors to today's hyped matchups. This time, it was Hank Luisetti, one of the early stars of the game, leading Stanford to victory over

A PIONEER: *Hank Luisetti stands as one of the early stars of the collegiate game.*

Long Island University and legendary coach Claire Bee.

That game very much was a jumping off point toward today's up-tempo game with Luisetti among the first practitioners of the one-handed shot, a staple of today's game

With a following cultivated, national tournaments soon were born, the National Invitational Tournament (NIT) at the Garden and a competing tournament that began in Chicago at Northwestern University under the auspices of the National Association of Basketball Coaches (NABC), which later grew into today's NCAA tournament, the event that has spawned the Final Four and March Madness.

While Luisetti was capturing the nation's imagination with a 50-point game that season against Duquesne, Temple would become the NIT's first champion in 1938, with Stanford not competing.

The following year, in the first NCAA championship, dubbed the Final Two, Oregon defeated Ohio State 46–33, in an era when the nation's best teams did not necessarily compete in the championship tournaments. The Oregon team was nicknamed the "Tall Firs" because of its exceptional height.

The first-ever game in the NCAA tournament was a 42–30 victory by Villanova over Brown on March 17, 1939 in Philadelphia.

The first telecasts of the collegiate game came on February 28, 1940, with a New York station showing a doubleheader at Madison Square Garden that featured Pittsburgh against Fordham, as well as Georgetown against New York University.

Among the notable factors in 1941 was who emerged as the scoring leader of the Pacific Coast Conference—Jackie Robinson, from UCLA, the player who six years later would break the color barrier in Major League Baseball.

The war years stunted the game's growth, with most of the older players called into service.

MJ MOMENT: *Michael Jordan wins the 1982 NCAA title for North Carolina.*

That youth movement spawned Utah's famed "Blitz Kids" in 1944, a team that went 21–4 with a starting five of Arnie Ferrin, Bob Lewis, Walt Misaka, Dick Smuin and Fred Sheffield that left the Utes with a lineup with an average age of 18½ years.

Although the competing NIT and NCAA tournaments left the nation with multiple champions, from 1943–45 the two titlists would square off in an unofficial national championship as a charity event to benefit the Red Cross during the later stages of World War II.

In the early stages of the tournaments, both the NIT and NCAA championship games were played at Madison Square Garden. The difference was the NIT staged its entire tournament at the site, while the NCAA only played its title game there.

By 1945, the college game had grown up, perhaps too much for some tastes. With Oklahoma A&M's 7-foot Bob Kurland and DePaul's 6-foot-10 George Mikan so dominating the game, goaltending rules were added to the sport. No longer could shots be swatted away randomly. No matter, Mikan and DePaul won the NIT and Kurland and Oklahoma A&M won the NCAA.

In 1946, the first championship game was telecast, as an estimated 500,000 in New York watched Oklahoma State defeat North Carolina 43-40 on WCBS-TV in New York.

Their service time completed, two Blitz Kids, Ferrin and Misaka, returned in 1947 to follow up their previous NCAA title with an NIT title, making them the first to win each tournament. When the two won their initial title, Utah was left without its home court, the Army having claimed the school's field house. Ironically, when the two were winning the NIT, the NCAA champion, Holy Cross, had to play its schedule on the road because the lack of a suitable venue in Worcester, Massachusetts.

In 1948, the legend of the University of Kentucky would become entrenched, when coach Adolph Rupp would guide the Fabulous Five of Cliff Barker, Ralph Beard,

TOO TALL?: *George Mikan was so dominating inside goaltending rules were added.*

BIG SHOT: *Oklahoma A&M's Bob Kurland was one of the game's first dominant big men.*

Alex Groza, Wah Wah Jones and Kenny Rollins to the NCAA title. The following year, Kentucky bid for both the NIT and NCAA titles, winning only the latter.

Among the Players of the Year in the '40s were North Carolina's George Glamack, Rhode Island State's Stan Modzelewski, St. Joseph's of Pennsylvania's George Senesky, DePaul's Mikan, Oklahoma A&M's Kurland, Oklahoma's Gerry Tucker, St. Louis' Ed Macauley and Yale's Tony Lavelli.

Final Four is born

Until 1952, the road to the Garden for the NCAA championship took teams through two regional sites. Thereafter, four NCAA regionals were staged, which, effectively, is when the Final Four was created.

The shift in power between the tournaments came in the mid-1950s, with the NCAA willing to accommodate a larger field, while the NIT remained limited to only 12 invitees.

Once the nation's most dominant team—the University of San Francisco, with future NBA legends Bill Russell and K.C. Jones—won the NCAAs in 1955 and 1956, the NIT had been cast aside to second-tier status.

Over the years, the NCAA would

increase its field to include not only league champions, but also the most successful at-large entrants.

The 1950s began with an NIT-NCAA double championship by Nat Holman's City College of New York. Out of nowhere, CCNY had burst upon the national scene with an unheralded roster.

The glory was short-lived.

In one of the most infamous cases in American sports, seven members of the CCNY roster and several others were arrested in a case that would result in proof that 86 college games from 1947 to 1951 had been fixed under the influence of 32 players. Even famed Beard, Groza and Bill Spivey from Kentucky were implicated.

That initial Final Four in 1952 in new basketball hotbed Seattle crowned Kansas as champion, an 80–63 winner over St. John's.

What gambling allegations couldn't do to the Kentucky program, recruiting irregularities did to Rupp and the Wildcats in 1952–53, when the school's program was shut down. Kentucky would rebound for a perfect 25–0 season in 1953–54, but with three of his players ruled ineligible to compete in the postseason, Rupp declined a tournament berth.

The championship game was televised nationally for the first time in 1954, with La Salle defeating Bradley 94–76 in Kansas City, Missouri.

Russell and Jones and their San Francisco Dons would dominate the following two seasons, with the lane widened in 1956 from six feet to 12 feet in a thinly veiled move to keep Russell from overwhelming the game.

In the 1956–57 season, North Carolina began to raise its voice as an NCAA champion, the success built off a recruiting pipeline from New York that remains in place to this day.

The later part of the 1950s proved to be a magical era for the game, when future NBA stars such as Jerry West, Oscar Robertson, Wilt Chamberlain and Elgin Baylor would emerge.

Among the Players of the Year in the '50s were Villanova's Paul Arizin, Duke's Dick Groat, Kansas's Clyde Lovellette, LaSalle's Tom Gola, San Francisco's Russell, North Carolina's Lennie

Rosenbluth, Cincinnati's Robertson and Seattle's Baylor.

Ohio State and center Jerry Lucas produced the first NCAA title of the 1960s, with the title remaining in the state but going to Robertson and Cincinnati the following season, as well as the year after. When Cincinnati and Ohio State met in the 1961 and 1962 title games, it marked the only times schools from the same states had played in the championship game.

The civil-rights movement resulted in incomplete tournaments early in the '60s, with Southeastern Conference power Mississippi State initially declining to play integrated schools. Ironically, when the school finally relented in 1963, Mississippi State lost to Loyola of Illinois, a team that started four black players.

The tournament had grown so popular that in 1963 sites for future competitions began to be selected two years in advance.

All the while, an emerging dynasty was gestating. UCLA, under legendary coach John Wooden, had advanced to its first Final Four in 1962. By 1964, the Bruins would reach great heights with a puny roster, a unit at 6-foot-5 and shorter giving the school its first title, defeating Duke 98–83 for the national championship.

The following two years produced two seminal moments for the game.

Early in the 1964–65 season, it was Cazzie Russell leading Michigan to a 93–76 victory over Princeton and Bill Bradley. The two collegiate legends soon would be teammates with the NBA's New York Knickerbockers.

The most momentous moment of the 1965–66 season came in the title game, when, at the height of the civil-rights movement, Texas-El Paso, starting an all-black lineup, defeated Kentucky and its all-white lineup in the NCAA title game. From that moment, the recruiting of black players seemingly became a nationwide passion, literally changing the complexion of the sport.

By the end of the 1966–67 season, UCLA was back on top and on January 20, 1998 the sport celebrated an electric moment, when UCLA's Lew Alcindor (later to change his name to Kareem Abdul-Jabbar) squared off before 52,693

PISTOL PETE: *LSU's Pete Maravich was more than a scorer, he was a true stylist.*

at Houston's Astrodome against the University of Houston's Elvin Hayes. Hayes won the battle, with 39 points in the Cougars' 71–69 victory. Alcindor won the war, his Bruins topping the Cougars in

the rematch during the NCAA Tournament on the way to another title.

ULCA also would win the title in 1969, but the scoring of Louisiana State guard "Pistol" Pete Maravich and the

rebounding of Detroit's Spencer Haywood prevented the game from settling into a malaise.

Among the players of the year in the 1960s were Cincinnati's Robertson, Ohio

State's Lucas, Duke's Art Heyman, UCLA's Walt Hazzard, Princeton's Bradley, UCLA's Gail Goodrich, Michigan's Russell, UCLA's Alcindor and Houston's Hayes.

UCLA rolls on

Maravich continued to dazzle with his scoring as the '70s began, and UCLA continued to role to NCAA titles. So dominant were the Bruins that Marquette instead elected to participate in the second-tier NIT instead in 1970, winning that tournament while UCLA rolled in the NCAA Tournament.

UCLA lost only one game the following season, to Austin Carr and Notre Dame, before rolling to another title. UCLA defeated Villanova for that title, but Wildcats forward Howard Porter was named Most Outstanding Player of the tournament. That honor was short-lived, with Porter stripped of the award when it was learned he had signed a professional contract before the tournament.

With Bill Walton taking over as UCLA's man in the middle, the Bruins went a perfect 30–0 on the way to the 1972 title. That 1972 title marked the third—and last—time a team won an NCAA title in its home city. The previous home-city winners had UCLA in Los Angeles in 1968 and CCNY in New York in 1950.

By that 1972 title, UCLA's dominance had taken a toll on the seemingly rigid infrastructure of the college game. For the next season, freshman were allowed to participate, leading to a more impassioned search for scholastic talent that was ready for college-level ball. Little matter, UCLA won another title, although Providence's Ernie DiGregorio did manage to dazzle the nation by leading the Friars to the Final Four with his ballhandling.

The 1973–74 season was humbling for the Bruins, at least by their standards. Not only did they lose for the first time in four seasons, a remarkable 88-game run ended, but North Carolina State went on to win the national title behind the dynamic leaping ability of David Thompson.

That 88-game string ended January 19, 1994 at Notre Dame, with the Irish winning 71–70. Gary Brokaw led the Fighting Irish with 25 points.

The following season would be a cur-

tain call for the retiring Wooden. He headed into retirement with a 10th title. Indiana and cantankerous coach Bob Knight would emerge as champions the following season. From there, colorful Al McGuire would guide Marquette to the 1977 title, Kentucky would win the title in 1978 only months after the passing of Rupp, and in perhaps the greatest showdown in Final Four history, Magic Johnson would lead Michigan State past Larry Bird and Indiana State in the 1979 championship game, with three-man officiating crew adopted for that tournament.

Among the Players of the Year in the 1970s were Louisiana State's Maravich, UCLA's Sidney Wicks, Notre Dame's Carr, UCLA's Walton, North Carolina State's Thompson, Kentucky's Kevin Greavey, UCLA's David Meyers, Indiana's Scott May, Indiana Kent Benson, Notre Dame's Adrian Dantley, UCLA's Marques Johnson, North Carolina's Phil Ford, Marquette's Butch Lee, Kentucky's Jack Givens and Indiana State's Bird.

The NCAA Tournament grew to 48 teams for the 1980 event, with 24 at-large berths now available. The previous

KING OF THE COURT: *John Wooden delivered championships with regularity to UCLA.*

College Basketball

season, the tournament had moved to 40 teams from 32.

Indiana's Hoosiers came back to win the NCAA Tournament in 1981. In 1982, with James Worthy overshadowing emerging teammate Michael Jordan, North Carolina took the title. The previous time the Tar Heels had won a title, Dean Smith was a member of that 1957 team that beat Kansas and Wilt Chamberlain in the title game in three overtimes. This time, Smith president over North Carolina's success as coach.

Mercifully, the NCAA abandoned its consolation game at the Final Four in 1982, mostly because of a lack of interest. Also eliminated, except for the start of games and overtimes, was the jump ball.

While North Carolina was dominant with a 32–2 record in winning its 1982 title, the Atlantic Coast Conference would produce another champion from the same state the following season, in one of the greatest Cinderella stories in the history of the game.

With a mediocre 17–10 record entering its conference tournament, North Carolina State hardly had the look of a champion. But with emotional coach Jim Valvano mixing strategy, luck and poor

SPELLING SUCCESS: *Akeem Olajuwon has since become Hakeem, but his game has remained.*

PAT ANSWER: *At both ends of the court, Patrick Ewing had what Georgetown needed.*

free-throw shooting by opponents, the Wolfpack made it all the way to the title game, where an airball by guard Dereck Whittenburg was turned into the winning basket against highly favored Houston by forward Lorenzo Charles at the buzzer.

The best game of that 1983 tournament, however, may have come in the national semifinals, when Houston produced a 94–81 victory over Louisville in one of the great dunking exhibitions in postseason lore. That year, it was determined because of the popularity of the event that future hosts of the Final Four must have at least 17,000 seats.

Houston would return to the title game the following season but lose the 1984 national championship to Georgetown 84–75, in a game that cen-

tered around the inside matchup of Houston's Akeem (later Hakeem) Olajuwon and Georgetown's Patrick Ewing. For the next two decades, the legendary big men would battle in the NBA, including in the 1994 NBA Finals won the Olajuwon and the Houston Rockets against Ewing's New York Knicks.

Ewing and the Hoyas would return to the championship game the following season, only to be victimized in one of the greatest title-game upsets, losing 66–64 to Villanova. The Wildcats had entered the tournament unranked and had lost both their regular-season matchups to Georgetown. In 1985, the tournament was expanded to its present 64-team format.

With the NCAA picking up the pace of its game for the 1985-86 season by adding a 45-second shot clock, Louisville proved to be a step ahead of the field, center Pervis Ellison and forward Billy Thompson leading the Wildcats to a championship-game victory over Duke.

The following season, the NCAA again tinkered with its game, adding the 3-point shot. Employing a bombs-away approach under the new rules, upstart Providence was able to make it to the Final Four, but Indiana emerged with the championship, defeating Syracuse in the title game.

In 1987, drug testing was introduced at the tournament.

The 1988 Final Four would provide a bittersweet result for Kansas. One on hand, the Jayhawks won the title over Oklahoma in the championship game. On the other hand, unranked Kansas was later found to have been guilty of recruiting violations and was prevented from a return trip to the 1989 tournament.

While there could be no repeat champion in 1989, that did not mean there would not be drama. For the first time in 26 years, the title game went into overtime, with Michigan emerging with an 80–79 victory over Seton Hall. The margin represented the first NCAA championship to be decided by a single point.

In 1989, it was decided a push would be made for larger host arenas for the Final Four, buildings that could seat at least 30,000.

Among the players of the year in the 1980s were DePaul's Mark Aguirre, Louisville's Darrell Griffith, Virginia's Ralph Sampson, North Carolina's Jordan, Georgetown's Ewing, Navy's David Robinson, Kansas' Danny Manning, Arizona's Sean Elliott and Duke's Danny Ferry.

1989–90: Rebel Yell

The 1989–90 college season was one played seemingly without conscience, Loyola Marymount setting an NCAA scoring record by netting an average of 122.4 points per game and Nevada-Las Vegas rolling to the national championship with a series of blowouts culminating in a 103–73 rout of Duke in the title game at the Final Four.

But a season marked by the first 100-point game in an NCAA final also was a somber season.

Forward Hank Gathers, the engine behind Loyola's scoring magnificence, died on the court of his league's post-season tournament of heart failure, his team enduring all the way to the finals of the West Regional behind close friend and emotionally drained guard Bo Kimble.

Also, the Rebels won their national

Race issues

As with so many other facets of American life, until the Civil Rights movement of the 1960s, college basketball only grudgingly moved toward integration.

Black players long had added to the game, most notable in the early years was the contribution of George Gregory, an All-Conference center at Columbia in the late 1920s. In the 1940s, Paul Robeson, the legendary actor and football player, would take the court for Rutgers.

But there still were schools that remained defiant. An example was Mississippi State's 1962 team, which was so set against playing schools with black players that the Bulldogs refused a berth in the NCAA Tournament that year because it meant having to play in desegregated games.

On March 19, 1966, though, everything changed. That's when No. 1 Kentucky played Texas Western for the national championship. The social significance of the game was it was the first championship matchup in which a team of five blacks started against a team of five whites.

"It was very significant later on down the road, that a great all-black team beat an all-white team," said Pat Riley, who started for that Kentucky team and later went on the become one of the preeminent coaches in the NBA. "Only years later do people understand the impact of that particular game, what it meant for college basketball, for players and recruiting."

Texas Western, now known as the University of Texas-El Paso, won 72–65.

Hate mail—from whites and blacks—soon streamed into El Paso. Coach Don "The Bear" Haskins, then a stern 36-year-old taskmaster, was accused alternately of exploiting and loving his black athletes, which, depending on the author of the letter, were grievous offenses. Later, Haskins would admit to occasionally wishing the Miners had finished second, so as not to stand as such a central figure in what otherwise had been a reserved lifestyle.

Though the Civil Rights movement was laced with rancor, violence and passion, this was a game that was, well, civil. Participants from both teams since have praised the level of sportsmanship and class that marked a game that, given the emotion of the times, could have deteriorated into an ugly spectacle.

"I hadn't thought of it as putting an all-black team on the court," Haskins said at the time of the team's 25th reunion in 1991. "I was simply playing the best players I had. It's what I had done all year."

Said legendary North Carolina star Bob McAdoo, "You never saw any black athletes on TV and that team was all black. You sat down and you took notice. I used to hear my father talk about Joe Louis, the champion. It was the same type of feeling."

Five years after that breakthrough game, McAdoo would become the first black North Carolinian to play for the Tar Heels.

Cincinnati and Loyola had utilized predominantly black starting lineups in earlier NCAA championship games. But before Hawkins' team, no team had started five blacks in a title game. In the Atlantic Coast Conference, Southeastern Conference and Southwest Conference, not one varsity player was black at the time of the 1966 championship game.

In the championship game, Kentucky, dubbed "Rupp's Runts" because of the undersized nature of coach Adolph Rupp's team, led once, at 1–0.

Said Texas Western guard Joe Hill, "The whole thing messed up Mr. Rupp's apple cart. He was a racist, but it was no big thing to us."

title in honor of former UNLV cheerleader Valerie Pida, who was recovering from a bone-marrow transplant.

The dominance of that UNLV roster would become apparent when forwards Larry Johnson and Stacey Augmon and guard Greg Anthony all would move on to lengthy NBA careers.

The consensus All-Americans that season were Syracuse forward Derrick Coleman, Louisiana State guard Chris Jackson (who later would change his name to Mahmoud Abdul-Rauf), Oregon guard Gary Payton, La Salle forward Lionel Simmons and UNLV's Johnson.

A season known for its scoring also would feature the first trio of players in the venerated Atlantic Coast Conference to average more than 20 points for the same team, with Dennis Scott, Brian Oliver and Kenny Anderson doing it at Georgia Tech.

But the ACC also would sustain a loss, when coach Jim Valvano, who led North Carolina State to that improbable 1983 title, was forced to resign. Valvano, a quick-witted likable personality, would be felled by cancer three years later.

1990–91: Duke's turn

In their fifth trip to the Final Four in six seasons, the Duke Blue Devils finally got it right with a 72–65 victory over Kansas in the championship game.

For Duke coach Mike Krzyzewski this was vindication, that a program run at such a high academic and ethical level could succeed at a time when scrutiny had been placed upon so many of the nation's basketball factories.

With one of his youngest rosters in years, Krzyzewski got his team to the title game with an upset of UNLV in the national semifinals, the same Rebels which had embarrassed the Wildcats in the title game a year earlier. That victory snapped UNLV's 45-game winning streak and prevented the Rebels from becoming the first team since the 1972–73 UCLA Bruins to repeat as champions.

The other national semifinal also sig-

naled a changing of the guard, with long-time North Carolina assistant coach Roy Williams beating the Tar Heels and venerated mentor Dean Smith to advance Kansas to the title game.

Stunning defense provided to be the difference for Duke, which was led by forward Christian Laettner and guard Bobby Hurley.

The consensus All-Americans that season were Georgia Tech's Anderson, Ohio State swingman Jim Jackson, UNLV's Johnson, Louisiana State center Shaquille O'Neal and Syracuse forward Billy Owens.

The season featured a 72-point effort from U.S. International's Kevin Bradshaw, who compiled his total against the no-defense, racehorse style of Loyola-Marymount. Considering the opposition's style, the effort hardly is considering one of the game's premier performances.

ALL-AMERICAN: *At LSU, Shaquille O'Neal gave a hint of the talent he would display as a pro.*

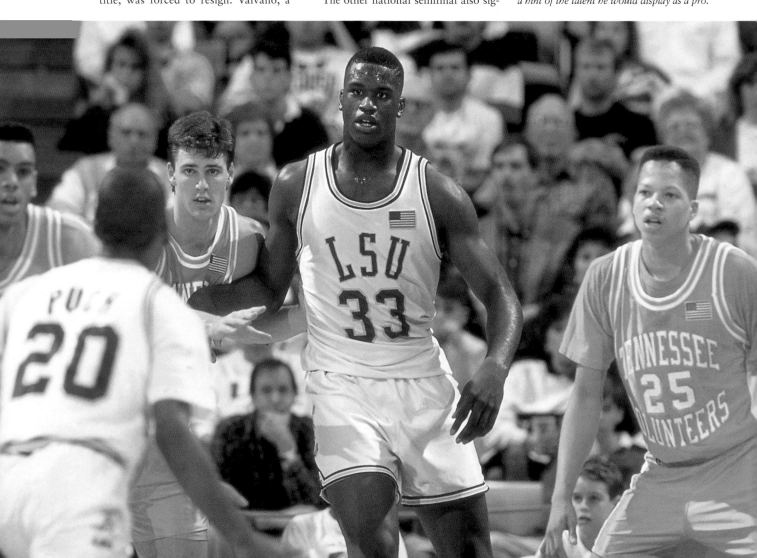

ents the Duke program would deliver to the NBA.

In its fifth consecutive visit to the Final Four, Duke was nothing short of overwhelming. The third consecutive appearance in the title game matched the records established by UCLA, Cincinnati and Ohio State.

In taking the title, Duke became the first team since North Carolina in 1982 to be ranked No. 1 all season and win the championship.

The consensus All-Americans that season were Ohio State's Jackson, Duke's Laettner, Southern Cal's Harold Miner, Georgetown's Alonzo Mourning and Louisiana State's O'Neal.

Further greatness also was on the way, with those title-game Wolverines led by the Fab Five freshmen: Chris Webber, Jalen Rose, Juwan Howard, Ray Jackson and Jimmy King.

1992–93: Webber's gaffe

Michigan's Fab Five freshman had turned sophomores, but the end result was the same, another appearance in the NCAA title game, this time against the famed North Carolina program.

The result also was the same, a loss.

But this championship game and 77–71 setback will be remembered for more than just Dean Smith's second national title as coach of the Tar Heels.

The Wolverines, down 73–71 with 11 seconds to play, were in position to at least tie when Webber was trapped along the sideline by North Carolina's George Lynch and Derrick Phelps. That's when Webber did what appeared to be the prudent thing, signaling for a time out.

Trouble was, Michigan did not have one left. Technical foul. Loss of possession. Four Donald Williams free throws later it was over.

Michigan coach Steve Fisher would take the blame, saying he must not have made the timeout situation clear to his players. For years, Webber would be tormented by opposing fans about his gaffe, jeers that would continue well into what turned into an illustrious NBA career.

1991–92: New dynasty?

Not since UCLA had won the 1973 title had a team repeated as NCAA champion. Duke would end the drought with a 71–51 pasting of Michigan in the 1992 finale of the Final Four.

But this was a season and a tournament not remembered as much for the title game as for how Duke managed to survive in the East regional.

Down one point and needing to go the full 94 feet in a matter of seconds in a dramatic overtime against Kentucky, Duke put together the ultimate play that resulted in the ultimate shot from Laettner, a jumper just beyond the foul line that somehow pushed Duke's Blue Devils past Kentucky's Wildcats 104–103, in what many consider the greatest play in tournament lore.

Laettner dominated the second half of the title game against the inexperienced Wolverines with 14 points over the final 20 minutes. The game also signaled the arrival of forward Grant Hill, who would emerge as one of the greatest tal-

476

Changing rules

College basketball has been a game in transition for more than a century, with rules changing faster seemingly than rules books can be printed.

In 1937–38, the center jump after each basket was rescinded. Later, in 1981–82, the jump ball was eliminated except for the starts of games and overtime periods.

In 1940–41, fan-shaped backboards were approved.

In 1944–45, unlimited substitution was allowed and defensive goaltending was banned. In 1948–49, coaches were allowed to have greater interplay with their players, in-game coaching having been previously frowned upon.

In 1951–52, a move was made to four 10-minute quarters, instead of two 20-minute halves. But in 1954–55, games reverted back to two 20-minute halves.

The lane was widened from six feet to 12 in 1956–57.

The dunk shot, previously considered an offensive-goaltending violation, was again allowed in 1976–77.

And if you're looking for reasons why a 45-second shot clock was implemented in 1985–86, look no further than the Dec. 15, 1973 game won 11–6 by Tennessee against Temple, the lowest scoring game since 1938. A total of 21 shots were taken. The shot clock later was reduced to 35 seconds in 1993–94.

As a further boost to scoring, the 3-point shot became a nationwide standard in 1986–87, established at 19 feet, 9 inches from the center of the basket.

save for forward Corliss Williamson. But what Scott Thurman, Corey Beck and Clint McDaniel did to opposing offenses was nothing short of torment.

Not even a 13–0 Duke rally in the second half could derail a system designed to throw waves and waves of pressure at the opposition. And, finally, when the ultimate moment of pressure arrived, Thurman responded with a 3-pointer with 50.7 seconds to play that gave the Razorbacks a 73–70 lead on the way to a 76–72 victory.

To put Arkansas' hustle into perspective, consider 6-foot-2 Beck had 15 rebounds in the championship game.

"We figured it was time for us to bring back the '40 minutes of hell' type of tempo and try to push the ball at them," coach Nolan Richardson said of how Arkansas put Duke away by forcing 23 Duke turnovers.

Duke, the previous national champion, this time failed to make it out of the Midwest Regional, its bid for a fifth consecutive berth in the Final Four derailed in the second round of the tournament by California. Had Duke advanced, point guard Bobby Hurley could have become the first player to start four consecutive NCAA Finals.

In 1993, it was determined that all tournament host venues would have to seat at least 12,000.

The consensus All-Americans that season were Indiana's Calbert Cheaney, Memphis State's Anfernee Hardaway, Duke's Hurley, Kentucky's Jamal Mashburn and Webber.

1993–94: Defense does it

Duke was back in the championship game in 1994, but what it encountered was nothing like those freewheeling offensive-oriented teams it had faced in its previous finals. This time it was Arkansas, a defensively driven whirlwind known for producing "40 minutes of hell."

Against a star-studded Duke roster, Arkansas would succeed behind a lineup that would make little noise in the NBA,

HELL BENT: *Arkansas delivered pure misery to opponents with its stifling defense on its way to winning the NCAA championship.*

PRESIDENTAL SEAL: *Arkansas native President Clinton followed his home-state Razorbacks through their glory years*

Duke coach Krzyzewski summed up the Arkansas experience in two words, "relentless pressure."

Bill Clinton, the former Arkansas governor, that year became the first sitting U.S. President to attend the tournament.

The consensus All-Americans that season were Duke's Hill, California's Jason Kidd, Connecticut's Donyell Marshall, Purdue's Glenn Robinson and Louisville's Clifford Rozier.

As if Arkansas did not do enough to pick up the pace of the game with its frenzied defense, this also was the season the NCAA reduced the shot clock from 45 seconds to 35 seconds per possession.

1994–95: UCLA returns

Ten championship banner hung in Pauley Pavilion on the campus of UCLA, all a tribute to coach John Wooden and his legendary Bruins of a previous era. This was a program with a legacy that slowly was fading from memory.

And here, again, was Arkansas, its frenzied approach in such stark contrast to what UCLA had advanced with during those championship seasons.

But, for one night, old school schooled the defending national champion, 89–78.

So much had changed since those previous UCLA titles. Broad television expo-

sure for so many more schools had made recruiting dominance far more difficult than during the Wooden era.

New conferences, such as the Big East, tempted players to stay closer to home, closer to the urban roots of the game. It was not as much that UCLA had failed itself, as the game had grown, taken the sport out of the province of a few fabled programs.

Having kindled a friendship with Wooden, UCLA coach Jim Harrick had restored tradition to the program. But it would take forward Ed O'Bannon and guard Toby Bailey to come through with championship-quality efforts against

478

Arkansas to send another title banner to the rafters at Pauley.

With point guard Tyrus Edney injured, UCLA was forced to play the title game basically with a six-player rotation, not exactly the math for success against "40 minutes of hell." But the Bruins held together to the tune of a 50–31 advantage in rebounds.

Also in 1995, CBS television paid $1.725 billion for the broadcast rights to the tournament through 2002.

The consensus All-Americans that season were UCLA's O'Bannon, Arizona's Damon Stoudamire, Maryland's Joe Smith, North Carolina's Jerry Stackhouse and Michigan State's Shawn Respert.

1995–96: 3-for-all

Like UCLA and its fabled program, Kentucky also had come to be viewed as a program that had failed its legacy, the school of Adoph Rupp having gone without a national championship since 1978. That would all end in 1996, but there was little resemblance between the team that defeated Syracuse 76–67 in the title game of the Final Four and previous Wildcat renditions.

Convinced, in this era of the shot clock and 3-point arc, that the game could be won with the longball and pressure defense, coach Rick Pitino arrived in Lexington in 1989 with very specific designs on how Kentucky again would rise.

Yet in the title game, Pitino's shooting

THE ANSWER: *Allen Iverson has solved defenses from Georgetown to the pros.*

stars proved to be anything but. Kentucky's game-winning .384 shooting percentage proved to be the lowest for the winning team in an NCAA title game since 1963, when Loyola of Chicago shot .274 and somehow still came out ahead against Cincinnati.

Kentucky had reached the title game by defeating Massachusetts 81–74, but, according to the NCAA, it is as if that game never happened. A series of gift-giving escapades exposed, the Minutemen were forced to relinquish their tournament earnings and their participation in the 1996 event since has been vacated by the NCAA.

For as much as has been made about Pitino's genius, starting with his extensive use of pro-style video scouting, he also had the benefit of a loaded roster, one that would march en masse to the NBA, players such as Antoine Walker, Ron Mercer, Derek Anderson and Tony Delk, who dropped seven 3-pointers on Syracuse in the championship game.

The consensus All-Americans that season were Massachusetts' Marcus Camby, Connecticut's Ray Allen, Georgetown's Allen Iverson, Seton Hall's Kerry Kittles and Wake Forest's Tim Duncan.

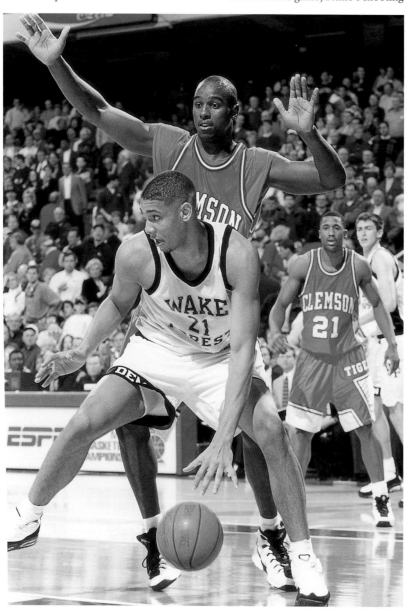

DUNCAN MACHINE: *Tim Duncan dominated at Wake Forest before turning pro.*

College basketball's smaller programs and their championships

The American college basketball landscape is not comprised solely of big-name programs, huge arenas and teams with the solitary goal of being one of the 64 selected in early March for the Division I NCAA Tournament.

Beyond the Division I schools that dream of the ultimate March Madness, there are smaller Division II, Division III, NAIA and junior-college schools that evoke equal passion as winter turns into spring, if only on a smaller basis.

Because of liberal transfer rules and, often, lower academic standards at the smaller institutions, it is not uncommon for some of the top Final Four talents to begin their journeys at these levels.

Indeed, schools that lack big-city recruiting bases often turn to junior colleges for seasoned talent. For Jerry Tarkanian and his highly successful program at Nevada-Las Vegas, such an approach allowed him to acquire mature talent, players who already had experienced two seasons of seasoning.

Among noted players who started their college careers on the junior-college level were Mitch Richmond, Dennis Rodman, Isaiah Rider, John Starks, Dennis Rodman, Kevin Willis and Bob McAdoo, the only junior-college player recruited by the famed program at North Carolina.

Nonetheless, among the reasons larger schools with lofty academic standards stay away from junior-college transfers is a graduation rate 10 percent below those who spend an entire collegiate career at a four-year institution.

FUTURE MENACE: *Before the tattoos, Dennis Rodman was a big-time presence at college.*

For Division II and Division III players, careers usually begin and end on the same level, only recently with their national championship games receiving widespread national television coverage.

In 1973, the NCAA formulated definitive standards for each of its divisions. Classified as Division III schools were institutions that did not offer scholarships, in other words, those players pay for the right to play. The first Division III tournament was contested in 1975, with North Park (Illinois) consistently among the most efficient performers at that level. The Division II tournament dates to 1957, with Kentucky Wesleyan and Evansville (Indiana) among the most successful at that level.

Among the most grueling of all post-season national championships is that of the NAIA (National Association of Intercollegiate Athletics). The tournament pits 32 of the best schools at this smaller-time level in a one week event that requires five victories. By contrast, NCAA Division I champions such as UCLA, Kentucky and Duke currently have to win six games in a three-week span. The NAIA, in fact, staged the first national tournament among the major basketball associations, in 1937.

In recent seasons, Oklahoma City has been among the NAIA powers.

To dismiss these lower levels of college basketball would be to overlook some of the greatest names in the sport. In addition to the aforementioned success stories, among those who also started at these lower levels were Zelmo Beaty, Walt Frazier, Phil Jackson, Scottie Pippen, Willis Reed, Truck Robinson, Jack Sikma and Jerry Sloan. While many of their institutions have since moved up to Division I status, at the times of those players' careers, there schools were lower in classification, if not talent.

1996–97: Raising Arizona

For years, the NBA had eaten away at the heart of college basketball. With underclassmen eligible to turn pro without limitation, the NCAA's best often would view major colleges as little more than way-stations, glorified junior colleges, if you will, with two years all the schooling accepted before moving to the next challenge.

This was an era when Kevin Garnett was going straight from high school to the NBA to the All-Star Game, a time when Stephon Marbury not only left

Georgia Tech after one season, but put together a rookie season in the NBA that made the decision appear wise.

Out of this morass emerged Arizona, a nice little team with nice little players, but a team that hardly evoked comparisons to some of the fabled institution that had emerged with NCAA championships. So be it. With an 84–79 overtime victory over Kentucky in the title game, the bottom line was that Lute Olson's team was No. 1 after defeating three No. 1 seeds.

While Kentucky was back in the title

game, Pitino this time was without Anderson, who had been sidelined at midseason by a knee injury.

The difference between this Kentucky loss and the previous season's title victory was an Arizona team loaded with the type of perimeter players able to deal with Kentucky's pressure defense and fleet enough to challenge shots at the 3-point arc, of which Kentucky launched an incredible 30. Paced by guards Mike Bibby and Miles Simon, who combined for 49 of Arizona's points, Lute Olson's

KIDD'S PLAY: *Point guard Jason Kidd was the driving force at Cal.*

team had the perfect counter to Kentucky's style.

The consensus All-Americans that season were Wake Forest's Duncan, Kentucky's Mercer, Kansas' Raef LaFrentz, Cincinnati's Danny Fortson and Utah's Keith Van Horn.

1997–98: Back at it

Kentucky returned for its third consecutive title game in 1998, defeating Utah 78–69 in the final. And while to term a title game anticlimactic would be over-

statement, the road to the Wildcats' second championship in three seasons was fought with sheer peril.

For starters, Kentucky had to reprise its tournament rivalry with Duke in the regional finals, emerging with an 86-84 victory that took some of the sting off of what Duke's Laettner had provided six years earlier. Then the Wildcats needed overtime to take Stanford 86–85 in the national semifinals.

But this also was a new experience for Kentucky. Pitino was gone to the NBA

and the Boston Celtics. Tubby Smith had been imported as coach from the University of Georgia.

Yet the Wildcats did not miss a beat.

A pair of scintillating national semifinals led to the championship game. Not only did Kentucky need overtime, but Utah advanced with a tight 65–59 victory over North Carolina.

The title game appeared headed toward a rout, with Rick Majerus' Utes up 10 at halftime. It would prove to be the largest halftime deficit overcome in a championship game, with Kentucky taking control in the second half through its suffocating defense. Instead of frenzied Pitino-style traps, Kentucky made the move to a more routine, but equally-as-intense defensive approach. In many ways, this was a no-name championship, with the majority of Kentucky's stars having followed Pitino to the pros, leaving behind the likes of Jeff Sheppard and Heshimu Evans.

"This is more than a basketball program, this is a way of life," Smith said of the Wildcats maintaining such a level of success in the midst of a coaching transition. "I'm just happy to be a small part of it."

By 1998, it was decided that future host venues for the Final Four must seat at least 30,000.

The consensus All-Americans that season were North Carolina's Antawn Jamison, Arizona's Simon, California's Jason Kidd and Kansas' LaFrentz and Paul Pierce.

1998–99: Yes, UConn

And there they were again, these cockroaches of college basketball, the Duke Blue Devils, back for another appearance in the championship game, Krzyzewski again spinning his March Madness.

On the other side stood coach Jim Calhoun and Connecticut, a school whose men's programs had been overshadowed by the women's program. The school greatest all-time basketball player? Arguably Rebecca Lobo.

Of course, there certainly could be an argument made in favor of guard Richard Hamilton, after he dropped 27 points on Duke in Connecticut's 77–74 victory over the Blue Devils in the title game. All were needed, as Connecticut sealed the victory only with two late free throws by guard Khalid El-Amin.

Having lost in regional finals three times in the '90s, Connecticut sweated its way thought the brackets, none of its final three victories by more than six points. Yet this Connecticut team demonstrated a perseverance that the Huskies had lacked in previous seasons, when talents such as Ray Allen, Donyell Marshall, Chris Smith, Scott Burrell and Donny Marshall were denied berths in the Final Four.

To produce a championship at the expense of the Blue Devils made the title all the more special. Closing with a 37–2 record, Duke had the opportunity to establish an NCAA single-season victory record. Yet the Huskies, the rare team with enough individual talent to challenge Duke, spread the Duke defense, attacked with unexpected success.

But Duke wasn't finished. A five-point deficit with 3:38 to play in the title game quickly turned into a one-point game, one settled by El-Amin's free throws.

The consensus All-Americans that year were Duke's Elton Brand, Connecticut's Hamilton, Utah's Andre Miller, Arizona's Jason Terry and Michigan State's Mateen Cleaves.

1999–00: Spartans again

Twenty-one years after Magic Johnson and Michigan State elevated the college game with a much-publicized championship victory against Larry Bird and Indiana State, the Spartans again were champions.

With Johnson looking on during the title game in Indianapolis, Michigan State, the only No. 1 regional seed to advance to the Final Four, blitzed Florida 89–76.

"It's been tough waiting these 21 years," Johnson said, "but they've been great the last couple of years, and I knew they were going to win it all."

The key to the championship may well have come a year earlier, when guard Mateen Cleaves, hyped as a pro prospect, opted to instead return to Michigan State for his senior season instead of turning to the NBA.

MORE MAGIC: *Like Magic Johnson, Mateen Cleaves won it all for Michigan State.*

482

1979 NCAA Finals

Before they changed the face of the NBA, invigorated a sagging professional league, Magic Johnson and Larry Bird provided college basketball with perhaps the greatest player-versus-player final in the history of the NCAA Tournament.

Each was about to play his final college game, even if it was not known at the time.

The two were among the greatest passers of their generations, passionate about the sport.

But they also were opposites.

Johnson expressed his joy for the game, his smile as bright as any on the college landscape.

Bird, by contrast, was soft-spoken, so out of place in the big time that he had transferred from the larger University of Indiana to smaller Indiana State as a freshman.

"To me," Bird would say, "it's a serious game."

Yet here they were, in the 1979 NCAA championship game in Salt Lake City— Indiana State vs. Michigan State, the sticks vs. the city.

Bird's Sycamores entered the Final Four 33–0. They had never been to a

Final Four. For the most part, the rest of the team was nondescript, save for guard Carl Nicks, who would play briefly in the NBA.

Michigan State took a more mundane 24–6 record into the Final Four, in what was only the school's second visit to the event. In addition to Johnson, the Spartans featured forward Greg Kelser, an intriguing NBA prospect who wore

the moniker "Special K", and center Jay Vincent, another future NBA player.

Michigan State blew out Penn 101–67 in one national semifinal, while Indiana State squeaked past DePaul 76–74 in the other.

Michigan State fans already were calling for Bird even before the conclusion of the Penn game.

The title game, as with so many championship matches, failed to live up to its billing, Michigan State rolling to a 75–64 victory over Indiana State, a matchup zone thwarting Bird.

Johnson would close with 24 points, Bird with 19.

But it was not the game itself, as much as the buildup, that excited the nation.

More than anything, a mutual admiration society was firmly established, one that would endure for years to come.

"I'm a fan of Larry Bird," Johnson would say. "You've got to be a fan of his if you like basketball."

Said Bird of Johnson, "He already plays like he's a graduate."

MAGIC'S MOMENT: *Johnson vs. Bird took root in the 1979 NCAA title game.*

"I knew they were going to win, especially when Mateen came back," Johnson said.

Cleaves provided an emotional boost in the title game, when he refused to remain in the locker room with a severely sprained ankle sustained in the second half.

"This is as storybook as it gets for Mateen," Spartans coach Tom Izzo said. "He has lived his dream."

Said Cleaves of his determination to return, "They would have had to amputate my leg to get me off the court, baby."

As Johnson was 21 years earlier in Salt Lake City, Cleaves was named the tournament's most outstanding player.

"He gave up a lot of money," Izzo said. "People should appreciate this kid."

While several top seeds fell early in the tournament, the Spartans marched through the event in style, winning every game by double-digit margins. Michigan

State also won the Big Ten regular-season and tournament titles.

The Spartans' 13-point margin of victory was the largest in a title game since Duke defeated Michigan by 20 in 1992.

The consensus All-Americans that year were Cincinnati's Kenyon Martin, Iowa State's Marcus Fizer, Stanford's Mark Madsen, Indiana's A.J. Guyton, Notre Dame's Troy Murphy and Texas' Chris Mihm.

The NIT

Now reduced to a consolation tournament, the National Invitation Tournament once stood as college basketball's premier championship tournament. During its inception, in fact, the NCAA Tournament was played after the NIT, so as not to be overshadowed.

As a matter of perspective, Utah was allowed to compete in the 1944 NCAA Tournament after being eliminated in the

first round of the NIT. Such double dipping continued through 1952.

In its early years, the NIT adopted a bent toward New York teams, with two or three of the city's teams included in the initial eight-team draws.

The local requirement eventually was dropped, as the event, now for NCAA Tournament non-qualifiers, was expanded to its current 32-team format. While the NCAA Tournament invites 64 teams before the NIT fills its field, the NCAA by no means fields the nation's top 64 teams. This is because champions from many smaller conferences may dilute the NCAA Tournament field.

By the 1950s, the NCAA required champions of its member conferences to participate in its own championship. Later, the NCAA mandated than any school extended an invitation to its tournament must accept it, or be banned from any other postseason competition.

With UCLA dominating the NCAA Tournament with consecutive championships from 1967–73, the NIT in many ways offered the more competitive event during that stretch.

The postseason competition between the tournaments became further muddled in 1974, when, for two years, a tournament was established that mandated participation from conference runners-up, further diluting the NIT fields.

In recent seasons, the NIT has served as a seasoning event for young teams on the verge of greater things in the NCAA Tournament in future seasons. The NIT, which still stages its final rounds in Madison Square Garden, which at one point hosted all games, tends to draw the greatest crowds when a New York-area school advances to the semifinals. A perennial favorite of the NIT selection committee is St. John's University, which plays its regular-season home game at Madison Square Garden.

In order to keep the NIT in the basketball lexicon, an NIT preseason tournament now also is staged at the start of the college season, with the final rounds of that event also contested at Madison Square Garden.

The coaches

Unlike in the pro game, where the players are the stars and the coaches seemingly are dismissed by whim, in the college game that coaches are the ones who provide the stability.

After four seasons of eligibility, college players either move on to the pros or real life. But coaches endure, the overseers of tradition and success.

Mention John Wooden and memories of the UCLA dynasty are rekindled. The same with Phog Allen at Kansas, Dean Smith at North Carolina, Claire Bee at Long Island University, Hank Iba at Oklahoma State, Nat Holman at City College of New York, Adolph Rupp at Kentucky and Bob Knight at Indiana.

For each legend there is a distinct personality. For Dale Brown, it was railing against the establishment at Louisiana State. For Pete Carril, it was pick-and-roll 'til you drop at Princeton. For Don Haskins, it was a gruff-but-homey approach at Texas-El Paso. For John Thompson, it seemingly was a career-long tribute to post play at Georgetown.

UCLA's Wooden not only won 10 NCAA Tournaments, but is one of only three coaches who left as coach of champion, joined by Marquette's Al McGuire in 1997 and Kansas' Larry Brown in 1988.

Of his success, Wooden admitted, "I don't know whether always winning is good. It breeds envy and distrust in others and overconfidence and a lack of appreciation very often in those who enjoy it."

The best tournament winning percentage, however, belongs to Cincinnati's Ed Jucker, who went 11–1 from 1961–63.

Several coaches have taken multiple schools to the NCAA Tournament, but Eddie Sutton is the only coach to do it four times, with visits with Creighton, Arkansas, Kentucky and Oklahoma State. Sutton also is one of only 11 coaches to take two schools to the Final Four, which he did with Arkansas and Oklahoma State. The only coaches to coach different schools in the championship game are Frank McGuire (St. John's, North Carolina) and Larry Brown (UCLA, Kansas). No coach has won with different schools.

Six coaches have played and coached in the Final Four: Vic Bubbas, Dick Harp, Bob Knight, Bones McKinney, Billy Donovan and Dean Smith.

Although he never made the big time and never was exposed at the Final Four, the biggest coaching name from small-school basketball arguably was Clarence

FOUR PLAY: *Eddie Sutton has guided four teams to the NCAA Tournament.*

"Big House" Gaines, who won 828 games in 47 seasons at Winston-Salem State in North Carolina and was the force behind the entrance of Earl "The Pearl" Monroe into the NBA.

In the earliest days of college basketball, coaches could not even coach. So limited were their roles that mythical national champions at the turn of the century, such as Yale, Columbia and Dartmouth, did not even list coaches.

To many of the great college coaches, the NBA never was considered a viable alternative.

Said Indiana's Knight, "If the NBA was on Channel 5 and a bunch of frogs were making love on Channel 4, I'd watch the frogs—even if (the picture) came in fuzzy."

Fantastic feats

No matter the level, one of the most remarkable feats in the college game was produced February 2, 1954 by Clarence "Bevo" Francis for Rio Grand (Ohio) College in a 134–95 victory over Hillsdale.

Francis, known for his innovative jump shot, scored 113 points in that game, with 38 baskets and 37 free throws.

A factory worker who never went on to play pro ball, the 6-foot-9 standout scored mostly on a variety of outside shots. He left school after two seasons to play with a team that opposed the comedic Harlem Globetrotters basketball team.

For Francis, the effort was preceded by a game when he scored 116 points against a junior-college team, a record that was not official because it came with his four-year school playing a two-year school.

Interestingly, Francis got into Rio Grand despite having no high school diploma (but with a wife and child in tow).

In the earliest stages of the college game, Wisconsin's Christian Steinmetz was the dominant player of his time, scoring 44 and 50 points in game when scores of many top matchups would not exceed 30 points per team.

While some derided the passive style of Midwest schools such as Wisconsin, Steinmetz nonetheless would be awarded

113 POINTS: *Bevo Francis reached the staggering total in a 1954 game.*

a spot in the Basketball Hall of Fame.

Stanford's Luisetti so shocked the East Coast establishment with his one-handed shooting style in the mid-1930s that some coaches, such as the legendary Nat Holman, claimed they never would teach the approach to their players. Nonetheless, Luisetti ended Long Island University's 43-game winning streak in 1935.

Luisetti later score 50 in a game as Stanford routed Duquesne 92–27 in 1938.

Another seminal moment would arrive on Feb. 13, 1954, when Furman forward Frank Selvy would score 100 points in a 149–95 victory over Newberry. Selvy would score 50 or more in seven games that season, at a time when teams averaged fewer than 70 points per game. In that 100-point game, Selvy scored 24 points in the first quarter, 13 in the second, 25 in the third and 38 in the fourth.

For dual excellence, there was the 1970 matchup between Louisiana State's Pete Maravich and Kentucky's Dan Issel. In that game, Maravich would win the battle with 64 points but Issel would win the war with 51 for Kentucky in the Wildcats' 121–105 victory.

Great teams

Among the first of the legendary teams in the era of the NCAA Tournament was the event's first winner, Oregon's legendary "Tall Firs."

In an era when the term "big man" was relative, Oregon could look down at the competition, with 6-foot-8 Urgel Wintermute at center and a pair of 6-foot-4 forwards in Laddie Gale and John Dick.

That Oregon team was one of the sport's great fast-break teams, as it rolled across the country on a 10-game, 22-day train expedition that built camaraderie and proved that a team from the West, with homegrown talent, could beat the Eastern establishment.

In 1944, Utah produced one of the most unlikely, and certainly unexpected NCAA champions. The Utes began their postseason odyssey in the NIT, only to lose in the first round to Kentucky. They then received a belated invitation to the NCAAs, when Arkansas withdrew because an auto accident had killed an assistant coach and player. The caveat

was Utah had to be in Kansas City within two days, forced to hop the next train out of New York.

So Utah, which did not have a home court that season because of the war effort, played on ... and on ... and on, until returning to New York for the NCAA championship game. A 42–40 victory over Dartmouth gave the Utes the NCAA title on the very Madison Square Garden court they had hoped to win the NIT title.

The following two seasons, legendary coach Hank Iba and legendary big man Bob Kurland would make Oklahoma A&M kings of the big dance.

Iba's approach was designed to get the most out of his 7-footer, with a slow-down offense and physical defense. The result was the first back-to-back NCAA champion.

To appreciate how rare a 7-footer was in those days, understand that Kurland preferred throughout his collegiate career to be listed at 6 feet, 11¾ inches.

Nearly five decades before Michigan would roll out its Fab Five Freshman, Kentucky in 1948 had the original Fabulous Five. With Alex Groza, Ralph Beard, Kenny Rollins, Wallace "Wah Wah" Jones and Cliff Barker, Kentucky began the legacy of coach Adolph Rupp with the '48 title.

This was a team of speed and ball-handling, and also of coaching detail, one so impressive that it came back and won the 1949 NCAA Tournament, as well.

The NCAA's first undefeated champion was the University of San Francisco in 1956. Led by irrepressible center Bill Russell, the Dons would win 60 consecutive games in rolling to the titles in 1955 and '56.

Russell credited much of the Dons' dominance to coach Phil Woolpert, who was ahead of his time when it came to the recruiting of black players.

Paired with future Boston Celtics teammate K.C. Jones, Russell would help the Dons finish 29–0 in 1955–56.

Ohio would become the center of the college-basketball universe in the early 1960s, the decade's first title going to Ohio State and a potent lineup that included Jerry Lucas, John Havlicek and Larry Siegfried and then Cincinnati win-

ning behind Oscar Robertson.

Arguably, that Ohio State team ranks as skilled as any. But behind Robertson, Cincinnati would win consecutive titles, also taking the 1962 title.

In 1964, all previous arguments about greatness ended. UCLA, under coach John Wooden, was in the verge of establishing a dynasty all of sports would envy, 10 championships in 12 years.

"Teams get scarred when they look at us," Wooden would say.

Walt Hazzard, Gail Goodrich, Lew Alcindor, Bill Walton, Sydney Wicks, Steve Patterson, David Meyers led the way.

There would nothing close thereafter.

Perfection was attained again in 1975-76, when Bob Knight's Indiana Hoosiers went 32–0 in winning the title, led by Scott May, Quinn Buckner, Bobby Wilkerson and Tom Abernethy. Ironically, Knights contends his team of the previous season was better and expressed disappointment after this championship that his Hoosiers did not have two.

The sleazy side

College basketball was forever tainted by the dumping of games by young players eager to reap rewards from an amateur endeavor. In 1945, two players from Brooklyn College would admit to rigging the score of a game against Akron for $1,000 total.

In 1951, three members of the City College of New York, a championship-level team, admitted to shaving points. That same year, players from powerful Long Island University were implicated in game fixing.

When the legendary University of Kentucky was discovered to have been party to such acts in 1951, the Southeastern Conference responded by suspending the school from basketball competition for the following season.

While point shaving apparently was at its height in the late 1940s and early '50s, the taint never would truly leave the game. In the early 1960s, several schools were implicated in smaller incidents. And in 1985, Tulane University in New Orleans took the dramatic step of disbanding its program in the wake of a conspiracy investigation into bribery charges.

In addition to gambling, racism sullied the sport in its early years.

In 1946, Tennessee refused to play Duquesne because it featured back player Chuck Cooper, who would go on to because the first black to play in the NBA. Even when Duquesne coach Chuck Davies said he would hold Cooper out, Tennessee nonetheless refuse to proceed.

Shortly thereafter, Duquesne also lost out on a game against Miami that same year, when an outdoor game at the famed Orange Bowl football stadium was canceled because of a local ordinance prohibiting blacks and whites from participating in the same athletic event.

And the widely respected NAIA tour-nament for small schools initially sought in 1948 to have schools agree not to play blacks, only to backtrack because of protests from schools in the more racially sensitive Northeast.

BETTER DAYS AHEAD: *The first black player in the NBA, Chuck Cooper suffered at college.*

UCLA's dynasty 1966–69

The greatest college team ever?

The argument certainly could be made for John Wooden's UCLA squads in 1966–67, 1967–68 and 1968–69.

Led by center Lew Alcindor (who later became Kareem Abdul-Jabbar), and coached Wooden, who, by then, was no stranger to dynasties, the two produced arguably the greatest of seasons for a school that had won 10 championships during a 12-year span.

Alcindor committed to the Bruins on May 4, 1965, out of New York prep powerhouse Power Memorial, a Manhattan Catholic school that had won 71 consecutive games during one stretch.

Under college rules at the time, freshmen were ineligible for varsity competition, so Alcindor did not play college ball in 1966–67. He would anchor a championship team for each of the next three seasons.

"At times he even frightens me," Wooden admitted during his time with Alcindor.

In his first game Alcindor displayed why, scoring 56 points in a victory over archrival Southern Cal.

Rounding out that powerhouse lineup were guards Lucius Allen and Mike Warren, and forwards Lynn Shackleford and Kenny Heitz.

The Bruins carried a 26-game winning streak into the 1967 NCAA Tournament and went on to defeat Dayton 79–64 for the national championship. The most anticipated matchup in that tournament was a 73–58 victory over center Elvin Hayes and Houston in the national semifinals.

In an apparent bid to neutralize Alcindor, the NCAA banned the dunk shot beginning the next season. That season, forwards Edgar Lacey and Mike Lynn were added to the mix, having missed the previous season due to injury.

The most significant regular-season game of Alcindor's second varsity season was a rematch with Houston, which drew 52,693 to the Astrodome. With Alcindor limited by an eye injury, Hayes dominated, with 39 points and 15 rebounds in a 71–69 victory, the Bruins' lone loss that season. Alcindor shot just 4 of 18.

The teams again would meet in the national semifinals at the NCAA Tournament, with the Bruins dominating 101–69. Alcindor outscored Hayes 19–10. A 92–72 victory over North Carolina followed in the national championship game.

For Alcindor's third and final season at UCLA, Allen, Lynn and Warren were gone, replaced by forwards Sidney Wicks and Curtis Rowe and guard John Vallely. In an anguishing season for Alcindor, when he was criticized for electing not to participate in the Olympics in support of a proposed boycott by black athletes, the Bruins' lone loss would come 46–44 to Southern Cal, to snap a 44-game winning streak.

UCLA would regroup to defeat Rick Mount and Purdue 92–72 for the Alcindor's third national championship. In his final collegiate game, Alcindor scored 37 points on 15-of-20 shooting and grabbed 15 rebounds, going out in much the same way he came in.

Roots of the game

So when did it really all begin, this frenzy that has led to March Madness, the Final Four and a sport that the biggest of universities and smallest of schools create such a passion with?

Try 1895, when Minnesota School of Agriculture defeated Hamline College 9–3 in a nine-on-nine game accepted as the first contest between two colleges (the University of Chicago claims a 6–1 record in 1894, as the first school to play a schedule of games, albeit against various club teams not affiliated with colleges).

As far as the five-on-five version, the thought is the first such college game took place in 1897, a 32–10 victory by Yale over Pennsylvania.

At its inception, the college game was both an indoor and outdoor sport, only adding to the urban legend of a decidedly city game.

Most of the early schools playing the game were located in the Northeastern sections of the United States, with the number pushing 100 institutions shortly after the turn of the century. By the 1910s, Midwestern schools added the sport and the number of participating colleges moved into the 100s.

During these years, basketball was a brutal endeavor. It was not until players were limited to five fouls per game that the sport was brought under control.

The precursors of today's Atlantic Coast, Big Ten, Big East and Pac-10 conferences came at the turn of the century, which such leagues became vehicles to promote rivalries and allow for championship competitions.

The status of the game would change at the start of the 1910s, when Phog Allen, an understudy to game inventor Dr. James Naismith at Kansas, would take over the Jayhawks and begin a relentless pursuit of the nation's top players, the precursor of today's rabid recruiting process.

The first known tie came on February 9, 1918, when an official scoring error was found and resulted in a 21–21 outcome between Kentucky and Kentucky Wesleyan.

The roaring '20s delivered fans in droves to the college game. The famed Palestra opened in Philadelphia in 1927. The passion was being kindled. Crowds in the 10,000s became common in New York in the early 1930s. A national obsession was about to change the face of college athletics, give birth to a winter passion on campuses across a nation.

The great teams of the sport's earliest era included the University of Chicago, which was dominant from 1907 to 1909 behind scoring leader John Schommer; the University of Kansas teams under Phog Allen, which won national titles in 1922 and 1923; the University of Pittsburgh teams that won titles in 1928 and 1930, behind forward Chuck Hyatt; and the Purdue team of the early 1930s the featured Wooden as its star player. The sport's earliest dynasty well may have been the University of Nebraska, which went 7–0 in 1898, 7–0 in 1899 and 5–0 in 1900.

From such limited roots has emerged a game that has captured an entire nation.

THE RULES OF BASKETBALL

When Dr. James Naismith drew up a list of 13 rules to govern his new game of "basket ball" in 1891, he provided the framework for an athletic phenomenon that would explode into worldwide prominence. Not only was the good professor uncanny in his assessment of the American sports psyche, he also was visionary in the fundamental guidelines that would survive the test of time.

Dr. Naismith simply provided the game's concepts and tools, letting the natural evolutionary process take care of details. It's fascinating, more than a century later, to examine Naismith's basic premises: a (peach) basket positioned at each end of a gymnasium, attached to a balcony 10 feet above the playing surface; players from competing teams trying to throw a round soccer ball into their respective baskets; a passing game (no running or moving with the ball) that promoted teamwork; limited contact between opposing players with "fouls" and penalties discouraging transgressions; a referee to call violations and fouls; two 15-minute halves, with a five-minute rest between.

Sound familiar? The rules have been fine-tuned, the players have become increasingly athletic and the game has risen from the floor to the stratosphere, but the basic tenets have remained remarkably entrenched. So entrenched that if Dr. Naismith could see a 1990s-style basketball game, he still would recognize the 1890s-era sport he invented—with some degree of open-mouthed amazement.

While the college and professional games have followed slightly different evolutionary trails, the basic focus of one has never strayed far from the other. Today's college and pro games differ only in customized playing rules, not in fundamentals, equipment or concepts. The basics are simple:

● The baskets, still 10-feet high, no longer are baskets. They are steel rims, attached to a rectangular backboard, with a net that hangs down and makes it easy to tell if a shot passes through. A field goal counts two points, a free throw (a 15-foot shot given to a player who has been fouled) counts one and a long field goal (23 feet, 9 inches from the top of the key in the NBA; 19 feet, 9 inches in college) counts three. The team that scores the most points in the specified time wins.

● The professional game is played in four 12-minute quarters with a 15-minute halftime. The college game is played in 20-minute halves. Any game that is tied after regulation is decided by one or more 5-minute overtime periods.

● The professional and college courts are a regulation 94 feet in length and 50 feet in width. After experimenting in the early years with court size and number of players, it was determined that five players to a team provided a comfortable fit with optimal strategic potential. Today's rules allow free substitution and professional rosters are allowed to contain 12 players.

The following sections will describe and analyze the positions, mechanics and strategies of basketball—professional and college.

The Positions

Most teams employ a lineup consisting of two guards, two forwards and a center. The non-center positions are broken down as point guard and shooting guard,

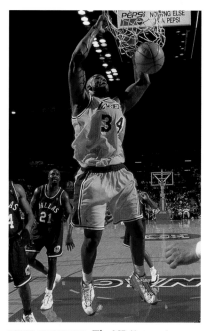

POWER PERSONIFIED: *The NBA's premier center, Shaquille O'Neal of the Lakers.*

small forward and power forward.

Because the center usually is the tallest player on the team, he mans the middle on both offense and defense and scores most of his points close to the basket. He can be a big scorer, but his most important functions are grabbing rebounds, defending the basket and discouraging would-be lane penetrators with his shot-blocking skills. The best NBA centers were, or are, intimidating: Wilt Chamberlain, Bill Russell and Kareem Abdul-Jabbar from the past; David Robinson, Shaquille

O'Neal, Hakeem Olajuwon and Alonzo Mourning in today's NBA.

The guards provide ballhandling and structure for the offense. The point guard primarily is a playmaker who handles the ball with error-free consistency and runs the offense. The shooting guard is more offensive, especially from long range. John Stockton is the NBA's premier point man; Michael Jordan and Clyde Drexler were classic shooting guards.

The forwards perform a variety of frontcourt duties. The power forward, big and physical, will spend much of the game close to the basket, battling for rebounds and defending key big men. The small forward is a shooter or slasher who usually can post big scoring numbers. He is not necessarily small, but he is usually mobile with outstanding athleticism. Former NBA greats Elgin Baylor and Adrian Dantley were small forwards. Utah's Karl Malone is one of today's best power forwards.

The Shot

Of all the game's mechanics, the methods for delivering ball to basket have evolved most dramatically. For years, basketball was played with feet glued firmly to the ground and those who showed upward mobility were chastised as showboats. Layups and hook shots were the primary scoring methods inside; two-handed set shots were the long-range weapon.

That all changed in the mid 1930s when Stanford University star Hank Luisetti introduced a one-hand shot that he got off with shocking quickness and accuracy. Other players were quick to copy and Luisetti's innovation evolved into the running one-hander, the jump shot (delivered with a flick of the wrist, hands extending ball above the head at the top of a jump) and a variety of moving jumpers from unusual angles, complete with mid-air adjustments and hang time.

As players grew taller and more athletic, the dunk shot became a powerful weapon. Players would simply leap high enough to slam the ball through the hoop—a high-percentage shot that pleases coaches and excites fans.

NOTHING BUT NET: *Denver's Raef LaFrentz shows great form with his jump shot.*

490

Modern creative players were masterful at finding new ways of getting the ball into the basket. And high-flying stars such as Anfernee Hardaway, Grant Hill and Michael Jordan constantly updated their arsenals with never-before-seen maneuvers that sometimes defy the imagination.

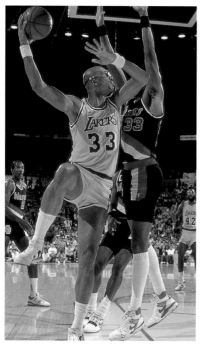

HOOKED: *Kareem Abdul-Jabbar elevated the game with his signature sky-hook move.*

The Dribble

This may be the least appreciated of the basketball player's tools. And its evolution was probably more painful than that of any other rule.

Early players were not permitted to dribble the ball— it was strictly a passing game. And the early ball, a crude leather cover over an inflatable bladder with an inflation tube sticking out, did not permit dribbling control anyway.

At various times and depending on whether you were watching the college or professional game, players were allowed one bounce; one bounce with no shot; two-handed, starting and stopping dribbles, and multiple dribbles with no progress toward the basket. The rule was not refined until the late 1930s, when the modern molded ball (without protruding stem) was introduced.

Since then, the dribble has become more than a tool—it's a weapon that can break

down defenses.

Nobody demonstrated that weapon better than the former Boston Celtics guard Bob Cousy, who dribbled the ball with amazing control, took it behind his back in traffic and either shot or passed without breaking stride. Today's NBA players, most of whom have grown up with a basketball in their hands, are proficient off the dribble— shooting, passing or leaping for a dunk. They go behind the back or between the legs with little thought and don't hesitate to put the ball on the floor in traffic.

Today's dribble rules are simple: one hand, no stopping and re-starting. The bouncing ball can be switched from one hand to the other without breaking dribble, but a player is never allowed to dribble with both hands. Once a player stops his dribble, he must either pass or shoot. Palming (bringing hand under ball in a semi-circular motion) is not allowed.

The NBA's best dribblers normally will be found at the point guard position.

The Rebound

While scorers win fan affection, rebounders win and lose games. The concept is simple: Rebounders position themselves near the basket and fight for missed shots. It's physical, it's intense and it is the survival of the fittest.

Rebounding on the defensive end of the court favors the defender, who has natural position between his man and the basket and needs only to block out for basket control. Offensive rebounding is more difficult for opposite reasons. Because the defender has superior position, it is necessary for the offensive player to fight his way around blocks and through traffic. Offensive rebounding often is a matter of intensity—wanting the ball more than an opponent—and it pays off with put-back chances and a lot of easy points.

Teams that win the rebounding wars often can win games even when they don't shoot well. Good teams usually will dominate the boards.

The Pass

Dr. Naismith wanted teamwork to be the strategic focus of his new game and his vision was fulfilled. NBA championships are won by teams built around unselfish players, and the heart and soul of every offense is crisp passing.

There's nothing complicated about the concept. The player with the ball looks for an open man and "passes" to him, hopefully advancing his team's strategic position. Good NBA offenses are built around quick passing by players who are constantly moving and setting screens to help each other get away from defenders.

There are four basic passes. The bounce pass limits the reach of defenders who cannot bend quickly enough to pick it off. Bounce passes are most effective in heavy traffic. The chest pass is delivered on a line to a man in an open area. The baseball pass is thrown long distance on a line, usually to someone on a fast break. And the lob pass is a high-arcing toss, usually over a defender to a center with his back to the basket.

There are variations. A lob pass can go deep over two or three defenders. Or it can be thrown as an "alley-oop" to a player who times his jump, catches the ball above the rim and slams it through the basket before returning to the floor.

The modern players will use creative behind-the-back and no-look passes to confound defenders, primarily on the fast break. Among the modern-day passing fancies are Isiah Thomas, John Stockton and Magic Johnson.

ON THE BOARDS: *Dennis Rodman's tenacity made him the game's dominant rebounder.*

492

The Free Throw

The free throw is a penalty assessed by the referee against those players who become too physical and use excessive contact, either accidentally or intentionally, to gain advantage over an opponent. The "free" or uncontested shot is taken by the "fouled" player from behind a line 15 feet from the basket.

Free throws are awarded in different ways. When a player makes illegal contact against a player in the act of shooting, two free throws are awarded if the shot does not go through the basket. If the player's shot does go in, the team is awarded the 2 points and the player gets one free throw. Players fouled in the act of shooting from 3-point range are awarded three free throws. Fouls committed against a player not in the act of shooting will result in an out-of-bounds throw in or free throws, depending on the number of fouls the team already has committed.

Free-throw shooting has evolved into an important element of the game. Teams that make a high percentage of free throws can score a lot of uncontested points and thus increase their chances for victory. Teams that miss a lot of free throws can lose games they probably should win. The most successful free-throw shooters (former players like Rick Barry and Larry Bird; such current stars as Reggie Miller and Mark Price) will make about 90 percent (9 of every 10) of their free throws. Poor free-throw shooters (for instance, Wilt Chamberlain and Shaquille O'Neal) might be in the 50 percent (5 of every 10) range.

Teams build game plans around free-throw shooting. It makes sense to force O'Neal to score his points from the line rather than get easy 2-point shots under the basket. Conversely, it's better to keep teams that make 75 percent of their free throws away from the line.

Free throws have always been an important part of basketball's end game. Teams trailing by two or three points in the final minute will commit fouls with the hope that the opposition will miss important free throws and give them a chance to catch up with 2 or 3-point baskets. Teams that cannot make their free throws have been known to lose good leads going into the final minutes of games because of it.

Defense

In simplest terms, defense means guarding your basket against opponents intent on scoring points. Those teams that limit

ON THE LINE: *Minnesota's Kevin Garnett prepares to shoot a free-throw.*

Naismith's Original 13 Rules of "Basket Ball"

The following rules, drafted by Dr. James Naismith for his new game of basket ball, were first published in January 1892 in *The Triangle*—the Springfield College newspaper.

1. The ball may be thrown in any direction with one or both hands.

2. The ball may be batted in any direction with one or both hands, never with the fist.

3. A player cannot run with the ball; the player must throw it from the spot where he catches it, allowance being made for a man who catches the ball when running at a good speed.

4. The ball must be held in or between the hands; the arms or body must not be used for holding it.

5. No shouldering, holding, pushing, tripping or striking in any way the person of an opponent is to be allowed. The first infringement of this rule by any person shall count as a foul; the second shall disqualify him until the next goal is made,

or if there was evident intent to injure the person, for the whole game; no substitute allowed.

6. A foul is striking the ball with the fist, violation of Rules 3 and 4, and such as described in Rule 5.

7. If either side makes three consecutive fouls it shall count for a goal for the opponents. (Consecutive means without the opponents making a foul.)

8. A goal shall be made when the ball is thrown or batted from the grounds into the basket and stays there, providing those defending the goal do not touch or disturb the goal. If the ball rests on the edge and the opponent moves the basket, it shall count as a goal.

9. When the ball goes out of bounds it shall be thrown into the field, and played by the person first touching it. In case of a dispute, the Umpire shall throw it straight into the field. The thrower is allowed five seconds; if he holds it longer, it shall go to the opponent. If any side persists in

delaying the game, the Umpire shall call a foul on them.

10. The Umpire shall be the judge of the men, and shall note the fouls, and notify the Referee when three consecutive fouls have been made. He shall have power to disqualify men according to Rule 5.

11. The Referee shall be judge of the ball, and shall decide when the ball is in play, in bounds, and to which side it belongs, and shall keep time. He shall decide when a goal has been made, and keep account of the goals, with any other duties that are usually performed by a Referee.

12. The time shall be two 15-minute halves, five minutes between.

13. The side making the most goals shall be the winner. In case of a draw, the game may, by agreement of captains, be continued until another goal is made.

---

scoring opportunities greatly increase their chance of winning.

College teams play two kinds of defense: the man-to-man, in which each player guards an opponent face to face, and the zone, in which players guard assigned areas of the court. Zones are outlawed in the NBA, a move that promotes more one-on-one moves and inside play.

While the basic principles of good defense are obvious—moving your feet, keeping your body between your opponent and the basket, forcing them to attempt difficult shots, deny them the ball, taking away passing lanes, don't foul—the intricacies of the man-to-man are more complicated. Forty-eight minutes of fighting through screens, diving for loose balls, expending energy chasing a quick opponent and banging bodies for position can take its toll. While basketball might be a non-contact sport in theory, it's a brutal physical game in practice.

STRONG MOVES: *The Suns' Penny Hardaway penetrates the Sonics defense.*

Winning teams usually are the ones that protect the ball on offense and force turnovers or other mental mistakes on defense.

Illegal defense

They don't play zone defense in the NBA. Everybody will tell you that.

It is one of the main differences between the collegiate game and the pros. That and the fact that NBA players get paid, of course.

But the fact of the matter is that they do play zone defense in the NBA. At least they try to get away with it. But every time a referee waves his arm horizontally in front of him, palm down, somebody else has gotten caught trying to bend the rules. That motion signals an illegal defense, better known as a zone.

In a zone defense, a player guards a certain area of the floor, as opposed to another player. In high school or college ball, a coach might employ a zone if his

THE GLOVE: *Gary Payton (right) shows classic man-to-man defense against Kobe Bryant (8).*

team is slower afoot than the opponent or if it is shorter in order to improve the chances for rebounds. A zone is also a good idea to try to stop penetration to the basket and force more jump shots.

All of that seems relatively clear cut, and one would think it would be fairly easy to recognize. But illegal defense calls are one of the most highly contested penalties in the NBA. In fact, try to think of the last time you saw an official signal an illegal defense when he didn't get an argument from the player involved. As soon as the referee motions the foul and blows his whistle, the player will rush up and point to exactly where he was and who he was guarding. Often, his coach is making the same argument—usually to no

avail. For their first violation, teams are given a warming. Subsequent violations earn technical fouls.

While the basics of the zone defense are fairly easy to understand, the specifics of the illegal defense are not. The NBA rules take up 25 pages at the end of the *Official NBA Guide* published by *The Sporting News*, and an entire one of those pages is dedicated to illegal defenses.

"Defenses which violate the rules and guidelines set forth are not permitted," it says under Rule No. 12—Fouls and Penalties—in the 1999–2000 edition. Plain and simple, right?

Now, here's the first guideline.

"The free throw lane is divided into the following areas: (1) The "outside"

lanes consist of two 2 feet x 19 feet areas which are adjacent and parallel to the college lane. (2) The "inside" lane consists of the 12 feet x 19 feet area which is the college lane. (3) The "posted-up" areas consist of two 3 feet x 19 feet areas which are adjacent and parallel to the free throw lane lines. A hashmark on the baseline denotes this area.

"If an offensive player's positioning permits, a defender may be positioned in the "outside" lane with no time limit. Defenders may be in a position within the "inside" lane for a tight 2.9 seconds. They must re-establish a position with both feet out of the "inside" lane, to be legally clear of the restricted area. A defender may be positioned within the "inside" lane with no time limitations, if an offensive player is positioned within the "posted-up" area." Got that?

Subsequent rules divide the frontcourt into strongside (with the ball) and weakside areas, as well as upper, middle and lower defensive areas. There are rules for defending and double-teaming within each area, all of which by covered by subsection x, which states: "Failure to comply with article k through article v above will result in an illegal defense violation."

No wonder there are so many challenges from players and coaches, especially considering the fouls are called in the heat of battle while all 10 players and the three officials are constantly on the move.

But, according to Harvey Pollack, longtime public relations director and now director of statistical information for the Philadelphia 76ers, the rules actually seem to be sinking in with players. In Pollack's 1999–2000 *NBA Statistical Yearbook*, he reports that there were 3,123 illegal defense calls in 1994–95, 2,300 in 1995–96, 2,161 in 1996–97 and 1,954 in 1997–98. There were only 972 called in 1998–99, but each team played only 50 games schedule because of the lockout. Still, if that total were projected out over 82 games, it would come to about 1,594, still a decline from the previous season.

The following definitions provide an insight into the rules and strategies that govern the game of basketball:

Assist: A player is credited with an "assist" when his pass leads directly to a basket by a teammate.

Backcourt: The court is divided in half by a center line. The backcourt area is where the opponent's basket is located when a team is on offense. If a team can't advance the ball out of its backcourt within 10 seconds after a throw-in, a violation is called and the ball goes to the opponent. Once across the center line, the offensive team cannot return to the backcourt area on that possession. "Backcourt" also can refer to a team's guard tandem.

Charge: A foul called against an offensive player for "charging" into a stationary defender who has established position.

Fast Break: A scoring strategy by a team that pushes the ball upcourt quickly before the defensive team can get set. A good fast break gives the offensive team an advantage in numbers.

Foul Lane: The area under the basket and extending from the base line to the free throw line. It is 16 feet wide and always painted a different color for contrast. An offensive player is allowed only 3 consecutive seconds in the lane on any possession—a rule designed to keep big men from camping under the basket.

Frontcourt: The area of the court where an offensive team's basket is located. A team has 10 seconds to advance the ball into its frontcourt after a backcourt throw in. "Frontcourt" also can refer to a team's front line—two forwards and a center.

Held Ball: When two players gain possession of the ball at the same time, the referee calls a held ball and possession is determined by a jump ball.

Jump Ball: Every game begins with a center jump—the two tallest players from each team's starting five contesting a ball tossed into the air between them by a referee. The players try to tap the ball to a teammate positioned around the center-court circle. Jump balls also occur when the referee calls a held ball, at the beginning of overtime, after a double foul, after a double free throw violation (players stepping into the foul lane before the ball is released), after an inadvertent whistle and other unusual instances specified in the NBA rules book.

Pivot Foot: When a player has possession of the ball but is not dribbling, passing or shooting, he must maintain contact with one foot on the floor. He can step with the opposite foot while "pivoting" around in a circular fashion to keep the ball away from defenders.

Referees: Each game is governed by a crew chief, a referee and an umpire. They call fouls, maintain order and make sure the games run smoothly and fairly.

Screen: The act of one player blocking the path of a defensive player so his teammate can get open to receive a pass. The screen, also called a pick, is legal as long as the screening player is stationary on contact.

Shot Clock: In the NBA, when a team gains possession, it has 24 seconds to get off a shot that touches the rim or goes into the basket. Failure to beat the clock results in a turnover. College clocks are set at 35 seconds.

Timeouts: Each NBA team can call seven regular timeouts and two 20-second time-outs during a regulation game. Timeouts are used to plan strategy, to regroup or to stop another team's momentum.

Turnover: A misplay by the offensive team that results in change of possession.

Walking: If a player takes excessive steps without dribbling or shuffles his pivot foot without passing or shooting, a violation is called and the other team gains possession. This violation also is called traveling.

FOUL PLAY: *L.A.'s Robert Horry (with ball) charges Portland's Scottie Pippen.*

496

New rules

The NBA knew it had to do something. After watching scoring and shooting percentages drop for years, the league commissioned a special committee to look into the problem and then take steps to rectify it.

The final straw seemed to be the lockout-shortened 1998–99 season, when Sacramento led the league averaging 100.2 points per game. The Kings were the only team to top the 100-point mark. With all of the advances and adjustments in defense, it was the eighth straight season scoring average dropped, and the total was the lowest since Fort Wayne's 92.4 average in 1954–55.

The scoring heyday in the league occurred in 1981–82, when the Denver Nuggets scored a whopping 126.5 points per game. Of course, back in those days almost every team scored more than 100 points per game. The two previous high scoring teams were the Philadelphia 76ers in 1961–62, who averaged 125.4 points per game, and the 1966–67 Sixers, who averaged 125.2.

Not so in the 1990s. After dismantling their championship team in the wake of Michael Jordan's retirement, the Chicago Bulls averaged 81.9 points per game under new coach Tim Floyd in the 50-game 1998–99 season. But the Bulls weren't the only team that suffered that season. With teams cramming 50 games into a 90-day span that often included as many as three games in three nights, the Atlanta Hawks, under Hall of Fame coach Lenny Wilkens, averaged just 86.3 points per game, and the New York Knicks, who advanced to the NBA Finals that season, averaged 86.4 points per game.

Those are the three lowest scoring averages in the history of the league. The post-lockout schedule can't be blamed for everything, however. In fact, three games in three nights were commonplace for much of the league's history. And in 1996–97, with teams never playing more than two consecutive games, the Cleveland Cavaliers averaged just 87.5 points per game.

What was the league to do?

After calling together some of the best and most respected minds in the game, including current and former players,

OPEN PLAY: *Denver's Nick Van Exel sinks a three-pointer.*

general managers, coaches and other experts, the league approved several rules modifications for the 1999–2000 season that were designed to improve the flow and the pace of the game and cut down on overly rough play.

"When we're talking about making the game less physical, we're not talking about violent physical, we're talking about rough-type physical," NBA senior vice president of basketball operations Rod Thorn. "We haven't had a real problem violence-wise, meaning fights or

crazy flagrant fouls, for several years, because we addressed that 10 years ago.

"You now hear words like 'impeding progress,' 'dislodging,' 'rerouting.' The clutching and grabbing and holding part of basketball were just getting to a level where we had to do something about it or strength and size were going to totally negate talent and basketball ability."

The changes:

● A defender may not make contact with his hands and/or forearms on an offensive player except below the free-throw line extended.

● If a player begins dribbling the ball with his back toward the basket below the free throw line, commonly referred to as "posting-up," must shoot, pass or pick up his dribble within five-seconds.

● To speed up play, the 24-second clock will be reset to 14 seconds if certain violations occur with 14 or fewer seconds left on the clock.

● No illegal defense guidelines will apply to a player who is defending an offensive player who is positioned on the strong side of the court.

"These rules will help us fine-tune and improve the look and flow of our game," Thorn said in a conference call with reporters at the end of the first season with the new rules. "We realize there will probably be a transitional period for everyone involved to get used to the changes, but we believe they will improve the game."

After a season of griping by players and coaches who sorely tested the patience of the league's referees, Thorn believed the rules did what they were supposed to do.

"There are several things that have transpired this year," he said. "Field-goal percentage is up, both two-point and three-point. Free-throw percentage is at 75 percent, which is the highest since 1992–93. Our scoring is up, and really the scoring part is ancillary. We were hoping maybe we would get some more points, but what we were really trying to do was to get some more movement, get some more fluidity and then, from an aesthetic standpoint and from a fan standpoint, to have a better flow to the game. I think that, by and large, that's what we've gotten.

"We've had seven teams average 100

points this year; last year we had one. We've got 10 teams giving up 100 points a game; last year we had two. (We had) the biggest scoring increase, 5.7 points at this time, in any one year in 40 years, since between 1958–59 and 1959–60. We're committed that we'll stay along this course.

"Right after the All-Star Game, we had a little slippage, so (director of officiating) Ed Rush and I had a talk with our crew chiefs and reaffirmed to them that we wanted to stay as we were. We didn't want to slip back into allowing the game to become too physical. Saying that, and from the league standpoint, that was the one area we really felt we could address as far as having a real impact on the game.

"I think the key statistic, when you're talking about keeping the scoring at a relatively high level, and when you talk about keeping the game flowing, is how many field goals are attempted. This year we're up to 82.1, which is up over three shots per team per game from last year, which is a big part of our scoring being higher.

"Whether that will stay there or not is problematic, because we're going to have to see what coaches are going to do and what teams are going to do as to what style they want to end up playing. Right now we've got some differences of style. We've got some teams that play quickly. We've got some teams that play a little slower. But most of them are somewhere in the middle and there's a good contrast. When you look at our game now relative to the last couple of years, I think we've got our game headed in the right direction. We're very happy with what has transpired on the court from the standpoint of the way the game is being played, and we think it's only going to get better as we go forward."

Of course, not everybody was as excited about the officiating as Thorn. Shawn Kemp, an 11-year veteran who played with the Cleveland Cavaliers, led the league with a whopping 371 fouls, far outdistancing Detroit's Christian Laettner, who had the next highest total- 326. They were two of the six players who had more than 300 fouls.

Not surprisingly, Kemp and Los Angeles Clippers rookie Lamar Odom fouled out more than anyone else in the league—13 times. But it was the veteran

who complained the most about the changes in the rules and the inconsistency of the officiating. After 11 years, Kemp expected the benefit of the doubt occasionally. But he rarely got it, and certainly not on the offensive end. It seemed as if half of his personals were offensive fouls. He refused to believe that was the case.

"If you have a guy out there who's aggressive ... for four quarters you have a team down there yelling at the officials 'Hey they're throwing the ball to him and this guy is overpowering people down low'," he said at season's end. "To officials, they might not see it as a foul but I'm sure they get tired of hearing them complain: 'Hey he's pushing. Offensive foul.'

"There's no way an individual can have as many offensive fouls as I've had this year. It was tough to swallow a lot of nights because I knew maybe it wasn't the right call. But when you're losing it's tough to say things to the officials. It's hard getting the respect you think you deserve."

According to Thorn, respect isn't the issue. Consistency is.

"That's what we strive for, is to try to get a consistency," Thorn admitted. "It's difficult. If you look at comments from virtually any year—and I've been in this league for over 30 years—every year you'll see a lot of comments from coaches, from GMs, sometimes even from owners that they'd like to see more consistency. That's what we're striving for.

"And we think that with the new rules that we put in place this year, that we have a better chance of consistency because there is a more literal interpretation. It's not so much subjective, and therefore you have better chance over the long haul of getting to that goal of becoming as consistent as you possibly can be."

Kemp, no doubt, would be pleased with that goal, and perhaps he can be relieved that the Cavaliers failed to make the playoffs after listening to the rest of the Thorn's comments.

"We've made it very clear that we expect to referee the playoffs exactly as we refereed the regular season," Thorn said, much to Kemp's chagrin. "We will not allow the game to become more physical in the playoffs than it is right now. I think there is a common misconception that fouls aren't called as frequently in the play-

offs as they are during the regular season.

"But if you look over the last four years, in the playoffs, there were more fouls called, and more fouls shot, in all of those playoffs than there were during the regular season. The one thing that is also very common is there are fewer shots taken. The games in the playoffs tend to slow down some as everybody has the ability to focus in on an opponent and take some of their pet offensive things away from them, because of this focus when you're playing someone either in a five-game or seven-game series.

"But we fully expect and will demand from our referees as they call the games, exactly as they have during the regular season."

The enforcers

How does the NBA enforce its rules on the court? The league sends three neutral officials to each game. Interestingly, the officials are on the road the entire season. They have no "home" games.

Designated as the crew chief, referee and umpire, they each have very specific duties and work in conjuction with an official scorer and two trained timers in each arena. One timer operates the game clock, and the other operates the 24-second clock. All of them must be approved by the league's Basketball Operations Department, which holds them to the highest standards of professionalism and neutrality.

In the case of any disagreements—whether between the officials or between the scorers and timers—the crew chief is the official in charge and has the final say. And while the officials generally are guided by the rule book, they also have the authority to make decisions not specifically covered in the rules. They must inform the league's Basketball Operations Department of any such decisions at the earliest possible moment.

The crew chief's authority also extends off the court and into the arena. If a spectator is verbally abusing players and/or coaches in a manner that prevents the coach from effectively communicating with his players, the crew chief will direct a building security officer to issue a warning to the fan. Should the fan persist after the warning, the crew chief has the authority to have the spectator ejected.

THE BUSINESS OF THE NBA

The popularity of basketball and its biggest stars has generated an entirely new business empire, making the NBA and its elite players a marketing man's dream. From sneakers to the Internet, basketball's bottom line is growing.

IF THE SHOE FITS: *Air Jordan shoes are just a small part of Nike's Jordan Brand empire, but Michael Jordan has been Nike's biggest pitchman.*

That Magic Touch

From not to hot, the NBA has become a marketing bonanza with an increasingly blurry line separating its sports and business personalities. When the 1980s dawned, the NBA was a star-depleted, uninteresting entity groping for direction. But after the arrival of Larry Bird and

Magic Johnson and the 1984 selection of David Stern as the league's fourth commissioner, the league vaulted into world prominence.

Stern's first order of business was to market the league's assets and he did so with a vengeance. He began lining up sponsors who accepted his pitch on the

marketability of players like Bird, Magic, Kareem Abdul-Jabbar, Dominique Wilkins, Charles Barkley and, of course, Michael Jordan. With creativity and purpose, the players were promoted, merchandised

(Opposite) AD MAN: *The Sixers' Allen Iverson has been featured in many commercials.*

STROE FRONT: *Charles Barkley looms large in a Nike Town display where the athlete's image is enough to sell ranges of merchandise.*

and packaged into international heroes and Stern used their prominence to propel the NBA—and basketball in general—toward global acceptance and recognition.

Youngsters in every corner of the world wanted to "Be Like Mike." They also wanted to soar in their Air Jordans, rebound like Sir Charles and pass like the Magic man. And as its individual players became international figures with spectacular athletic skills and deep pockets, the NBA's prominence began to grow by leaps and bounds.

Jordan at his peak was reported to be

pulling in $35 million annually in endorsements alone. Other players such as Barkley, Shaquille O'Neal and Hakeem Olajuwon have ridden the NBA's popularity wave to fame and fortune beyond the basketball court and that's fine with Stern, who knows that player success rubs off on the league he is trying to energize.

Before the 1992 Olympic Games in Barcelona, the NBA's international efforts were handled as part-time projects by a handful of employees. Now the league has regional offices with full-time staffers in Geneva, Hong Kong, Tokyo, Toronto,

Sydney, Mexico City, Barcelona and Miami (serving the Latin American countries). One of their primary duties is assisting global sponsors like Coca-Cola, McDonald's, Reebok and Nike in formulating NBA-theme promotions and projects.

But what Jordan and the Dream Team provided more than anything else was a lust for everything that carried an NBA logo, team logos and colors or player likenesses. Since Stern's first year as commissioner, the NBA's gross from the sale of team merchandise has increased from $10 million to about $3 billion.

Nothing, it seems, is sacred. Everything from T-shirts to coffee mugs, from trash cans (with nets) to license plates, from caps to posters bear the NBA touch. Sponsors like Reebok and Nike vie for the licensing rights to the NBA's clothing and apparel business, which has become enormous both in the U.S. and abroad.

The Big-Money Game

Business or pleasure? The answer, of course, is both. The NBA still is about competition and entertainment, but now it has a bottom line—an impressive and ever-growing bottom line.

Players still soar above the rim, dribble behind their back and drop long-range bombs on opponents. But now they do it while modeling their sponsor-labeled shoes, wristbands and other paraphernalia. Players and coaches sign autographs and appear away from the court in designer clothing. Sponsors are everywhere—signing players to hefty endorsement contracts, buying name association with NBA awards and products, getting involved with special NBA promotions and paying high prices for licensing rights.

It all adds up to big money and big questions that filter through the very fibers of the game. Can sport retain its competitive purity in a big-money atmosphere? Can its players perform with hunger and intensity with long-term, multi-million-dollar contracts and endorsement deals?

The answers are not easy and the money-versus-sport questions are only going to get more complicated. Business or pleasure? Just keep your eye on the bouncing ball.

NBA store

It's where "I Love This Game" meets "Shop 'til You Drop."

Its exact address is on Fifth Avenue in New York City, in the heart of one of the biggest shopping districts in the world, certainly the most well-known in the United States.

But the NBA store is about much more

BE LIKE MIKE: *His No.45 jersey was a hot item when Michael Jordan un-retired.*

No bird soars too high
If he soars with his own wi[ngs]
—William Blake

than merchandise—as extensive and impressive as its selection may be.

Walking into the door off 52nd Street in midtown Manhattan is like a trip back in time. On the video scoreboard hanging in the middle, a tape is playing from the 50th anniversary All-Star game held in Cleveland's Gund Arena in 1997. At halftime of that game, amid fireworks and flashbulbs, the league saluted its brightest stars—from Michael Jordan to George Mikan and everybody in between.

Watching the tape is almost like reliving the moment, goosebump by goosebump.

In fact, it's possible to stand perfectly still for some time before even beginning to browse through the fantastic collection of NBA clothing and memorabilia in the 35,000-square-foot, three-level store, the first retail establishment owned, operated and merchandised by a North American sports league. Almost everything you can think of is available here with the NBA, WNBA or an individual team logo on it.

Want a leather jacket? No problem. How about a nice warmup suit? There are dozens to choose from. Need a souvenir from your trip to the big city or a birthday present for your favorite sports-crazed niece or nephew? You can pick from sweatshirts, T-shirts, hats, ties, pajamas, shorts. If you can wear it, it's here—likely in men's, women's and children's sizes.

There's a library full of basketball books and videos, and a china cabinet full of glassware—and we're not talking about just coffee mugs. There are glasses, as well as plates and bowls. There are one-of-a-kind items like beaded jackets and purses, and every conceivable form of jewelry.

Even those who don't like to shop can occupy themselves by watching live games or highlights on the big-screen television sets scattered throughout the store or by taking advantage of the interactive displays.

For special occasions, the NBA can use the halfcourt, complete with bleachers, to hold all sorts of events and, in fact, the league regularly schedules appear-

ances by NBA and WNBA players, coaches, legends and other celebrities.

Why, in one year alone, the store was the setting for guest appearances by Karl Malone, Keith Van Horn, Ray Allen, Mark Jackson, Felipe Lopez, Doc Rivers, Jeff Van Gundy, Lisa Leslie, Michele Timms, Natalie Williams, Chamique Holdsclaw, Vickie Johnson, Cynthia Cooper, Sheryl Swoopes, Nykesha Sales, Rebecca Lobo, Bill Bradley and Bill Cosby—among others.

NBA city

After a day (or more) at Disney World, a trip through the Everglades, a tour of NASA, an evening on South Beach and some shopping in Boca Raton or Coconut Grove or Coral Gables, the savvy tourist in Florida, no matter how weary (or broke) undoubtedly is heading for Universal Studios, where one of the newest attractions is NBA City.

Located at Universal Studios Citywalk, a collection of themed restaurants and stores for which there is no separate admission charge, NBA City is a joint venture between the NBA and Hard Rock Cafe International. It's the first NBA restaurant and it's the first time in the Hard Rock's 29-year history it has leveraged its expertise to launch a new dining concept.

Despite the fact that the building is set back a bit off the main street, it's impossible to miss the three-story high bronze sculpture of a basketball player, complete with ball, that seems to be emerging from the building.

Inside, there's a 350-seat, 17,000-square-foot, two-story restaurant that has the feel of an old fieldhouse, right down to the old bricks, wooden floors and worn leather seats. Scattered throughout the building are old pictures and memorabilia. "Hoosier-esque" is how director of marketing Chris Havlicek described it, referring to the classic sports movie.

Havlicek is the son of former Boston Celtics star John Havlicek. Chris Havlicek played basketball at the University of Virginia and was working for Coca-Cola in Atlanta when the opportunity arose to take over NBA City.

"The NBA was looking for a marketing guy who had a basketball back-

ground, and I fit the bill," Havlicek said.

The whole project got off to a rocky start when Hurricane Floyd swept through and wiped out the grand opening ceremonies in September of 1999. But the event was rescheduled and business picked up during the NBA season and the traditionally busy spring.

In fact, many of the teams that came in to play the Orlando Magic made the trek out to Universal Studios to check out the food and the fun.

According to Havlicek, there was an equal emphasis placed on both, unlike many theme restaurants where the food is secondary. The menu features contemporary American cuisine with a wide range of choices from soups and salads to pizzas, sandwiches, pasta, hamburgers, chicken and seafood.

For a change of pace, there's an upscale lounge called the NBA City Club, where fans can watch live games on television or pick from a selection of video highlights.

Before or after dinner, there's plenty to look at, from the historic displays to the interactive video games. In fact, while waiting for dinner, many booths feature video monitors playing NBA highlights. In the NBA City Playground, fans can test their skills and/or knowledge of the game.

There's also a gift shop, with a wide variety of items featuring the NBA City logo, as well as regular NBA or individual team merchandise. Also available are personalized NBA or WNBA jerseys.

New league

At the dawn of the 21st century, NBA Commissioner David Stern announced plans for the league's newest venture–a developmental league in North America starting play in the fall of 2001.

The subject was raised for the first time publicly in a conference call with reporters before the 2000 playoffs began.

"We think the basketball community is still a vibrant, interested and actually a growing community, because there are more people playing this sport than any other sport," Stern said. "So long term, we're very optimistic about our prospects and continuing to try to develop long-term plans to further grow the sport."

To that end, Stern said, the league was

Michael Jordan—a walking, talking business empire

IN HIS SHOES: *Young players can wear Jordan brand shoes, to say nothing of his brand of underwear, toiletries, etc.*

The numbers are only estimates but when Michael Jordan contemplated retirement after the 1998 Finals, it was Wall Street economists and share dealers who showed as much concern as the average sports fan in the street.

A report, published in the prestigious *Forbes* business magazine shortly before the start of the Bulls' series with the Jazz, estimated that Jordan had been worth a staggering $310 billion to the US economy during his career.

After years of being comparatively underpaid, Jordan finally started earning his market value from Bulls owner Jerry Reinsdorf in the 1996–97 and 1997–98 seasons. After lengthy negotiations, his contract in the latter campaign was a basic $34 million, the biggest individual contract in the history of team sports.

Thanks to Jordan, Reinsdorf had seen his team's value rise to in excess of $200 million—not a bad return for the $9.2 million Reinsdorf spent in buying 56 per cent of the club the year after Jordan arrived. That figure is only the tip of the iceberg as far as Jordan's personal wealth is concerned. Companies like Nike, Oakley, Rayovac, General Mills (Wheaties cereal) and Quaker Oats (Gatorade sports drink) typically pay the former Bull between $2–5 million a year to add his name to their product. Industry experts estimate that Jordan has earned around $240 million in endorsement money in the 1990s, a figure that made his basketball playing contract look insignificant.

But, in reaching their magical $10 billion figure, *Forbes* unearthed some other incredible Michael money facts:

● Jordan made an impact of $165.5 million on attendance at NBA games—including $135 million in Chicago.

● His personal effect on TV revenues has been worth $366 million.

● His worldwide fame has added $3.1 billion to the NBA's colossal global merchandising sales.

● His movie *Space Jam* grossed $230 million worldwide, with his other sports videos generating revenue of $80 million.

● His four books have generated nearly $17 million in sales.

● Want to smell like Michael? Jordan cologne has worldwide sales of $155 million. Wear his underwear? Predictions are for annual sales of $10 million.

● Sportswear company Nike, possibly the biggest winners from the effects of the Jordan phenomenon, have gained to the tune of $5.2 billion.

moving forward with a plan for a developmental league. According to the commissioner, the new league had been proposed several years ago, but it was put on the back burner while the NBA turned its attention to the WNBA.

With the women's league up and running, though, Stern has refocused on the developmental league in an effort to recognize local basketball stars, take advantage of their followings and utilitize some of the beautiful new arenas that are being built. He wants to identify players who might be all-conference or even All-Americans who think their careers are

over or that they'll have to go overseas to continue playing.

"There is a real opportunity here to do something that I would call grassroots, in terms of developing the sport around the country further and to create a pool of players that we could use for some more dynamic international development since there are limits to the way that we can increase our global participation beyond the McDonald's Championship, the opening games in Japan, the Mexican exhibition game and a few others," Stern said. "We can develop both players, who will be getting additional skills and be

available for the NBA, and non-playing personnel in terms of the coaching, assistant coaching, general managing, marketing and public relations. It's a win-win in the classic sense of being a developmental league."

Ever since the landmark 1971 ruling that allowed underclassmen to join the NBA before their college classes graduated, the league has been struggling with how to handle the influx of underclassmen that has grown larger and larger in recent years. In fact, where it once was the rare exception for a player to come into the league right from high school,

OUR TOWN: *The attractive Nike Town entrance invites shoppers, with basketball an integral part of its stores.*

Surfin' the Net makes the NBA accessible all around the world

The NBA's ever-extending tentacles now are reaching through cyberspace, feeding news and information to millions of fans on the Internet's World Wide Web.

The NBA, never missing an opportunity to market its product to the global community, reinforced its already powerful world presence in November, 1995, when the league opened its web site at NBA.com and began offering a package of basketball information designed to satiate the appetite of its hungriest fans.

Among the offerings: Home pages (or Home Courts) for all 29 teams with basic information like player biographies, rosters, arena charts and transactions; player features and regular chat sessions with players, coaches and general managers; photos, video clips and audio clips of great players and plays; All-Star ballots that allow fans around the world to cast votes for their favorite players; and information designed for the international fan who wants to learn more about the game.

Not surprisingly, the NBA site was an immediate winner, generating more than a million file requests over its first weekend and attracting more than 200,000 fans in its first week. Quick contact was made with fans in Canada, Mexico, Colombia, Costa Rica, Greece, Indonesia, Korea, Singapore, Taiwan, Brazil, Argentina, Australia, New Zealand and numerous other countries.

now there are a few players who make that leap every year.

The league really is powerless to stop them, despite the fact that their skills are not fully developed. "We recognize that, as a pure business matter, it would be great to keep kids in college," Stern said. "It would be good for them, good for the colleges and good for us. We've tried, within limits, to address the issue. We asked the (NBA) Players' Association to sit down and come up with a program where we could agree that perhaps players would earn more if they played their full four years because they had more value, and it would be reduced if they didn't. And after originally indicating to us that seemed to be a good idea from their perspective, the Players' Association said no. That's their right, and that's fine.

"Then we went to the NCAA (which prohibits athletes from making money from their sports) and said, rather than you accusing us of taking away your players, could we agree that we will do something at your direction so that young men who are in school and playing, who you identify as potential future draft picks, could receive additional loans, a stipend, however you want to do it, so that the reason for them leaving wouldn't be that they just couldn't make ends meet? The answer from the NCAA on that was that they couldn't consider that

for a variety of reasons that may be good. We don't even want to argue about that anymore. For us, this is not an assault on the collegiate system."

The commissioner also stressed that, in addition to not being a substitute for college, the new league would not be equivalent to major-league baseball's minor leagues, where young athletes, drafted out of high school, are brought up through an organization with the goal of eventually making that team's major-league roster. "Frankly, its not going to be our initial target to get kids to come pouring out of the high school and come into this league," said Stern, who insisted that would be made clear in the new league's charter. "That's not where we're going to be ... Our present plan is not to have a league full of 18-year-olds. It may be, because this will be run as a single enterprise, that we'll have some youngsters because it would seem to be unfair not to, but it would be reluctantly, I assure you.

"I'm not sure we're the right substitute for some of the other opportunities they might have. Anything we will do will have significant continuing education. I don't mean degree completion, but life skills and the like, because we think there's a real opportunity for that."

Stern is confident athletes will take advantage of the new opportunity.

"The numbers are virtually unlim-

ited," he said. "This is a very popular and growing sport. America literally populates leagues around the world, with players playing America's game overseas. There have been leagues that have come and leagues that have gone. And we would like to see that there's a league here that is well-funded, well-thought-out and will be here forever. We think it's all about structure, economic support and a good operational and selling philosophy.

"But the last problem is players who have committed themselves to our game. In some cases it may even be a youngster who has played through four years (of college) and who may not quite be ready for (the pros) and might decide it's time to go into some other field but would like to play for a couple of years, to play off some of the fame he acquired in college and see the world a little bit, on some tours that the players might take, and go on with the skills he's acquired on and off the court to the rest of his life. So we think there are ample scores of very competent players who can play at this level.

"In small cities where there are buildings and the opportunity to involve the city, and the community and the sport, and there are young men who have spent the better part of their lives playing basketball and developing reputations, maybe we can be constructive in helping them make that final judgment about whether they are ready for the pros, and provide some continual support that enables them to move on to their non-basketball life. The NBA is in a particularly good position, with our coaching staffs and our professional basketball people, to help kids definitively evaluate their future. This is not going to be a league where players play in it for 10 years. This is going to be a league of young people making both career and life decisions over a period of time."

It will be several years before the NBA can evaluate the success of its development league and of some of is other ventures as well.

Of course by that time, there is no telling what else the league will have branched off into.

(Opposite) HAPPY MAN: *The league's progress pleases NBA Commissioner David Stern.*

THE HALL OF FAME

The idea for a basketball memorial took root in the 1940s, spread slowly with nourishment from dedicated coaches and officials and blossomed into a state-of-the-art, high-tech, crowd-pleasing testimonial to the elegant athletes, past and present, who perform for the modern fan.

From Dr. James Naismith's 1891 invention of basketball to his death in 1939, he could never have imagined a game that has soared into the stratosphere of worldwide popularity, much less the Springfield, Mass., shrine that bears his name and helps visitors form a lasting bond with its greatest players and most memorable moments.

The first Hall of Fame class was elected in 1959, and the first Hall of Fame museum was dedicated February 18, 1968—a two-story, red-brick building on the Springfield College campus. That humble abode stood in stark contrast to the expanded $11.5 million, three-story, 54,000-square-foot structure that replaced it in 1985, sitting majestically off Interstate 91, on the banks of the Connecticut River near downtown Springfield.

Where Legends Live Forever

The Hall of Fame visitor gets a large dose of basketball history and nostalgia, but the primary attractions are interactive videos, shooting and jumping arcades and three movie theaters that highlight such memorable moments as NBA All-Star Weekends, NBA Finals, NCAA Final Fours and Olympic Games. The museum is a wide-ranging tribute to the game on every level—men and women, professional and amateur, American and foreign—and more than 150,000 visitors pass through its turnstiles annually.

The first class of 18 inductees featured Naismith, George Mikan and two teams—Naismith's "first" 1891 team and the Original Celtics of the 1920s and

'30s. By the 1968 building dedication, the Hall already had a 66-member roster that has since grown to 217 men and women and four teams. Anybody is eligible, but potential inductees have to be nominated on special ballots, pass through a screening committee and receive 18 votes from the 24-member Honors Committee. Players and referees are eligible five years after retirement; coaches after 25 years in the game, or five years of retirement; and contributors can be elected after retirement. Induction ceremonies are held every May.

The class of 1998, indicative of the international nature of basketball, included only three men with an NBA background, a women's coach, and a Yugoslav.

The following Hall of Fame players, coaches and contributors have been associated with the NBA.

HALL OF FAME ENSHRINEES

NBA-Associated Personnel

Kareem Abdul-Jabbar: 7–2, 267-pound center. Born April 16, 1947, at New York. Attended UCLA. Played 20 seasons with Bucks, Lakers. Member of Bucks' 1971 and Lakers' 1980, 1982, 1985, 1987, 1988 championship teams. Scoring champion 1971 (31.7), 1972 (34.8). Rebounding champion 1976 (16.9). Rookie of the Year 1970. Regular-season MVP 1971, 1972, 1974, 1976, 1977, 1980. NBA Finals MVP 1971, 1985. Career totals: 38,387 points, 17,440 rebounds, 5,660 assists. Member of 35th

Anniversary All-Time Team. Included in 50 greatest players in NBA History. Elected 1995.

Nate (Tiny) Archibald: 6–1, 160-pound point guard. Born September 2, 1948, at New York. Attended Arizona Western, Texas-El Paso. Played 13 seasons with Royals/Kings, Nets, Celtics, Bucks. Member of Celtics' 1981 championship team. Scoring champion 1973 (34.0). Assist champion 1973 (11.4). All-Star Game MVP 1981. Career totals: 16,481 points, 6,476 assists. Included in 50 greatest players in NBA History. Elected 1991.

Paul Arizin: 6–4, 200-pound guard/foward. Born April 9, 1928, at Philadelphia. Attended Villanova. Played 10 seasons with Warriors. Member of Warriors' 1956 championship team. Scoring champion 1952 (25.4), 1957 (25.6). All-Star Game MVP 1952. Career totals: 16,266 points, 6,129 rebounds. Member of the 25th Anniversary All-Time Team. Included in 50 greatest players in NBA History. Elected 1977.

Rick Barry: 6–7, 220-pound forward. Born March 28, 1944, at Elizabeth, N.J. Attended Miami (Fla.). Played 14 seasons with Warriors, Oaks/Capitols/Squires (ABA), Nets (ABA), Rockets. Member of Oaks' 1969, Warriors' 1975 championship teams. Scoring champion 1967 (35.6), 1969 (34.0, ABA). Rookie of the Year 1966. NBA Finals MVP 1975. All-Star

(Opposite) CLEAR SKIES: *Kareem Abdul-Jabbar made the sky hook famous.*

Game MVP 1967. Career totals ABA/ NBA: 25,279 points, 6,863 rebounds, 4,952 assists. Included in 50 greatest players in NBA History. Elected 1987.

Elgin Baylor: 6–5, 225-pound forward. Born September 16, 1934, at Washington, D.C. Attended College of Idaho, Seattle. Played 14 seasons with Lakers. Rookie of the Year 1959. All-Star Game co-MVP 1959. Career totals: 23,149 points, 11,463 rebounds, 3,650 assists. Member of the 35th Anniversary All-Time Team. Included in 50 greatest players in NBA History. Coached 4 NBA seasons (86–135). Elected 1976.

Walt Bellamy: 6–11, 245-pound center. Born July 24, 1939, at New Bern, N.C. Attended Indiana. Played 14 seasons with Packers/ Zephyrs/Bullets, Knicks, Pistons, Hawks, Jazz. Rookie of the Year 1962. Career totals: 20,941 points, 14,241 rebounds. Elected 1993.

Dave Bing: 6–3, 185-pound guard. Born November 24, 1943, at Washington, D.C. Attended Syracuse. Played 12 seasons with Pistons, Bullets, Celtics. Scoring champion 1968 (27.1). Rookie of the Year 1967. All-Star Game MVP 1976. Career totals: 18,327 points, 5,397 assists. Included in 50 greatest players in NBA History. Elected 1990.

Larry Bird: 6–9, 220-pound forward. Born December 7, 1956, at West Baden, In. Attended Indiana State. Played 13 seasons with Celtics. Member of Celtics' 1981, 1984, 1986 championship teams. Rookie of the Year 1980. Regular-season MVP 1984, 1985, 1986. NBA Finals MVP 1984, 1986. All-Star Game MVP 1982. Career totals: 21,791 points, 8,974 rebounds, 5,695 assists. Included in 50 greatest players in NBA history. Coached 3 NBA seasons with Pacers (147–67). Elected 1998.

Bill Bradley: 6–5, 205-pound forward. Born July 28, 1943, at Crystal City, Mo. Attended Princeton. Played 10 seasons with Knicks. Member of Knicks' 1970,

LARRY LEGEND: *The Celtics' Larry Bird helped the Boston franchise to much success in the '80s.*

1973 championship teams. Career totals: 9,217 points, 2,533 assists. Elected 1982.

Al (Digger) Cervi: 5–11, 185-pound guard. Born February 12, 1917, at Buffalo, N.Y. Played 5 NBL seasons with Buffalo, Rochester, Syracuse; 4 NBA seasons with Nationals. Career NBA totals: 1,591 points. Coached 9 NBA seasons (326–241). Elected 1984.

Wilt (the Stilt) Chamberlain: 7–1, 275-pound center. Born August 21, 1936, at Philadelphia. Attended Kansas. Played 14 seasons with Warriors, 76ers, Lakers. Member of 76ers' 1967 and Lakers' 1972 cham-pionship teams. Scoring champion 1960 (37.6), 1961 (38.4), 1962 (50.4), 1963 (44.8), 1964 (36.9), 1965 (34.7), 1966 (33.5). Rebounding champion 1960 (27.0), 1961 (27.2), 1962 (25.7), 1963 (24.3), 1966 (24.6), 1967 (24.2), 1968 (23.8), 1969 (21.1), 1971 (18.2), 1972 (19.2), 1973 (18.6). Rookie of the Year 1960. Regular-season MVP 1960, 1966, 1967, 1968. NBA Finals MVP 1972. All-Star Game MVP 1960. Career totals: 31,419 points, 23,924 rebounds, 4,643 assists. Member of 35th Anniver-sary All-Time Team. Included in 50 greatest players in NBA History. Elected 1978.

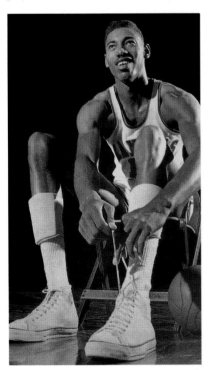

THE STILT: *Wilt Chamberlain was one of the best ever to lace up a pair of sneakers.*

TAKING A PASS: *Boston's Bob Cousy made passing an art form.*

Bob Cousy: 6–1, 175-pound point guard. Born August 9, 1928, at New York. Attended Holy Cross. Played 14 seasons with Celtics, Royals. Member of Celtics' 1957, 1959, 1960, 1961, 1962, 1963 championship teams. Assist champion 1953 (7.7), 1954 (7.2), 1955 (7.8), 1956 (8.9), 1957 (7.5), 1958 (7.1), 1959 (8.6), 1960 (9.5). Regular-season MVP 1957. All-Star Game MVP 1954, 1957. Career totals: 16,960 points, 4,786 rebounds, 6,955 assists. Member of 25th and 35th Anniversary All-Time Teams. Included in 50 greatest players in NBA History. Coached 5 NBA seasons (141–209). Elected 1970.

Dave Cowens: 6–9, 230-pound center. Born October 25, 1948, at Newport, Ky. Attended Florida State. Played 11 seasons with Celtics, Bucks. Member of Celtics' 1974, 1976 championship teams. Co-Rookie of the Year 1971. Regular-season MVP 1973. All-Star Game MVP 1973. Career totals: 13,516 points, 10,444 rebounds. Included in 50 greatest players in NBA History. Coached 2 NBA seasons (83–67). Elected 1991.

Billy Cunningham: 6–7, 210-pound forward. Born June 3, 1943, at Brooklyn, N.Y. Attended North Carolina. Played 11 seasons with 76ers, Cougars (ABA). Member of 76ers' 1967 championship team. Regular-season MVP 1973 (ABA). Career totals ABA/NBA: 16,310 points, 7,981 rebounds, 3,305 assists. Included in 50 greatest players in NBA History. Coached 8 NBA seasons (454–196). Elected 1986.

Bob Davies: 6–1, 175-pound guard. Born January 15, 1920, at Harrisburg, Pa. Attended Franklin & Marshall, Seton Hall. Played 3 NBL seasons with Rochester; 7 BAA/NBA seasons with Royals. Member of Royals' 1951 champ-ionship team. Assist champion 1949 (5.4). Career NBA totals: 6,594 points. Member of 25th Anniversary All-Time Team. Elected 1969.

Dave DeBusschere: 6–6, 235-pound forward. Born October 16, 1940, at Detroit. Attended Detroit. Played 12 seasons with Pistons, Knicks. Member of

Knicks' 1970, 1973 championship teams. Career totals: 14,053 points, 9,618 rebounds. Included in 50 greatest players in NBA History. Coached 3 NBA seasons (79–143). Elected 1982.

Alex English: 6–7, 190-pound forward. Born January 5, 1954, at Columbia, S.C. Attended South Carolina. Played 15 seasons with Bucks, Pacers, Nuggets. First NBA player to score 2,000 points eight straight seasons. Eight-straight All-Star games. Led NBA scoring, 1982–83 (28.4 ppg). Career totals: 25,613 points, 6,538 rebounds, 4,351 assists. Elected 1997.

Julius (Dr. J) Erving: 6–7, 210-pound forward. Born February 22, 1950, at Roosevelt, N.Y. Attended Massachusetts. Played 16 seasons with Squires (ABA), Nets (ABA), 76ers. Member of Nets' 1974 (ABA), 1976 (ABA) and 76ers' 1983 championship teams. Scoring champion 1973 (31.9, ABA), 1974 (27.4, ABA), 1976 (29.3, ABA). Regular-season MVP 1974 (ABA), 1975 (ABA), 1976 (ABA), 1981. Playoff MVP 1974 (ABA), 1976 (ABA). All-Star Game MVP 1977, 1983. Career totals ABA/NBA: 30,026 points, 10,525 rebounds, 5,176 assists. Included in 50 greatest players in NBA History. Elected 1993.

Walt (Clyde) Frazier: 6–4, 205-pound point guard. Born March 29, 1945, at Atlanta, Ga. Attended Southern Illinois. Played 13 seasons with Knicks, Cavaliers. Member of Knicks' 1970, 1973 champ-ionship teams. All-Star Game MVP 1975. Career totals: 15,581 points, 4,830 rebounds, 5,040 assists. Included in 50 greatest players in NBA History. Elected 1987.

Joe Fulks: 6–5, 190-pound forward/center. Born October 26, 1921, at Birmingham, Ky. Attended Murray State. Played 8 seasons with Warriors. Member of Warriors' 1947 championship team. Scoring champion 1947 (23.2), 1948

(22.1). Career totals: 8,003 points. Member of 25th Anniversary All-Time Team. Elected 1977.

Harry Gallatin: 6–6, 215-pound forward/center. Born April 26, 1927, at Roxana, Ill. Attended Northeast Missouri State. Played 10 seasons with Knicks, Pistons. Rebounding champion 1954 (15.3). Career totals: 8,843 points. Coached 4 NBA seasons (136–120). Elected 1991.

George Gervin: 6–7, 185-pound guard. Born April 27, 1952, at Detroit. Attended Long Beach State, Eastern Michigan. Played 14 seasons for Virginia Squires (ABA), Spurs (ABA, NBA), Bulls. Scoring champion 1978 (27.2), 1979 (29.6), 1980

(33.1), 1982 (32.3). All-Star Game MVP 1980. Career totals ABA/NBA: 26,595 points, 5,602 rebounds, 2,798 assists. Included in 50 greatest players in NBA History. Elected 1996.

Tom Gola: 6–6, 205-pound guard/forward. Born January 13, 1933, at Philadelphia. Attended La Salle. Played 10 seasons with Warriors, Knicks. Member of Warriors' 1956 championship team. Career totals: 7,871 points, 5,605 rebounds. Elected 1975.

Gail Goodrich: 6–1, 175-pound guard. Born April 23, 1943, at Los Angeles. Attended UCLA. Played 14 seasons for Lakers, Suns, Jazz. Member of Lakers'

(*Opposite*) **SPEAKING ENGLISH:** *Alex English let his offense do his talking for him.*

(*Right*) **HOUSE CALL:** *Philadelphia's Julius "Dr. J" Erving cured all the 76ers' ailments.*

1972 championship team. Career totals: 19,181 points, 4,805 assists. Elected 1996.

Hal Greer: 6–2, 175-pound guard. Born June 26, 1936, at Huntington, W. Va. Attended Marshall. Played 15 seasons with Nationals/76ers. Member of 76ers' 1967 championship team. All-Star Game MVP 1968. Career totals: 21,586 points, 5,665 rebounds, 4,540 assists. Included in 50 greatest players in NBA History. Elected 1981.

Cliff Hagan: 6–4, 215-pound forward. Born December 9, 1931, at Owensboro, Ky. Attended Kentucky. Played 13 seasons with Hawks, Chaparrals (ABA). Member of Hawks' 1958 championship team. Career totals ABA/NBA: 14,870 points, 5,555 rebounds. Elected 1977.

John (Hondo) Havlicek: 6–5, 205-pound guard/forward. Born April 8, 1940, at Martins Ferry, OH. Attended Ohio State. Played 16 seasons with Celtics. Member of Celtics' 1963, 1964, 1965, 1966, 1968, 1969, 1974, 1976 championship teams. NBA Finals MVP 1974. Career totals: 26,395 points, 8,007 rebounds, 6,114 assists. Member of 35th Anniversary All-Time Team. Included in 50 greatest players in NBA History. Elected 1983.

Connie Hawkins: 6–8, 215-pound forward/ center. Born July 17, 1942, at Brooklyn, N.Y. Attended Iowa. Played 9 seasons with Pipers (ABA), Suns, Lakers, Hawks. Member of Pipers' 1968 championship team. Scoring champion 1968 (26.8, ABA). Regular-season MVP 1968 (ABA). Career totals ABA/ NBA: 11,528 points, 5,450 rebounds, 2,556 assists. Elected 1992.

Elvin Hayes: 6–9, 235-pound forward / center. Born November 17, 1945, at Rayville, La. Attended Houston. Played 16 seasons with Rockets, Bullets. Member of Bullets' 1978 championship team. Scoring champion 1969 (28.4). Rebounding champion 1970 (16.9), 1974 (18.1). Career totals: 27,313 points, 16,279 rebounds. Included in 50 greatest players in NBA History. Elected 1990.

TOMMY BOY: *Boston's Tom Heinsohn.*

Tom Heinsohn: 6–7, 218-pound forward. Born August 26, 1934, at Jersey City, N.J. Attended Holy Cross. Played 9 seasons with Celtics. Member of Celtics' 1957, 1959, 1960, 1961, 1962, 1963, 1964, 1965 championship teams. Rookie of the Year 1957. Career totals: 12,194 points, 5,749 rebounds. Coached 9 NBA seasons (427– 263). Elected 1986.

Bailey Howell: 6–7, 220-pound forward. Born January 20, 1937, at Middleton, Tenn. Attended Mississippi State. Played 12 seasons with Pistons, Bullets, Celtics, 76ers. Member of Celtics' 1968, 1969 championship teams. Six-time NBA All-Star. Career totals: 17,770 points, 9,383 rebounds, 1,853 assists. Elected 1997.

Dan Issel: 6–9, 240-pound forward. Born October 25, 1948, at Batavia, Ill. Attended Kentucky. Played 15 seasons with Colonels (ABA), Nuggets (ABA, NBA). Member of Colonels' 1975 championship team. Scoring champion 1971 (29.9, ABA). Co-Rookie of the Year 1971 (ABA). All-Star Game MVP 1972 (ABA). Career totals ABA/NBA: 27,482 points, 11,133 rebounds. Coached 3 NBA seasons (96–102). Elected 1993.

Buddy Jeannette: 5–11, 175-pound point guard. Born September 15, 1917, at New Kensington, Pa. Attended Washington & Jefferson. Played 7 NBL seasons with Warren, Cleveland, Detroit, Sheboygan, and Fort Wayne; 3 BAA/NBA seasons with Bullets. Member of 1948 championship team. Career NBA totals:

997 points. Coached 6 NBA seasons (136–173). Elected 1994.

Neil Johnston: 6–8, 210-pound center. Born February 4, 1929, at Chillicothe, Ohio. Attended Ohio State. Played 8 seasons with Warriors. Member of Warriors' 1956 championship team. Scoring champion 1953 (22.3), 1954 (24.4), 1955 (22.7). Rebounding champion 1955 (15.1). Career totals: 10,023 points, 5,856 rebounds. Coached 2 NBA seasons (95–59). Elected 1990.

K.C. Jones: 6–1, 200-pound point guard. Born May 25, 1932, at Taylor, Tex. Attended San Francisco. Played 9 seasons with Celtics. Member of Celtics' 1959, 1960, 1961, 1962, 1963, 1964, 1965, 1966 championship teams. Career totals: 5,011 points, 2,908 assists. Coached 10 NBA seasons (522–252). Elected 1989.

Sam Jones: 6–4, 205-pound guard. Born June 24, 1933, at Wilmington, N.C. Attended North Carolina Central. Played 12 seasons with Celtics. Member of Celtics' 1959, 1960, 1961, 1962, 1963, 1964, 1965, 1966, 1968, 1969 championship teams. Career totals: 15,411 points, 4,305 rebounds, 2,209 assists. Member of 25th Anniversary All-Time Team. Included in 50 greatest players. Elected 1983.

Bob Lanier: 6–11, 265-pound center. Born September 10, 1948, at Buffalo, N.Y. Attended St. Bonaventure. Played 14 seasons with Pistons, Bucks. All-Star Game MVP 1974. Career totals: 19,248 points, 9,698 rebounds, 3,007 assists. Coached 1 NBA season (12–25). Elected 1992.

Joe Lapchick: 6–5, 185-pound center. Born April 12, 1900, at Yonkers, N.Y. Playing career was pre-BAA/NBA. Coached 9 NBA seasons (326–247). Elected 1966.

Clyde Lovellette: 6–9, 235-pound forward/center. Born September 7, 1929, at Petersburg, Ind. Attended Kansas. Played 11 seasons with Lakers, Royals, Hawks, Celtics. Member of Lakers' 1954 and Celtics' 1963, 1964 championship teams. Career totals: 11,947 points, 6,663 rebounds. Elected 1988.

Jerry Lucas: 6–8, 235-pound forward / center. Born March 30, 1940, at Middletown, Ohio. Attended Ohio State. Played 11 seasons with Royals, Warriors, Knicks. Member of Knicks' 1973 championship team. Rookie of the Year 1964. All-Star Game MVP 1965. Career totals: 14,053 points, 12,942 rebounds. Included in 50 greatest players in NBA History. Elected 1979.

(Easy) Ed Macauley: 6–8, 190-pound forward/center. Born March 22, 1928, at St. Louis. Attended St. Louis University. Played 10 seasons with Bombers, Celtics, Hawks. Member of Hawks' 1958 championship team. All-Star Game MVP 1951. Career totals: 11,234 points. Coached 2 NBA seasons (89–48). Elected 1960.

(Pistol) Pete Maravich: 6–5, 200-pound guard. Born June 22, 1947, at Aliquippa, Pa. Attended Louisiana State. Played 10 seasons with Hawks, Jazz, Celtics. Scoring champion 1977 (31.1). Career totals: 15,948 points, 3,563 assists. Included in 50 greatest players in NBA History. Elected 1987.

Slater Martin: 5–10, 170-pound point guard. Born October 22, 1925, at Houston. Attended Texas. Played 11 seasons with Lakers, Knicks, Hawks. Member of Lakers' 1950, 1952, 1953, 1954 and Hawks' 1958 championship teams. Career totals: 7,337 points, 3,160 assists. Coached 1 NBA season (5–3). Elected 1981.

Dick McGuire: 6–0, 180-pound point guard. Born January 25, 1926, at Huntington, N.Y. Attended St. John's, Dartmouth. Played 11 seasons with Knicks, Pistons. Assist co-champion 1951 (6.3). Career totals: 5,921 points, 4,205 assists. Coached 7 NBA seasons (197–260). Elected 1993.

Kevin McHale: 6–10, 225 pounds. Born December 19, 1957, in Hibbing, Minnesota. Elected in 1999. Attended University of Minnesota. Teamed with Larry Bird and Robert Parish to form one

WELL-ARMED: *Kevin McHale's long arms were key to his success.*

of the greatest frontlines in professional basketball history with the Boston Celtics. In a 12-year span, McHale's Celtics compiled a 690–276 record, won nine Atlantic Division titles and six Eastern Conference championships. With a variety of almost-unstoppable low-post moves, McHale revolutionized pivot play and helped lead Boston to three NBA championships (1981, 1984 and 1986). Named to the NBA's 50th Anniversary Team in 1996 and seven NBA All-Star Teams (1984, 1986–91), McHale was an All-NBA first-team selection in 1987. He won the league's Sixth Man Award in 1984 and 1985.

George Mikan: 6–10, 245-pound center. Born June 18, 1924, at Joliet, Ill. Attended DePaul. Played 2 NBL seasons with Chicago, Minneapolis; 7 BAA/NBA seasons with Lakers. Member of Lakers' 1949, 1950, 1952, 1953, 1954 championship teams. Scoring champion 1949 (28.3), 1950 (27.4), 1951 (28.4), 1952 (23.8). Rebounding champion 1952 (13.5), 1953 (14.4). All-Star Game MVP 1953. Career totals: 10,156 points, 4,167 rebounds. Coached 1 NBA season (9–30). Member of 25th and 35th Anniversary All-Time Teams. Included in 50 greatest players in NBA History. Elected 1959.

Vern Mikkelsen: 6–7, 230-pound forward/ center. Born October 21, 1928, at Fresno, Calif. Attended Hamline. Played 10 seasons with Lakers. Member of Lakers' 1950, 1952, 1953, 1954 championship teams. Career totals: 10,063 points. Elected 1995.

Earl (the Pearl) Monroe: 6–3, 190-pound guard. Born November 21, 1944, at Philadelphia. Attended Winston-Salem State. Played 13 seasons with Bullets, Knicks. Member of Knicks' 1973 championship team. Rookie of the Year 1968. Career totals: 17,454 points, 3,594 assists. Included in 50 greatest players in NBA History. Elected 1990.

Calvin Murphy: 5–9, 165-pound guard. Born May 9, 1948, at Norwalk, Conn. Attended Niagara. Played 13 seasons with Rockets. Career totals: 17,949 points, 4,402 assists. Elected 1993.

Bob Pettit: 6–9, 215-pound forward. Born December 12, 1932, at Baton Rouge, La. Attended Louisiana State. Played 11 seasons with Hawks. Member of Hawks' 1958 championship team. Scoring champion 1956 (25.7), 1959 (29.2). Rookie of the Year 1955. Regular-season MVP 1956, 1959. All-Star Game MVP 1956, 1958, 1962. Career totals: 20,880 points, 12,849 rebounds. Coached 1 NBA season (4–2). Member of 25th and 35th Anniversary All-Time Teams. Included in 50 greatest players in NBA History. Elected 1970.

Andy Phillip: 6–2, 195-pound point guard. Born March 7, 1922, at Granite City, Ill. Attended Illinois. Played 11 seasons with Stags, Warriors, Pistons, Celtics. Member of Celtics' 1957 championship team. Assist champion 1950 (5.8), 1951 (6.3), 1952 (8.2). Career totals: 6,384 points, 3,759 assists. Elected 1961.

Jim Pollard: 6–5, 185-pound forward. Born July 9, 1922, at Oakland, Calif. Attended Stanford. Played 1 NBL season with Minneapolis; 7 BAA/NBA seasons with Lakers. Member of Lakers' 1949, 1950, 1952, 1953, 1954 championship teams. Career totals: 5,762 points. Coached 2 NBA seasons (32–87). Elected 1977.

Frank Ramsey: 6–3, 190-pound guard. Born July 13, 1931, at Corydon, Ky. Attended Kentucky. Played 9 seasons with Celtics. Member of Celtics' 1957, 1959, 1960, 1961, 1962, 1963, 1964 championship teams. Career totals: 8,378 points, 3,410 rebounds. Elected 1981.

Willis Reed: 6–10, 240-pound center. Born June 25, 1942, at Hico, La. Attended Grambling State. Played 10 seasons with Knicks. Member of Knicks' 1970 and 1973 championship teams. Rookie of the Year 1965. Regular-season MVP 1970. NBA Finals MVP 1970, 1973. All-Star Game MVP 1970. Career totals: 12,183 points, 8,414 rebounds. Included in 50 greatest players in NBA History. Coached 4 NBA seasons (82–124). Elected 1981.

Arnie Risen: 6–9, 200-pound forward. Born October 9, 1924, at Lexington, Ky.

Attended Kentucky State, Ohio State. Played 1 NBL season with Indianapolis; 12 NBA seasons with Rochester, Celtics. Member of Rochester's 1951 championships team, Celtics' 1957 championship team. Career totals: 7,633 points, 5,011 rebounds 1,058 assists. Elected 1998.

Oscar (Big O) Robertson: 6–5, 220-pound guard. Born November 24, 1938, at Charlotte, Tenn. Attended Cincinnati. Played 14 seasons with Royals, Bucks. Member of Bucks' 1971 championship team. Scoring champion 1968 (29.2). Assist champion 1961 (9.7), 1962 (11.4), 1964 (11.0), 1965 (11.5), 1966 (11.1), 1967 (10.7), 1968 (9.7), 1969 (9.8). Rookie of the Year 1961. Regular-season MVP 1964. All-Star Game MVP 1961, 1964, 1969. Career totals: 26,710 points, 7,804 rebounds, 9,887 assists. Member of 35th Anniversary All-Time Team. Included in 50 greatest players in NBA History. Elected 1979.

John (Honey) Russell: 6–1, 195-pound guard. Born May 31, 1902, at Brooklyn, N.Y. Attended Seton Hall. Playing career was pre-BAA/NBA. Coached 2 NBA seasons (42–66). Elected 1964.

Bill Russell: 6–10, 220-pound center. Born February 12, 1934, at Monroe, La. Attended San Francisco. Played 13 seasons with Celtics. Member of Celtics' 1957, 1959, 1960, 1961, 1962, 1963, 1964, 1965, 1966, 1968, 1969 championship teams. Rebounding champion 1957 (19.6), 1958 (22.7), 1959 (23.0), 1964 (24.7), 1965 (24.1). Regular-season MVP 1958, 1961, 1962, 1963, 1965. All-Star Game MVP 1963. Career totals: 14,522 points, 21,620 rebounds, 4,100 assists. Coached 8 NBA seasons (341–290). Member of 25th and 35th Anniversary All-Time Teams. Included in 50 greatest players in NBA History. Elected 1974.

Dolph Schayes: 6–8, 220-pound forward/ center. Born May 19, 1928, at New York. Attended New York University. Played 1 NBL season with Syracuse; 15 seasons with Nationals/76ers. Member of Nationals' 1955 championship team.

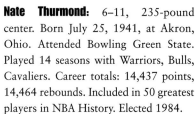

Rebounding champion 1951 (16.4). Career totals: 18,438 points, 11,256 rebounds. Coached 5 NBA seasons (151–172). Member of 25th Anniversary All-Time Team. Included in 50 greatest players in NBA History. Elected 1972.

Bill Sharman: 6–1, 190-pound guard. Born May 25, 1926, at Abilene, Tex. Attended Southern California. Played 11 seasons with Capitols, Celtics. Member of Celtics' 1957, 1959, 1960, 1961 championship teams. All-Star Game MVP

1955. Career totals: 12,665 points, 2,779 rebounds. Coached 7 NBA seasons (333–240). Member of 25th Anniversary All-Time Team. Included in 50 greatest players in NBA History. Elected 1975.

David Thompson: 6–5, 195-pound guard/forward. Born July 13, 1954, at Shelby, N.C. Attended North Carolina State. Played 9 seasons with Nuggets (ABA, NBA), Super-Sonics. Career totals ABA/ NBA: 13,422 points, 2,446 rebounds, 1,939 assists. Elected 1996.

Nate Thurmond: 6–11, 235-pound center. Born July 25, 1941, at Akron, Ohio. Attended Bowling Green State. Played 14 seasons with Warriors, Bulls, Cavaliers. Career totals: 14,437 points, 14,464 rebounds. Included in 50 greatest players in NBA History. Elected 1984.

Jack Twyman: 6–6, 210-pound guard/forward. Born May 11, 1934, at Pittsburgh, Pa. Attended Cincinnati. Played 11 seasons with Royals. Career totals: 15,840 points, 5,424 rebounds. Elected 1982.

Wes Unseld: 6–7, 245-pound center. Born March 14, 1946, at Louisville, Ky. Attended Louisville. Played 13 seasons with Bullets. Member of Bullets' 1978 championship team. Rebounding champion 1975 (14.8). Rookie of the Year 1969. Regular-season MVP 1969. NBA Finals MVP (1978). Career totals: 10,624 points, 13,769 rebounds, 3,822 assists. Coached 7 NBA seasons (202–345). Included in 50 greatest players in NBA History. Elected 1988.

Bill Walton: 6–11, 235-pound center. Born November 5, 1952, at La Mesa, Calif. Attended UCLA. Played 10 seasons with Trail Blazers, Clippers, Celtics. Member of Trail Blazers' 1977, Celtics' 1986 championship teams. Rebounding champion 1977 (14.4). Regular-season MVP 1978. NBA Finals MVP 1977. Career totals: 6,215 points, 4,923 rebounds. Included in 50 greatest players in NBA History. Elected 1993.

Bobby Wanzer: 6–0, 170-pound guard. Born June 4, 1921, at New York. Attended Seton Hall. Played 1 NBL season with Rochester; 9 seasons with Royals. Member of Royals' 1951 championship team. Career totals: 6,924 points. Coached 4 NBA seasons (98–136). Elected 1987.

Jerry West: 6–2, 185-pound guard. Born May 28, 1938, at Cheylan, W.V. Attended West Virginia. Played 14 seasons with Lakers. Member of Lakers'

WESTERN UNION: *Jerry West was a perfect fit for the Los Angeles Lakers.*

518

1972 championship team. Scoring champion 1970 (31.2). Assist champion 1972 (9.7). NBA Finals MVP 1969. All-Star Game MVP 1972. Career totals: 25,192 points, 5,376 rebounds, 6,238 assists. Coached 3 NBA seasons (145–101). Member of NBA 35th Anniversary All-Time Team. Included in 50 greatest players in NBA History. Elected 1979.

Lenny Wilkens: 6–1, 180-pound guard. Born October 28, 1937, at Brooklyn, N.Y. Attended Providence. Played 15 seasons with Hawks, SuperSonics, Cavaliers, Trail Blazers. All-Star Game MVP 1971. Career totals: 17,772 points, 5,030 rebounds, 7,211 assists. Coached 27 NBA seasons (1,179–981). Included in 50 greatest players in NBA History. Elected 1989.

George Yardley: 6–5, 195-pound forward. Born November 23, 1928, at Hollywood, Calif. Attended Stanford. Played 7 seasons with Pistons, Nationals. Scoring champion 1958 (27.8). Career totals: 9,063 points, 4,220 rebounds. Elected 1996.

Non-NBA Players

Thomas B. Barlow: 6–1, 190 pounds. Born July 9, 1896 at Trenton, N.J. Elected in 1981. Attended Rider Moore Stewart Business College. Barlow is best known for contributions to the Trenton Tigers of the Eastern League, the SPHAs of the Philadelphia League and the Philadelphia Warriors of the ABL. He played under Hall of Fame coach Eddie Gottlieb with the SPHAs and Warriors. Barlow and his SPHAs were among the best in the nation in 1926. He played in the first professional game at the old Madison Square Garden. While playing at Madison Square Garden with the Trenton Tigers, promoters would display a seven-foot cutout photograph of Barlow with the wording, "Caveman Barlow plays here tonight."

MARQUEE ATTRACTION: *"Caveman Barlow plays here tonight."*

basketball. A four-time Olympian and member of several European Championship teams, Belov is considered among the greatest international players of all time. With his induction, he became the first international player elected into the Basketball Hall of Fame. So deft with the basketball and such a prolific scorer, he earned the nickname, "the Jerry West of Russia." Belov not only led the Soviet Union to the 1972 Olympic gold in

Munich, but also to bronze medals in the 1968, 1976 and 1980 Games. Belov also led the Russian National Team to four European championships and two World Championships.

Carol Blazejowski: 5–10. Born September 29, 1956, in Elizabeth, N.J. Elected in 1994. Attended Montclair State. Known as "The Blaze," she scored 3,199 points at Montclair State from

TRUE LEGEND: *John Beckman was considered the Babe Ruth of basketball by some.*

John Beckman: 5–8, 165 pounds. Born October 22, 1895, at New York, N.Y. Elected in 1972. Did not play college basketball. Having played for 27 years, Beckman, in his era, was considered the "Babe Ruth of Basketball." A tough-minded player and accurate free-throw shooter, he toured with several teams before joining the Original Boston Celtics, a virtual all-star collection of talent. A prototype team player because of his team defense and passing abilities, he later became captain of the Celtics in 1922. In addition to his player capacities, he also served as coach for the Baltimore Orioles, Detroit Cardinals and Nanticoke Nans.

Sergei Belov: 6–3, 175 pounds. Born January 23, 1944, in Nashevoko, Russia. Elected in 1992. Did not play college

WORLD RENOWN: *Russia's Sergei Belov has been compared favorably to Jerry West.*

1974–78. She became the first recipient of the Wade Trophy, as the 1978 Women's Basketball Player of the Year. She also was a three-time All-America selection (1976, 1977, 1978) and was named Converse Women's Player of the Year in 1977. A member of the 1979 World University team that won the gold medal in Mexico City, she also earned a silver medal as a member of the 1979 Pan American Team. She was selected to the 1980 Olympic Team that did not participate in the Moscow Games because of the U.S. boycott. She also played with the New Jersey Gems of the Women's Basketball League and was the league's leading scorer in 1981.

Bennie Borgmann: 5–8, 170 pounds. Born November 21, 1899, in Haledon, N.J. Elected in 1961. Did not play college basketball. Routinely selected to various All-Pro teams, Borgmann was a double-figure scorer at a time when teams rarely would score more than 30 points per game. Among his pro teams were the Kingston Colonels, Fort Wayne Hoosiers, Chicago Bruins, Original Celtics, Brooklyn Americans and Newark Mules. A skilled baseball player, he spent several years in the Boston Red Sox farm system and eventually broke into the major leagues in 1932 with the St. Louis Cardinals. In all, he participated in 5,000 combined professional basketball and baseball games.

Joseph Brennan: 5–11, 175 pounds. Born November 15, 1900, in Brooklyn, N.Y. Elected in 1974. Did not play college basketball. Nicknamed "Poison Joe," Brennan went directly from high school to a 17-year professional career. Among his most renown play came while with the all-Irish Brooklyn Visitations. He was the Metropolitan Basketball League's leading scorer in 1922, and led the Brooklyn Dodgers to Met League championships in 1922 and 1923, and the Visitations to ABL championships in 1929, 1931 and 1935. Able to mix speed and savvy, he was a consistent shooter with either hand. Also coached at Manhattan College and St. Francis.

(**Opposite**) **THE BLAZE:** *Carol Blazejowski was the first player to win the Wade Trophy.*

ALL-AMERICAN: *Cosic became the first foreign player to become a collegiate All-American.*

Charles Cooper: 6–4, 215 pounds. Born August 30, 1907, in Newark, Delaware. Elected in 1977. Did not play college basketball. Known as "Tarzan," Cooper was called the best center to play the game by legendary coach and basketball pioneer Joe Lapchick. In a 20-year career, Cooper had his greatest moments with the New York Renaissance and Chicago Bears. Cooper's potent inside play and rebounding proved to be the perfect complement to the Rens' remarkable outside shooting. While with the Rens, he led the team to 88 consecutive victories

and the 1939 World Professional Tournament title. Cooper also served as player-coach of the Bears for two seasons.

Kresimir Cosic: 6–11. Born November 26, 1948 in Zagreb, Croatia. Elected in 1996. Attended Brigham Young University. Cosic's decision to attend BYU paved the way for other international basketball players to play on the U.S. collegiate level. Cosic arrived at BYU after leading Yugoslavia to the 1968 Olympic silver medal. He became the first foreign player to

DUAL DETERMINATION: *Joe Crawford also has made it into two other Halls: AAU Hall of Fame and Women's Basketball Hall of Fame.*

earn All-America honors. Cosic elected to remain an amateur to retain his Olympic eligibility and also participated in the 1972, '76 and '80 Games, leading Yugoslavia to the gold medal in the 1980 Moscow Games. Cosic then emerged as a leading coach, guiding Yugoslavia to a silver medal in 1988 at the Seoul Games.

Joan Crawford: 5–10. Born August 22, 1937, in Fort Smith, Arkansas. Elected in 1997. Attended Clarendon College. A veteran of 14 seasons in the Amateur Athletic Union, the deft passer and rebounder was named to 13 consecutive AAU All-America teams and won 10 AAU championships with Nashville Business College. In addition, she was named Most Valuable Player in the 1963 and 1964 National AAU Tournaments. In international play, Crawford led the United States to a gold medal in the 1959 and 1963 Pan American Games. She also was a member of the 1957 USA World Championship team that defeated Russia for the gold medal. She also is a member of AAU Hall of Fame and Women's Basketball Hall of Fame.

Denise Curry: 6–1. Born August 22, 1959, in Fort Benton, Montana. Elected in 1997. Attended UCLA. A three-time All-America at UCLA, Curry led the Bruins to the 1978 AIAW National Championship. She led UCLA in scoring each of her four seasons and set 14 school records. A 1994 inductee into the UCLA Athletic Hall of Fame, Curry had her jersey number 12 retired along with those of Kareem Abdul-Jabbar, Bill Walton and

(Opposite) RECORD SETTER: *Denise Curry set 14 records during her four years at UCLA.*

Ann Meyers at the 25th anniversary of Pauley Pavilion. Curry also was a member of UCLA's 1978 National Championship softball team. In basketball, she was on gold-medal teams at the 1984 Olympics, the 1983 Pan American Games and the 1979 World Championships. She also was selected to the 1980 Olympic Team that did not participate in the Moscow Games. She played eight professional seasons in Germany, France and Italy.

Forrest S. DeBernardi: 6–1, 172 pounds. Born February 3, 1899, in Nevada, Missouri. Elected in 1961. Attended Westminster College. In addition to playing as a two-time All-America at Westminster College in 1920 and 1921, he was a star on the Kansas City Athletic Club (KCAC) basketball team that finished third in the AAU national tournament in 1920 and won the tournament in 1921. When he retired in 1929, he had participated in 10 national AAU tournaments and was named to the AAU All-American team eight times. Five times he was a member of a national championship team. A versatile player, he was named an AAU All-America at guard, forward and center.

H.G. "Dutch" Dehnert: 6–0, 190 pounds. Born April 5, 1898, in New York, N.Y. Elected in 1969. A member of the Original Celtics, Dehnert was among the innovators of pivot play. His ability to excel with the maneuvers soon had the Celtics using the option as the focus of their attack. His ballhandling and defense helped the Celtics to more than 1,900 victories. When the Celtics joined the American Basketball League in 1926, Dehnert soon led them to titles in 1927 and 1928. From there, he led the Cleveland Rosenblums to two more ABL championships, in 1929 and 1930. He also served as coach of five professional teams.

Anne Donovan: 6–8. Born November 1, 1961 in Ridgewood, N.J. Elected in 1995. Attended Old Dominion. Considered the best player in women's college basketball from 1979 to 1983, Donovan was a

(Opposite) **DID IT ALL:** *Anne Donovan dominated at both the college and professional levels.*

three-time All-America at Old Dominion University. Donovan so dominated the paint that she averaged double figures in points and rebounds over her college career. She ended her career at Old Dominion as the Lady Monarchs' all-time leading scorer (2,719 points), rebounder (1,976) and shot blocker (801). She also thrived in international play. A three-time Olympian (1980, 1984, 1988), she led the United States to gold medals in 1984 and 1988. She played professionally for five years in Japan and one year in Italy. She also has coached at the college and pro levels of the women's game.

Paul Endacott: 5–10, 167 pounds. Born July 3, 1902, in Lawrence, Kansas. Elected in 1972. Attended the University of Kansas. Known for his aggressive defense, Endacott was a two-time All-Missouri Valley Conference team selection at the University of Kansas. Playing under legendary coach Phog Allen, Endacott led Kansas to two national titles and the

DEFENSIVE DERVISH: *Max Friedman may have been the best defensive guard of his era.*

first-ever Missouri Valley Conference undefeated record. He was named to the Associated Press all-time All-American second team. He was named Player of the Year as a senior. He later would play for AAU Phillips Petroleum Company, the team that later became legendary the Phillips 66 unit that dominated AAU competition.

Harold "Bud" Foster: 6–3, 185 pounds. Born May 30, 1906, in Newton, Kansas. Elected in 1964. Attended the University of Wisconsin. An All-Conference player in 1929 and 1930, Foster was the on-court leader for the Wisconsin team that compiled a 43–8 three-year record for Hall of Fame coach Walter Meanwell. Foster briefly then played professionally, before returning to Wisconsin in 1935 to serve as coach, where he compiled a 265–267 record and won three Big Ten Conference titles. His crowning achievement was leading the Badgers to the 1941 NCAA title. He also served as a president of the National Association of Basketball Coaches.

Max "Marty" Friedman: 5–7, 138 pounds. Born July 12, 1889, in New York, N.Y. Elected in 1971. Did not play college basketball. Perhaps the greatest defensive guard of his era, Friedman played professionally from 1910 to 1927 in almost every league in the East. In 1921, he played with the New York Whirlwinds, a team considered one of the greatest professional teams of all time. Among his teammates were Hall of Fame players Barney Sedran and Nat Holman. He closed his playing career as captain of the 1926 American Basketball League champion Cleveland Rosenblums, before emerging as an international promoter of the sport.

William Gates: 6–3, 196 pounds. Born August 30, 1917, in Decatur, Alabama. Elected in 1989. Did not play college basketball. A skilled player from an early age, Pop Gates went directly from a high school championship team (Benjamin Franklin, New York, 1938) to a World Professional Champion (New York Renaissance, 1939). In his second season with the Rens, Gates was named World Tournament All-Pro, an honor he earned

526

eight times in a 12-year professional career. Gates later played for the Long Island Grumman Flyers, coached by Hall of Famer Clair Bee. Gates later would serve as a successful player-coach at several stops, including a five-year run as player-coach of the Harlem Globetrotters.

Robert "Aces" Gruenig: 6–8, 220 pounds. Born March 12, 1913, in Chicago, Illinois. Elected in 1963. Attended Northwestern University. Renown for his dynamic hook shot, Gruenig was among the sport's first great big men. He led the Denver Safeway (1937), Denver Nuggets (1939) and Denver American Legion (1942) teams to AAU championships. In 1948, at the age of 35, he scored 104 points in five AAU tournament games. He was named to AAU All-America first teams 10 times (1937–40, 1942–46, 1948) and to the second team once (1933). Although he briefly attended Northwestern, he never suited up for the Illinois school.

Victor Hanson: 5–10, 175 pounds. Born July 30, 1903, in Watertown, N.Y. Elected in 1960. Attended Syracuse University. Not merely a basketball star, Hanson became the first player also inducted into the College Football Hall of Fame. He also was signed by the baseball Yankees, playing two seasons for New York. On the court, Hanson was part of the 1925–26 Syracuse team that went 19–1 and was named national champion. As a senior, Hanson was named Player of the Year, scoring 280 points, a single-season school record that stood for two decades. Hanson played professionally with the Cleveland Rosenblums and then returned to Syracuse to form his own team, "The All-Americans of Syracuse."

Lusia Harris: 6–3. Born February 10, 1955, in Minter City, Mississippi. Elected in 1992. Attended Delta State University. Considered one of the greatest centers ever to play women's basketball, Harris was a member of the first-ever women's Olympic team in 1976, and scored the game's first points. She ended her career with a silver medal in those Montreal Games and then the 1977 AIAW national championship. While playing for Hall of Fame coach Margaret Wade, the three-time All-America led the Lady Statesmen to three consecutive AIAW national championships (1975, 1976 and 1977) and a remarkable 109–6 overall record. She spent one season playing for the professional Houston Angels.

Marques Haynes: 6–0, 160 pounds. Born October 3, 1926, in Sand Springs, Oklahoma. Elected in 1998. Attended Langston University. Perhaps the finest ballhandler in the history of the sport, and certainly the most colorful, Haynes

(*Left*) **POPS WAS TOPS:** *William Gates thrived with a variety of professional teams.*

(*Right*) **DOUBLE THREAT:** *Victor Hanson also left his mark on the football field.*

STANDING TALL: *Lusia Harris is considered one of the greatest centers in women's basketball.*

528

spent most of his 40-year career with trick-shot teams such as the Harlem Globetrotters and Harlem Magicians. Haynes caught the attention of Harlem Globetrotters owner Abe Saperstein in 1946, during a game Haynes' college team defeated the Globetrotters. Haynes then helped lead the Globetrotters to two victories over George Mikan and the Minneapolis Lakers. Haynes is the first Globetrotter player elected into the Basketball Hall of Fame.

JUST FOR FUN: *Marques Haynes was a skilled player and entertainer.*

Nat Holman: 5–11, 165 pounds. Born October 19, 1896, in New York, N.Y. Elected in 1964. Attended Savage School for Physical Education. A remarkably accurate outside shooter, Holman played most of his career with the Original Celtics. Holman's contributions to the game were the efficient execution of the pivot game and switching man-to-man defense. During his playing career, Holman also was displaying his basketball acumen as coach at City College of New York. In one game, Holman scored 23 points in a 28–25 Hoboken victory. Holman also authored four basketball books: *Scientific Basketball* (1922), *Winning Basketball* (1933), *Championship Basketball* (1942) and *Holman On Basketball* (1950).

Robert J. Houbregs: 6–8, 225 pounds. Born March 12, 1932, in Vancouver, British Columbia. Elected 1987. Attended University of Washington. Renown for his hook shot, Houbregs averaged a school-record 25.6 points per game in 1953 on the way to being selected national Player of the Year. He also was named to the 1953 NCAA All-Tournament team. During his time in college, he had games of 49, 45 and 32 points. Selected by Milwaukee in the NBA draft, he played five seasons with the Hawks, Baltimore Bullets, Boston Celtics, Fort Wayne Pistons and Detroit Pistons. In 1979, he became the first basketball player elected into Washington's Sports Hall of Fame.

Charles "Chuck" Hyatt: 5–11, 160 pounds. Born February 28, 1908, in Syracuse, N.Y. Elected in 1959. Attended University of Pittsburgh. An accurate outside shooter, Hyatt scored 880 points in three seasons at Pittsburgh, as he led the Panthers to the 1928 and 1930 national championships. During those seasons while playing under Hall of Fame coach Dr. Henry Clifford Carlson, he also finished first, second and third in the country in scoring. Player of the Year in 1930, Hyatt went on to a successful AAU career. He coached the Kansas City Blues and Pittsburgh Raiders professional teams, as well as the Universal Pictures and Phillips 66ers amateur teams.

William C. Johnson: 6–4, 185 pounds. Born August 16, 1911, in Oklahoma City, Oklahoma. Elected in 1977. Attended the University of Kansas. Nicknamed "Skinny," Johnson was known for his jumping ability. A three-year starter at Kansas under Hall of Fame coach

Phog Allen in the early 1930s, Johnson led the Jayhawks to a 41–12 record and three Big Six Conference titles. He was named All-Big Six in 1932 and 1933 and All-America in 1933. Johnson went on to a highly successful amateur career, named second-team AAU All-America in 1934. He went on to become coach at Cleveland Chiropractic College.

Edward "Moose" Krause: 6–3, 220 pounds. Born February 2, 1913, in Chicago, Illinois. Elected in 1976. Attended Notre Dame. Among the preeminent big men of his era, Krause dominated the post to the degree that he provided the impetus for the three-second rule. A lineman for Knute Rockne's legendary football teams with the Fighting Irish, he played his basketball at Notre Dame under Hall of Fame coach George Keogan. In an era of dirt courts, Krause led Notre Dame to a 54–12 record in three seasons. A three-time All-America, he was one of the first players to average over 10 points a game. As a coach, Krause later guided the Irish to a 98–48 record.

Robert "Bob" Kurland: 6–10, 230 pounds. Born December 23, 1924, in St. Paul, Minnesota. Elected in 1961. Attended Oklahoma A&M. Among the game's all-time great big men, Kurland

QUICK STUDY: *Nancy Lieberman became the youngest basketball Olympic medal winner.*

HUGE PRESENCE: *Bob Kurland was so imposing he led to a rules change.*

proved so adept at the blocked shot that he emerged as a changing force for the rule outlawing goaltending. In leading Oklahoma A&M to back-to-back national championships in 1945 and 1946, Kurland became the first player to win back-to-back NCAA Tournament MVP awards. Opting against a professional career, he joined the AAU Phillips 66 Oilers and in six seasons led the 66ers to three national championships and a remarkable 369–26 record. In 1948 and 1952, Kurland played on gold-medal-winning Olympic teams, becoming the first player in history to do so.

Nancy Lieberman: 5–10. Born July 1, 1958, in Brooklyn, N.Y. Elected in 1996. Attended Old Dominion. An aggressive point guard who played with a physical nature emulated by few in the women's game, Lieberman, at age 18, became the youngest basketball player in Olympic history to win a medal, as she helped the United States finish second in the 1976 Montreal Olympics. A three-time All-America at Old Dominion University, Lieberman led the Lady Monarchs to back-to-back AIAW National Championships in 1979 and 1980. She was twice named as the Wade Trophy

MAKING INNOVATIONS SINGLE-HANDEDLY: *Hank Luisetti helped deliver the one-handed shot to he sport.*

winner. In 1985, she made history by playing in a men's professional league, with the Springfield Fame of the United States Basketball League.

Angelo "Hank" Luisetti: 6–3, 175 pounds. Born June 16, 1916, in San Francisco, California. Elected in 1959. Attended Stanford. One of the game's great innovators, Luisetti became the sport's first successful practitioner of the one-handed running shot. Twice in his three seasons at Stanford he was named Player of the Year. He averaged 16.1 points and led Stanford to three consecutive Pacific Coast championships. In 1936, in a game at famed Madison Square Garden, he scored 15 points to help Stanford snap Long Island University's 43-game winning streak. Luisetti became the first college player to score 50 points in a game when Stanford defeated Duquesne 92–27 on Jan. 1, 1938.

Branch McCracken: 6–4, 200 pounds. Born June 9, 1908, in Monrovia, Indiana. Elected in 1960. Attended Indiana University. During a fabled career at Indiana, McCracken played center, forward and guard, leading the school in scoring all three of his seasons. Known as "Big Bear" because of his build and continence, he set a Big Ten record as a senior with 147 points. He enjoyed an equally successful coaching career, compiling a 450–231 record in 32 seasons at Indiana and Ball State. He coached Indiana, known as the "Hurrying Hoosiers," to NCAA championships in 1940 and 1953. He also played professionally for four teams.

Jack McCracken: 6–2, 190 pounds. Born June 15, 1911, in Chickasha, Oklahoma. Elected in 1962. Attended Northwest State Teachers College. Known as "Jumping Jack," he was a nationally recognized amateur. In fact, in

FAST TRACK: *Bobby McDermott went to the pros after just one season of high-school ball.*

1939, he was named the greatest player ever by the AAU. He led Denver Safeway to the 1937 championship, the first of three national titles he would garner. As a collegian at Northwest Missouri State Teachers College, McCracken starred for Henry Iba, leading the team to 43 consecutive victories and a perfect 31–0 record in 1929–30. Iba said he considered McCracken one of the finest players he had coached.

Bobby McDermott: 5–11, 180. Born January 7, 1914, in Whitestone, N.Y. Elected in 1988. Did not play college basketball. A premier practitioner of the two-handed set shot, McDermott was voted the "Greatest Player of all-time" in 1946 by National Basketball League coaches. He turned professional after just one year of high school, and starred in the ABL and NBL for 17 years. After leading the Brooklyn Visitations to the ABL title in 1935, he played for the Original Celtics from 1936 to 1939 and 1940 to 1941. In five seasons with the Fort Wayne Zollner Pistons, McDermott won consecutive NBL titles. He would become the only player to lead three leagues (ABL, NYSL, NBL) in scoring.

Ann Meyers: 5–9. Born March 26, 1955, in San Diego, California. Elected in 1993. Attended UCLA. Meyers was the first high school player to make a United States National Team. She was the first woman to receive a full athletic scholarship from UCLA. She was the first women's player named to Kodak's All-America team four straight seasons and the first woman elected to the UCLA Athletic Hall of Fame. She played on the first women's Olympic team, which earned a silver medal at the Montreal

TREND SETTER: *Ann Meyers became the first female player to earn a scholarship to UCLA.*

POINTS WELL MADE: *Before arriving at USC, Cheryl Miller once scored 105 points in a high school game.*

534

Games in 1976. She also was the first woman to earn a tryout with an NBA team, cut early by the Indiana Pacers.

Cheryl Miller: 6–2. Born January 3, 1964 in Riverside, California. Elected in 1995. Attended Southern Cal. At Riverside, Calif., Poly High School, Miller scored 105 points in a game against Notre Vista in 1982. She would eventually guide her school to a 132–4 record. At Southern Cal, Miller scored 3,018 career points and was a four-time All-America. Miller led the Trojans to a 112–20 record and NCAA titles in 1983 and 1984. She also guided the United States to a gold medal in the 1984 Olympics, and gold medals at the 1983 Pan American and 1986 Goodwill Games. She eventually became coach of the WNBA's Phoenix Mercury, and in the 1998 season, led Phoenix to the WNBA Finals against eventual champion Houston.

Charles "Stretch" Murphy: 6–6, 200 pounds. Born April 10, 1907, in Marion, Indiana. Elected in 1960. Attended Purdue. Another of the game's initial great big men, Murphy teamed with John Wooden to form a powerful tandem under Hall of Fame coach Ward "Piggy" Lambert at Purdue. Murphy was considered an elite defender, yet a player also dangerous with the ball. His outlet passes were the key to the development of Purdue's potent running game. He led Purdue to conference titles in 1928 and 1929. He later would play for three professional teams: the Chicago Bruins, Indianapolis Kautskys and Oshkosh All-Stars.

H.O. "Pat" Page: 5–9, 155 pounds. Born March 20, 188,7 in Watervliet, Michigan. Elected in 1962. Attended University of Chicago. Among the game's first defensive specialists, Page, a three-time All-America, led Chicago to three Western Conference titles, a national AAU title and three national collegiate championships. Undersized, Page used his guile to earn the Player of the Year Award in 1901. His savvy later paid off in a successful college coaching career at

QUICK TRIGGER: *Charles Murphy was known for his passes that drove Purdue's attack.*

Butler, University of Chicago and The College of Idaho. As a college coach, he went 267–149, leading Butler to a championship in 1924 and Chicago to the national title game in 1920.

Col. John S. Roosma: 6–1, 188 pounds. Born September 3, 1900, in Passaic, N.J. Elected in 1961. Attended Army. Urged in 1921 to attend the U.S. Military Academy by General Douglas MacArthur, Roosma earned 10 athletic letters in four sports at Army. On the court, he played under Hall of Fame coach Harry Fisher, scoring 1,126 points in 74 games and leading the Cadets to an undefeated 17–0 season in 1923. He was selected All-American three times. He is believed to be the first in college history to score 1,000 points in a career. Among his victories at Army were by 53–8 against Trinity and 66–5 against St. John's College.

Ernest J. Schmidt: 6–3, 180. Born February 12, 1911, in Nashville, Kansas. Elected in 1974. Attended Kansas State Teachers College. A pivot scorer with a wide range of moves, Schmidt was a four-time All-Conference center, as he led Kansas State to four consecutive conference titles. He was nicknamed "One Grand" because he closed his college career with exactly 1,000 points. He led Kansas State to 47 consecutive victories and was selected an All-America in 1932. He also played amateur ball for the Reno Creameries and the Denver Piggly Wiggly. As a prep player, he led his high school to three consecutive state championships.

John J. Schommer: 6–1, 175 pounds. Born January 29, 1884, in Chicago, Illinois. Elected in 1959. Attended the University of Chicago. Nicknamed "Mr. Everything" at the University of Chicago for his excellence in football, basketball, baseball and track, the four-time basketball All-America was an intense competitor. In four years, Schommer's teams lost only seven games, as he led Chicago to three straight Big Ten titles. In 1908 his 80-foot shot with only seconds remaining to help Chicago defeat the University of Pennsylvania and win the national championship. He eventually

would rewrite the basketball rules book and also officiate Big Ten games from 1911 to 1940.

Barney Sedran: 5–4, 115 pounds. Born January 28, 1891, in New York, N.Y. Elected in 1962. Attended City College of New York. The smallest player enshrined in the Basketball Hall of Fame, Sedran earned the nickname "The Mighty Mite of Basketball." Quick and with great court vision, Sedran turned professional in 1912 with the Newburgh Club of the Hudson River League. He then

starred with the Utica team of the New York State League. For nearly two decades, Sedran was considered one of the early game's best players and was one of the few able to figure how to beat the Original Celtics. He went on to stellar coaching career.

Uljana Semjonova: 7–0. Born March 9, 1952 in Daugavpils, Latvia. Elected in 1993. Did not play college basketball. From 1970 to 1985, Semjonova was voted the most popular athlete in Latvia 12 times. Her credentials include an 18-

MR. EVERYTHING: *John J. Schommer excelled in most every sport at the turn of the century.*

year career in which she never lost a game playing in international basketball competition. She won 45 medals in international events, including three gold medals from the World Championships and two gold medals playing for the Soviet Union in the 1976 and 1980 Olympics. In the '76 Games, she scored 32 points against a U.S. team featuring Hall of Famers Ann Meyers and Lusia Harris-Stewart. Her professional career included stints in Russia, Spain and France.

Christian Steinmetz: 5–9, 137 pounds. Born June 28, 1887, in Milwaukee, Wisconsin. Elected in 1961. Attended the University of Wisconsin. In an era when points were hard to come by, Steinmetz established himself as one of the premier scorers in college basketball's early days. In 1904–05, he scored 23 more points than all opposing teams tallied against the Badgers. He scored a remarkable 462 of Wisconsin's 681 points, including a 50-point outburst against Sparta. His impressive totals came despite his diminutive stature. In 1905, he led Wisconsin to an undefeated regular season, with the lone loss to Columbia for the national championship.

John A. "Cat" Thompson: 5–10, 160 pounds. Born February 10, 1906, in St. George, Utah. Elected in 1962. Attended Montana State. A quick and agile performer, he was nicknamed "The Cat" by Montana State coach G. Ott Romney. At Montana State, Thompson led the Golden Bobcats to a 72–4 record over two seasons. The three-time All-America averaged 15.4 points a game at a time when the national scoring average was 40 points per team. He led Montana State to the national championship with a 36–2 record in 1929. He briefly played professionally for the Pacific Coast Athletic Club. Later, he would serve as a high school coach in Montana and Idaho.

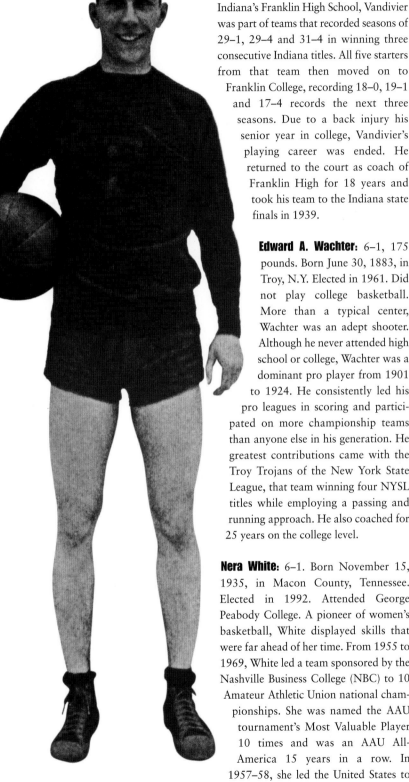

(Opposite) **LATVIAN LEGEND:** *Uljana Semjonova won 45 medals in international competitions.*

PREP PRODIGY: *Robert Vandivier's high school team stayed together for college.*

Robert "Fuzzy" Vandivier: 6–0, 170 pounds. Born December 26, 1903, in Franklin, Indiana. Elected in 1975. Attended Franklin College. A captain at Indiana's Franklin High School, Vandivier was part of teams that recorded seasons of 29–1, 29–4 and 31–4 in winning three consecutive Indiana titles. All five starters from that team then moved on to Franklin College, recording 18–0, 19–1 and 17–4 records the next three seasons. Due to a back injury his senior year in college, Vandivier's playing career was ended. He returned to the court as coach of Franklin High for 18 years and took his team to the Indiana state finals in 1939.

Edward A. Wachter: 6–1, 175 pounds. Born June 30, 1883, in Troy, N.Y. Elected in 1961. Did not play college basketball. More than a typical center, Wachter was an adept shooter. Although he never attended high school or college, Wachter was a dominant pro player from 1901 to 1924. He consistently led his pro leagues in scoring and participated on more championship teams than anyone else in his generation. He greatest contributions came with the Troy Trojans of the New York State League, that team winning four NYSL titles while employing a passing and running approach. He also coached for 25 years on the college level.

Nera White: 6–1. Born November 15, 1935, in Macon County, Tennessee. Elected in 1992. Attended George Peabody College. A pioneer of women's basketball, White displayed skills that were far ahead of her time. From 1955 to 1969, White led a team sponsored by the Nashville Business College (NBC) to 10 Amateur Athletic Union national championships. She was named the AAU tournament's Most Valuable Player 10 times and was an AAU All-America 15 years in a row. In 1957–58, she led the United States to the World Basketball Championship, where she was named MVP. She also toured on all-star teams to Russia, West

WHITE FLAG: *Nera White carried the banner for women's basketball at the beginning.*

Germany, France, Brazil, Venezuela and Great Britain.

John R. Wooden: 5-10, 185. Born: October 14, 1910, in Martinsville, Indiana. Elected in 1960 as a player and 1973 as a coach. Attended Purdue. Although inducted first as a player, it was coaching that cemented the Wooden legacy. With Wooden as coach, UCLA set all-time records with four perfect 30-0 seasons, 88 consecutive victories, 38 straight NCAA Tournament victories, 20 conference championships, and 10 national championships, including seven in a row. Wooden first learned the game when he was eight years old in 1918, 27 years after the invention of basketball, shooting at a tomato basket attached to a barn. The 1932 Player of the Year at

Purdue, Wooden learned his lessons well under Hall of Fame coach Ward "Piggy" Lambert.

NBA-Associated Coaches

Red Auerbach: Born September 20, 1917, at Brooklyn, N.Y. Coached 20 BAA/NBA seasons (938–479) with Capitols, Blackhawks, Celtics. Coached Celtics' 1957, 1959, 1960, 1961, 1962, 1963, 1964, 1965, 1966 championship teams. NBA Coach of the Year 1965. Coach of 25th Anniversary All-Time Team. Elected 1968.

Chuck Daly: Born July 20, 1930, at St. Mary's, Pa. Coached 12 NBA seasons (564–379) with Cavaliers, Pistons, Nets.

Coached Pistons' 1989, 1990 championship teams. Coached U.S. Dream Team to Olympic gold medal in 1992. Coached 8 college seasons (151–62) at Boston College, Pennsylvania. Elected 1994.

Alex Hannum: Born July 19, 1923, at Los Angeles. Coached 16 NBA/ABA seasons (649–564) with Hawks, Syracuse, Warriors, 76ers, San Diego, Oakland, Nuggets. Coached Hawks' 1958 championship team, 76ers' 1967 championship team and Oakland's 1969 ABA championship team. NBA Coach of the Year 1964. ABA Coach of the Year 1969. Elected 1998.

Red Holzman: Born August 10, 1920, at Brooklyn, N.Y. Coached 18 NBA seasons (696–604) with Hawks, Knicks. Coached Knicks' 1970, 1973 championship teams. NBA Coach of the Year 1970. Elected 1986.

Alvin (Doggie) Julian: Born April 5, 1901, at Reading, Pa. Coached 2 NBA seasons (47–81) with Celtics. Coached Holy Cross to 1947 NCAA Tournament championship. Also coached at Albright, Muhlenberg, Dartmouth. Elected 1967.

Ken Loeffler: Born April 14, 1902, at Beaver Falls, Pa. Coached 3 BAA seasons (79–90) with Bombers, Steamrollers. Coached La Salle to 1954 NCAA Tournament championship and 1952 NIT title. Coached Geneva, Yale, La Salle and Texas A&M to 310 victories. Elected 1964.

Frank McGuire: Born November 8, 1916, at New York. Coached 1 NBA season (49–31) with Warriors. Coached North Carolina to 1957 NCAA Tournament championship. Coached St. John's, North Carolina and South Carolina to 550–235 record. NCAA Coach of the Year three times. Elected 1976.

Jack Ramsay: Born February 21, 1925, at Philadelphia. Coached 21 NBA seasons (864–783) with 76ers, Braves, Trail Blazers, Pacers. Coached Trail Blazers' 1977 championship team. Coached 11 college seasons (234–72) with St. Joseph's. Elected 1992.

(Above) **DOG DAYS:** *Alvin "Doggie" Julian.*

(Below) **BOMBS AWAY:** *Ken Loeffler led the Bombers, Steamrollers and four college teams.*

Lenny Wilkens: Born October 28, 1937, at Brooklyn, N.Y. Coached 25 NBA seasons (1,120–908) with Supersonics, Trail Blazers, Cavaliers, Hawks. Coached Supersonics' 1979 championship team. Coached U.S. team to gold medal at 1996 Olympic Games. NBA Coach of the Year 1994. Elected 1998, joined John Wooden as only two-time inductee, player and coach.

Non-NBA Coaches

Phog Allen: Born November 18, 1885, in Jamesport, Missouri. Elected in 1959. Initially a player under basketball founder James Naismith at Kansas, Allen would emerge as the "Father of Basketball Coaching." Allen coached 48 seasons at four schools, compiling a 746–264 record and retired as the winningest coach in collegiate basketball history. In 39 seasons at Kansas, he won 590 games, leading Kansas to the 1952 NCAA national championship. A founder of the National Association of Basketball Coaches, he served as the organization's first president. He pushed for basketball's inclusion as an Olympic sport and then guided the United States to the gold in 1952 in Helsinki.

Harold Anderson: Born September 11, 1902, in Akron, Ohio. Elected in 1985. Among the first coaches in college basketball to win 500 games, Anderson recorded his greatest accomplishments at Bowling Green State University, from 1942 to 1963. He produced a 362–185 record that included six NIT tournament appearances and three trips to the NCAA Tournament. Throughout the success, he was considered one of the game's true sportsmen. He also was among the pioneers of the running game and oversaw the initial stages of the career of Hall of Fame center Nate Thurmond. As a player at Otterbein College, he twice was named All-Conference.

Sam Barry: Born December 17, 1892, in Aberdeen, South Dakota. Elected in 1979. After a four-year stint at Knox College, Barry coached Iowa for seven seasons, leading the Hawkeyes to the 1923 Big Ten championship and a share of the 1926 title. He then coached USC for 18 years, leading the Trojans to a 260–138 record, a record that included winning Pacific Coast Conference titles in 1930, 1935 and 1940. Under Barry, USC won the conference's Southern Division seven times and finished third in the 1940 NCAA Tournament. In 1948, Barry, adept at teaching many sports, led the USC baseball team to an NCAA title, and also served as an assistant football coach.

Ernest A. Blood: Born October 4, 1872 in Manchester, New Hampshire. Elected in 1960. A success at every coaching level, Blood coached for 51 years, compiling a 1,268–165 record. An advocate of offensive-driven basketball, from 1915 to 1924 he coached the Passaic, N.J., High School "Wonder Teams" to a 200–1 record that included a high school-record 159-game winning streak over five seasons. Blood's Passaic teams won seven

New Jersey championships. His 1921–1922 team, which won 33 consecutive games, outscored its opposition 2,293–612. He also coached at Army and Clarkson University. His college teams had a combined 56–7 record in his two seasons at that level.

Howard G. Cann: Born October 11, 1895, in Bridgeport, Connecticut. Elected in 1968. A coach whose teams were fundamentally sound and well prepared, he proved to be a dominant figure at New York University. Aided by rabid crowds when his team's games were played at Madison Square Garden, in 35 seasons Cann coached NYU to a 409–232 record. He led the Violets to an undefeated season in 1933–34, a trip to the NCAA final in 1945, and to the NIT final in 1948. He was named national Coach of the Year in 1947. A respected player, he was named Player of the Year in 1920 when he led the Violets to the AAU championship. He also was an Olympic shot-putter.

Dr. H. Clifford Carlson: Born July 4, 1894, in Murray City, Ohio. Elected in 1959. A practicing physician in addition to serving as a coach, Carlson was an intriguing personality. An offensive-minded zealot, he devised the Figure 8 offense, an innovation that many other coaches copied. In 1922, Carlson designed the offense as coach at the University of Pittsburgh. In 1928, Pittsburgh went a perfect 21–0 and won the national championship. Carlson's Panthers would also win another title, in 1930. He also was among the first coaches to take his teams west for competition. He played collegiately at Pittsburgh, earning letters also in baseball and football.

Lou Carnesecca: Born January 5, 1925, in New York, N.Y. Elected in 1992. An icon at St. John's, Carnesecca guided each of his St. John's teams to postseason appearances. His 1985 Redmen advanced to the Final Four, and his 1979 and 1991 teams competed in NCAA Regional Finals. He became the 30th coach in NCAA history to reach the 500-victory mark. He had eighteen 20-victory seasons at St. John's and averaged more than 20 a

year. He was voted national Coach of the Year in 1983 and 1985. From 1970 to 1973, Carnesecca coached the New Jersey Nets of the ABA, taking the Nets to the 1972 Finals. He was known for the eye-catching sweaters he would wear on the sidelines later in his career.

Ben Carnevale: Born October 30, 1915, in Raritan, N.J. Elected in 1970. Perhaps no coach in the Hall had to make the accommodations made by Carnevale. While it is impressive enough that in 20 seasons at Navy he compiled a 257–160 record, consider that, at the time, Naval Academy restrictions meant the school could not feature a player 6 feet 4 or taller. Carnevale began his college-coaching tenure at North Carolina, where he led the Tar Heels to the finals of the 1946 NCAA Tournament. His teams were known for disciplined, aggressive defense. Five of his teams qualified for the NCAA Tournament, and two others appeared in the NIT. He was named College Coach of the Year in 1947.

Pete Carril: Born July 10, 1930, in Bethlehem, Pennsylvania. Elected in 1997. Carril took over the basketball program at Princeton University in 1967 and became the first Division I coach to record 500 victories (525–273) without the ability to provide a scholarship, because of his school's Ivy League status. With lesser talents on his rosters, Carril devised a wonderful pick-and-roll strategy that played to the strengths of his shooters. Carril's teams led the nation in scoring defense 14 of his final 21 seasons. Over Carril's 29 seasons, Princeton won 514 games, recorded only one losing season, won 13 Ivy League Championships and earned 13 postseason tournament bids.

Everett Case: Born June 21, 1900, in Anderson, Indiana. Elected in 1982. Among the earliest of sideline motivators, the "Old Grey Fox" worked the sidelines with a fervor. In 21 seasons at four high schools, Case compiled a 467–124 record. He then moved on to North Carolina State for 18 seasons. From 1946 to 1964, Case's teams there went 376–133, winning six straight Southern Conference titles and four Atlantic

Conference titles. Case three times was voted ACC Coach of the Year. Under Case, the Wolfpack finished third in the 1947 NIT and third in the 1950 NCAA Tournament.

Jody Conradt: Born May 13, 1941, in Goldthwaite, Texas. Elected in 1998. When Conradt's Texas team defeated Northwestern, 89–86, on Dec. 18, 1997, she became only the eighth coach in Division I men's and women's basketball history to win 700 games. She became Texas coach in 1976 and achieved unparalleled success. Conradt has coached four Olympians, 20 All-Americas, six Southwest Conference Players of the Year, two Wade Trophy winners, two National Players of the Year, one Broderick Award winner and 20 players who have gone on to professional basketball careers. She has served as women's athletic director at Texas since 1992 and has been inducted into the Texas Women's (1986), International Women's Sports (1995), Texas Sports (1998) and Women's Basketball (1999) Halls of Fame.

Denny Crum: Born March 5, 1937, in San Fernando, California. Elected in 1994. An icon at the University of Louisville, Crum has taken his Cardinals to more Finals Fours than all but three coaches. In addition to producing those six appearances, Crum guided Louisville to the 1980 and 1986 NCAA championships. An assistant under John Wooden at UCLA for three NCAA titles, Crum in 1993 became the second fastest coach to win 500 games. He has been named College Coach of the Year three times. Crum coached the 1977 USA World University Team to a gold medal and the 1987 Pan American team to a silver medal.

Everett S. Dean: Born March 18, 1898, in Livonia, Indiana. Elected in 1966. After a three-year playing career at Indiana University and being named to the 1921 All-America team, Dean started his coaching career at Carleton College, where he compiled a 45–4 record. Dean returned to coach his alma mater in 1924, and in 1926, led the Hoosiers to their first Big Ten championship. In 14 seasons at Indiana, Dean won 163 games while losing 93 and shared three Big Ten titles. He then moved on to have comparable success at Stanford, leading the Cardinal to the 1942 national championship.

Antonio Diaz-Miguel: Born July 6, 1933, in Alcazar de San Juan, Ciudad Real, Spain. Elected in 1997. Coach of the Spanish National Team from 1965 to 1992, Diaz-Miguel guided the squad to six Olympic berths, including a silver medal in the 1984 Games in Los Angeles. His teams also participated in 14 European Championships and four World Championships. He coached the European All-Star team six times and was named the "Best Spanish Coach" of the 1980s. In addition to coaching a team strong on fundamentals, he also was keenly aware of the need for sportsmanship on the international level, spending much of his time lecturing on the subject.

Edgar A. Diddle: Born March 12, 1895, in Gradyville, Kentucky. Elected in 1972. As coach at Western Kentucky for 42 seasons, Diddle was known for his impassioned approach on the sidelines. From 1922 to 1964, he won 759 of 1,061 games at Western Kentucky. He became the first coach to coach 1,000 games at one school. His teams won or shared 31 conference titles in three separate leagues and competed in 11 postseason tournaments. He is considered one of the pioneers of the fast-paced approach. From 1934 to 1949 and 1947 to 1954, the Hilltoppers won 20 games or more in all but one season.

Bruce Drake: Born December 5, 1905, in Gentry, Texas. Elected in 1973. As coach at Oklahoma for 17 seasons from 1938 to 1955), Drake led the Sooners to six Big Six titles. Guiding mostly undersized players, Drake's team innovated a weave that came to be known as the "Drake Shuffle." A two-time All-America as a player at Oklahoma, he returned to his alma mater and coached the freshman team for 10 years before being named head coach in 1938. He led Oklahoma's varsity to a 200–181 record and three NCAA Tournament appearances. His 1947 team lost in the NCAA final to Holy Cross.

Clarence Gaines: Born May 21, 1923, in Paducah, Kentucky. Elected in 1982. Known as "Big House," Gaines retired in 1993 with 828 victories. Over a record 47 years at Winston-Salem State University, his teams won 20 or more games 18 times, capturing the Central Intercollegiate Athletic Association (CIAA) champion-ship 12 times. Gaines stressed a fast-paced, athletic game that played into the hands of arguably his greatest product, guard Earl "The Pearl" Monroe. In 1967, the Rams compiled a 31–1 record and Gaines was named Coach of the Year. In 1989, he was elected president of the National Association of Basketball Coaches.

Jack Gardner: Born March 29, 1910, in Texico, New Mexico. Elected in 1984. "The Fox" guided both Kansas State and Utah into the Final Four. In 28 years of coaching at the major college level, Gardner's teams compiled a 486–235 record. Factor in his 10 years (1933–43) of coaching in amateur, high school, junior-college and military ball, and his record stands at 649–278. Gardner coached Kansas State to Final Four appearances in 1948 and 1951. He then coached Utah to the Final Four in 1961 and 1966. Another proponent of the running game, Gardner was able to find success with his lineups regardless of height.

Amory T. "Slats" Gill: Born May 1, 1901, in Salem, Oregon. Elected in 1968. Gill's Oregon State teams were known as much for their sportsmanship as skill. In 36 seasons at Oregon State, he compiled a 599–392 record and captured five Pacific Coast Conference titles. His 1949 and 1963 teams placed fourth in the NCAA Tournament. A past president of the National Association of Basketball Coaches, he coached in the 1964 NABC All-Star Game. He also served as athletic director at Oregon from 1964 to 1966. The coliseum on Oregon State's campus is named in Gill's honor. He played at Oregon State from 1920 to 1924.

Aleksandr Gomelsky: Born January 18, 1928, in Leningrad, Russia. Elected in 1995. Gomelsky is known as the father of Soviet men's basketball. In 29 years of coaching, he compiled a 490–177 record. His Soviet National Team won seven European Championships (1959, 1963, 1965, 1967, 1969, 1979, and 1981) and two World Championships (1967, 1982). Gomelsky established his international prowess in the Olympic Games. He led the Soviet Union to a pair of bronze medals in 1968 and 1980, the silver medal in 1964, and most notably, the 1988 gold medal in Seoul. Gomelsky was renown for his coaching clinics and has authored 10 books on basketball strategy, tactics and techniques.

Marv Harshman: Born October 4, 1917, in Eau Claire, Wisconsin. Elected in 1985. From 1945 to 1985, Harshman compiled 642 victories at Pacific Lutheran (241–121), Washington State University (155–181) and the University of Washington (246–146). At Pacific Lutheran, he coached four NAIA District I basketball champions. At the University of Washington, he was selected NCAA Division I Coach of the Year in 1984 and Pac-10 Coach of the Year in 1982 and 1984. Four of his Washington teams won 20 or more games. He served as a member of the U.S. Olympic Committee from 1975 to 1981 and coached the United States to a gold medal in the 1975 Pan American Games. He served as president of the NABC in 1981.

Don Haskins: Born March 14, 1930, in Enid, Oklahoma. Elected in 1997. In 1966, Haskins' all-black Texas Western team upset the all-white Kentucky team coached by Adolph Rupp for the NCAA championship. In 38 seasons at what would become Texas-El Paso, Haskins had only four losing seasons. His record included seven Western Athletic Conference championships, four WAC tournament titles, 14 NCAA Tournament berths and seven trips to the NIT. A gruff personality known as "The Bear," Haskins served as an assistant Olympic coach in 1972. After playing under legendary Hank Iba at Oklahoma A&M, Haskins used his coaching skills to prepare Tiny Archibald and Tim Hardaway for the NBA.

Edgar S. Hickey: Born December 20, 1902, in Reynolds, Nebraska. Elected in 1979. Known as "The Little General" during a 35-year coaching career, Hickey found success at Creighton, St. Louis University and Marquette. A strategist who often would draw plays out with chalk on the sideline, he compiled a 212–89 record at St. Louis, and, along with Hall of Famer "Easy" Ed Macauley, led St. Louis to a 24–3 record and the NIT title in 1947–48. Hickey and Macauley became known at St. Louis as "Mutt & Jeff" for their disparate builds. An NABC president in 1954, he was voted Coach of the Year in 1959.

Howard A. Hobson: Born July 4, 1903, in Portland, Oregon. Elected in 1965. A star player at Oregon, Hobson was among the first to take a western power to the East Coast. From 1933 to 1956, Hobson coached at Southern Oregon College, Oregon and Yale. His 27-year overall record was 495–291, a record that included leading Oregon to the first-ever NCAA title in 1939, as well as three Pacific Coast Conference titles. His Yale teams won or shared five Big Three crowns. Also known as a distinguished writer, he authored several basketball tomes. He conducted clinics in 16 countries and was a member of the U.S. Olympic Basketball Committee for 12 years.

Hank Iba: Born August 6, 1904, in Easton, Missouri. Elected in 1969. A true sideline legend. Behind dominating 7-foot center Bob Kurland, Iba's Oklahoma A&M (later Oklahoma State) teams became the first to win consecutive NCAA titles, in 1945 and 1946. His Oklahoma A&M teams won 14 Midwestern Valley titles, and were largely responsible for generating most of Iba's 767 victories. He also coached at Maryville College and the University of Colorado. He is the only coach in U.S. Olympic history to win two Olympic gold medals (1964 in Tokyo; 1968 in Mexico City). Dishearteningly, he also was victimized by shaky officiating in the 1972 Olympics, left with a silver medal his team refused to accept.

Frank W. Keaney: Born June 5, 1886, in Boston, Massachusetts. Elected in 1960.

Among the pioneers of aggressive, up-tempo offense, Keaney's tactics enabled his 1939 Rhode Island unit to become the first college team to average more than 50 points per game. In 1943, Rhode Island averaged over two points a minute, at 80.7 points, to earn the nickname, "The Firehouse Gang." In 27 seasons at Rhode Island, Keaney never had a losing season, in going 403–124 and leading his team to four NIT appearances. He also became the first coach ever signed by the Boston Celtics, but Keaney's doctor did not allow him to take the job.

George E. Keogan: Born March 8, 1890, in Minnesota Lake, Minnesota. Elected in 1961. Passionate about man-to-man defense and post play, Keogan arrived at Notre Dame in 1923 as head basketball and baseball coach, as well as assistant to legendary football coach Knute Rockne. In 20 seasons, Keogan compiled a 327–97 record at Notre Dame and never had a losing season. Keogan's greatest player, three-time All-America and Hall of Famer Edward "Moose" Krause, was named as his successor. Before arriving at Notre Dame, at Superior State, St. Louis, St. Thomas, Allegheny and Valparaiso, he had a combined record of 85–28.

Bob Knight: Born October 25, 1940, in Massillon, Ohio. Elected in 1991. An icon at Indiana, known for his driving style, Knight produced three NCAA championships (1976, 1981, 1987) at Indiana. Knight learned the game at Ohio State, as a player under Hall of Fame coach Fred Taylor, and was on the team that won the 1960 NCAA championship. Knight then guided Army to a 102–50 record. More than 15 of Knight's former assistant coaches have become head coaches at the collegiate level, including Duke's Mike Krzyzewski. A four-time national Coach of the Year, in 1984 Knight became one of only three coaches to win titles at the Olympic Games, NCAA Tournament and NIT.

Ward L. Lambert: Born May 28, 1888, in Deadwood, South Dakota. Elected in 1960. With an All-America lineup of future Hall of Famers Charles "Stretch" Murphy and John Wooden, Lambert

achieved great success at Purdue. In 29 seasons of preaching an attacking style, Lambert compiled a 371–152 record at Purdue, including the 1932 national championship. Overall, he led the Boilermakers to 11 Big Ten titles and a 228–105 Big Ten record. He also authored the book, Practical Basketball, one of the early guides of the game. He also served as Commissioner of the National Professional Basketball League from 1946 to 1949.

Harry Litwack: Born September 20, 1907, in Austria. Elected in 1976. A two-time captain of Temple's basketball team, Litwack played seven seasons with the professional Philadelphia SPHAs from 1930 to 1936 and helped the team capture championships in both the Eastern Basketball League and American Basketball League. He then coached Temple's freshman team to a 181–32 record from 1931 to 1951, and even doubled as Eddie Gottlieb's assistant coach with the Philadelphia Warriors in 1950–51. He became Temple's head coach in 1952 and compiled a 373–193 record. He directed the Owls to 13 postseason tournaments, including the NIT championship in 1969 and third-place NCAA finishes in 1956 and 1958.

A.C. "Dutch" Lonborg: Born March 16, 1898, in Gardner, Illinois. Elected in 1973. A second-team All-America selection at Kansas under legendary Phog Allen, Lonborg coached for 29 years at McPherson College, Washburn University and Northwestern University. In 1925, Lonborg's Washburn team won the national AAU title and became the last college team to do so. After compiling a 63–15 four-year record at Washburn, Lonborg enjoyed his greatest coaching success at Northwestern. In 23 years there, he won 237 games and directed Northwestern to the Big Ten title in 1931. In 1950, Lonborg returned to Kansas as athletic director for 14 years.

Arad A. McCutchan: Born July 4, 1912, in Evansville, Indiana. Elected in 1981. A legendary coach at the University of Evansville, he compiled a 515–313 record at the school. During his 31 years at his alma mater, where he starred and led the Purple Aces in scoring three years, McCutchan won 14 Indiana conference titles and five NCAA smaller-school championships. His 1965 team went 29–0, earning McCutchan his second consecutive honor as NCAA Coach of the Year Award. He coached teams at the Olympic trials in 1960 and 1968 and was an assistant coach for the U.S. Pan American team in 1971.

Al McGuire: Born September 7, 1928, in New York, N.Y. Elected in 1992. As the Marquette coach from 1964 to 1977, McGuire won both NCAA (1977) and NIT (1970) championships. In 1971, he was named Coach of the Year following Marquette's 28–1 season. He first compiled a 109–64 record at Belmont Abbey, including five tournament appearances. He led Marquette to 11 straight postseason appearances and a 295–80 record. Prior to his coaching career, he captained the 1951 St. John's team that finished 26–5 and in third place in the NIT. He also played professionally with the New York Knicks and the Baltimore Bullets.

Dr. Walter E. Meanwell: Born January 26, 1884, in Leeds, England. Elected in 1959. Known as everything from "Doc" to "Little Doctor" to "Napoleon of Basketball" to "The Little Giant" to "The Wizard," Meanwell was among the first coaches to instill a sense of order in the game, designing precise actions to a game that had run amok in its initial years. He implemented those measures as the first coach at the University of Wisconsin in 1912. In his first three seasons at Wisconsin, his Badgers won 44 of 45 games, and in 20 seasons, won 70 percent of their games. Before retiring in 1934, Meanwell had coached the University of Wisconsin to eight conference championships.

Ray Meyer: Born December 18, 1913, in Chicago, Illinois. Elected in 1979. Through 42 seasons, Meyer compiled a 724–354 record at DePaul, guiding the Blue Demons to 21 postseason appearances. Meyer recorded 37 winning

seasons and twelve 20-victory seasons, including seven straight from 1978 to 1984. Two Meyer-coached DePaul teams reached the Final Four. Meyer was named Coach of the Year four times, guiding such future NBA stars as Mark Aguirre and Terry Cummings. Meyer also coached a College All-Star team that played a nationwide tour against the Harlem Globetrotters. As a player, Meyer was a captain under Hall of Fame coach George Keogan at Notre Dame.

Ralph Miller: Born March 9, 1919, in Chanute, Kansas. Elected in 1988. As a player at the University of Kansas, Miller learned the game from Hall of Fame coach Phog Allen. Miller then began a 38-year collegiate coaching career in Division I at Wichita State University in 1951, continuing on to Iowa and Oregon State. While at Wichita State, Miller won

220 games, one conference title and received one NCAA and three NIT bids. While at Iowa, he recorded 95 wins, including a 14–0 Big 10 Conference record in 1970 and an NCAA bid. Miller departed Iowa for Oregon State after winning the Big 10 title in 1970. From 1980 to 1982, Miller's Beavers captured three consecutive Pac-10 Conference titles, won 77 of 88 games and compiled a 49–5 conference record.

Billie Moore: Born May 5, 1943, in Westmoreland, Kansas. Elected in 1999. The first coach in women's basketball history to lead two schools to national championships, she achieved the feat at Cal State-Fullerton and UCLA. In 1970, her first season at California State-Fullerton, Moore led her team to the 1970 Association of Intercollegiate Athletics for Women (AIAW) national

TWIN TITLES: *Billie Moore led two schools to women's collegiate titles, the first to do so.*

title. In her eight seasons at Fullerton (1969–77), she compiled a 140–15 record. She continued her coaching successes at UCLA for 16 seasons (1977–93), where she compiled a 296–181 record and led her team to the 1978 AIAW national title.

Aleksandar Nikolic: Born October 28, 1924 in Sarajevo, Yugoslavia. Elected in 1998. The "Father of Yugoslavian Basketball," Nikolic took over the Yugoslavian National Team in 1953 and won silver medals in the 1961 and 1965 European Championships and a bronze in 1963. In 1969, Nikolic took over Italian club team Ignis Varese and over a four-year span won three national titles, three European titles, three Italy Cups and two International Cups. After an 11-year stretch away from the Yugoslavian National Team, Nikolic returned in 1976 and coached the squad to the 1977 European Championship and the 1978 World Championships. He died in 2000.

Cesare Rubini: Born November 2, 1923, in Trieste, Italy. Elected in 1994. As both a player and a coach from 1941 to 1978, Rubini methodically built the Simmenthal Club of Milan and Italian national basketball program from scratch. Rubini won 15 Italian Basketball Championships, five as a player (1950–55) and 10 as a coach. During his 31 years as head coach of the Simmenthal Club of Milan, Rubini compiled a 322–28 record. A graduate of the University of Trieste, Rubini has been a member of FIBA's Central Board since 1984, and has served as president of the World Association of Basketball Coaches since 1979.

Adolph Rupp: Born September 2, 1901, in Halstead, Kansas. Elected in 1969. In winning 875 games in 41 years of coaching, Rupp took more than 80 percent of his players from the state of Kentucky and built the program at the University of Kentucky. His teams won four NCAA championships (1948, 1949, 1951, 1958), one NIT title in 1946, appeared in 20 NCAA Tournaments and

(Opposite) **CENTER STAGE:** *John Thompson's Georgetown won the 1984 NCAA title.*

captured 27 Southeastern Conference titles. Twenty-four of his players earned All-American honors, seven captured Olympic gold medals and 28 played professionally. He was a four-time Coach of the Year. He also co-coached the 1948 U.S. Olympic team to a gold medal; five members of that Olympic team were from the University of Kentucky.

Leonard D. Sachs: Born August 7, 1897, in Chicago, Illinois. Elected in 1961. In an era when goaltending was allowed, Sachs devised his strategies around pivot play and a 2–2–1 zone that left a player almost as a defender of the basket. Sachs played professional football for the Chicago Cardinals before moving on to become basketball coach at Loyola University from 1923 to 1942. In 19 seasons at the school, Sachs compiled a 224–129 record, including a 31-game winning streak from 1928 to 1930. Sachs also was a member of the Illinois Athletic Club team that won the national amateur title in 1917.

Everett F. Shelton: Born May 12, 1898, in Cunningham, Kansas. Elected in 1980. Over 46 years, Shelton coached at the high school, college and AAU levels and compiled an 850–437 record. His best seasons were at the University of Wyoming from 1939 to 1959. In 19 seasons, he compiled a 328–200 record, and led the Cowboys to eight conference championships, eight NCAA Tournament appearances and the 1943 NCAA championship. In 1932, he developed a five-man weave, an offense that he later used to capture the 1937 AAU championship with the Denver Safeways. As president of the NABC (1959–1960), Shelton was instrumental in launching the National Interpreter of Basketball Rules for Officials.

Dean Smith: Born February 28, 1931, in Emporia, Kansas. Elected in 1983. Smith began coaching North Carolina in 1962 and reached the Final Four 11 times and won the NCAA championship in 1982 and 1993. Following a 94–74 victory over Louisville in the 1997 NCAA Tournament, Smith became the NCAA's all-time winningest coach, at 879–254, topping Hall of Famer Adolph Rupp's

875 victories. A four-time national Coach of the Year, Smith played on the Kansas Jayhawks' NCAA championship team in 1952 with Hall of Famer Clyde Lovellette and under the legendary coach Phog Allen. He also coached the 1976 U.S. Olympic Team to a gold medal.

Fred R. Taylor: Born December 3, 1924, in Zanesville, Ohio. Elected in 1986. A starting forward on Ohio State's Big 10 championship team that finished third nationally in 1950, Taylor then played three years of professional baseball in the Washington Senators' organization. He was named head coach of his alma mater in 1958 and in his 18 years in Columbus, the Buckeyes won the 1960 NCAA championship, were finalists in 1961 and 1962 and finished third in 1968. He compiled a 297–158 record as the Buckeyes coach. Among those Taylor coached were Hall of Famers Jerry Lucas, John Havlicek and Bob Knight.

John Thompson: Born September 2, 1941, in Washington, D.C. Elected in 1999. In 27 years as coach at Georgetown, Thompson compiled a 596–239 record. His teams appeared in three NCAA Final Fours (1982, 1984, 1985), played in 14 consecutive NCAA Tournaments (1979–92), made 24 consecutive postseason appearances (20 NCAA, 4 NIT) and won seven Big East Tournament championships. He won seven Coach of the Year Awards. Thompson also led the United States to a bronze medal in the 1988 Seoul Olympics and was an assistant coach for the 1976 gold medal-winning team. As a member of the Boston Celtics, Thompson was the back-up center for Bill Russell on two NBA championship teams (1965 and 1966).

Margaret Wade: December 30, 1912, in McCool, Mississippi. Elected in 1985. In 1959, Wade returned to her alma mater as head of the women's physical education department at Delta State. Fourteen years later, Delta State resurrected its women's basketball program, and, at age 60, Wade met the challenge of developing an elite national basketball program. Her first team compiled a 16–2 record. The next three seasons produced an unprecedented three AIAW national championships

(1975–77) and a 93–4 record that included a 51-game winning string. Wade's Delta State teams were led by fellow Hall of Famer Lusia Harris. In 1979, Wade retired with a 157–23 record. Each year, women's basketball presents the Wade Trophy, awarded to the top women's collegiate player.

Stanley H. Watts: Born August 30, 1911 in Murray, Utah. Elected in 1986. Watts became the sixth coach in history to win 100 games in his first five years. In 23 seasons at Brigham Young University, Watts compiled a 371–254 (.594) record. His Cougars teams won eight conference titles, appeared in 11 postseason tournaments and captured the 1951 and 1966 National Invitation Tournament championships. Watts was chosen as BYU's freshman coach in 1947 and inherited the varsity team in 1949. Watts' book, Developing an Offensive Attack in Basketball (1958), became a standard manual on fast-break offense, something that his BYU teams played with aplomb.

Phil Woolpert: Born December 19, 1915 in Danville, Kentucky. Elected in 1992. One of only six coaches in NCAA history to win back-to-back national championships, Woolpert accomplished that feat by leading the University of San Francisco, with Hall of Famers Bill Russell and K.C. Jones, to the 1955 and 1956 titles. In 1955, Woolpert, then 40, became the youngest coach in NCAA history to win the title. Woolpert compiled a 153–78 record at USF, and the Dons led the nation in defense in 1955, 1956 and 1958. He was named Coach of the Year in 1955 and 1956. Under Woolpert, USF won 60 straight games from 1955 to 1957.

Teams

First team: Elected in 1959. These were the members of the gym class taught by Dr. James Naismith at what now is Springfield College. The roster: Lyman W. Archibald, Franklin Everets Barnes, Wilbert Franklin Carey, William Richmond Chase, William Henry Davis, George Edward Day, Benjamin Snell French, Henry Gelan, Ernest Gotthold

Hildner, Genzabaro Sadakni Ishikawa, Raymond Pimlott Kaighn, Eugene Samuel Libby, Finlay Grant MacDonald, Frank Mahan, Thomas Duncan Patton, Edwin Pakenham Ruggles, John George Thompson and George Radford Weller. The 18 were training to become executive secretaries at the International YMCA Training School and were given 13 rules devised by Naismith.

Original Celtics: Elected in 1959. A collection of the finest basketball players from the early 1900s, the team routinely would draw 4,000 to the Central Opera House in New York. After playing in various leagues, the Original Celtics opted to barnstorm, returning with a 193–11–1 record. From there, the team would play about 140 games per year. The roster of the first rendition: George (Horse) Haggerty, Chris Leonard, John Beckman, Dutch Dehnert, Nat Holman, Pete Barry, Dave Banks, Ernie Reich, Benny Borgmann, Joe Lapchick, Elmer Ripley, George Whitty, Eddie Burke and Mike Smolick. On April 10, 1921, the Celtics and the New York Whirlwinds played before 11,000 fans at the 71 Reg. Armory in New York, at the time the largest basketball crowd ever.

Buffalo Germans: Elected in 1961. A collection of players from a YMCA in Buffalo, N.Y., these childhood friends would go on to win the 1901 Pan American championship and the 1905 Olympic title in St. Louis, when the game was still a demonstration sport. The group routinely defeated the nation's top professional and amateur teams. The team disbanded in 1929 with a 792–86 record. The coach was Dr. Fred Burkhardt and the players were Philip Dischinger, Henry J. Faust, Alfred A. Heerdt, Edward Linneborn, John I. Maier, Albert W. Nanweiler, Edward C. Miller, Harry J. Miller, Charles P. Monahan, George L. Redlein, Dr. Edmund Reimann, Williams C. Rhode and George Schell.

New York Renaissance: Elected in 1963. This limited-roster, all-black team from New York played the game with such style and flair and cunning that opponents often were left dazed and confused. From their founding in 1922 to

their disbanding in 1949, the Rens barnstormed to a 2,588–539 record. In one remarkable 86–day stretch during the 1932–33 season, the Rens won 88 consecutive games. Each player excelled in his role. "Wee" Willie Smith and Charles "Tarzan" Cooper were rebounding specialists. Clarence "Fat" Jenkins was the fleet guard and "Pop" Gates guided the offense. Also on the team were John Holt, James "Pappy" Ricks, Eyre Saitch and Bill Yancey

Other NBA Contributors

Clair Bee: Former NBA coach and innovator. Instrumental in development of 3-second rule and 24-second clock. Elected 1967.

Walter Brown: One of NBA's founding fathers and organizer of Boston Celtics franchise. Elected 1965.

Larry Fleisher: General counsel of NBA Players Association for more than 25 years. Elected 1990.

Eddie Gottlieb: One of NBA's founding fathers and coach of the league's first champion, the Philadelphia Warriors, in 1947. Elected 1971.

Lester Harrison: Long-time owner and coach of Rochester Royals; led team to 1951 NBA championship. Elected 1979.

Ned Irish: One of NBA's founding fathers and organizer of New York Knickerbockers franchise. Long-time basketball director of New York's Madison Square Garden. Elected 1964.

J. Walter Kennedy: Commissioner of NBA, 1963–75. Elected 1980.

Larry O'Brien: Commissioner of NBA, 1975–84. Elected 1991.

Maurice Podoloff: President of BAA/NBA from its founding in 1946 until 1963. Elected 1973.

(Opposite) BROWN DERBY: *Walter Brown was one of the NBA's founding fathers.*

NBA Career Leaders

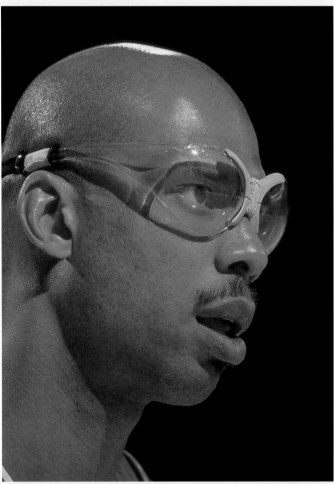

IRON MAN: *No one logged more court time than Kareem Abdul-Jabbar.*

Regular Season

Scoring

Player	Pts.
1. Kareem Abdul-Jabbar	38,387
2. Wilt Chamberlain	31,419
3. Karl Malone	31,041
4. Michael Jordan	29,277
5. Moses Malone	27,409
6. Elvin Hayes	27,313
7. Oscar Robertson	26,668
8. Dominique Wilkins	26,534
9. John Havlicek	26,395
10. Hakeem Olajuwon	25,822

Per Game Scoring Average
(minimum 10,000 points)

Player	Avg.
1. Michael Jordan	31.5
2. Wilt Chamberlain	30.1
3. Shaquille O'Neal	27.5
4. Elgin Baylor	27.4
5. Jerry West	27.0
6. Bob Pettit	26.4
7. George Gervin	26.2
8. Karl Malone	26.0
9. Oscar Robertson	25.7
10. Dominique Wilkins	24.8

Field Goals Made

Player	No.
1. Kareem Abdul-Jabbar	15,837
2. Wilt Chamberlain	12,681
3. Karl Malone	11,435
4. Elvin Hayes	10,976
5. Michael Jordan	10,962
6. Alex English	10,659
7. John Havlicek	10,513
8. Hakeem Olajuwon	10,272
9. Dominique Wilkins	9,913
10. Robert Parish	9,614

Free Throws Made

Player	No.
1. Moses Malone	8,531
2. Karl Malone	8,100
3. Oscar Robertson	7,694
4. Jerry West	7,160
5. Dolph Schayes	6,979
6. Adrian Dantley	6,832
7. Michael Jordan	6,798
8. Kareem Abdul-Jabbar	6,712
9. Charles Barkley	6,349
10. Bob Pettit	6,182

Games

Player	No.
1. Robert Parish	1,611
2. Kareem Abdul-Jabbar	1,560
3. Moses Malone	1,329
4. Buck Williams	1,307
5. Elvin Hayes	1,303
6. John Havlicek	1,270
7. John Stockton	1,258
8. Paul Silas	1,254
9. Sam Perkins	1,222
10. Dale Ellis	1,209

Minutes

Player	No.
1. Kareem Abdul-Jabbar	57,446
2. Elvin Hayes	50,000
3. Wilt Chamberlain	47,859
4. John Havlicek	46,471
5. Robert Parish	45,704
6. Moses Malone	45,071
7. Karl Malone	44,608
8. Oscar Robertson	43,866
9. Buck Williams	42,464
10. Hakeem Olajuwon	41,299

Rebounds

Player	No.
1. Wilt Chamberlain	23,924
2. Bill Russell	21,620
3. Kareem Abdul-Jabbar	17,440
4. Elvin Hayes	16,279
5. Moses Malone	16,212
6. Robert Parish	14,715
7. Nate Thurmond	14,464
8. Walt Bellamy	14,241
9. Wes Unseld	13,769
10. Buck Williams	13,017

Assists

Player	No.
1. John Stockton	13,790
2. Magic Johnson	10,141
3. Oscar Robertson	9,887
4. Isiah Thomas	9,061
5. Mark Jackson	8,574
6. Maurice Cheeks	7,392
7. Lenny Wilkens	7,211
8. Bob Cousy	6,955
9. Guy Rodgers	6,917
10. Rod Strickland	6,723

Steals

Player	No.
1. John Stockton	2,844
2. Maurice Cheeks	2,310
3. Michael Jordan	2,306
4. Clyde Drexler	2,207
5. Alvin Robertson	2,112
6. Hakeem Olajuwon	2,018
7. Scottie Pippen	1,986
8. Derek Harper	1,913
9. Mookie Blaylock	1,888
10. Isiah Thomas	1,861

Blocked Shots

Player	No.
1. Hakeem Olajuwon	3,652
2. Kareem Abdul-Jabbar	3,189
3. Mark Eaton	3,064
4. Patrick Ewing	2,758
5. Tree Rollins	2,542
6. David Robinson	2,506
7. Dikembe Mutombo	2,443
8. Robert Parish	2,361
9. Manute Bol	2,086
10. George T. Johnson	2,082

CHAIRMAN OF THE BOARDS: *Wilt Chamberlain was the rebound king.*

NBA Career Leaders

Playoffs

Scoring

Player	Pts.
1. Michael Jordan	5,987
2. Kareem Abdul-Jabbar	5,762
3. Jerry West	4,457
4. Karl Malone	4,203
5. Larry Bird	3,897
6. John Havlicek	3,776
7. Hakeem Olajuwon	3,727
8. Magic Johnson	3,701
9. Elgin Baylor	3,623
10. Wilt Chamberlain	3,607

Per Game Scoring Average (Minimum 1,000 points)

Player	Avg.
1. Michael Jordan	33.4
2. Jerry West	29.1
3. Shaquille O'Neal	27.7
4. Elgin Baylor	27.0
5. George Gervin	27.0
6. Hakeem Olajuwon	26.9
7. Karl Malone	26.6
8. Bob Pettit	25.5
9. Dominique Wilkins	25.4
10. Rick Barry	24.8

Field Goals Made

Player	No.
1. Kareem Abdul-Jabbar	2,356
2. Michael Jordan	2,188
3. Jerry West	1,622
4. Karl Malone	1,532
5. Hakeem Olajuwon	1,492
6. Larry Bird	1,458
7. John Havlicek	1,451
8. Wilt Chamberlain	1,425
9. Elgin Baylor	1,388
10. Scottie Pippen	1,292

Free Throws Made

Player	No.
1. Michael Jordan	1,463
2. Jerry West	1,213
3. Karl Malone	1,134
4. Magic Johnson	1,068
5. Kareem Abdul-Jabbar	1,050
6. Larry Bird	901
7. John Havlicek	874
8. Elgin Baylor	847
9. Kevin McHale	766
10. Wilt Chamberlain	757
Scottie Pippen	757

Games

Player	No.
1. Kareem Abdul-Jabbar	237
2. Scottie Pippen	198
3. Danny Ainge	193
4. Magic Johnson	190
5. Robert Parish	184
6. Byron Scott	183
7. Dennis Johnson	180
8. Michael Jordan	179
9. John Havlicek	172
10. Kevin McHale	169
Dennis Rodman	169

Minutes

Player	No.
1. Kareem Abdul-Jabbar	8,851
2. Scottie Pippen	7,814
3. Wilt Chamberlain	7,559
4. Magic Johnson	7,538
5. Bill Russell	7,497
6. Michael Jordan	7,474
7. Dennis Johnson	6,994
8. Larry Bird	6,886
9. John Havlicek	6,860
10. Karl Malone	6,556

Rebounds

Player	No.
1. Bill Russell	4,104
2. Wilt Chamberlain	3,913
3. Kareem Abdul-Jabbar	2,481
4. Wes Unseld	1,777
5. Karl Malone	1,769
6. Robert Parish	1,761
7. Elgin Baylor	1,724
8. Larry Bird	1,683
9. Dennis Rodman	1,676
10. Hakeem Olajuwon	1,573

Assists

Player	No.
1. Magic Johnson	2,346
2. John Stockton	1,716
3. Larry Bird	1,062
4. Michael Jordan	1,022
5. Scottie Pippen	1,011
6. Dennis Johnson	1,006
7. Isiah Thomas	987
8. Jerry West	970
9. Bob Cousy	937
10. Kevin Johnson	935

Steals

Player	No.
1. Scottie Pippen	383
2. Michael Jordan	376
3. Magic Johnson	358
4. John Stockton	309
5. Larry Bird	296
6. Maurice Cheeks	295
7. Clyde Drexler	278
8. Dennis Johnson	247
9. Hakeem Olajuwon	238
10. Julius Erving	235

Blocked Shots

Player	No.
1. Kareem Abdul-Jabbar	476
2. Hakeem Olajuwon	468
3. Robert Parish	309
4. Patrick Ewing	299
5. Kevin McHale	281
6. David Robinson	247
7. Julius Erving	239
8. Caldwell Jones	223
9. Elvin Hayes	222
10. Mark Eaton	210

NBA Finals

Scoring

Player	Pts.
1. Jerry West	1,679
2. Kareem Abdul-Jabbar	1,317
3. Michael Jordan	1,176
4. Elgin Baylor	1,161
5. Bill Russell	1,151
6. Sam Jones	1,143
7. Tom Heinsohn	1,035
8. John Havlicek	1,020
9. Magic Johnson	971
10. James Worthy	754

Per Game Scoring Average (Minimum 225 points)

Player	Avg.
1. Rick Barry	36.3
2. Shaquille O'Neal	34.0
3. Michael Jordan	33.4
4. Jerry West	30.5
5. Bob Pettit	28.4
6. Hakeem Olajuwon	27.5
7. Elgin Baylor	26.4
8. Julius Erving	25.5
9. Joe Fulks	24.7
10. Clyde Drexler	24.5

Field Goals Made

Player	No.
1. Jerry West	612
2. Kareem Abdul-Jabbar	544
3. Sam Jones	458
4. Michael Jordan	438
5. Elgin Baylor	442
6. Bill Russell	415
7. Tom Heinsohn	407
8. John Havlicek	390
9. Magic Johnson	339
10. James Worthy	314

Free Throws Made

Player	No.
1. Jerry West	455
2. Bill Russell	321
3. Magic Johnson	284
4. Elgin Baylor	277
5. George Mikan	259

PASS MASTER: *Magic Johnson is the all-time leader for playoffs assists.*

NBA Career Leaders

	Player	No.
6.	Michael Jordan	258
7.	John Havlicek	240
8.	Kareem Abdul-Jabbar	229
9.	Sam Jones	227
	Bob Pettit	227

Games

	Player	No.
1.	Bill Russell	70
2.	Sam Jones	64
3.	Kareem Abdul-Jabbar	56
4.	Jerry West	55
5.	Tom Heinsohn	52
6.	Magic Johnson	50
7.	John Havlicek	47
	Frank Ramsey	47
9.	Michael Cooper	46
10.	Elgin Baylor	44
	K.C. Jones	44

Minutes

	Player	No.
1.	Bill Russell	3,185
2.	Jerry West	2,375
3.	Kareem Abdul-Jabbar	2,082
4.	Magic Johnson	2,044
5.	John Havlicek	1,872
6.	Sam Jones	1,871
7.	Elgin Baylor	1,850
8.	Wilt Chamberlain	1,657
9.	Bob Cousy	1,639
10.	Tom Heinsohn	1,602

Rebounds

	Player	No.
1.	Bill Russell	1,718
2.	Wilt Chamberlain	862
3.	Elgin Baylor	593
4.	Kareem Abdul-Jabbar	507
5.	Tom Heinsohn	473
6.	Bob Pettit	416
7.	Magic Johnson	397
8.	Larry Bird	361
9.	John Havlicek	350

	Player	No.
10.	Sam Jones	313

Assists

	Player	No.
1.	Magic Johnson	584
2.	Bob Cousy	400
3.	Bill Russell	315
4.	Jerry West	306
5.	Dennis Johnson	228
6.	Michael Jordan	209
7.	Scottie Pippen	207
8.	John Havlicek	195
9.	Larry Bird	187
10.	Kareem Abdul-Jabbar	181

Steals

	Player	No.
1.	Magic Johnson	102
2.	Scottie Pippen	67
3.	Larry Bird	63
4.	Michael Jordan	62
5.	Michael Cooper	59
6.	Dennis Johnson	48
7.	Danny Ainge	46
8.	Kareem Abdul-Jabbar	45
9.	Julius Erving	44
10.	Maurice Cheeks	38

Blocked Shots

	Player	No.
1.	Kareem Abdul-Jabbar	116
2.	Hakeem Olajuwon	54
	Robert Parish	54
4.	Kevin McHale	44
5.	Caldwell Jones	42
6.	Julius Erving	40
7.	Dennis Johnson	39
	Scottie Pippen	39
9.	Darryl Dawkins	35
	Elvin Hayes	35

STAT MAN: *Jerry West scored more NBA Finals points than anyone else.*

All-Time Team Victories

Regular Season

	Team	No.
1.	Boston Celtics	2,527
2.	Los Angeles Lakers	2,507
3.	Philadelphia 76ers	2,165
4.	New York Knicks	2,156
5.	Atlanta Hawks	2,049
6.	Golden State Warriors	1,967
7.	Detroit Pistons	1,945
8.	Sacramento Kings	1,863
9.	Chicago Bulls	1,477
10.	Washington Wizards	1,467

Playoffs

	Team	No.
1.	Los Angeles Lakers	332
2.	Boston Celtics	272
3.	Philadelphia 76ers	184
4.	New York Knicks	177
5.	Chicago Bulls	147
6.	Atlanta Hawks	119
7.	Detroit Pistons	116
8.	Houston Rockets	100
9.	Golden State Warriors	99
	Seattle SuperSonics	99

NBA Finals

	Team	No.
1.	Boston Celtics	70
	Los Angeles Lakers	70
3.	Chicago Bulls	24
4.	Philadelphia 76ers	23
5.	New York Knicks	20
6.	Golden State Warriors	17
7.	Detroit Pistons	15
8.	Houston Rockets	12
9.	Atlanta Hawks	11
10.	Seattle SuperSonics	9

NBA Championships

	Team	No.
1.	Boston Celtics	16
2.	Los Angeles Lakers	12
3.	Chicago Bulls	6
4.	Golden State Warriors	3
	Philadelphia 76ers	3
6.	Detroit Pistons	2
	Houston Rockets	2
	New York Knicks	2

NOTE: *These are franchise records.*

NBA Career Leaders

Regular Season (ABA/NBA)

Scoring

Player	Pts.
1. Kareem Abdul-Jabbar	38,387
2. Wilt Chamberlain	31,419
3. Karl Malone	31,041
4. Julius Erving	30,026
5. Moses Malone	29,580
6. Michael Jordan	29,277
7. Dan Issel	27,482
8. Elvin Hayes	27,313
9. Oscar Robertson	26,710
10. Dominique Wilkins	26,668

Per Game Scoring Average
(Minimum 14,000 points)

Player	Avg.
1. Michael Jordan	31.5
2. Wilt Chamberlain	30.1
3. Shaquille O'Neal	27.5
4. Elgin Baylor	27.4
5. Jerry West	27.0
6. Bob Pettit	26.4
7. Karl Malone	26.0
8. Oscar Robertson	25.7
9. George Gervin	25.1
10. Dominique Wilkins	24.8

Field Goals Made

Player	No.
1. Kareem Abdul-Jabbar	15,837
2. Wilt Chamberlain	12,681
3. Julius Erving	11,818
4. Karl Malone	11,435
5. Elvin Hayes	10,976
6. Michael Jordan	10,962
7. Alex English	10,659
8. John Havlicek	10,513
9. Dan Issel	10,431
10. George Gervin	10,368

Free Throws Made

Player	No.
1. Moses Malone	9,018
2. Karl Malone	8,100
3. Oscar Robertson	7,694
4. Jerry West	7,160
5. Dolph Schayes	6,979
6. Adrian Dantley	6,832
7. Michael Jordan	6,798
8. Kareem Abdul-Jabbar	6,712
9. Dan Issel	6,591
10. Charles Barkley	6,349

Games

Player	No.
1. Robert Parish	1,611
2. Kareem Abdul-Jabbar	1,560
3. Moses Malone	1,455
4. Artis Gilmore	1,329
5. Buck Williams	1,307
6. Elvin Hayes	1,303
7. Caldwell Jones	1,299
8. John Havlicek	1,270
9. John Stockton	1,258
10. Paul Silas	1,254

Minutes

Player	No.
1. Kareem Abdul-Jabbar	57,446
2. Elvin Hayes	50,000
3. Moses Malone	49,444
4. Wilt Chamberlain	47,859
5. Artis Gilmore	47,134
6. John Havlicek	46,471
7. Robert Parish	45,704
8. Julius Erving	45,227
9. Karl Malone	44,608
10. Oscar Robertson	43,886

Rebounds

Player	No.
1. Wilt Chamberlain	23,924
2. Bill Russell	21,620
3. Moses Malone	17,834
4. Kareem Abdul-Jabbar	17,440
5. Artis Gilmore	16,330
6. Elvin Hayes	16,279
7. Robert Parish	14,715
8. Nate Thurmond	14,464
9. Walt Bellamy	14,241
10. Wes Unseld	13,769

Assists

Player	No.
1. John Stockton	13,790
2. Magic Johnson	10,141
3. Oscar Robertson	9,887
4. Isiah Thomas	9,061
5. Mark Jackson	8,574
6. Maurice Cheeks	7,392
7. Lenny Wilkens	7,211
8. Bob Cousy	6,955
9. Guy Rodgers	6,917
10. Rod Strickland	6,723

Steals

Player	No.
1. John Stockton	2,844
2. Maurice Cheeks	2,310
3. Michael Jordan	2,306
4. Julius Erving	2,272
5. Clyde Drexler	2,207
6. Alvin Robertson	2,112
7. Hakeem Olajuwon	2,018
8. Scottie Pippen	1,986
9. Derek Harper	1,957
10. Mookie Blaylock	1,888

WHO ELSE?: *It's no surprise that MJ leads in career scoring average.*

NBA Career Leaders

Blocked Shots

Player	No.
1. Hakeem Olajuwon	3,652
2. Kareem Abdul-Jabbar	3,189
3. Artis Gilmore	3,178
4. Mark Eaton	3,064
5. Patrick Ewing	2,758
6. Tree Rollins	2,542
7. David Robinson	2,506
8. Dikembe Mutombo	2,443
9. Robert Parish	2,361
10. Caldwell Jones	2,297

NBA All-Star Game

Scoring

Player	Pts.
1. Kareem Abdul-Jabbar	251
2. Oscar Robertson	246
3. Michael Jordan	234
4. Bob Pettit	224
5. Julius Erving	221
6. Elgin Baylor	218
7. Wilt Chamberlain	191
8. Isiah Thomas	185
9. John Havlicek	179
10. Magic Johnson	176

Field Goals Made

Player	No.
1. Kareem Abdul-Jabbar	105
2. Michael Jordan	97
3. Oscar Robertson	88
4. Julius Erving	85
5. Bob Pettit	81
6. Isiah Thomas	76
7. John Havlicek	74
8. Wilt Chamberlain	72
9. Elgin Baylor	70
10. Magic Johnson	64

Free Throws Made

Player	No.
1. Elgin Baylor	78
2. Oscar Robertson	70
3. Bob Pettit	62
4. Julius Erving	50
5. Wilt Chamberlain	47
6. Bob Cousy	43
7. Dolph Schayes	42
8. Kareem Abdul-Jabbar	41
9. Moses Malone	40
10. David Robinson	39

Games

Player	No.
1. Kareem Abdul-Jabbar	18
2. Wilt Chamberlain	13
Bob Cousy	13
John Havlicek	13
5. Elvin Hayes	12
Hakeem Olajuwon	12
Oscar Robertson	12
Bill Russell	12
Jerry West	12
10. Nine players tied	11

Minutes

Player	No.
1. Kareem Abdul-Jabbar	449
2. Wilt Chamberlain	388
3. Oscar Robertson	380
4. Bob Cousy	368
5. Bob Pettit	360
6. Bill Russell	343
7. Jerry West	341
8. Magic Johnson	331
9. Michael Jordan	324
10. Elgin Baylor	321

Rebounds

Player	No.
1. Wilt Chamberlain	197
2. Bob Pettit	178
3. Kareem Abdul-Jabbar	149
4. Bill Russell	139
5. Moses Malone	108
6. Dolph Schayes	105
7. Elgin Baylor	99
8. Hakeem Olajuwon	94
9. Elvin Hayes	92
10. Dave Cowens	81

Assists

Player	No.
1. Magic Johnson	127
2. Isiah Thomas	97
3. Bob Cousy	86
4. Oscar Robertson	81
5. John Stockton	71
6. Gary Payton	60
7. Jerry West	55
8. Kareem Abdul-Jabbar	51
9. Michael Jordan	49
10. Larry Bird	41

Steals

Player	No.
1. Michael Jordan	33
2. Isiah Thomas	31
3. Larry Bird	23
4. Magic Johnson	21
5. Julius Erving	18
6. Scottie Pippen	17
7. Rick Barry	16
George Gervin	16
John Stockton	16
10. Hakeem Olajuwon	15

Blocked Shots

Player	No.
1. Kareem Abdul-Jabbar	31
2. Hakeem Olajuwon	23
3. Patrick Ewing	16
4. David Robinson	13
5. Kevin McHale	12
6. Julius Erving	11
Shaquille O'Neal	11
8. George Gervin	9
9. Robert Parish	8
10. Magic Johnson	7
Jack Sikma	7

Career Coaching Leaders

Regular Season

Victories

Coach	No.
1. Lenny Wilkens	1,179
2. Pat Riley	999
3. Bill Fitch	944
4. Red Auerbach	938
5. Dick Motta	935
6. Don Nelson	926
7. Jack Ramsay	864
8. Cotton Fitzsimmons	832
9. Gene Shue	784
10. Larry Brown	707

Games

Coach	No.
1. Lenny Wilkens	2,160
2. Bill Fitch	2,050
3. Dick Motta	1,952
4. Don Nelson	1,678
5. Jack Ramsay	1,647
6. Gene Shue	1,645
7. Cotton Fitzsimmons	1,607
8. Pat Riley	1,433
9. Red Auerbach	1,417
10. John MacLeod	1,364

Winning Percentage (Minimum 450 games)

Coach	Pct.
1. Phil Jackson	.746
2. Billy Cunningham	.698
3. Pat Riley	.697
4. Red Auerbach	.662
5. K.C. Jones	.643
6. Jerry Sloan	.636
7. Paul Westphal	.635
8. Lester Harrison	.620
9. Tom Heinsohn	.619
10. George Karl	.596

Playoffs

Victories

Coach	No.
1. Pat Riley	155
2. Phil Jackson	126
3. Red Auerbach	99
4. K.C. Jones	81
5. Chuck Daly	75
6. Jerry Sloan	74
7. Lenny Wilkens	72
8. Billy Cunningham	66
9. John Kundla	60
10. Red Holzman	58

Games

Coach	No.
1. Pat Riley	252
2. Phil Jackson	175
3. Red Auerbach	168
4. Lenny Wilkens	157
5. Jerry Sloan	144
6. K.C. Jones	138
7. Chuck Daly	126
Dick Motta	126
9. Don Nelson	112
10. Bill Fitch	109

Winning Percentage (Minimum 50 games)

Coach	Pct.
1. Phil Jackson	.720
2. Gregg Popovich	.667
3. Butch Van Breda Kolff	.636
4. John Kundla	.632
5. Billy Cunningham	.629
6. Larry Costello	.617
7. Larry Bird	.615
. Pat Riley	.615
9. Chuck Daly	.607
10. Red Auerbach	.589

NBA Single-Game Highs

Regular Season

Points

Player/Team	Date	Pts.
1. Wilt Chamberlain, Phil.	3–2–62	100
2. Wilt Chamberlain, Phil.	12–8–61	78
	(3 OT)	
3. Wilt Chamberlain, Phil.	1–13–62	73
Wilt Chamberlain, S.F.	11–16–62	73
David Thompson, Den.	4–9–78	73
6. Wilt Chamberlain, S.F.	11–3–62	72
7. Elgin Baylor, Lakers	11–15–60	71
David Robinson, S.A.	4–24–94	71
9. Wilt Chamberlain, S.F.	3–10–63	70
10. Michael Jordan, Chi.	3–28–90	69
	(OT)	
11. Wilt Chamberlain, Phil.	12–16–67	68
Pete Maravich, N.O.	2–25–77	68
13. Wilt Chamberlain, Phil.	3–9–61	67
Wilt Chamberlain, Phil.	2–17–62	67
Wilt Chamberlain, Phil.	2–25–62	67
Wilt Chamberlain, S.F.	1–11–63	67
17. Wilt Chamberlain, Lakers	2–9–69	66
18. Wilt Chamberlain, Phil.	2–13–62	65
Wilt Chamberlain, Phil.	2–27–62	65
Wilt Chamberlain, Phil.	2–7–66	65
21. Elgin Baylor, Minn.	11–8–59	64
Rick Barry, G.S.	3–26–74	64
Michael Jordan, Chic.	1–16–93	64
24. Joe Fulks, Phil.	2–10–49	63
Elgin Baylor, Lakers	12–8–61	63
Jerry West, Lakers	1–17–62	63
Wilt Chamberlain, S.F.	12–14–62	63
Wilt Chamberlain, S.F.	11–26–64	63
George Gervin, S.A.	4–9–78	63
30. Wilt Chamberlain, Phil.	1–14–62	62
Wilt Chamberlain, Phil.	1–17–62	62
	(OT)	
Wilt Chamberlain, Phil.	1–21–62	62
	(OT)	
Wilt Chamberlain, S.F.	1–29–63	62
Wilt Chamberlain, SF	11–15–64	62
Wilt Chamberlain, Phil.	3–3–66	62

Field Goals Made

Player/Team	Date	No.
1. Wilt Chamberlain, Phil.	3–2–62	36
2. Wilt Chamberlain, Phil.	12–8–61	31
	(3 OT)	
3. Wilt Chamberlain, Phil.	12–16–67	30
Rick Barry, G.S.	3–26–74	30
5. Wilt Chamberlain, Phil.	1–13–62	29
Wilt Chamberlain, S.F.	11–3–62	29
Wilt Chamberlain, S.F.	11–16–62	29
Wilt Chamberlain, Lakers	2–9–69	29
9. Elgin Baylor, Lakers	11–15–60	28
Wilt Chamberlain, Phil.	12–9–61	28
Wilt Chamberlain, S.F.	1–11–63	28
Wilt Chamberlain, Phil.	2–7–66	28
David Thompson, Den.	4–9–78	28
14. Joe Fulks, Phil.	2–10–49	27
Wilt Chamberlain, Phil.	3–9–61	27
Wilt Chamberlain, Phil.	1–14–62	27
Wilt Chamberlain, S.F.	11–21–62	27

Wilt Chamberlain, S.F.	12–11–62	27
Wilt Chamberlain, S.F.	1–29–63	27
Wilt Chamberlain, S.F.	3–10–63	27
Wilt Chamberlain, S.F.	11–26–64	27
Michael Jordan, Chi.	1–16–93	27
	(OT)	
23. Wilt Chamberlain, Phil.	2–21–60	26
Wilt Chamberlain, Phil.	2–17–62	26
Wilt Chamberlain, S.F.	12–18–62	26
Wilt Chamberlain, S.F.	2–16–63	26
	(2 OT)	
Wilt Chamberlain, S.F.	11–15–64	26
Wilt Chamberlain, Phil.	3–3–66	26
Wilt Chamberlain, Phil.	2–13–67	26
Pete Marvavich, N.O.	2–25–77	26
David Robinson, S.A.	4–24–94	26

Free Throws Made

Player/Team	Date	No.
1. Wilt Chamberlain, Phil.	3–2–62	28
Adrian Dantley, Utah	1–4–84	28
3. Adrian Dantley, Utah	11–25–83	27
4. Adrian Dantley, Utah	10–31–80	26
Michael Jordan, Chi.	2–26–87	26
6. Frank Selvy, Mil.	12–2–54	24
Willie Burton, Phil.	12–13–94	24
8. Dolph Schayes, Syr.	1–17–52	23
	(3 OT)	
Nate Archibald, Cin.	2–5–72	23
Nate Archibald, K.C./Oma.	1–21–75	23
Pete Maravich, N.O.	10–26–75	23
	(2 OT)	
Kevin Johnson, Phoe.	4–9–90	23
Dominique Wilkins, Atl.	12–8–92	23
14. Larry Foust, Minn.	11–30–57	22
Richie Guerin, N.Y.	2–11–61	22
Oscar Robertson, Cin.	12–18–64	22
Oscar Robertson, Cin.	12–27–64	22
Oscar Robertson, Cin.	11–20–66	22
John Williamson, N.J.	12–9–78	22
World B. Free, S.D.	1–13–79	22
Bernard King, N.Y.	12–25–84	22
Rolando Blackman, Dal.	2–17–86	22
Eric Floyd, Houston	2–3–91	22
	(2 OT)	
Detlef Schrempf, Indiana	12–8–92	22
Charles Barkley, Phoe.	12–20–95	22
Latrell Sprewell, G.S.	3–10–97	22
Michael Jordan, Chi.	4–18–98	22

Rebounds

Player/Team	Date	No.
1. Wilt Chamberlain, Phil.	11–24–60	55
2. Bill Russell, Boston	2–5–60	51
3. Bill Russell, Boston	11–16–57	49
Bill Russell, Boston	3–11–65	49
5. Wilt Chamberlain, Phil.	2–6–60	45
Wilt Chamberlain, Phil.	1–21–61	45
7. Wilt Chamberlain, Phil.	11–10–59	43
Wilt Chamberlain, Phil.	12–8–61	43
	(3 OT)	
Bill Russell, Boston	1–20–63	43

Wilt Chamberlain, Phil.	3–6–65	43
11. Wilt Chamberlain, Phil.	1–15–60	42
Wilt Chamberlain, Phil.	1–25–60	42
Nate Thurmond, S.F.	11–9–65	42
Wilt Chamberlain, Phil.	1–14–66	42
Wilt Chamberlain, L.A.	3–7–69	42
16. Bill Russell, Boston	2–12–58	41
Wilt Chamberlain, S.F.	10–26–62	41
Bill Russell, Boston	3–14–65	41
19. Bill Russell, Boston	12–12–58	40
Wilt Chamberlain, Phil.	11–4–59	40
Bill Russell, Boston	2–12–61	40
Jerry Lucas, Cin.	2–29–64	40
Wilt Chamberlain, S.F.	11–22–64	40
Wilt Chamberlain, Phil.	12–28–65	40
25. Neil Johnston, Phil.	12–4–54	39
Bill Russell, Boston	1–25–59	39
Bill Russell, Boston	12–19–59	39
Wilt Chamberlain, Phil.	12–28–59	39
Wilt Chamberlain, Phil.	1–13–60	39
	(OT)	
Wilt Chamberlain, Phil.	1–29–60	39
Wilt Chamberlain, Phil.	11–4–60	39
Bill Russell, Boston	12–21–61	39

Assists

Player/Team	Date	No.
1. Scott Skiles, Orlando	12–30–90	30
2. Kevin Porter, N.J.	2–24–78	29
3. Bob Cousy, Boston	2–27–59	28
Guy Rodgers, S.F.	3–14–63	28
John Stockton, Utah	1–15–91	28
6. Geoff Huston, Cleveland	1–27–82	27
John Stockton, Utah	12–19–89	27
8. John Stockton, Utah	4–14–88	26
9. Ernie DiGregorio, Buff.	1–1–74	25
Kevin Porter, Detroit	3–9–79	25
Kevin Porter, Detroit	4–1–79	25
Isiah Thomas, Detroit	2–13–85	25
Nate McMillan, Seattle	2–23–87	25
Kevin Johnson, Phoenix	4–6–94	25
Jason Kidd, Dallas	2–8–96	25
	(2 OT)	
16. Guy Rodgers, Chicago	12–21–66	24
Kevin Porter, Washington	3–23–80	24
John Lucas, S.A.	4–15–84	24
Isiah Thomas, Detroit	2–7–85	24
	(2 OT)	
John Stockton, Utah	1–3–89	24
Magic Johnson, Lakers	11–17–89	24
Magic Johnson, Lakers	1–9–90	24
	(OT)	
23. Jerry West, Lakers	2–1–67	23
Kevin Porter, Detroit	12–27–78	23
Kevin Porter, Detroit	3–30–79	23
Nate Archibald, Boston	2–5–82	23
Magic Johnson, Lakers	2–21–84	23
Magic Johnson, Lakers	4–20–88	23
Fat Lever, Denver	4–21–89	23
John Stockton, Utah	4–12–90	23
John Stockton, Utah	12–8–90	23
John Stockton, Utah	12–29–91	23
John Stockton, Utah	4–17–92	23

NBA Single-Game Highs

Mookie Blaylock, Atlanta	3–6–93	23
Nick Van Exel, Lakers	1–5–97	23

Steals

Player/Team	Date	No.
1. Larry Kenon, S.A.	12–26–76	11
Kendall Gill, New Jersey	4–13–99	11
3. Jerry West, Lakers	12–7–73	10
Larry Steele, Portland	11–16–74	10
Fred Brown, Seattle	12–3–76	10
Gus Williams, Seattle	2–22–78	10
Eddie Jordan, N.J.	3–23–79	10
Johnny Moore, S.A.	3–6–85	10
Fat Lever, Denver	3–9–85	10
Clyde Drexler, Portland	1–10–86	10
Alvin Robertson, S.A.	2–18–86	10
Alvin Robertson, S.A.	11–22–86	10
Ron Harper, Cleveland	3–10–87	10
Michael Jordan, Chicago	1–29–88	10
Alvin Robertson, S.A.	1–11–89	10
		(OT)
Alvin Robertson, Mil.	11–19–90	10
Kevin Johnson, Phoenix	12–9–93	10
Clyde Drexler, Houston	11–1–96	10
Mookie Blaylock, Atl.	4–14–98	10
19. Calvin Murphy, Hou.	12–14–73	9
Larry Steele, Portlan	3–5–74	9
Rick Barry, G.S.	10–29–74	9
Don Watts, Seattle	2–23–75	9
Larry Steele, Portland	3–7–75	9
Larry Steele, Portland	3–14–76	9
Quinn Buckner, Mil.	1–2–77	9
Don Watts, Seattle	3–27–77	9
Earl Tatum, Detroit	11–28–78	9
Gus Williams, Seattle	1–23–79	9
Ron Lee, Detroit	3–16–80	9
Dudley Bradley, Indiana	11–10–80	9
Dudley Bradley, Indiana	11–29–80	9
Micheal Ray Richardson, N.Y.	12–23–80	9
Johnny High, Phoenix	1–28–81	9
Magic Johnson, Lakers	11–6–81	9
Jack Sikma, Seattle	11–27–82	9
Rickey Green, Utah	11–10–82	9
Rickey Green, Utah	11–27–82	9
Micheal Ray Richardson, G.S.	2–5–83	9
Darwin Cook, N.J.	12–3–83	9
		(OT)
Gus Williams, Wash.	10–30–84	9
Johnny Moore, S.A.	1–8–85	9
Larry Bird, Boston	2–18–85	9
Micheal Ray Richardson, N.J.	10–30–85	9
		(3 OT)
Maurice Cheeks, Phil.	1–5–87	9
T.R. Dunn, Denver	1–6–88	9
Michael Jordan, Chicago	11–9–88	9
Hersey Hawkins, Phil.	1–25–91	9
John Stockton, Utah	2–12–91	9
Michael Adams, Wash.	11–1–91	9
Doc Rivers, Clippers	11–6–91	9
Michael Jordan, Chicago	4–2–93	9

Fat Lever, Dallas	2–10–94	9
Scottie Pippen, Chicago	3–8–94	9
Eric Murdock, Mil.	4–2–94	9
Mookie Blaylock, Atl.	2–17–97	9
Doug Christie, Toronto	2–25–97	9
		(OT)
Eddie Jones, Charlotte	11–4–99	9
Paul Pierce, Boston	12–3–99	9
Allen Iverson, Phil.	3–19–00	9

Blocked Shots

Player/Team	Date	No.
1. Elmore Smith, Buffalo	10–28–73	17
2. Manute Bol, Wash.	1–25–86	15
Manute Bol, Wash.	2–26–87	15
Shaquille O'Neal, Orl.	11–20–93	15
5. Elmore Smith, Buffalo	10–26–73	14
Elmore Smith, Buffalo	11–4–73	14
Mark Eaton, Utah	1–18–85	14
Mark Eaton, Utah	2–18–89	14
9. George Johnson, S.A.	2–24–81	13
Mark Eaton, Utah	2–18–83	13
Darryl Dawkins, N.J.	11–5–83	13
Ralph Sampson, Hou.	12–9–83	13
		(OT)
Manute Bol, G.S.	2–2–90	13
Shawn Bradley, Dallas	4–7–98	13
15. Nate Thurmond, Chi.	10–18–74	12
George Johnson, N.J.	3–21–78	12
Tree Rollins, Atlanta	2–21–79	12
Mark Eaton, Utah	2–5–83	12
Mark Eaton, Utah	3–17–84	12
Mark Eaton, Utah	2–26–85	12
Manute Bol, Wash.	12–12–85	12
		(OT)
Mark Eaton, Utah	11–1–86	12
Manute Bol, Wash.	2–5–87	12
Hakeem Olajuwon, Hou.	3–10–87	12
		(2 OT)
Manute Bol, Wash.	3–26–87	12
Manute Bol, G.S.	2–22–89	12
Hakeem Olajuwon, Hou;	11–11–89	12
David Robinson, S.A.	2–23–90	12
Dikembe Mutombo, Den.	4–18–93	12
Shawn Bradley, N.J.	4–17–96	12
Vlade Divac, Charlotte	2–12–97	12

Playoffs

Scoring

Player/Team	Date	Pts.
1. Michael Jordan, Chi.	4–20–86	63
		(2 OT)
2. Elgin Baylor, Lakers	4–14–62	61
3. Wilt Chamberlain, Phil.	3–22–62	56
Michael Jordan, Chi.	4–29–92	56
Charles Barkley, Phoe.	5–4–94	56
6. Rick Barry, S.F.	4–18–67	55
Michael Jordan, Chi.	5–1–88	55
Michael Jordan, Chi.	6–16–93	55
Michael Jordan, Chi.	4–27–97	55
10. John Havlicek, Boston	4–1–73	54
Michael Jordan, Chi.	5–31–93	54

Field Goals Made

Player/Team	Date	No.
1. Wilt Chamberlain, Phil.	3–14–60	24
John Havlicek, Boston	4–1–73	24
Michael Jordan, Chi.	5–1–88	24
4. Charles Barkley, Phoe.	5–4–94	23
5. Wilt Chamberlain, Phil.	3–22–60	22
Wilt Chamberlain, Phil.	3–22–62	22
Elgin Baylor, Lakers	4–14–62	22
Wilt Chamberlain, S.F.	4–10–64	22
Rick Barry, S.F.	4–18–67	22
Billy Cunningham, Phil.	4–1–70	22
Michael Jordan, Chi.	4–20–86	22
		(2 OT)
Michael Jordan, Chi.	4–27–97	22

Free Throws Made

Player/Team	Date	No.
1. Bob Cousy, Boston	3–21–53	30
		(4 OT)
2. Michael Jordan, Chi.	5–14–89	23
3. Michael Jordan, Chi.	5–5–89	22
		(OT)
Karl Malone, Utah	5–3–92	22
5. Oscar Robertson, Cin.	4–10–63	21
Derrick Coleman, N.J.	5–6–94	21
Kevin Johnson, Phoe.	5–20–95	21
8. Bob Cousy, Boston	3–17–54	20
		(OT)
Jerry West, Lakers	4–3–62	20
Jerry West, Lakers	4–5–65	20
Magic Johnson, Lakers	5–8–91	20
Karl Malone, Utah	5–9–91	20

FROM THE LINE: *Bob Cousy set a FT record in '53.*

NBA Single-Game Highs

Rebounds

Player/Team	Date	No.
1. Wilt Chamberlain, Phil.	4–5–67	41
2. Bill Russell, Boston	3–23–58	40
Bill Russell, Boston	3–29–60	40
Bill Russell, Boston	4–18–62	40
		(OT)
5. Bill Russell, Boston	3–19–60	39
Bill Russell, Boston	3–23–61	39
Wilt Chamberlain, Phil.	4–6–65	39
8. Bill Russell, Boston	4–11–61	38
Bill Russell, Boston	4–16–63	38
Wilt Chamberlain, S.F.	4–24–64	38
Wilt Chamberlain, Phil.	4–16–67	38

Assists

Player/Team	Date	No.
1. Magic Johnson, Lakers	5–15–84	24
John Stockton, Utah	5–17–88	24
3. Magic Johnson, Lakers	5–3–85	23
John Stockton, Utah	4–25–96	23
5. Doc Rivers, Atlanta	5–16–88	22
6. Magic Johnson, Lakers	6–3–84	21
Magic Johnson, Lakers	4–27–91	21
Magic Johnson, Lakers	5–18–91	21
John Stockton, Utah	4–24–92	21
10. Many players tied		20

Steals

Player/Team	Date	No.
1. Allen Iverson, Phil.	5–13–99	10
2. Rick Barry, G.S.	4–14–75	8
Lionel Hollins, Portland	5–8–77	8
Maurice Cheeks, Phil.	4–11–79	8
Craig Hodges, Mil.	5–9–86	8
Tim Hardaway, G.S.	5–8–91	8
Tim Hardaway, G.S.	4–30–92	8
Mookie Blaylock, Atl.	4–29–96	8
9. Many players tied		7

Blocked Shots

Player/Team	Date	No.
1. Mark Eaton, Utah	4–26–85	10
Hakeem Olajuwon, Hou.	4–29–90	10
3. Kareem Abdul-Jabbar, L.A.	4–22–77	9
Manute Bol, Wash.	4–18–86	9
Hakeem Olajuwon, Hou.	4–29–93	9
Derrick Coleman, N.J.	5–7–93	9
Greg Ostertag, Utah	5–12–97	9
		(OT)
Alonzo Mourning, Mia.	4–22–00	9

NBA Finals

Scoring

Player/Team	Date	Pts.
1. Elgin Baylor, Lakers	4–14–62	61
2. Rick Barry, S.F.	4–18–67	55
Michael Jordan, Chi.	6–16–93	55
4. Jerry West, Lakers	4–23–69	53
5. Bob Pettit, St.Louis	4–12–58	50
6. Michael Jordan, Chi.	6–12–92	46
7. Jerry West, Lakers	4–19–65	45
Jerry West, Lakers	4–22–66	45

TEAM PLAYER: *Utah's John Stockton dished out 24 assists to equal Magic's single-game high.*

Wilt Chamberlain, Lakers	5–6–70	45
Michael Jordan, Chi.	6–14–98	45

Field Goals Made

Player/Team	Date	No.
1. Elgin Baylor, Lakers	4–14–62	22
Rick Barry, S.F.	4–18–67	22
3. Jerry West, Lakers	4–23–69	21
Michael Jordan, Chi.	6–16–93	21
Shaquille O'Neal, Lakers	6–7–00	21
6. Wilt Chamberlain, Lakers	5–6–70	20
7. Bob Pettit, St.Louis	4–12–58	19
Jerry West, Lakers	4–22–66	19
K. Abdul-Jabbar, Lakers	5–7–80	19
Michael Jordan, Chi.	6–13–93	19
		(3 OT)
Shaquille O'Neal, Lakers	6–19–00	19

Free Throws Made

Player/Team	Date	No.
1. Bob Pettit, St.Louis	4–9–58	19
2. Shaquille O'Neal, Lakers	6–9–00	18
3. Cliff Hagan, St.Louis	3–30–58	17
Elgin Baylor, Lakers	4–14–62	17
Jerry West, Lakers	4–21–65	17
Jerry West, Lakers	4–25–69	17
7. Bob Pettit, St.Louis	4–11–57	16
Michael Jordan, Chi.	6–12–92	16
9. 7 players tied		15

Rebounds

Player/Team	Date	No.
1. Bill Russell, Boston	3–29–60	40
Bill Russell, Boston	4–18–62	40
		(OT)
3. Bill Russell, Boston	4–11–61	38

Bill Russell, Boston	4–16–63	38
Wilt Chamberlain, S.F.	4–24–64	38
Wilt Chamberlain, Phil.	4–16–67	38
7. Bill Russell, Boston	4–9–60	35
8. Wilt Chamberlain, Phil.	4–14–67	33
		(OT)

Assists

Player/Team	Date	No.
1. Magic Johnson, Lakers	6–3–84	21
2. Magic Johnson, Lakers	6–4–87	20
Magic Johnson, Lakers	6–12–91	20
4. Bob Cousy, Boston	4–9–57	19
Bob Cousy, Boston	4–7–59	19
Walt Frazier, N.Y.	5–8–70	19
Magic Johnson, Lakers	6–14–87	19
Magic Johnson, Lakers	6–19–88	19
9. Jerry West, Lakers	5–1–70	18
		(OT)
10. Many players tied with 17; Last:		
Magic Johnson, Lakers	6–16–88	17

Steals

Player/Team	Date	No.
1. Robert Horry, Houston	6–9–95	7
2. John Havlicek, Boston	5–3–74	6
Steve Mix, Philadelphia	5–22–77	6
Maurice Cheeks, Phil.	5–7–80	6
Isiah Thomas, Detroit	6–19–88	6
6. Many players tied with 5; Last:		
Ron Harper, Lakers.	6–11–00	5

Blocked Shots

Player/Team	Date	No.
1. Bill Walton, Portland	6–5–77	8
Hakeem Olajuwon, Hou.	6–5–86	8
Patrick Ewing, N.Y.	6–17–94	8
4. Dennis Johnson, Seattle	5–28–78	7
Patrick Ewing, N.Y.	6–12–94	7
Hakeem Olajuwon, Hou.	6–12–94	7
7. K. Abdul-Jabbar, Lakers	5–4–80	6
Patrick Ewing, N.Y.	6–10–94	6
9. Many players tied with 5; Last:		
David Robinson, S.A.	6–9–99	5
		(OT)

Most Times Leading League

Scoring	Michael Jordan, 10
Field Goal Percentage	Wilt Chamberlain, 9
Field Goals	Michael Jordan, 10
Free Throw Percentage	Bill Sharman, 7
Free Throws	Karl Malone, 8
Rebounds	Wilt Chamberlain, 11
Assists	John Stockton, 9
Steals	Micheal Ray Richardson, 3
	Alvin Robertson, 3
	Michael Jordan, 3
Blocked Shots	Kareem Abdul-Jabbar, 4
	Mark Eaton, 4

Yearly Statistical Leaders

Scoring

Year	Points	Player
1946–47	1389	Joe Fulks, Philadelphia
1947–48	1007	Max Zaslofsky, Chicago
1948–49	1698	George Mikan, Minn.
1949–50	1865	George Mikan, Minn.
1950–51	1932	George Mikan, Minn.
1951–52	1674	Paul Arizin, Phil.
1952–53	1564	Neil Johnston, Phil.
1953–54	1759	Neil Johnston, Phil.
1954–55	1631	Neil Johnston, Phil.
1955–56	1849	Bob Pettit, St. Louis
1956–57	1817	Paul Arizin, Phil.
1957–58	2001	George Yardley, Detroit
1958–59	2105	Bob Pettit, St. Louis
1959–60	2707	Wilt Chamberlain, Phil.
1960–61	3033	Wilt Chamberlain, Phil.
1961–62	4029	Wilt Chamberlain, Phil.
1962–63	3586	Wilt Chamberlain, S.F.
1963–64	2948	Wilt Chamberlain, S.F.
1964–65	2534	Wilt Chamberlain, S.F./Phil.
1965–66	2649	Wilt Chamberlain, Phil.
1966–67	2775	Rick Barry, S.F.
1967–68	2142	Dave Bing, Detroit
1968–69	2327	Elvin Hayes, San Diego

(*converted to average per game from 1969–70)

Year	Ave.	Player
1969–70	31.2	Jerry West, Lakers
1970–71	31.7	Kareem Abdul-Jabbar, Mil.
1971–72	34.8	Kareem Abdul-Jabbar, Mil.
1972–73	34.0	Nate Archibald, K.C./Oma.
1973–74	30.6	Bob McAdoo, Buffalo
1974–75	34.5	Bob McAdoo, Buffalo
1975–76	31.1	Bob McAdoo, Buffalo
1976–77	31.1	Pete Maravich, N.O.
1977–78	27.2	George Gervin, S.A.
1978–79	29.6	George Gervin, S.A.
1979–80	33.1	George Gervin, S.A.
1980–81	30.7	Adrian Dantley, Utah
1981–82	32.3	George Gervin, S.A.
1982–83	28.4	Alex English, Denver
1983–84	30.6	Adrian Dantley, Utah
1984–85	32.9	Bernard King, N.Y.
1985–86	30.3	Dominique Wilkins, Atl.
1986–87	37.1	Michael Jordan, Chicago
1987–88	35.0	Michael Jordan, Chicago
1988–89	32.5	Michael Jordan, Chicago
1988–90	33.6	Michael Jordan, Chicago
1990–91	31.5	Michael Jordan, Chicago
1991–92	30.1	Michael Jordan, Chicago
1992–93	32.6	Michael Jordan, Chicago
1993–94	28.9	David Robinson, S.A.
1994–95	29.3	Shaquille O'Neal, Orl.
1995–96	30.4	Michael Jordan, Chicago
1996–97	29.6	Michael Jordan, Chicago
1997–98	28.7	Michael Jordan, Chicago
1998–99	26.8	Allen Iverson, Phil.
1999–00	29.7	Shaquille O'Neal, Lakers

Field Goal Percentage

Year	Pct.	Player
1946–47	.401	Bob Feerick, Wash.
1947–48	.340	Bob Feerick, Wash.
1948–49	.423	Arnie Risen, Roch.
1949–50	.478	Alex Groza, Indiana
1950–51	.470	Alex Groza, Indiana
1951–52	.448	Paul Arizin, Phil.
1952–53	.452	Neil Johnston, Phil.
1953–54	.486	Ed MacAuley, Boston
1954–55	.487	Larry Foust, Fort Wayne
1955–56	.457	Neil Johnston, Phil.
1956–57	.447	Neil Johnston, Phil.
1957–58	.452	Jack Twyman, Cin.
1958–59	.490	Ken Sears, New York
1959–60	.477	Ken Sears, New York
1960–61	.509	Wilt Chamberlain, Phil.
1961–62	.519	Walt Bellamy, Chicago
1962–63	.528	Wilt Chamberlain, S.F.
1963–64	.527	Jerry Lucas, Cincinnati
1964–65	.510	Wilt Chamberlain, S.F.–Philadelphia
1965–66	.540	Wilt Chamberlain, Phil.
1966–67	.683	Wilt Chamberlain, Phil.
1967–68	.595	Wilt Chamberlain, Phil.
1968–69	.583	Wilt Chamberlain, Lakers
1969–70	.559	Johnny Green, Cin.
1970–71	.587	Johnny Green, Cin.
1971–72	.649	Wilt Chamberlain, Lakers
1972–73	.727	Wilt Chamberlain, Lakers
1973–74	.547	Bob McAdoo, Buffalo
1974–75	.539	Don Nelson, Boston
1975–76	.561	Wes Unseld, Washington
1976–77	.579	K. Abdul-Jabbar, Lakers
1977–78	.578	Bobby Jones, Denver
1978–79	.584	Cedric Maxwell, Boston
1979–80	.609	Cedric Maxwell, Boston
1980–81	.670	Artis Gilmore, Chicago
1981–82	.652	Artis Gilmore, Chicago
1982–83	.626	Artis Gilmore, S.A.
1983–84	.631	Artis Gilmore, S.A.
1984–85	.637	J. Donaldson, Clippers
1985–86	.632	Steve Johnson, S.A.
1986–87	.604	Kevin McHale, Boston
1987–88	.604	Kevin McHale, Boston
1988–89	.595	Dennis Rodman, Detroit
1989–90	.625	Mark West, Phoenix
1990–91	.602	Buck Williams, Portland
1991–92	.604	Buck Williams, Portland
1992–93	.576	Cedric Ceballos, Phoenix
1993–94	.599	Shaquille O'Neal, Orl.
1994–95	.633	Chris Gatling, G.S.
1995–96	.584	Gheorghe Muresan, Wash.
1996–97	.604	Gheorghe Muresan, Wash.
1997–98	.584	Shaquille O'Neal, Lakers
1998–99	.576	Shaquille O'Neal, Lakers
1999–00	.574	Shaquille O'Neal, Lakers

Free-throw percentage

Year	Pct.	Player
1946–47	.811	Fred Scolari, Wash.
1947–48	.788	Bob Feerick, Wash.
1948–49	.859	Bob Feerick, Wash.
1949–50	.843	Max Zaslofsky, Chi.
1950–51	.855	Joe Fulks, Phil.
1951–52	.904	Bob Wanzer, Rochester
1952–53	.850	Bill Sharman, Boston
1953–54	.844	Bill Sharman, Boston
1954–55	.897	Bill Sharman, Boston
1955–56	.867	Bill Sharman, Boston
1956–57	.905	Bill Sharman, Boston
1957–58	.904	Dolph Schayes, Syracuse
1958–59	.932	Bill Sharman, Boston
1959–60	.892	Dolph Schayes, Syracuse
1960–61	.921	Bill Sharman, Boston
1961–62	.896	Dolph Schayes, Syracuse
1962–63	.881	Larry Costello, Syracuse
1963–64	.853	Oscar Robertson, Cin.
1964–65	.877	Larry Costello, Phil.
1965–66	.881	Larry Siegfried, Boston

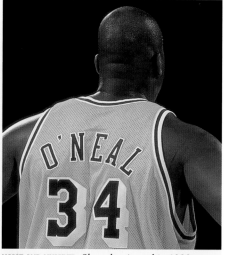

NAME AND NUMBER: *Shaq dominated in 1999–2000, finishing as the season's scoring leader.*

NEXT QUESTION? *Allen Iverson silenced defenders in 1998–99, leading the NBA in scoring.*

Yearly Statistical Leaders

1966–67	.903	Adrian Smith, Cincinnati
1967–68	.873	Oscar Robertson, Cin.
1968–69	.864	Larry Siegfried, Boston
1969–70	.898	Flynn Robinson, Mil.
1970–71	.859	Chet Walker, Chicago
1971–72	.894	Jack Marin, Baltimore
1972–73	.902	Rick Barry, Golden State
1973–74	.902	Ernie DiGregorio, Buffalo
1974–75	.904	Rick Barry, Golden State
1975–76	.923	Rick Barry, Golden State
1976–77	.945	Ernie DiGregorio, Buffalo
1977–78	.924	Rick Barry, Golden State
1978–79	.947	Rick Barry, Houston
1979–80	.935	Rick Barry, Houston
1980–81	.958	Calvin Murphy, Houston
1981–82	.899	Kyle Macy, Phoenix
1982–83	.920	Calvin Murphy, Houston
1983–84	.888	Larry Bird, Boston
1984–85	.907	Kyle Macy, Phoenix
1985–86	.896	Larry Bird, Boston
1986–87	.910	Larry Bird, Boston
1987–88	.922	Jack Sikma, Milwaukee
1988–89	.911	Magic Johnson, Lakers
1989–90	.930	Larry Bird, Boston
1990–91	.918	Reggie Miller, Indiana
1991–92	.947	Mark Price, Cleveland
1992–93	.948	Mark Price, Cleveland
1993–94	.956	Mahmoud Abdul-Rauf, Denver
1994–95	.934	Spud Webb, Sacramento
1995–96	.930	Mahmoud Abdul-Rauf, Denver
1996–97	.906	Mark Price, Golden State
1997–98	.939	Chris Mullin, Indiana
1998–99	.915	Reggie Miller, Indiana
1999–00	.950	Jeff Hornacek, Utah

Three-point field-goal percentage

Year	Pct.	Player
1979–80	.443	Fred Brown, Seattle
1980–81	.383	Brian Taylor, San Diego
1981–82	.439	Campy Russell, N.Y.
1982–83	.345	Mike Dunleavy, S.A.
1983–84	.361	Darrell Griffith, Utah
1984–85	.433	Byron Scott, Lakers
1985–86	.451	Craig Hodges, Milwaukee
1986–87	.481	Kiki Vandeweghe, Port.
1987–88	.491	Craig Hodges, Mil./Pho.
1988–89	.522	Jon Sundvold, Miami
1989–90	.507	Steve Kerr, Cleveland
1990–91	.461	Jim Les, Sacramento
1991–92	.446	Dana Barros, Seattle
1992–93	.453	B.J. Armstrong, Chicago
1993–94	.459	Tracy Murray, Portland
1994–95	.524	Steve Kerr, Chicago
1995–96	.522	Tim Legler, Washington
1996–97	.470	Glen Rice, Charlotte
1997–98	.464	Dale Ellis, Seattle
1998–99	.476	Dell Curry, Milwaukee
1999–00	.491	Hubert Davis, Dallas

Minutes

Year	Mins.	Player
1951–52	2939	Paul Arizin, Philadelphia
1952–53	3166	Neil Johnston, Phil.
1953–54	3296	Neil Johnston, Phil.
1954–55	2953	Paul Arizin, Philadelphia
1955–56	2838	Slater Martin, Minnesota
1956–57	2851	Dolph Schayes, Syracuse
1957–58	2918	Dolph Schayes, Syracuse
1958–59	2979	Bill Russell, Boston
1959–60	3338	Wilt Chamberlain, Phil.
	3338	Gene Shue, Detroit
1960–61	3773	Wilt Chamberlain, Phil.
1961–62	3882	Wilt Chamberlain, Phil.
1962–63	3806	Wilt Chamberlain, S.F.
1963–64	3689	Wilt Chamberlain, S.F.
1964–65	3466	Bill Russell, Boston
1965–66	3737	Wilt Chamberlain, Phil.
1966–67	3682	Wilt Chamberlain, Phil.
1967–68	3836	Wilt Chamberlain, Phil.
1968–69	3695	Elvin Hayes, San Diego
1969–70	3665	Elvin Hayes, San Diego
1970–71	3678	John Havlicek, Boston
1971–72	3698	John Havliceck, Boston
1972–73	3681	Nate Archibald, K.C./Oma.
1973–74	3602	Elvin Hayes, Washington
1974–75	3539	Bob McAdoo, Buffalo
1975–76	3379	K. Abdul-Jabbar, Lakers
1976–77	3364	Elvin Hayes, Washington
1977–78	3638	Len Robinson, N.O.
1978–79	3390	Moses Malone, Houston
1979–80	3226	Norm Nixon, Clippers
1980–81	3417	Adrian Dantley, Utah
1981–82	3398	Moses Malone, Houston
1982–83	3093	Isiah Thomas, Detroit
1983–84	3082	Jeff Ruland, Washington
1984–85	3182	Buck Williams, N.J.
1985–86	3270	Maurice Cheeks, Phil.
1986–87	3281	Michael Jordan, Chi.
1987–88	3311	Michael Jordan, Chi.
1988–89	3255	Michael Jordan, Chi.
1989–90	3238	Rodney McCray, Sac.
1990–91	3315	Chris Mullin, G.S.
1991–92	3346	Chris Mullin, G.S.
1992–93	3323	Larry Johnson, Charlotte
1993–94	3533	Latrell Sprewell, G.S.
1994–95	3361	Vin Baker, Milwaukee
1995–96	3457	Anthony Mason, N.Y.
1996–97	3362	Glen Rice, Charlotte
1997–98	3394	Michael Finley, Dallas
1998–99	2060	Jason Kidd, Phoenix
1999–00	3464	Michael Finley, Dallas

Rebounding

Year	No.	Player
1950–51	1080	Dolph Schayes, Syracuse
1951–52	880	Larry Foust, Fort Wayne
	880	Mel Hutchins, Milwaukee
1952–53	1007	George Mikan, Minn.
1953–54	1098	Harry Gallatin, N.Y.
1954–55	1085	Neil Johnston, Phil.
1955–56	1164	Bob Pettit, St. Louis
1956–57	1256	Maurice Stokes, Roch.
1957–58	1564	Bill Russell, Boston
1958–59	1612	Bill Russell, Boston
1959–60	1941	Wilt Chamberlain, Phil.
1960–61	2149	Wilt Chamberlain, Phil.
1961–62	2052	Wilt Chamberlain, Phil.
1962–63	1946	Wilt Chamberlain, S.F.
1963–64	1930	Bill Russell, Boston
1964–65	1878	Bill Russell, Boston
1965–66	1943	Wilt Chamberlain, Phil.
1966–67	1957	Wilt Chamberlain, Phil.
1967–68	1952	Wilt Chamberlain, Phil.
1968–69	1712	Wilt Chamberlain, Lakers

(*coverted to average per game from 1969–70)

Year	Ave.	Player
1969–70	16.9	Elvin Hayes, San Diego
1970–71	18.2	Wilt Chamberlain, Lakers
1971–72	19.2	Wilt Chamberlain, Lakers
1972–73	18.6	Wilt Chamberlain, Lakers
1973–74	18.1	Elvin Hayes, Washington
1974–75	14.8	Wes Unseld, Washington
1975–76	16.9	K. Abdul-Jabbar, Lakers
1976–77	14.4	Bill Walton, Portland
1977–78	15.7	Len Robinson, N.O.
1978–79	17.6	Moses Malone, Houston
1979–80	15.0	Swen Nater, San Diego
1980–81	14.8	Moses Malone, Houston
1981–82	14.7	Moses Malone, Houston
1982–83	15.3	Moses Malone, Phil.
1983–84	13.4	Moses Malone, Phil.
1984–85	13.1	Moses Malone, Phil.
1985–86	13.1	Bill Laimbeer, Detroit
1986–87	14.6	Charles Barkley, Phil.
1987–88	13.03	Michael Cage, Clippers
1988–89	13.5	Hakeem Olajuwon, Hou.
1989–90	14.0	Hakeem Olajuwon, Hou.
1990–91	13.0	David Robinson, S.A.
1991–92	18.7	Dennis Rodman, Detroit
1992–93	18.3	Dennis Rodman, Detroit
1993–94	17.3	Dennis Rodman, S.A.
1994–95	16.8	Dennis Rodman, S.A.
1995–96	14.9	Dennis Rodman, Chi.
1996–97	16.1	Dennis Rodman, Chi.
1997–98	15.0	Dennis Rodman, Chi.
1998–99	13.0	Chris Webber, Sac.
1999–00	14.1	Dikembe Mutombo, Atl.

Assists

Year	No.	Player
1946–47	202	Ernie Calverly, Prov.
1947–48	120	Howie Dallmar, Phil.
1948–49	321	Bob Davies, Rochester
1949–50	396	Dick McGuire, N.Y.
1950–51	414	Andy Phillip, Phil.
1951–52	539	Andy Phillip, Phil.
1952–53	547	Bob Cousy, Boston
1953–54	518	Bob Cousy, Boston
1954–55	557	Bob Cousy, Boston
1955–56	642	Bob Cousy, Boston
1956–57	478	Bob Cousy, Boston
1957–58	463	Bob Cousy, Boston
1958–59	557	Bob Cousy, Boston
1959–60	715	Bob Cousy, Boston
1960–61	690	Oscar Robertson, Cin.
1961–62	899	Oscar Robertson, Cin.

Yearly Statistical Leaders

Year		Player
1962–63	825	Guy Rodgers, S.F.
1963–64	868	Oscar Robertson, Cin.
1964–65	861	Oscar Robertson, Cin.
1965–66	847	Oscar Robertson, Cin.
1966–67	908	Guy Rodgers, Chicago
1967–68	702	Wilt Chamberlain, Phil.
1968–69	772	Oscar Robertson, Cin.

*(*converted to average per game from 1968–69)*

Year	Ave.	Player
1969–70	9.1	Lenny Wilkens, Seattle
1970–71	10.1	Norm Van Lier, Cin.
1971–72	9.7	Jerry West, Lakers
1972–73	11.4	Nate Archibald, K.C./Oma.
1973–74	8.2	Ernie DiGregorio, Buffalo
1974–75	8.0	Kevin Porter, Washington
1975–76	8.1	Don Watts, Seattle
1976–77	8.5	Don Buse, Indiana
1977–78	10.2	Kevin Porter, Det.-N.J.
1978–79	13.4	Kevin Porter, Detroit
1979–80	10.1	Micheal Ray Richardson, N.Y.
1980–81	9.1	Kevin Porter, Washington
1981–82	9.6	Johnny Moore, S.A.
1982–83	10.5	Magic Johnson, Lakers
1983–84	13.1	Magic Johnson, Lakers
1984–85	13.98	Isiah Thomas, Detroit
1985–86	12.6	Magic Johnson, Lakers
1986–87	12.2	Magic Johnson, Lakers
1987–88	13.8	John Stockton, Utah
1988–89	13.6	John Stockton, Utah
1989–90	14.5	John Stockton, Utah
1990–91	14.2	John Stockton, Utah
1991–92	13.7	John Stockton, Utah
1992–93	12.0	John Stockton, Utah
1993–94	12.6	John Stockton,Utah
1994–95	12.3	John Stockton, Utah
1995–96	11.2	John Stockton, Utah
1996–97	11.4	Mark Jackson, Den./Ind.
1997–98	10.5	Rod Strickland, Wash.
1998–99	10.8	Jason Kidd, Phoenix
1999–00	10.1	Jason Kidd, Phoenix

Personal Fouls

Year	Fouls	Player
1946–47	208	Stan Miasek, Detroit
1947–48	231	Charles Gilmur, Chicago
1948–49	273	Ed Sadowski, Phil.
1949–50	297	George Mikan, Minn.
1950–51	308	George Mikan, Minn.
1951–52	286	George Mikan, Minn.
1952–53	334	Don Meineke, Fort Wayne
1953–54	303	Earl Lloyd, Syracuse
1954–55	319	Vern Mikkelsen, Minn.
1955–56	319	Vern Mikkelsen, Minn.
1956–57	312	Vern Mikkelsen, Minn.
1957–58	311	Walter Dukes, Detroit
1958–59	332	Walter Dukes, Detroit
1959–60	311	Tom Gola, Philadelphia
1960–61	335	Paul Arizin, Philadelphia
1961–62	330	Tom Meschery, Phil.
1962–63	312	Zelmo Beaty, St. Louis
1963–64	325	Wayne Embry, Cincinnati
1964–65	345	Bailey Howell, Baltimore
1965–66	344	Zelmo Beaty, St. Louis
1966–67	344	Joe Strawder, Detroit
1967–68	366	Bill Bridges, St. Louis
1968–69	329	Billy Cunningham, Phil.
1969–70	335	Jim Davis, Atlanta
1970–71	350	Dave Cowens, Boston
1971–72	314	Dave Cowens, Boston
1972–73	323	Neal Walk, Phoenix
1973–74	319	Kevin Porter, Washington
1974–75	330	Bob Dandridge, Mil.
	330	Phil Jackson, N.Y.
1975–76	356	Charlie Scott, Boston
1976–77	363	Lonnie Shelton, N.Y.
1977–78	350	Lonnie Shelton, N.Y.
1978–79	367	Bill Robinzine, K.C.
1979–80	328	Darryl Dawkins, Phil.
1980–81	342	Ben Poquette, Utah
1981–82	372	Steve Johnson, K.C.
1982–83	379	Darryl Dawkins, N.J.
1983–84	386	Darryl Dawkins, N.J.
1984–85	344	Hakeem Olajuwon, Hou.
1985–86	333	Charles Barkley, Phil.
1986–87	340	Steve Johnson, Portland
1987–88	332	Patrick Ewing, N.Y.
1988–89	337	Grant Long, Miami
1989–90	328	Rik Smits, Indiana
1990–91	338	Sam Mitchell, Minnesota
1991–92	315	Tyrone Hill, G.S.
1992–93	332	Stanley Roberts, Clippers
1993–94	312	Shawn Kemp, Seattle
1994–95	338	Shawn Bradley, Phil.
1995–96	300	Elden Campbell, Lakers
	300	Otis Thorpe, Detroit
1996–97	320	Shawn Kemp, Seattle
1997–98	321	Ervin Johnson, Mil.
1998–99	212	Danny Fortson, Denver
1999–00	371	Shawn Kemp, Cleveland

Steals

Year	Ave.	Player
1973–74	2.68	Larry Steele, Portland
1974–75	2.85	Rick Barry, Golden State
1975–76	3.18	Don Watts, Seattle
1976–77	3.47	Don Buse, Indiana
1977–78	2.74	Ron Lee, Phoenix
1978–79	2.46	M.L. Carr, Detroit
1979–80	3.23	Micheal Ray Richardson, N.Y.
1980–81	3.43	Magic Johnson, Lakers
1981–82	2.67	Magic Johnson, Lakers
1982–83	2.84	Micheal Ray Richardson, Golden State/New Jersey
1983–84	2.65	Rickey Green, Utah
1984–85	2.96	Michael Ray Richardson, N.J.
1985–86	3.67	Alvin Robertson, S.A.
1986–87	3.21	Alvin Robertson, S.A.
1987–88	3.16	Michael Jordan, Chicago
1988–89	3.21	John Stockton, Utah
1989–90	2.77	Michael Jordon, Chicago
1990–91	3.04	Alvin Robertson, Mil.
1991–92	2.98	John Stockton, Utah
1992–93	2.83	Michael Jordan, Chicago
1993–94	2.96	Nate McMillan, Seattle
1994–95	2.94	Scottie Pippen, Chicago
1995–96	2.85	Gary Payton, Seattle
1996–97	2.72	Mookie Blaylock, Atlanta
1997–98	2.61	Mookie Blaylock, Atlanta
1998–99	2.68	Kendall Gill, N.J.
1999–00	2.67	Eddie Jones, Charlotte

Blocked Shots

Year		Player
1973–74	4.85	Elmore Smith, Buffalo
1974–75	3.26	Kareem Abdul-Jabbar, Milwaukee
1975–76	4.12	Kareem Abdul-Jabbar, Lakers
1976–77	3.25	Bill Walton, Portland
1977–78	3.38	George Johnson, N.J.
1978–79	3.95	Kareem Abdul-Jabbar, Lakers
1979–80	3.41	Kareem Abdul-Jabbar, Lakers
1980–81	3.39	George Johnson, S.A.
1981–82	3.12	George Johnson, S.A.
1982–83	4.29	Tree Rollins, Atlanta
1983–84	4.28	Mark Eaton, Utah
1984–85	5.56	Mark Eaton, Utah
1985–86	4.96	Manute Bol, Wash.
1986–87	4.06	Mark Eaton, Utah
1987–88	3.71	Mark Eaton, Utah
1988–89	4.31	Manute Bol, G.S.
1989–90	4.59	Hakeem Olajuwon, Hou.
1990–91	3.95	Hakeem Olajuwon, Hou.
1991–92	4.49	David Robinson, S.A.
1992–93	4.17	Hakeem Olajuwon, Hou.
1993–94	4.10	Dikembe Mutombo, Den.
1994–95	3.91	Dikembe Mutombo, Den.
1995–96	4.49	Dikembe Mutombo, Den.
1996–97	3.40	Shawn Bradley, N.J.-Dallas
1997–98	3.65	Marcus Camby, Toronto
1998–99	3.91	Alonzo Mourning, Miami
1999–00	3.72	Alonzo Mourning, Miami

Ejections

Year	No.	Player
1950–51	19	Cal Christensen, Tri-Cities
1951–52	18	Don Boven, Milwaukee
1952–53	26	Don Meineke, Fort Wayne
1953–54	12	Earl Lloyd, Syracuse
1954–55	17	Charley Share, Milwaukee
1955–56	17	Vern Mikkelsen, Minn.
	17	Arnie Risen, Boston
1956–57	18	Vern Mikkelsen, Minn.
1957–58	20	Vern Mikkelsen, Minn.
1958–59	22	Walter Dukes, Detroit
1959–60	20	Walter Dukes, Detroit
1960–61	16	Walter Dukes, Detroit
1961–62	20	Walter Dukes, Detroit
1962–63	13	Frank Ramsey, Boston
1963–64	11	Zelmo Beaty, St. Louis
	11	Gus Johnson, Baltimore
1964–65	15	Tom Sanders, Boston
1965–66	19	Tom Sanders, Boston
1966–67	19	Joe Strawder, Detroit

Yearly Statistical Leaders

1967–68	18	John Tresvant, Det./Cin.
	18	Joe Strawder, Detroit
1968–69	14	Art Harris, Seattle
1969–70	18	Norm Van Lier, Cin.
1970–71	16	John Trapp, San Diego
1971–72	14	Curtis Perry, Hou./Mil.
1972–73	16	Elmore Smith, Buffalo
1973–74	15	Mike Bantom, Phoenix
1974–75	12	Kevin Porter, Washington
1975–76	19	Bill Robinzine, K.C.
1976–77	21	Joe Merriweather, Atlanta
1977–78	20	George Johnson, N.J.
1978–79	19	John Drew, Atlanta
	19	Tree Rollins, Atlanta
1979–80	12	Tree Rollins, Atlanta
	12	James Edwards, Indiana
	12	George McGinnis, Den/Ind
1980–81	18	Ben Poquette, Utah
1981–82	25	Steve Johnson, K.C.
1982–83	23	Darryl Dawkins, N.J.
1983–84	22	Darryl Dawkins, N.J.
1984–85	16	Ken Bannister, N.Y.
1985–86	13	Joe Barry Carroll, G.S.
	13	Steve Johnson, S.A.
1986–87	16	Steve Johnson, Portland
1987–88	11	Jack Sikma, Milwaukee
	11	Frank Brickowski, S.A.
1988–89	14	Rik Smits, Indiana
1989–90	11	Grant Long, Miami
	11	Rik Smits, Indiana
	11	LaSalle Thompson, Ind.
1990–91	15	Blair Rasmussen, Denver
1991–92	13	Shawn Kemp, Seattle
1992–93	15	Stanley Roberts, Clippers
1993–94	11	Shawn Kemp, Seattle
	11	Rik Smits, Indiana
1994–95	18	Shawn Bradley, Phil.
1995–96	11	Matt Geiger, Charlotte
1996–97	11	Shawn Kemp, Seattle
	11	Walt Williams, Toronto

1997–98	15	Shawn Kemp, Cleveland
1998–99	9	Danny Fortson, Denver
	9	Otis Thorpe, Washington
1999–00	13	Shawn Kemp, Cleveland
	13	Lamar Odom, Clippers

Top winning percentages

Regular season

	Pct.	Year	Team	Record
1.	.878	1995–96	Chicago	(72–10)
2.	.841	1971–72	L.A. Lakers	(69–13)
	.841	1996–97	Chicago	(69–13)
4.	.840	1966–67	Phil. 76ers	(68–13)
5.	.829	1972–73	Boston	(68–14)
6.	.8171	1985–86	Boston	(67–15)
	.8171	1991–92	Chicago	(67–15)
	.8171	1999–00	L.A. Lakers	(67–15)
9.	.8167	1946–47	Wash. Caps.	(49–11)
10.	.805	1970–71	Milwaukee	(66–16)

Home

1.	.976	1985–86	Boston	(40–1)
2.	.971	1949–50	Rochester	(33–1)
3.	.969	1949–50	Syracuse	(31–1)
4.	.968	1949–50	Minneapolis	(30–1)
5.	.967	1946–47	Wash. Caps	(29–1)
6.	.951	1986–87	Boston	(39–2)
		1994–95	Orlando	(39–2)
		1995–96	Chicago	(39–2)
		1996–97	Chicago	(39–2)
10.	.944	1970–71	Milwuakee	(34–2)

Road

1.	.816	1971–72	L.A. Lakers	(31–7)
2.	.805	1995–96	Chicago	(33–8)
3.	.800	1972–73	Boston	(32–8)
4.	.780	1974–75	Boston	(32–9)
		1996–97	Miami	(32–9)
6.	.765	1966–67	Phil. 76ers	(26–8)
7.	.756	1991–92	Chicago	(31–10)

		1999–00	L.A. Lakers	(31–10)
9.	.732	1982–83	Phil. 76ers	(30–11)
		1996–97	Chicago	(30–11)

Top single-game crowds

Regular season

	Att.	Date/Teams/Arena
1.	62,046	March 27, 1998 Chi. at Atlanta (Georgia Dome)
2.	61,983	January 29, 1988 Boston at Detroit (Silverdome)
3.	52,745	February 14, 1987 Phil. at Detroit (Silverdome)
4.	49,551	April 17, 1990 Den. at Minnesota (Metrodome)
5.	47,692	March 30, 1988 Atl. at Detroit (Silverdome)
6.	45,790	November 7, 1997 Chi. at Atlanta (Georgia Dome)
7.	45,458	April 13, 1990 Orl. at Minnesota (Metrodome)
8.	44,970	February 21, 1987 Atl. at Detroit (Silverdome)
9.	44,180	February 15, 1986 Phil. at Detroit (Silverdome)
10.	43,816	February 16, 1985 Phil. at Detroit (Silverdome)

Playoffs

	Att.	Date/Teams/Arena/Round/Game
1.	41,732	June 16, 1988 Lakers at Detroit (Silverdome) 1988 NBA Finals, Game 5
2.	40,172	April 15, 1980 Mil. at Seattle (Kingdome) 1980 Western Conference Semifinals, Game 5
3.	39,554	June 18, 1999 N.Y. at S.A.(Alamodome) 1999 NBA Finals, Game 2
4.	39,514	June 16, 1999 N.Y. at S.A.(Alamodome) 1999 NBA Finals, Game 1
5.	39,457	May 30, 1978 Wash. at Seattle (Kingdome) 1978 NBA Finals, Game 4

All-Star Games

	Att.	Date/City/State/Arena
1.	44,735	February 12, 1989 Houston, Texas (Astrodome)
2.	43,146	February 10, 1985 Indianapolis, Ind. (Hoosier Dome)
3.	36,037	February 11, 1996 San Antonio, Texas (Alamodome)
4.	34,275	February 8, 1987 Seattle, Washington (Kingdome)
5.	31,745	February 4, 1979 Pontiac, Michigan (Silverdome)

DYNAMIC DUO: *Coach Phil Jackson (left) and Michael Jordan celebrate the Bulls' fifth NBA title.*

CHRONOLOGY OF PROFESSIONAL BASKETBALL

1891 (December) Dr. James Naismith introduces his new game of "basket ball" to a physical education class at the Springfield Men's Christian Association Training School at Springfield, Mass.

1892 (March 11) The first public basketball game is played between students and teachers at the Springfield Christian Association Training School. Football coaching great Amos Alonzo Stagg scores the teachers' only goal in a 5–1 loss.

1893 Backboards are introduced to protect the ball from spectator interference.

1894 Free throws are introduced and the free-throw line is moved from 20 to 15 feet.

1895 The point value of field goals is changed from three to two and free throws from three to one.

1896 The first known professional basketball game is played in Trenton, N.J., by teams trying to pay rent for the local armory.

1897 Five players to a team—the game gains structure.

1898 The six-team National Basketball League is introduced as the game's first professional circuit.

1925 The American Basketball League, the first attempt at a national professional circuit, is organized with teams ranging from New York to Chicago.

1927 (January 7) Abe Saperstein organizes the Harlem Globetrotters, a barnstorming team that will gain international acclaim and popularity.

1929 The professional cage, a court surrounded by rope or chicken wire, is eliminated.

1932 Basketball courts are divided into frontcourt and backcourt and the new three-second rule limits time in the lane.

1936 (August) Basketball is played for the first time as an official Olympic sport.

1936 (December 30) During a college contest at New York's Madison Square Garden, Stanford star Hank Luisetti introduces his one-handed shot, an innovation that would speed the evolution of the game.

1937 (March 17) The center jump after each basket is eliminated, a far-reaching decision that speeds up the game at all levels of play. The 10-second rule also is introduced.

1937 The National Basketball League, with 13 teams stretching from Buffalo and Pittsburgh in the East to Kankakee, Ill., and Oshkosh, Wis., in the Midwest, begins play.

1939 (November 28) Dr. James Naismith, basketball's inventor, dies in Lawrence, Kan., triggering a drive that eventually leads to creation of a basketball Hall of Fame in his honor.

ORIGINAL IDEA: *Dr. James Naismith invented the game that has become so popular around the world.*

FIVE-ON-FIVE: *The Minneapolis Lakers became the National Basketball Association's first back-to-back champions in 1950.*

1946 (June 6) The Basketball Association of America, the forerunner to the National Basketball Association, is organized with Maurice Podoloff as its president.

1946 (November 1) The New York Knickerbockers defeat the Toronto Huskies 68–66 in the first BAA game. The contest, ironically, is played on Canadian soil in Toronto.

1947 (January 11) The BAA outlaws zone defenses.

1947 (April 22) Joe Fulks scores 34 points and the Philadelphia Warriors clinch the BAA's first champion-ship series with an 83–80 Game 5 victory over the Chicago Stags.

1949 (August 3) When six National Basketball League teams and the newly formed Indianapolis Olympians merge into the BAA, the new 17-team circuit is renamed "National Basketball Association".

1950 (April 23) George Mikan scores 40 points and the Minneapolis Lakers become the NBA's first back-to-back champions with a 110–95 Game 6 triumph over the Syracuse Nationals.

1950 (October 31) Washington's Earl Lloyd becomes the first black player in NBA history when he plays in a game against Rochester.

1950 (November 22) Fort Wayne defeats Minneapolis 19–18 in the lowest-scoring game in NBA history.

1951 (January 6) Indianapolis defeats Rochester 75–73 in six overtimes – the longest game in NBA history.

1951 (March 2) East 111, West 94 in the NBA's first All-Star Game at Boston Garden.

1952 The NBA foul lane is widened from 6 to 12 feet, a move designed to neutralize the dominance of Minneapolis big man George Mikan.

562

1954 (April 12) Jim Pollard scores 22 points and the Minneapolis Lakers defeat the Syracuse Nationals 87–80 in Game 7 of the NBA Finals, becoming the first team to win three straight championships.

1954 (October 30) Rochester defeats Boston 98–95 in the first NBA game played with a 24-second shot clock.

1957 (April 13) Boston defeats St. Louis 125–123 in a double-overtime Game 7 classic, winning the first of 11 championships the Celtics would capture in a 13-year period.

1959 The first Hall of Fame class is enshrined—15 individuals and two teams.

1959 (April 9) The Boston Celtics overpower the Minneapolis Lakers 118–113, completing the first NBA Finals sweep in history and winning the first of eight straight championships.

1960 (October 19) The "Los Angeles Lakers" open their first West Coast season with a 140–123 loss at Cincinnati.

1960 (November 15) Lakers forward Elgin Baylor erupts for an NBA-record 71 points in a 123–108 victory over the New York Knicks in a game at Madison Square Garden.

1960 (November 24) Philadelphia center Wilt Chamberlain sets a single-game rebounding record when he grabs 55 in a 132–129 loss to Boston.

1961 The NBA expands to nine with the addition of the Chicago Packers—a team that would move to Baltimore after two seasons.

1962 (March 2) Chamberlain scores an incredible 100 points in the Warriors' 169–147 victory over New York.

1962 (April 14) Lakers star Baylor scores a still-standing NBA Finals record 61 points in a 126–121 Game 5 victory over Boston.

1963 (September 1) Walter Kennedy becomes the NBA's second president—a title that would be changed to commissioner four years later.

1964 The NBA widens its foul lane from 12 to 16 feet.

1964 (November 13) St. Louis Hawks forward Bob Pettit becomes the NBA's first 20,000-point scorer in a 123–106 loss to Cincinnati.

1965 (January 15) San Francisco trades Chamberlain to the Philadelphia 76ers for $150,000 and three players.

1966 (February 14) Chamberlain passes Pettit as the NBA's all-time leading scorer when he notches his 20,881st point in a game against Detroit.

1966 (April 28) The Boston Celtics win their eighth straight championship. The seventh-game 95–93 victory over the Lakers marks Red Auerbach's last game as Boston coach and sets the stage for center Bill Russell to become the NBA's first black coach.

1966 The NBA expands to 10 with the addition of the Chicago Bulls.

1967 Two more expansion teams: the San Diego Rockets and Seattle SuperSonics bring the NBA field to 12.

1967 (February 2) The rival American Basketball Association begins operation with former NBA great George Mikan as its commissioner.

1967 (April 24) The Philadelphia 76ers complete an amazing 79–17 season with a six-game victory over San Francisco in the NBA Finals, officially ending Boston's eight-year title reign.

1967 (October 13) The ABA begins play with the Oakland Oaks recording a 134–129 victory over the Anaheim Amigos.

1967 (November 19) Indiana's Jerry Harkness connects on a 92-foot shot in an ABA game against Dallas—the longest basket in professional history.

1968 The Milwaukee Bucks and Phoenix Suns expansion teams bring the NBA roster to 14.

1968 (February 17) The Naismith Memorial Basketball Hall of Fame opens in Springfield, Mass.—the site where Dr. James Naismith invented the game more than three-quarters of a century earlier.

1968 (May 4) The Pittsburgh Pipers record a 122–113 Game 7 victory over the New Orleans Buccaneers and win the ABA's first championship.

1968 (April 2) UCLA star Lew Alcindor spurns the ABA and signs a five-year contract with the NBA's Milwaukee Bucks.

1968 (July 5) The Philadelphia 76ers trade Chamberlain to the Los Angeles Lakers for three players and cash.

1969 (May 5) The Celtics earn their 11th championship in 13 years and officially close out the "Bill Russell Era" with a 108-106 Game 7 victory over Los Angeles.

1970 The NBA expands to 17 with the addition of teams in Buffalo, Cleveland and Portland and realigns into four divisions—the Atlantic, Central, Midwest and Pacific.

1971 (March 9) The Bulls end Milwaukee's record 20-game winning streak with a 110–103 victory at Chicago.

1972 (January 9) The Los Angeles Lakers, winners of a professional-sports record 33 straight games, drop a 120–104 streak-ending decision at Milwaukee.

1972 (February 16) Lakers center Wilt Chamberlain becomes the first NBA player to reach 30,000 points during a 110–109 victory at Phoenix.

1972 (March 26) The Los Angeles Lakers complete the NBA's most successful regular season (69–13) with a 124–98 victory over the Seattle SuperSonics.

1974 (March 7) The New Orleans Jazz begins operation as the NBA's 18th franchise.

1974 (August 29) The ABA's Utah Stars sign Moses Malone, the first high school player to jump directly to the professional level.

1975 (February 14) The ABA's San Diego Conquistadors defeat New York in the highest scoring game in professional history, 176–166.

1975 (June 1) Larry O'Brien succeeds Walter Kennedy as NBA commissioner.

1975 (June 16) The Milwaukee Bucks change the NBA's balance of power when they send 7-foot-2 center Kareem Abdul-Jabbar to Los Angeles in a blockbuster six-player trade.

1976 (June 17) The 9-year-old ABA goes out of business and the NBA absorbs four teams—the Denver Nuggets, Indiana Pacers, San Antonio Spurs and New York Nets—raising membership to 22.

1976 (October 21) The Philadelphia 76ers purchase the rights to forward Julius Erving from the cash-depleted New York Nets for $3 million.

1978 (April 9) In a season-closing scoring title duel, Denver's David Thompson scores 73 points in one game and San Antonio's George Gervin notches 63 in another. Gervin wins the title, 27.22 to 27.15.

1978 (July 7) An NBA franchise swap: John Y. Brown and Harry Mangurian trade their Buffalo Braves team to Irv Levin for the Boston Celtics.

1978 The NBA adds a third referee.

1979 The NBA adopts the 3-point field goal and eliminates the third referee.

1979 (October 12) The first 3-point field goal: Chris Ford connects for Boston in a game against Houston.

1980 (May 1) The Dallas Mavericks organize as the NBA's 23rd franchise.

1983 (December 13) The highest scoring game in NBA history lasts three overtimes and ends Detroit 186, Denver 184.

1984 (February 1) David Stern succeeds Larry O'Brien as NBA commissioner.

1984 (April 5) Lakers center Kareem Abdul-Jabbar becomes the NBA's all-time leading scorer when he surpasses Chamberlain's career total of 31,419 points in a game against Utah.

1985 (June 18) The New York Knicks, winner of the NBA's first Draft Lottery, select Georgetown center Patrick Ewing with their first pick.

LEADING SCORER: *Kareem Abdul-Jabbar becomes the all-time points leader in NBA history, L.A. Lakers vs. Utah, April 5, 1984.*

564

DEAL MAKERS: *Billy Hunter (left) and David Stern announce an end to the first lockout in NBA history in January 1999.*

1985 (June 30) The new Naismith Hall of Fame is dedicated in Springfield, Mass.

1986 (April 20) Chicago's Michael Jordan scores a playoff-record 63 points in a 135–131 double-overtime loss to Boston in a first-round game.

1987 (March 1) The Boston Celtics become the first team to reach 2,000 regular-season victories.

1987 (April 22) An NBA record crowd of 61,983 watches the Pistons beat the Celtics at Detroit's Pontiac Silverdome.

1988 (June 21) The Los Angeles Lakers become the first repeat champions in 19 years with a 108–105 Game 7 victory over the Detroit Pistons—their fifth title of the 1980s.

1988 (June 28) The annual draft is reduced from seven to three rounds.

1988 The NBA returns to its once abandoned three-referee plan. More expansion sees the arrival of the Charlotte Hornets and Miami Heat.

1989 (June 27) The draft is reduced from three rounds to two.

1989 League membership expands to 27 as the Minnesota Timberwolves and Orlando Magic begin play.

1990 (November 3) Phoenix defeats Utah 119–96 in a game at Japan's Tokyo Metropolitan Gymnasium—the first regular-season NBA game played outside North America.

1991 (November 7) Magic Johnson, one of the NBA's greatest stars, announces his retirement from the Los Angeles Lakers because he has tested positive for HIV.

1992 (August 8) The NBA-powered Dream Team, representing the U.S. in the Olympic Games at Barcelona, Spain, defeats Croatia 117–85 and captures the gold medal.

1993 (June 20) John Paxson's 3-point basket gives Chicago a 99–98 victory over Phoenix and the Bulls become the first team in 27 years to win three consecutive championships.

1993 The NBA announces its expansion to 28 teams with the addition of the Canadian city of Toronto.

1993 (October 6) Michael Jordan, saying he has no more basketball worlds to conquer after leading the Bulls to three straight NBA championships, retires.

1994 (April 27) The NBA awards its 29th franchise to Vancouver. The Grizzlies and Toronto Raptors will start playing in the 1995–96 season.

1995 (February 1) Utah guard John Stockton records career assist 9,922 in a game against Denver, replacing Magic Johnson as the NBA's all-time leader.

1996 (January 30) Magic Johnson begins his comeback attempt at age 36 in a game against Golden State. He would retire again after the season.

1996 (February 21) Stockton breaks another all-time NBA record when he intercepts a Boston pass for career steal No. 2,311, passing former star Maurice Cheeks.

1996 (March 1) When the Atlanta Hawks defeat the Cleveland Cavaliers, 74–68, Lenny Wilkens becomes the first NBA coach to reach 1,000 victories.

1996 (April 21)The Chicago Bulls complete the greatest regular season in NBA history when they defeat Washington 103–93 on the final day, lifting their record to an unprecedented 72–10.

1997 (June 19) The Chicago Bulls make it five titles in the 1990s by beating Utah Jazz. Michael Jordan is named Finals MVP for the fifth time.

1998 (June 14) The Chicago Bulls collect their sixth title with another win over Utah. Jordan wins a record tenth scoring title, a record-equalling fifth League MVP award and a sixth Finals MVP as the Jazz are downed in six.

1999 (January 13) Michael Jordan announces retirement as a player.

1999 (January 20) NBA and NBA Players Association sign new collective bargaining agreement.

1999 (February 5) Season begins after the first three months were lost because of the owners lockout.

1999 (June 25) San Antonio wins its first NBA championship, beating the New York Knicks in six games. Tim Duncan is the Finals MVP.

1999 (October 12) Wilt Chamberlain dies of a heart attack.

2000 (June 19) Los Angeles Lakers win their 12th NBA title, beating the Indiana Pacers in six games. Shaquille O'Neal earns the Finals MVP.

(Opposite) ADMIRAL SAILS: *The San Antonio Spurs' David Robinson celebrates winning the 1999 NBA Championship.*

Every sport has its own language and basketball is no exception. A few terms have been discussed from a technical point of view in the *Rules* chapter, pages 494–5, but if the language of an announcer leaves you confused, this may be of help.

Airball When a player shoots a shot that doesn't touch the rim it is sarcastically referred to as an "airball."

Alley-oop pass The pass is thrown as a player runs toward the basket. The receiving player catches the ball in the air and either dunks or lays it in the hoop without touching the ground.

Assist A player earns an assist when his pass to another player leads directly to a basket.

Backcourt As it refers to players, backcourt generally means guards. A team with a great backcourt would have two very talented guards.

Basket The orange hoop through which the ball must go for a player to score. A net underneath slows the ball, to confirm that the ball has indeed passed through the hoop. The net is made of white cord hanging from small orange metal rings. A basket is also the name given to the score awarded for putting the ball through the hoop, worth two points on most shots.

Bench Where substitutes and coaches reside during games. A "bench" player is another term for a reserve.

Blocking An illegal move by a defender to impede the ballhandler by making contact.

Bounce pass: Passing the ball from one player to another by bouncing it on the floor.

Bucket Slang term to describe a basket.

Center Usually the tallest player on a team's starting unit with a variety of skills that sometimes include shotblocking, rebounding and scoring. Patrick Ewing, David Robinson, Shaquille O'Neal and Alonzo Mourning are examples of top-flight centers.

Charity stripe Another name for the free-throw line.

Court The size of the court varies according to the level at which the game is being played, but the features of the court remain the same for all. The court is split into two by a center line, around which are two center-circles. Each end of the court has a free-throw line, bordered by free-throw lanes. These lanes both have a semi-circle with a 6ft radius from the center of the free-throw line. The boundaries of the court are marked by the sidelines and end lines, and there should be at least 3ft of unobstructed space beyond them. The court must have a hard surface.

Double dribble This ballhandling offence occurs when a player dribbles the ball, stops dribbling by holding the ball with one or both hands, then resumes dribbling. The opposing team is awarded possession of the ball.

Double foul When two players commit a foul at the same time, resulting in a jump ball.

Downtown The slang name given to the area outside the three point arc. Placed 7.25m from the basket, shots from this area are worth three points.

Draft A selection process to determine on which NBA teams the top newcomers will play.

Dunk The act of slamming the ball through the basket with one or two hands.

Fake When a player feigns to make one move but actually makes another to trick an opponent.

Fast break A play that occurs when the offensive team quickly gets the ball out ahead of the defensive team. The offensive team usually has a one- or two-man advantage as it goes in for a score.

Field goal Either a two-point or three-point basket can also be referred to as a field goal.

Forwards Aim to score as many baskets as possible during a game. Forwards play close to the basket, and must be good shooters and rebounders. They are usually taller than guards, but shorter than centers.

Foul A violation commited by one player against another player. On accumulating six personal fouls in a game, a player is disqualified for the rest of the game.

Free throw When a foul is commited in the act of shooting, the player fouled gets to take shots from the free-throw line, which is 15 feet from the basket. The number of shots depends on the situation of the foul, but free throws are always worth one point each.

Frontcourt As it refers to players, frontcourt usually means forwards and centers.

Goaltending Defensive: If a defending player blocks the ball after it has been shot and it is directly above the basket, on its way down toward the basket, or on the rim, this is illegal. The penalty is that the offensive team gets an automatic two points. Offensive: This occurs when an offensive player touches the ball as it is directly above the basket or on the rim. The penalty for offensive goaltending is loss of possession of the ball.

Guards Usually the shortest players on the court, but also the quickest. They need to shoot from long distance, and excel in dribbling and passing.

Halftime The time in between the first half and the second half. In the NBA each half consists of two 12-minute quarters. Teams break between the second and third quarters and change the baskets at which they shoot.

Hook shot The player starts with his back to the basket, quickly pivots around in a continuous movement before jumping and extending his shooting arm to flick his wrist to release the shot towards the basket.

Jump ball The ball is thrown into the air by an official between two opposing players to start the first or second half, after a double foul has been committed or if two players from opposing teams have gained possession of the ball at the same time. The two players must stand in the half of the circle nearest to their own baskets.

Jump shot A shot taken away from the basket. Players usually jump into the air, set themselves and take the shot. Sometimes referred to as a "jumper."

Key The keyhole-shaped area extending from the baseline under the basket.

Lane The painted area running from the end line under the basket out to the free-throw line. Offensive players cannot be in the lane more than three seconds.

Lottery The process that determines the order of selection at the start of the NBA Draft.

Man-to-man A defensive strategy in which a player directly marks an opponent instead of an area on the court.

No-look pass A flashy play where an offensive player looks in one direction as a fake, then throws a pass in another direction without looking at his target.

Officials The referees, the scorer, the timekeeper and the shot-clock operator.

One-on-one A single offensive player taking on a single defender during play.

Outlet pass Develops a defensive rebound into a fast break.

Out of bounds A player is out of bounds if he touches or goes beyond the boundary lines. The ball is deemed out of bounds if it touches any player or object in this area. The ball is then awarded to the team not in contact with the ball before it went out.

Overtime When a game is tied at the end of regulation play the two teams play a five-minute overtime period. A game can include as many overtime periods as are necessary to determine a winner.

Paint The area under the basket, and extending to the foul line. Also called the "lane," it is always painted a different color from the rest of the floor.

Pivot This takes place when a player who is holding the ball steps and turns once or more than once in any direction with the same foot, while the other foot—called the pivot foot—is being kept at its point of contact on the floor.

Point guard Usually a team's main ball-handler. He leads the offense and distributes the ball to the team's best scorers. John Stockton, Anfernee Hardaway and Gary Payton are among the NBA's best point guards.

Power forward Usually occupies one of two forward spots on a five-man unit. Known primarily for their rebounding and defensive skills. Karl Malone, Horace Grant and Chris Webber are examples of power forwards.

Quadruple-double Refers to a player who accumulates 10 or more in at last four of five statistical categories—points, rebounds, steals, blocked shots, assists—in a single game. These are very rare.

Rebound The gathering or controlling of a missed shot.

Screen This is a legal action by a player who, without causing undue contact, delays or prevents an opponent from reaching a desired position.

Shot clock The 24-second clock used to time possessions. The offensive team has 24 seconds in which to get off a shot.

Shooting guard Occupies one of two guard positions and usually is one of the team's primary offensive weapons. Michael Jordan was a shooting guard. Others include Reggie Miller, Latrell Sprewell and John Starks.

Sixth man Usually refers to a team's top reserve.

Slam dunk A player jumps spectacularly into the air at a considerable height and throws the ball down hard into the basket to perform a slam dunk (see also "Dunk").

Small forward Occupies one of two forward spots, the small forward is most often known for his scoring. Though not necessarily smaller in size, these players are better known for shooting and scoring skills than rebounding or defensive skills. Grant Hill and Scottie Pippen are considered small forwards.

Steal The act of a defensive player either taking the ball away from an offensive player or intercepting a pass is known as stealing.

Substitutes Substitutes are allowed to sit on the bench. They can enter play only during a dead ball and when the clock has been stopped. Substitutes are not allowed to take over from a player shooting a free throw unless he is injured.

Technical foul Assessed for a number of violations including fighting, verbal abuse of a referee, a second illegal defense call and flagrant foul.

10-second rule A team in possession of the ball in the backcourt has 10 seconds in which to move forward with the ball into the frontcourt. They are not allowed to return to the backcourt with the ball.

Three-second rule No player is permitted to stay in the restricted area between the opposing team's end line and free-throw line for longer than three seconds at a time when his team is in possession.

Traveling When a player carries the ball rather than dribbling it correctly.

Time The game is split into two halves of equal time with a break for half time. If the game ends in a tie, then an extra five minutes are added at the end.

Triple-double Refers to a player who accumulates double figures, 10 or more, in at least three of five statistical categories—points, rebounds, steals, blocked shots, assists—in a single game.

Turnover A play that results in a change of possession with the control of the ball going from one team to the other.

Verticality Used to ensure that a player has a legal position. A defender who already has moved into a position and raises his arms and hands within the vertical plane is in legal position, and therefore should not be charged with a foul if an attacking player comes into contact with them.

Violations When a player breaks the rules without physical contact being involved, such as a double dribble or kicking the ball. No foul is charged for a violation, but the offending team loses possession of the ball.

Weak side Describes the side of the key area on which the attacking team does not have the ball.

Zone Used as a defensive strategy to cover areas of the court rather than individual players.

A

Abdul-Jabbar, Kareem 21, *21*, 22, *24*, 32, 58, 62, 92, 94–5, *94*, 118, 128, 131, 135, 152, 161, 168, 185, 266, 269, 290, 332, 338, 340, 341, 342, 342, 343, *343*, 345, *345*, 346, 347, 363, *363*, 364, 372, 373, *373*, 379, 383, 388, 391, 456, 488, *490*, 498, 508, *508*, 548, *563 see also* Lew Alcindor
Abdul-Rauf, Mahmoud 47, 474
Abdul-Wahad, Tariq 47, 422, 433
Abdur-Rahim, Shareef 88, 89, *89*, 146, *146*, 153, 381
Abernethy, Tom 485
Ackerman, Val 447, 448, 449, 450, 461, *461*, 463, 464, 465
Adams, Alvan 74, 146–7, 334
Adams, Michael 147, *147*
Adelman, Rick 77, 79
Adubato, Richie 71, 118, 462, *462*
Aguirre, Mark 44, 48, 148, *148*, 276, 420, 473
Ainge, Danny 36, 74, 75, 148, *148*, 196, 343, 350
Air Canada Center, Toronto 400–401, *400*, 404, 405
Akron University 485
Alamodome, San Antonio 400, 403, 404, 405
Albright, Jane 296
Alcindor, Lew 62, 74, 94, 117, 170, 301, 329, *329*, 371, 377, 381, 383, 416, 469, 470, 471, 485, 487 *see also* Kareem Abdul-Jabbar
Alexander, Leslie 450
Alexeeva, Lidia 462
All American Red Heads 451, 460
Allen, Lucius 62, 301, 329, 487
Allen, Phog 212, 280, 293, 483, 487, *539*
Allen, Ray 63, *63*, 148–9, *149*, 164, 368, 381, 410, 478, 481, 503
Amaechi, John 422, 433
America West Arena, Phoenix 399
American Basketball Association 21–2, 31
American Basketball Council 444
American Basketball League (1925–31) 16
American Basketball League (women) 446, 451, 453, 454, *464*
AmericanAirlines Arena, Miami 397, *397*, 405, *405*
Anderson (Indiana) Packers 30,
Anderson Packers 160
Anderson, Derek 57, 478, 479
Anderson, Harold 539
Anderson, Kenny 23, 38, 67, 77, 149, *149*, 440, 474
Anderson, Nick 70, 71, 150, 353
Anderson, Willie 81
Anthony, Greg 255, 474

Arapovic, Franjo 428
Arcain, Janeth 461
Archibald, Nate (Tiny) 79, 150, 162, 364, 371, 508
Arco Arena, Sacramento 399–400
Arena in Oakland, The 396, *396*
Arizin, Paul 18, 50, 150, 185, 204, 314, 364, 369, *376*, 377, 469, 508
Arizona State University 249
Armstrong, B.J. 39, 192
Armstrong, Darrell 150, *151*
Artest, Ron 41, *41*
Assist 494–5
Astrodome, Houston 402
Atlanta Hawks 30, 34–5, 152, 155, 161, 167, 188, 192, 197–9, 199, 209, 217, 225, 228, 243, *243*, 252, 257, 266, 267, 268, 269, 298, 299, 362, 381, 392, 404, 405, 410, 426, *426*, 427, *427*, 428, *428*, 436, 496 *see also* Milwaukee Hawks, St. Louis Hawks, Tri-Cities Blackhawks
Attles, Al 50, 333
Auerbach, Arnold (Red) 18, *18*, 19, 20, 32, 36, 102, 103, 106, 112, 114, 138, 212, 231, 237, 240, 270, 272–3, *272*, *273*, 298, 305, 316, 320, 321, 322, 324, 360, 376, *376*, 383, 386, 388, 460, 538
Augmon, Stacey 474
Auriemma, Geno 297, 464.
Austin, Isaac 60
Avery, William 381
Azzi, Jennifer 449

B

Backcourt 495
Baer, Clara Gregory 451
Bailey, Thurl 86
Bailey, Tony 477
Baker, Vin 63, *82*, 83, 123, 151, *151*, 246, 374, 410
Baltimore Bullets 30, 90, 91, 117, 183, 197, 200, 201, 206, 212, 225, 239, 251, 260, 278, 306, *306*, 329, 370, 381 *see also* Capital Bullets, Chicago Packers/ Zephyrs, Washington Bullets/ Wizards
Banks, Davey 15
Barker, Cliff 468, 485
Barkley, Charles 23, 52, 53, 72, 72, 74, 75, 96–7, *96*, 97, 128, 182, 216, 217, 238, 268, 277, 351, 364, 373, 408, 410, 427, 498, *500*
Barlow, Thomas (Caveman) 518, *518*
Barnes, Jim 416
Barnes, Marvin 152
Barnett, Dick 68, 112, 278, 328, 331
Barros, Dana 152, *152*
Barry, Pete 15
Barry, Rick 22, 50, 66, 98–9, *98*,

99, 266, 325, 333, 364, 370, 492, 508–10
Barry, Sam 539
Basketball Association of America 18, 20, 28
Battie, Tony 261
Battle, John 243
Baylor, Elgin 21, 58, 98, 100–101, *100*, 128, 143, 284, 317, 320, 321, *321*, 323, 324, 326, 327, 328, 330, 364, 369, 370, *370*, 388, 439, 469, 489, 510
Beard, Butch 98, 333
Beard, Ralph 468, 485
Beaty, Zelmo 34, 152, 479
Beck, Corey 476
Beck, Ernie 314
Beckman, Johnny 15, 519, *519*
Bee, Claire 467, 483, 546
Bellamy, Walt 90, 152, 370, 510
Belov, Aleksander 418
Belov, Sergei 519, *519*
Bender, Jonathan 247
Benson, Kent 471
Berensen, Senda 451, 452, 462
Bertka, Bill 59, 118
Best, Travis 247
Biasetti, Hank Arcado 422, 424, 433, 441
Biasone, Danny 19, 313
Bibby, Henry 153, 301
Bibby, Mike 153, *153*, 479
Bickerstaff, Bernie 91, 116, 197
Binelli, Augusto 428
Bing, Dave 21, 48, 153–4, 364, 371, 381, 510
Birdsong, Otis 154–5
Biriukov, Jose 409
Blackman, Rolando 44, *154*, 155, 191, 372
Blair, Bill 64
Blake, Marty 380
Blaylock, Mookie 35, 155, *155*, 252
Blazejowski, Carol 453, 462, 519–21, *521*
Blood, Ernest 539–40
Boe, Roy 66
Bogues, Tyrone (Muggsy) 157, *157*, 381
Bol, Manute 157, 158, 228
Bolton-Holifield, Ruthie 446, 448, 455
Boone, Ron 157
Borgmann, Bennie 521
Borrell, Lazaro 422, 433, *433*
Boston Celtics 19, *19*, 20, 21, 22, 22, 28, 30, 32, 34, 35, 36–7, 100, 102, 104, 106, 107, 112,

114, 115, 117, 118, 132, 133, 138, 143, 148, 149, 150, 152, 154, 165, 168, 178, 181, 185, 188, 190, 193, 195, 197, 200, 205, 211, 212, 215, 222, 224, 231, 232, 235, *235*, 237, 240, 249, 250, 250, 261, 262, 262, 263, 265, *265*, 270, 271, 272, *272*, 275, 284, 286, 312, 315, *315*, 316, 317, *317*, 318, *318*, 319, *319*, 320, 320, 321, *321*, 322, 323, *323*, 324, *324*, 325, 326, *326*, 327, *327*, 331, 332, *332*, 334, 339, *339*, 342, *342*, 343, 344, *344*, 346, 350, 353, 360, 362, 364, 368, 369, 370, 371, 372, 376, 383, *383*, 386, *386*, 388, 391, 392, *392*, 401, 415, 430, 435, 439, 460, 480, 485, 490
Boston College 276
Boston Garden 386, *386*, 388, 389, 391, 392, 401, 403, 405
Bowie, Sam 77, 378
Bowling Green State University 258
Bowman, Nate *328*
Bracker, Joanne 462
Bradley Center, Milwaukee 398, *398*
Bradley University 192, 262, 469
Bradley, Bill 21, 68, *112*, 157, *157*, 278, 328, 330, 331, 416, 469, 503, 510–11
Bradley, Harry Lynde 398
Bradley, Shawn 45, 157–8, *158*, 228, 259
Bradshaw, Kevin 474
Bradtke, Mark 420
Brand, Elton 40, 158, *158*, 368, 369, 381, 481
Brandon, Terrell 63, *64*, 65, 160, *160*, 224, 365
Brennan, Joseph 521
Brewer, Jim 42
Brewer, Ron 80
Brian, Frank 160, 313
Bridgeman, Junior 62, 287
Bridges, Bill 34, 160
Briggs, Gary 26
Brigham Young University 148
Brokaw, Gary 471
Brooklyn College 485
Brooks, Scott 128
Brooslin, Mike 432
Brovelli, Bruce 197
Brovelli, Jim 91
Brown University 467
Brown, "Downtown" Freddie 82, 160–61, 336, 337
Brown, Dale 483
Brown, John Y. 56
Brown, Larry 47, 55, 56, 57, 73, 81, 295, 483
Brown, Renee 448
Brown, Roger 54, 170
Brown, Walter 360, 388, 546, *546*
Brown, Warren 411
Bryant, Joe 431

Bryant, Kobe *5*, 59, *59*, 161, 173, 181, 192, 241, 358, 365, *365*, 375, 429, *430*, 431, *494*
Bubbas, Vic 483
Buckner, Quinn 62, 401, 485
Buffalo Braves 30, 56, 125, 152, 164, 171, 219, 288, 371, 381, 391, *see also* Los Angeles Clippers, San Diego Clippers
Buffalo Germans 15, 546
Burrell, Scott 481
Burton, Willie 382
Buse, Don 55
Buss, Jerry 290, 391
Byers, Walter 462

C

Caldwell, Joe 34, 416, *416*
Calhoun, Jim 480, 481
Calipari, John 67
Camby, Marcus 84, 233, 381, 478
Campbell, Edna 449
Campbell, Elden *38*, 241
Cann, Howard 540
Capital Bullets 30, 91, *see also* Baltimore Bullets, Chicago Packers/Zephyrs, Washington Bullets/Wizards
Caputo, Pasquale 431
Carlesimo, P.J. 51, 77, 253
Carlson, Don 305, 307
Carlson, Dr. H. Clifford 540
Carnesecca, Lou 66, 540
Carnevale, Ben 540
Carr, Antoine 161–2, *162*
Carr, Austin 42, 471
Carr, Joe 16
Carr, M.L. 343
Carril, Pete 483, 540
Carroll, Joe Barry 51, 430
Carter, Butch 84
Carter, Donald 44
Carter, Vince *4*, 84, *85*, 85, 149, 162, *162*, 366, *366*, 367, 410
Cartwright, Bill 68, 162, *162*, 233
Case, Everett 540
Casey, Don 67
Cassell, Sam 149, 162–4, 353
Cavalli, Gary 447, 451
Ceballos, Cedric 74, 164, *165*, 360
Centenary University 235
Cervi, Al (Digger) 164–5, 313, *313*, 511
Chamberlain, Wilt (The Stilt) 20–21, *20*, 32, 50, 51, 58, 72, 92, 99, 104–5, *104*, *105*, 128, 130, 131, 136, 138, 152, 167, 169, 188, 240, 247, 258, 262, 263, 322, *322*, 325, *325*, 327, 328, 329, 330, 331, *363*, 363, 364, 365, 370, 377, 388, 391, 469, 472, 488, 492, 511, *511*, *548*
Chambers, Tom 56, 74, 75, 82, 165, *165*, 372
Chancellor, Van 446, 456, *456*, 460
Chaney, Don 165–7
Chapman, Rex 202
Charge *495*, 495
Charles, Lorenzo 472
Charlotte Coliseum 393
Charlotte Hornets 38–9, 167, 168, 169, 173, 184, 192, 202, 227, 235, 241, 298, 381, 393,

429, 434, 441
Charlotte Sting 393, 455, 462
Cheaney, Calbert 476
Cheeks, Maurce 72, 167, *167*, 275, 338, 391
Chenier, Phil 91
Cheyney State University 452
Chicago Bulls 23, 24, 32, 40–41, 110, 120, 121, 136, 137, 141, 158, *158*, 162, 184, 185, 187, 192, 195, 196, 205, 206, 209, *209*, 212, 220, 233, 235, 238, *238*, 247, 250, 251, 256, 258, 262, 282, *282*, 283, 298, *302*, 332, 349, *349*, 350, *350*, 351, *351*, 353, 354, *354*, 355, *355*, 356, *356*, 368, 373, 374, 377, 378, 379, *379*, 381, 388, 389, *389*, *393*, *393*, 400, 401, 404, 429, 460, 496, 504, *559*
Chicago Gears 17, 18, 284
Chicago Hustle 452
Chicago Packers 30, 90, 152 *see also* Baltimore Bullets, Chicago Zephyrs, Capital Bullets, Washington Bullets/Wizards
Chicago Stadium 389, *389*
Chicago Stags 30, 106, 237, 269, 305, 306, 307
Chicago Zephyrs 30, 90 *see also* Baltimore Bullets, Chicago Zephyrs, Capital Bullets, Washington Bullets/Wizards
Childs, Chris 68
Chones, Jim 42
Christie, Doug 84
Christodoulou, Theo 428
Cibona Zagreb 439
Cincinnati Royals 30, 78, 134, 170, 212, 247, 259, 321, 329, 370, 371, 377 *see also* Kansas City/Kansas City-Omaha Kings, Sacramento Kings
City College of New York 19, 469, 471, 483, 485
Clark, Archie 167
Cleaves, Mateen 481, *481*, 482
Clemson University 171, 187, 230, 300
Cleveland Cavaliers 31, 42–3, 112, 151, 160, 171, 178, 180, 187, 192, 202, 206, *206*, 211, 224, 230, 237, 239, *239*, 258, 276, *277*, 298, 365, 368, 374, 379, 380, 381, *381*, 404, 426, 428, 430, 431, 433, 496, 497, 455
Cleveland Rebels 30,
Cleveland Rockers 393
Cleveland Rosenblums 16
Clifton, Nat (Sweetwater) 19, 20
Clinton, President Bill 477, *477*
Cobbs, Mary 456
Cohen, Haskell 360
Coin flip 377, 381
Colangelo, Jerry 442
Coleman, Derrick 39, 66–7, 167, *167*, 440, 474
Coleman, Jack 309, 315
Coles, Bimbo 155
Colgate University 435, *435*
Coliseum, Indiana 402
Collins, Doug 48, 275, 282, 335, 365, 418
Columbia University 473, 484

Compaq Center, Houston 396
Conner, Lester 141
Conradt, Jody 462, 540
Conseco Fieldhouse, Indiana 401–2
Continental Airlines Arena, New Jersey 398
Cooke, Jack Kent 391
Cooper, Charles 521
Cooper, Chuck 20, 486, *486*
Cooper, Cynthia 367, 396, 447, *447*, 455, *455*, 456, 459, 460, *460*, 503
Cooper, Michael 58, 120, 167–8, *167*, 343, 345, 463
Cosic, Kresimir 521–2, *521*
Costello, Larry 168, 287, 325, 329
Cousy, Bob 18, 19, 20, 36, 92, 102, 106–7, *106*, *107*, 138, 212, 215, 237, 246, 249, 272, 315, 316, *316*, 317, 318, *318*, 319, 321, 322, 360, 364, 369, 388, 490, 511, *511*, *554*
Cowens, Dave 36, 38, 39, 51, 102, 168, 225, 250, 265, 332, 364, 371, 511
Crawford, Joan 462, 522, *522*
Creighton University 250, 483
Cremins, Bobby 239
Croce, Pat 379
Crum, Denny 540
Cummings, Terry 56, 62, 81, 168, 381
Cunha, Victorino 409
Cunningham, Billy 21, 60, 72, 168–9, *168*, 188, 205, 262, 270, 274–5, *274*, *275*, 276, 325, 364, 391, 511
Curry, Dell 168, *168*
Curry, Denise 462, 522–5, *522*

D

D'Antonio, Mike 47
DeBernardi, Forrest 525
DeBusschere, Dave 48, 68, 112, 157, 173, *173*, 278, 328, 331, 364, 370, 511–3
DiGregorio, Ernie 56, 471
Dallas Chaparrals 30, 80, 157, 190 *see also* San Antonio Spurs
Dallas Diamonds 454
Dallas Mavericks 44–5, 118, 137, 148, 155, 171, 191, 192, 207, 219, 231, 232, 236, 248, *248*, 256, 259, 287, 346, 365, 368, 373, 394, *394*, 430, 431, 432, *432*, 462
Dallmar, Howie 305
Daly, Chuck 48, 66, 70, 71, 97, 137, 191, 270, 276–7, *276*, 298, 409, 439, 440, 538
Dampier, Louie 170
Dandridge, Bob 62, 91, 170, 329, 336, *336*, 337
Daniels, Mel 22, 54, 170
Danilovic, Sasha 410
Dantley, Adrian 86, 170–1, *170*, 276, 346, 471, 489
Dartmouth University 484, 485
Daugherty, Brad 42, 171, *171*, 298
Davies, Bob 17, 19, 28, 78, 171, 263, 309, *309*, 369, 511
Davies, Chuck 486

Davis, Dale 171–2
Davis, Kenny 420
Davis, Walter 172, *172*
Dawkins, Darryl 172, *172*, 205, 275, 338, 340, *340*
Dayton University 487
Dean, Everett S. 540–41
Defense 492–3, *493*, *494*
Dehnert, H.G. (Dutch) 15, 525
Delk, Tony 478
Delta Center, Utah 401, 404
Denver Nuggets (*formerly* Denver Rockets) 30, 46–7, 147, 172, 178, 193, 199, 205, 211, 222, 228, 258, *260*, 261, 369, 371, *394*, 427, 433, 436, *489*, 496, *496*
DePaul University 127, 148, 168, 468, 469, 473, 482
Detroit Falcons 30,
Detroit Pistons 30, 48–9, 137, 148, 152, 153, 162, 167, *167*, 171, 173, 174, *175*, 181, 183, 192, 195, 196, 197, 204, 207, 209, 211, *211*, 215, 222, 239, 244, 254, *254*, 257, *257*, 276, 298, 298, 346, 347, *347*, 348, *348*, 350, 353, 362, 370, 371, 372, 381, 382, 391, 394, *395*, 409, 462, 497 *see also* Fort Wayne Pistons
Detroit Shock 396, 449, 454, 455
Detroit University 470
Developmental league 503–5
Diaz-Miguel, Antonio 541
Dick, John 485
Dickerson, Michael 88, 89
Diddle, Edgar 541
Dischinger, Terry 48, 90
Divac, Vlade 38, 39, 173, *173*, 267, 410, 420, 429, 433–5, 440
Donaldson, James 44
Donovan, Anne 453, 462, 525
Donovan, Billy 483
Draft rules 380–82
Drake, Bruce 541
Dream Team 97, 102, 118, 123, 131, 141, 209, 227, 238, 246, 277, 406–11, *408*, 420, 427, 439, 500
Drew, John 86
Drexler, Clyde 23, 52, 77, 97, 128, 174, *174*, 206, 239, 348, 350, 364, 367, 408, 489
Dribble 490
Duckworth, Kevin 244
Dudley, Chris 441
Duke University 158, 180, 187, 209, 276, 294, 381, *381*, 408, 430, 469, 471, 473, 473, 474, 475, *475*, 476, 477, 479, 480, 481
Dukes, Walker 48
Dumars, Joe 48, *167*, 174–5, *175*, 204, 215, 276, 347, 348
Dumas, Richard 351
Duncan, Tim 81, *81*, 175, *175*, 244, 246, 357, *357*, 375, *375*, 410, 459, 478, *478*, 480
Dunleavy, Mike 77
Dunn, T.R. 462–3
Duquesne University 231, 467, 485, 486
Durbin, Mark 292
Dydek, Margo 455

E

Eastern Michigan University 184
Eaton, Mark 158, 228
Eckman, Carol 462
Edeshko, Dvorni 418
Edney, Tyrus 478
Edwards, James 48, 276, 346, 347
Edwards, Teresa 451, 464, *464*
El-Amin, Khalid 481
Elie, Mario 177, *177*
Elliott, Sean 81, 177, *177*, 473
Ellis, Dale 82, 177–8, *178*, 187, 217, 373
Ellis, LaPhonso 35, 47
Ellis, LeRoy 323, *323*, *324*
Ellison, Pervis 473
Embry, Wayne 78, 178, 380
Endacott, Paul 525
English, Alex 46, 47, 178, *178*, 513, *513*
Erickson, Keith 301
Erving, Julius (Dr J) 22, *31*, 66, 72, 92, 96, 97, 108–9, *108*, *109*, 125, 167, 205, 212, 268, 274, 275, 335, *335*, 338, 340, *340*, 341, 362, 364, 365, 366, 371, 372, *372*, 391, 439, 513, *513*
Evans, Heshimu 480
Evansville University 251, 479
Ewing, Patrick 68, 69, 110–11, *110*, *111*, 131, 161, 171, 187, 202, 225, 254, 290, 352, 357, 364, 374, 378, 379, 408, 420, *422*, 424, 472, *472*, 473

F

Farmer, Larry 301
Fast break 495
Ferrell, Duane 155
Ferrin, Arnie 468
Ferry, Bob 180, 430
Ferry, Danny 26, 180, *180*, 430, 473
Finley, Michael 44, *44*, 365, 375
First team 508, 546
First Union Center, Philadelphia 398–9
Fisher, Scott 443, 475
Fitch, Bill 36, 42, 57
Fitzsimmons, Cotton 74,
Fizer, Marcus 385, 482
FleetCenter 386, 388, 392, *392*
Fleisher, Larry 546
Florida Atlantic University 457
Florida State University 162–4, 168
Floyd, Sleepy 180–81, *181*
Floyd, Tim 41, 496
Forbes, Jim 418
Ford, Chris 57, 63, 181
Ford, Phil 79, 381, 471
Fordham University 467
Fort Wayne Pistons 17, 30, 48, 126, 160, 181, 237, 269, 313, 314, 347, 496 *see also* Detroit Pistons
Fortson, Danny 480
Foster, Bill 300, 301
Foster, Harold 525
Foul lane 495
Foust, Larry 48, 126, 181, 313
Fox, Rick 181, *181*, 424, *434*, *435*
Foyle, Adonal 422, 435–6, *435*

Franchise expansion and movement 28–30
Francis, Clarence (Bevo) 484, *484*
Francis, Steve 52, *53*, 158, 182, *182*, 368
Fratello, Mike 35, 42, 43, 426, 428, 430
Frazier, Walt (Clyde)21, 68, 92, 112–3, *112*, *113*, 157, 225, 278, 328, 330, *330*, 331, 364, 371, 479, 513
Free Throw 492, *492*
Free, World B. (*also* Lloyd Free) 51, *56*, 182–3, 335
Friedman, Max (Marty) 525, *525*
Frontcourt 495
Fulks, Joe 18, 50, 183, 305, *305*, 360, 369, 513
Furey, Jim 15, 16
Furman University 485

G

Gabor, Billy 312
Gaines, Clarence (Big House) 483–4, 541
Gale, Laddie 485
Gallatin, Harry 19, 183, 513
Gallatin, Larry 309
Gardner, Jack 541
Garnett, Kevin 64, 65, 183–4, *183*, 218, 222, 366, 375, 410, 479, *492*
Garrity, Pat 71, 75, 191, 217
Gaston, Paul 388
Gates, William 525–6, *526*
Gathers, Hank 473
Gatling, Chris 47, 217
Gavitt, Dave 409
Gaze, Andrew 420, 443
Geiger, Matt 38, 61
General Motors Place, Vancouver 401, *401*
Gentry, Alvin 48, 131
George Washington University 376
Georgetown University 110, 120, 181, 225, 228, 295, 378, 379, 424, 436, 467, 472, *472*, 473, 475, 478, *478*, 483
Georgia Dome, Atlanta 404
Georgia Tech 149, 239, 474, 479
Gervin, George 22, 80, 154, 184, *184*, 364, 371, 372, 513
Gill, Amory 541
Gill, Kendall 67, 184–5, *184*, 192
Gilliam, Armen 217
Gillom, Jennifer 367
Gilmore, Artis 22, 170, 185
Givens, Jack 471
Glamack, George 469
Glouchkov, Georgi 428, *428*, 441–2, *441*
Gnad, Hansi 409
Gola, Tom 185, 204, 211, 370, 469, 513
Golden State Warriors 30, 50–51, 99, 117, 155, 160, 168, 181, 189, 196, 199, 202, 209, 227, *227*, 231, 235, 239, 242, 251, 253, 254, 265, *265*, 266, 267, 286, 287, 333, *333*, 368, 374, 396, *396*, 400, 409, 422, 427, 430, 435 *see also* Philadelphia Warriors

Gomelsky, Aleksander 541
Gomez, Calderon 409
Goodrich, Gail 58, 185, 301, 324, 330, 331, 471, 485, 513–4
Gottlieb, Eddie 18, 50, 305, 546
Graber, Betty Jo 462
Graboski, Joe 314
Grambling State University 240
Granik, Russ 379
Grant, Brian 77, 185–7, *185*
Grant, Horace 40, 70, 120, *186*, 187, 187, 282, 351
Great Western (*also* Los Angeles) Forum 390, 391
Greavey, Kevin 471
Green, A.C. 131, 157, 187, *187*, 251
Green, Sihugo 20
Greer, Hal 21, 72, 167, 169, 188, 205, 262, 325, 364, 370, 391, 514
Gregory, George 473
Grevey, Kevin 91
Griffith, Darrell 86, 188, *188*, 381, 473
Griffith, Yolanda 449, 457, *457*, 465
Griffiths, Michelle *444*
Grimstead, Swede 15
Groat, Dick 469
Gross, Bobby 76, 335
Groza, Alex 369, 469, 485
Gruenig, Robert 526
Grunfeld, Ernie 188
Guerin, Richie 35, 188–9, *189*
Guglliotta, Tom 64, 65, *74*, 75, 184, 189, *189*, 411
Guilford College 182
Gund Arena, Cleveland 393, 401, 404
Gund, George and Gordon 42
Guthridge, Bill 295
Guyton, A.J. 482

H

Hagan, Cliff 20, 34, 35, 36, 133, 160, 190, 197, 215, 218, 272, 292, 293, 315, 316, 318, 319, 377, 514
Haggerty, Horse 15
Hairston, Harry 330
Haley, Jack 136
Hall of Fame Museum 508
Hameline College 487
Hamilton, Leonard 197
Hamilton, Richard 480
Hamline University 222
Hannum, Alex 19, 72, 283, 315, 325, 388, 538
Hanson, Victor 526, *526*
Hardaway, Anfernee (Penny) 23, 70, 71, 75, 190–91, *190*, 265, 368, 383, 410, *410*, 476, 490, *493*
Hardaway, Tim 51, 60, 61, 191, *191*, 218, 219, 290, 365, 411
Harlem Globetrotters 15, 16, 20, 104, 192, 390, 449, 452, 454, 484
Harp, Dick 483
Harper, Derek 44, 68, 155, 191, *192*
Harper, Ron 41, 42, *56*, 57, 180, 192, 430

Harrick, Jim 477
Harrington, Al 247
Harris (Stewart), Lusia 453, 462, *526*, *528*
Harris, Del 59, 63, 137
Harrison, Les 78, 127, 546
Harrison, Tiger 308
Harshman, Marv 541
Hartman, Jack 280
Haskins, Clem 192
Haskins, Don (The Bear) 280, 473, 483, 541
Havlicek, Chris 503
Havlicek, John 20, 36, 92, 114–5, *114*, *115*, 168, 212, 250, 265, 272, 321, 324, 326, *326*, 327, *327*, 332, 334, 364, 371, 388, 415, 485, 503, 514
Hawkins, Connie 22, 74, 192, 514
Hawkins, Hersey 184, 192, *193*
Hayes, Elvin 52, 91, 116–7, *116*, *117*, 122, 136, 170, 333, *333*, 337, 364, 371, 416, 470, 471, 487, 514
Haynes, Marques 15, 526–8, *528*
Haywood, Spencer 22, 46, 193, 371, 378, 418, *419*, 470
Hazzard, Walt 301, 471, 485
Head, John 462
Heard, Garfield 56, 74, 91, 197, 334, 388
Heinsohn, Tom 19, 20, 36, 114, 115, 193–5, 212, 272, 315, 316, 317, 318, 319, *319*, 321, *321*, 322, 377, 514, *514*
Heitz, Kenny 487
Held ball 495
Henderson, Gerald 342
Heyman, Art 470
Hickey, Edgar 542
Hilkene, John 401–2,
Hill, Bob 81, 137
Hill, Brian 71, 88, 89
Hill, Grant 23, 48, *48*, 49, 70, 71, 175, 195, *195*, 254, 365, 410, 459, 475, *475*, 477, 490
Hill, Joe 473
Hill, Tyrone 63, 195
Hillhouse, Art 305
Hillsdale College 484
Hobson, Howard 542
Hodges, Craig 360
Hoefer, Charlie 424
Hoffman, Paul 306
Holdsclaw, Chamique 455, 457, 459, *459*, 503
Hollins, Lionel 76, 89, *338*
Holman, Nat 15, 17, 469, 483, 485, *528*, *528*
Holy Cross University 106, 193, 195, 377, 468
Holzman, Red 17, 19, 68, 270, 278, *278*, 282, 283, 282, 328, 538
Hopkins, Bob 82
Hornacek, Jeff 86, 87, *87*, 195, *195*, 367, 368, *368*
Horry, Robert 75, 195–6, *196*, 353, *495*
Hortencia 432
Houbregs, Robert 528
Houston Angels 453
Houston Comets 367, 396, *444*, 446, 447, *447*, 450, 455, *455*,

456, *456*, 457, 459, 460, *460*, 461, 462, 465, *465*
Houston Rockets 30, 52–3, 97, 110, 117, 125, 128, 141, 162, 167, 174, 177, *177*, 182, *182*, 195, 201, 202, 220, 228, *228*, 238, 254, 290, *302*, 339, *339*, 344, *344*, 352, *352*, 353, *353*, 367, 368, 371, 372, *377*, 378, *378*, 396, *422*, 436, 439, 450, 455, 472 *see also* San Diego Rockets
Houston, Allan 68, 69, 196, *197*, 411
Houston, Wade 196
Howard, Juwan 91, *91*, 196–7, *197*, 265, 475
Howell, Bailey 48, 197, 326, *326*, 514
Hudson, "Sweet" Lou 34, 35, 197–9
Hughes, Larry 51
Hundley, Hot Rod 320
Hunter, Billy 25, *25*, 564
Hurley, Bobby 474, 476
Hutchins, Mel 313
Hyatt, Charles 528
Hyatt, Chuck 487

I

Iba, Henry (Hank) 270, 280–81, *280*, *281*, 292, 418, 420, 483, 485, 542
Idaho State University 157
Il Messaggero, Rome 430
Ilgauskas, Zydrunas 43, 424, 426, 428, 431–2
Illegal defenses 493–4
Illinois Wesleyan University 250
Indiana Fever 456
Indiana Pacers 30, 31, 54–5, 102, 111, 120, 161, 170, 171, 178, 201, 202, 222, 224, *224*, 227, 236, 241, 246, 247, *247*, 248, *248*, 249, 252, 253, 257, 259, 277, 283, 288, 358, *358*, 401, 402, 452, 453
Indiana State University 22, 102, 118, 301, 383, 471, 481, 482
Indianapolis Jets 30
Indianapolis Olympians 30
Indianapols Indians 369
Iona College 189
Iowa State University 195, 385, 482
Irish, Ned 16, 390, 466, 546
Irvine, George 48
Issel, Dan 22, 46, 47, 109, 170, 199, 485, 514
Iverson, Allen 26, 73, *73*, 199, *199*, 209, 218, 254, 366, 381, *478*, *478*, *490*, *498*, *556*
Izzo, Tom 482

J

Jackson, Chris 474, 475, (*see also* Mahmoud Abdul-Rauf)
Jackson, Jim 35, 44, 199, *199*, 251, 299, 474
Jackson, Lucious (Luke) 72, 188, 325, 416
Jackson, Mark 47, 55,172, 199–200, *200*, 247, 503

Jackson, Phil 40, 59, 136, 137, 161, 270, *270*, 282–3, *282*, *283*, 331, 356, 357, 389, 460, 479, *559*
Jackson, Ray 475
Jamison, Antawn 51, *51*, 84, 480
Jeannette, Buddy 200, 306, 514
Johnson, (Magic) Earvin 21, 22, *23*, 58, 92, 94, 102, 118–9, *118*, 128, 154, 161, 168, 209, 211, 232, 249, *249*, 252, 266, 269, 277, 290, 338, *338*, 340, 342, 343, 345, *345*, 347, 349, 364, 372, 373, *373*, 377, 378, 379, 388, 391, 406, *408*, 410, 409, 427, 456, 463, 471, 481, *481*, 482, *482*, 491, 498, *549*
Johnson, Avery *80*, 81, 357
Johnson, Charles 336
Johnson, Dennis 36, 82, 200, 267, 298, 336, 337, 342, 343, 345, 371
Johnson, Eddie 74, 82, 201
Johnson, Gus 90, 201, 329, 370
Johnson, John 42, 201–2, *336*
Johnson, Kevin 74, 75, 202, *202*, 217, 224, 351
Johnson, Larry 38, 68, 202, *202*, 474
Johnson, Marques 62, 202, 287
Johnson, Vickie *444*, 503
Johnson, Vinnie 48, 161, 204, *204*, 276, 347, 348
Johnson, William 528–9
Johnston, Neil 18, 50, 150, 185, 204–5, 314, *314*, 369, 514
Jones, Bobby 72, 205, *205*, 275, 391
Jones, Caldwell 205
Jones, Charles 205
Jones, Dwight 418
Jones, Eddie 39, 59, 241, 249
Jones, K.C. 20, 36, 205, 272, 323, 343, 344, 415, 469, 485, 514
Jones, Major 205
Jones, Popeye 44
Jones, R. William 418
Jones, Sam 20, 36, 114, 205, 272, 316, 319, 320, 322, 323, 324, 327, 364, 388, 514
Jones, Wali 21, 72, 188, 325
Jones, Wallace (Wah Wah) 469, 485
Jones, Wilbert 205
Jordan, Michael 6, 23, 24, *25*, 26, 32, 40, 41, 91, 92, 120–21, *120*, *120*, 131, 141, 158, *158*, 161, 162, 174, 192, 195, 209, 212, 233, 238, 253, 270, 277, 282, *282*, 294, 295, *302*, 349, 350, *350*, 351, 351, 354, *354*, 355, *355*, 356, *356*, 358, 360, *360*, 363, 366, 373, 374, 375, 378, 388, 389, 392, 406, 408, 420, *420*, 427, 429, 448, 459, 460, 465, 467, 472, 473, 489, 490, 496, 498, *498*, 500, *501*, 503, *503*, 504, *504*, 551, *559*
Joyce, Kevin 418
Jucker, Ed 134, 483
Julian, Alvin (Doggie) 538, *539*
Jump ball 495

K

Kahn David 402
Kaner, Richard 427, 428
Kansas City/Kansas City-Omaha Kings 30, 79, 150, 154, 157, 201, 256, 265, 371, 381 *see also* Rochester Royals, Sacramento Kings
Kansas State University 155, 242
Karl, George 63, 82, 83, 149, 184, 246, 430
Karnisovas, Arturas 409
Kasten, Stan 298, 426, *426*, 427
Keaney, Frank 542
Keller, Billy 54
Kellogg, Clark 55
Kelser, Greg 482
Kemp, Shawn 23, *42*, 43, 82, 151, 187, 206, *206*, 236, 354, *374*, 497
Kennedy, J. Walter 21, 546
Kenon, Larry 66, 80
Kentucky Colonels 170, 185, 199
Kentucky Wesleyan University 479, 487
Keogan, George 542
Kerner, Ben 34, 132
Kerr, Johnny (Red) 206, 389
Kerr, Steve 355
Kersey, Jerome 206–7, *207*, 239
Key Arena, Seattle 400, 403, *403*
Kidd, Jason 44, 75, *75*, 131, *144*, 153, 202, 207, *208*, 367, 411, 480, *480*
Kiley, John 388
Kimble, Bo 473
Kinder Bologna 433
King, Bernard 188, 209, *209*
King, George 312, 313
King, Jimmy 475
Kingdome, Seattle 402, 403, *403*
Kittles, Kerry 67
Knight, Billy 55
Knight, Bob 280, 281, 294, 295, 297, 420, 471, 483, 484, 485, 542
Knight, Brevin 43, 224
Kratter, Marvin 388
Krause, Edward 529
Krause, Jerry 209, 379, *379*
Kruger, Lon 35
Kruminsh, Jan 415
Krzyzewski, Mike 474, 477, 480
Kukoc, Toni 41, 73, 209, *209*, 354, 420, 428, 429, *429*
Kundla, John 58, 100, 270, 284, *284*, 308
Kupchak, Mitch 91
Kurland, Bob 280, 281, 412, *413*, 468, 469, *469*, 485, 529, *529*

L

La Salle University 181, 185, 469, 474
Lacey, Edgar 487
Lacey, Sam 79
Laettner, Christian 64, 209, *210*, 408, 474, 475, 480, 497
LaFrentz, Raef *46*, 47, 369, 480, *489*
Laimbeer, Bill 48, 204, 211, *211*, 276, 346
Lambert, Ward (Piggy) 301, 542

Langdon, Trajan 381, *381*
Lanier, Bob 48, 62, 94, 211, 371, 514
Lapchick, Joe 14, 15, 16, 17, 18–19, 68, 127, 211, *211*, 284, 514
Layden, Frank 86, 104, 140, 459, 462
Leaventhal, Don 382
Lee, Butch 419, 471
Lemon, Meadowlark 15
Lenard, Voshon 60, 192
Leonard, Bob (Slick) 54
Leonard, Chris 15
LeRoux, Buddy 388
Leslie, Lisa 455, 456, 459, *459*, 464, 503
Lever, Lafayette (Fat) 47, 211, *212*
Levin, Irv 56
Levingston, Cliff 243
Lewis, Bob 468
Lewis, Freddie 54, 170
Lewis, Guy 128
Liberty Basketball Association 451, 452
Lieberman (Cline), Nancy 454–5, *454*, 449, *449*, 452, 464, 529–31, *529*
Litwack, Harry 542
Lloyd, Earl 20, 312
Lobo, Rebecca 444, *444*, 446, 448, 459, 480, 503
Locke, Bernadette 452
Lockout 24–5, *25*, 357, 366, 367, 368, 375, *564*
Loeffler, Ken 538, *539*
Lonborg, A.C. (Dutch) 542
Long Island Knights 454
Long Island University 19, 467, 483, 485, 514
Long, Grant 60
Longley, Luc 64, 420, 424, 432
Los Angeles (*also* Great Western) Forum 390, 391
Los Angeles Clippers 30, 56–7, 167, 180, 181, 192, 200, 202, 217, 233, 234, 243, 249, 261, 288, 369, 379, *383*, 396, *397*, 430, 439, 497 *see also* Buffalo Braves, San Diego Clippers
Los Angeles Lakers 21, 22, 30, 32, 58–9, 94, 100, 103, 104, 112, 113, 118, 120, 121, 130, 131, 137, 142, 143, 152, 157, 160, 161, 167, 168, 173, 181, *181*, 185, 187, *187*, 192, *192*, 193, 196, 197, 199, 207, 219, 224, 231, *231*, 236, 238, 241, *241*, 248, 249, 253, 259, 260, *260*, 266, 269, 269, 275, 276, 278, 282, 283, 290, 320, 321, *321*, 323, *323*, 324, *324*, 326, 327, *327*, 328, 329, 330, *330*, 331, *331*, 338, *338*, 340, 341, *341*, 342, *342*, 343, *343*, 345, *345*, 346, 346, 347, 349, 349, 350, 353, 356, 357, 358, 365, 370, 371, 372, 373, 377, 379, 388, 390, 391, 397, *397*, 400, 402, 405, 429, 431, 433, 434, *434*, 456, 459, 460, 463, *488*, *495* see also Minneapolis Lakers
Los Angeles Sparks 455, 456, 459, 463

572

Loscutoff, Jim 20, 211, 315
Lottery picks 378, 379, 384
Loughery, Kevin 60, 66, 90, 114, 135, 212
Louisiana State Univeristy 160, 133, 217, 470, *470*, 471, 474, *474*, 475, 483, 485
Louisiana Tech 122, 448, 452
Love, Bob 40, 212
Lovellette, Clyde 212, 312, 318, 469, 514
Lowe, Sidney 64, 89
Loyola-Illinois University 469, 478
Loyola-Marymount University 473, *474*
Lucas, Jerry 21, 78, 112, 212–3, 259, 278, 330, 364, 370, 377, 415, 469, 471, 485, 515
Lucas, John 286, 287
Lucas, Maurice 76, 124, 213, *213*, 288, 335
Lue, Tyronn 261
Luisetti, Hank *16*, 16, 466, *466*, 467, 485, 489, *530*, 531
Lynam, Jim 197
Lynch, George 475
Lynn, Mike 487
Lyon, Bill 443

M

McAdoo, Bob 56, 68, 219, *219*, 288, 341, 364, 371, 381, 430, 473, 479
Macauley, Ed 18, 19, 34, 35, 36, 133, 215, 218, 272, 316, 360, 369, 377, 469, 515
McCarthy, John *318*
McClain, Katrina 451
McCracken, Branch 531
McCracken, Jack 531
McCray, Nikki 444, 446, *446*
McCray, Rodney 52, 220
McCray, Scooter 220
MacCulloch, Todd 424
McCutchan, Arad A. 542
McDaniel, Clint 476
McDaniel, Xavier 82, 220, *220*
McDermott, Bobby 17, 531, *531*
McDonald, Glenn 334, 388
McDonald's Open 426, 432, 441, 505
McDyess, Antonio 5, 47, 220–222, *220*
McGinnis, George 22, 54, *55*,170, 222, *222*, 275, 335,]
McGlocklin, Jon 62
McGrady, Tracy *84*, 85, 366
McGuire, Al 222, 471, 483, 543
McGuire, Dick 222, 237, 278, 515
McGuire, Frank 104, 483, 538
McHale, Kevin 22, 36, 181, 200, 222, 343, 344, 345, 364, 388, 435, 515–6, *515*
McHugh, Howie 388
McIlvaine, Jim 67
McKey, Derrick 82
McKinney, Bones 483
McKinney, Jack 290
MacLean, Don 187
MacLeod, John 44, 74, 148, 334, 442
McMillen, Tom 418, 420

McMillian, Jim *56*, *330*
Madison Square Garden, New York 16, 390, *390*, 391, 393, 402, 403, 405, 453, 456, 466, 467, 483, 485
Madsen, Mark 482
Maggette, Corey 187, 381
Mahorn, Rick 215, *215*, 346
Majerle, Dan 26, 74, 215–6, *215*, 351
Majerus, Rick 480
Malone, Brendan 84
Malone, Jeff 216, 217
Malone, Karl 23, 24, 86, 87, 122–3, *122*, *123*, 140, *140*, 141, 195, 217, 355, 356, 363, 364, 373, 374, 378, 408, 409, 410, 489, 503
Malone, Moses 22, 52, 72, 96–7, 124–5, *124*, *125*, 136, 167, 205, 275, 339, 341, *341*, 364, 391
Man defense 493, *494*
Manhattan College 19
Mankato State University 382
Manning, Danny 57, 71, 74, 75, 191, 217, 442, 473
Maravich, Pete 34, 86, 217, 268, 364, 470, *470*, 471, 485, 515
Marbury, Stephon 64, *65*, 67, *67*, 164, 184, 217–8, *217*, 381, 479
Marciulionis, Sarunas 409, 420, 424, *424*, 426, 427, 430
Marcopolos, Tony 439
Marin, Jack 90
Marist College 252, 424
Marquette University 471, 483
Marshall University 188
Marshall, Donny 481
Marshall, Donyell 64, 189, 477, 481
Martin, Kenyon 385, *385*, 482
Martin, Slater 18, 58, 106, 127, 218, 222, 237, 238, 284, 308, 312, 316, 515
Mashburn, Jamal 23, *32*, 44, 61, 218–9, *218*, 476
Mason, Anthony 38, 39, *39*
Maxwell, Cedric 102, 339, 342, 343
Maxwell, Vernon 352
May, Darlene 462
May, Scott 471, 485
Mayzel, Harry 424
MCI Center, Washington 401
Meanwell, Dr. Walter 543
Medalha, Jose 409
Melvin, Chasity 449
Memorial Coliseum, Portland 391
Memphis Sounds 170
Memphis State University 368, 476
Memphis University 190
Menedez, Al 442
Meneghin, Dino 427
Mercer, Ron 36, 47, 478, 480
Metrodome, Minnesota 403
Meyer, Ray 543
Meyers, Ann 452, 453, 455, 462, 531–4, *532*
Meyers, Dave 301, 453, 471, 485
Miami Heat *32*, 60–61, 110, 136, 184, 187, 190, 191, 216, 218, 219, 227, 239, 241, 252, 275, 277, 290, *290*, 294, 374, 397, 405

Miami Sol 397, 455
Michigan State University 22, 102, 118, 252, 385, 471, 478, 481, *481*, 482
Mihm, Chris 482
Mikan, George 17, *17*, 18–9, 20, 21, 28, 31, 58, 64, 92, 104, 126–7, *126*, *127*, 181, 204, 212, 218, 222, 238, 284, *284*, 307, *307*, 308, 310, 311, *311*, 312, *312*, 313, 360, 364, 369, *369*, 468, *468*, 469, 503, 508, 516
Mikkelsen, Vern 18, 58, 127, 218, 222, 238, 284, 308, *308*, 310, 312, *317*, 377, 516
Miller, Andre 43, *43*, 153, 222–4, *224*, 368, 481
Miller, Cheryl 448, 453, *453*, 459, 463, *463*, *533*, 534
Miller, Mike 385, *385*
Miller, Oliver 74, 84
Miller, Ralph 543
Miller, Reggie 23, 54, 55, *154*, 171, 200, 224, *224*, 247, 358, *358*, 402, 410, 453, 492
Milton, DeLisha 449
Milwaukee Bucks 21, 62–3, 94, 115, 135, 148, 149, 151, 160, 164, 168, 169, 170, 171, 178, 181, 188, 202, 211, 217, 224, 231, 232, 237, 244, 246, 247, 250, 278, 286, 287, 329, *329*, 330, 332, *332*, 368, 371, 374, 377, 383, 396, 398, *398*, 426, 430, 432
Milwaukee Does 452
Milwaukee Hawks 30, 34, 133
see also Atlanta Hawks, St. Louis Hawks, Tri-Cities Blackhawks
Miner, Harold 475
Minneapolis Lakers *12*, 17, 18, 19, 30, 58, 100, 106, 127, 133, 142, 181, 183, 212, 218, 222, 238, 255, 263, 270, 284, 307, *307*, 308, *308*, 309, 310, *310*, 311, *311*, 312, *312*, 313, 317, *317*, 350, 353, 369, 377, 460, 561 see also Los Angeles Lakers
Minnesota Lynx 455
Minnesota Muskies 170
Minnesota School of Agriculture 487
Minnesota Timberwolves 64–5, 160, 183, 184, 189, 209, 218, 222, 239, *243*, 251, *251*, 299, 357, 381, 398, 403, *492*
Misaka, Walt 468
Mississippi State University 197, 217, 469, 473
Missouri State Teachers College 183
Mitchell, Mike 80
Mitchell, Sam 430
Modzelewski, Stan 469
Moe, Doug 47, 178, 261
Moncrief, Sidney 62, 224–5, *225*, 287
Monroe, Earl (The Pearl) 68, 90, 112, 157, 212, 225, 278, 329, 331, 364, 371, 381, 439, 484, 516
Montclair State University 453
Monter, Chris 382
Montero, Jose-Antonio 428

Moore, Billie 463, 543–5, *543*
Morandoti, Ricardo 428
Morgan State University 381
Morris, Chris 441
Most, Johnny 388
Motta, Dick 40, 44, 91, 148, 161, 212
Mount University 487
Mourning, Alonzo 5, 23, 38, 60, *60*, 61, 131, *144*, 225–7, *225*, 228, 290, 411, 448, 475, 489
Mullin, Chris *50*, 51, 55, 227, *227*, 401, 408, 420
Mullins, Jeff 325
Murdock, Eric 130
Muresan, Gheorghe 227–8, *227*, 436, *436*
Murphy, Calvin 52, 195, 228, *228*, 516
Murphy, Charles 534, *534*
Murphy, Troy 482
Musselman, Bill 64
Mutombo, Dikembe 25, 35, *35*, 47, 228, *228*, 424, 436, *436*

N

Naismith, Dr. James 12, 14, *14*, 422, 451, 487, 488, 491, 493, 508, *560*
Nance, Larry 42, 74, 230, *230*, 298, 360, 362, 366
Nash, John 207
Nash, Steve 424
National Basketball League (1898–1903) 14
National Basketball League (1937–49) 17, 28
Natt, Calvin 47
NBA City 503
NBA Finals 1947 – 305, *305*
1948 – 306, *306*
1949 – 307, *307*
1950 – 308, *308*
1951 – 309, *309*
1952 – 310, *310*
1953 – 311, *311*
1954 – 312, *312*
1955 – 313, *313*
1956 – 314, *314*
1957 – 315, *315*
1958 – 316, *316*
1959 – 317, *317*
1960 – 318, *318*
1961 – 319, *319*
1962 – 320, *320*
1963 – 321, *321*
1964 – 322, *322*
1965 – 323, *323*
1966 – 324, *324*
1967 – 325, *325*
1968 – 326, *326*
1969 – 327, *327*
1970 – 328, *328*
1971 – 329, *329*
1972 – 330, *330*
1973 – 331, *331*
1974 – 332, *332*
1975 – 333, *333*
1976 – 334, *334*
1977 – 335, *335*
1978 – 336, *336*
1979 – 337, *337*
1980 – 338, *338*
1981 – 339, *339*

1982 – 340, *340*
1983 – 341, *341*
1984 – 342, *342*
1985 – 343, *343*
1986 – 344, *344*
1987 – 345, *345*
1988 – 346, *346*
1989 – 347, *347*
1990 – 348, *348*
1991 – 349, *349*
1992 – 350, *350*
1993 – 351, *351*
1994 – 352, *352*
1995 – 353, *353*
1996 – 354, *354*
1997 – 355, *355*
1998 – 356, *356*
1999 – 357, *357*
2000 – 358, *358*
NBA Store 501–3
NBA, birth of 18, 20
NBA.com 506
NCAA (National Collegiate Athletic Association) 17
NCAA Final Four 469–82, 483, *483*, 485, 487
Neal, Jim 312
Nelson, Don 20, 36, 44, 45, 51, 62, 137, 231, 232, *232*, 265, 270, 286–7, *286*, 287, 272, 324, 326, 388
Nelson, Donn 44, 287, 430, 431
New Jersey Nets (*formerly* New Jersey Americans) 30, 66–7, 149, 154, 155, 164, 167, 181, 184, *184*, 185, 199, 209, 218, 249, 257, 261, *261*, 266, 277, 398, 427, 436, *436*, 439, 440, 441, 442 *see also* New York Nets
New Orleans Jazz 30, 86, 185, 217, 403, 453 *see also* Utah Jazz
New Orleans Superdome 403
New York Knickerbockers (Knicks) 19, 20, 21, 28, 30, 68–9, 100, 103, 104, 110, 112, 127, 143, 155, 157, 161, 162, 167, 168, 173, 183, 185, 188, 189, 191, 193, 196, 202, 207, 209, 211, 212, 219, 220, 222, 224, 225, 233, 240, *240*, 241, *241*, 243, 246, 253, 254, 261, 265, 266, 269, 278, 282, *283*, 284, 286, 287, *287*, 290, 298–9, 305, 309, 310, 311, 312, 328, 330, *330*, 351, *352*, 352, 357, 371, 374, 378, 390, 422, *422*, 441, 453, 456, 469, 472, 496
New York Liberty 448, 449, 453, 455, 456, 462
New York Nets 22, 30, 66, 109, 170, 212, 268 *see also* New Jersey Nets
New York Renaissance 16, 546
New York University 19, 248, 466, 467
Newberry College 485
Newell, Pete 295, 415
Niagara University 168, 228
Nicks, Carl 482
Nike *498*, 501, 504
Nike Town *500*, *505*
Nikolic, Aleksandar 545
NIT 390, 467, 482–3, 485
Nixon, Norm 231–2, *231*, 340, 341

Norman, Ken 57
Norris, Dr. Anna J. 451
North Carolina Central College 205
North Carolina State University 258, 294, 381, 471, 472, 474
North Park (Illinois) University 479
Northwestern University 467
Nowitzki, Dirk 45, *45*, 232, *232*, 368, 385, 432, *432*

O

O'Bannon, Ed 477, *477*
O'Brien, Larry 22, 546
O'Neal, Shaquille 23, *26*, 58, *58*, 59, 70, 71, 130–31, *130*, *131*, 161, 181, 187, 192, 196, 225, 253, 259, 283, *302*, 241, 353, 358, *358*, 364, 366, 374, 375, *375*, 383, 410, 448, 459, 474, *474*, 475, 488–9, *488*, 492, 500, *556*
Oakland Oaks 99
Oakley, Charles 68, 161, 233, *233*, *422*
Obras Sanitarias 433
Odom, Lamar 57, 158, 233–4, *234*, 369, 497
Offensive foul 497
Ohio State University 114, 199, 204, 212, 467, 469, 470–71, 474, 475, 485
Oklahoma A & M (*later* State) University 280, 281, 468, 469, *469*, 485
Oklahoma City University 479
Oklahoma State (*formerly* A & M) University 280, 468, 483
Olajuwon, Hakeem (*formerly* Akeem) 23, 52, 53, *53*, 97, 128–9, *128*, 136, 171, 182, 225, 238, *302*, 344, 352, *352*, 353, *353*, 364, 377, 378, *378*, *409*, 410, *422*, 432, 436–9, *439*, 472, *472*, 489, 500
Old Dominion University 453
Olimpia Milano *430*, 431
Oliver, Brian 474
Olowokandi, Michael 56, 57, 383, *383*, 439
Olson, Lute 479
Olympic Games 1936 – 412
1948 – 292, 412, *412*
1952 – 212, 413, *413*
1956 – 20, 138, 205, 409, 415, *415*
1960 – 142, 415, *415*
1964 – 157, 281, 409, 416, *416*
1968 – 281, 416–8, *419*
1972 – 281, 406, 418, *418*, 420
1976 – 170, 172, 295, 297, 419, 452, 453, 454
1980 – 419, 453
1984 – 110, 227, 236, 239, 258, 420, *420*, 452, 453
1988 – 406, 409, 409–10, *409*, 420, 426, 443, 452
1992 – 97, 102, 123, 141, 174, 209, 227, 238, 246, 277, 406, *406*, 408, *408*, 409, 427, 439, 452, 500,
1996 – 123, 131, 141, 238, 298, 409, *409*, 410, *410*, 436, 439,

442, 443, 446, 452, 459, 461
2000 – 149, 175, 189, *220*, 227, 410, 411, *411*
Omni, Atlanta 404
Oregon State University 235
Original Celtics 15–6, *15*, 211, 508, 546
Original Rules of Basket Ball 493
Orlando Centroplex 398, *399*
Orlando Magic 70–71, 130, 150, *151*, 187, 190, 191, 195, 199, 217, 239, 243, 257, 265, 266, 277, 290, *302*, 353, 368, 374, 379, 383, 398, *399*, 410, 433, 462, 503
Orlando Miracle 398, 455
Owens, Billy 60, 187, 474

P

Page, H.O. (Pat) 534–5
Paige, Woody 365–6
Palace of Auburn Hills, The 394–6, *395*
Palacio, Milt 422
Panathinaikos 433
Parish, Robert 22, 36, 51, 102, 181, 200, 222, 235, *235*, 342, *342*, 343, 344, *344*, *345*, 364, 371, 435
Park, Sinja 463
Paspalj, Zarko 410, 420, 427
Pass *490*, 491
Patterson, Steve 485
Paultz, Billy, 80
Paxson, Jim 379
Paxson, John 120–21, 192, 282, 349, 351
Payne, Tom 293
Payton, Gary 82, 83, *83*, 235–6, *235*, 374, 375, 410, 474, *494*
Penn State University 433
Peoria Caterpillars 413
Pepperdine University 200
Pepsi Center, Denver 394, *394*
Percudani, Dick 441, 442
Perkins, Sam 44, 82, 236, *236*, 294, 349, *349*
Perrot, Kim 450, *450*
Perry, Curtis 74, 334
Person, Chuck *236*, 237
Person, Wesley 43
Peterson, Morris 385
Petrov, Alexander 416
Petrovic, Drazen 67, 420, 427, 439–41, *440*
Pettit, Bob 20, 34, 35, 122, 132–3, *132*, *133*, 160, 190, 197, 215, 218, 315, 316, *316*, 318, 319, 363, 364, 369, 370, 388, 516
Pettit, Jane 398
Pettit, Lloyd 398
Pfund, Randy 118
Phelps, Derrick 475
Philadelphia 76ers 21, 30, 72–3, 96, 99, 152, 104, 109, 118, 125, 160, 165, 167, 168, 169, 172, 182, 188, 192, 195, 199, 205, 206, 209, 211, 217, 219, 222, 251, 254, 262, 274, 275, 276, 283, 286, 288, 325, *325*, 326, 335, *335*, 338, *338*, 340, 341, *341*, 370, 371, 372, 373, 379, 388, 398–9, 428, *429*, 430, 496,

498 see also Syracuse Nationals
Philadelphia Hustle 453
Philadelphia Rage 453, *464*
Philadelphia Spectrum 391
Philadelphia Warriors 20, 28, 30, 50, 104, 150, 168, 183, 185, 204, 205, 237, *246*, 247, 305, 314, *314*, 306, 369, 370, *376*, 377 *see also* Golden State Warriors, San Francisco Warriors
Philips Arena, Altanta 392, 404, 405
Phillip, Andy 106, 237, 360, 516
Phillips 66ers *412*, 413
Phills, Bobby 39, 441
Phoenix Mercury 367, 399, *444*, 448, 454, 455, 456
Phoenix Suns 74–5, 97, 121, 131, 146, 147, 148, 165, 172, 185, 189, 191, 192, 195, 196, 200, 201, 202, 206, 207, 215, 216, 217, 222, 230, 244, 246, 250, 265, 282, 290, 334, 340, 351, 367, 371, 377, 388, 391, 399, 422, 441, 442, 455, 456, *493*
Pida, Valerie 474
Pierce, Paul 37, *37*, 368, 480
Pierce, Ricky 47, 82, 237, *237*
Pippen, Scottie 40, 52, 53, 77, 120, 158, 162, 187, 195, 238, *238*, 270, 282, 349, *349*, 350, 351, 354, *354355*, *355*, 356, 364, 374, 380, 408, 410, 479, *495*
Pitino, Rick 36, 149, 152, 232, 452, 478, 479, 480
Pittsburgh Ironmen 30,
Pittsburgh Pipers 192
Pivot foot 495
Podoloff, Maurice 18, 28, 360, 546
Point-shaving scandal 19
Pollard, Jim 18, 28, *29*, 58, 127, 218, 222, 238, 284, 308, 310, *310*, 312, 369, 516
Popovich, Gregg 81
Porter, Howard 471
Porter, Kevin 239
Porter, Terry 77, 206, 239, *239*
Portland Fire 456
Portland Memorial Coliseum 391
Portland Trail Blazers 76–7, 121, 125, 148, 149, 172, 174, 187, 199, 205, 206, 213, 238, *238*, 239, *243*, 244, *244*, 248, *248*, 252, 255, *255*, 259, 261, 263, *263*, 266, 266, 276, 288, *288*, 298, 299, 335, *335*, 348, 350, 351, 357, 378, 381, 391, 399, 427, 428, 439, *495*
Potapenko, Vitaly 37, 431, *431*, 432
Pressey, Paul 232
Price, Mark 42, 224, 239, *239*, 298, 374, 492
Princeton University 157, 469, 483
Providence Steamrollers 30,
Providence University 152, 265–6, 381, 471
Purdue University 246, 300, 477, 487

574

R

Radja, Dino 420
Rambis, Kurt 59, *341*
Ramsay, Dr. Jack 8–11, *8, 9, 56,* 76, 77, 109, 270, 288, *288*, 538
Ramsey, Frank 20, 240, 293, 317, *317*, 318, 319, 320, 322, 388, 516
Real Madrid 430, 439
Rebound 490–91, *491*
Recasner, Eldridge 39, 167
Redin, Harley 463
Reebok 501
Reed, Willis 21, 68, 112, 157, 240, *240*, 278, 328, 330, 331, *331*, 358, 364, 371, 439, 440, 441, 479, 516
Reeves, Bryant 88, 240, *241*
Reeves, Khalid 38
Referees 495, 497
Reich, Ernie 15
Reid, J.R. 39, 81
Reinhart, Bill 19, 376
Reinsdorf, Jerry 504
Respert, Shawn 478
Reunion Arena, Dallas 394, *394*
Rhode Island State University 469
Rice University 487
Rice, Glen 38, 39, 60, 61, 181, 241, *241*, 365, 374
Richardson, Nolan 476
Richardson, Pooh 64
Richmond, Mitch 51, 79, 91, 196, 242, *242*, 265, 374, 410, 479
Rickard, Tex 390
Rider, Isaiah *34*, 35, 64, 77, 199, 243, *243*, 299, 479
Riley, Pat 58, 60, 61, 68, 110, 131, 136, 216, 219, 227, 270, 274, 287, 290, *290*, 294–5, 343, 346, 362, 379, 456, 460, 463, 473
Rio Grande (Ohio) College 484
Risen, Arnie 19, 28, 78, 181, 263, 309, 316, 516
Rivers, Glenn (Doc) 71, 243, 503
Robertson, Alvin 80, 243–4, *244*
Robertson, Oscar (Big O) 21, 32, 62, 78, 92, 128, 134–5, *134, 135*, 178, 199, 211, 212, 259, 329, 363, 364, 370, 371, 377, 415, 439, 469, 470, 485, 516
Robeson, Paul 473
Robinson, Cliff 26, 75, 244, *244*
Robinson, Crystal 449
Robinson, David 23, 80, 81, *81*, 171, 175, 225, 244–6, *246*, 357, *357*, 364, 375, 383, 408, 410, 442, 473, 488, *564*
Robinson, Glenn *62*, 63, 149, 164, 246, 477
Robinson, Jackie 467
Robinson, Truck 74, 136, 479
Rocha, Red 313
Rochester Royals 17, 18, 19, 30, 78, 127, 164, 171, 183, 222, 254, 259, 263, 278, 307, 309, 310, 369 *see also* Kansas City/ Kansas City-Omaha Kings, Sacramento Kings
Rodgers, Guy 246–7, *246*, *376*, *377*
Rodgers, Jimmy 64
Rodman, Dennis 26, 40, 45, 48,

81, 136–7, *136, 137, 151*, 204, 268, 270, 276, 346, 354, 364, 479, *479*, *491*
Rogers, Rodney 75
Rollins, Kenny 469, 485
Rollins, Tree 243
Roosma, Col. John 535
Rose Garden, Portland *386*, 391, 399
Rose, Jalen 47, 227, 247, *247*, 358, 475
Rose, Malik *357*
Rosenbluth, Lennie 469
Rothstein, Ron 60, 462
Rowe, Curtis 301, 487
Rozier, Clifford 477
Rubini, Cesare 545
Rudoy, Herb 424
Ruland, Jeff 215
Rule changes 496–7
Rules of Basket Ball, Original 493
Rupp, Adolph 190, 240, 270, 292–3, *292, 293*, 280, 468, 469, 471, 473, 478, 483, 485, 545
Rush, Ed 497
Russell, Bill 19, *19*, 20, 32, 35, 36, 82, 92, 104, 105, 114, 115, 128, 131, 132, 136, 138–9, *138*, 152, 165, 178, 190, 193, 205, 212, 215, 227, 231, 240, 244, 263, 272, 273, 315, 316, 317, 318, 319, 320, *321*, 322, *322*, 323, 324, *324*, 325, 326, 327, 364, 370, 376, 388, 415, *415*, 439, 469, 485, 488, 516
Russell, Campy 42, 68
Russell, Cazzie 469, 471
Russell, John "Honey" 16, 516
Rutgers University 452, 473

S

Sabonis, Arvydas 77, 420, 424, 427, 428, *428*
Sachs, Leonard 545
Sacramento Kings 30, 78–9, 173, 187, 188, 196, 242, 256, 265, 267, 368, 374, 399–400, 427, 429, 433, 434, 455, 496 *see also* Cincinnati Royals, Kansas City/ Kansas City Omaha Kings, Rochester Royals
Sacramento Monarchs 400, 446, 457, 465
Sadowski, Ed 424
St. Francis University (Pa.) 239
St. Jean, Gary 51
St. John's University 211, 222, 227, 269, 466, 469, 483
St. Joseph's (Penn) University 469
St. Joseph's College 288
St. Louis Bombers 30, 305, 377
St. Louis Hawks 20, 30, 34, 132, 133, 152, 160, 181, 183, 188, 189, 190, 197–9, 215, 218, 250, 266, 272, 278, 283, 315, 316, 317, 318, *318*, 319, 363, 369, 370, 377, 388 *see also* Atlanta Hawks, Milwaukee Hawks, Tri-Cities Blackhawks
St. Louis Spirits 125, 152, 157, 165
St. Louis University 215, 293, 469
St. Thomas College 284
Sakandelidze, Sako 418
Sales, Nykesha 503

Salley, John 48, 204, 276, 346
Sampson, Ralph 51, 52, 128, 344, 372, *372, 377, 378*, 381, 461, 473
San Antonio Spurs 26, 30, 80–81, 111, 136, 137, 161, 167, 168, 170, 175, 177, *177*, 184, 185, 202, 204, 205, 207, *207*, 239, 243, 244, *244*, 246, *246*, 253, 255, 266, 340, 357, *357*, 371, 372, 383, 400, 403, *404*, 405, 427, *564 see also* Dallas Chaparrals
San Diego Clippers 30, 56, 231, 381 *see also* Buffalo Braves, Los Angeles Clippers
San Diego Rockets 30, 52, 82, 117, 371 *see also* Houston Rockets
San Francisco Warriors 30, 50, 98, 104, 212, *246, 247*, 258, 283, 322, 325, *325*, 370 *see also* Golden State Warriors, Philadelphia Warriors
San Jose State University 433
Sanders, Tom 20, 36, 98, 272, *323*, 324
Saperstein, Abe 15
Sauldsberry, Woody *319*
Saunders, Flip 64, 65
Schaefer, Herm 307
Schanwald, Steve 136
Schaus, Fred 58, 133, 142, 143
Schayes, Dolph 18, 19, 72, 181, 248, 312, 313, 360, 364, 516–7
Schmidt, Ernest 535
Schmidt, Oscar 420, 432, 442–3, *443*
Schommer, John 487, 535, *535*
Schrempf, Detlef 44, 77, 248, *248*, 424, *424*
Scorer 497
Scott, Byron 58, 249, *249*, 346, *346*, 347, 349
Scott, Charlie 36, 74, 334
Scott, Dennis 70, 474
Screen 495
Seattle Storm 456
Seattle SuperSonics 82–3, 111, 117, 123, 151, 152, 160, 161, 162, 165, 178 178, 184, 187, 192, 193, 200, 201, 204, 206, 220, 235, 236, 246, 248, *248*, 250, 258, 265, 266, 267, 283, 288, 298, 336, *336*, 337, *337*, 354, 371, 372, 373, *374*, 381, 400, 402, *403*, 401, 422, 427, 433, *493*
Seattle University 469
Sedran, Barney 535
Seikaly, Rony 60
Selvy, Frank 320, 388, 485
Semjonova, Uljanna 463, 535–7, 537
Senesky, George 469
Seton Hall University 171, 263, 473, 478
Seymour, Paul 308, 312
Shackleford, Lynn 487
Sharman, Bill 18, 19, 20, 36, 106, 138, 212, 215, 249–50, 272, 315, 316, 317, 318, 319, 364, 369, 517
Shaw, Brian 430
Sheboygan Redskins 30,

Sheehan, Pat 424
Sheffield Sharks 433
Sheffield, Fred 468
Shelton, Everett 545
Shelton, Lonnie 201
Sheppard, Jeff 480
Sherman, Maude 451
Short, Purvis 51
Shot *489*, 489–90
Shot clock 19 313, 476, 495
Shue, Gene 48, 90, 275
Sibenka 439
Siegfried, Larry 388, 485
Sikma, Jack 82, 201, 250, *250*, 267, 298, 337, 479
Silas, Paul 36, 39, 74, 250, 334
Simmons, Connie 309
Simmons, Lionel 474
Simon, Miles 479, 480
Skansi, Peter 409
Skiles, Scott 75
Skoog, Whitey 311
SkyDome, Toronto 404
Sloan, Jerry 40, 86, 122, 123, 250–51, 479
Smiddy, Jim 463
Smith College 451
Smith, Adrian 370
Smith, Chris 481
Smith, Dean 270, 280, 293, 294–5, *294, 295*, 296, 297, 472, 474, 475, 483
Smith, Greg 62, 329
Smith, Joe 251, *251*, 478
Smith, Kenny 52, 353
Smith, Margaret 545
Smith, Phil 333
Smith, Randy 56, 251, 288, 371
Smith, Steve 35, 60, 76, 77, 252, *252*, 299, 411
Smith, Tubby 480
Smits, Rik 54, *54*, 55, 171, 224, 247, 252–3, *252*, 424
Smolick, Mike 15
Smuin, Dick 468
Snow, Eric 72
Snyder, Dick 42
Sobers, Rickey *334*
Sophia Newcomb College 451
Spectrum, Philadelphia 391
Spencer, Felton 64
Spivey, Bill 469
Sprewell, Latrell 51, *68*, 69, 196, 253, *253*, 254, 374
Springfield (Mass.) College 508
Springfield Fame 452
Staak, Bob 197
Stackhouse, Jerry 49, *49*, 73, 253–4, *254*, 478
Staley, Dawn 451
Stanford University 451, 466, 467, 480, 482, 485, 489
Stankovic, Boris 409, 426
Staples Center, Los Angeles 391, 396, 397, *397*, 405
Starbird, Kate 451
Starks, John 51, 254, *254*, 352, 479
Steele, Larry 76
Steinmetz, Christian 484, 537
Stepien, Ted 42, 276
Stern, David 23, 25, 136–7, 362, 367, 375, 379, 382–3, *385*, 426, 449, 461, 464, 498, 500, 503, 505, 506, *506*, *564*

Stockton, John 23, 24, 86, *86*, 87, 123, 140–41, *140*, *141*, 195, 217, 356, 363, *364*, 364, 374, 408, 410, 489, 491, *555*
Stoev, Stefko Stanev 442
Stokes, Maurice 136, 254–5, 259, 369
Stoudamire, Damon 77, 84, 252, 255, *255*, 478
Strickland, Rod *90*, 91, 255, 431
Summit, The, Houston 396
Summitt, Pat 270, 296–7, *296*, *297*, 463
Sura, Bob 365
Sutton, Eddie 280, 281, 483, *483*
Swoopes, Sheryl 444, 450, 460, 465, *465*, 503
Syracuse Nationals 19, 21, *28*, 30, 72, 164, 165, 168, 188, 206, 248, 269, 308, 312, 313, *313*, 314 *see also* Philadelpha 76ers
Syracuse University 153, 167, 473, 474, 478
Szczerbiak, Wally 65, *65*

T

Takev, Bozhidar 442
Tao, Song 428
Target Center, Minnesota 398, 403
Tarkanian, Jerry 479
Tarpley, Roy 44, 256, *256*
Tatum, Goose 15
Taylor, Fred 545
Taylor, Maurice 57, 130
TD Waterhouse Centre, Orlando 398, *399*
Teague, Bertha 452, 463
Temple University 247, *376*, 467, 476
Terry, Jason 481
Texas Tech University 444
Texas Western University (*also* UTEP) 473
Theus, Reggie 79, 256–7, *257*
Thomas, Isiah 23, 48, 84, 174, 207, 215, 257, *257*, 276, 346, 347, *347*, 348, *348*, 362, 364, 366, 372, 378, 420, 491
Thompson, Billy 473
Thompson, David 46, 47,154, 257–8, 371, 381, 471, 517
Thompson, John 295, 483, 537, 545, *545*
Thompson, Mychal 97
Thompson, Tina *444*, 450, 455, *455*, 459, 460
Thorn, Rod 411, 496–7
Thorpe, Otis 52, 79, 242, 265
Three-point shot 22, *496*
Thurman, Scott 476
Thurmond, Nate 21, 51, 99, 258, 325, 364, 517
Tikhonenko, Valery 428
Timekeeper 497
Timeout 495
Timms, Michele 448, 455, 503
Tisdale, Wayman 258–9, *258*
Todd, Jim 57
Toler, Penny 456
Tomjanovich, Rudy 52
Toney, Andrew 72, 275, 340, 341, 391
Toronto Huskies 30, 88, 422, 441
Toronto Raptors 84–5, 149, 161,

161, 162, 169, 233, 236, 244, 255, 257, *299*, 366, 400, *400*, 404
Traveling 495
Traylor, Robert 432
Trent, Gary 259, *259*
Tri-Cities Blackhawks 30, 34, 106, 272 *see also* Atlanta Hawks, Milwaukee Hawks, St. Louis Hawks
Trippe, Joe 15
Tripucka, Chris 26
Tsioropoulos, Lou 293
Tucker, Gerry 469
Tulane University 485
Turnover 495
Twardzik, Dave 76
Twyman, Jack 78, 178, 255, 259, 517

U

U.S. International University 474
U.S. Naval Academy 244, 383, 473
UCLA (California-Los Angeles) 94, 117, 140, 185, 202, 224, 261, 263, 266, 292, 294, 297, 299, 299, 300, 329, 377, 449, 452, 453, 467, 469, 470, 471, *471*, 475, 477–8, 479, 483, 485, 487
United Center, Chicago 389, 393, *393*, 405
United States Basketball League 452
University of Arizona 153, 255, 473, 478, 479, 480, 481
University of Arkansas 225, 243, 476, *476*, 477, *477*, 478, 483, 485
University of California 146, 202, 207, 295, 451, 476, 477, 480, *480*
University of Central Arkansas 238
University of Chicago 487
University of Cincinnati 134, 259, 261, 329, 385, *385*, 469, 470, 475, 480, 482, 483, 485
University of Connecticut 244, 297, 444, *444*, 464, 477, 478, 480, 481
University of Detroit 193, 418
University of Florida 267, 385, 481
University of Georgia 266, 480
University of Hartford 151
University of Houston 117, 128, 154, 167, 174, 439, 470, 471, 472, *472*, 487
University of Idaho 201
University of Illinois 150, 184,201, 237
University of Indiana 152, 222, 257, 280, 294, 471, 472, 473, 476, 482, 483, 484, 485
University of Iowa 192
University of Kansas 160, 212, 217, 219, 265, 293, 377, 413, 418, 452, 469, 472, 473, 474, 480, 483, 487
University of Kentucky 170, 190, 199, 240, 292, 293, *412*, 413, 452, 468, 469, 471, 473, 475, 476, 478, 479, 480, 483, 485, 485, 487

University of Louisville 188, 220, 472, 473, 477, 260
University of Maryland 251, 266, 294, 478
University of Massachusetts 109, 161, 478
University of Miami 98, 300, 486
University of Michigan 196, 241, 247, 264, 265, 368, 469, 471, 473, 475, 485
University of Minnesota 192, 197, 222, 382
University of Nebraska 487
University of New Mexico 170, 424
University of North Carolina 120, 168, 171, 172, 181, 205, 219, 253, 269, 293, 294, 366, 402, 435, 467, 468, 469, 472, 473, 474, 475, 478, 479, 480, 483, 487
University of Notre Dame 170, 211, 466, 471, 482
University of Ohio 259
University of Oklahoma 147, 155, 258, 469, 473
University of Oregon 467, 474, 485
University of Pacific 439
University of Penn 482
University of Pennsylvania 276, 469, 487
University of Pittsburgh 467, 487
University of Rhode Island 233
University of San Francisco 19, 138, 162, 205, 376, 415, 469, 485
University of Seattle 100
University of South Carolina 178
University of Southern California 249, 267, 453, 475, 487
University of Tennessee 188, 196, 296, *296*, 452, 459, 476, 486
University of Texas 218, 452, 482
University of Utah 224, 261, 468, 480, 481, 482, 485
University of Virginia 294, 461, 473, 503
University of Washington 248, 424
University of West Virginia 142, 143
University of Wisconsin 296, 484
University of Wisconsin–Stevens Point 239
UNLV (Nevada-Las Vegas) 202, 257, *257*, 473, 474, 474, 479
Unseld, Wes 21, 90, 91, 170, 201, 225, 260, 329, 336, 337, 364, 381, 517
Utah Jazz 30, 86–7, 104, 121, 122, 123, 140, 141, 151, 157, 161–2, 165, 171, 188, 195, *195*, 201, 209, 217, 251, *254*, 265, 283, 346, 355, 356, 363, 364, 367, 368, 373, 374, 381, 401, 404, 455, 489, 504, *555 see also* New Orleans Jazz
Utah Stars 125, 152, 157
Utah Starzz 367, 455, 465
UTEP (Texas-El Paso, *formerly* West Texas State University) 150, 469, 483

V

Vallely, John 487
Valvano, Jim 472, 474
Van Arsdale, Dick 74, 334
Van Exel, Nick 47, *47*, *144*, 260–61, *260*, *496*
Van Gundy, Jeff 68, 69, 503
Van Horn, Keith 66, 67, 261, *261*, 480, 503
Van Lier, Norm 40
Vancouver Grizzlies 88–9, 146, 153, 182, 240–41, *241*, 249, 277, 379, 401, *401*, 422
Vandeweghe, Ernie 261
Vandeweghe, Kiki 47, 261, *261*
Vandivier, Robert 537, *537*
Varchev, Simeon Nanev 442
Vaught, Loy 57
Versace, Dick 89, 120
Villanova University 150, *376*, 467, 469, 471, 472
Vincent, Jay 44, 482
Virginia Squires 109, 184
Vlahov, Andrew 410
Volkov, Alexander 420, 427, *427*, 428
Vrankovic, Stojan 420

W

Wachter, Edward 537
Wade, Margaret 452, 463, 545–6
Wake Forest University 478, *478*, 480
Walk, Neil 74
Walker, Antoine 36, 262, *262*, 478
Walker, Chet 21, 40, 72, 168, 188, 262, 325
Walker, Darrell 84, 91, 197
Walker, Jimmy 381
Walking 495
Wall, Bill 281
Wallace, Rasheed 77, *77*, 187, 262–3, *263*
Walsh, Donnie 402
Walton, Bill 56, 76, 77, 263, 288, 301, 335, *335*, 344, 364, 471, 485, 517
Wanzer, Bobby 19, 78, 263–4, 517
Ward, Charlie 69
Warren, Mike 301, 487
Washington Bullets 30, 90, 91, 99, 117, 147, 154, 170, 187, 189, 192, 193, 196, 201, 207, 209, 212, 215, 217, 239, 265, 267, 298, 333, 336, *336*, 337, 371, 381, 403, 430, 436, *436* *see also* Baltimore Bullets, Capital Bullets, Washington Wizards
Washington Capitols 18, 20, 30, 272, 305, 307
Washington Generals 449, 452, 454
Washington Mystics 401, 444, 446, 455, 459
Washington Wizards 30, 90–91, 121, 196, 228, 242, 255, 265, 298, 401, 431 *see also* Baltimore Bullets, Capital Bullets, Washington Bullets
Washington, Ora 453

Washington, Richard 301
Waterloo (Iowa) Hawks 30.
Watts, Stanley 546
Weatherspoon, Clarence 73, 251
Weatherspoon, Teresa 448, *448*, 449, 451
Webb, Spud 264, *264*, 362
Webber, Chris 23, 51, 70, 79, *79*, 91, 189, 196, 222, 242, 247, 264–5, *264*, 267, 368, 375, 475
Webster, Marvin 82, 381
Wedman, Scott 79, 342, 343
Welts, Rick 367
Wennington, Bill 409, 424
Wesley, David 39
West Texas State University (*later* UTEP) 167
West, Jerry 21, 58, 92, 100, 130, 142–3, *142*, *143*, 167, 205, 320, 321, 323, 324, 326, 327, 328, *328*, 330, *330*, 331, 364, 371, 388, 415, 456, 469, 517–8, *517*, *550*
Western Kentucky University 192
Western Illinois University 382
Westhead, Paul 290, 338
Westminster College 466
Westphal, Paul 74, 75, 83, 151, 265, 334, 371, 401
White, Eddie 15

White, Jo Jo 36, 168, 250, 265, *265*, 332, 334, *334*, 418,
White, Maurice 18
White, Nera 463, 537–8, *538*
Whitsitt, Bob 288
Whittenburg, Dereck 472
Wicks, Sidney 301, 381, 471, 485, 487
Wilkens, Lenny 35, 42, 82, 155, 265–6, 270, 290, 298–9, *298*, *299*, 364, 371, 410, 411, 443, 496, 518. 539
Wilkes, Jamaal (*formerly* Keith) 58, 266, 301, 333, *333*, 338, 340, *340*
Wilkins, Dominique 23, 34, 35, 86, 243, 266, *266*, 268, 362, 364, 378, 426, 498
Willerson, Bobby 485
Williams, Buck 77, 206, 244, 266–7, *267*, 420
Williams, Donald 475
Williams, Freeman 56, 86
Williams, Gregg 297
Williams, Gus 82, 267, 298, 337, *337*, 371
Williams, Hot Rod 42
Williams, Jason *11*, 78, 79, 153, 267–8, *267*, 368
Williams, Jayson 25, 67, 268, *268*

Williams, Natalie 367, 449, 503
Williams, Pat 70
Williams, Reggie 430
Williams, Roy 295, 474
Williamson, Corliss 476
Williamson, John 66, 268
Willis, Kevin 60–61, 243, 268–9, *268*, 479
Windsor and Assumption College 422, 424
Winston-Salem State University 225, 381, 484
Winter, Tex 52
Wintermute, Urgel 485
Winters, Brian 88
Wittman, Randy 43
WNBA 505
Wolters, Kara 451
Women's Basketball Association 452
Women's Basketball League 451, 453, 454
Women's Professional Basketball League 452
Woodard, Lynette 452, 455
Wooden, John 140, 270, 280, 287, 292, 294, 296, 297, 300–301, *300*, *301*, 449, 469, 471, *471*, 477, 483, 485, 487, 538

Woolpert, Phil 546
Worthy, James 23, 58, 118, 168, 266, 269, *269*, 290, 294, 341, 342, 343, 345, *345*, 346, 349, 364, 378, 388, 391, 472
Wright State University *431*
Wright, Larry 337
Wright, Sharone 84

X

Xavier University 187

Y

Yale University 469, 484, 487
Yardley, George 48, 269, 313, 314, 518
YMCA 12, 14, *14*
Young Men's Christian Training Centre 12, *14*

Z

Zaslofsky, Max 18, 19, 48, 106, 160, 269, 305, 309
Zimbalist, Andy 404
Zollner, Fred 48
Zone defense 493

Picture credits

Carlton Books Limited would like to thank the following sources for their kind permission to reproduce the pictures in this book:

Allsport UK Ltd
AP Photo
Basketball Hall of Fame, Springfield, MA
Corbis/Bettmann/UPI
The Sporting News

Every effort has been made to acknowledge correctly and contact the source and/or copyright holder of each picture, and Carlton Books Limited apologises for any unintentional errors or omissions which will be corrected in future editions of this book.